CYBERSPACES AND GLOBAL AFFAIRS

Cyberspaces and Global Affairs

Edited by

SEAN S. COSTIGAN
MIT CogNet and The New School, USA

and

JAKE PERRY
Independent scholar

ASHGATE

Published by
Ashgate Publishing Limited
Wey Court East
Union Road
Farnham
Surrey, GU9 7PT
England

Ashgate Publishing Company
Suite 420
101 Cherry Street
Burlington
VT 05401-4405
USA

www.ashgate.com

British Library Cataloguing in Publication Data
Cyberspaces and global affairs.
1. Cyberspace. 2. International relations--Technological innovations.
I. Costigan, Sean S. II. Perry, Jake.
303.4'833-dc22

Library of Congress Cataloging-in-Publication Data
Cyberspaces and global affairs / [edited] by Sean S. Costigan and Jake Perry.
p. cm.
Includes bibliographical references and index.
ISBN 978-1-4094-2754-4 (hbk.) -- ISBN 978-1-4094-2755-1 (ebook)
1. Technology and international relations. 2. Internet and international relations. 3. Mass media and international relations. 4. International relations--Technological innovations. 5. Information technology--Political aspects. 6. Internet--Political aspects. I. Costigan, Sean S. II. Perry, Jake.
JZ1254.C73 2012
327.0285'4678--dc23

2011024565

ISBN 9781409427544 (hbk)
ISBN 9781409427551 (ebk)

MIX
Paper from responsible sources
FSC® C018575

Printed and bound in Great Britain by the MPG Books Group, UK

Contents

List of Figures

List of Tables

Notes on Contributors

Sujit Bhar, with 25 years of journalistic experience under his belt, is currently a consultant with an international industrial group based out of Kolkata (earlier Calcutta), India. His journalistic activity started in Kolkata and moved to New Delhi, the time being spent with sport, social issues, the environment and business-related coverage. He was born and educated in Kolkata, graduating from the University of Calcutta. He also runs his own business, involving schools and external activity.

Madeline Carr is a doctoral candidate at Australian National University where she researches the political history of the Internet. Previously she was Director at Fearless Media and a State Manager at AFTRS Tasmania. Madeline's research interests include American foreign policy, international relations theory, the philosophy of technology and the nexus between the media and politics. She tutors for AusAID in the Graduate Studies in International Affairs program at ANU.

Sean S. Costigan is Project Leader at MIT Cognet and part-time faculty at The New School. In 2010 he was a fellow at the University of Calcutta's Institute of Foreign Policy Studies, prior to which he taught at The New School and was Director for Strategic Initiatives, Center for Security Studies, ETH Zurich. He is co-chair of the Economics of Security Study Group and chair of the editorial board, Partnership for Peace Consortium of Defense Academies and Security Studies Institutes. He previously served as executive editor of Columbia International Affairs Online, Research Associate for Science and Technology at the Council on Foreign Relations, and on the staff of the Center for International Affairs, Harvard University.

Erica Dingman is a research associate at the World Policy Institute in New York City. Her research focuses on the Arctic, Inuit, and Canada/U.S. relations. She holds a Masters in International Affairs from The New School. Erica was born and raised in Canada and is a long-time resident of the U.S., a duality that greatly influences her research.

Lida Khalili Gheidary is currently a freelance researcher and translator. Previously, she worked as a research assistant for the BBC World Service Trust. She graduated with a Master of Research (MRes) from the Management department and the Information Systems group of the London School of Economics.

Fotios C. Harmantzis is Affiliate Professor at the School of Technology Management, Stevens Institute of Technology, where he teaches courses in financial engineering and telecommunications management. His research interests are in the areas of quantitative investments under uncertainty, valuation of real options, risk management, and economic/financials of high-tech and telecom. His degrees include a Ph.D. in Electrical Engineering and a Finance MBA from the University of Toronto, and a Master's in Operations Research from the University of Pennsylvania.

Jeffrey A. Hart is Professor of Political Science at Indiana University in Bloomington, Indiana. He specializes in the study of international politics and international political economy, and specifically international competition in high technology industries.

Tim Junio is a researcher with the National Defense University regarding information technology and national security and a doctoral candidate at the University of Pennsylvania. His related publications recently appeared in *Joint Force Quarterly*, *Armed Forces Journal*, and *C4ISR Journal*. Additionally, he has worked on information operations for the U.S. military, Defense Department, and Intelligence Community.

Nat Katin-Borland works at the Open Society Institute's (OSI) New York Office in the Information Systems Department, helping to manage OSI's web-based social networking and online collaboration platforms and strategizing with programs about how they can use tools on the internet to do their work more effectively. Nat is passionate about exploring the potential for Web 2.0 technologies to act as a catalyst for social change. Nat also worked at OSI's Washington, DC Office with the Middle East and Africa Programs, helping to raise awareness with policy-makers on Capitol Hill on key human rights issues from these regions. Nat received his Master's degree in International Affairs from the New School University in New York City in 2009 and his Bachelor's degree in 2002 from Wesleyan University, where he pursued a double-major in History and Science in Society.

Kenneth H. Keller is Director of the Bologna Center; Professor of Science and Technology Policy, Johns Hopkins SAIS; President Emeritus of the University of Minnesota; was Professor of Chemical Engineering and Materials Science, Department Chair, Academic Vice President and President of the University of Minnesota for more than three decades; was Senior Fellow for Science and Technology and Senior Vice President of Programs at the Council on Foreign Relations in New York; member of the National Academy of Engineering; fellow of the American Association for the Advancement of Science; founding fellow of the American Institute of Medical and Biological Engineering; member of the Council on Foreign Relations; former member and chairman of the National Research Council's Board on Assessment of National Institute of Standards and Technology Programs and NASA Astrophysics Performance Committee; former member of the Board of Life Sciences, of the Commission on Physical Sciences, Mathematics and Applications, and of the Science and Technology Advisory Panel to the Director of Central Intelligence; and past chair of the Medical Technology Leadership Forum. He obtained his Ph.D. in chemical engineering from The Johns Hopkins University.

Ryan Kiggins is a doctoral candidate at the University of Florida Department of Political Science in Gainesville, FL. His dissertation, supervised by Professor Ido Oren, investigates the formation of U.S. Internet governance policy, arguing that U.S. policy-makers viewed the Internet as the technological key for opening overseas markets and political institutions to American commercial and political expansion in the post-Cold War era. He specializes in Internet governance issues, cyber security policy, global electronic commerce policy, global political economy, especially U.S. foreign economic policy, U.S. foreign policy, and U.S. national security interests.

Anthony Lopez is a writer and broadcast journalist based out of New York City. He has an M.A. in International Affairs from the New School, where he concentrated primarily on issues of conflict and security.

Shriya Malhotra has a B.A. in international development from McGill University and an M.A. in International Affairs: Cities and Urbanization from the New School. Her research explores the intersection of art, design and IT to promote urban sustainability. Her specific focus is on the role of visual and spatial analysis for improved urban population health and better cities. She believes in the power of maps, the Internet and chocolate.

Fabien Miard grew up in Switzerland with a Swiss, French and Brazilian background. He earned an M.Phil. in Political Science from the University of Oslo, Norway, and a B.A. in Political Science and Scandinavian Studies from the University of Zurich, Switzerland. At the University of Oslo his studies focused on development studies, peace and conflict studies, and political economy. Fabien Miard now works in a small, international web marketing company based in Oslo that does multilingual search engine optimization and profile filtering for universities.

David Millman is the Director of Digital Library Technology Services at New York University. His group, part of both the NYU Libraries and the University IT unit, creates digital collections and builds infrastructure to enable long-term digital preservation and new forms of scholarly communication. He previously held several roles at Columbia University, most recently as Senior Director of Research, Teaching and Learning Technologies in the central IT division.

Emily Molfino is a doctoral student in political science at Arizona State University. Emily's research examines the role of information and communication technologies at regional, national, and global levels on various types of conflict and conflict resolution. With this in mind, Emily is actively involved with the Consortium for Science, Policy, and Outcomes at Arizona State University. Emily received her M.A. in International Affairs from The New School in 2010. Her Bachelor's degree came from San Diego State University in 2007. In 2008, Emily worked with African Services Committee, an NGO working to improve the health and self-sufficiency of those in Ethiopia and African communities in New York City. While with African Services Committee, she worked as a program assistant helping with research, evaluation, and management.

Chris Pallaris is the Director and Principal Consultant of i-intelligence. He leads and coordinates the company's research, training and consulting activities in Switzerland and beyond. In addition to his formal duties, Chris serves on the board of the European Open Source Intelligence (EUROSINT) Forum, where he chairs a working group on best practices in OSINT. He is a regular speaker at conferences on security and intelligence.

Jake Perry is a media-everyman with experience in evaluating, directing, and assessing multiple media campaigns across varied mediums. He is also a seasoned researcher specializing in media, corporate, and legal information. His current work concerns new media planning and strategy, social media campaigns and outreach, as well as other technological advances that impact social relations and issues. He graduated with an MA in 2010 from the Graduate Program in International Affairs at the new school in Manhattan while working for the *World Policy Journal* and *Threatened Voices*, an advocacy project of Globalvoicesonline.org. Prior to that he was a Managing Editor at the PenguinGroup, USA, and also worked at Houghton Mifflin in Boston, MA.

Hannes R. Richter is Deputy Director of the Austrian Press and Information Service at the Embassy of Austria in Washington, DC, where he specializes in the intersection of new media, political communication, and public diplomacy. He is also an Austrian Marshall Plan Visiting Research Fellow at the University of California, Berkeley, and a Permanent Fellow with Center Austria at the University of New Orleans. He has taught American government and voting behavior at New Orleans and at the Free University Berlin. He is the co-founder of Campaign Digital Inc., an NGO specializing in new media services in public and cultural diplomacy, and a founding member of the Netzdemokraten, an online political participation group in Berlin. He holds degrees from the University of Innsbruck and the University of New Orleans.

Hannes Steen-Thornhammar was born in Stockholm and has a B.B.A. in Design and Management from Parsons School of Design and an M.Sc. in Information Systems from the London School of Economics. He is currently working as a consultant on social media strategies for businesses in Stockholm, London and New York.

Christoph Stork is Senior Researcher at Research ICT Africa. He holds a Ph.D. in financial economics from London Guildhall University, UK, a Diplom Kaufmann (M.A.) from the University of Paderborn, Germany, and a B.A. Economics from the Nottingham Trent University, UK. He has more than 10 years of research experience in Africa and has led continent-wide household and small business surveys, providing the only multicountry demand-side data and analysis of information and communications technology (ICT) access and usage on the continent, for use by regulators, policy-makers and multilateral agencies such as the OECD and the ITU. His research has informed policies, laws and regulations in the ICT field, specifically in Namibia, where he has provided technical advice to the Namibian Communications Commission and Namibian Government on ICT policy and regulation, including a ground-breaking benchmarking study on interconnection termination rates.

Natalya Sverjensky works in communications and sustainable development and is a graduate of the Design and Management B.B.A. program at Parsons School of Design in New York. Her interests are in the role of IT in corporate social responsibility and political change.

Venkata Praveen Tanguturi, a member of the Deloitte Research team, focuses on cross-industry research and the TMT industry. His main research interests are in real options, investment decisions, technology adoption, evolution of wireless networks, mobile security, strategies, and socio-economic analysis. His work has been published in the *Journal of Telecommunications Policy*, *Journal of Technology in Society*, *International Journal of Mobile Communications*, and by Deutsche Bank. Praveen has a Ph.D. in Technology Management from the Stevens Institute of Technology, New Jersey; a Master's in Telecommunications from University of Pittsburgh, Pennsylvania; and a Bachelor's in Electronics and Telecommunications from the University of Mumbai, India.

Tony Vetter is currently an Associate with IISD's Global Connectivity program, after having been a Project Manager from 2007 to 2010. He has over 10 years of experience in the telecommunications sector, having worked in product manager, technical marketing, and advisory roles at Ciena, Roshnee and Nortel. After completing a Master's degree in international development, Tony launched a new career focusing on the role ICTs can play in achieving sustainable development. Tony now works at Digital Opportunity Trust as their Senior Director, Operations. His research interests include ICTs as a tool for creating educational, economic and entrepreneurial opportunities in developing countries; ICTs and the environment; and ICT governance and innovation for sustainable development.

Eddie Walsh is completing post-M.A. coursework at The Paul H. Nitze School of Advanced International Studies, The Johns Hopkins University. He previously served as a senior consultant on foreign affairs to the U.S. federal government and program manager for cyber security at one of the world's largest software companies. His research interests include the impact of nontraditional security issues on foreign policy.

Daniel Wehrenfennig, Ph.D. is the director of the Certificate Program in Conflict Analysis and Resolution at the University of California, Irvine (UCI). He also directs yearly educational fact-finding trips with Muslim, Jewish, Christian and unaffiliated UCI students and community members to Israel/Palestine (the Olive Tree Initiative). He has produced a documentary film for civic education in Malawi/Africa. His recent work has been published by *Peace Review*, *Communication Theory*, the University of California Press, Lexington Books and *Studies in Ethnicity and Nationalism*.

Deborah L. Wheeler is an assistant professor of Political Science at the United States Naval Academy. She has written extensively on the development and impact of the Internet in the Arab World. She has conducted fieldwork in Kuwait, Oman, United Arab Emirates, Jordan, Egypt, Tunisia and Morocco.

Foreword

Kenneth H. Keller, Director and Professor, Bologna Center and
Paul H. Nitze School of Advanced International Studies, The Johns Hopkins University

One of the challenges for scholars and policymakers in recent years has been to understand the implications of the assertion—really the cliché—that we live in a "technological age." Almost everyone, certainly those in the developed world, experiences in daily life or is at least aware of the manifestations of new scientific understanding and resulting technological developments—the innovations—in devices for communication, computation, and control, in medical care, in energy systems, in military weaponry, in manufacturing, in agriculture and the food supply, to name some of the more obvious examples. Those who have looked more closely at the trends have done so generally within the framework of the dynamics of scientific and technological development, explaining that these innovations are the products of disruptive technologies that have arisen from molecular and cellular understanding of biological phenomena, from the ability to create new materials with unique properties and, of course, from the creative combination of hardware and software, of sensors, computer chips, and signal transmission devices, which we call information technology.

Yet a narrow focus on what new technologies "do" or how they are developed, while clearly important, comes up short in helping us to understand their full impact on society or, as much to the point, the impact of society on the pathways of technology development. Without a more comprehensive look at how significant new technologies affect the social, cultural, and political, as well as the economic aspects of communities, nations, and the relations among nations, we are vulnerable to surprises and we miss the opportunity to make compensating adjustments that leverage the positive aspects of the new developments and reduce the negative aspects. Indeed, we create a situation in which it is easy for the public to become divided into "technophiles" and "technophobes," the utopians and the dystopians, those who believe technology can solve most or all of society's problems, and those who see technology as the fundamental cause of our problems.

The task, then, is to develop a framework for analyzing the interactions between science and technology on the one hand and, on the other hand, the formal and informal institutions of society. The interactions, it is important to emphasize, are bi-directional: technology affects society; society affects technology. When we talk about a comprehensive look at the subject, we mean that we must cast the net wide, looking beyond first-order effects. If information technology changes the ways that people obtain information and communicate with each other, we need to look not only at how that affects more traditional information transmission systems, but also at how it affects the workplace and the marketplace, political organization of a culture, the civic infrastructure of a community, art forms, learning systems, and a society's values from privacy to freedom of speech to freedom of information to intellectual property.

One way of looking at these issues is to categorize them along a spectrum from "technology push" to "societal pull." In the former case, technology is itself the driving force for changing the structure of society—inexorably and deterministically. At the other extreme, it is asserted that the direction of technology development is primarily responsive to the needs and desires of society; societal signals guide the innovations that are made possible by new technologies. However, of course, in almost every instance the reality lies between those extremes and only by examining the trajectory of technology development and societal change from a systemic perspective can we come to understand and, importantly, guide or at least influence that development.

The exercise of examining these interactions can take surprising turns. For example, in the case of information technology, it raises normative questions about such issues as the socially and politically appropriate boundary between public and private spaces, the rights that are associated with privacy, the limits we should impose, if any, on free speech, the structure and regulation of the marketplace, and even the balance of civil rights and national security. When these issues are examined through the lens of international affairs, they come into even sharper focus because they highlight fundamental value differences between otherwise very similar nations, in the very meaning of such concepts as privacy and free speech. We face the quandary of WikiLeaks, the divergence in national treatment of hate speech, and the challenge of virtual, rather than physical, movement of labor across national boundaries.

As many of the articles in this impressive volume point out, one of the recurring themes in the analysis of the influences of information technology is that of power and its shifts between groups and institutions. Although all organizations at every level have access to the new information technologies, the timely availability of information and the ability to organize and analyze it at relatively low (and increasingly lower) cost has, generally, shifted power from governments to other groups and institutions: multinational corporations, nongovernment organizations, epistemic communities, and individuals. Yet it is not always easy to understand the implications of those shifts. For example, in many people's view, the growth of single issue groups has coarsened political discourse by leaving less room for compromise and, in many cases, reducing democratic accountability. Some suspect that the growth of virtual communities has weakened the cohesiveness of physical communities. Although some traditional information intermediaries—newspapers, broadcast networks—may have lost influence, new intermediaries—search engines, blogs, information aggregators—have been enabled by the new technologies, so that the increasing power of individuals may be more theoretical than real. It has been frequently argued that power depends on an "informed public." Historically, the limitation or bottleneck to an "informed public" was access to information, whereas the new limitation may well be the ability to sort through a surfeit of information of varying quality.

Still another recurrent theme is the counterintuitive observation that the more that information gives us the tools of control—over power grids, just-in-time manufacturing, complex derivatives, integrated record systems, the battlefield—the more it makes our society vulnerable to disruptions and instabilities. Thus, we encounter the new security threats and, as a consequence, the blurring of lines between the institutional structures of defense and civic society.

These are only a few examples of the rich landscape examined in this book. It is ambitious and comprehensive, and yet it can be no more than a chapter in what must inevitably be an ongoing examination of the constantly expanding interactions between information technology and society. Where international affairs is concerned, understanding these interactions plays a key role in clarifying how information technology constrains certain diplomatic choices, enables others, and introduces new issues to the international negotiation agenda. In that respect, it is a new subject for leaders and diplomats to address in a "technological age." It is also one that will inevitably grow as other scientific advances and disruptive technologies change our politics, our economy, and our culture, and this volume, insightful and useful in its own right, will serve as a useful model for other efforts in the future.

Preface

It seems to go without saying that information technologies are changing the ways in which states, institutions and people interact. Whether it is the WikiLeaks release of classified U.S. diplomatic cables or Twitter breaking news of humanitarian crises, mobile phones employed to alleviate suffering, Wikipedia's goal of democratizing knowledge, Google's audacious attempt to organize the world's information or a state's creation of malware, parallels are everywhere. Dispelling the hype surrounding information technologies while also challenging dystopian points of view, this collection of studies and viewpoints examines information and communications technologies and international affairs, moving across the spheres of the private, state and global.

Attempting to give a comprehensive view in this fast-changing field is in itself an audacious act. Indeed, in this effort we were reminded of the humbling comment from Friedrich Nietzsche from his "On the Future of Our Educational Institutions," "in order that a future possibly very remote generation may come face to face with that towards which we are blindly and instinctively groping." So, to help us and future generations come face-to-face with the wild world of information technology and international affairs—as it currently stands—we sought to explore such issues as networks and networked thinking, social networks and state power, military modernization, information ownership, digital divides, censorship, neutrality, cyberwars, humanitarian needs, terrorism, privacy and rebellion. As such, the authors in this volume address critical questions of our time, many of which are not yet considered in traditional international relations programs. New scholars will surely surmount present day orthodoxies and this book should help in particular by examining such questions as: what, if anything, is the value of information for states and societies? What differences exist in local and state behavior and policies worldwide and why? How have social networks affected state behavior? How do different types of governments respond to information flows and in what ways have information technologies changed the loci of power? Who owns and regulates information? What constitutes a state's information technology policy? How have information technologies changed national and international security, privacy and free speech? And in what ways are security, the state and information technology intertwined?

From the outset of this endeavor, we intended to create a primer on information technology and international affairs, to be read by scholars, students and lay people with an interest in this emerging and increasingly salient field. It is worth noting that, while this book was developed in a global distributed environment, using networked tools, with people in far-flung places, *physical interaction* and the *face-to-face debate* that ensued were crucial. Without it, this book would not have seen completion. We also recognized that in the digital world, readers now sample books chapter by chapter, on their own. Few read from start to finish. Furthermore, no book on such a fluid topic as information technology could be exhaustive. Taking these realities into account—and like the technologies and forms of communication that we discuss—there are many points of entry into this work and so this book is meant to be sampled.

Our efforts resulted in this book being organized into research chapters and viewpoints that are compiled into three sections: the first section deals with issues of security, defense, and threats to states, such as cyberwar and cyberterror. The second section offers insights into challenges confronting individuals, the body politic, and societies, considering such issues as combating censorship abroad as a pillar of foreign policy or social networks, and regime change and what that might portend. The third section addresses growing challenges, to include the vast amount of information that is being created and the difficulties inherent in using it to solve problems, and the growing and varied "digital divide" that has deep consequences in a world that is ever more IT-centered. Throughout each section, viewpoint chapters add to the discussion by taking positions and making claims—sometimes unconventionally—concerning developments in IT that have markedly affected international affairs. Additionally, each section is preceded by a word cloud that acts as a visual summary.

It is crucial to note that information technology and international affairs share dynamism in common. By the publication date, the pace of change will surely make some of the facts in this volume seem passé, but each chapter was written to consider long-standing concerns. Finally, the IT world does not recognize such designations as junior or senior: awareness makes relevance, and the ability to put thoughts into action is most highly prized. As such, our work has aimed to capture that spirit.

Sean S. Costigan and Jake Perry

Acknowledgments

We are especially thankful to all who made this book possible. At the New School, many people introduced us to new ideas and helped challenge our points of view. In addition to those who authored chapters in this book, we would like to thank Michael Auerbach, Jonathan Bach, Elizabeth Buckley, Stephen Collier, Patrick Corcoran, Max Fraad-Wolff, David Gold, Mansura Khanam, Anthony Lopez, Sandra Nurse, Everita Silina, and Matthew Schwartz. Sean's colleagues and students at the Institute for Foreign Policy Studies, University of Calcutta, contributed numerous invaluable insights. In Kolkata, particular thanks go to Kingshuk Chaterjee and Shantanu Chakrabarti for generously offering the space and time to consider the issues freely with a healthy dose of jocularity and another dose of "biscoots" at the faculty club. Ambassadors Amitava Tripathi and Pram Rath shared their incomparable knowledge during network down (and up) times, and in New York, Peter Dimock and Anne Routon offered solid editorial advice just when it was needed most. This book would not have been possible without the keen editorial vision of Kirstin Howgate, Dymphna Evans and Margaret Younger at Ashgate. Finally, we wish to thank our parents for having the foresight to buy the crazily expensive, new-fangled devices called "home computers" for their children—all without a clear plan for recouping those investments!

Glossary

3G	Mobile Third Generation—International Mobile Telecommunications-2000 (IMT-2000).
4GW	Fourth Generation Warfare—conflict characterized by blurring of lines between war and politics, civilian and soldier (source: Wikipedia).
Botnet	A collection of software agents, or robots, that run autonomously and automatically.
CNA	Cyber network attack.
CND	Cyber network defense.
CNO	Cyber network operations.
DDoS	Distributed denial of service (attack).
Digital divide	The gap between people with effective access to digital and information technology and those with very limited or no access at all.
Disruptive technology	Technological innovation that disrupts an existing market.
e-learning	Comprises all forms of electronically supported learning and teaching.
Flash mob	A group of people who assemble suddenly in a public place.
GIGO	"Garbage in, garbage out."
ICANN	Internet Corporation for Assigned Names and Numbers.
ICT	Information and communication technology.
IGF	Internet Governance Forum.
IMSI	International mobile subscriber identity.
Internetworking technology	Internetworking is a term used by Cisco, BBN, and other providers of network products and services as a comprehensive term for all the concepts, technologies, and generic devices that allow people and their computers to communicate across different kinds of networks (source: SearchNetworking.com).
IO	Information operations.
IP	Intellectual property.
ISDN	Integrated Services Digital Network.
ISP	Internet service provider.
IT	Information technology.
ITU	International Telecommunication Union.
Long tail	The statistical property that a larger share of population rests within the tail of a probability distribution than observed under a "normal" or Gaussian distribution.
Malware	Malicious software.
NCW	Network centric warfare.
OLPC	One Laptop Per Child (Project).
RSS	Really simple syndication.
SaaS	Software as a service.

SCADA	Supervisory control and data acquisition.
SCOT	Social construction of technology.
SIM	Subscriber identity module or subscriber identification module.
SMS	Short message service.
Teledensity	The number of landline telephones in use for every 100 individuals living within an area. A teledensity greater than 100 means there are more telephones than people. Third-world countries may have a teledensity of less than 10 (source: PCMag.com).
Tweet	A post on Twitter.
VoIP	Voice Over Internet Protocol.
W3C	World Wide Web Consortium.
Web 2.0	Term used to describe the evolution of the Web and the Internet in recent years from primarily a desktop tool where users consume information to an interactive platform where they are creating it and contributing their own content. Examples of Web 2.0 are modern blogs and social networking destinations such as Facebook and YouTube.
Wi-Fi	Wireless fidelity.
WIMAX	Worldwide Interoperability for Microwave Access.

PART I

management
military
communication
cyber
security
conflict
attacks
Google
accessed
countries
government
States
United
NCW
ICT
China
computer
networks
non-official
University
one
infrastructure
technology
Online
world
Ireland
Northern
Belfast
international
cyberwar
systems
online
cyberterrorism
transformation
different
York
network
technologies
global
digital
data
Israel
critical
attack
groups
Security
private
Chinese
threat
dialogue
warfare
National
Military
Israel/Palestine
people
Defense
Technology
war
like
cyberspace
power
potential
possible
mobile
threats
Cyber
hackers
individuals
states
militaries
diffusion
May
2001
1999
Jerusalem
Stuxnet
Estonia
operations
important
political
access
phone
research
websites
development
first
social
International
culture
public
around
well
War
April
future
example
must
time
system

Chapter 1
Cyberwar: A Real and Growing Threat

Nat Katin-Borland

> Major cyberspace vulnerabilities will be used against us. For many, the cyber threat is hard to understand. They think that these cyber attacks are unfortunate, but are just a cost of doing business, just a minor nuisance … No one has ever died in a cyber attack, after all, there has never been a smoking ruin for cameras to see. Such reasoning is dangerous. Implicit in such thinking is the unarticulated notion that the only cyber attacks that can happen in the future are those similar to what has happened in the past. (Clarke 2003: 1–2)
>
> Richard Clarke, former Counter-Terrorism Official, U.S. National Security Council

> Like nuclear radiation, cyberwar doesn't make you bleed, but it can destroy everything. (cited by Davis 2007)
>
> Ene Ergma, Speaker of the Estonian Parliament

Introduction

Cyberspace is an ever-expanding global digital network that links many aspects of life, including social, business and military communications. The Internet has collapsed boundaries and empowered individuals in previously unimaginable ways. While new technologies allow for enormous gains in efficiency, productivity and communications, they also create new vulnerabilities and threats for technologically advanced nations and their citizens. Many computer systems around the world are interconnected through mostly public telecommunications infrastructure. Thus, the digital tools used by individuals, companies and states are vulnerable to infiltration by groups seeking to compromise the security of computerized systems. The modern global computer networks that enable instant communication and rapid digital transactions also present a back door into the inner workings of state activities. To penetrate the network of another state is to unlock its secrets and control its critical infrastructure. Today, cyberspace is rapidly becoming both the new battleground for conflicts between states and the next frontier that needs to be secured in the name of national security.

The U.S. military and security services have long incorporated notions of "information warfare" into military doctrine and operational planning. John Alger, a former dean of the School of Information Warfare and Strategy at National Defense University, has written that information warfare "consists of those actions intended to protect, exploit, corrupt, deny, or destroy information or information resources in order to achieve a significant advantage, objective, or victory over an adversary" (Schwartua 1996: 12). An August 2006 directive from the Secretary of Defense (Department of Defense Directive S-3600.1: 3) argues that information warfare "contributes to information superiority by both defending military decision-making from adversary attacks and by influencing and degrading an adversary's decision-making capability, thereby producing an information advantage. [Information Operations] contributes directly to the national security strategy, which uses all elements of national power in a synchronized and coordinated manner to influence adversary perceptions and behavior." The directive continues:

> In peacetime, IO supports national objectives primarily by influencing adversary perceptions and decision-making. In crises short of hostilities, IO can be used as a flexible deterrent option to demonstrate resolve and communicate national interest to affect adversary decision-making. In conflict IO may be applied to achieve physical and psychological results in support of military objectives. During post conflict or stability operations, IO continues to support national objectives and influence foreign perceptions. (DOD Directive S-3600.1: 3)

For the purposes of this chapter, these definitions are rather unhelpful. To begin with, they assume that information operations take place against a specific adversary, in a definable battle space and in conjunction with on-the-ground operations in an actual war. Furthermore, these conceptions of information warfare assume that a clear line can be drawn between wartime and peacetime. I prefer John Arquilla and David Ronfeldt's more fluid notions of cyberwar and netwar: "Netwar refers to information-related conflict at a grand level between nations or societies. It means trying to disrupt or damage what a target population knows or thinks it knows about itself and the world around it. A netwar may focus on public or elite opinion … It may involve, diplomacy, propaganda and psychological campaigns … or infiltration of computer networks and databases" and cyberwar "refers to conducting military operations according to information-related principles. It means disrupting or destroying information and communications systems. It means trying to know everything about an adversary while keeping the adversary from knowing much about oneself. It means turning the 'balance of information and knowledge' in one's favor, especially if the balance of forces is not" (Arquilla and Ronfeldt 1995). Cyberwar and netwar are as much intellectual challenges as they are military classifications. In a cyberwar, success comes to those who embrace the decentralized power of the Internet, challenge existing command hierarchies and "redraw the boundaries around which institutions and their offices are normally built" (Arquilla and Ronfeldt 1995). These terms also imply that, in the digital wars of the future, many conflicts may fall short of actual armies meeting on the battlefield.

In reality, a cyber attack can occur at any time and may not always be associated with political or economic activities or any actual military operations. Additionally, because identity can be concealed so easily online, it is unlikely that the source of an attack will be readily apparent. That being said, as recent U.S. action in Iraq and Russian action in Georgia have demonstrated, it is now common practice to bring down the network of a country prior to invasion with actual ground troops (McWilliams 2003; Danchev 2008). Still, the primary concern of this chapter is cyberwar—actions that use computers and computer networks to inflict damage against the recipient. This is not to imply that causalities cannot occur in a cyberwar. On the contrary, one can imagine a scenario where an attack takes place against a hospital's computer network, for example, and in the resulting chaos patients die as heart monitors go offline and medical records disappear. In a cyberwar, the traditional dichotomies of wartime and peacetime, civilian and military, and battlefield and home front are collapsed. When cyberspace is the battlefield, all members of society can potentially be drawn in. These primarily web-based actions can be perpetrated by a variety of actors—including individual hackers, terrorists, criminal syndicates and states, just to name a few—for a variety of reasons. This chapter focuses primarily on state-centric cyber actions, that is, cyber attacks perpetrated by one state against another.

Unfortunately, it is not a question of *if* a serious cyber attack will occur in the U.S., but a question of *when*. Estonia, for example, has already experienced a mild cyberwar. Each year, the Pentagon fends off tens of thousands of hackers (in 2007, 43,880 "malicious incidents" were reported; Wagley 2008). Even if the vast majority of these incidents were the work of amateur hackers and not foreign governments, there is clearly a vulnerability of crucial digital infrastructure in the U.S. The time to act is now, before the network is seriously attacked. In 1996, the President's Commission on Critical Infrastructure Protection warned,

> In the past we have been protected from hostile attacks on the infrastructures by broad oceans and friendly neighbors. Today, the evolution of cyber threats has changed the situation dramatically. In cyberspace, national borders are no longer relevant. Electrons don't stop to show passports. Potentially serious cyber attacks can be conceived and planned without detectable logistic preparation. They can be invisibly reconnoitered, clandestinely rehearsed, and then mounted in a matter of minutes or even seconds without revealing the identity and location of the attacker. (Denning 1999: 75)

Similar to terrorism, the threat has long been identified, but clear action on cyber security has yet to take place.

This chapter proceeds by first identifying instances of cyberwar, with a focus on the 2007 attacks against Estonia. Then, to emphasize the potential threat of cyberwar, state-sponsored cyber actions against the U.S. will be reviewed. The third section will document how the U.S. has handled cyber security in the past and will discuss new changes by the Obama administration on the cyber security front. Finally, by way of a conclusion, an international cyber security regime will be discussed as a possible way forward for the U.S. and its allies to shore up cyber security and prepare for a potential cyber attack.

From Cyber Protests to Cyberwar

Advanced, post-industrial societies and economies are critically dependent on networked computer information and communication systems. This information infrastructure helps to drive globalization and knit various states together within a globally interdependent economic system (Castells 1999: 10). This economic and social interconnectedness probably acts as a deterrent against more widespread use of cyberwar tactics since bringing down the network of a trade partner does not make good economic sense. The sophistication and importance of the IT infrastructure that modern society rests upon has itself become a form of vulnerability. Disruption of civilian or government infrastructures is an attractive option for countries that want to engage in asymmetric warfare and lack the capacity to compete with larger powers on the traditional battlefield, or for more powerful countries that want to intimidate weaker competitors. Indeed, so important are information infrastructures in the twenty-first century that an attack against them is at minimum considered a strategic strike and potentially an act of war (DeCenso 2000).

To date, many incidents labeled as cyberwar are better characterized as cyber harassment, cyber graffiti or cyber protests. Cyberwar, however, goes beyond the defacement of websites owned by a rival nation or political movement. Instances of website defacement are probably the work of hacktivists (i.e. overzealous hackers responding to political events) and do not necessarily indicate the involvement of government forces. For example, during the Taiwanese presidential elections in August and September of 1999, pro-Chinese hacktivists defaced approximately 165 Taiwanese websites (Jame 1999). Another example is India and Pakistan engaging in cyber protests caused by national and ethnic differences. After a 2000 ceasefire in the Kashmir Valley, hacktivists took it upon themselves to continue the hostilities and pro-Pakistani hackers defaced more than 500 Indian websites (Wallia 2001). A similar flare-up between nationalist hackers from both countries occurred in 2008, with Indian hacktivists actually taking over several low-level Indian government sites, demanding that the sites be made more secure (Barak 2008).

In October 2000, Israeli and Palestinian hackers engaged in adversarial hacking when the prolonged peace talks between the two groups broke down. During this difficult time, hackers from each side seized the opportunity to attack websites belonging to the opposition. Beginning on 6 October 2000, 166 Israeli websites and at least 15 Palestinian websites suffered defacements at the hands of opposing hackers. In this case, the cyber harassment coincided with physical violence in the region, but there is no evidence that governments were behind the actions (Israeli–Palestinian Cyber Conflict 2001: 9). A similar pattern repeated itself with hostilities in 2006 and 2009 (Harwood 2009).

In the past few years, Japan has been targeted several times in online protests. During the first week of April 2001, pro-Korean hackers attacked Japanese organizations responsible for the approval of a new history textbook. The textbook glossed over atrocities committed by Japan during World War II and the occupation of China and South Korea. The perceived reluctance of Japan to accept responsibility for its actions triggered the protests. The main participants in this incident were Korean university students, who used email bombs in a denial of service (DOS) attack. A DOS attack is designed to bring a network to its knees with an overwhelming amount of traffic. The students crashed several websites, including that of Japan's Education Ministry and that of the controversial textbook's publishing company (McMillan 2001). These attacks were neither long-lasting nor organized. In 2001, 2004 and 2008, pro-Chinese hackers targeted Japanese websites after Japan's Prime Minister visited a controversial war memorial (Heike 2009). The worst attacks occurred in 2001, when hackers defaced several websites belonging mostly to Japanese companies and research institutes. Pro-Chinese hackers have become adept at using cyberspace as a platform for protests and cyber civil disobedience, as well as for displaying a strong sense of patriotic nationalism, but these examples do not necessarily point to Chinese government involvement.

In 2007, Russian-sponsored agents began what has been widely called the first "real" cyberwar against Estonia (Farivar 2007). Starting in late April, websites of various Estonian government entities, the nation's largest bank and several media outlets were targeted with heavy DOS attacks, grinding traffic on their network to a halt. The attack was in response to the removal of a bronze statue of a World War II-era Soviet soldier from a public park. Estonian authorities were expecting street protests by citizens of Russian descent, but they were not prepared for sustained cyber attacks against their critical network infrastructure. Attribution for the Estonian attacks was made difficult by the fact that a large "botnet" (short for robotic network) was utilized for the attacks, harnessing the power of thousands of computers located around the world. Eventually, Estonian authorities traced the attacks to various rogue Russian nationalist hackers and several computers inside the Kremlin, pointing to Russian government involvement in the attacks (Farivar 2007). Russian officials quickly denied any role in the cyber attacks against Estonia and warned the Estonian government "to be extremely careful when making accusations" (Landler and Markoff 2007). The use of a botnet and the sustained nature of the attacks against Estonia (they peaked on 9 May, Victory Day in Russia, but continued until 18 May), place the incident several degrees of severity above the cyber protests and cyber vandalism described in other contexts. Botnets are also expensive, making it likely that, even if Russian agents did not participate directly in the attacks, they at least provided financial backing. In addition, there was evidence that Russian agents visited chat rooms frequented by nationalist hackers to incite anger against the Estonian government. These forums contained clear instructions on how to send a DOS attack and which Estonian websites to target (Landler and Markoff 2007). Denis Bilunov, executive director of the United Civil Front, a Russian opposition party, confirmed Estonian suspicions of Russian involvement,

"There is a specific department with the FSB—the successor to the KGB—that specializes in coordinating Internet campaigns against those they consider a threat. They have attacked Chechen rebel sites, us, and now it appears they have attacked Estonia" (Davis 2007).

Another reason why the cyber attacks against Estonia are unique is because of the role the Internet plays in Estonian life. Estonia, or "eStonia" as some citizens prefer, is known as the most "wired" nation in Europe. All citizens have access to free Wi-Fi, voting in national elections happens online and parliamentary and cabinet-level discussions sometimes take place in Internet chat rooms (Davis 2007). Disabling websites in Estonia is not simply a matter of slowing down networks or blocking access to email, but more like a digital invasion that threatens the government's ability to provide essential services to its citizens. Estonian Defense Minister Jaak Aaviksoo explained, "The attacks were aimed at the essential electronic infrastructure … All major commercial banks, telcos, media outlets, and name servers—the phone books of the Internet—felt the impact, and this affected the majority of the Estonian population. This was the first time that a botnet threatened the national security of an entire nation" (Davis 2007). Journalist Tuuli Aug reports the loss of control she felt when the attacks started, "It was extremely frightening and uncontrollable because we are used to having Internet all the time and then suddenly it wasn't around anymore. You couldn't get information; you couldn't do your job. You couldn't reach the bank … It was just confusing and frightening, but we didn't realize it was a war because nobody had seen anything like it before" (Mite 2007). All told, the worst effects of the attack were the economic losses, probably in the millions. Estonia's Hansabank, the nation's largest, reported losses of over $1 million (Mite 2007).

Although Estonia's reliance on the Internet made it vulnerable to sustained cyber attacks, it also meant that the government's response was rapid and professional, facilitated by an informal network from the Internet security community, including a Computer Emergency Response Team (CERT), which assembled immediately for a coordinated response (Kasekamp 2008: 158). Experts were flown in from other countries and firewalls were assembled and monitored around the clock (Davis 2007). Although the DOS attacks overwhelmed many of Estonia's digital defenses, the rapid response probably prevented the damage from being much worse. Estonia's impressive response to these attacks raised their status in the eyes of the international community. NATO allies praised the country for its response to the attacks and established the first NATO Cyber Defense Centre in Tallin, Estonia's capital (DPA 2008). Additionally, Estonian cyber security experts are in demand at military and security conferences around the world. When Georgia suffered cyber attacks from Russian forces during the summer of 2008, Estonia sent in members of its CERT to assist the Georgian government, and even offered its servers to host the Georgian Foreign Ministry's website (Tubalkain-Trell 2008).

Could the U.S. be Next?

From a U.S. perspective, the attacks against Estonia appeared to be a watershed moment. U.S. Homeland Security Secretary Michael Chertoff commented at the time,

> Estonian government websites that usually received 1,000 visits a day were inundated with 2,000 visits a second. This attack went beyond simple mischief. It represented an actual threat to national security and the ability of the Estonian government to govern its country. We face in the 21st century a very difficult problem: a single individual, a small group of people and certainly a nation state can potentially exact the kind of damage or disruption that in years past only came when you dropped bombs or set off explosives. (Espiner 2008)

After Estonia's experience, governments can no longer talk in potentialities.

It is widely agreed by security experts that, at the state level, China is the U.S.'s biggest cyber threat (Bruno 2008). Cyber tensions between the two countries have been steadily on the rise for a decade, gradually moving from relatively harmless cases of cyber vandalism to more serious incidents. Tensions can be traced back to May 1999 after the U.S. accidentally bombed the Chinese embassy in Belgrade, Yugoslavia during the NATO air campaign. U.S. websites were defaced in the name of China and massive email campaigns were executed to gain sympathy and support for the Chinese cause. U.S. government websites were primarily targeted, including the Departments of Energy and the Interior, and the National Park Service, which all suffered web page defacements. In addition, the White House website was taken down for three days after it was continually mail bombed (Denning 2008).

In response to an incident in the spring of 2001 in which a Chinese fighter jet was lost at sea after colliding with a U.S. naval reconnaissance plane, pro-Chinese hacktivists and cyber protesters began a cyber assault on U.S. websites. The attacks also coincided with the two-year anniversary of the Chinese embassy bombing by the U.S. in Belgrade and the traditionally celebrated May Day and Youth Day in China. Led by the uniquely named Honker Union of China, pro-Chinese hackers defaced or crashed over 100 seemingly random websites, mainly with .gov and .com URLs, through DOS attacks and similar measures. Although some of the tools used were sophisticated, they were readily available to both sides on the Internet, and so could not be easily traced back to the Chinese government (Tang 2001). Many rogue postings on U.S. sites included pictures of the dead Chinese fighter pilot and messages calling for the downfall of the United States. Pro-U.S. hackers responded with similar defacements and messages, causing damage to several hundred Chinese websites (Costello 2001). Although an annoyance, these types of attacks were not considered dangerous or out of the ordinary by U.S. officials.

Recently, however, the Chinese have stepped up their activities against U.S. cyber assets. In June 2007, Chinese hackers broke into a Pentagon network that serves the Office of the Secretary of Defense, briefly disabling the system. In the immediate aftermath of the security break, Deputy Under Secretary of Defense Richard Lawless informed the House Armed Services Committee: "Chinese capabilities in this area [cyberwarfare] have evolved from defending networks from attack to offensive operations against adversary networks" (Lawless 2007: 7–8). China's People's Liberation Army (PLA) has had its own cyberwarfare units since at least 2003 and the PLA plans to "reach the strategic goal of building informationalized armed forces and being capable of winning informationalized wars by the mid-21st century" (*China's National Defense in 2006*: Sec. II). PLA cyberwarfare units are both active and highly sophisticated. They are apparently the only PLA units that regularly target enemy military assets in the course of their duties. Pentagon computer security personnel have been monitoring PLA cyber activities for several years, including one instance in 2004 when Chinese cyber agents, traced to a network in Central China, unleashed a "scanner program" on U.S. military computer systems, ripping data from several "secure" systems. The coordination and sophistication of the operation caused several analysts to flag it as the work of the PLA. The hackers "were in and out with no keystroke errors and left no fingerprints, and created a backdoor in less than 30 minutes. How can this be done by anyone other than a military organization?" (Brenner 2005).

In the spring of 2009 intelligence reports indicated that Chinese cyber spies had infiltrated several U.S. electrical grid systems and controls. The goal of the intruders seemed to be to map and document the inner workings of the grid, rather than inflict immediate damage. U.S. authorities investigating the security breach found software tools left behind that could be used to destroy infrastructure components at a later date. A U.S. intelligence official familiar with the investigation noted, "If we go to war with them [China], they will try to turn them on" (Gorman 2009). Officials worry that other critical infrastructure systems such as sewage and nuclear power plants and financial networks are similarly at risk to outside attack. After the infiltration, Director of National Intelligence Dennis Blair reported to Congress, "Over the past several years, we have seen cyber attacks against critical infrastructures abroad, and many of our own infrastructures are as vulnerable as their foreign counterparts. A number of nations, including Russia and China, can disrupt elements of the U.S. information infrastructure" (Gorman 2009). Chinese authorities immediately denied any involvement in the electrical grid security breach. A spokesman for the Chinese Embassy in Washington, DC said the Chinese government "resolutely oppose[s] any crime, including hacking, that destroys the Internet or computer network" and complained that "some people overseas with [a] Cold War mentality are indulged in fabricating the sheer lies of the so-called cyberspies in China" (Gorman 2009).

This discussion of the escalation of cyber activity by the Chinese against the U.S. is not meant to imply that these nations are in a cyberwar. At this time, the simmering cyber feud has not escalated beyond isolated actions by hacktivists and espionage activities that that are fairly common for foreign militaries to mount against each other. It is likely that the U.S. is penetrating PLA firewalls as well, but information on these activities and capabilities is highly classified, so public information is scarce. *Washington Post* defense analyst William Arkin has reported that the U.S. military's "ability to penetrate into enemy computer networks, our ability to exploit communication networks, to manipulate digital information, is real" (Bruno 2008). Rather, the discussion is meant as a reminder that other nations are seeking to penetrate critical U.S. information systems and that they are finding vulnerabilities. The Department of Defense (DOD) reported 43,880 "incidents of malicious activity" against its networks in 2007 alone, a 31% increase from 2006 (Wagley 2008). More recent data indicate that a cyber attack in 2008 caused the DOD to take as many as 1,500 computers offline for an "unspecified" amount of time and that, in the first few months of 2009, the Pentagon has spent more than $100 million "responding to and repairing damage from cyber attacks and other computer network problems" (Associated Press 2009).

The United States and Cyber Security

The U.S. government has long been aware of the danger of vulnerabilities in its information technology infrastructures. In recent decades, the issue of cyber security has waxed and waned depending on world events and political priorities. After gaining momentum in the late 1990s under the Clinton administration, 9/11 and the global threat of terrorism unseated cyberwar as the threat de jour (Vijayan 2008). In the wake of the 2007 cyberwar against Estonia, however, the U.S. seems to be taking the issue more seriously. It is beyond the scope of this chapter to discuss every U.S. initiative to bolster information security, particularly the countless cyber security-focused commands and offices within the intelligence services and military, but there are several important programs worth discussing. The first is the Computer Emergency Response Team Coordination Center (CERT/CC) at Carnegie–Mellon University. CERT/CC was established in 1988 following a major incident on the Internet that disrupted thousands of computers with a particularly vicious worm code (a self-replicating computer code that infects a computer and then sends copies of the virus to other machines on the network). The DOD's Defense Advanced Research Projects Agency, which pioneered the Internet in the 1960s, created the CERT/CC so that the U.S. would be better prepared for future incidents. CERT/CC offers a 24-hour point of contact and acts a central clearing house for information on computer vulnerabilities (*CERT Coordination Center*). Over time,

CERT/CC came to focus on private sector issues, while U.S.-CERT, an independent government agency, focuses on emergency response for U.S. government entities (*U.S.-CERT: About Us*). The CERT model has been replicated in many countries around the world and helps to link a network of security specialists available to respond to cyber security emergencies (*About CERT*).

Another cyber security initiative was the formation of the President's Commission on Critical Infrastructure Protection (PCCIP) in July 1996. The PCCIP was asked to study the critical infrastructures that constitute the life support systems of the nation, determine their vulnerabilities to a wide range of threats and propose a strategy for protecting them in the future (*Protecting America's Critical Infrastructures: PDD 63*). Eight infrastructures were identified as key vulnerabilities: telecommunications, banking and finance, electrical power, oil and gas distribution/storage, water supply, transportation, emergency services and government services. In their final report, issued in October of 1997, the commission reported that the threats to critical infrastructures were real and that, through mutual interconnectedness, they could be vulnerable in new ways.

> Intentional exploitation of these new vulnerabilities could have severe consequences for our economy, security, and way of life ... Physical means to exploit physical vulnerabilities probably remain the most worrisome threat to our infrastructures *today*. But almost every group we met voiced concerns about the new cyber vulnerabilities and threats. They emphasized the importance of developing approaches to protecting our infrastructures against cyber threats *before* they materialize and produce major system damage. (Denning 1999: 75)

In the wake of the PCCIP report, President Clinton released Presidential Decision Directive 63, establishing the National Infrastructure Protection Center and calling on the federal government "to serve as a model to the rest of the country for how infrastructure protection is to be attained" (*Protecting America's Critical Infrastructures: PDD 63*).

Despite early indications that U.S. officials understood the danger cyber threats pose to critical physical and digital systems, a report by the CIA in 2008 revealed that hackers had succeeded in infiltrating electric companies in undisclosed locations inside and outside the U.S., and in at least one instance, shut off power to multiple U.S. cities (Bridis 2008). Scott Borg, director of the U.S. Cyber Consequences Unit, a nonprofit research institute that studies cyber threats commented, "The [U.S.] government is scrambling to try and protect its own systems, to try and check the Chinese from reading government email, but the focus probably needs to be critical infrastructure. That's what we need to defend" (Bruno 2008).

In 2007, the Department of Homeland Security released information documenting 37,258 attacks on government and private networks, compared with only 4,095 in 2005, the first year the agency began tracking such data (Gorman 2008). This prompted President Bush to call on the National Security Agency (NSA) and Homeland Security to coordinate to protect government and civilian communication networks from hackers. Originally unveiled as a $144 million plan in 2008, the White House's 2009 budget called for an additional $6 billion to build a secretive system to protect U.S. communications networks (Gorman 2008). In a recent editorial, *The Economist* speculates that the recent surge in cyber threat "scare stories" has less to do with a real change in the threat pattern and more do with a bureaucratic

> turf war between American government agencies over who should oversee the nation's cyber-security. In one corner is the Department of Homeland Security, which operates the National Cyber Security Center (NCSC), a body set up to coordinate American's various cyber-security efforts. In the other corner is the ... NSA, which thinks it ought to be in charge. At stake are tens of billions

> of dollars in funding promised for a multi-year cyber security initiative. ("Cyberwar: Battle is Joined" 2009)

Adding to the Beltway intrigue, Rod Beckstrom resigned in March of 2009 as director of Homeland Security's National Cyber Security Center, worrying that the NSA's push for a greater role in guarding the government's computer systems could give it the power to collect and analyze every email message, text message and Google search conducted by every employee in every federal agency. Beckstrom indicated that he thought the NSA's sole focus should be on foreign targets, not the U.S. government, "I have very serious concerns about the concentration of too much power in one agency. Power over information is so important, and it is so difficult to monitor, that we need to have checks and balances" (Risen and Lichtblau 2009).

In characteristic fashion, the Obama administration has played its hand close to the vest. Rather than step into the middle of ugly agency turf battles, the White House announced in February 2009 that it was mounting a 60-day interagency review of the federal government's various cyber security programs (Corbin 2009). The Obama team's statement about the review indicated that they were taking the issue seriously, "The national security and economic health of the United States depend on the security, stability, and integrity of our nation's cyberspace, both in the public and private sectors. The president is confident that we can protect our nation's critical cyber infrastructure while at the same time adhering to the rule of law and safeguarding privacy rights and civil liberties" (Corbin 2009). Melissa Hathaway, a former consultant with Booz Allen Hamilton who worked under the Director of National Intelligence in the Bush administration, headed the review. Hathaway's main goal was to coordinate with the relevant agencies, Congress and the private sector to evaluate how the government's cyber security initiatives are being managed, and develop a framework to streamline the fragmented operations. After Rod Beckstrom's resignation in March, Hamilton was promoted to acting senior Director for Cyberspace Security. Although the cyber security review is now finished, Obama's exact plan is still unclear. In a recent public statement, Hamilton admitted that the administration has a lot of heavy lifting to do in shoring up the nation's network security: "Cyberspace won't be secured overnight and on the basis of one good plan. As they say, this is a marathon, not a sprint. But with this review, we have taken the first steps to make real and lasting progress" (Patrizio 2009).

To make matters more confusing, Congress has also become involved in cyber security planning. In April 2009 Senators Jay Rockefeller (D-WV) and Olympia Snowe (R-ME) introduced the Cybersecurity Act of 2009. Echoing early White House efforts in the late 1990s, the legislation seeks to address America's vulnerability to massive cyber crime, global cyber espionage, and cyber attacks that could cripple critical infrastructures by:

> 1) Significantly raising the profile of cybersecurity within the Federal government and streamlining cyber-related government functions and authorities. 2) Promoting public awareness and protecting civil liberties. 3) Remaking the relationship between government and the private sector on cybersecurity. 4) Fostering innovation and creativity in cybersecurity to develop long-term solutions. (Rockefeller and Snowe 2009)

The House easily passed the bill in February 2010 with overwhelming bi-partisan support (Lorber 2010). During his floor speech in support of the bill, Representative Michael Arcuri (D-NY) remarked that, "Investing in cybersecurity is the Manhattan Project of our generation, but this time around we are facing far greater threat. Nearly every high school hacker has the potential to hamper our unfettered access to the Internet. Just imagine what a rogue state could do." Representative

Arcuri also emphasized that, if the U.S. hopes to secure its critical cyber infrastructure, the government has to add more "cyber warriors" to keep up with potential enemies because troops active in cyber security "are every bit as important to our security as a soldier" on a physical battlefield (Lorber 2010).

Although on its face, it seems like a step in the right direction for bringing cyber security issues to the top of the public agenda, civil liberty advocates warn that the Cybersecurity Act lacks privacy safeguards like clear standards or judicial review. The Electronic Frontier Foundation worries about one particularly broad provision that allows the Department of Commerce to gain access "to all relevant data concerning (critical infrastructure) networks without regard to any provision of law, regulation, rule, or policy restricting such access" if a cyber attack is underway (Granick 2009). Besides the obvious civil liberty implications, "it isn't clear whether this provision would require systems to be designed to enable access, essentially a back door for the Secretary of Commerce that would also establish a primrose path for any bad guy to merrily skip down as well" (Granick 2009).

Another bill was recently drafted by Senator Tom Carper (D-DE)—the U.S. Information and Communications Enhancement Act of 2009 (U.S. ICE)—which calls for the creation of "hacker squads to test the defenses of federal agency networks. In addition, agencies would be required to show that they can effectively detect and respond to the latest cyber attacks on their information systems" (Krebs 2009). This is a welcomed step because government agencies are probably much less secure in reality than they are on paper, as criminal and especially state-sponsored hackers are improving their attack techniques far faster than the U.S. government is improving its defenses. Allan Paller, director of research for the SANS Institute, a security-training group, has warned, "Hackers and nation states have more deeply penetrated civilian government agencies and the critical national infrastructure computer networks than the public and most members of Congress have been told" (Krebs 2009). U.S. ICE also calls for a National Office for Cyberspace within the Executive Office of the President, responsible for "achieving an assured, reliable, secure, and survivable global information and communications infrastructure and related capabilities" (Krebs 2009).

Much less is known about the U.S. military's offensive cyber capabilities, which remain highly classified. A recent report in the *New York Times* reveals that there has been a "huge increase in the sophistication of American cyberwarfare" tactics (Sanger and Markoff 2009).

> The most exotic innovations under consideration would enable a Pentagon programmer to surreptitiously enter a computer server in Russia or China, for example, and destroy a "botnet" … before it could be unleashed in the United States. Or American intelligence agencies could activate malicious code that is secretly embedded on computer chips when they are manufactured, enabling the United States to take command of an enemy's computers by remote control over the Internet. That, of course, is exactly the kind of attack officials fear could be launched on American targets, often through Chinese-made chips or computer servers. (Sanger and Markoff 2009)

Issues like government-sanctioned hacking of foreign networks and pre-emptive cyber operations were so thorny that the Bush administration concluded they lacked "the credibility or the political capital to deal with the subject" (Sanger and Markoff 2009).

A 2009 report from the National Academy of Sciences, titled "Technology, Policy, Law, and Ethics regarding U.S. Acquisition and Use of Cyber Capabilities," has concluded that the veil of secrecy that has surrounded cyberwar planning is actually detrimental to U.S. military policy: "Today's policy and legal framework for guiding and regulating the U.S. use of cyberattack is ill-formed, underdeveloped, and highly uncertain. Secrecy has impeded widespread understanding and debate about the nature and implications of U.S. cyberattack" (Markoff and Shanker 2009). As a result, many nuances of cyberwar have remained poorly understood, even as the military actively prepares for it. In a recent war game in April 2009 at West Point, cadets who were computer science and information technology majors competed against "enemy" hackers stationed at the NSA (Kilgannon and Cohen 2009). Mimicking a response to an actual cyber attack, teams were judged by how effectively they identified threats from the NSA hackers and neutralized them. The Pentagon is also reviewing plans for the creation of a National Cyber Range, a replica of the "Internet of the future" that military planners can use to simulate cyber attacks (Sanger and Markoff 2009).[1]

Even with effective models of the Internet and realistic war games, uncertainties remain. One especially problematic issue surrounding cyberwar is the high degree of anonymity of those who carry out such attacks, making it hard to identify the perpetrators. Additionally, cyber operations result in much more uncertain outcomes than even traditional warfare, making it hard to predict success or collateral damage. Early in the Obama administration's tenure, Secretary of State Hillary Rodham Clinton made the most comprehensive effort to date to explicitly warn potential adversaries that cyber attacks would not be ignored. Drawing on the language of nuclear deterrence, Secretary Clinton cautioned: "States, terrorists and those who would act as their proxies must know that the United States will protect our networks. Those who disrupt the free flow of information in our society or any other pose a threat to our economy, our government and our civil society" (Markoff et al. 2010). Clinton, however, did not elaborate how the U.S. would respond, beyond suggesting that countries that knowingly permit cyber attacks to be launched from their territories would suffer damage to their reputations, and could be frozen out of the global economy. In striking contrast to Clinton's blunt warning, the National Academy of Sciences report cautions that traditional notions of deterrence through "enduring unilateral dominance in cyberspace is neither realistic nor achievable" (Markoff and Shanker 2009). This is largely because, in comparison to financing conventional military forces, improving cyber capabilities is relatively inexpensive, so dominance in cyberspace is not reserved for only the world's leading powers.

Stuxnet: The First "Cyber Missile"?

Since it was first discovered in June of 2010, Stuxnet, a highly sophisticated malicious software program, or malware, has created a huge stir throughout the computer security industry (Clayton 2010). Most malware is used by cyber criminals to steal proprietary data such as credit card information and business plans or to harness groups of computers together for use in a botnet. What sets Stuxnet apart and makes it a deadly new breed of malware is that Stuxnet is designed to silently sabotage infected computers. Specifically, Stuxnet targets Siemens software systems, a company that designs operating systems for large industrial facilities like nuclear power plants (McMillan 2010).

Stuxnet worms its way into a computer and looks for very specific Siemens Programmable Logic Controller (PLC) settings, a digital fingerprint that tells the malware that it has found its target, and then injects its own code into the operating system. If Stuxnet determines that the system is not its target, then it moves on causing no damage. Once Stuxnet injects its new code into the PLC device, it causes silent failure of crucial aspects of the plant's systems, such as

1 It is rumored that the NSA already has a similar model of the Internet, but it is on a smaller scale than the system under development by the Pentagon.

centrifuges or heating and cooling systems that are undetectable until the damage is already done. In other words, Stuxnet was not an indiscriminant killer, it was searching for a very specific real-world target, "a cyber weapon created to cross from the digital realm to the physical world—to destroy something" (Clayton 2010). Ralph Langer, a highly respected cyber-security researcher, was one of the first experts to reverse engineer the Stuxnet code. Langer was stunned by what he discovered, "Until a few days ago, people did not believe a directed attack like this was possible … Stuxnet is a 100-percent-directed cyber attack aimed at destroying an industrial process in the physical world. This is not about espionage, as some have said. This is a 100 percent sabotage attack" (Clayton 2010).

Although experts have been able to glean what Stuxnet does once it infects a computer, it remains unknown who created the malware and what its target was. Most security experts agree that Stuxnet is probably the work of a nation-state or at least sponsored by a nation-state. Its code is complex and it was expensive to create. Experts estimate that it took a highly knowledgeable team of eight to 10 people about six months to write the code (Schneier 2010). The malware was then probably rigorously tested in a sophisticated laboratory, pointing towards the work of a skilled and well-financed government agency. Other clues emerge from where the computers infected by Stuxnet were found. Of the 100,000 or so machines reportedly infected by Stuxnet to date, 60% are located in Iran (Halliday 2010). This had led to speculation that Israel or the U.S. unleashed Stuxnet in an effort to sabotage Iran's nuclear facilities. This theory is popular because, in August of 2010, at the height of the Stuxnet infection rate, Iran's Bushehr nuclear processing plant in Natanz was mysteriously taken offline. In November, Iranian President Mahmoud Ahmadinejad seemed to confirm that Stuxnet did in fact infect the Natanz facility when he announced at a press conference that computer code launched by "enemies of the state" had sabotaged centrifuges used in Iran's nuclear enrichment program (Zetter 2010b).

Several prominent features in Stuxnet's code point to Israeli involvement in particular. After all, Israel has long openly speculated about a pre-emptive strike against Iranian nuclear facilities. A 2009 article released by *Israel News*, with no byline, even went so far as to state, "As Iran's nuclear assets would probably be isolated from outside computers, hackers would be unable to access them directly … Israeli agents would have to conceal the malware in software used by the Iranians or discreetly plant it on portable hardware brought in, unknowingly, by technicians" (*Israel News* 2009). Looking back, this article has raised eyebrows as it is widely assumed that Russian contractors operating in nuclear facilities around the world, including Iran, probably unwittingly spread Stuxnet through infected portable USB thumb drives (Halliday 2010).

The first clue implicating Israel involves two file directory names—myrtus and guava—that appear in the Stuxnet code. Some suggest that the name myrtus could refer to the biblical Jewish Queen Esther, also known as Hadassah, who saved Persian Jews from destruction after alerting King Ahasuerus of a plot to massacre them. Hadassah means myrtle in Hebrew and guavas are in the myrtle, or myrtus family of fruit (Zetter 2010a). Another clue lies with a "do not infect" marker in the code. Stuxnet conducts checks on infected machines to determine if it has reached its intended target. If it finds the correct configuration, it executes its program, if not, then it halts infection. One marker that the malware uses to determine if it should cease infection is the numerical string "19790509" (Zetter 2010a). Some researchers suggest that the value refers to a date, 9 May 1979, that marks the day Habib Elghanian, a Persian Jew, was executed in Tehran, which prompted many other Jews to flee the country (Zetter 2010a). While such clues may point to Israel, they could also easily be red herrings planted in the code to increase suspicion of Israel and mask the true perpetrators. The seemingly damning clues could just be coincidences, reinforcing a popular theory, but not actually based in hard facts. Many researchers, for example, believe that "myrtus" could just as easily stand for "my remote terminal units," referring to components contained in the control systems targeted by Stuxnet (Mills 2010). While the true source of Stuxnet remains a mystery, one thing is clear: the age of highly customizable, weaponized computer software capable of hitting specific targets without outside detection has arrived.

A Global Cyber Treaty?

As the U.S. enters the era of cyberwar, it cannot rely on the strength of its conventional military forces to act as an effective deterrent. Certainly, the development of effective cyber security policies and early warning methodologies will be important because of the difficulties inherent in identifying and assessing a sophisticated cyber attack. Differentiating a cyber attack originating from a rival state from accidental factors (such as a surge in demand for certain information on a network), implementation mistakes (such as server errors brought on by human error), or simple cyber vandalism by low-level hacktivists, will not be an easy task. Moreover, even if it is clear that an actual cyber attack is underway, U.S. officials will have to correlate multiple pieces of information, many of dubious quality, to gain a better understanding of the actions involved in the attack and the extent of the damage. As the Estonian experience demonstrated, even a relatively minor cyber attack can degrade network service, data quality and capacity, making rapid response difficult.

Preventative or deterrent measures are frequently untenable in cyberspace, partly because of the ability of attackers to remain anonymous. One of the key issues for decision-makers in the future will be whether cyber attacks lead only to cyber retaliation or to retaliatory actions in the physical world, or both. Notions of escalation and deterrence that were familiar during the Cold War have to be re-examined in light of the new realities brought on by cyberwar and will probably unearth thorny issues revolving around civil liberties and the existing laws of war. The U.S. can also reinforce and isolate essential network services and create firewalls and intrusion detection systems to provide warning in the event of a security breach. Still, numerous dangers remain with a go-it-alone approach.

Former "cyber czar" for the Clinton Administration Richard Clarke warns that the U.S. is more vulnerable than most nations when it comes to cyber security and cyberwar, stemming from several "asymmetrical vulnerabilities" beyond the control of U.S. officials. Clarke outlines four main vulnerabilities:

> First … the United States has a greater dependency upon cyber-controlled systems than potential adversary nations … Second, few nations … have more of their essential national systems owned and operated by private enterprise companies. Third, in no other major industrialized and technologically developed nation are those private owners and operators of infrastructure so politically powerful that they can routinely prevent or dilute government regulation of their operations … Fourth, the U.S. military is highly vulnerable to cyber attack. The U.S. military is "netcentric," bringing access to databases and information further down into the operation of every imaginable type of military organization. (Clarke 2010: 226–7)

Given these asymmetries, Clarke insists that pursuing "cyber peace" should be a U.S. priority.

In the wake of the 2007 cyber attacks, Estonia re-evaluated its cyber security strategy, offering important lessons to U.S. policy-makers and military planners. To reduce vulnerabilities in cyberspace and protect critical infrastructure and information systems, Estonia reorganized their cyber security strategy around four broad principles designed to:

1. improve interdepartmental coordination mechanisms for prevention, rapid response and recovery from attacks;
2. advance legal mechanisms and revise existing laws to support cyber security goals;
3. launch awareness programs on cyber security for the whole society, breaking down barriers between the public and private sectors;
4. enhance international cooperation, promoting cyber security culture and international agreements. (Kasekamp 2008: 171–2)

Estonia's first three principles are certainly wise, but echo strategies that the U.S. is already slowly implementing. The last pillar of its cyber strategy, enhancing international cooperation, however, is worth exploring in more detail. Estonia's cyber strategy recognizes that vulnerabilities and threats overlap in cyberspace. International communications networks are connected through a series of switches and routers, so a serious cyber attack against one country can have far-reaching ramifications.

Threats in cyberspace offer a unique challenge to the international community for several reasons:

- *Absence of traditional borders*: traditional borders separating international and domestic, and external and internal domains are blurred in cyberspace.
- *No clearly demarcated line between public and private spheres*: it is impossible to neatly divide cyberspace between public and private sectors; they are both connected.
- *Collapsed distance and time horizons*: cyber attacks can occur from huge geographic distances, at high speeds, at any time with very little warning.
- *No established rules*: domestic cyber security laws can be uneven and there are few international regulations or global rules established for cyberwar.

The cyber security problem is global and will not be resolved by the efforts of just one state or group of states. The Internet knows no frontiers and attacks may come from distant and undisclosed locations, or out of countries where the regulatory framework is insufficient.

Heli Tiirmaa-Klaar, an official in Estonia's Ministry of Defense, argues, "Securing global cyberspace is possible only if there is general international awareness of the potential threat, and condemnation of cyber attacks that disrupt the normal functioning of society" (Kasekamp 2008: 169). For Tiirmaa-Klaar, the specter of cyberwar mirrors other shared global threats such as terrorism, nuclear proliferation or global warming. "If actors at all levels of cyber threats and vulnerabilities take necessary security measures, it will be possible to shape a more secure global cyber space … In this respect, there is a clear analogy with anti-pollution and environmental issues. In order to achieve a healthier environment, we have created numerous regimes and international laws. A similar regulatory regime is necessary, if we are to cope successfully with the growing threats in cyberspace" (Kasekamp 2008: 169–70).

To date, an international regime to govern cyberspace has yet to emerge. Several regional regimes have been implemented including NATO's Cyber Defense Centre in Tallin and the Council of Europe's Convention on Cybercrime, but these institutions and agreements lack the global reach and norm changing power of a truly international approach.

One of the primary obstacles to establishing an effective international framework for cooperation in cyberspace is that existing alliances such as NATO and the UN are extremely slow in responding to a call to action. The ability and willingness for UN member states to respond to genocide in Darfur is a recent example of this problem. To be truly effective, defense against cyber attack will require an instant response. Still, the UN can begin to encourage international cooperation by creating a clearing house of cyber threat data, similar to what it has created with ReliefWeb (http://www.reliefweb.int), a website that collects key documents relating to humanitarian and emergency response. A so-called "CyberThreatWeb" would act as a central repository for member states to report suspicious activities and attacks on information infrastructure to help effectively monitor growing threats and track and apprehend bad actors. This type of global cooperation would facilitate the creation of best practices on cyber security and response to cyber threats, and open lines of communication between nations to help fill gaps in cyber security, especially in developing countries with nascent IT sectors.

In 2001, the World Federation of Scientists (WFS) first made the case for a "universal order of cyberspace" as the most effective tool to control the threat of cyberwar (World Federation of Scientists 2003: 7–8). The WFS report recommends,

> Because of its universal character, the United Nations system should have the leading role in inter-governmental activities for the functioning and protection of cyberspace so that it is not abused or exploited by criminals, terrorists, and states for aggressive purposes. In particular it should: (a) respond to an essential and urgent need for a comprehensive consensus Law of Cyberspace; (b) advance the harmonization of national cybercrime laws through model prescription; and (c) establish procedures for international cooperation and mutual assistance. (World Federation of Scientists 2003: 15)

This concept has since been elaborated further in a publication from the UN Institute for Training and Research, which makes the argument that cyberspace is part of the common heritage of mankind and that unimpaired access to its benefits is a legitimate and non-negotiable global right (Kamal 2005).

The biggest barrier to a global cyber treaty will be the development of international law to encapsulate cyberwar. It is presently unclear how established international law pertains to cyber attacks and how cyberwar is to be dealt with by the laws of armed conflict (Barkham 2001). The cyber security issue may require re-examination and reinterpretation of the UN Charter, which was not drafted with twenty-first-century cyber threats in mind. A key Charter term in need of clarification is of course "armed attack." A comprehensive Law of Cyberspace could go along way to help iron out these issues within the UN system.

Given these thorny international issues, Richard Clarke envisions a system in which each UN member state is responsible for policing behavior, upholding international standards and insuring "security of their piece of cyberspace" (Clarke 2010: 249). Clarke refers to such an international standard as National Cyberspace Accountability, which in addition to obligating a nation to police their own activity, would also imply an "obligation to assist" (Clarke 2010: 250). This obligation would require participant states to "respond quickly to inquiries in international investigations, seize and preserve server or router records, host and facilitate international investigators, produce their citizens for questioning, and prosecute citizens for specified crimes" (Clarke 2010: 250).

Of course, a global agreement on cyber security will gain little traction if its primary proponents on the international stage are Estonia and the WFS. The U.S. should join this debate and begin advocating for an international compact on cyberspace. This is in the U.S.'s strategic interest as it is likely to be one of the first nations to engage in active cyber combat, both offensively and defensively. Presently, the world is full of failed cyber states, countries that are not dependent on technology to the same degree as the U.S. and have little at stake in the cyberwar debate. These failed cyber states, suffering from corruption, poverty and poor governance, are exactly the locations where cyber threats will grow exponentially in the near future, as terrorist and other nonstate actors increase their cyberwar capabilities. A global cyber treaty would bring developing and failed cyber states into the community of established cyber states, further cementing the global economic and political interdependence that helps to stabilize the current international system. It is much better to confront the thorny issues of global governance of cyberspace in a time of relative cyber peace, when the U.S.'s primary adversaries in cyberspace are still other nations. A global agreement would only serve to augment, not replace, the cyber defense and cyber security planning the U.S. has already begun. The threat of cyberwar is real and growing and the time to act is now.

References

About CERT [Online: CERT]. Available at: http://www.cert.org/meet_cert/ [accessed: 1 January 2011].

Arquilla, J.J. and Ronfeldt, D.F. 1995. Cyberwar and Netwar: New Modes, Old Concepts, of Conflict. *Rand Review* [Online, Fall]. Available at: http://www.rand.org/publications/randreview/issues/RRR.fall95.cyber/cyberwar.html [accessed: 14 April 2009].

Associated Press 2009. Cyber Attacks are Costly for Pentagon. *Los Angeles Times* [Online, 8 April]. Available at: http://www.latimes.com/news/nationworld/nation/la-na-cyber-attacks8-2009apr08,0,6224986.story [accessed: 1 January 2011].

Barak, S. 2008. India and Pakistan Hack it Out Online. *Secure Computing Magazine* [Online, 28 November]. Available at: http://www.securecomputing.net.au/News/129656,india-and-pakistan-hack-it-out-online.aspx [accessed: 1 January 2011].

Barkham, J. 2001. *Information Warfare and International Law on the Use of Force* [Online: New York University School of Law]. Available at: http://www3.law.nyu.edu/journals/jilp/issues/34/pdf/34_1_b.pdf [accessed: 1 January 2011].

Brenner, B. 2005. Titan Rain Shows Need for Better Training. *SearchSecurity.com* [Online, 11 December]. Available at: http://searchsecurity.techtarget.com/news/article/0,289142,sid14_gci1151715,00.html# [accessed: 1 January 2011].

Bridis, T. 2008. CIA: Hackers Demanding Cash Disrupted Power. *MSNBC* [Online, 18 January]. Available at: http://www.msnbc.msn.com/id/22734229/ [accessed: 1 January 2011].

Bruno, G. 2008. The Evolution of Cyber Warfare. *Council on Foreign Relations* [Online, 27 February]. Available at: http://www.cfr.org/publication/15577/evolution_of_cyber_warfare.html [accessed: 1 January 2011].

Castells, M. 1999. *Information Technology, Globalization and Social Development: Discussion Paper No. 114* [Online: United Nations Research Institute for Social Development]. Available at: http://www.unrisd.org/80256B3C005BCCF9/(httpAuxPages)/F270E0C066F3DE7780256B67005B728C/$file/dp114.pdf [accessed: 1 May 2009].

CERT Coordination Center [Online: CERT]. Available at: http://www.cert.org/certcc.html [accessed: 1 January 2011].

China's National Defense in 2006 [Online: China.org]. Available at: http://www.china.org.cn/english/features/book/194421.htm [accessed: 1 January 2011].

Clarke, R.A. 2003. *Major Cyberspace Vulnerabilities will be Used Against U.S. Testimony to the Committee on Government Reform, Subcommittee on Technology, Information Policy, Intergovernmental Relations and the Census* [Online, 8 April]. Available at: http://www.au.af.mil/au/awc/awcgate/congress/clarke_8apr03.pdf [accessed: 1 May 2009].

Clarke, R.A. 2010. *Cyberwar: The Next Threat to National Security and What to Do About It*. New York: Harper Collins.

Clayton, M. 2010. Stuxnet Malware is 'Weapon' Out to Destroy … Iran's Bushehr Nuclear Plant? *Christian Science Monitor* [Online, 21 September]. Available at: http://www.csmonitor.com/U.S.A/2010/0921/Stuxnet-malware-is-weapon-out-to-destroy-Iran-s-Bushehr-nuclear-plant [accessed: 1 December 2010].

Corbin, K. 2009. Obama Calls for Cybersecurity Review. *InternetNews.com* [Online, 10 February]. Available at: http://www.internetnews.com/security/article.php/3801846/Obama+Calls+for+Cybersecurity+Review.htm [accessed: 1 January 2011].

Costello, S. 2001. Analysis: U.S.–China 'Cyberwar' Fires Blanks. *CNN* [Online, 11 May]. Available at: http://archives.cnn.com/2001/TECH/internet/05/11/china.cyberwar.idg/index.html [accessed: 1 January 2011].

Cyberwar: Battle is Joined. *The Economist* [Online, 23 April 2009]. Available at: http://www.economist.com/opinion/displaystory.cfm?story_id=13527677 [accessed: 1 January 2011].

Danchev, D. 2008. Coordinated Russia vs. Georgia cyber attack in progress. *ZDNet* [Online, 11 August]. Available at: http://blogs.zdnet.com/security/?p=1670 [accessed: 1 January 2011].

Davis, J. 2007. Hackers Take Down the Most Wired Country in Europe. *Wired Magazine* [Online, 21 August]: Available at: http://www.wired.com/politics/security/magazine/15-09/ff_estonia [accessed: 1 January 2011].

DeCenso, D.J. 2000. Information Operations: An Act of War? *Air & Space Power Chronicles* [Online, 31 July]. Available at: http://www.iwar.org.uk/iwar/resources/airchronicles/dicenso1.htm [accessed: 1 January 2011].

Denning, D.E. 1999. *Information Warfare and Security*. Reading, MA: Addison Wesley.

Denning, D.E. 2008. The Web Ushers in New Weapons of War and Terrorism. *Scientific American* [Online, 18 August]. Available at: http://www.scientificamerican.com/article.cfm?id=web-brings-new-weapons-of-war [accessed: 1 May 2009].

Department of Defense Directive S-3600.1. 2006 [Online, 14 August]. Available at: http://www.fas.org/irp/doddir/dod/info_ops.pdf [accessed: 1 May 2009].

DPA 2008. Estonia sends experts to Georgia to help combat cyber attacks. *Earth Times* [Online, 11 August]. Available at: http://www.earthtimes.org/articles/show/224942,estonia-sends-experts-to-georgia-to-help-combat-cyber-attacks.html [accessed: 1 January 2011].

Espiner, T. 2008. Estonia's Cyberattacks: Lessons Learned, a Year on. *ZDNet* [Online, 30 April]. Available at: http://news.zdnet.co.uk/security/0,1000000189,39408158,00.htm [accessed: 1 January 2011].

Farivar, C. 2007. Cyberwar I, *Slate* [Online, 22 May]. Available at: http://www.slate.com/id/2166749/ [accessed: 1 January 2011].

Gorman, S. 2008. Bush Looks to Beef Up Protection Against Cyberattacks. *Australian IT* [Online, 28 January]. Available at: http://www.australianit.news.com.au/story/0,23121680-5013044,00.html [accessed: 1 January 2011].

Gorman, S. 2009. Electricity Grid in U.S. Penetrated by Spies. *Wall Street Journal* [Online, 8 April]. Available at: http://online.wsj.com/article/SB123914805204099085.html [accessed: 1 January 2011].

Granick, J. 2009. Federal Authority Over the Internet? The Cybersecurity Act of 2009. *Electronic Frontier Foundation* [Online, 10 April]. Available at: http://www.eff.org/deeplinks/2009/04/cybersecurity-act [accessed: 1 January 2011].

Halliday, J. 2010. Stuxnet Worm is the 'Work of a National Government Agency.' *Guardian* [Online, 24 September]. Available at: http://www.guardian.co.uk/technology/2010/sep/24/stuxnet-worm-national-agency [accessed: 1 January 2011].

Harwood, M. 2009. Hackers Take the Fight Over Gaza Online. *Security Management* [Online, 7 January]. Available at: http://securitymanagement.com/news/hackers- take-fight-over-gaza-online-005063 [accessed: 1 January 2011].

Heike 2009. Chinese hackers deface Yasukuni Shrine website … again. *The Dark Visitor* [Online, 1 January]. Available at: http://www.thedarkvisitor.com/2009/01/chinese-hackers-deface-yasukuni-shrine-websiteagain/ [accessed: 1 January 2011].

Israel News 2009. Wary of Naked Force, Israel Eyes Cyberwar on Iran. *YnetNews.com* [Online, 7 July]. Available at: http://www.ynetnews.com/articles/0,7340,L-3742960,00.html [accessed: 1 January 2011].

Israeli–Palestinian Cyber Conflict (IPCC). *iDefense* [Online, 3 January]. Available at: http://ddanchev.blogspot.com/2006/07/hacktivism-tensions-israel-vs.html [accessed: 1 January 2011].

Jame, F. 1999. China, Taiwan in Web hacking 'war.' *ZDNet* [Online, 11 August]. Available at: http://news.zdnet.com/2100-9595_22-103001.html [accessed: 1 January 2011].

Kamal, A. 2005. *The Law of Cyber-Space: An Invitation to the Table of Negotiations* [Online: United Nations Institute for Training and Research]. Available at: http://www.un.int/kamal/thelawofcyberspace/index.htm [accessed: 1 January 2011].

Kasekamp, A. (ed.) 2008. *The Estonian Foreign Policy Yearbook: 2008*. Tallin: The Estonian Foreign Policy Institute.

Kilgannon, C. and Cohen, N. (2009). Cadets Trade the Trenches for Firewalls. *New York Times* [Online, 11 May]. Available at: http://www.nytimes.com/2009/05/11/technology/11cybergames.html?ref=global-home [accessed: 1 January 2011].

Krebs, B. 2009. Proposal Would Shore Up Govt. Cyber Defenses. *Washington Post* [Online, 27 April]. Available at: http://voices.washingtonpost.com/securityfix/2009/04/proposal_would_shore_up_uncle.html [accessed: 1 January 2011].

Landler, M. and Markoff, J. 2007. Digital Fears Emerge After Data Siege in Estonia. *New York Times* [Online, 29 May]. Available at: http://www.nytimes.com/2007/05/29/technology/29estonia.html [accessed: 1 January 2011].

Lawless, R.P. 2007. *China: Recent Security Developments*. Prepared Statement of the Deputy Under Secretary of Defense for Asian and Pacific Security Affairs before the House Armed Services Committee [Online, 13 June]. Available at: http://armedservices.house.gov/pdfs/FC061307/Lawless_Testimony061307.pdf [accessed: 1 May 2009].

Lorber, J. 2010. House Passes Cybersecurity Bill. *New York Times* [Online, 4 February]. Available at: http://thecaucus.blogs.nytimes.com/2010/02/04/house-passes-cybersecurity-bill/ [accessed: 1 January 2011].

Markoff, J. and Shanker, T. 2009. Panel Advises Clarifying U.S. Plans on Cyberwar. *New York Times* [Online, 30 April]. Available at: http://www.nytimes.com/2009/04/30/science/30cyber.html [accessed: 1 January 2011].

Markoff, J., Sanger, D.E. and Shanker, T. 2010. In Digital Combat U.S. Finds No Easy Deterrent. *New York Times* [Online, 26 January]. Available at: http://www.nytimes.com/2010/01/26/world/26cyber.html [accessed: 1 January 2011].

McMillan, R. 2010. Was Stuxnet Built to Attack Iran's Nuclear Program? *PC World* [Online, 21 September]. Available at: http://www.pcworld.com/businesscenter/article/205827/was_stuxnet_built_to_attack_irans_nuclear_program.html [accessed: 1 January 2011].

McMillan, S. 2001. Cyber Attackers Remind Japan of its Infamous Past. *The National Business Review* (4 April).

McWilliams, B. 2003. Iraq's Crash Course in Cyberwar. *Wired Magazine* [Online, 22 May]. Available at: http://www.wired.com/politics/law/news/2003/05/58901?currentPage=2 [accessed: 1 January 2011].

Mills, E. 2010. Stuxnet: Fact vs. Theory. *CNET News* [Online, 5 October]. Available at: http://news.cnet.com/8301-27080_3-20018530-245.html [accessed: 1 January 2011].

Mite, V. 2007. Estonia: Attacks Seen as First Case of "Cyberwar." *Radio Free Europe/Radio Liberty* [Online, 30 May]. Available at: http://www.rferl.org/content/article/1076805.html [accessed: 1 January 2011].

Patrizio, A. 2009. Obama's Cybersecurity Reviewer: Long Road Ahead. *InternetNews.com* [Online, 22 April]. Available at: http://www.internetnews.com/government/article.php/3816846/Obamas%20Cybersecurity%20Chief%20Long%20Road%20Ahead.htm [accessed: 1 January 2011].

Protecting America's Critical Infrastructures: PDD 63. 1999 [Online: U.S. Department of Justice]. Available at: http://www.usdoj.gov/criminal/cybercrime/factsh.htm [accessed: 1 January 2011].

Risen, J. and Lichtblau, E. 2009. Control of Cybersecurity Becomes Divisive Issue. *New York Times* [Online, 17 April]. Available at: http://www.nytimes.com/2009/04/17/us/politics/17cyber.html [accessed: 1 January 2011].

Rockefeller, R. and Snowe, O. 2009. *Chairman Rockefeller and Senator Snowe Introduce Comprehensive Cybersecurity Legislation*. U.S. Senate Committee on Commerce, Science and Transportation [Online, 1 April]. Available at: http://commerce.senate.gov/public/_files/Cyberbillsummaryonepagerplusthreepagesummarypressrelease1Apr090.pdf [accessed: 28 April 2009].

Sanger, D.E. and Markoff, J. 2009. U.S. Steps Up Effort on Digital Defenses. *New York Times* [Online, 28 April]. Available at: http://www.nytimes.com/2009/04/28/us/28cyber.html [accessed: 1 January 2011].

Schneier, B. 2010. Stuxnet. *Schneier on Security* [Online, 7 October]. Available at: http://www.schneier.com/blog/archives/2010/10/stuxnet.html [accessed: 1 January 2011].

Schwartua, W. 1996. *Information Warfare*. New York: Thunder's Mouth Press.

Tang, R. 2001. China–U.S. Cyber War Escalates. *CNN* [Online, 1 May]. Available at: http://archives.cnn.com/2001/WORLD/asiapcf/east/04/27/china.hackers/index.html [accessed: 1 January 2011].

Tubalkain-Trell, M. 2008. Super Cyber Villains. *The Baltic Times* [Online, 11 September]. Available at: http://www.baltictimes.com/news/articles/21332/ [accessed: 1 January 2011].

U.S.-CERT: About Us [Online: U.S.-CERT]. Available at: http://www.us-cert.gov/aboutus.html [accessed: 1 January 2011].

Vijayan, J. 2008. Obama Administration to Inherit Cybersecurity Challenges. *IDG News Service* [Online, 20 November]. Available at: http://news.idg.no/cw/art.cfm?id=BA5D79CA-17A4-0F78-31AE05464647DF69 [accessed: 1 January 2011].

Wagley, J. 2008. Foreign Hackers are Overwhelming U.S. Government Computers, Says Analyst. *Security Management* [Online, 19 December]. Available at: http://www.securitymanagement.com/news/foreign-hackers-are-overwhelming-u-s-government-computers-says-analyst-005019 [accessed: 1 January 2011].

Wallia, K. 2001. Indians, Pakistanis Play Patriotic Games on Net. *The Times of India* (6 January).

World Federation of Scientists 2003. *Toward a Universal Order of Cyberspace: Managing Threats from Cybercrime to Cyberwar*, Permanent Monitoring Panel on Information Security [Online, August]. Available at: http://eproceedings.worldscinet.com/9789812702753/9789812702753_0044.html [accessed: 1 January 2011].

Zetter, K. 2010a. New Clues Point to Israel as Author of Blockbuster Worm, or Not. *Wired Magazine* [Online, 1 October]. Available at: http://www.wired.com/threatlevel/2010/10/stuxnet-deconstructed/ [accessed: 1 January 2011].

Zetter, K. 2010b. Iran: Computer Malware Sabotaged Uranium Centrifuges. *Wired Magazine* [Online, 29 November]. Available at: http://www.wired.com/threatlevel/2010/11/stuxnet-sabotage-centrifuges/ [accessed: 1 January 2011].

Chapter 2
From an Analog Past to a Digital Future: Information and Communication Technology in Conflict Management

Daniel Wehrenfennig

Introduction

Global transformations in the last decades have been closely connected with technical evolution (Dicken 2003; Held et al. 1999). Advances in communication technology have led to increasing worldwide reach and connectivity, and mobile phone technology has led to more mobility. This has triggered many changes in socialization and communication patterns in today's so-called Network Society[1] (Castells 1996), and consequently in the existing conflict environments. Modern information and communication technologies (ICT) hold much potential to be used positively to enhance conflict management[2] practices. However, they also have limits. Nevertheless, conflict management approaches and practices have only recently started to make more use of the new communication capabilities, with varying degrees of success. Owing to the recent development and the generally lacking analysis of these developments, few case studies have been done on this issue, especially in the realm of citizen or nonofficial conflict management. More recently analysis is emerging on the role of professional news media in conflict environments (Gilboa 2006). For the most part it shows the challenges to traditional diplomacy and the attempts of adaptations by official actors through digital diplomacy, or net diplomacy (Bollier 2003). However, the use of ICT in nonofficial conflict management has been hardly studied.

Therefore the focus of this chapter will be to study and evaluate the early use of modern ICTs in citizen peace-building and conflict management. Starting (1) with a more general theoretical discussion of the changes, chances and challenges in the developments of ICT to show the relevance for today's conflicts and their resolution, this will be followed by a discussion of (2) examples of ICT usage in incidental, indirect and direct conflict communication based on field research in Northern Ireland and Israel/Palestine. The purpose of these examples is to show the use of ICT in conflict management. This leads into (3) the evaluation, which will take a more aggregated perspective on ICT use and impact on nonofficial conflict management in both case regions. In order to do this, a framework of conflict levels and stages to analyze the ICT in the specific conflict

1 A further development from the earlier notion of the *Information Age*, with, however, stronger emphasis on the impact of changes on today's societies and their organization.

2 When using conflict management in a general definition the author is alluding to a very broad definition of dealing with any kind of conflict environment, acknowledging the different pre-, current and post conflict and violence stages and the often used categorization of, for example, conflict prevention or resolution, which will be discussed more in depth in the evaluating chapters and the conclusion. However, the focus of this chapter will be on nonofficial actors and groups and less on official diplomacy or professional media, two areas that also have been changed dramatically by the emergence of new ICTs.

context of Northern Ireland and Israel/Palestine will first be established. Finally, the gathered information on the ICT changes in the region, the ICT uses for nonofficial conflict management and the expectations based on the conflict phase will be combined, in order to come to a final evaluation and to shed some light on the strengths and the weaknesses of ICT usage for nonofficial conflict management and citizen peace-building purposes in current conflict environments.

Although this chapter mainly concentrates on the possible positive changes the use of ICTs can bring to conflict environments, the author is aware of the negative side to this development as well. For two reasons this will not be a major part of this chapter and will be only briefly discussed. First, the interviews focused on the positive use of ICTs and their degree of success and applicability (based on the questions asked—see Appendix). Second, to further discuss the possible negative impact of ICTs on conflict environments would require significant broadening of the theory and analysis of this chapter, which is a worthwhile effort but beyond the context of this work.

Changes and Chances

Within the last decade, there has been an enormous transformation in the way people socialize and communicate, driven or manifested by technical evolution and progress, especially in the telecommunication sector. Modes of communication have important consequences for society (Deibert 1997). Telecommunication has expanded dramatically, further manifesting its social networking status and power around the world (Barabasi 2003). Regardless of the discussion of whether technical determinism shapes society and speeds globalization or vice versa (Preston 2001: 110), most researchers seem to agree that these changes in ICT initiate new forms of interaction and create new kinds of relations and power structures between participants (Poster 2001: 100–1). This then defines the framework for future political and cultural developments (Preston 2001: 121). At the same time, it affects social, political and personal interaction. Thus, ICT also strongly affects existing conflict situations in their varying stages around the world and, consequently, impacts the models and practices of conflict prevention, management and resolution. This provides, at least theoretically, new chances for positive engagement on different levels.

Increasing Capacity and Connectedness

The explosive growth of governmental and trans-governmental communication and interaction, as well as nongovernmental interaction, brings many opportunities and challenges to conflict management (Held et al. 1999). These networks are extensive and highly active on a day-to-day basis, facilitated increasingly by electronic communication, which dramatically alters the nature of political communication and gives rise to new network capacities and developments (Held et al. 1999).

> The new communication systems create new experiences, new modes of understanding and new frames of political reference independently of direct contact with particular people or issues. (Meyrowitz 1985: 7)

Previously existing hierarchies and privileges are called into question through the new horizontal and vertical connectedness and capacities of these networks (Barabasi 2003: 162–9, 201–4, 233; Lederach and Jenner 2002: 40). This development has challenged and in part changed the communication and organization culture in traditional diplomacy and conflict management from vertical paradigms toward more horizontal connectedness, and dramatically increased the numbers and capacity of nonofficial actors and groups. The new media work as an integrating force, providing new platforms of involvement in forms of Habermasian political and cultural digital public spheres, centered around open-access egalitarian and transparent debate (Preston 2001: 94–100, 209). This in return leads to potentially more participatory societal structures—empowering and including disenfranchised groups to contribute to peace-building (Avnon). One can already see this development in the mobilization and empowerment of international groups and individuals (global civil society). It can also be observed in local groups in the area of crisis monitoring, where critical developments are made instantly available to the global community through various forms of ICT (Deibert 1997: 79). Internet chat rooms and blogs as well as private websites have become major news sources, often providing faster and sometimes more reliable information than the major news services (e.g. during the Iraq War). Furthermore, the Internet as a tool for democratization has had a major impact on secluded societies and has invoked desperate reactions by the reigning regimes (e.g. Iran and China). The technical capacities today have altered the power of governments[3] and the military to contain and control crisis and conflicts. This, in many ways, has made conflict situations more transparent and has opened up new ways of support and intervention, especially powerful alliances between official and unofficial actors[4] (Bollier 2003: 16–26). However, this uncontrolled rise in capacity also increases the chances for more chaos (Cincotta 2002).

Global Reach and Proximity

Through expanding networks and global connectedness, the world has become a smaller place. The vision of McLuhan and Powers (1989) of a global village seems to be becoming true. Telecommunication networks are expanding around the world even faster than computer networks (Preston 2001: 214–15) and telecommunication activities have increased immensely everywhere (cf. data in Held et al. 1999: 344). In particular, mobile communication through satellites is now able to reach areas in the world that cannot yet be reached by conventional phone lines. This development carries with it the chance to bring the world together.

> In the more optimistic, utopian variant, new ICT based developments are leading to a much more open and egalitarian communication system and culture defined around greater individual freedom, reflexivity and expression. (Preston 2001: 216)

Through global communication capacities, new forms of conferencing and "meetings" are possible. Phone conferences (sometimes accompanied by real time digital videos) have become a very viable form of interaction (Held et al. 1999: 19). People working and living in remote societies do not need to travel to communicate with people elsewhere in the world anymore; it can be done through telecommunication, creating a distant proximity (Rosenau 2003). One can handle

3 David Bollier remarks, "diasporic communities around the world affect the internal politics and external policy positions of their homeland through emails and websites. The rapid transmission of news directly from the source allows world players to bypass formal diplomatic channels, requires quicker and perhaps less considered responses by government officials and enables NGO's to express and impress their positions more widely" (Bollier 2003).

4 A great example of this capacity is newly founded Peace NGO Forum in Israel/Palestine, connecting over 120 peace NGOs from both sides with each other, including 12 bi-partisan organizations (Baskin, Husseini, Perlman).

a situation without being physically present ("absent presence"), which becomes very attractive in the context of the physical separation and segregation characteristic of many conflicts today. Even if this form of communication is not as strong as face-to-face meetings, through the digitalization of our world, it has become more and more credible and is increasingly adopted as a "normal"[5] form of communication (at least in the Western networked society). This can provide new possibilities for conflict management through better observation and communication technology. Thus, the potential is there for conflict management approaches to immensely benefit from the new ICT capacity to globally connect people and to create a distant proximity between them by overcoming physical constraints and drawing in global attention and expertise. ICTs can be very helpful when used constructively.

Total Accessibility and Immediate Response

Mobility has become the highest commodity in our media age. It is part of the global paradigm but also results from the immense privatization of technology, especially through the spread of the mobile phone. The mobile phone is a communication device that normally travels very close to its owner and is everywhere that he or she is (Katz and Aakhus 2002: 194). Today, people can be reached at all times and everywhere, or can access information[6] themselves at any time—at least this is what people believe. This paradigm has changed our communication habits and expectations (Katz and Aakhus 2002: 182), and has also influenced the way people communicate in conflict situations. Through the multiple connectednesses of actors' rapid reporting of events, incidents and catastrophes can generate almost immediate regional or global ramifications (Poster 2001: 59). This allows for immediate reaction and intervention. From a preemptive perspective, it has the potential to hinder the outbreak of a conflict or crisis when signs of rising tension can be detected earlier and response applied faster. Accessibility of the right people and a quick response can hinder potential crises or limit their effect by providing assistance or starting appropriate counter-actions.

Perpetual Communication

Increasing connectedness through new technologies, with the new level of accessibility, has increased the dynamics of daily communication. Communication in the network society has become more flexible and faster but also shorter, which might be a form of reaction to the information overload discussed earlier. Katz and Aakhus call this phenomenon "perpetual contact"; people are in a mode of "perpetual communication," organizing their lives by brief communications. This is the day of the "Instant Messaging" generation, where short and precise messages by email, instant messenger, mobile phone (Blackberry) or pager structure people's lives. In particular, the younger generations increasingly rely on personal technological devices like mobile phones to define themselves and create social circles (Holson 2008). Communication seems always available, so people communicate more often than they used to, but the communication is briefer. According to Katz and Aakhus, mobile communication in particular has become an "instrument for managing practical affairs. The mobile phone is praised as a means to handle or avoid the emergencies and

5 New studies have shown that, especially for younger people, the media reality of chat-rooms, platonic web-contacts in Facebook, etc., is not much different from the reality of physical contacts.

6 As Mark Poster describes, "information is now instantly available all over the globe and may be stored as long as electricity is available" (Poster 2001: 3).

crises that otherwise disrupt the smooth flow of every life [and has become] a means to facilitate the planning and coordination of everyday matters" (Katz and Aakhus 2002: 5).

This creates new opportunities for conflict management practices to efficiently connect conflict parties. The new technologies, which train us in brief and precise communication, can also increase social performance and decrease misunderstanding if used wisely.[7] Perpetual contact serves the need of the fast and multi-connected world in the network society. However, can it substitute for or enhance the needed human component of conflict management? Another question is whether perpetual communication in blogs, chat rooms or on the mobile phone (e.g. text messaging) can generate similar bonding or transforming emotions to face-to-face interaction, since this remains one of the main means of conflict management? The use of perpetual communication through ICTs is becoming a major part of daily societal organization and interaction, and provides many potential benefits to better and faster deal with differences and misconceptions.

Some of these propositions, predictions or questions maybe seem to be far-fetched or very Westernized. This is probably true, given that most studies on developing trends are conducted in the context of the more developed countries in the West and are very often from a hyperglobalist perspective. However, historically there is a strong indication that these trends in the more developed countries will also replicate themselves in less developed parts of the world, but in varying degrees. In the context of a more globalized world, these developments are already affecting current conflict environments (and former ones) as the following analysis of ICT usage in nonofficial conflict management practices in the case of Northern Ireland and Israel/Palestine will show.

Challenges

Even though this chapter is about the use of modern communication technology for nonofficial conflict management, the other side of the coin needs to be discussed at least briefly. Thinking through the theoretical potential of ICTs can also reveal the potential downside.

> Growing interconnectedness may be both a source of intense conflict (rather than cooperation) as well as a product of shared fears and deeply held animosities. (Held et al. 1999: 28)

Increased interconnectedness through modern communication can create resistance, especially when it happens almost exclusively on an in-group level.[8] Such use can bring forth or exacerbate animosity to the others, further alienating people and groups from each other (Castells 2001: 65–7). Besides the use of ICTs (especially websites) for untouchable terror mobilization, the technology is also massively used by resistance movements worldwide.[9] Furthermore, new capacities built by empowering nonstate actors in particular through ICTs can also lead to a void of power and structures (Bollier 2003: 25–7) which can be dangerous because it limits the sometimes necessary

7 Business experiences have shown that the use of more condensed, shorter and immediate modes of communication has decreased misunderstanding and increased creativity and performance.

8 An example has been the decision of the Palestinian Non-governmental Network to stop all people-to-people programs with the start of the Second Intifada, which had a final detrimental effect on the peace work in the region, forcing most of the last organizations to abandon their work (Zoughbi).

9 In the case of Palestine, the formation of rapid response and resistance is one of the major ways that mass-mobile communication is used, getting people to create barricades and act as "human shields" against approaching Israeli army troops (Rishmawi). This has often caused the Israeli army to suspend cell-phone reception in certain areas at times.

ability of governments to intervene (Cooper 2002). In terms of global reach and proximity, the flipside is a potentially growing digital divide (May 2002: 88–92; Preston 2001: 216–20) between those who have access to modern information technology and those who are left out (Cincotta 2002: 8; May 2002: 88–92). This could create a critical new global and inter-societal bi-polarity between people and groups that are connected and the ones who are left out (Schuler and Day 2004: 61–5). In terms of total accessibility and fast response, immediate reaction by a multitude of parties can also complicate conflicts by adding more unpredictable and uncontrollable reactions (Bollier 2003: 38). Wrong or misleading information, often solicited through modern communication (websites, blogs, email, text messages) provokes direct reaction and consequences. As Madeline Albright notes: "You don't know to whom you are really speaking, I mean, just send out words, and you don't know how they will be taken" (Bollier 2003: 31).

Conflict parties are often forced to react instantly and to deal with the pressure coming from all sides as a consequence of information appearing in the global networks, without having time to counter-check or verify the information given to them. This opens up new power for the intentional misuse of communication and propaganda, potentially hurting the peace process more than positive ICT use could help it (Gilboa 2006). When thinking of perpetual communication, this seems to be the other major negative point, besides the potential inability to bring out the human dimension. In fast, perpetual communication, information often lacks depth and is usually not well researched. How can one assess the reliability of all these new sources, which are often the basis of far-reaching political and social decisions (Bollier 2003: 10)? Given that perpetual communication structures do not just decrease the quality but also increase the quantity, this can lead to a total overabundance of this type of communication. People may feel unable to deal with the information overload (Barabasi 2003: 114–19; Rosenau 1999: 8) and are potentially less informed (or their information is more overly specialized) than before. This is a structural dilemma that is difficult to solve (Lederach 1997: 130–33).

Thus, is has to be acknowledge that there is also a flipside to new communication technologies that is already being exploited by people and groups to cause more conflict. However, that is not very surprising. Throughout history, extremists have always understood the power of new media and communication to shape opinion and to mobilize the masses (e.g. the propaganda machine in the Nazi reign), which, in a weird sense, supports the claim for the huge potential of ICTs in conflict management.

Case Studies

Field research in Northern Ireland (2005, 2008) and Israel/Palestine (2006, 2007, 2008) resulted in about 120 interviews with conflict management experts and groups (see the list of participants in the Appendix, pages 44–8). A major part of each semi-structured interview dealt with the importance of ICT in conflict management and discussion of the strengths and weaknesses of these approaches (see interview questions in the Appendix, page 43). The following analysis is based on these preliminary interviews as well as further information acquired about the usage of ICTs in nonofficial conflict management and citizen peace-building approaches. Instead of discussing all ICT applications found,[10] and to provide a better overview, some exemplary applications are introduced that stand for whole groups of similar usages of ICTs in nonofficial conflict management

10 Which even in the context of the many direct and indirect data and examples I have acquired will still be incomplete and only give partial justice to the whole topic.

and citizen peace-building. Therefore this analysis is divided into three parts, each representing a different intentionality in the use of ICTs and their applications. This differentiation is important to better understand the chosen application of ICTs and to better put its strengths and weaknesses into context.

Incidental Communication

The first category of approaches is the most difficult, even though there is much potential for it. It is labeled incidental communication, meaning an irregular use of ICT for conflict management and peace-building purposes. This kind of ICT usage is more sporadic and occasional, used to warn the other side or acquire important information. It has been frequently used in diplomacy, where diplomats or government leaders use "emergency-channels" of communication to de-escalate situations. The most famous example is the creation of the "red-phone" between the White House and the Kremlin as a consequence of the Cuban missile crisis. Other examples can be found in the early warning literature and its practices, applying mechanisms (technology applications) to deal with famine, genocide and other fast-erupting crises mainly in Africa and East Asia (CEWARN/IGAD Report 2000). Through modern communication capabilities, ICTs have been used in the cases noted, although only rarely and without much documentation. However, with the emergence of ICTs and their application in the private sectors and lifestyles of people living in conflict zones, especially the rise of private computing and mobile telecommunication, more unofficial forms and usage of ICTs in conflict management and peace-building can be found.

Pre-emptive Communication: Mobile Phone Interface Network, Belfast A major example in the Northern Ireland conflict was the use of mobile phone networks between Protestant and Catholic neighborhoods (often called Interfaces) in and around the Shankill and Falls Road in Belfast in the 1990s. The first Interface network was set up in north Belfast in the summer of 1997. Nongovernmental organizations (NGOs) equipped community leaders and members on both sides with mobile phones and trained them to preemptively inform the other side when tension was rising in one's own group (O'Halloran, Magowan). Community leaders on each side of the interface contacted each other to obtain information on what was happening (e.g. a noise might be just a kids' party where they are setting off fireworks, and not an attack, or some people may have got drunk in a local pub, gone over to the other neighborhood and started provocation). This simple, incidental de-escalation communication was so successful that it seriously decreased tension on both sides in many incidents and then turned into what Chris O'Halloran (director of the Interface Project in Belfast) calls arms-length communication, periodic secret and private communication between the community leaders on both sides of the Interface in order to decrease tension and to inform each other on the current issues and changes in each community.

> Essentially a phone network is a way of creating the beginning of trustful relationships … the main thing we have been seeing that helps the people here is to understand the situation they are living in and that means to gather factual information about the conflict. (O'Halloran)

This de-escalated many crisis situations before they happened and ultimately changed attitudes of the two sides towards each other. The success of these mobile phone networks was not well received by either Protestant or Catholic paramilitaries, which capitalized on the tension between the communities. Some tried to discourage the use of the mobile phone networks and in some cases initially confiscated the mobile phones (Magowan). However, this tension was soon overcome and today basically all interface areas in Belfast now have mobile phone networks, some with a long-standing history of excellent interaction and communication (O'Halloran). Mobile phone networks are as small as three on three, or even two on two, or as large as 12. For the smaller networks, phones are often provided, while members of the larger networks often use their own phones and receive refunds of their phone bill (O'Halloran). However as O'Halloran emphasizes, these mobile phone networks should not stand alone but need to be reinforced by personal face-to-face contacts.

Back-channel Communication A similar use of ICTs for early warning purposes is a standard procedure between security experts in many crises. Because the stakes are so high and a major incident can destabilize a whole region, security experts engage in incidental back-channel communication to warn of coming events or to offer information on events that have taken place. In Israel/Palestine, with its legacy of suicide attacks and army invasions, this communication is often used to hinder the outbreak of a bigger crisis (Alpher). Because of the need for immediacy, this communication is mostly done through ICTs.

Back-channel dialogues in general are some of the most secret and ongoing dialogues in most conflicts, and make much use of ICTs, which overcomes the challenges of being seen to openly communicate with the enemy. This was true for dialogue between the paramilitary leadership and the British government in the Northern Ireland conflict (Duddy, Oliver), and is true today for the Palestinian Liberation Organization (PLO), Hamas, the Israeli government and the security apparatus (Nusseibeh). These dialogues are by nature secret and occur "on a basis that their existence could be denied" (Tonge 2002: 146), which again makes ICTs a key instrument. In the Northern Ireland context, all key back-channel dialogues[11] were mostly face-to-face, but early phone communication served as an important element to organize and follow up on these meetings. However, today, with increasing technical capabilities and changing technology perception (e.g. truthfulness), whole back-channel talks might be digital (Baskin). Yet back-channel talks are not limited only to key actors; they have also been increasingly adopted by nonofficial actors, including personal exchanges by community and religious leaders as well as neighborhood talks, which with the existence of mobile phone networks today are getting increasingly easier (Yellin).

Event Coordination: Orange Marches in Northern Ireland and Religious Holidays in Israel/ Palestine Incidental communication can also be found in the context of planned events that need a flexible reaction structure. This followed years of clashes at the Orange Marches in many Northern Ireland cities, especially in Derry and Belfast. In addition to many other preemptive de-escalation measures, like avoiding certain roads and areas and pre-event talks with radicals on both sides, incidental communication is used during the event itself (Conere, Hewitt). Because emotions change very quickly and uncooperative groups still enter the picture, leaders on both sides as well as the security apparatus have established mobile communication networks to inform and react very flexibly, avoiding major clashes and surprises. This is at least one reason (besides a general de-escalation) for the recent peaceful history of the marches in Northern Ireland.

Other uses of incidental ICT for preventative purposes include privately run radio programs (and in some cases even TV programs) in Israel/Palestine before the major religious holidays of all the religions in the regions, using ICT to raise awareness and educate the general population on the

11 Between IRA leadership and British Government facilitated by Brendan Duddy ("The Link") starting in the 1970s, between Irish and British Government facilitated by Father Alex Reid from the late 1980s and later in the 1990s civil society and paramilitaries dialogue facilitated by Professor Paul Arthur and others.

traditions and rituals involved, to avoid misunderstanding and bewilderment as well as to support more inter-group understanding (Weissman).

Further examples of ICT use in incidental nonofficial conflict management practices can be found in oral accounts of many activists in both cases. In particular, people living in areas affected by violence, such as the rocket and fighter attack-stricken cities of Gaza and Sderot in Israel/Palestine, are often more involved in this kind of communication to check up on each other's well-being (Zion).

Indirect Communication

The difference between indirect communication and incidental communication is the fact that it is not sporadic but permanently accessible. Because of this, we only find this kind of ICT usage in the context of openly accessible Internet-based websites and platforms. This kind of indirect communication is mostly used to provide information and, as the legacy of the "third power," to control and counter-balance government and legislature by information and mobilization. Within the last decade, the use of Internet-based media has increased dramatically and traditional information and news services have either vanished or switched to an Internet-based format.[12] This digital information revolution creates great opportunities for the use of indirect information in nonofficial conflict management.

Specified Nonofficial News Service: www.mideastweb.org The Mideastweb website is one among many typical news media websites dealing with the Israel/Palestine conflict. News or thematic websites are the most common use of ICTs for conflict management purposes. Mideastweb provides updated news about the developments in and around the Israel/Palestine conflict. The website was planned as an umbrella website for all the different groups active in dialogue in the region and also to provide an e-dialogue forum for them. However, the owner of the website, Ami Isseroff, believes that competition between the different dialogue groups for funding prevented this feature from taking off, which is a typical dialogue industry problem in his perception. Therefore, despite a small interactive dialogue part of the website, it mostly gathers different news stories and makes them available in a structured form, sometimes with additional comments. There are many of these websites, all in a way claiming objectivity and full information for the readership, which in practice will never be achieved. However, amongst the overwhelming mass of information and news appearing every day, these web-based platforms can be a useful resource for orientation and staying updated and informed.

Indirect Conflict Data Management: CAIN Internet Portal and Data Archive CAIN is a conflict archive accessible for everyone online. The online portal runs through the University of Ulster and provides probably the largest conflict glossary on the events in Northern Ireland from 1968 until today. While there is hardly any interactive functionality in this portal, its complexity and the vastness of information on the evolving of the Northern Ireland conflict is astonishing. The large number of perspectives and opinions presented in the database minimizes partiality. Furthermore, the close ties with the University of Ulster system guarantees a more academic approach to the use of the data archives. CAIN gives everyone interested in the Northern Ireland conflict the opportunity to access a wealth of information free of charge.

12 A powerful example is the *New York Times*, whose online readership has already passed the paper-based readership by far.

Indirect Digital Dialogue: www.bitterlemons.org A different but very interesting web-based platform is Bitterlemons. It is an Internet-based discussion forum that brings together experts from both sides to voice their different opinions on a given issue in the form of short essays. The website is owned and maintained by a prominent and respected Jew and a prominent and respected Palestinian, who both always take one of the sides. As Yossi Alper, the Jewish editor, explicitly states, the website does not try to mediate the different opinions or to find common ground. The website wants people to address their differences and articulate questions and aspirations without the fear of being excluded from the dialogue or being pushed to change their opinion. This kind of bitter dialogue is important and missing in the often very soft and dishonest communication between the Jewish and Palestinian leadership and is much more helpful in understanding the other (Alpher). The website is one of a kind and has a vast readership in and outside of the region. The essays and discussions posted on the website are very often reprinted in major newspapers in Israel, Egypt, Jordan and across the region (Alpher).

Media Monitoring: MIFTAH and Keshev Another very interesting web-based initiative is the media-monitoring unit, a cooperative venture between the Palestinian Initiative for the Promotion of Global Dialogue and Democracy, MIFTAH, and the Center for the Protection of Democracy in Israel, Keshev. In cooperation with the European Union these two organizations monitor the different kinds of media in the region (including online media) and provide evaluation and reports on their actions. Their mission statement is:

> To contribute to developing professional, brave, critical and free media. Such a media is capable of providing better press and media services … according to scientific and professional standards that would contribute to strengthening the credibility of this media and enhance its impact, as well as assist in establishing the role of media as a watchdog over the executive power. (MIFTAH-Media Monitoring Report 2006: 3)

The evaluations of the initiative are accessible online as well as immediate information on questionable news. MIFTAH and Keshev furthermore contact the media (in each society) when they find reports insufficient and try to get them changed (Bathish). This cooperation is very unique and shows another valuable way how ICTs can be used for conflict management.

Other interesting forms of indirect communication used for conflict management include the development of the computer game *Global Conflicts: Palestine* by the Danish software company Serious Games Interactive ("Global Conflicts: Palestine": 5). The player is given a glimpse of the complexity of the conflict by taking on the role of a young reporter in a very Jerusalem-like interactive city, with the mission to create objective journalism out of the many personal stories he or she receives from interactive characters. This computer game is another very creative way to use ICT applications to better inform people about the conflict.

Direct Communication

The third category of ICT usage for conflict management is direct communication, or more accurately, technically mediated direct communication. This category is distinctive from the other two approaches in that there is an attempt to establish a sustainable interaction via different kinds of ICTs. In the legacy of Allport's contact hypothesis (1954), connecting people on a continuing basis furthers understanding and creates trust. While Allport gives much importance to the human factor in that kind of interaction, newer research like Amichai-Hamburger and McKenna's

"The Contact Hypothesis Reconsidered: Interacting via the Internet" (2006) also sees similar effects possible through computer-mediated interaction. While theoretically very stimulating, examples of this kind of interaction have been rare.

E-Dialogue: Aida Refugee Camp Student-learning Center Projects of Internet-based dialogue between different student groups have been tried before. Professor Miles Hewstone tried to create a program to connect Protestant and Catholic school children in Northern Ireland via an Internet-based platform, but it was canceled by British authority and law (Kalman 2006: 3). The same has happened to many other attempts.[13] However, a more private and surprising kind of e-dialogue has succeeded, as Ayed Al Azzeh, a teacher in the Aida Refugee Camp Student-learning Center, told me. The center has been equipped with a couple of Internet accessible computers and the students were taught to surf the Internet and to contact other people via online forums. Students connected with other students online, initially not knowing that they were chatting with Jews. Many interesting e-chats developed and critical questions were discussed. However, being based on a voluntary and noncommittal platform, this e-dialogue was not sustained for a long time. Azzeh was surprised, though, how open his students were to discussions with Jews on the Internet (Azzeh). Similar experiences were found in the y-peace program, sponsored by the American embassy, connecting young people in Gaza and Israel through email dialogues (Mghari). This more formalized e-dialogue again created some surprisingly open discussions, but again did not prove to be very sustainable.

Peres Center Internet Project The most extensive and probably also most effective program on Internet use for direct conflict communication purposes found in this research was created by the Peres Center for Peace in Israel/Palestine. After it was initially started in 2003, but failed to launch, the project finally began in early 2006. The Peres Center built Internet centers in Gaza, the West Bank and Israel through a virtual interface where teenagers from all these areas met online. Under the oversight of professional staff in each center, the teenagers involved took part in virtual activities and programs. Surprisingly the teenagers developed relationships and openly shared very personal information with each other, without having ever met in person (Zion). In June 2006, the teenagers involved met face-to-face, further strengthening their relationships. The success of this program can be seen in the fact that many of the participants stayed in contact (via email and/or online forums) after their term in the program officially ended (Zion). However, it also reveals some of the challenges and limits to exclusively online contacts. After half a year of digital relationship-building and dialogue, some of the Palestinian students prepared a guide to their Palestine as a PowerPoint presentation about their future dreams, calling Haifa the most northern city of Palestine, Jerusalem the capital and Eilat the most southern city and showing maps without any mentioning of Israel. Despite these eye-opening experiences on the limitations of online dialogue, this program has been very successful in connecting teenagers of whom a majority had never before met someone from the other group. More centers, especially in the West Bank, are currently being built (Zion).

13 Videoconference projects between youth living in the main Belfast crisis neighborhoods on the Shankill and the Falls Road in Northern Ireland were discussed a couple of years ago. It was planned to have them first "meet" online and overcome their still existing prejudices toward each other, but these projects never took off and were soon cancelled (O'Halloran).

ICT Expertise: The OneVoice Movement Probably the group making most use of the many capabilities of modern ICTs is the OneVoice movement, with offices in Tel Aviv (OneVoice Israel) and Ramallah (OneVoice Palestine). The movement is a relative young initiative that tries to connect and mobilize moderates on both sides against the societal influence of extremists. They try to specifically connect youth leaders with each other and engage in many public campaigns to make the moderate voices in both societies heard (Balderman, Shaheen). The members are very young and ICT-savvy. Living with the restriction of not being able to easily visit each other's offices, they engage in regular multi-media phone conferences, linking cameras, computers and phone-lines in both offices with each other to have interactive meetings (Balderman). In their approaches to building more dialogue between young people on both sides, they also make very good use of popular Internet contact platforms like Facebook. They provide open online discussions and forums between interested students in the region and worldwide (Asnes). In another example of their multiple ICT usage, which may fit better in the category of incidental communication, they addressed the world economic forum meeting on 25 January 2007 via a multi-media, multi-location phone conference and engaged in an interactive discussion with their own political leadership (most notably Tzipi Livni, Mahmoud Abbas and Shimon Peres). The OneVoice Movement is an inspiration in seeing what is possible when making good use of modern ICT capabilities.

Besides the use of computer-based direct communication, the interviewees shared some examples based on the use of mobile telecommunication via mobile phones for nonofficial conflict management. However, the reported applications are not systematic or regular[14] (ongoing) which makes them rather forms of incidental crisis communication.

Evaluation

Following the differentiation of ICT usage in nonofficial conflict management into incidental, indirect and direct communication and the discussion of specific examples from the cases studies of Northern Ireland and Israel/Palestine, the next step is to focus on the evaluation of ICT use as a whole. First we will try to gauge the strengths and weaknesses of ICT for nonofficial conflict management in the cases discussed by first establishing an expectation and context framework based on conflict phases, before discussing the actual development and social penetration of ICTs in Northern Ireland and Israel/Palestine, and evaluating their use for nonofficial conflict management in these regions based on the actual practices compared with the developed expectations.

Concepts and Phases

In order to evaluate and critique ICT use in nonofficial conflict management in Northern Ireland and Israel/Palestine, we need to place it in a contextual framework of expectations and predictions. In this step the different stages of the conflict and resolution process need to be taken into account. This brings new challenges and opportunities to use of ICTs in nonofficial conflict management. For this contextual framework Eytan Gilboa's (2006) categorization on the varying uses and objectives of media in the different phases of a conflict and its resolution will be adopted. While Gilboa discusses the role and use of media, his findings on what is assumed to be the most effective use of

14 Which can be still connected to the fear of eavesdropping by outside parties, a capability and method the Israeli military has openly admitted. In the past cell-phone usage has also been used to locate the user and, in the case of "political targets," to eliminate him/her, further sparking the fear of this media.

media in the different phases of the conflict and resolution process are very adaptable to ICT use in nonofficial conflict management and peace-building, and will serve as an evaluation tool for our case studies. Gilboa distinguishes between four stages—onset–prevention, escalation management, de-escalation–resolution and termination–reconciliation—as meaningful concepts for conflicts and its resolution instead of just time frames to describe the pre- and post-conflict phases (Gilboa 2006: 599). He attaches specific goals and predictions about media use and effectiveness to each of these phases, which can be adapted to this research.

As indicated in the name, conflict management in the *onset–prevention phase* is mostly concerned with the prevention of violence, which includes the use of ICT for this purpose. This includes trying to engage the parties in the crisis from a very early stage, through the use of Internet or telecommunications, trying to establish forms of information exchange and dialogue that can work to de-escalate the conflict. Especially in an area of widespread Internet use, the dissemination of different positions in order to prevent growing prejudice or offer clarification to misused and misinterpreted events (e.g. on blogs, or through email lists or text messages) can have a key preventive effect (Stauffacher et al. 2005: 10ff). Furthermore, the use of early warning tools is very important.

In the circumstances of a conflict (violence) eruption *escalation management* becomes central; here incidental communication plays a key role. Immediacy becomes a factor and ICT use can serve as an important warning or reporting tool. Given the generally high animosity between the groups in this phase, groups or individuals shy away from cooperating with the other side, either because of personal differences or from fear of the consequences from their own people. Regular ICT use for nonofficial conflict management is most often in the realm of indirect communication, e.g. making statements on one's own website and writing articles for online publications. This kind of balanced information management through ICT usage is very important for conflict management, because many people look to online news as their source of knowledge and motivation. However, since escalation management is the phase with the least use of direct communication through ICTs, in some long-term conflicts, back-channel communications have proven to be very effective. Slowly re-engaging certain groups[15] and key decision-makers with each other (e.g. intentional secret dialogue) prepares for de-escalation.

Once the immediate violence has ceased and a standstill or equilibrium in the conflict has been achieved, we enter the *de-escalation–resolution* phase. While in the escalation management phase ICT use was much more reactive, the de-escalation phase offers the opportunity for much more proactive use. Here direct communication should be very strong, using ICTs for different forms of nonofficial negotiation and diplomacy (Second Track Diplomacy). Particularly in the context of separation between the conflict parties, ICT use like videoconferences and e-dialogues can be employed to limit the alienation effect. In particular, forms and applications of direct ICT-assisted telecommunication (e.g. phone conferences) have proven to be very effective. ICTs are important in this phase to assist with the mass integration and mobilization of many people on both sides into the conflict resolution process (Kronish, Hewitt). ICTs can help form a connected critical mass (e.g. peace constituency) working towards peace. While incidental communication is still very important, it should be more and more embedded in forms of ongoing direct communication. Nonofficial conflict management can be very effective in disseminating information to the

15 Thinking about the new phenomena of social interactive networks with new chat functions, e.g. Facebook or Myspace, there seemed to be at least the theoretical possibilities to use them as a means of mobilization of the general public towards de-escalation.

wider public through ICT and create feedback to the political level to support the official negotiation process.

Once an official peace agreement has been reached and/or a process of next steps to end the conflict has been agreed on, the *termination–reconciliation* phase starts. This phase is one of the most interesting and sadly one of the least studied phases in nonofficial conflict management. In theory the use of ICTs for nonofficial conflict management purposes should look very similar to the de-escalation–resolution phase, based on mostly direct communication and backed by indirect information management to further strengthen and build relationships between the former adversary groups. Here ICTs can be used to create shared digital life-worlds and social communication networks to stipulate the new one-group feeling and behavior. Reconciliation is a long-term process and ultimately should develop into normality, transcending ICT use for nonofficial conflict management purposes into the common use of ICT in a reconciled society.

After creating the expectation and context framework for the use of ICTs in the different phases of nonofficial conflict management, they have to be applied to the cases of Northern Ireland and Israel/Palestine. While arguably Northern Ireland would be at the beginning of the termination–reconciliation stage, Israel/Palestine is still in the escalation management phase. Although historically both conflicts have been through different stages in the recent past, both have made use of different ICT applications. However, before taking an in-depth look at both cases, the general development of ICT penetration and use in both regions needs to be established.

Northern Ireland

The data collection for Northern Ireland consists of 15 interviews conducted in the summer of 2005 and 44[16] more interviews conducted in the spring of 2008 in Northern Ireland and the Republic of Ireland, as well as supporting archival research. Preliminary evaluation of the data provides some interesting findings.

The *increasing capacity and connectivity* through ICTs in Northern Ireland is prevalent. With the increasing economic success and simultaneously decreasing costs for ICTs, personal computers and mobile phones and their various forms of adaptations (e.g. Blackberry, iPhone) have become the norm in communication. A major part of the population is connected through the Internet[17] and mobile telecommunication use is very high, with nearly one mobile phone per capita.[18] This allows for *global reach and proximity* through ICTs as well as *total accessibility* and *immediate response*. In Northern Ireland, as in much of the Western world, people are very engaged in forms of *perpetual communication* through modern ICTs such as mobile phones and computers. However, despite these trends, the use of modern ICTs for nonofficial conflict management in total remains more limited than might be expected.

In terms of *incidental communication*, while all 55 interviews supported the fact that ICTs are an important means of communication, the "meaningful" examples they described mostly fall into the category of incidental communication. Furthermore, a majority of these examples are historical.

16 Two interviews were conducted in the U.S. with visitors from Northern Ireland, one with Professor Paul Arthur (2008) and one with Professor Colm Campbell (2007).

17 With estimates from Ireland having a public penetration rate of 50.1% and the UK 66.4%, we can estimate that more then half of the population in Northern Ireland is effectively connected through the Internet (for more information on this subject see http://www.internetworldstats.com/stats4.htm#europe).

18 See statistics at http://www.infoplease.com/ipa/A0933605.html—even though Northern Ireland is not mentioned as a separate country or region, the numbers for Ireland and the UK (from 2005) allow for the same conclusion, that mobile phone use is very high with an estimated penetration rate of ca. 100%.

However, interviewees who personally participated in them (e.g. back-channel communication) acknowledged that ICTs played a minor, although very important, role in arranging for face-to-face meetings and passing on important messages quickly. However, the most successful use of ICTs in Northern Ireland continues to be the many mobile phone networks in Interface areas, which continue to prove an essential tool for de-escalation and trust-building between communities in tension (O'Halloran). In terms of *indirect communication*, there are very professional websites [e.g. INCORE and CAIN archives, Northern Ireland Council for Voluntary Action (NICVA), Community Foundation for Northern Ireland (CFNI) and Community Relations Council (CRC)] that provide much well-structured information on the Northern Ireland and other conflicts. Most of the NGOs have a web presence; however, the standards vary. Some organizations provide daily updates on events and have an easily accessible and well-connected web presence, while other web presences lag behind modern standards and in some cases are not updated. In the current post-conflict context of Northern Ireland, this can be seen as an indicator on the position and survival chances of many NGOs in the years to come and in the context of ending EU funding (Bloomfield, McAleavey). None of the groups and individuals interviewed engaged in any form of structured and regular (ongoing) *direct* form of ICT assisted digital communication like chats, online dialogue forums or video-conferencing, and they were not aware of this use of ICTs for conflict management in the Northern Ireland context.[19] Some mentioned the use of this technical capability in the educational and health sector, but *direct* communication in the form of ongoing dialogue and information exchange is still going on in the mobile phone interface projects where, starting from incidental communication, stronger, more regular (and ongoing) forms of information sharing and dialogue were established. This has played and still plays a major role in the de-escalation and conflict management efforts in most interface areas (O'Halloran).

Northern Ireland: ICT Use in the Termination–Reconciliation Process Based on the conflict phase contextual framework, ICT use for nonofficial conflict management in the *escalation management* and in *de-escalation–resolution* phases of the 1990s meets, in part, the expectations. Given the early development phase of modern ICT applications, Northern Ireland was in the forefront of some innovative ways of using early Internet capabilities and especially mobile phone technology for back-channel communication and interface work. However, after the Good Friday Agreement and the conflict resolution process that followed (*termination–reconciliation* phase), there has been much less ICT use for nonofficial conflict management than expected. As stated above, none of the interviewees could point to any computer-assisted direct digital communication and the use of direct mobile phone networks is mostly limited to interface areas. However, based on the termination–reconciliation phase categorization, this should be the phase that most uses direct communication. There are many possible reasons for this absence; one could be the decline of nonofficial conflict management and citizen peace-building activities in general (Acheson). The added dimension of declining funds and the lesser "immediacy" of a need for dialogue after the peace agreement may give a further explanation, which might explain why ICT-assisted dialogue only seems to happen in interface areas in the main cities, where groups are still clashing with each other (Hewitt). Also, the high costs involved for ICT-assisted direct communication may explain why we only find video-conferencing in more professionalized areas like health systems. Furthermore, in line with the theories of conflict management presented earlier, the use of ICTs is much more necessary in the context of massive segregation and limitations of mobility, which

19 James Magowan (CFNI) and Chris O'Halloran (Interface project) had heard about a computer-assisted videoconference and chat project for conflict management purposes, but had no more information on it.

one could argue is not the case in Northern Ireland today. Consequently, the use of ICTs might no longer be needed and has given way to direct face-to-face peace-building, as Chris O'Halloran states: "mobile phones can only do so much, also they are very good, but they are no substitute for personal contact."

However, while these arguments may have some validity, the region is again facing increasing prejudice between the former conflict parties (Hewitt, McAleavey). This can, at least in part, be linked to the decrease in dialogue between the groups. Large parts of the country still live in *de facto* segregation; and since there is no apparent need for communication, the groups are again hardly talking with each other (Oliver, Conere, Jarman). Contexts calling again for more dialogue combined with the widespread ICT possibilities that now exist should make the greater use of ICT in nonofficial conflict management a logical choice.

Israel/Palestine

In the summer of 2006 (25) and 2007 (43), 68 semi-structured expert interviews in Israel/Palestine were conducted for this research as well as archival research in the region. In general the use of ICT in Israel/Palestine is in very high demand and *connectivity and capabilities* seem to have increased rapidly in recent years. The country is leading in mobile phone use in the wider region with 7.757 million mobile phones in use in Israel with a population of 6.426 million (which means that there are more mobile phones being used than there are people). There are over a million further users in the West Bank and Gaza, with a combined population of about 4 million.[20] In terms of Internet use, Israel has a high public penetration of 57.6% (December 2007) that is steadily rising. As the Palestinian media monitoring organization MIFTHA observed, the use of the Internet increased dramatically after the start of the Second Intifada in 2000 (Bathish). With an estimated public penetration rate of 38% in 2007, Internet literacy is increasing and reaches beyond educated elite (Thabit). This can be seen as a logical reaction to the massive physical mobility limitations imposed, causing groups and individuals to rely on new ICTs for communication and *global reach* with supporters around the world to create a *proximity* to the events in the West Bank and Gaza (Amayreh 2007). In general, ICTs have played a tremendous role in linking local nongovernmental groups on both sides with an international constituency, through which groups and individuals have been able to bypass local media restrictions and blockades, raise funds and organize activities on a global scale. The new ways of *total accessibility* and *immediate response* through ICTs have further professionalized and empowered nonofficial groups, like the current peace-building resistance movements, to better organize and respond to events (Rishmawi, Zoughbi). The same can be said in Israel, especially in the rocket-attacks stricken region (e.g. Sderot), where new ICTs are used extensively to warn people of immediate attacks and inform others afterwards (Yellin, Zion). New forms of *perpetual communication* can mostly be found in young people in the region, who use mobile phones and the Internet to organize their day-to-day lives.[21] While high-end usage of ICTs (fast Internet) is common for most people in Israel, is it more difficult to come by in the Palestinian regions, where the more low-tech uses are very common. However, outside of the main metropolitan areas of Bethlehem, Ramallah and Nablus, many of the rural areas in the West Bank are not well connected to computer services yet. However, similar to other conflict regions, despite

20 See all the statistical data from 2007 at http://www.infoplease.com/ipa/A0933605.html.

21 In terms of *perpetual communication* habits, another interesting issue observed is the strong "story-culture" in the region, which seems to be in contradiction with perpetual communication. Future development will determine if this important cultural aspect can be preserved in the rush towards more globalized perpetual communication structures.

the major technical possibilities, the use of modern ICTs for nonofficial conflict management is very limited.

The most common use of ICTs for nonofficial conflict management in Israel/Palestine is *incidental*, which is not surprising given the vast privatization of ICT applications. All 62 interviews were arranged through email and then confirmed via mobile telecommunication. The Internet and mobile phone have become the major means of communication, making it logical that, in times of crisis, these are the means are used. However, these forms of ICT applications are neither formalized nor used regularly in a proactive way as a nonofficial conflict management tool, but rather are reactive forms of private (crisis) communication building on already existing personal networks between players from the different conflict groups. In terms of *indirect communication* use, nearly all organizations and individuals interviewed have their own website, but they are mostly passive web applications[22] to display relevant information with occasional "discussion forums." However, the recent evolution of computer application to more *direct communication* applications in the form of live blogs or chats, with an increasing digital community attached to it, has not yet entered the realm of nonofficial conflict management. Only two (OneVoice Israel and OneVoice Palestine) out of the 62 organizations and individuals interviewed use ICTs (e.g. phone conferences, online video conferences) for regular direct conflict management communication and another three had heard of it. All others (which means over 90%) have never even heard about the use of modern ICTs for direct communication and dialogue efforts in conflict management.

Israel/Palestine: ICT Use in the Escalation Management Phase Following the contextual conflict phase framework, rising use of ICT-assisted communication in this current *escalation management* phase in Israel/Palestine is to be expected. The major use of ICTs for nonofficial conflict management has been in indirect communication. While this follows the expectations of the early conflict and resolution phases, it is much less frequent than expected. The escalation management use of ICTs peaked around the Oslo process but then stagnated along with the general peace process and had little to no effect on the crisis of the late 1990s and the Second Intifada since 2001. The picture is even darker for indirect communication and direct communication use of ICT use as analyzed above. This development is surprising given the general increasing use and penetration of ICT in the region since 2000. Furthermore, the context of increasing segregation between the parties who mostly only know each other through the media should produce a higher use of ICTs for nonofficial conflict management (Bessiso-Naji), to continue or renew contacts and relationships in order to counteract the existing misconceptions on both sides. Often missing capacity and technical knowledge is given as a reason for the lack of development. However, given the statistics of the increased use of the Internet and mobile phones, this does not seem likely. Also more extremist organizations and individuals on both sides seem to bridge the knowledge gap, relying heavily on the Internet and mobile communication capacities to inform and organize their supporters. One could make the argument that the general marginalization of the peace-building activities on both sides, now often attached to the negative connotation "peace industry," has not allowed for the utilization of modern technical capacities. On the Palestinian side modern technology approaches to conflict management are often seen as Westernized (e.g. funded by foreigners) and are therefore rejected (Rishmawi), and on the Israeli side the peacenik categorization keeps many people from participating (Isseroff). Also, involvement in peace-

22 Which in a twisted way often takes away another chance for personal face-to-face communication, because the information can be acquired otherwise. Interviewees often commented "I do not know what they (another organization I inquired about) are doing right now, but just check out their website."

building through the use of ICTs might be more private than traditional conflict management approaches (e.g. going to seminars or participating in open demonstrations), because it is based around private (more secret) communication applications. There are some indications that less formal ICT-moderated conflict management dialogues and communication are happening in open digital social networks like Facebook or Myspace, but again on a very noncommitted, informal and private basis. In summary, the use of ICT for nonofficial conflict management in Israel/Palestine seems to follow the same trajectory as the peace-building and dialogue efforts in general. Most ICT use is in-group communication, in which the communication between very reactive groups is linked to the current official relations between the groups. This means that, if relations are improving (e.g. the Oslo process), there is a greater chance of ICT use for conflict management along the line of general peace-building activities. However, in times of crisis (e.g. the Second Intifada), ICT usage for these purposes hardly exists besides incidental use, which leads to lost opportunities to bridge the segregated groups and continue the dialogue and communication even in times of crisis. Unfortunately, it seems that the hardliners and extremists on both sides seem to have the monopoly on using new ICTs proactively.

Limitations and Challenges

The field research in Northern Ireland Israel/Palestine also revealed some challenges and limitations in the use of modern ICT for nonofficial conflict management that need to be mentioned. Besides the fact that new ICTs are used to promote sustainable peace and conflict reconciliation, they are also misused by more extreme elements in both societies.

The most basic and fundamental critique is that, while ICTs might be helpful in connecting people, they cannot (and in the eyes of most people interviewed, will never) replace the need for face-to-face communication in nonofficial conflict management. This sentiment found wide support in all of the interviews and was generally combined with a more cynical attitude towards people who see in ICT the solution to the conflict (Frankenthal, Ryan). Nearly everyone emphasized the idea that face-to-face communication is still essential, but also indicated that it should be supplemented with the capabilities of ICTs if possible (O'Halloran). The strength of ICTs is more at the grass-roots and civil society level, helping people to stay in contact in the period between the face-to-face interactions. The official political-level digital dialogue is more difficult and it was described by many interviewees as a constant challenge to get access while not being co-opted (Perlman, Isseroff, Hewitt).

Other limitations or challenges discussed involve social components, such as the higher foreign language competence of Israelis, which alienates many Palestinians in digital dialogue because they cannot express themselves on the same level (Zang), as well as in general the different communication styles and traditions[23] (Husseini). This may be a problem that is, in many ways, connected to age demographics. Mostly older people run into these language barriers (Baskin). Another issue, which became apparent in the Northern Ireland research, is that, even with the decreasing costs of ICT usage, there is still a digital gap between different classes of society. While more affluent people easily navigate through the opportunities provided by ICTs and are able to use

23 As examples, issues of accuracy and detail are in general very different in the communication styles between Palestinians and Israelis. Also the more story-telling culture of the Palestinians and the in general more direct communication of the Israelis can cause challenges when dialoguing with each other.

them for peace-building purposes, lower and working class communities are often left out because of economic disadvantages (Dougherty, O'Halloran).

Last but not least, a general observation about ICT use in direct communication reveals that the language used in unsupervised open online Internet forums, blogs and social networks is much more extreme and offending than in normal "difficult" dialogue. While this phenomenon seems to be true for the general sphere of Internet communication, it is potentially much more damaging for digital dialogue in conflict zones (Baskin). Despite these limitations, a majority of the experts and practitioners interviewed believed in the positive potential of ICT use for nonofficial conflict management, but also acknowledged that the current use is far from optimum.

Digital Diplomacy as an Example

An example of an impressive turnaround to make the use of ICTs for conflict management more optimal can currently be seen in the new digital or net diplomacy. Following the analysis of Sheryl J. Brown, accompanying the accelerated diffusion of information and communication technologies globally, we are witnessing a parallel diffusion of the practice of diplomacy[24] among nonstate actors who have access to these technologies. As Jeffery R. Cooper describes, "Responding to the technologically changing conflict environment new forms of Virtual Diplomacy or Net Diplomacy have been developed in an attempt to make better use of ICTs for diplomacy" (Smith 1999).

Conflict groups are being connected directly through the Internet or Internet applications (programs) and online platforms work as a mediator between groups. This is already visible in Northern Ireland, where official offices (like the Borough Council) are trying to become more transparent and accessible (Moore). Modern information networks have superseded traditional diplomacy as the venue for reliable and specific information (Bollier 2003: 4) and furthermore help groups involved in the process to create global constituencies for specific issues (Brown 2001: 1). It is also a major tool for mobilization as Don McAleer and Paul Pringle, responsible for communication in the Office of the First Minister and the Deputy First Minister in the Northern Ireland Parliament, explained. Governments are starting their own media campaigns to point out and explain their politics to counter fundamentalist critiques. Yet, despite these hopeful developments, governments in both regions, with their vast capacity, have yet to initiate more forms of ICT-aided direct communication through models of e-governance and build an e-constituency as seen in other western countries (Lo, Hanna).

All in all, it seems that governments are making more use of ICTs for conflict management purposes (especially proactively) than the nonofficial actors in the civil society do, although they are also not using the available ICT capabilities to their fullest potential. However, the trend set by many governments to proactively communicate with and better inform their constituency through the use of ICTs is a path nonofficial conflict management can learn from and adapt to their own needs and potential.

---

24 At another point Brown puts it even more directly: "It is safe to say that diplomacy's theater of operation, its tools, and its practitioners have changed fundamentally to meet the demands of flatter, more responsive, more information-equipped and demanding global publics, who include everyone from Mom and Pop in Mule Shoe, Texas, to Jiang Zemin in Beijing" (Brown 2001: 5).

Conclusion

> The information age is more than just the technology that delivers the avalanche of information and in turn feeds the individual and organizational thirst for more information. The information age brings social, cultural, psychological, and legal changes to the way we live. (Jauch 1997: 1)

This chapter has analyzed the use of ICT for nonofficial conflict management. It has outlined some theory behind it and looked at examples from Northern Ireland and Israel/Palestine. It has discussed the vast potential for ICTs to advance the mission and work of nonofficial conflict management in the future. Based on the evaluation of the current use of ICTs for nonofficial conflict management, despite some hopeful exceptions discussed, the capacity for use is underutilized. This is true for the post-conflict reconciliation phase in Northern Ireland as well as for the current de-escalation management in Israel/Palestine. This underdevelopment comes at a high price—extremist factions have claimed the ICT market and are using and exploiting it skillfully. The challenge for the future will be to take away the initiative and competitive advantage of these extremist groups by increasingly using ICTs for conflict management purposes, to limit the influence of extremists in these new ICT spheres.

Nevertheless, echoing the observation of most of the experts interviewed, even with all the potential that ICTs bring to conflict management practices, they cannot replace face-to-face dialogue[25] (Cooper 2002: 6). Howard Cincotta argues:

> Despite the pervasive impact of the new media, any expectations that it would replace confidential negotiations and personal exchanges … missed the point. Neither a Middle East settlement nor a trade deal on computer software would be resolved in a public press conference or an electronic chat room. But on the other hand, neither agreement could be sustained for a nanosecond without the engagement, understanding, and support of a transformed world networked and empowered by information technology. (Cincotta 2002: 9)

Here, combined models of face-to-face dialogue mixed with intermediate computer or telecommunication dialogue seem to be very promising,[26] especially in the context of the growing digital life-world for people in today's societies who are spending much of their time using ICTs. In particular, the use of mobile telecommunication and information for nonofficial conflict management purposes needs to be much more developed. With nearly every person in Northern Ireland and Israel/Palestine using mobile phones and their spinoffs for most daily communication, these spheres need to be more explored for conflict management purposes. Summarizing, the major strength of ICTs use for nonofficial conflict management lies in the exacerbation of traditional approaches, meaning that modern ICTs enhance communication when there is a personal contact (O'Halloran). In particular, they have the power to connect, mobilize and organize the many

25 Credibility and trust are the keys to power in the new information age, which has flooded us with information that is often inaccurate, unreliable, or simply irrelevant. However, face-to-face interaction remains still the primary method of gaining and developing this trust and credibility.

26 Based on Howard Cincotta's and others' prediction "There is usually no greater mistake than to make straight-line projections from your baseline outwards. Nevertheless, we can assume that, over the next decades or so, information technology will continue to expand and proliferate, creating a networked, broadband world that, whatever its conflicts and tensions, is even more interconnected than today" (2002: 7). This means that diplomacy needs to be more active in this new technological network.

dispersed peace-building actors and groups to build an informed critical mass needed to bring major change.

Academics and practitioners will hopefully find this analysis helpful and keep on exploring and using modern ICT for nonofficial conflict management. As Stewart Brand puts it: "once a new technology rolls over you, if you're not part of the steamroller, you're part of the road" (Brand 2004: 43). This does not mean that one should not be cautious about it, but one should also not wait so long that the chance to be at the forefront of influence and impact through new ICTs has been wasted. As often happens in conflicts, the new ICTs spheres and markets are dominated by extremists who set and control the agendas with their messages and applications. Modern information and communication technologies are the future of conflict management, because, despite their many critics, transformations are conceived as having been underway for many decades and are likely to continue into the foreseeable future (Rosenau 1999: 4). Therefore, there is no better time to start moving from the analog past into the digital future of conflict management.

Appendix

1. *Questions from semi-structured interviews in Israel/Palestine (adapted for Northern Ireland questionnaire) who deal with communication and ICTs.*

I. Communication in the Israel/Palestine Conflict
   a. From your perspective, what role did communication between the parties play in the Israel/Palestine peace process? Please compare the importance of communication to other issues like economic interests or religious beliefs.
   b. What is/was the "relative" importance of dialogue?
   c. How was/is you/your organization involved in dialogue processes? Could you evaluate the importance/effectiveness of it?

II. Personal Experiences with the Communication Process
   a. Were you part of communication or dialogue processes (official or un-official)? If yes, what was your experience?
   b. Did communication with the other party help you better deal with the conflict on a day-to-day basis? Yes or no, why and how?
   c. What were the greatest difficulties when communicating with the other party? When (if ever) and how did this change?

Parts III and IV dealt more specifically with issues of second track diplomacy and citizen dialogue/ action.

V. Technology and the Communication Process
   a. Besides face-to-face meetings, what other forms of communication between the parties took place? Phone conversations/emails/chats? Please describe.
   b. How did the use of technology change over the years? What do you think are the advantages or disadvantages of it?
   c. Please comment on the potential of technical communication to overcome the existing "physical" separation.

2. *List of conducted expert interviews (each lasting 60–90 minutes).*

Equally representing each conflict party (plus observers/third party) and different levels of society to get a full impression.

Northern Ireland

Protestants and Unionists:

Professor Arthur Williamson (Department of Sociology, University of Ulster and Director of Center for Voluntary Action), 07/31/05 in Coleraine.
Wavell Moore (Chief Executive Coleriane Borough Council), 07/27/05 in Coleraine.
Martin Snoddon (Director Trauma Therapy Resource Center), 07/28/05 in Belfast.
Andrew Wiliamson (government employee), Coleraine.
Sammy Johnston (Project Manager, Belfast Unemployment Centre), 04/24/08 in Belfast.
Rev. Tom Hannon (Cornerstone Community), 04/17/08 in Belfast.
David Stevens (Director, Corrymeela Community), 04/10/08 in Belfast.
Joe Camplisson (Chairman, FARCET), 04/23/08 in Belfast.
Jackie Hewitt (Director, FARCET), 04/25/08 in Belfast.
Brian Dougherty (Director, St. Columbs Park House Derry/Londonderry), 04/11/08 in Derry/Londonderry.
Quintin Oliver (Director, Strategem and Yes Campaign for Referendum).
Professor Nicholas Acheson [University of Ulster, Belfast (Jordanstown)], 04/23/08 in Belfast.
Bill Smith (former government employee), 09/04/08 in Belfast.
Alex (Ozo) Calderwood (EX-PARAMILITARY), 04/18/08 in Belfast.

Catholic and Nationalists:

Chris O'Halloran (Director Belfast Interface Project), 04/22/08 in Belfast.
Father Gerry Reynolds (Clonard Monastery), 07/28/05 in Belfast.
Joe Conere (Seeds of Hope), 07/28/05 in Belfast.
Dr. James Magowan (Fund Development Manager, The Community Foundation for Northern Ireland), 07/29/05 and 04/17/08 in Belfast.
Professor Paul Arthur [Political Science, University of Ulster, Magee Campus (Derry/Londonderry), Director Graduate Program on Peace and Conflict Studies], 07/29/05 and 04/10/08 in Belfast and 5/17/07 in Irvine, U.S.A.

Liam Maskey (Executive Director, Intercomm), October 2004 Irvine, U.S.A.
Damien McIlroy [former community worker, Community Relations Council (CRC)], 04/11/08 in Belfast.
Martin McGuinness (3rd Deputy First Minister of Northern Ireland, MLA, MP for Sinn Fein), 04/23/08 near Belfast.
Carmel Hanna [Northern Ireland Legislative Assembly member (MLA) for SDLP], 04/17/08 in Belfast.
Francee Broly [Northern Ireland Legislative Assembly member for (MLA) Sinn Fein], 04/23/08 near Belfast.
Alex Maskey [Northern Ireland Legislative Assembly member (MLA) for Sinn Fein], 04/23/08 near Belfast.
Paul O'Conner (Pat Finucane Centre), 04/18/08 in Derry/Londonderry.
Anne Gallagher (Director, Seeds of Hope), 2005 and 04/18/04 in Belfast and 04/29/04 in Dublin.
Gerry Adams (President Sinn Fein, MLA, MP), 04/23/08 near Belfast.
Sean Mclynches (community worker, Sinn Fein Center Dongiven), 04/18/08 in Dongiven.
Colin White (community worker, Sinn Fein Dongiven), 04/18/08 in Dongiven.
Professor Stephen Ryan [Political Science, University of Ulster, Magee Campus (Derry/Londonderry)], 04/11/08 in Derry/Londonderry.
Paul McKenna (ex-paramilitary), 04/18/08 in Belfast.
Patrick McGee (ex-paramilitary), 04/26/08 in Belfast.
Paul McLynches (ex-paramilitary and former Sinn Fein Politician—now had founded own party), 04/27/08.
Brendan Duddy (businessman and secret link between IRA and British Government), 04/25/08 in Derry/Londonderry.

Others:

Clem MacCartney (negotiator), 07/26/05 in Coleraine.
Don McAleer (Principal Information Officer Executive Information Service, Office of the First Minister and Deputy First Minister), 08/01/05 in Belfast.
Paul Pringle (Senior Information Officer, Office of the First Minister and the Deputy First Minister), 08/01/05 in Belfast.
Professor Colm Campbell (Head of Transitional Justice Institute, University of Ulster), 02/19/06 in Irvine, U.S.A. and 04/18/08 in Belfast.
Neil Jarman (Conflict Research Institute), 04/24/08 in Belfast.
Dr David Bloomfield (Director, Glencree), 04/29/08 near Dublin (Republic of Ireland).
Jacintia (Program Manager, Glencree), 04/29/08 near Dublin (Republic of Ireland).
Dr Matt Cannon (Director, Irish Peace Institute), 04/15/08 in Limerick (Republic of Ireland).
Seamus McAleavey [Director, Northern Ireland Council for Voluntary Action (NICVA, former NICSS)], 04/15/08 in Belfast.
Anna Lo [Northern Ireland Legislative Assembly member (MLA) for the Alliance Party], 04/25/08 in Belfast.
Olive Hobson (Director, Quaker House Belfast), 04/24/08 in Belfast.
Professor Beverly Milton-Edwards (Queens University Belfast), 04/24/08 in Belfast.
Professor Orla Muldoon (University of Limerick), 04/15/08 in Limerick (Republic of Ireland).

Professor Cathy Gormley Heenan [University of Ulster, Belfast (Jordanstown)], 04/24/08 in Belfast.
Jerry Carla, Ciaven Nujent, Seamus and Mark Kelly (Protestant and Catholics at WAVE in Belfast), 04/23/08 in Belfast.
Bronagh Hinds (co-founder, Women's Coalition), 04/14/08 in Belfast.

Israel/Palestine

Israeli:

Hagit Ra'anan (Bridges of Peace), 09/09/06 in Tel Aviv.
Ami Isseroff (Middle East Web), 09/09/06 in Tel Aviv.
Melissa Boskovich (Peace Child Israel), 09/11/06 in Tel Aviv.
Adi Balderman (OneVoice Israel), 09/12/06 in Tel Aviv.
Yossi Alpher (bitterlemons.org, Mossad), 09/13/06 in Tel Aviv.
Yehuda Stolov (Interfaith Encounter), 09/20/06 in Jerusalem.
Professor Ephraim Kleiman (Emeritus Hebrew University, Madrid Conference participant), 09/20/06 in Jerusalem.
Samuel Smadja (SarElTours), 09/21/06 in Jerusalem.
Moshe Berger (Motivation Circle, graduate student Herbrew University), 09/21/06 in Jerusalem.
Lee Perlman (Abraham Fund, Coexistence Network), 09/25/06 in Jerusalem and 09/24/07 in Neve Ilan.
Sagi Rasmovich (former officer IDF, OneVoice Israel), 03/08/07 in Irvine, U.S.A. and 09/12/07 by phone.
Rabbi Mordechai Piron, 09/09/07 in Jerusalem.
Dr Deborah Weissman (co-chair Interreligious Coordinating Council Israel), 09/10/07 in Jerusalem.
Yitzhak Frankenthal (Founder Parents Circle and Arik Institute), 09/10/07 in Jerusalem.
Professor Samuel Peleg (Netanja College, advisor to Yossi Beilin, academic chairman, OneVoice), 09/11/07 in Herzlia.
Esther Golan (Holocaust survivor), 09/12/07 in Jerusalem.
Nomika Zion (Kibbutz Migvan), 09/17/07 in Sderot.
Eric Yellin (Kibbutz Migvan), 09/14/07 in Sderot.
Gershon Baskin (CEO Israel/Palestine Center for Research and Information), 09/17/07 in Jerusalem.
Judith Green (Rapprochement Dialogue Center), 09/18/07 in Jerusalem.
Professor Eythan Gilboa (Chair Communications Program Bar-Ilan University), 09/18/07 in Jerusalem.
Professor Galia Golan-Gild (Diplomacy and Strategy, Herzlia Interdisciplinary Center, co-founder Peace Now), 09/19/07 in Herzlia.
Rabbi Ron Kronish (Director Interreligious Coordinating Council Israel), 09/20/07 in Jerusalem.
Professor Dan Avnon (Political Science, Hebrew University, Head of Gilo Center), 09/23/07 in Jerusalem.
Yehoshua Ratz (teacher), 09/23/07 in Jerusalem.

Eldad Joffe (Administrative Director Gilo Center Hebrew University), 09/23/07 in Jerusalem.
Tali Yariv-Mashal (Gilo Center Research Fellow, Lecturer Hebrew University), 09/23/07 in Jerusalem.
Professor Tamar Hermann (Director Peace Research Center Tel Aviv University), 09/23/07 by phone.
Professor Daniel Bar-Tal (Political Psychology Tel Aviv University), 09/26/07 in Herzlia
Ami Isseroff (Middle East Web), 09/27/07 by phone.

Palestinians (some Israeli citizens/Israeli-Arabs):

Nasireen Shaheen (OneVoice Palestine), 09/18/06 in Ramallah.
Zoughbi Zoughbi (Wi'am Palestinian Conflict Resolution Center), 09/19/06 in Bethlehem.
Lourdes B. Habash (Holy Land Trust), 09/19/06 in Bethlehem.
George Rishmawi (Rapprochement Center, former International Solidarity Movement [ISM]), 09/19/06 in Bethlehem.
Ayed Al Azzeh (Teacher Aida Refugee Camp), 09/19/06 in Bethlehem.
Professor Amad Jamal (Chair Political Science Department, Tel Aviv University), 09/14/06 in Tel Aviv.
Rami Bathish (MIFTAH), 09/21/06 in East-Jerusalem.
Dalia Labadi (Student, OneVoice Palestine), 03/08/07 in Irvine, U.S.A and 09/12/07 in Ramallah.
Hekmat Bessiso-Naji (AFSC-Quakers), 09/12/07 in Ramallah.
Husan H. El Mghari (Palestinian Youth Union of Cooperation for peace, Palestinian Dialogue Center Gaza), 09/12/07 in Ramallah.
Ekrema A. Thabit (Palestinian Youth Union Ramallah), 09/12/07 in Ramallah.
Esam Said (Palestinian Dialogue Center Ramallah), 09/12/07 in Ramallah.
Zaki Issa Awwad (teacher Talita Kumi school Bethlehem), 09/19/07 in Bethlehem.
Suleiman Abu-Dayyeh (Friedrich Naumann Stiftung), 09/20/07 in Bethlehem.
Jonny Shahwan (Beit Liqa), 09/20/07 in Bethlehem.
Professor Sari Nusseibeh (Director Al-Quds University, delegate Madrid Conference and Oslo Peace Process), 09/23/07 in Beit Haninia/East-Jerusalem.
Nijmeh Ali (student Hebrew University), 09/23/07 in Jerusalem.
Salim Manayer (Director of Musalaha), 09/24/07 in Jerusalem.
Kamel Husseini (Peace Negotiation Team in Madrid and Oslo).

Others:

Petra Held (Ecumenical Fraternity), 09/20/06 in Jerusalem.
Cedar Duaybis (Saabel), 09/21/06 in East-Jerusalem.
Benjamin Pogrund (Yakar), 09/21/06 in Jerusalem.
Guido Baltes (Johanniter Hospitz), 09/21/06 in Jerusalem and 09/24/07 in Jerusalem.
Miriam Asnes (OneVoice, Intl Coordinator), 03/08/07 in Irvine, U.S.A.
Jörg Bremer (Correspondent Frankfurter Allgemeine Zeitung), 09/05/07 in Jerusalem.
Probst Gräbe (Head of German church in Israel), 09/09/07 in Jerusalem.
Johannes Zang (freelance journalist), 09/10/07 in Jerusalem.

Anja Michalke (teacher Talita Kumi school), 09/14/07 in Bethlehem.
Johannes Gerloff (journalist for Israelnet), 09/18/07 in Jerusalem.
Rebecca Volkerson (Women for Peace), 09/25/07 in Tel Aviv.

References

Allport, G.W. 1954. *The Nature of Prejudice*. Cambridge, MA: Addison-Wesley.

Amayreh, K. 2007. "Internet use High Among Palestinians." Available at: Aljazeera.net; http://english.aljazeera.net/English/archive/archive?ArchiveId=14979 [accessed: March 2008].

Amichai-Hamburger, Y. and K.Y. McKenna. 2006. "The Contact Hypothesis Reconsidered: Interacting via the Internet." *Journal of Computer-Mediated Communication*, 11(3), article 7. Available at: http://jcmc.indiana.edu/vol11/issue3/amichai-hamburger.html [accessed: 1 August 2011].

Barabasi, A.-L. 2003. *Linked*. New York: Plume/Penguin Group.

Bollier, D. 2003. *The Rise of Netpolitik—How the Internet is Changing International Politics and Diplomacy*. The Aspen Institute Communication and Society Program.

Brand, S. 2004. "The Media Lab: Inventing the Future at MIT." In: D. Schuler and P. Day. *Shaping the Network Society—The New Role of Civil Society in Cyberspace*. Cambridge, MA: The MIT Press, p. 43ff.

Brown, S.J. 2001. "The Diffusion of Diplomacy." *Magazine on Information Impacts*, co-authored with Margarita Studemeister, pp. 1–6.

Castells, M. 1996. *The Information Age—Economy, Society and Culture, Vol 1: The Rise of the Network Society*. Oxford: Blackwell.

Castells, M. 2001. *The Internet Galaxy, Reflections on the Internet, Business and Society*. Oxford: Oxford University Press

Cincotta, H. 2002. "Postmodern Diplomacy and the New Media." In: B. Fulton, ed., *Net Diplomacy I: Beyond Foreign Ministries*. Washington, DC: United States Institute of Peace.

Cooper, J.R. 2002. "Diplomacy in the Information Age: Implications for Content and Conduct." In: B. Fulton, ed., *Net Diplomacy I: Beyond Foreign Ministries*. Washington, DC: United States Institute of Peace.

Deibert, R.J. 1997. *Parchment, Printing, and Hypermedia: Communication in World Order Transformation*. New York: Columbia University Press.

Dicken, P. 2003. *Global Shift: Reshaping the Global Economic Map in the 21st Century*. New York: The Guilford Press.

Gilboa, E. 2006. "Media and International Politics." In: J.G. Oetzel and S. Ting-Toomey (eds). *The Sage Handbook of Conflict Communication: Integrating Theory, Research, and Practice*. Thousand Oaks, CA: Sage, pp. 595–626.

"Global Conflicts: Palestine." Israelnetz report 06/2006, p. 5; http://www.israelnetz.de [accessed: February 2007].

Held, D., A. McGrew, D. Goldblatt and J. Perraton Mark. 1999. *Global Transformations*. Stanford, CA: Stanford University Press.

Holson, L.M. 2008. "Text Generation Gap: U R 2 old." *The New York Times online*, 9 March 2008.

Jauch, D.M. 1997. "The Enterprise of Diplomacy in the Information Age." Presented at USIP Virtual Diplomacy Conference April 1997.

Kalman, M. 2006, "Using Power of the Internet to Promote Peace." *San Francisco Chronicle*. Available at: http://articles.sfgate.com/2006-10-08/opinion/17314206_1_northern-ireland-rival-groups-conflict-resolution [accessed: 1 August 2011].

Katz, J.E. and M.A. Aakhus. 2002. *Perpetual Contact—Mobile Communication, Private Talk, Public Performance*. Cambridge: Cambridge University Press.

Lederach, J.P. 1997. *Building Peace*. Washington, DC: United States Institute of Peace Press.

Lederach, J.P. and J.M. Jenner. 2002. *Into the Eye of the Storm: A Handbook of International Peacebuilding*. San Francisco, CA: Jossey-Bass.

May, C. 2002. *The Information Society—A Skeptical View*. Cambridge: Polity Press and Blackwell.

McLuhan, M. and B.R. Powers. 1989. *The Global Village: Transformations in World Life and Media in the 21st Century*. New York: Oxford University Press.

Meyrowitz, J. 1985. *No Sense of Place: The Impact of Electronic Media on Social Behaviour*. Oxford: Oxford University Press.

MIFTAH-Media Monitoring Report. 2006. "The Palestinian-Israeli Conflict in the Media Coverage of the 17th Israeli Knesset Elections." Sixth Report. Ramallah (Palestine).

Poster, M. 2001. *The Information Subject*. Amsterdam: Gordon and Breach.

Preston, P. 2001. *Reshaping Communications*. London: Sage.

Rosenau, J. 1999. "States, Sovereignty, and Diplomacy in the Information Age." Available online at www.usip.org, 25 February 1999.

Rosenau, J.N. 2002. *Information Technologies and the Skills, Networks, and Structures that Sustain World Affairs*. In: J.N. Rosenau and J.P. Singh (eds). *Information Technologies and Global Politics*. New York: State University of New York Press, pp. 275–88.

Rosenau, J.N. 2003. *Distant Proximity: Dynamics beyond Globalization*. Princeton, NJ: Princeton University Press.

Schuler, D. and P. Day. 2004. *Shaping the Network Society—The New Role of Civil Society in Cyberspace*. Cambridge, MA: The MIT Press.

Smith, G.S. 1999. "Reinventing Diplomacy: A Virtual Necessity." Available at: www.usip.org, 25 February 1999 [accessed: 1 August 2011].

Stauffacher, D., W. Drake, P. Currion and J. Steinberger. 2005. *Information and Communication Technology for Peace: The Role of ICT in Preventing, Responding to and Recovering from Conflict*. New York: United Nations Information and Communication Technology Task Force.

Tonge, J. 2002. *Northern Ireland: Conflict and Change*, 2nd edn. Essex: Pearson Education.

Chapter 3
Marching Across the Cyber Frontier: Explaining the Global Diffusion of Network-centric Warfare

Tim Junio

Introduction

In recent years, the question of how militaries may transform the use of information technology (IT)—and how IT may transform militaries—has resulted in a growing body of inconclusive research (Adamsky 2010; Adamsky and Bjerga 2010; Arquilla and Ronfeldt 1997, 2001; Cohen 1996; Farrell 2010; Goldman 2004; Goldman and Mahnken 2004; Latham 2003; Nye and Owens 1996; Russell 2010; Sloan 2002). Part of the problem lies in identifying exactly how a transformed military will look and fight. While extensive progress has been made in developing new IT for warfare, no one appears to know what organization and doctrine will characterize a networked force. This frustrating state of military analysis may be likened to a similar phenomenon in the private sector during the late 1980s, when a prominent economist remarked that computers were visible everywhere—except in productivity statistics (Solow 1987). Similarly, one may say that IT is visible everywhere in modern militaries—except in the doctrine of a few states. After a lag time of about a decade, IT measurably improved business productivity and affected corporate organization (Brynjolfsson and Hitt 2000, 2003; Cummins 2004). How long a lag time will militaries bear before IT fundamentally alters warfare, if it does so at all?

Another part of the problem of analyzing IT-based change is the puzzling spread of military desires to develop networked forces. Over two dozen countries have stated that they want to transform their forces in a manner resembling the U.S. concept of network-centric warfare (NCW). These countries exhibit dramatic differences on variables that might cause them to have similar visions of future warfare, such as culture, perceptions of threat, regional power dynamics, geographic situation, history, organization, regime type, alliance commitments, and political objectives. Why are countries as disparate as the Netherlands, United Arab Emirates, France, Australia, Brazil, Italy, Israel, the UK, New Zealand, Russia, China, Hungary, Sweden, Malaysia, and India, among others, calling for similar approaches to the conduct of war?

My objective is to answer this question by seeking causal explanations common to as many of the NCW transformers as possible. Among the countries that claim they want a networked force, only 12 are actually transforming, according to my review of these countries' defense strategies, system acquisitions, network deployments, experimentation with networking concepts, and doctrinal developments. Eleven of the 12 countries—Australia, France, Germany, Israel, Italy, the Netherlands, Singapore, South Korea, Sweden, the U.S., and the UK—share a unique characteristic: compared along 13 variables, on average, they are remarkably more advanced in the use of IT than the rest of the world. This coding refers to countries that are attempting *force-wide* military transformations. A limited development with IT, such as the creation of niche modernized units, does not qualify a military as an NCW transformer. Some countries of great interest to readers, such as China and Russia, are, therefore, not considered among the transforming militaries.

The 13 variables, selected as indicators of the states' social and economic saturation with IT, suggest a modest affirmation of the hypothesis that militaries reflect the societies they come from. The NCW approach to defense planning appears to be common among these countries because their militaries perceive great value in a particular set of capabilities that have already transformed their societies and economies. A reasonable extension of this claim is that social and economic IT transformation has led to the development of an IT networking culture that is influencing military personnel to think differently about warfare. While a partial explanation at best, this claim is the only one that establishes a causal relationship regarding the diffusion of NCW among countries with dramatically variant contexts.

To establish this argument, I first offer background information on force transformation and NCW, the concepts underlying this chapter's analysis. I then examine six theoretical frameworks of military diffusion and assess their explanatory power. The most promising approach is a modified cultural argument, in which culture is treated as social behaviors, including those created by the broad distribution of new technologies. I test this claim by examining qualitative evidence of how IT changes human behavior, and how those behaviors may be spilling over from societies into their militaries. I further support my analysis by reviewing quantitative data on countries transforming with NCW to determine whether or not they are more saturated with IT than the rest of the world. I close the chapter with prospects for further research, particularly regarding other causal arguments.

Force Transformation and Information Technology

I define "force transformation" as the process of a military changing how it trains and equips to fight, particularly in regard to its organization, doctrine, and technology. Transformation is a concept distinct from "modernization," which refers to qualitative improvements in how a military already plans and organizes to fight. Transformation also is distinct from "innovation"; innovations are technological or behavioral changes that, once acted upon by a military, may result in a transformation or modernization. For instance, the development of the M-4 rifle may be considered a modest innovation in infantry operations, for its smaller size and lighter weight relative to the M-16 allow for improved maneuver in close quarters. The smaller and lighter assault rifle does not, however, fundamentally alter how infantry forces operate. On the other hand, the development of breech-loading rifles was a transformative innovation because it enabled infantry forces to reload their weapons while lying prone, rather than standing. This shift in technology led to changes in basic infantry tactics by allowing for cover, concealment, and reorganization away from tiered columns (Ropp 2000).

The most common driver of transformation is when technology makes existing ways of war so vulnerable to defeat that new concepts of operations must be created to overcome the technology. This concept is akin to "disruptive" or "displacing" technologies in the private sector. Such technologies render a firm's core competencies obsolete and require the firm to develop new practices and organization to remain competitive (Christensen 1997; Christensen and Bower 1995; Golder and Tellis 1997; Henderson 1993; Tushman and Anderson 1986). Technological development may be one of two kinds: a breakthrough or a new employment. Breakthroughs are new technologies that are consequential on their own merits, such as atomic fission, while employments are new ways of using existing technology, such as the effects of railroads on manned power deployment and logistical support during the American Civil War and World War I. Drivers other than technology also may prove transformative to warfare. A prominent example is Napoleon's transformation of the French armed forces with the concept of the *levée en masse*. This transformation showed dramatic organizational and doctrinal change that resulted from a nontechnological development: the emergence of French nationalism. The strength of the new identity resulted in increased trust within the army; Napoleon was able to adopt mission-type orders and deploy skirmishers because he could reasonably expect to maintain cohesion of the force without the coercive discipline common to other European militaries at the time. In response to Napoleon's transformation of warfare, other states replicated the French model and created nationalisms of their own to compete (Herrera and Mahnken 2003; Posen 1993).

Throughout this chapter, I focus on the strategic level of transformation, a force's overall vision of what concepts of operations will result in superior performance in the next war.[1] Information technologies are not breakthrough technologies that independently transform warfare, but the broad category of IT does contain many new force employments that together suggest the potential for transformation. To date, the most dramatically new employment technologies have been the microprocessor, networking hardware, and software. The microprocessor allows for unprecedented computation that is applicable to a very wide range of military behaviors, from the simplest aggregation of inputs (e.g. the status of soldiers in a sensor network) to highly advanced algorithms that optimize processes.[2] Computer networking technology most fundamentally changes communication and situational awareness. The speed of communication is not unique; the telegraph allowed for nearly instantaneous command and control from afar. Rather, IT dramatically increases the amount of information that may be transmitted at once and extends by several orders of magnitude the distance of instantaneous communication. This, in turn, has the potential to revolutionize command and control by allowing senior leaders to closely follow changes at the lowest levels of warfare; the bandwidth available over fiber optic and satellite networks can carry real-time video and sensor data on the battlespace.[3] Superior battlespace awareness also strongly affects the lower levels of military command, as officers are able to use this data to better synchronize responses to changing conditions.

Finally, software is an important and understudied variable underlying the modernization and transformation of military forces with IT. Before long, one may hear the phrase "bad code loses wars" invoked regularly within the military and defense contractor community.[4] The hardware deployed in new IT systems necessarily runs off computer code, and the quality of this code affects

1 Conceptually, transformation may occur at any of the three levels of combat (tactical, operational, and strategic). I caution readers to observe carefully how others use the phrase "force transformation"; many writers and officials tend not to distinguish between levels of warfare. For example, the Air Force has advertised the F-22 as "transformational" technology. This claim is true at the *tactical* level of air combat operations; testing of the F-22 against other aircraft demonstrates the overwhelming advantage of the F-22's stealth and battlespace awareness capabilities. The F-22 alone, however, is an insufficiently unique technology to completely change how the entire Air Force fights, much less the entire U.S. military. The U.S. has enjoyed air superiority in all of its conflicts since World War II, and the benefit of uber-superiority is not strategically transformational.

2 "Genetic algorithms," or other adaptive algorithms, are an excellent example. For an example relevant to warfare, consider the ability of advanced algorithms to reduce satellite blackout time.

3 At least one prominent author, retired Navy Admiral William A. Owens, has referred to the ability of militaries to "lift the fog of war." While even he would almost certainly agree that this view is hyperbolic, the potential to dramatically increase knowledge of developments during war—with practically perfect knowledge of the disposition of at least friendly forces—is real (Owens 2001).

4 Consider spectacular public failures of software written for complex U.S. weapon systems, such as the F-22. During a flight several years ago, an F-22 squadron's advanced electronic systems—the best in the

the utility and efficiency of the hardware. Speed is a factor of the code: better written software runs more quickly. In an exchange between militaries that are highly developed with IT, the edge of superior software could prove decisive. This is a particularly noteworthy point regarding large militaries such as that of the U.S., because the cost of changing or upgrading software is much greater than that of a small force. Issues like interoperability between platforms compound the problem. The example of the U.S. Army's Future Combat System (FCS) helps to illustrate these points. The Government Accountability Office concluded in spring 2008 that the Army's transformation program could "collapse under the weight of its poor software design." According to the report, the lines of software code in FCS had reached 95.1 million, almost triple the original estimate (Government Accountability Office 2008).

Software is also highly important in the independent information realm for several reasons. By the "independent information realm," I mean the data carried over networks without regard to the hardware carrying the data. One reason is that militaries need to operate in the broader cyberspace to conduct operations, which may include missions such as computer network attack against foreign adversaries. Another reason is that the militaries and governments have an interest in reaching foreign populations through cyberspace, such as in Western states trying to influence young Muslims not to engage in external jihad. A third is that the militaries' use of a common, global IT infrastructure renders operations susceptible to foreign network attacks, creating massive new defensive missions that are necessary for the implementation of NCW. Finally, as the general interconnectivity of societies increases and economies become more dependent on IT networks, classic threats in cyberspace—such as piracy and criminal hackers—may become of far greater security interest to states. This, in turn, may lead governments to undertake "policing" or "patrolling" behavior in cyberspace in a manner conceptually similar to defending otherwise ungoverned spaces, such as sea lines of communication.

Unlike most employment breakthroughs in warfare, IT *followed* in the private sector, rather than originated in it. The first computers, preceding the microprocessor, were designed for decryption and to help the U.S. military compute missile trajectories, and the most important networking technology, Internet Protocol, was developed by the Defense Department for continuity of operations during nuclear war (Agar 2003). Advancement with these technologies then occurred in the private sector—far outpacing the military—and the U.S. military is now catching up to where its own technology has evolved.

What is Network-centric Warfare?

Network-centric warfare is a broad term for a group of operational concepts that, together, are intended to enable a military to conduct missions quicker and more effectively. It is not, as its U.S. Department of Defense (DoD) proponents claimed, a theory of modern warfare (Office of Force Transformation 2005). The link between the operational concepts comprising NCW is that each is enabled by the integration of IT within the force; NCW is the U.S. DoD's answer to the question of how to seize the advantages of the IT revolution and catch up with advancements in the private sector. These concepts include self-synchronization, which is the ability of joint forces to react simultaneously and in a coordinated manner without waiting for central direction; the organization of military forces in a network whereby each constituent part—down to the level of individual

world—were disabled when the aircraft crossed the international time zone, thereby tripping a flaw in the on-board software (*Defense Industry Daily* 2007).

soldiers—is both a sensor and receiver of information in the network; increased speed of decision-making; enhanced battlespace awareness; and downward delegation of decision-making authority.

These concepts result in a vision of an NCW force that is able to execute combat operations extremely quickly and with very good battlespace awareness. Exactly how quickly and how aware are not defined, but examples of what a "network-centric" force ought to look like, such as the U.S. Army's experimentation with IT-enabled and reorganized Stryker combat brigades, suggest an objective of completing combat missions in well below a third of the time before the transformation and with fewer casualties (Gonzales et al. 2005). In terms of battlespace awareness, the U.S. military appears to have chosen as its threshold near-complete knowledge of friendly and enemy force disposition at the operational level, and the objective at the tactical level is at least complete knowledge of the location of friendly forces and minimal information on their status (DATL 2004; Kime 2004; Office of Force Transformation and Office of the Assistant Secretary of Defense for Networks and Information Integration 2003).

Navy Vice Admiral Arthur Cebrowski and a DoD civilian, John Garstka, formally introduced the term "network-centric warfare" in a 1998 U.S. Naval Institute Proceedings article.[5] Subsequently, much theoretical heavy lifting regarding NCW was done by two entities within the U.S. Department of Defense—the Office of Force Transformation (disbanded in 2006) and the office of the Assistant Secretary of Defense for Networks and Information Integration (Alberts et al. 2000; Alberts and Hayes 2003; Office of Force Transformation 2003, 2005; Office of Force Transformation and Office of the Assistant Secretary of Defense for Networks and Information Integration 2003). The concept faced significant backlash from defense commentators and retired military officers, many of whom argued that NCW is an overly technological vision of future warfare that neglects the "human element" of combat, but NCW has remained the dominant vision for U.S. force transformation.[6] No ideational competitor has emerged to displace NCW, and the defense press has observed U.S. military services acquiring IT, particularly new networks and command, control, communications, computation, intelligence, surveillance, and reconnaissance (C4ISR) systems, to improve combat operations (Fulghum 2005; Kasales 2002; Peck 2008; Sherman 2005; Singer 2009; Tuttle 2004; Wall 2003).

The NCW concept has spread widely during the time the U.S. has been grappling with how to transform in the midst of its wars.[7] Foreign defense civilians and military officers, such as

---

5 Cebrowski and Garstka (1998). For an insider's account of the development of NCW within the Defense Department, see Blaker (2007). While NCW is a relatively new term, the policy and academic discourse regarding IT-based military change stretches back for decades. As early as the 1970s, Soviet authors coined the phrase "military–technical revolution" to describe how the advent of advanced IT would result in a new organizational paradigm that they called "reconnaissance–strike complexes." Discussion among policy-makers, historians, and academics of how to systematically analyze the potential for IT to change the character of warfare developed under the heading of a "revolution in military affairs" (Adamsky 2008; Cohen 1996; Gray 2004; Knox and Williamson 2001; Krepinevich 1992; Marshall 1992, 1993).

6 For example, Hoffman and Van Riper (1998). Lieutenant Colonel Hoffman (U.S. MCR) and Retired Lieutenant General Van Riper (U.S. MC) suggest that the military should focus on creating better leaders instead of better technology. For similarly sweeping criticisms of NCW, see Cimbala (2005) and Vego (2003). Finally, a competing theory of future warfare, "Fourth Generation Warfare," argues that interstate wars are on the decline in favor of small-scale insurgency-like conflicts. Its proponents claim that the DoD's planned NCW transformation is inappropriate to such conflicts. For a summary and criticism of 4GW, see Junio (2009).

7 Ongoing combat operations in Iraq and Afghanistan have had mixed effects on the progress of NCW; current mission needs have detracted from the military's ability to prepare for the future, but experimentation with new concepts and technologies in wartime may prove to be a large influence on force transformation. As

those of Australia and Singapore, cite the original U.S. authors of NCW when discussing plans to transform their own forces (Evans 2006; Ming 2002). Other countries describe their interest in developing capabilities nearly identical to those of the U.S., but invoke different terminology. The British, for instance, say they are seeking a "network-enabled capability," rather than network-centric warfare (Barrielondon 2002). Many of these states, such as India, use U.S. terminology but pledge to adapt NCW to local circumstances (Press Trust of India 2005). In his book on NCW, *Transforming Military Force*, Jim Blaker writes, "Sweden, Singapore, and Australia … have made impressive strides … each matches or exceeds the United States technically in some key military areas. Sweden has developed what may be the world's best coastal surveillance system. The local air and sea surveillance and tracking systems developed by Singapore and Australia match and probably exceed those of the United States in reliability and sophistication" (Blaker 2007: 139).

Among these competing perspectives on how NCW will evolve, for clarity in this chapter, I will refer to NCW as the abstracted American "basket of concepts" definition. I will return to this question of country-specific transformations later, and now seek to examine more closely the issue of why the concept of NCW spread—diffused—around the world.

Analyzing NCW through Existing Prisms of Diffusion

Simply stated, military diffusion is the spread of a technology or behavior from one military to another. The explanation of how, why, and under what circumstances this occurs is not a simple matter, however. The study of diffusion is small relative to other fields of security studies, but like any branch of social science, there is no academic consensus on causal processes, and the truth for any given diffusion probably is a combination of factors. The analytic prisms used by academics—I use the words "prisms" or "paradigms" because only some are proper theories—include competition/neorealism, power relationships, offense–defense theory, organization, culture, and macro-level economic and social trends. Below, I briefly describe each prism and its applicability to NCW. In developing this overview of the field of diffusion, I borrow heavily on the work of Joao Resende-Santos, Emily Goldman, Rich Andres, and Colin Elman (Elman 1999; Goldman and Andres 1999; Resende-Santos 1996).

The competition/neorealist view of diffusion is that states will emulate each other in military practices owing to the structural pressures of the international system. The state of anarchy incentivizes states to prepare constantly for war, as they are unable to rely on a higher authority for their security, and the effectiveness of a state's armed forces is therefore of paramount importance. A state's observation of others in the international system will lead it to derive best practices and technologies to improve its own competitiveness. States most often will focus on the efforts of the most powerful state or states in the system for the obvious reason that the practices of the strongest are most likely to make others stronger. Practically every article or book noting this view of diffusion attributes its root to a quote from Kenneth Waltz, the father of the Neorealist School. In his *Theory of International Politics*, Waltz writes:

> The possibility that conflict will be conducted by force leads to competition in the arts and instruments of force … Contending states imitate the military innovations contrived by the country

Stephen Peter Rosen (1991) argues in *Winning the Next War*, many military innovations occur as lower-level officers become convinced of the utility of a new technology or practice and go on to use the technology or practice throughout their careers.

> of greatest capability and ingenuity. And so the weapons of the major contenders, even their military strategies, begin to look much the same all over the world.[8] (Waltz 1979: 127)

The diffusion of NCW appears to follow the basic logic of the neorealist theory; the most powerful military in the international system, that of the U.S., has embraced NCW as the best solution to preparing for future conflict. The competition/neorealist paradigm would suggest that the NCW model of the U.S. is being copied because other states perceive it as of the "greatest capability and ingenuity"; however, the U.S. NCW transformation is still in its early stages. The U.S. military has not yet written an NCW doctrine, and at the time it first demonstrated *early* concepts related to NCW in Operations Enduring Freedom and Iraqi Freedom, several states had already latched on to the NCW model. Therefore, there could not have been a demonstration effect of NCW in the international system. The only demonstration effect may have been from the *modernization* of forces using IT, but a foreign military's decision to pattern the use of IT is altogether different from a conscious decision to use *network-centric* warfare concepts. States face a variety of choices regarding what sort of IT military they would like to create; NCW is but one option.[9] Perhaps one may make an extended argument that, by virtue of past successes, the current U.S. military and defense bureaucracy have demonstrated their ability to do good future warfare strategy. However, while this sort of reputational demonstration effect may be plausible, it makes little sense within the neorealist paradigm, which focuses on the dire state of anarchy and states' strong motivations to have effective armed forces. For instance, Resende-Santos writes, "[s]tates are concerned with proven effectiveness, with those institutions or technologies that have been proven to work" (Resende-Santos 1996: 210). Staking one's future on another's past reputation—rather than on the proven effectiveness of a military system—is not a prediction that is consistent with the Neorealist School.

A second paradigm, closely related to neorealists' analysis of system structure, is that of power relationships determining military diffusion; for instance, states may be coerced to emulate a foreign military or may choose to bandwagon with a perceived threat (Eyre and Suchman 1996; Wendt and Barnett 1993). These arguments, too, are inapplicable to the NCW case. The states declaring intent to transform do not perceive the U.S. as threatening, and many are allies. One possible causal explanation is that states are transforming to maintain interoperability with the

8 Waltz (1979). Joao Resende-Santos and Colin Elman sought to modify Waltz's model of diffusion. Resende-Santos claims that variation in diffusion is due to states' relative vulnerability, and Resende-Santos believes a state's vulnerability is determined by the external balance of power—in other words, perceived threats, such as the likelihood of war—and the offense–defense balance. Colin Elman contradicts Waltz's "military strategies begin to look much the same all over the world" prediction, arguing that: states' factor endowments and geography make them more or less well suited to a particular practice; how states learn about foreign military innovation (such as through war) matters in how they emulate; and, the immanency and probable severity of war affects diffusion rates. The competition/neorealist model always will be incorrect if it is used as originally articulated by Waltz, Elman argues, because weapons and strategies never come to look the same around the world. I find these modifications are also unable to explain NCW. I discuss power balances and the offense–defense balance as separate diffusion paradigms in this chapter, and Elman's views regarding geography suffer the problem of highly variant geographical contexts among the NCW transformers (Elman 1999: 55–6, 375; Resende-Santos 1996: 195, 213, 215).

9 Even if networking were a universal concept for IT-based warfare, the design of any particular military network could differ greatly from that of any other. John Arquilla and David Ronfeldt, foundational scholars of networked warfare theory, describe different network organizations in their work *Networks and Netwars* (2001: 7–10). Many issues persist following network design, such as determining how much bandwidth to produce at each level within a military hierarchy.

U.S., as they see the U.S. as a guarantor of their security. Unfortunately, this argument is terribly inconsistent across cases: some close allies, such as Japan, are not transforming owing to domestic political constraints; some transforming allies pride themselves on having an independent security posture, such as Israel; and some transformers, like India, do not rely on the U.S. to defend them.

A third diffusion paradigm, offense–defense theory (ODT), suggests that states' perception of the offense–defense balance may motivate them to increase or decrease the pace and scope of their military emulation (Jervis 1978; Levy 1984; Lynn-Jones 1995; Quester 1977). I consider ODT as a separate theoretical framework, although Resende-Santos treats it as a supplement to the neorealist approach (Resende-Santos 1996: 215–16). Scholars of ODT fall into two camps, one of which views the offense–defense balance as a dyadic relationship that may be analyzed by a net assessment of two military powers (Glaser and Kaufmann 1998; Quester 1977; Van Evera 1999). The other groups of scholars describe a global character of military technology that may be offense- or defense-dominant, thereby increasing or decreasing the probability of war among an era's great powers (Adams 2003; Hopf 1991; Jervis 1978; Lynn-Jones 1995; Snyder 1994). For purposes of analyzing NCW, neither ODT approach is satisfying: NCW does not lend an inherent advantage to either offensive or defensive warfare. The concepts that NCW encapsulates—speed in operations and decision-making, devolved command and control, self-synchronization, and improved battlespace awareness—are equally important to attacking or defending forces.[10]

Another prism for analyzing military diffusion is organization theory, a view which focuses on how "the interests and empowerment of members of military organizations," and "existing values, past experiences, and needs," affect military responses to foreign developments (Elman 1999: 79; Goldman and Andres 1999: 9; Rogers 2003). While other prisms for military diffusion at least appear plausible, on its face the organization model seems an unlikely candidate, as the states pursuing NCW have very different military organizations. The only potential application of the organization model would be an extended argument that the military bureaucracies of transforming countries have strong incentive structures to use more IT; I have found no evidence that this is the case, however, other than the prospect that individual military personnel may be IT-savvy and thereby seek a networked force. This is an argument more consistent with a cultural view of diffusion.

Cultural perspectives on military diffusion present a fifth possible explanation for the diffusion of NCW. The cultural prism of diffusion suggests that cultural traits from a given society—extant outside of its military—cause members of the military to make judgments in ways distinct from other cultures. Only a handful of works look at how culture affects the incorporation of new technologies and practices into a force, and diffusion sometimes is discussed tangentially in works on strategic cultures (Fischerkeller 1998; Goldman 2006; Johnston 1995; Katzenstein 1996; Kier 1995; Wright 1955). Work in this subfield of diffusion studies focuses on the traditional political science view of culture, as a system of symbols, meanings, and norms. This approach to analyzing diffusion has little promise regarding NCW, as the states seeking NCW transformations

10 This is a simplistic statement of a long thought process. One can consider that, since distance is often a powerful obstacle for an attacking force to overcome, the logistical improvements enabled by NCW may give a strong offensive advantage. On the other hand, one may claim that a lack of information on an impending attack is a powerful obstacle for defending forces, and the improvement in battlespace awareness thereby is a strong defensive advantage. Similarly, the present relative weakness of network defenses suggests that NCW leads to more vulnerabilities for the attacking force; one may counter this claim by pointing out that the defending force is equally vulnerable to network attacks. Having considered many such scenarios, I reached the early conclusion that NCW is neither inherently offensive or defensive, and I hope future work may more rigorously address the issue.

stem from societies with very different cultures. Another view, however, may give some insight into NCW diffusion: if culture is viewed more broadly as loosely codified practices, there may be an independent culture of IT that has diffused through the societies in question.[11] I will, therefore, retain a "loose" cultural argument as a possible explanation for NCW diffusion and return to it later in this chapter.

The final prism through which scholars examine military diffusion may be called macro-social/economic. The basic argument behind this view is that broad changes in societies and economies with new technology eventually lead to new methods of military organization. A popular aphorism, that the way states make war reflects how they make wealth, is a manifestation of this perspective (Toffler and Toffler 1993). Few scholars adhere to this view, as it is usually associated with analysis of the industrial revolution in Western Europe, and has not proven nearly as successful at explaining other diffusions.[12] The argument sounds promising regarding the information revolution, for the widespread use of IT could spill over into military behavior. Unfortunately, this approach shares a similar problem to the competition/neorealist approach: while IT-based modernization probably could be partially explained by the model, NCW transformations—a much more precise answer to how to use IT—remains an open question. The perspective also lacks specificity regarding which elements of macro-social/economic change will affect military operations.

The existing literature on diffusion, therefore, does not have a complete model for analyzing the spread of NCW; the competition/neorealist and macro-social/economic approaches are promising only in the abstract. An untraditional cultural explanation appears to have greater explanatory power; the states pursuing NCW come from very different cultures, but perhaps the development of a *new* culture as a result of IT has made these societies more prone to follow the model of the U.S. To examine whether or not this is the case, I must first establish which countries are transforming with NCW (rather than merely claiming to want NCW), and then compare these countries along indicators of social and economic development with IT.

A First Look at Who is Transforming with IT

To determine which militaries are transforming with IT, I conducted searches on "network centric" and "military network" in Lexis-Nexis and EBSCO. In addition to news, these databases contain articles from academic journals, defense press, specialized trade publications, nonacademic defense journals, and press releases. I combed through the several thousand article hits for evidence of countries seeking technology for NCW and for countries' statements of transformation strategies. For all countries that appeared in the search, I maintained running folders with both affirming and refuting evidence regarding NCW transformation. Among several dozen countries of interest, I narrowed the list to 22 countries for which multiple reports suggested an interest in NCW. Next, I conducted country-specific searches for the countries with the fewest hits, to ensure that these militaries do not use alternative terminology that may not have returned results during my early searches.

11 This is not an entirely new perspective on "culture"; in fact, it follows Douglass North's view of culture as informal constraints on behavior. This view allows for culture to have been created from practically any source, not merely ethnic-oriented origins like tradition. See Chapter 5, "Informal Constraints," in North (1990).

12 See Goldman and Andres's (1999) overview of this model, which they call the "power-transitions theory." Goldman and Andres mostly attribute the perspective to Organski and Kugler (1980).

The important next step was to determine which countries are *really* transforming with NCW, as opposed to just saying so or acquiring new IT strictly for modernization. Among many possible variables, I chose five indicators of transformation that I consider most relevant. I limited the number of variables to five because, with 22 countries, conducting a truly complete review of each country's military dispositions would take literally years for one person to complete. The variables are whether or not each country has an articulated transformation *strategy* (rather than a mere statement of intent); is acquiring new IT specifically for NCW; is developing or deploying new military networks; is experimenting with NCW war fighting concepts and technology; or is developing new doctrine for NCW. These five indicators are shorthand of a framework for analyzing the state of a military's implementation of an innovation presented in Tom Mahnken's *Uncovering Ways of War*. Mahnken breaks the stages of innovation (the word is not used in the same manner as in this chapter; the "innovations" he analyzes are equivalent to "transformations" here) into three: speculation, experimentation, and implementation. Mahnken uses 14 indicators, however, a list too long to review given the large number of states potentially transforming with NCW (Mahnken 2002). I read through the data I had recorded for each country and conducted additional searches, including reviewing the public websites of each military, to look for transformation strategies and white papers. I coded a country's military as transforming if I recorded at least three positives among these five variables.

The results are a modest first approximation of which countries around the world are transforming in pursuit of NCW. These 12 countries are Australia, France, Germany, India, Israel, Italy, the Netherlands, Singapore, South Korea, Sweden, the U.S., and the UK. This finding alone is striking. As noted earlier, the countries claiming that they are interested in pursuing NCW are dramatically different from one another. The countries that are *really* transforming are similarly distinct; the coding did not indicate that only West European forces seek NCW, for example. Instead, militaries facing different future threats, stemming from various cultures and histories, and situated in unique institutional and political contexts all share a similar vision of what they want their future militaries to look like. Part of the surprise of these results is that NCW is a capabilities-based approach to defense planning; as opposed to, say, an anti-access strategy, NCW does not lend itself to fighting a particular adversary. This means that the transformers similarly perceive that the basket of NCW concepts will help them to win although each has a unique vision of their most likely next war. Another highly noteworthy finding is that practically no countries are in the process of developing NCW doctrine. Instead, even the most advanced countries, such as the U.S., have been seeking doctrinal insights from military experimentation. Only France has articulated a vision, which it calls a "space bubble," for its NCW doctrine.

Table 3.1 Coding of countries transforming in pursuit of network-centric warfare

Country	Strategy	Acquisition	New networks	Experimenting	Doctrine
Australia	1	1	1	1	0
Brazil	0	1	0	0	0
Brunei	0	1	0	0	0
China	0	1	0	0	0
Czech Republic	1	1	0	0	0
Finland	0	1	0	0	0
France	0	1	1	1	1
Germany	1	1	1	1	0
India	0	1	1	1	0
Israel	0	1	1	1	0
Italy	1	1	0	1	0
Malaysia	0	1	0	0	0
Netherlands	1	1	1	1	0
New Zealand	1	1	0	0	0
Norway	0	1	0	0	0
Russia	0	0	0	0	0
Singapore	1	1	1	1	0
South Korea	1	1	1	0	0
Sweden	1	1	0	1	0
United Arab Emirates	0	1	0	0	0
UK	1	1	1	1	0
U.S.	1	1	1	1	0

Before further examining the transforming countries, it is important to note several caveats about the coding process. First, the coding involved some abstraction. As described in the "What is Network-centric Warfare?" section, I use the general U.S. Defense Department approach to NCW that is academically and professionally useful, but other transformers may very well achieve the new war-fighting effects in different ways. For example, while all NCW militaries seek superior intelligence, surveillance, and reconnaissance systems, some may place a greater emphasis on unmanned aerial vehicles while others focus on satellite systems or land-based fixed infrastructure. Second, since NCW transformation is in its early-to-intermediate stages in even the most advanced militaries, such as that of the U.S., the threshold for coding a country as transforming is necessarily low. Many of the countries coded as transformers are still at the very beginning of the transformation process. India's military, for example, suffers from serious problems of disjointedness, and the pace of development with IT varies tremendously between services.[13]

A third caveat regarding the coding of transformers is the possibility that some countries, such as Russia and China, are particularly good at maintaining military secrets. If this is the case, then researchers will be unable to determine the degree to which these militaries are changing. Unfortunately, there is no way to get around this problem without throwing one's hands up in despair with any research endeavor into current military planning. The data I reviewed is as good as it can be to researchers outside the intelligence community, and I strove to make my research as replicable as possible. In my opinion, the data is not skewed by inaccessible information, for two reasons. First, I found extensive commentary on *modernization* efforts in some militaries suspected of transforming, such as that of China. These forces are attempting to "catch up" to the rest of the world with niche advanced IT capabilities and, on a force-wide basis, are unable to compete technologically with the most advanced forces.[14] Second, a broad trend in military technology is that militaries are no longer self-sufficient in force development. Practically every country has a supply chain of hardware and expertise that crosses borders. The defense press is thereby able to catch glimpses of countries' developments with IT. Similarly, the sending and receipt of military advisers is frequently announced for political purposes, such as to demonstrate improving relations between two states. The exception may be niche technologies that remain highly secretive; the record, however, suggests that even these transfers often do not remain secret for very long (Griffin and Lin 2008; U.S. Congress 1999).

Socialization with Information Technology

I now return to the research question of why these very different countries have militaries pursuing very similar concepts of future warfare. What is common to all of these countries? Could whatever makes them similar be causing them to seek similar transformations? One quality follows from a large literature in the social sciences: extensive penetration with IT changes societies and economies (Doueihi 2008; Joinson et al. 2007; Jordan 1999; Lessig 1999; Mitchell 2003; Renninger and Shumar 2002; Thomas 2002; Walker and Herrmann 2005). This should be an uncontroversial hypothesis, as anyone residing in an IT-rich society may observe the penetration of IT in practically every aspect of one's life. The single most important aspect

13 I thank Anit Mukherjee for our conversations regarding this point.

14 This conclusion appears consistent with other secondary source accounts that specifically review IT-based military change, such as the discussions of Chinese and Japanese military modernization in Goldman and Mahnken (2004) and chapter 7, "Chinese Network-centric Warfare," in Mulvenon et al. (2006).

is the interconnectivity of individuals within IT-rich societies. A "connected" person is able to access a large portion of the accumulated wisdom of mankind via the World Wide Web, and may communicate instantaneously with any other connected person in real time with voice, text, or (bandwidth-permitting) video. The low cost and high accessibility of the technology makes this fundamental social reordering widespread in the NCW transforming countries. This is nothing less than a complete change in how individuals network, and to those who have grown up in the networked world, a world without the network is difficult to conceive. The ability to network with others—including developing new relationships in online networks for the full range of human behaviors—has become second nature to those of the networked generation.

Perhaps the best way to understand how IT can change societies is to look past our own societies and instead examine those that are more remote and culturally unique. Ethnographers have chronicled how becoming "networked" into the rest of the world has caused social and cultural shocks. While this trend may partially be associated with the more general process of globalization, some recent work, such as that chronicled in the edited volume *Native on the Net: Indigenous and Diasporic Peoples in the Virtual Age*, focuses specifically on IT. For example, one essay in this book describes how youth in the remote island nation of Tonga have spurred a generational change as a result of online interaction with the Tongan diaspora in the West. According to ethnographer Helen Lee, online conversation has led to the opening of physical world conversation on topics traditionally considered taboo within Tongan culture, and as Tongan youth learn about the lives of diaspora Tongans, their social and economic expectations have become elevated. This case, and other cases in the book, demonstrates how technology is able to change societies—and one may plausibly assume that the effect is exaggerated as a society is further saturated with the new technology.

The economies of networked societies have been transformed in ways similar to the recognized social changes. One example is the measured shift in favor of service sectors; ideas are the most important new product in advanced economies (Bell 2007). Another shift, obvious but not as clearly measured, is the ubiquity of IT in the workplace and the organizational consequences that follow. In the NCW transformer countries—and niche elements of countries such as India—it is inconceivable to think of any major business not being saturated with IT and IT processes. Jobs increasingly—almost universally—involve using a computer or some other IT, and it is difficult to meet a college graduate who does not own a personal computer, use it at least daily, and expects to have a computer at their place of business. The ideational hegemony of IT networking is nearly complete in countries that are saturated with IT.

New cultures also have developed within cyberspaces. Some of these norms emerged over time based on the preferences of users while the designers of cyberspaces centrally created others. Some examples of these cyberspaces include text-based chat rooms, virtual worlds, discussion boards, and online games. Each has a range of practices that are considered acceptable by its members, and each has software limitations on what users are able to do. For instance, chat rooms have unique vocabulary, language, and norms (Haythornthwaite 2007; Holt 2004). How the cultures of these new cyberspaces may spill over into military behavior is less clear than the examples of how IT has created new physical world cultures, but one aspect of cyber culture that subtly affects military behavior is language. I have heard face-to-face requests to continue a conversation "offline" countless times in intelligence agencies and the Pentagon. While examples such as this do not demonstrate a causal link between IT culture and military transformation, of course, they are weak data on how IT culture pervades all aspects of societies.

If one accepts my qualitatively supported assertion that widespread use of IT results in different human behaviors—particularly in social networking—then it stands to reason that these behavioral changes are spilling over into how military personnel think through and solve problems. A *direct* causal argument, however, is extremely difficult to make, particularly given the absence of any large data set on the use of IT by officers and enlisted in any military.[15] This is also a tough causal argument to make because the military personnel under examination may not themselves be aware of the origins of their behavior, requiring an interpretivist explanation that will never be wholly satisfying to all readers. The link between IT societies and IT militaries is not impossible to divine, however: having coded the militaries transforming with IT, one can examine data on the saturation of these societies with IT. If the data are consistent, then the hypothesis that social and economic development with IT spills over into military behavior at least remains viable and further research should target a possible IT culture.[16] If the data are inconsistent with the hypothesis, then scholars must begin anew the search for causal explanations of the diffusion of NCW transformation.

The Transformers' IT Saturation Convergence

To analyze levels of social and economic saturation with IT, I used the World Bank's World Development Indicators (WDI) database, one of the few data sets that contains variables specifically on development with information and communication technology. A previous study, authored by Chris Demchak, attempted to answer a similar research question to the one posited here (although she focuses on modernization rather than transformation), but did not use direct IT indicators. Only one of Demchak's variables, electricity per capita, could have pointed to social development with IT (Demchak 2003). WDI data, including variables like bandwidth and personal computers per capita, provide a far more accurate look at how IT is used throughout a society or economy. I compiled descriptive statistics of states' saturation with IT, and did not perform more advanced statistical analysis for two simple and unavoidable reasons. First, 12 is too small a sample of transforming countries to produce meaningful regression analysis.

15 The closest research that has been done in this direction is Tom Mahnken and James FitzSimonds's *The Limits of Transformation: Officer Attitudes Toward the Revolution in Military Affairs* (2003), in which the authors' survey data supports the expectations presented here. Mahnken and FitzSimonds conclude that "85 percent of the officers [they] surveyed believed that forces employing information-age technology, doctrine, and organizations would enjoy a substantial edge over those that do not. Seventy-five percent felt that new ways of war would give the U.S. dominance over the full range of adversaries … Eighty-five percent believed that within [the next twenty years] computer network attack would become a central feature of military operations." On the other hand, the surveyed officers viewed "transformation" conservatively relative to the arguments I have presented (pp. 105–6).

16 Few political scientists have systematically studied how broad social traits are reflected in military behavior and organization. Most military historians, however, do not even question that militaries must reflect the societies whence they came. For example, in *War in European History*, Sir Michael Howard (1976) argues that the British and French refused to believe Hitler intended to wage war because of a process of social learning in which, generally, the memory of World War I in these populations made them more pacific. *Arabs at War*, by Kenneth Pollack (2002), makes a powerful argument that local culture is strongly causal in military effectiveness. A broader argument, made or alluded to in a large number of histories, is the claim that World War I military technology and organization reflected large-scale social and economic changes following the industrial revolution (Keegan 1994; Ropp 2000; Van Creveld 1989).

Second, attempts to compensate for the small "*n*," such as with re-sampling techniques or treating a "transformation year" as an observation, would in my view warp the data to the point of the result being practically useless.

Settling on a plan to produce descriptive statistics, I reviewed data on the entire world for 13 variables chosen to indicate how widely IT is diffused throughout the societies and economies of those countries experiencing NCW military transformation in comparison to those that are not transforming.[17] Arranging the data in a comparative table produces striking results. The countries coded as transforming with NCW have superior results on nearly all the WDI IT indicators compared with the rest of the world. The transformers also have far superior results compared with two random samples per variable taken from the rest of the world, indicating that the transformers are far more advanced with IT—and, presumably, more changed with IT—than any random handful of countries in the world (random sampling in the statistical software package "R"). The most indicative variables are those that show social saturation with IT, that is, the variables capturing a country's average levels of access to transnational networks and computers. For example, the NCW transformers have over six times the amount of bandwidth per capita than does the average person in the rest of the world, and the figure is nearly identical when compared with a random sample. Similarly, the transformers have five times as many computers per capita as the average country in the world or in random samples of countries. Aggregate sums, rather than per capita data, are even more telling: the transformers on average have over *20 times* the total bandwidth of nontransforming countries, and over *12 times* the average number of Internet users. The economic indicators are also impressive; the transformers' economies derive many more of their exports from computer and communication services and high-technology exports than does the rest of the world or random samples.

17 I did not tally data on countries that do not maintain independent security postures, as recorded in the CIA World Factbook. The WDI database was missing data for some countries in the year of analysis (either 2006 or 2005, depending on the variable). In these instances, I ran a linear regression based on historical (and future, if available) data to create a point estimate of the variable measure for that year. Any countries that were missing too much data to create a fair approximation for the base year (e.g. fewer than five data points), were excluded.

Table 3.2 Comparison of information technology integration indicators between NCW transformers and the rest of the world (all data for 2006, except those indicated with an asterisk, which are from 2005)[a]

Variable	Transformers' average	Transformers low[b]	Transformers high	World average	Random sample 1	Random sample 2
International Internet bandwidth per capita*	6,730.57	766.45 (Australia, projected)	20,501.59 (Netherlands)	1,156.33	2,693.05	801.95
Total international Internet bandwidth*	286,435.22	17,000 (Israel)	1,074,047.96 (U.S., projected)	10,590.4	5,821.7	11,179.14
Broadband subscribers per 100 population	19.94	14.66 (Italy)	31.76 (Netherlands)	3.63	4.62	4.60
Internet users per 100 population	55.14	26.94 (Israel)	85.65 (Netherlands)	18.14	29.09	17.95
Total Internet users	44,805,354.17	1,899,060 (Israel)	210,200,000 (U.S.)	5,980,213.5	3,483,803.43	1,973,950.53
Personal computers per 100 population*	58.32	29.64 (Israel, projected)	85.44 (Netherlands)	11.16	12.92	11.97
Total personal computers*	38,781,331.46	2,960,000 (Singapore)	230,400,000 (U.S.)	2,561,690.28	5,925,915.88	6,505,772.67
Secure Internet servers	30,019.92	1,286 (Israel)	259,881 (U.S.)	781.83	2,368.46	607.73
Mobile phone subscribers per 100 of population	95.87	80.76 (U.S.)	133.3 (Italy)	49.29	39.22	43.05
Total mobile phone subscribers	66,129,700.75	4,788,600 (Singapore)	241,800,000 (U.S.)	12,844,888.3	16,067,354.6	5,067,869
Computer services as a percentage of commercial exports	47.01	21.39 (Australia)	73.69 (India)	28.31	37.73	27.76
Computer services as a percentage of commercial imports	40.09	23.56 (Australia)	53.68 (Netherlands)	28.57	31.65	33.02
High-tech exports as a percentage of manufactured exports*	22.49	7.77 (Italy)	56.58 (Singapore)	8.74	6.38	9.12

Note: [a] Each variable excludes countries for which the reported data was too poor to create a point prediction for 2006 or 2005. The original data spreadsheets are available by subscription to the World Bank Development Indicators Database (accessible through the electronic resources of most university libraries).

[b] India excluded from ranges.

The data indicate, therefore, that the countries transforming with NCW are far more saturated with IT than the rest of the world. India is a partial exception: on per capita indicators, India falls far short of the other transforming countries. In aggregate measures, however, India is on par with the transformers. This finding is remarkable, as it suggests that a common causal process is underway in the diffusion of NCW, as opposed to random convergence or a unique causal argument for each country. *If one accepts my conclusion that IT has had dramatic effects on social and economic behavior, then the strong implications of my data analysis are that these new behaviors are spilling over into military practices and that a high degree of IT saturation is a necessary precondition for the development of NCW.*

Despite the strong correlation in the data regarding IT saturation and NCW transformation, two inconsistencies suggest that the IT culture spillover process is insufficient to fully explain NCW diffusion. The first inconsistency is the exceptional case of India. Based on the available data and coding scheme adopted for this study, India's military is in the early stages of a transformation, but its saturation with IT is far lower than the rest of the transformers on a per capita basis. The obvious answer to why India is an exception is that the country has extremely high-tech niches; Western countries heavily rely on India for information support services, and, economically speaking, Indian cities bear a resemblance to Western cities. The WDI indicators cannot identify militaries that are likely to transform based on a minority of the society that has transformed owing to a new IT culture. While this does not disprove my argument, it suggests that global analyses of saturation metrics will not suffice to identify all imminent transformations. The case of China is an important one in this regard; China's military is rapidly modernizing, and niche units are focused on the exploitation of IT for warfare. A reasonable argument may be made that, in the foreseeable future, China will attempt a force-wide transformation that takes advantage of these as well as other new technologies. The basic IT culture argument may apply, but would not be reflected in per capita data. China's enormous rural population, almost completely unexposed to the transformation of Chinese cities, skews the country's IT saturation metrics and suggests alternative measures are needed to analyze China's potential to seek NCW or another IT transformation.

A second, more challenging problem for the IT culture argument is that many countries have high levels of saturation with IT on the WDI data, but these countries are not transforming. This shows—very importantly—that one of three trends is occurring. First, other causal processes may be contributing to NCW transformation. Identifying these other causes is obviously challenging, as I have demonstrated that almost none of the academic arguments regarding diffusion are able to account for the spread of NCW. Having researched the NCW phenomenon a great deal, I believe I have the latitude to make some informed speculation about these possible additional causes. A powerful one that merits further investigation is the possibility that the defense contractor community has marketed NCW as a popular commodity—or has simply foreclosed options by offering NCW services rather than others. Many of the militaries under analysis buy hardware and defense consulting expertise from the same firms. Lockheed Martin, for example, has opened an NCW development facility in India, clearly with an intent to sell NCW products and concepts to the Indian military (Lockheed Martin 2008). Based on the available evidence, therefore, it is possible that the causal arrow points from the market to the state.

Similarly, alliance relationships may affect the diffusion of NCW. To some degree this may be a question of formal compliance with interoperability requirements within an alliance such as NATO. NATO maintains an Allied Transformation Headquarters based in Norfolk, Virginia—coincidentally or not, the same location as the U.S. Joint Forces Command's experimentation branch, one of the most forward-leaning agents of U.S. defense transformation. Alliance relationships may exhibit a follow-the-leader phenomenon that is partially consistent with the neorealist explanation:

some U.S. security partners may seek their future warfare advice from the U.S. to maintain close relations or simply for lack of better alternatives. Both proposed additional causes—choices between the defense contractor and allied advisory communities—fail to explain in a general way why some countries choose NCW and others do not, however. Tacking on more explanations than my IT culture claim may make the causal process more complete on a case-by-case basis, but generalization beyond the necessary condition of IT saturation appears to be an unlikely prospect.

A second possible reason is that other factors may be hindering countries that otherwise would seek military transformation. Most prominent among these hindrances are domestic politics and resource constraints. Almost all of the countries with high IT saturation statistics are in Western Europe, with the exception of Japan. These countries either lack the political will to increase defense spending or simply cannot afford to, as evidenced by a cursory glance at their military spending as a part of GDP. Indeed, re-reviewing the data in light of this question, I find that many of these countries are among those that I noted as declaring an interest in NCW; they are thinking about future warfare in the same terms as the transformers, but are not transforming.

Third, it is possible that different IT cultures are developing owing to interaction with local culture, or that some local cultures are interfering with the adoption of an IT because these cultures are less compatible with IT than others. This analysis follows some work from the private sector. One book using contrasting case studies of British and Japanese networking argues that preexisting cultural predilections in favor of decentralization and centralization, respectively, affected how firms developed their IT architectures (Kambayashi 2003). A more hierarchical society, therefore, may become saturated with IT, but not with the social networking IT culture, because of a combination of cultural deference to authority and government actions to control the flow of information within its borders.

Conclusion

This chapter has offered a first answer to the question of why NCW is spreading around the world. I used data on military trends and social and economic development with IT to stake a claim that high penetration with IT leads to a new culture of social networking, and that over time, this new culture spills over into military behavior. While this argument is compelling—and, by far, comports more closely with reality than any existing model of military diffusion—several gaps remain in the causal narrative. The evidence is sufficiently strong to merit follow-on research, and I dedicate the remainder of this chapter to highlighting the most promising lines of future research and the reasons why NCW diffusion is important to the broader study of military change.

A first prospect for additional work is to develop a formal model or theory of how technology cultures affect military diffusion. Such a model or theory would reverse the traditional analysis of culture; most of the time, analysts consider how an existing culture affects the use of a new technology. *The argument of this chapter implies that technologies may have their own cultures based on what those technologies make possible.* A second line of research is comparative case studies of the causal process underlying several countries' choices of NCW and decisions on how to implement their transformations. A third clearly important research project would be one that more closely examines the relationship between IT-heavy societies and their militaries. What is the IT culture of transforming militaries? One powerful data set would be surveys of military officer and enlisted use of IT; this would give insight into the subtle ways in which IT is altering human behavior with spillover consequences for the conduct of warfare. Finally, as argued in this chapter, NCW is but one approach to how to transform a military with IT. A fascinating future research project could look at alternative organizational models for IT-rich militaries; for example, while NCW focuses on delegating decision-making authority downward, IT could just as easily empower centralized control of a force.

The question of how IT is changing military behavior remains inconclusive. This study, however, helps to delineate where scholars should draw, or redraw, the boundaries of the debate regarding future warfare. In particular, my data and argumentation give modest credence to the view of those who focus on analyzing technological change. While the fields of political and military science have been unable to produce a diagram of what background and qualities produce superior leadership, technology-focused research has been able to show the potential for unique and superior combat operations. The utility of these technologies always will depend on the quality of integration and training, of course, but critics who claim these issues are paramount tend to ignore the basic and incontrovertible point that inventions and innovations create possibilities where none existed before. These possibilities are subject to human choice, but the qualities of new technologies constrain what choices are possible. Focusing on what new military behaviors are made possible by IT is a necessary starting point for the later analysis of how best to incorporate those technologies to achieve the world's next militaries.

References

Adams, Karen Ruth. 2003. "Attack and Conquer? International Anarchy and the Offense–Defense–Deterrence Balance." *International Security* 28(3): 45–83.

Adamsky, Dima. 2008. "Through the Looking Glass: The Soviet Military–Technical Revolution and the American Revolution in Military Affairs." *Journal of Strategic Studies* 31(2): 257–94.

Adamsky, Dima. 2010. *The Culture of Military Innovation: The Impact of Cultural Factors on the Revolution in Military Affairs in Russia, the U.S., and Israel*. Stanford, CA: Stanford University Press.

Adamsky, Dima and Kjell Inge Bjerga. 2010. "Introduction to the Information-Technology Revolution in Military Affairs." *Journal of Strategic Studies* 33(4): 463–8.

Agar, Jon. 2003. *The Government Machine: A Revolutionary History of the Computer*. Cambridge: MIT Press.

Alberts, David S., John J. Garstka, and Frederick P. Stein. 2000. *Network Centric Warfare: Developing and Leveraging Information Superiority*, 2nd edition. Washington, DC: Department of Defense Command and Control Research Program.

Alberts, David S. and Richard E. Hayes. 2003. *Power to the Edge*. Washington, DC: Department of Defense Command and Control Research Program.

Arquilla, John and David Ronfeldt (eds). 1997. *In Athena's Camp: Preparing for Conflict in the Information Age*. Santa Monica: RAND.

Arquilla, John and David Ronfeldt (eds). 2001. *Networks and Netwars: The Future of Terror, Crime, and Militancy*. Santa Monica: RAND.

Barrielondon, Douglas. 2002. "Britain Determines Military Net Value." *Aviation Week and Space Technology* 157(26): 53.

Bell, Daniel. 2007. *The Coming Postindustrial Society*. New York: McGraw Hill.

Blaker, James R. 2007. *Transforming Military Force: The Legacy of Arthur Cebrowski and Network Centric Warfare*. Westport, CT: Praeger.

Brynjolfsson, Erik and Lorin M. Hitt. 2000. "Beyond Computation: Information Technology, Organizational Transformation, and Business Performance." *Journal of Economic Perspectives* 14(4): 23–48.

Brynjolfsson, Erik and Lorin M. Hitt. 2003. "Computing Productivity: Firm-Level Evidence." *Review of Economics and Statistics* 85(4): 793–808.

Cebrowski, Arthur K. and John J. Garstka. 1998. "Network-Centric Warfare: Its Origins and Future." *U.S. Naval Institute Proceedings* 124(1): 28–35.

Christensen, Clayton. 1997. *The Innovator's Dilemma: When New Technologies Cause Great Firms to Fail*. Cambridge, MA: Harvard Business Press.

Christensen, Clayton and Joseph L. Bower. 1995. "Disruptive Technologies: Catching the Wave." *Harvard Business Review* January–February: 43–53.

Cimbala, Stephen J. 2005. "Transformation in Concept and Policy." *Joint Force Quarterly* 38: 28–33.

Cohen, Eliot A. 1996. "A Revolution in Warfare." *Foreign Affairs* 75: 37–54.

Cummins, Jason G. 2004. *A New Approach to the Valuation of Intangible Capital*. FEDS working paper no. 2004-17 (April).

DATL. 2004. "DoD List of Force Transformation Case Studies." *Defense Acquisition, Technology and Logistics* September–October: 74–5.

Defense Industry Daily. 2007. "F-22 Squadron Shot Down by International Date Line." *Defense Industry Daily*. Available at: http://www.defenseindustrydaily.com/f22-squadron-shot-down-by-the-international-date-line-03087/ [accessed: 1 August 2011].

Demchak, Chris C. 2003. "Creating the Enemy: Global Diffusion of the Information Technology-based Military Model." In *The Diffusion of Military Technology and Ideas*, ed. Emily Goldman and Leslie Eliason. Stanford, CA: Stanford University Press.

Doueihi, Milad. 2008. *La Grande Conversion Numerique*. Paris: Seuil.

Elman, Colin. 1999. *The Logic of Emulation: The Diffusion of Military Practices in the International System*. New York: Department of Political Science, Columbia University.

Evans, Michael. 2006. "Australia and Defense Transformation." *Defence Studies* 6(2): 133–49.

Eyre, Dana P. and Mark C. Suchman. 1996. "Status, Norms, and the Proliferation of Conventional Weapons: an Institutional Theory Approach." In *The Culture of National Security*, ed. Peter J. Katzenstein. New York: Columbia University Press.

Farrell, Theo. 2010. "Improving in War: Military Adaptation and the British in Helmand Province, Afghanistan, 2006–2009." *Journal of Strategic Studies* 33(4): 567–94.

Fischerkeller, Michael P. 1998. "David Versus Goliath: Cultural Judgments in Asymmetric Wars." *Security Studies* 7(4): 1–43.

Fulghum, David A. 2005. "Wireless War." *Aviation Week and Space Technology* 163(10): 48–50.

Government Accountability Office. 2008. *Defense Acquisitions: 2009 Review of Future Combat System is Critical to Program's Direction*. Testimony to the United States Congress. Document no. GAO-08-638T, 10 April.

Glaser, Charles L. and Chaim Kaufmann. 1998. "What is the Offense–Defense Balance and Can We Measure it?" *International Security* 22(4): 44–82.

Golder, Peter N. and Gerard J. Tellis. 1997. "Will It Ever Fly? Modeling the Takeoff of Really New Consumer Durables." *Marketing Science* 16(3): 256–70.

Goldman, Emily O. 2004. "Introduction: Information Resources and Military Performance." *Journal of Strategic Studies* 27(2): 195–219.

Goldman, Emily O. 2006. "Cultural Foundations of Military Diffusion." *Review of International Studies* 32: 69–91.

Goldman, Emily O. and Richard B. Andres. 1999. "Systemic Effects of Military Innovation and Diffusion." *Security Studies* 8(4): 79–125.

Goldman, Emily O. and Thomas G. Mahnken (eds). 2004. *The Information Revolution in Military Affairs in Asia*. New York: Palgrave MacMillan.

Gonzales, Daniel et al. 2005. *Network-centric Operations Case Study: The Stryker Brigade Combat Team*. Santa Monica: RAND.

Gray, Colin. 2004. *Strategy for Chaos: Revolutions in Military Affairs and the Evidence of History*. London: Frank Cass.

Griffin, Christopher and Joseph E. Lin. 2008. "China's Space Ambitions." *Armed Forces Journal* 145(9): 18–21.

Haythornthwaite, Caroline. 2007. "Social Networks and Online Community." In *The Oxford Handbook of Internet Psychology*, ed. Adam N. Joinson, Katelyn Y.A. McKenna, Tom Postmes, and Ulf-Dietrich Reips. Oxford: Oxford University Press.

Henderson, Rebecca. 1993. "Underinvestment and Incompetence as Responses to Radical Innovation." *RAND Journal of Economics* 24(2): 248–70.

Herrera, Geoffrey L. and Thomas G. Mahnken. 2003. "Military Diffusion in Nineteenth-Century Europe: The Napoleonic and Prussian Military Systems." In *The Diffusion of Military Technology and Ideas*, ed. Emily O. Goldman and Leslie C. Eliason. Stanford, CA: Stanford University Press.

Hoffman, Frank and Paul K. Van Riper, 1998. "Pursuing the Real Revolution in Military Affairs: Exploiting Knowledge-Based Warfare." *National Security Studies Quarterly* 4(3): 1–20.

Holt, Richard. 2004. *Dialogue on the Internet: Language, Civic Identity, and Computer-Mediated Communication*. Westport, CT: Praeger.

Hopf, Ted. 1991. "Polarity, The Offense Defense Balance, and War." *The American Political Science Review* 85(2): 475–93.

Howard, Michael. 1976. *War in European History*. Oxford: Oxford University Press.

Jervis, Robert. 1978. "Cooperation Under the Security Dilemma." *World Politics* 30(2): 167–214.

Johnston, Alastair Iain. 1995. "Thinking About Strategic Culture." *International Security* 19(4): 35.

Joinson, Adam N., Katelyn Y.A. McKenna, Tom Postmes and Ulf-Dietrich Reips (eds). 2007. *The Oxford Handbook of Internet Psychology*. Oxford: Oxford University Press.

Jordan, Tim. 1999. *Cyberpower: The Culture and Politics of Cyberspace and the Internet*. London: Routledge.

Junio, Timothy J. 2009. "Military History and Fourth Generation Warfare." *Journal of Strategic Studies* 32(2): 243–69.

Kambayashi, Norio. 2003. *Cultural Influences on IT Use: A UK–Japanese Comparison*. New York: Palgrave Macmillan.

Kasales, Michael C. 2002. "The Reconnaissance Squadron and ISR Operations." *Military Review* 82(3): 52–8.

Katzenstein, Peter J. (ed.). 1996. *The Culture of National Security*. New York: Columbia University Press.

Keegan, John. 1994. *A History of Warfare*. New York: Knopf.

Kier, Elizabeth. 1995. "Culture and Military Doctrine: France Between the Wars." *International Security* 19(4): 65–93.

Kime, Patricia. 2004. "OFT Case Studies Aim to Codify Tenets of Networked Operations." *Sea Power* March: 21–2.

Knox, MacGregor and Murray Williamson. 2001. *The Dynamics of Military Revolution, 1300–2050*. Cambridge: Cambridge University Press.

Krepinevich, Andrew F. 1992. "The Military-Technical Revolution: A Preliminary Assessment." Washington, DC: Department of Defense Office of Net Assessment (released by Center for Strategic and Budgetary Assessments under the same name in 2002).

Latham, Robert. 2003. *Bombs and Bandwidth: The Emerging Relationship Between Information Technology and Security*. New York: Free Press.

Lessig, Lawrence. 1999. *Code, and Other Laws of Cyberspace*. New York: Basic Books.

Levy, Jack S. 1984. "The Offensive/Defensive Balance of Military Technology: A Theoretical and Historical Analysis." *International Studies Quarterly* 28(2): 219–38.

Lockheed Martin. 2008. "Lockheed Martin Showcases Proven Performance, Global Partnerships and Innovation at DEFEXPO India 2008."

Lynn-Jones, Sean. 1995. "Offense–Defense Theory and Its Critics." *Security Studies* 4(4): 660–91.

Mahnken, Thomas G. 2002. *Uncovering Ways of War: U.S. Intelligence and Foreign Military Innovation, 1918–1941*. Ithaca, NY: Cornell University Press.

Mahnken, Thomas and James R. FitzSimonds. 2003. *The Limits of Transformation: Officer Attitudes Toward the Revolution in Military Affairs*. Newport, RI: Naval War College.

Marshall, Andrew. 1992. *The Military–Technical Revolution: A Preliminary Assessment*. ed. Office of Net Assessment Department of Defense.

Marshall, Andrew. 1993. *Some Thoughts on Military Revolutions—Second Version*. Office of Net Assessment Department of Defense.

Ming, James Tan Chong. 2002. "Embracing Network-Centric Warfare in the Information Age." *Pointer [Official Journal of the Singapore Armed Forces]* 28(2).

Mitchell, William. 2003. *Me++: The Cyborg Self and the Networked City*. Cambridge, MA: MIT Press.

Mulvenon, James et al. 2006. *Chinese Responses to U.S. Military Transformation and Implications for the Department of Defense*. Santa Monica, CA: RAND.

North, Douglass C. 1990. *Institutions, Institutional Change, and Economic Performance*. Cambridge: Cambridge University Press.

Nye, Joseph S. and William A. Owens. 1996. "America's Information Edge." *Foreign Affairs* 75(2): 20–36.

Office of Force Transformation. 2003. *Military Transformation: A Strategic Approach*. Government document. U.S. Department of Defense.

Office of Force Transformation. 2005. *The Implementation of Network-centric Warfare*. Government document. U.S. Department of Defense.

Office of Force Transformation and Office of the Assistant Secretary of Defense for Networks and Information Integration. 2003. *[Network-Centric Operations] Conceptual Framework Case Study Template Illustrative Example*. Government document (PowerPoint presentation). U.S. Department of Defense.

Organski, A.F.K. and Jacek Kugler. 1980. *The War Ledger*. Chicago, IL: University of Chicago Press.

Owens, William A. 2001. *Lifting the Fog of War*. Baltimore, MD: Johns Hopkins University Press.

Peck, Allen G. 2008. "Airpower's Crucial Role in Irregular Warfare." *Military Technology* 32(3): 16–23.

Pollack, Kenneth M. 2002. *Arabs at War*. Lincoln, NE: University of Nebraska Press.

Posen, Barry R. 1993. "Nationalism, the Mass Army, and Military Power." *International Security* 18(2): 80–124.

Press Trust of India. 2005. *Do Not Copy West Blindly on Net-Centric Warfare: Army Chief*. Press Trust of India.

Quester, George H. 1977. *Offense and Defense in the International System*. New York: John Wiley & Sons.
Renninger, K. Ann and Wesley Shumar (eds). 2002. *Building Virtual Communities: Learning and Change in Cyberspace*. Cambridge: Cambridge University Press.
Resende-Santos, Joao. 1996. "Anarchy and the Emulation of Military Systems: Military Organization and Technology in South America." *Security Studies* 5(3): 193–260.
Rogers, Everett. 2003. *The Diffusion of Innovations*, 5th edition. New York: Free Press.
Ropp, Theodore. 2000. *War in the Modern World*. Baltimore, MD: Johns Hopkins University Press.
Rosen, Stephen Peter. 1991. *Winning the Next War: Innovation and the Modern Military*. Ithaca, NY: Cornell University Press.
Russell, James A. 2010. "Innovation in War: Counterinsurgency Operations in Anbar and Ninewa Provinces, Iraq, 2005–2007." *Journal of Strategic Studies* 33(4): 595–624.
Sherman, Jason. 2005. "The Drone Wars." *Bulletin of the Atomic Scientists* 61(5): 28–37.
Singer, P.W. 2009. *Wired for War: The Robotics Revolution and Conflict in the Twenty-first Century*. New York: Penguin Press.
Sloan, Elinor. 2002. *The Revolution in Military Affairs*. Montreal: McGill-Queen's University Press.
Snyder, Jack. 1994. "Civil–Military Relations and the Cult of the Offensive, 1914 and 1984." *International Security* 9(1): 108–46.
Solow, Robert M. 1987. "We'd Better Watch Out." *New York Times*, 12 July, p. 36.
Thomas, Douglas. 2002. *Hacker Culture*. Minneapolis, MN: University of Minnesota Press.
Toffler, Alvin and Heidi Toffler. 1993. *War and Anti-war*. New York: Warner Books.
Tushman, Michael L. and Philip Anderson. 1986. "Technological Discontinuities and Organizational Environments." *Administrative Science Quarterly* 31: 439–65.
Tuttle, Rich. 2004. "Beyond Blue Force Tracker." *Aviation Week and Space Technology* 160(8): 84.
U.S. Congress. 1999. *Report of the Select Committee on U.S. National Security and Military/Commercial Concerns with the People's Republic of China*. ("The Cox Report.") U.S. Congress.
Van Creveld, Martin L. 1989. *Technology and War: From 2000 B.C. to the Present*. New York: Free Press.
Van Evera, Stephen. 1999. *Causes of War*. Ithaca, NY: Cornell University Press.
Vego, Milan. 2003. "Net-Centric is Not Decisive." *U.S. Naval Institute Proceedings* 129(1).
Walker, W. Richard and Douglas J. Herrmann. 2005. *Cognitive Technology: Essays on the Transformation of Thought and Society*. Jefferson, NC: McFarland.
Wall, Robert. 2003. "Finding the Needle." *Aviation Week and Space Technology* 159(25): 28–9.
Waltz, Kenneth. 1979. *Theory of International Politics*. Reading, MA: Addison-Wesley.
Wendt, Alexander and Michael Barnett. 1993. "Dependent State Formation and Third World Militarization." *Review of International Studies* 19: 321–47.
Wright, Quincy. 1955. *The Study of International Relations*. New York: Appleton-Century-Crofts.

Chapter 4
VIEWPOINT: Cyberterrorism: Cyber "Pearl Harbor" is Imminent

Emily Molfino

Terrorism has evolved partly as a consequence of absorbing technological advances. Defining contemporary terrorism is challenging owing to the sheer breadth of actions included under the single term (German 2007). Even with this lack of agreement, various academic and policy definitions do converge on some basic elements. As defined by Bruce Hoffman in *Inside Terrorism*, terrorism is violence or the threat of violence "used and directed in pursuit of, or in service of, a political aim." Terrorism is a premeditated act enmeshed in politics and power focused on the goal of generating fear and changing the current system (Hoffman 1998: 15, 41–3). Moreover, where traditional war is between nation states, terrorism is conducted by assorted nonstate actors—state-sanctioned or not—against a state, community or other civilian targets. These qualifiers help distinguish terrorism from other types of violent acts. Yet, this definition is not comprehensive enough in regard to the cyber world. As cyberterrorism does not wage physical violence, a comprehensive definition for terrorism must not be solely based in the physical world. Mike German, an FBI investigator, saw it as essential to highlight the criminal properties of terrorism: terrorism is a war crime without a war. Terrorism is fundamentally a criminal act (German 2007). With no international authority, this criminal quality is an important component of terrorism in regard to prevention and prosecution at the domestic level.

Not only are terrorists' motivations different than "typical" criminals, so are the influences in their decision-making. The specific strategies and targets of terrorism are a function of ideology, organization, leading members, perceived audience, and various internal and external stimuli. Contrary to what some might initially believe, terrorists are rational beings whose targets are chosen based on their view of expected rewards while strategies must align with the terrorist's political aim. Additionally, terrorist groups are dependent on the support of their audience financially and psychologically; the costs of an act of terror must be within the threshold the terrorist group's audience is willing to accept (Hoffman 1998).

Yet what triggered this seemingly sudden upsurge in terrorist threats and acts? Is it merely coincidence that terrorism entered into everyday language around the world at the same time advances in information and communication technologies grew exponentially? In his popular books, Thomas Friedman includes the Internet as one of the many reasons terrorist organizations like Al-Qaeda emerged and grew in followers. As technologies like the Internet shrank the world, cultures increasingly found themselves frustrated and angry. People started comparing themselves with others around the world, leading to a collective feeling of humiliation (Friedman 2005). This humiliation led some individuals into anti-West ideologies and organizations that supported terrorism, including cyberterrorism.

Terrorist Use of Technology

The National Commission on Terrorist Attacks underscored the relationship between terrorism and technology: "Terrorists … have benefited from this same rapid development of communication technologies" (National Commission on Terrorist Attacks 2004: 88). Terrorists frequently employ information and communication technologies (ICTs) as a tool in planning and executing operations. For instance, the Internet provides users access to a multitude of information—such as bomb-making manuals—alongside the numerous digital communication tools, both of which potential terrorists can exploit (Hoffman 1998). Yet, if contemporary terrorism is frequently used against Western norms and ideals, why then is modern technology, born in these very same cultures, such an advantageous tool for these organizations and individuals? The answer can be pared down to the fundamental structures of terrorist organizations and the digital world. Compared with previous eras, modern-day terrorist groups are decentralized, international, and dynamic in structure, have greater ability for destruction, and are no longer dependent on state sponsorship (National Commission on Terrorist Attacks 2004). The structure of the Internet fits perfectly with these characteristics: the Internet is decentralized and naturally unfiltered unless an outside entity intervenes, and the Internet is international and dynamic with a constant flood of new and potential users, websites, and digital postings.

Moreover, as technology rapidly advances, terrorist organizations must try to keep one step in front of the game in regard to their use of technology. This includes finding the best ways to employ technologies while also finding and exploiting potential vulnerabilities (Hoffman 1998). Take Louis Beam, former Klansman and Aryan Nations ambassador, who was pivotal in taking the white supremacist movement in America into the digital era. His "leaderless resistance"—a term coined in a 1983 article well before the World Wide Web—became possible with the rise of modern information and communication technologies. Beam's "leaderless resistance" was originally created to support white supremacist terrorism and centered around "phantom cell networks" and "autonomous leadership units" whose leaders and members were independent of each other. Their individual acts of terror would reinforce each other, leading to an ensuing revolution (Hoffman 1998: 117–18; German 2007: 11–12). This structure requires a way to communicate messages and plans remotely and in varying locations; the Internet is able to provide these things. This potential utility is still recognized today with Al-Qaeda calling on its supporters to learn and exploit ICTs: "We strongly urge Muslim Internet professionals to spread and disseminate news and information about the jihad through email lists, discussion groups and their own Websites … We must make the Internet our tool" (Weimann 2006: 28).

Both the direct uses and indirect influences of the Internet are key to understanding how technologies shape contemporary terrorism. The Internet has allowed increased isolation of individuals and increased connectedness to an outside identity (Bjorn-Andersen et al. 1982). It can be said that it is the result of Internet technology that a particular form of Muslim identity and solidarity—not the only identity, however—sympathetic to terrorist organizations (Friedman 2005) has been able to grow in supporters and influence. In a direct sense, individuals and groups can access needed information to act upon their grievances: propaganda, recruitment, psychological warfare, and fundraising efforts are quickly spread by use of the Internet (Costigan 2007); websites and chat-rooms disseminate dogma and potential terrorists plan and execute future attacks. Furthermore, the structure of the Internet allows for the quick evasion of investigators credited to the ability to relocate websites and change Internet Service Providers (ISPs) at record speeds (Weimann 2006). Along with this, terrorist groups have access to encryption tools, creating "virtual safe houses" for communication (Costigan 2007). All this can be done at a distance out of the reach of law enforcement (Schneier 2009). This is important as rising threats make international travel to certain areas in the world more difficult for some individuals if not nearly impossible. Yet, there are few borders in the virtual world, and the borders that do exist can be easily infiltrated. This anonymity, evasiveness, and dissemination power increases the uncertainty behind potential threats on the web.

As technology rapidly infiltrates society, governments must react just as quickly to ensure the proper evolvement and utilization of security policy. This requires governments being able to predict future consequences of future technological advancements (Bjorn-Andersen et al. 1982) just as quickly, if not more quickly, than terrorists' use of these advancements—a difficult task in a security environment concerned with the present. Security policy has long been dependent on technology (Johnson 1998). However, today's threats are not based on weapon technology as it was during the Cold War, but rather on ICTs. This alters how states will react to threats: "The [Defense Intelligence Agency] acknowledges that key trends in military technology have the potential to change the nature of warfare and the characteristics of that threat" (Johnson 1998: 1). Militaries often claim that security will drift toward those states that embrace civilian and military technologies and place them into their own systems and models (Johnson 1998). Upcoming chapters will cover such issues in regard to cyberwar. Yet, dependency on technology—especially on ICTs—has its downsides. On the Internet, groups and individuals can be perceived as a bigger threat than they are in reality (Weimann 2006), which encourages overreaction. It is easy to post videos and blogs, and communicate with like-minded groups; it is another to have the capability to follow through with terror plans. As terrorist organizations recruit more tech-savvy members, we cannot rely on this lack of ability much longer.

National security is no longer threatened by terrorists' physical existence; we must also consider terrorists' cyber existence. Osama bin Laden long ago identified cyberspace as "a means to damage both our economy and our psyche—and countless extremists have taken this to heart," said FBI Director Robert S. Muller at the RSA Conference in San Francisco (Nakashima 2010). It needs to be emphasized, though, that terrorist use of Internet technology as a tool for their activities is not cyberterrorism (Stohl 2006). Nevertheless, terrorists are now using the cyber world not only as tool but also as their arena for attack, thus conducting cyberterrorism.

Defining Cyberterrorism?

Almost everything we do every day is somehow connected and/or dependent on virtual networks (Verton 2003). Therefore, we are susceptible to cyber attacks in all directions—unless you are a true Luddite or hermit. It needs to be noted that cyberterrorism did not appear out of thin air. Cybercrime has been occurring for most of the period of computer networks' existence. In fact, over $48 billion is lost annually as a result of cybercrime (Council of Europe Staff 2007). Yet, this does not mean cybercrime is the same thing as cyberterrorism, just as international crime is a different entity than international terror. The term "cyberterrorism" comes from combining the cyberspace with terrorism. Just as there are countless of definitions of terrorism, there is yet to be an official definition of cyberterrorism. Essentially, as defined in Jonathan Matusitz's article, cyberterrorism is an act of terror that is conducted via computer network technology—like the Internet—against computer and/or network infrastructure that takes place in a virtual world. Some brief examples include destroying technological infrastructure via virtual tools, breaking into the controls of top clearance areas like nuclear power plants, using computers to break into and shut off power grids, and creating disruptions in federal networks (Matusitz 2008; Pollitt n.d.).

Cyberterrorism is ultimately the convergence of the symbolic, virtual world with the physical world—a union that is growing in complexity every day as our drive towards access, control, and mining increases (Collin n.d.). As this convergence grows, the fears of an "Electronic Pearl Harbor" also intensify (Stohl 2006: 223–4). Such an attack will not be with "normal" weapons: what the bomb is to conventional warfare, the virus is to cyberterrorism. As of 2003, over 50,000 computer viruses and over 30,000 hacker-related websites existed (Verton 2003). Problems and fears are multiplied when cyber experts are unsure about the purpose of a discovered virus, which can lie latent for years before found or activated (Matusitz 2008). Similar to viruses, but more controlled, botnets can be programmed and released around the Internet without notice. When the services of the botnet are needed, the bots can be activated to conduct massive attacks. An additional well-known cyber-tool to be exploited by terrorists is hacking (Council of Europe Staff 2007): hacking is when a person breaks into an unauthorized network by the use of cyber-tools. Nonetheless, it is important to distinguish between hacking activities and cyberterrorism. Hacking by itself is different from cyberterrorism because damage caused by hacking is not premeditated and the act itself is not malevolent (Matusitz 2008). The same thing goes with "hacktivism," which is hacking for political activism. The actual strategies of activism also differ compared with cyber terrorism with hacktivists conducting virtual sit-ins, email bombs, web hacks, and viruses/worms (Stohl 2006). Increasing the potential risks of cyberterrorism, cascading failures occur when parts of a network are interconnected and dependent on each other: when a precedent part goes out, the next part goes out, causing a chain reaction of failures. This structure increases the vulnerability of access points where terrorist can use cyber-tools to begin their attack (Matusitz 2008).

Examples of Cyberterrorism

Whether or not cyberterrorism has already occurred is strongly debated (Council of Europe Staff 2007). Researchers and policy actors rarely agree on whether a cyber attack was merely a form of cybercrime, cyberwar, or an act of cyberterrorism. Take an example from 2000, committed in Australia by an Australian citizen: after being denied a job at a water treatment facility, a cyberterrorist accessed the computer network of Maroochy Shire Council's sewage treatment plant from outside the system and released 264,000 gallons of raw sewage into the Sunshine Coast (Matusitz 2008). Some might counter this by noting that the attack lacked the fear motivation required for cyberterrorism. Another example is found in May 2000 with the Love Bug—officially the "I Love You" virus—that eventually caused damage to the value of over $10 billion worldwide. Not only were individual computers infected, but also large networks such as the Pentagon, parliaments, banks, and corporations. The man charged with creating and releasing the virus was released owing to the lack of cyberterrorism laws in the Philippines. Some thought that he could have been charged for a type of credit card fraud or for malicious mischief related to the case, but the obscurity of the legal constraints prevented any charges being filed. All this occurred with less than a hundred keystrokes (Matusitz 2008). Yet again, this example does not fit perfectly within a cyberterrorism definition as it lacks a political element.

This disputed cyberterrorism definition has come into play more recently with the 2010 WikiLeaks posting of confidential military documents and diplomatic cables obtained through the help of an enlisted soldier. Owing to the lack of laws concerning cyberterrorism and cyber attacks, the U.S. government wavered on deciding if it had the jurisdiction to prosecute the founder, Julian Assange, under existing laws. Many, including then possible Republican presidential candidate Rick Santorum, viewed the releasing of these confidential documents as a terrorist act that permanently undermined U.S. national security and thought Assange ought to be extradited and prosecuted as a terrorist. Moreover, after the arrest of Assange for unrelated sex charges in London, an independent grassroots group, Anonymous, digitally rallied its supporters and shut down sites like Amazon and MasterCard after these companies pulled their connections with WikiLeaks. Some might call this cyberterrorism; others might view it as hacktivism.

An act of cyber terror does not need to be extravagant. As described by Barry Collin, a cyberterrorist can access a cereal manufacturere's computer system and increase the iron supplement level to lethal levels for children (Pollitt n.d.; Collin n.d.). Neither does an attack need to physically destroy to be successful; an attack must "only" cause enough fear and impairment for society and consumers to lose confidence in the system (Verton 2003).

Although there are few concrete and universally agreed upon examples, we should not be complacent. What these past events tell us is that cyberterrorism is possible. Imagine if a terrorist organization acquired the necessary skills and strategy plans to conduct such a cyber attack.

Why We Need Protection

If something were an actual threat, one might assume it would be fairly effortless to convince the population that they needed protection from it. Such is not the case with cyberterrorism. What constitutes as a security threat varies between individuals owing to security's subjective and personal nature. Moreover, assessing potential threats is not a straightforward process. People have a hard time calculating risks that are not normal or well known: cyberterrorism does not fall into "traditional" security realms and is commonly misrepresented in literature and media. Thus, the public is left uninformed and with unrealistic perceptions of cyberterrorism risks. People also underestimate risks that they are prepared to take: individuals in the U.S. frequently access and depend on the Internet, making them more prone to taking risks so that they may continue using the Internet as they always have. Lastly, risks that are personalized seem greater than the anonymous risks: cyberterrorism on the Internet is bodiless and virtual (Schneier 2009).

There are also issues with technology itself. As information and communication technologies grow in complexity, the attackers benefit by being able to hide in its many layers—defenders are left being reactive, playing a game of cat-and-mouse (Schneier 2009). Traditional concepts of time and place are not followed in the cyber world: time is "aperspectival" and fluid (Matusitz 2008: 183). In short, cyberterrorist attacks are quick, unpredictable, and incomprehensible (Council of Europe Staff 2007; Matusitz 2008). Cyberterrorism involves a multitude of seemingly unconnected actors who make multiple moves at the same time while in a single location (Stohl 2006). "The possibilities in cyberspace and cyberterrorism are quasi unlimited and far more complex" (Matusitz 2008: 181). The populace fears technology owing to this complexity, obscurity, and ability to control (Pollitt n.d.). This fear distorts and even prevents proper action against cyberterrorism.

These negative characteristics are not new, but are embedded deep within Internet technology. When the Internet was created, its architects had reliability on their mind, not security; they were concerned with getting the packets of information to their destination rather than with the potential risks of improper use and malicious intrusion. They originally thought the Internet would be a tool of government, science, and corporations, and not necessarily individuals (Matusitz 2008). Whether this lack of foresight was preventable or not is a moot point now, but the consequence must be dealt with.

As commented by General Habriger in a white paper about the threat of cyberterror, "The unfettered access to cyber weapons systems (i.e. computers and Internet access) and armies (i.e. botnets that can be captured or rented), coupled with the capacity for such attacks to strike at our nation's strategic vulnerabilities presents a uniquely dangerous threat" (Habiger 2010: 4). Terrorist organizations have also recognized the importance of computing skills and have been actively recruiting people with such skills (Verton 2003). "Smart attackers look for ways to make their attack as effective as possible and technology can give the leverage and more ambition" (Schneier 2009: 526). Computer knowledge is spreading fast and is highly accessible for anyone to learn. Terrorist organizations have the motivation; all they need are the skills.

Can Technology Protect Against Technology?

Security involves trade-offs: a security gain—perceived or actual—means giving something up, whether it is financial resources, convenience, privacy, and/or personal space (Schneier 2009). Terrorism in general is located in a category separate from *traditional* threats, which disposes people to view and react to such risks differently. The same is true when terrorists go online. Intensifying after 9/11, it is commonly believed by some policy-makers that the best path towards security is through technology. Although this has been successful in many cases, using technology to protect against technology is not always the best option. At the very basic level, technology enables and empowers individuals while security is a preventer whose goal is to stop people from performing certain acts (Schneier 2009). The question must be asked if an enabler tool can prevent and stop attacks?

Bruce Schneier briefly addressed this issue when he described so-called bad security, which is when technology is employed in order to gain security, yet is unsuccessful and possibly even making the population less secure. The decision must be made whether this trade-off and the costs are worth the costs and risk of bad security: sometimes it is, and sometimes it is not (Schneier 2009). Accordingly, finding acceptable trade-offs will require an effort to marry security perceptions. In an effort to spotlight federal policy towards preventing cyber attacks like cyberterrorism, Secretary of State Hillary Clinton underscored how the severity of cyber attacks has led the U.S. towards a policy of deterrence through retribution, where "countries or individuals that engage in cyber attacks should face consequences and international condemnation" (Habiger 2010: 2–3).

What to do About This?

The current system of defending against cyberterrorism is flawed. Policies created to prevent cyberterror act merely as window dressing for security, rarely addressing the underlining issues as discussed here (Habiger 2010). Computers do not independently control human lives to cause a classical risk (Pollitt n.d.). Moreover, "the face of terrorism is changing … the methods of counter-terrorism that our world's specialists have honed over the years are ineffectual against this enemy" (Collin n.d.). Counter-terrorism measures in place today must adapt to these new threats and weapons; traditional policies will not work. The events of 9/11 proved that it can happen and we cannot be complacent and wait for attack before defending ourselves. There are steps that can be taken to effectively protect us from cyberterrorism:

1. *Technological education is needed*: a national campaign must begin to spread the truth about cyber risks. The populace must be accepting of the needed trades-offs to ensure their security. The inconvenience of practising secure cyber actions—using complex passwords

and reporting possible hacking—is worth the peace of mind that it brings (Habiger 2010; Pollitt n.d.).

2. *Laws and policies need to be redesigned or created*: governments must be willing to invest time and financial resources to learn more and protect themselves against cyberterrorism. Deterrence and preemption are key components in the U.S.'s national security plans. However, are these methods productive in the cyber world? How can one preempt an unknown attacker who can attack from any computer around the world? How can one deter if the attacker has no basis to judge the risk of retaliation, let alone has nothing to lose? These tactics must be redesigned to address virtual enemies. Domestic cyberterrorism laws are also needed so there is a clear basis for understanding what cyberterrorism is and how it will be criminally handled (Habiger 2010; Verton 2003).
3. *International agreements are needed*: the Cybercrime Convention and the Convention on the Prevention of Terrorism must be revised to accurately represent modern threats and advancing technologies. After this, states must sign and ratify these two international treaties. States will then be able to combine their efforts to fight cyberterrorism, just as they have done for other types of terrorism. (Council of Europe Staff 2007).
4. *Use the hackers*: instead of shunning harmless hackers, they should be utilized. They possess the skills and knowledge needed in this fight and are the most skilled at finding cyber vulnerabilities that terrorists can exploit (Collin n.d.).
5. *The human element needs to remain*: emotions and perceptions are key to understanding the motivation behind terrorism threats. Technology can only take us so far and is unable to properly assess these invisible qualities. We cannot be dependent on technology; there needs to be human oversight and intervention capability.
6. *Private industry needs to be involved*: the government cannot provide complete security on its own—a majority of the network lies in private hands. Companies must be willing to report attacks and proactively protect themselves. They must be ready to help investigators looking into possible acts of terror that might require a level of information sharing between federal and private actors that some are uncomfortable with (Nakashima 2010; Habiger 2010).

Although the threat is imminent and outwardly invisible, we should not act as if we have been defeated (Habiger 2010). Now is the time to start to act, before terrorist organizations have the full capacity to conduct cyberterrorism.

References

Bjorn-Andersen, Niels, Michael Earl, Olav Holst, and Enid Mumford. *Information Society: For Richer, for Poorer*, Vol. 2. Amsterdam: North-Holland, 1982.

Collin, Barry C. *The Future of Cyberterrorism: Where the Physical and Virtual Worlds Converge*. n.d. Available at: http://afgen.com/terrorism1.html [accessed: 1 January 2011].

Costigan, Sean S. "Terrorists and the Internet: Crashing or Cashing In?" In *Terrornomics*, edited by Sean S. Costigan and David Gold, 113–28. Aldershot: Ashgate, 2007.

Council of Europe Staff. *Cyberterrorism: The Use of the Internet for Terrorist Purposes*. Council of Europe, 2007.

Friedman, Thomas L. *The World is Flat*. New York: Picador, 2005.

German, Mike. *Thinking Like a Terrorist*. Washington, DC: Potomac Books, 2007.

Habiger, Eugene E. *Cyberwarfare and Cyberterrorism: The Need for a New U.S. Strategic Approach*. White Paper, The Cyber Secure Institute, 2010.

Hoffman, Bruce. *Inside Terrorism*. New York: Columbia University Press, 1998.

Johnson, Wayne M. *Seller Beware: U.S. International Technology Transfer and Its Impact on National Security*. Maxwell Paper no. 16. Maxwell Air Force Base, AL: Air War College, 1998.

Matusitz, Jonathan. "Cyberterrorism: Postmodern State of Chaos." *Information Security Journal: A Global Perspective* 17 (2008): 179–87.

Nakashima, Ellen. "FBI Director Warns of 'Rapidly Expanding' Cyberterrorism Threat." *The Washington Post*, 4 March 2010. Available at: http://www.washingtonpost.com/wp-dyn/content/article/2010/03/04/AR2010030405066.html [accessed: 1 January 2011].

National Commission on Terrorist Attacks. *The 9/11 Commission Report: Final Report of the National Commission on Terrorist Attacks*. New York: W.W. Norton, 2004.

Pollitt, Mark M. "Cyberterrorism—Fact or Fancy?," n.d. Available at: http://www.cs.georgetown.edu/~denning/infosec/pollitt.html [accessed: 1 January 2011].

Schneier, Bruce. "'Security Trade-offs are Subjective' and 'Technology Creates Security Imbalances'." In *Technology and Society: Building Our Sociotechnical Future*, edited by Deborah G. Johnson and Jameson M. Wetmore, 515–36. Cambridge, MA: MIT Publishing, 2009.

Stohl, Michael. "Cyber Terrorism: a Clear and Present Danger, the Sum of all Fears, Breaking Point or Patriot Games?" *Crime, Law and Social Change* 46 (2006): 223–38.

Verton, Dan. *Black Ice: The Invisible Threat of Cyber-Terrorism*. Emeryville, CA: McGraw-Hill, 2003.

Weimann, Gabriel. *Terror on the Internet: The New Arena, the New Challenges*. Washington, DC: U.S. Institute of Peace Press, 2006.

Chapter 5
VIEWPOINT:
Protecting Google. Is an Attack Against Google, an Attack Against the U.S.?

Nat Katin-Borland

> This cyber domain is exponentially expanding our ability to create and share knowledge, but it is also enabling those who would steal, corrupt, harm or destroy the public and private assets vital to our national interests. The recent intrusions reported by Google are a stark reminder of the importance of these cyber assets, and a wake-up call to those who have not taken this problem seriously. Companies who promptly report cyber intrusions to government authorities greatly help us to understand and address the range of cyber threats that face us all. (Blair 2010: 2)
>
> Dennis C. Blair, United States Director of National Intelligence

> It's important for the public to understand that there is a lot at risk. We need to be realistic about the fact that it's not just military networks that are at risk, it's all networks. And we realize that military networks are built on the networks of industry. (cited by Corrin 2010)
>
> General John Davis, Director of Operations, United States Army Cyber Command

Google, the web search giant, is one of the most successful companies of the past decade. There are even acronyms capturing Google's ubiquity: WIDGI ("when in doubt, Google it"). It is no wonder then that, for many web users, Google is synonymous with finding content online. Google is their gateway to the Internet, where they turn to find information and connect with other people online. Google, however, is much more than just the industry leader in Internet search, it is also a leader in mapping (Google Maps), satellite imagery (Google Earth), mobile devices (Android), photo sharing (Picasa), video sharing (YouTube and Vimeo), email (Gmail), web advertising (AdWords), cloud computing, social networking (Orkut) and blogging (Blogger; *Google Milestones* n.d.). The web data tracking site Alexa consistently ranks Google.com as far and away the most visited website in the world (Alexa 2010).

Google's popularity and wide range of products has brought the company huge financial rewards. In 2009, a time when most businesses were struggling through a recession, Google posted revenues of well over $6 billion, a 17% rise over its 2008 earnings (Oreskovic 2010). Google's large user base and high profile have also made it a target for malicious attacks, most notably when hackers based in China penetrated Google's security to spy on the company and its users (McMillan 2010). This has led many to ask the question: how important is Google to the U.S. and its economy? Is maintaining access to Google on a par with keeping other critical infrastructure systems like electricity and water online? Finally, what is the U.S. government willing to do to protect the Internet operations of large corporations like Google?

Luckily, we do not have to speculate on answers to these questions. The December 2009 attacks against Google and 30 other corporations (the attacks were not made public until January 2010) were a watershed moment for the U.S. and how it deals with cyber security. In the 2010 *Annual*

Threat Assessment of the U.S. Intelligence Community, Director of National Intelligence Dennis Blair identified "cyber threats" as one of the key security vulnerabilities facing the nation: "The national security of the United States, our economic prosperity, and the daily functioning of our government are dependent on a dynamic public and private information infrastructure, which includes telecommunications, computer networks and systems, and the information residing within. This critical infrastructure is severely threatened" (Blair 2010: 2). Secretary of State Hilary Clinton made it equally clear that the U.S. will seek to ensure freedom of expression on the Internet just as vehemently as it protects its economic and political interests:

> Because amid this unprecedented surge in connectivity, we must also recognize that these technologies are not an unmitigated blessing. These tools are also being exploited to undermine human progress and political rights … On their own, new technologies do not take sides in the struggle for freedom and progress, but the United States does. We stand for a single Internet where all of humanity has equal access to knowledge and ideas. And we recognize that the world's information infrastructure will become what we and others make of it. Now, this challenge may be new, but our responsibility to help ensure the free exchange of ideas goes back to the birth of our republic. The words of the First Amendment to our Constitution are carved in 50 tons of Tennessee marble on the front of this building. And every generation of Americans has worked to protect the values etched in that stone … So as technology hurtles forward, we must think back to that legacy. We need to synchronize our technological progress with our principles …
>
> There are many other networks in the world. Some aid in the movement of people or resources, and some facilitate exchanges between individuals with the same work or interests. But the Internet is a network that magnifies the power and potential of all others. And that's why we believe it's critical that its users are assured certain basic freedoms. Freedom of expression is first among them. This freedom is no longer defined solely by whether citizens can go into the town square and criticize their government without fear of retribution. Blogs, emails, social networks, and text messages have opened up new forums for exchanging ideas, and created new targets for censorship …
>
> Governments and citizens must have confidence that the networks at the core of their national security and economic prosperity are safe and resilient. Now this is about more than petty hackers who deface websites. Our ability to bank online, use electronic commerce, and safeguard billions of dollars in intellectual property are all at stake if we cannot rely on the security of our information networks. Disruptions in these systems demand a coordinated response by all governments, the private sector, and the international community …
>
> Now, ultimately, this issue isn't just about information freedom; it is about what kind of world we want and what kind of world we will inhabit. It's about whether we live on a planet with one Internet, one global community, and a common body of knowledge that benefits and unites us all, or a fragmented planet in which access to information and opportunity is dependent on where you live and the whims of censors.
>
> Information freedom supports the peace and security that provides a foundation for global progress. Historically, asymmetrical access to information is one of the leading causes of interstate conflict. When we face serious disputes or dangerous incidents, it's critical that people on both sides of the problem have access to the same set of facts and opinions. (Clinton 2010)

As Secretary Clinton makes clear, protecting Internet freedoms and upholding confidence in global information systems and networks are key to continued U.S. prosperity and global leadership in the twenty-first century.

The Internet as Critical Infrastructure

Traditionally, the critical infrastructure of a nation was thought of as the system of highly complex and interdependent physical assets essential to the minimum operations of a nation's economy and government. It included communications, energy, banking and finance, transportation, water supply, and emergency services. Increasingly, however, a nation counts its information and data networks as key elements of its essential infrastructure (Moteff and Parfomak 2004: 1–4). For critical infrastructure systems, they could be owned and operated by the government or the private sector, or both. Much of any nation's critical infrastructure has historically been physically and logically separated; they were systems that had little interdependence. In the modern world, as a result of advances in information technology over the past several decades and the necessity of improved efficiency, these crucial systems and assets have become increasingly automated and interlinked.

Simultaneously, these same advances have created new vulnerabilities to equipment failure, human error, weather, and of course physical and cyber attacks. For the U.S., imbalances in military strengths will probably lead its future enemies—including other nations, nonstate actors, and individuals—to inflict harm in nontraditional ways, such as attacks within the country against critical infrastructure targets. The U.S. economy is increasingly reliant upon interdependent and cyber-supported infrastructures, making attacks on its infrastructure and information systems capable of significantly harming both the nation's military power and its economy. Most experts agree that addressing these vulnerabilities requires flexible approaches that span both the public and private sectors in order to best ensure both domestic and international security:

> Securing cyberspace requires government and the private sector to work together. The private sector designs, deploys, and maintains much of the nation's critical infrastructure. This is important because unlike certain other elements of national security, the government alone cannot secure cyberspace. There is a bifurcation of responsibility (the government must protect national security) and control (it does not manage the asset or provide the function that must be protected). (Langevin et al. 2008: 43)

Furthermore, two global trends in the information technology arena increase the stakes for companies who oversee the networks and systems governing critical infrastructure. The first is "network convergence," or the merging of voice, video and data communications over a common network (Whitney 2010a). While convergence increases efficiency and services for users, it also increases the costs and consequences of cyber attacks and network outages, because virtually all communication types travel on the same networks. If an attack brings down one part of the network, the entire system could fail and bring down all associated communications services with it. The second trend is "channel consolidation," or "the concentration of data captured on individual users by service providers through emails or instant messaging, Internet search engines, Web 2.0 social networking … and geographic location of mobile service subscribers, which increases the potential and consequences for exploitation of personal data by malicious entities" (Blair 2010: 3). Web users are placing more and more of their critical data online, using fewer and fewer separate services. For example, Google is the first place where most individuals turn to access information in the event of an emergency. However, many users do not solely depend on Google's search engine; they also use its email client, phone service, web browser and social networking applications, potentially placing mountains of private and proprietary data in the hands of hackers or foreign spies. Protecting companies like Google will increasingly become a necessity for the U.S. government to both protect personal data and secure communications infrastructure.

Google and China

Access to China's booming economy and growing middle class customer base has long been the goose that laid the golden egg for technology companies. Almost as soon as Google was founded in 1999, it offered a Chinese language version of its regular www.google.com search engine. Then, in 2002, users in China began to report prolonged site outages and missing information in search results, particularly when queries involved politically sensitive topics such as, "freedom of speech" or "Tibet" (Schrage 2006). Google executives stated the following: "We faced a choice at that point: hold fast to our commitment to free speech (and risk a long-term cut-off from our Chinese users), or compromise our principles by entering the Chinese market directly and subjecting ourselves to Chinese laws and regulations" (Schrage 2006). Ultimately, Google decided that it was in the best interests of its users to not only continue operations in China, but to expand its services. A Google executive elaborated, "Our search results were being filtered; our service was being crippled; our users were flocking to local Chinese alternatives; and, ultimately, Chinese Internet users had less access to information than they would have had" (Schrage 2006). In other words, even a filtered Google was better than no Google at all.

Starting in July of 2005, Google commenced research and development operations on the ground in China. They quickly followed in January of 2006 with the launch of a Chinese language search portal, www.google.cn. A crucial provision that paved the way for Google.cn was the agreement that Google respect all "local conditions," meaning that Google subject itself to self-censorship by complying with Chinese laws and regulating all "illegal content," including an unspecified list of politically sensitive search terms. To keep customers informed, Google promised to notify users when search results were being filtered and protect its users by not hosting any services involving personal data, like email or blogging tools, on the ground in China (Schrage 2006). In testimony before Congress, Google Vice President for Global Communications and Public Affairs, Elliot Schrage, summed up Google's plan in China this way:

> Our hope is that our mix of measures, though far from our ideal, would accomplish more for Chinese citizens' access to information than the alternative. We don't pretend that this is the single 'right' answer to the dilemma faced by information companies in China, but rather a reasonable approach that seems likely to bring our users greater access to more information than any other search engine in China. And by serving our users better, we hope it will be good for our business, too, over the long run … Looking ahead, we will carefully monitor conditions in China, including new laws and other restrictions on our services. If we determine that we are unable to achieve the objectives I've outlined above, we will not hesitate to reconsider our approach to China. (Schrage 2006)

In January of 2010, Google took the unusual step of announcing that it had been subjected to an advanced cyber attack originating from inside China in mid-December of 2009 (Drummond 2010).

Most companies that are victims of cyber crime or other attacks do no come forward out of fear that the publicity will damage their reputations, scare away customers, and endanger future profits (Bartz and Finkle 2009). Google felt the need to come forward because of the brazen nature of the attacks and the targets. Through its investigation of the attacks, Google discovered that the goal of the attacks seemed to be to compromise the email accounts of human rights activists working in China. Although only two accounts were hacked by attackers, deeper investigation determined that "the accounts of dozens of U.S.-, China- and Europe-based Gmail users who are advocates of human rights in China appear to have been routinely accessed by third parties. These accounts have not been accessed through any security breach at Google, but most likely via phishing scams or malware placed on the users' computers" (Drummond 2010). Phishing is a popular technique employed by scam artists to gain access to someone's computer: a recipient receives a seemingly benign email from a known contact, asking the user to open an attachment or access a link, containing a "sleeper" program that embeds itself on the computer. Once the malware is downloaded, the program can be controlled remotely, allowing an attacker to access email and documents on the computer's hard drive. Such a coordinated attack on Google's servers and users took the company by surprise and made them realize that their engagement in China may be causing more harm than good.

In the wake of the incident Google announced,

> These attacks and the surveillance they have uncovered—combined with the attempts over the past year to further limit free speech on the web—have led us to conclude that we should review the feasibility of our business operations in China. We have decided we are no longer willing to continue censoring our results on Google.cn, and so over the next few weeks we will be discussing with the Chinese government the basis on which we could operate an unfiltered search engine within the law, if at all. We recognize that this may well mean having to shut down Google.cn, and potentially our offices in China. (Drummond 2010)

In April, after failing to reach an adequate agreement with Chinese authorities, Google began to redirect its Google.cn search traffic to servers in Hong Kong, effectively ending voluntary censorship of its Chinese portal (Nakashima 2010a).

As the dust settled, it became apparent that Google was not the only company targeted by Chinese-based attacks. At least 34 other companies were also attacked, including Yahoo, Symantec, Adobe and Dow Chemical. The attacks on the other companies followed the same pattern as those on Google—network architecture probes and phishing scams designed to fool employees intro downloading malware to give outside access to their computer's network drives. It was clear that Google's ongoing standoff with China over privacy and security issues had widespread ramifications, some of which affected the already sensitive relations between the U.S. and China. White House spokesman Nick Shapiro stated that "The recent cyber-intrusion that Google attributes to China is troubling" and that President Obama considers Internet freedom "a central human rights issue."

More recently, diplomatic cables disclosed on the site WikiLeaks revealed that orders for the attacks on Google came from the very top echelon of the Chinese government. One cable described how Li Changchun, the country's senior propaganda official and a member of China's ruling body, the Politburo Standing Committee, was shocked to discover negative information about himself on the Internet: "A well placed contact claims that the Chinese government coordinated the recent intrusions of Google systems. According to our contact, the closely held operations were directed at the Politburo Standing Committee level" (Glanz and Markoff 2010). A 3 November 2008 cable also revealed additional attacks on Google that were not publicly reported, including an attack in 2008, code-named "Byzantine Candor" by investigators, that compromised more than 50 megabytes of emails and a "complete list of user names and passwords from an American government agency" (Glanz and Markoff 2010).

Although the Chinese government quickly refuted all accusations of government-sponsored cyber attacks and espionage on American companies, many security experts do not give such denials any credence. An unidentified spokesman for the China's Ministry of Industry and Information Technology released a statement declaring an "accusation that the Chinese government participated in [any] cyberattack, either in an explicit or inexplicit way, is groundless and aims to denigrate China" (Musil 2010). National security expert James Lewis, on the other hand, identifies state-sanctioned cyber attacks as part of "a big espionage program aimed at getting high-tech information and politically sensitive information—the high-tech information to jump-start China's economy and the political information to ensure the survival of the regime. This is what China's leadership is after. The Chinese have been good at mixing economic and political espionage. This reflects China's national priorities" (Cha and Nakashima 2010).

Google and the National Security Agency

Despite Google's public disclosure of the 2009 cyber attacks, very few details on what exactly the attackers accessed and whether the compromised data also included information about Google's highly confidential search engine source code were made available. Buried in the initial disclosure was an admission that Google was cooperating with "relevant U.S. authorities" (Drummond 2010). This was the first clue as to how seriously both Google and the U.S. government were taking the Chinese attacks. The full extent of the partnership was not made public until February of 2010 when the *Washington Post* reported that Google had turned to the National Security Agency (NSA) for help after the cyber attacks (Nakashima 2010b). The NSA, which conducts surveillance and code breaking for the Federal government, does not usually operate on American soil, but because of NSA experience in protecting government networks from similar attacks, Google reached out for assistance.

Virtually nothing is known about the Google–NSA partnership, as both sides have declined to provide details, but anonymous *Washington Post* sources revealed that "the alliance is being designed to allow the two organizations to share critical information without violating Google's policies or laws that protect the privacy of American's online communications … [T]he deal does not mean the NSA will be viewing users' searches or e-mail accounts or that Google will be sharing proprietary data" (Nakashima 2010b). The collaboration, formally known as a "cooperative research and development agreement," reportedly only concentrates on creating better defenses for Google's networks and on evaluating Google software and hardware for potential vulnerabilities (Gorman and Vascellaro 2010). A brief NSA statement identified its work with Google "as part of its information-assurance mission," through which the "NSA works with a broad range of commercial partners and research associates to ensure the availability of secure tailored solutions for Department of Defense and national security systems customers" (Nakashima 2010b).

The Google–NSA partnership was even more surprising since Google refused to cooperate with the NSA in 2008 for the NSA's Terrorist Surveillance Program (Nakashima 2010b). The NSA has also been embroiled since 2005 in allegations that the agency violated federal law in conducting illegal surveillance of Americans' phone and Internet communications (Savage and Risen 2010).

Many observers worry that any NSA involvement in the telecom sector will put the agency in a position once again to surreptitiously monitor legitimate communications by U.S. citizens. The Electronic Privacy Information Center, an Internet privacy organization, has tried in vain to get more details on the Google–NSA partnership and worries that the secret agreement could "impact the privacy of millions of users of Google's products and services around the world" (Gabbatt 2010). Others speculate that Google reached out to the NSA for strategic reasons, in order to avoid the disclosures associated with regulation as part of the nation's critical infrastructure (Markoff 2010). Partnership with the Department of Homeland Security, for example, may have funneled Google into the same category as energy and water distribution systems and opened the company to increased government regulation and monitoring. Ultimately, Google's agreement with the NSA may have had more to do with avoiding stringent government oversight and regulation than with protection from cyber attacks.

Conclusion

Regardless of the reasons behind Google's decision to reach out to the NSA, the government's reaction made it clear that it will take steps to protect technology firms like Google. From the NSA's perspective, all networks are connected, so it is not worth attempting to differentiate where on the national cyber ecosystem an attack occurred. Public sector agencies rely on private sector tools to keep their critical systems up and running, and it is frequently impossible to draw strict lines on where government networks end and private networks begin. Following this logic, the NSA has stepped up its efforts to monitor the networks of private companies in a program they call "Perfect Citizen" (Whitney 2010b). Reports of this secret program indicate that the $100 million initiative will develop technologies to monitor the networks of utilities and other companies serving the needs of the nation's critical infrastructure, scanning them for any sign of cyber attacks (Whitney 2010b). The NSA has countered that Perfect Citizen is "purely a vulnerabilities-assessment and capabilities-development contract. This is a research and engineering effort. There is no monitoring activity involved, and no sensors are employed in this endeavor" (Wolf 2010). Whether Perfect Citizen is a monitoring system, as some reports indicate, or simply research and development, as defined by the NSA, the threat of cyber attacks against the U.S. and its citizens remains real.

The December 2009 Chinese attacks against Google only scratched the surface of what a serious cyber attack against the nation's infrastructure could mean. In Google's case, individual accounts were breached, but a large-scale failure of the system was avoided. In the case of a full-scale outage to even a small section of Google's infrastructure, the results could be very damaging for both Google and the hundreds of millions of users around the globe who rely on Google products. Despite privacy concerns, because the U.S. depends so strongly on the continuous and reliable performance of its networked infrastructure, most cyber security experts agree that an active partnership between the public and private sector is the only way to shore up defenses and coordinate responses in the event of an attack or other emergency. Both private firms and the government will benefit by having more information about how networks are being infiltrated and affected by a range of cyber security threats. In a world where technology and networks yield as much power as traditional militaries, intellectual property and access to proprietary systems will become increasingly important and governments will seek to protect those resources, whether controlled by the public or private sector (Lynn 2010).

The U.S. has also made it clear that the ability to operate in cyberspace with freedom and confidence is a key right in a modern society with a global economy. As statements by Secretary Clinton indicate, in the future, the U.S. may defend transnational attacks on privacy and freedom of speech the same way it defends transnational shipping lanes. Nations like China may see the stance of the U.S. on Internet freedom as just another tactic to preserve Western hegemony, but in our increasingly wired world where access to information technology and networked data determine the future of governments and businesses alike, those assets will be defended vigorously. Security expert James Lewis argues,

> Economic strength, technological leadership and the ability to innovate will be as important as military force in creating national power, particularly in competition with rising nations who wish to reduce U.S. influence without resorting to open military conflict. The primary damage to U.S. national security and economic strength from poor cybersecurity comes from the theft of intellectual property and the loss of advanced commercial and military technology to foreign competitors. A failure to secure America's information infrastructure weakens the U.S. and makes our competitors stronger. (Lewis 2009: 3)

The coordinated response by U.S. government agencies and Google to China's cyber attacks is only the beginning of these types of partnerships.

References

Alexa. 2010. *Google.com.* [Online: Alexa: The Web Information Company]. Available at: http://www.alexa.com/siteinfo/google.com [accessed: 11 December 2010].

Bartz, D. and Finkle, J. 2009. Cyber Breaches are a Closely Kept Secret. *Reuters* [Online, 24 November]. Available at: http://www.reuters.com/article/idU.S.TRE5AN4YH20091124 [accessed: 1 January 2011].

Blair, D.C. 2010. *Annual Threat Assessment of the U.S. Intelligence Community for the Senate Select Committee on Intelligence*. Office of the Director of National Intelligence [Online, 2 February]. Available at: http://www.dni.gov/testimonies/20100202_testimony.pdf [accessed: 1 December 2010].

Cha, A.E. and Nakashima, E. 2010. Google China Cyber Attack Part of Vast Espionage Campaign, Experts say. *Washington Post*. 14 January 2010.

Clinton, H.R. 2010. *Remarks on Internet Freedom*. U.S. Department of State [Online, 21 January]. Available at: http://www.state.gov/secretary/rm/2010/01/135519.htm [accessed: 1 January 2011].

Corrin, A. 2010. Cyber Risks Place New Demands on Public/Private Partnership. *Federal Computer Week* [Online, 26 July]. Available at: http://fcw.com/Articles/2010/07/26/FEAT-Cybersecurity-requires-new- cooperation-with-industry.aspx [accessed: 1 December 2010].

Drummond, D. 2010. A New Approach to China. *Official Google Blog* [Online, 1 January 2011]. Available at: http://googleblog.blogspot.com/2010/01/new-approach-to-china.html [accessed: 11 December 2010].

Gabbatt, A. 2010. Google Teams Up with National Security Agency to Tackle Cyber Attacks. *Guardian* [Online, 5 February]. Available at: http://www.guardian.co.uk/technology/2010/feb/05/google-national-security-agency-cyber-attack [accessed: 1 December 2010].

Glanz, J. and Markoff, J. 2010. Vast Hacking by a China Fearful of the Web. *New York Times* [Online, 4 December]. Available at: http://www.nytimes.com/2010/12/05/world/asia/05wikileaks-china.html [accessed: 6 December 2010].

Google Milestones. n.d. [Online: Google Cooperate Information]. Available at: http://www.google.com/corporate/milestones.html [accessed: 11 December 2010].

Gorman, S. and Vascellaro, J.E. 2010. Google Working With NSA to Investigate Cyber Attack. *Wall Street Journal* [Online, 4 February]. Available at: http://online.wsj.com/article/SB100014240527487040415045750449209056899 5 4.html [accessed: 1 December 2010].

Langevin, J.R. et al. 2008. *Securing Cyberspace for the 44th Presidency: A Report of the CSIS Commission on Cybersecurity for the 44th Presidency*. Center for Strategic and International Studies [Online, December]. Available at: http://csis.org/files/media/csis/pubs/081208_securingcyberspace_44.pdf [accessed: 1 December 2010].

Lewis, J.A. 2009. *Cybersecurity—Assessing Our Vulnerabilities and Developing an Effective Defense*. U.S. Senate Committee on Commerce, Science, and Transportation [Online: Center for Stategic and International Studies, 19 March 2009]. Available at: http://csis.org/testimony/cybersecurity-assessing-our-vulnerabilities-and-developing-effective-defense [accessed: 11 January 2011].

Lynn, W.J. 2010. *Remarks on Cyber at the Council on Foreign Relations*. U.S. Department of Defense [Online, 30 September]. Available at: http://www.defense.gov/speeches/speech.aspx?speechid=1509 [accessed: 11 January 2011].

Markoff, J. 2010. Google Asks Spy Agency for Help with Inquiry into Cyberattacks. *New York Times* [Online, 5 February]. Available at: http://www.nytimes.com/2010/02/05/science/05google.html [accessed: 1 December 2010].

McMillan, R. 2010. Google Attack Part of Widespread Spying Effort. *PC World* [Online, 13 January]. Available at: http://www.pcworld.com/businesscenter/article/186786/google_attack_part_of_widespread_spying_effort.html [accessed: 11 December 2010].

Moteff, J. and Parfomak, P. 2004. *Critical Infrastructure and Key Assets: Definition and Identification*. Congressional Research Service Report for Congress, Library of Congress [Online, 1 October]. Available at: http://www.fas.org/sgp/crs/RL32631.pdf [accessed: 11 December 2010].

Musil, S. 2010. China Denies Involvement in Google Cyberattacks. *CNET News* [Online, 24 January]. Available at: http://news.cnet.com/8301-1009_3-10440208- 83.html [accessed: 1 December 2010].

Nakashima, E. 2010a. Chinese Leaders Ordered Google Hack, U.S. Cable Quotes Source as Saying. *Washington Post* [Online, 4 December]. Available at: http://www.washingtonpost.com/wp-dyn/content/article/2010/12/04/AR2010120403323.html [accessed: 6 December 2010].

Nakashima, E. 2010b. Google to Enlist NSA to Help it Ward off Cyberattacks. *Washington Post* [Online, 4 February]. Available at: http://www.washingtonpost.com/wp-dyn/content/article/2010/02/03/AR2010020304057.html [accessed: 1 December 2010].

Oreskovic, A. 2010. Google Profit Rises, Revenue Misses Some Forecasts. *Reuters* [Online, 22 January]. Available at: http://www.reuters.com/article/idU.S.TRE60K33U20100122 [accessed: 11 December 2010].

Savage, C. and Risen J. 2010. Federal Judge Finds N.S.A. Wiretaps were Illegal. *New York Times* [Online, 31 March]. Available at: http://www.nytimes.com/2010/04/01/us/01nsa.html [accessed: 11 December 2010].

Schrage, E. 2006. *Testimony of Google Inc. before the Subcommittee on Asia and the Pacific, and the Subcommittee on Africa, Global Human Rights, and International Operations*. Committee on International Relations, U.S. House of Representatives [Online: Official Google Blog, 15 February]. Available at: http://googleblog.blogspot.com/2006/02/testimony-internet-in-china.html [accessed: 11 December 2010].

Whitney, L. 2010a. Government Warns of Looming Cyberthreats. *CNET News* [Online, 3 February]. Available at: http://news.cnet.com/8301-1009_3-10446647-83.html [accessed: 1 December 2010].

Whitney, L. 2010b. Report: NSA Initiating Program to Detect Cyberattacks. *CNET News* [Online, 8 July]. Available at: http://news.cnet.com/8301-1009_3-20009952-83.html [accessed: 11 December 2010].

Wolf, J. 2010. U.S. Eavesdropping Agency Says Private Citizen is Purely R&D. *Reuters* [Online, 9 July]. Available at: http://www.reuters.com/article/idU.S.TRE66807I20100709 [accessed: 11 December 2010].

Chapter 6
VIEWPOINT: Invisible Threats

Jake Perry

Cyberwar is a real and pressing global threat. Just as the activity of commerce, communications, and industry has gone online, so have military and security operations. Evidence of this point of view is clear: as of November 2010, the Cyber Command of the U.S. became operational, prepared to defend as well as perform offensive tactical missions in cyberspace; China, in July 2010, announced the creation of a military unit dedicated to the "new cyber threat" (Branigan 2010); and then there are the private defense contractors "scrambling" to hire employees and "fill massive cyber security contracts" (Byrt 2010). As an international concern, militaries, countries, and the private sector should be invested in combating and protecting against this technological threat. Yet, with all of the press coverage and the ratcheting up of resources and rhetoric, some very fundamental questions still lurk in terms of cyberwar. For instance, what does it look like? How does it start, or end? When do countries and governments respond once it is identified? But most importantly, is it *the most pressing* online threat?

Questions like these, it seems, almost cannot be answered now that it's apparent that cyberspace is the next theater of war and combat. In the place of answers are exaggeration, confusion, and hyperbole. Terms like "Cyber Pearl Harbor" and "Cyber Katrina" are used to sum up what are, in reality, very complex and multi-faceted actions. Put "cyber-" in front of anything and you're likely to scare someone, somewhere.

To be clear, cyberspace presents and acts as the conduit for myriad threats, perhaps war, and possibly as a tactic in a larger, real-world conflict. However, by far the most pressing threat to citizens on the Internet around the world is crime: identity theft, fraud, email scams, extortion—these are the everyday hazards of operating and communicating online. Cyber-espionage, basically spying via a variety of means, is also a threat and can be sponsored by a government but may also be carried out by a loose group of hackers looking to sell passwords or bank accounts. Then cyber-activism—or hacktivism—could ruin your servers, corrupt your data or, à la WikiLeaks, dump it for the world to see. Even plain old hacking, completely self- or purpose-motivated as opposed to profit-driven, could affect your online experience and have repercussions offline. And of course, this list of hazards is hardly exhaustive.

With such diverse threats, from so many different actors and locations, via a multitude of ways, for all sorts of reasons, you begin to see how easy it might be to (mis)label reported computer-related shenanigans as "cyberwar." The Estonia attacks in 2007, referred to by journalist Cyrus Farivar (2007) as "Cyberwar I [one]," which shut down government and financial websites, were plain and simple distributed denial of service attacks (or DDoS, where a website is overloaded with traffic to the point of shutting down) head-started by ethnic Russians unhappy with Estonia's policies. Denial of service attacks, while disruptive, hardly add up to war—as Kevin Poulsen (2007) says in an article in response to the coverage of the Estonia attacks, "there are good reasons to reject the idea that timeout errors are an act of war." There is a difference between merely flooding the system (like Estonia) and actually having a target and engaging it (closer to "war").

Yet, thanks to media overstatement and security experts around the globe, cyberwar remains the online menace that receives the most ink, and possibly, therefore, the majority of government spending. Yet it is cybercrime that is currently, and most clearly, affecting individuals and the networks they course through everyday. With all the emphasis on war, simple and basic and everyday online enforcement stands to lose. Because what good can a crime-fighting effort do if the majority of resources are employed to fight a rhetorical war?

The Problem

The threats that cyberspace and our technological interconnectedness present are invisible to the public at large. When your credit card number is stolen in real life, your wallet is taken or your purse is snatched and generally it quickly becomes obvious that your property is gone. The scenario plays out on a different timetable online and is less obvious. On a larger scale, if foreign agents crossed a nation's border, broke into a high-profile defense firm and began downloading intellectual property secrets, many levels of enforcement would be alerted. When this happens online, the response is a bit muddied. There is also a good chance that the populace will never know about it when high-level pilfering occurs online.

Yet governments do know about such attacks and are concerned. In a May 2009 speech, U.S. President Barack Obama said, "This cyber threat is one of the most serious economic and national security challenges we face as a nation," while also framing the protection of the U.S. digital infrastructure as a "national security priority" (Obama 2009). Michael McConnell, a former National Security Agency (NSA) director and current cyberwar contractor, proclaimed in early 2010, "The United States is fighting a cyberwar today, and we are losing" (McConnell 2010). This isn't just a Western concern. In 2008, the Indian government passed the Technology Amendment Act, which put its Computer Emergency Response Team (CERT-In) in charge of both gathering information on and conducting analysis of "cyber incidents," as well as coordinating "emergency measures for handling cyber security" (CERT-In 2010).

Attach to this worry the vulnerability of the computer network and the computer itself. The layers upon layers of complexity in the hardware and operating software—added to an Internet connection and the endless and intricate daisy chains of other computers and servers—all create nooks and crannies for the hacker, or whoever, to exploit. Along with the billions of lines of code, the potential for unforeseen mistakes and lapses in security are staggeringly high. All of this complexity allows for breaches, for some agent to manipulate a system that, again, is almost unknown to the everyday user.

As listed above, these threats can come in a variety of shapes, sizes, and methods, but to simplify a bit, there are generally two "kinds:"

- *cyber attacks*—a targeted act that looks to damage, change, or make less useful the computer systems, or the information within those systems, of a foe or target. Disruption is the key element here.
- *cyber exploitations*—various acts of monitoring and/or espionage on computer systems, as well as copying and pilfering the data within those systems. Disruption is not intended, as the ability to steal from these systems—and therefore keeping them operational to do so—is paramount.

Cyber attacks lend themselves to warfare or conflict, like taking over an electric grid or manipulating official governmental/military lines of communication. Cyber exploitations, on the other hand, are more fit for crime where an agent is stealing personal information or intercepting lines of communication. One kind of threat is concerned with rendering systems "dead"; the other wants to keep the systems "alive" but unaware of the threat's presence in order to thieve as much potentially valuable information as possible.

Either way, both of these threats are incredibly hard to defend against, partly because of the aforementioned complexity factor—that covering *all* of the security bases is incredibly difficult—but mostly because an attacker needs to discover one or at most a couple of vulnerabilities in the system to cause problems. In a cyber security situation, the burden is on the defender to find *all* of the weak points in a particular system, while the attacker need only discover one. The maths is on the attacker's side that he will find something the defender failed to spot.

Other conventional and traditional lines of defense fall short as well. Distance, something that so obviously thwarts traditional, real-world attacks, actually helps an aggressor in cyberspace. An agent can route and channel Internet activity through dozens of countries, servers, and telecommunications networks, making an attack seem to come from China, or Russia, or Indonesia, or even Nashville. Those doing the forensic work on such an attack need a huge amount of time and resources—as well as a high level of international cooperation for most incidents—to retrace these cyber-steps, usually allowing the source to slip away.

In addition to the complexity and difficulty involved in securing swathes of cyberspace, another factor is how largely undetectable these attacks often are. Malware can be downloaded and installed without knowledge; a computer can become a zombie, another node in a remotely controlled botnet sending out spam emails or the like, without the slightest acknowledgment. Illicit programs can sit dormant on a user's system or in a network for months or even years before being remotely sprung into action—suddenly recording keystrokes and passwords. Usually these things do become known after the fact, after something has gone wrong or damage has been done. Google experienced this, apparently, at the beginning of 2010, when it announced that Chinese-sponsored operatives had hacked into its corporate digital infrastructure, an action that "resulted in the theft of intellectual property from Google" (Drummond 2010). Even one of the biggest in cyberspace can fall victim to a menace it cannot see.

If the activity is somehow accurately traced, and a location or country is identified, the Attribution Issue still exists. Trying to truly nail down the origin of a sophisticated cyber attack/exploitation is like trying to find a particular needle in a stack of needles. Even if the computer is found, it does not quite implicate a person, or a country, for the action. In 2009, The Information Warfare Monitor conducted a study to trace what became known as "GhostNet"—an extensive cyber scheme that targeted Tibetan officials and their computers, and included "a network of over 1,295 infected hosts [computers] in 103 countries" (I.W. Monitor 2009: 1). Furthermore, up to 30% of the computers affected were considered "high-value targets", including those of "ministries of foreign affairs, embassies, international organizations, news media, and NGOs", where these computers were being profiled and sensitive documents and data were being taken without knowledge (ibid.). What makes this study so important is not only the extensive detective work undertaken to track the GhostNet virus, but also that the ultimate origin of the virus could not be adequately determined. The virus was most likely launched from China, but the study *could not* ascertain if the Chinese government was controlling the effort. It possibly could have been a group of patriotic hackers, making it similar to what happened in Estonia in 2007, or maybe even a Chinese criminal syndicate—the study could not even rule out the prospect of a country other than China being behind the assault. Other countries could have been used to "deliberately mislead observers as to the true operator(s) and purpose of the GhostNet system" (ibid.: 49).

So in addition to the increasing complexity of these computer systems—both individually and as a part of a network—and the increasing reliance technologically advanced societies have on these networks, there is also the problem of the anonymity that they can provide. Without being able to pinpoint where, from whom, or why an action was deployed, an official national response will always be a few steps behind, and hampered from doing much of anything at first—let alone declare war. All of these factors display in their own way that it has become easier than ever for individuals to do harm to computer systems, and the data and information flowing between them, from anywhere, almost instantly, and with an incredibly low detection or trace rate. Yet does this add up to warfare?

Crime versus War

In March 2010, the FBI's Internet Crime Complaint Center (IC3) announced that the 2009 monetary losses attributed to cybercrime in the U.S. had doubled from the previous year to $559 million (AFP 2010). This is most likely a conservative number. The IC3 survey only covers the "complaints reporting monetary loss that were referred to law enforcement" (ibid.). In other words, these numbers are limited to individuals and only those individuals who were motivated to get official enforcement involved—businesses, companies, organizations, etc., are largely absent from these figures. Much like a citizen never reporting that their car was vandalized, thinking that local law enforcement will not put in the necessary time to find the perpetrators, many cybercrimes—if not most—go unreported.

Yet even with these limited numbers, other trends are apparent. Cybercrime is being carried out at an alarmingly increasing rate, with a 22% jump in complaints being reported to IC3 from 2008 to 2009. Donald Brackman, director of the National White Collar Crime Center, which runs the IC3 with the FBI, explained that cybercriminals "are also developing increasingly sophisticated means of defrauding unsuspecting consumers," and that "Internet crime is evolving in ways we couldn't have imagined just five years ago" (ibid.). In the U.S.—which could serve as a good Petri dish with the high level of dependence the country's services and operations, public and private, have on computer systems and networks—not only is the number of incidents of cybercrime rising, but they are also evolving at a staggering rate.

The U.S. is but one example. The fiscal damage cybercrime is bringing to global markets and economies is enormous—and basically an inexact science. In that same May 2009 speech, President Obama claimed that, in 2008, "cyber criminals stole intellectual property from businesses worldwide worth up to one trillion dollars" (Obama 2009). Again, these numbers could be far from reality as the cyber security community has yet to discover a metric, as well as the ability to verify the data that is being collected, to accurately report the damages of online criminal activity.

In an essay titled "The Economics of Online Crime," authors Moore, Clayton, and Anderson conclude: "Since about 2004, online crime has become organized and industrialized like no other crime, with the possible exception of the drugs trade" (2009: 17). To the point of being able to collect accurate information concerning online security failures or breaches, they explain that a major problem with these statistics is that they are being reported by agencies or entities that have incentives to over- or underreport. For example, a security survey from McAfee, a U.S.-based computer security firm that produces anti-virus software, might inflate their domestic estimates of online crime and theft in the interest of justifying and promoting the need for their products. A multinational bank or a telecommunications company, in contrast, would provide deflated figures in the interest of managing customer/investor worry, professional reputation and, possibly, a fluctuating stock price. Governments, in the interest of lessening concern while boosting perceived capability, might also underreport (or effectively manage the figures of) data thefts or digital infrastructure violations.

However, even with the issues of (in)accurate reporting, at least cybercrime has figures to debate. For example, Panda Security, an online security firm, claimed in their 2010 annual report that "46.8 percent of computers around the world have been infected by some kind of malware," usually with the intent of stealing personal information (Panda Labs 2010). While these figures can be brought into question in terms of Panda Security's intent and motive as a business invested in providing security solutions, the information this company reports is staggering and reflects, at least, that an online crime ecosystem—complete with recruiters, managers, research and development, and just plain clever individuals—is in robust health. To cite more examples from the Panda report (2010): the year 2010 saw the creation and distribution of "one third of all viruses that exist" and are classified by Panda Security; "[t]he average number of new threats created every day has risen from 55,000 to 63,000"; and "an average of 53 percent of computer users have been infected at some time by some type of malware, even with protection installed and up-to-date."

For a concrete example of these figures in practice, in October 2010 more than 100 people were arrested or charged for participating in a global bank hack where "[a]t least $3 million was stolen from U.S. accounts from about May of last year to this September [2010]" (Bray et al. 2010). These arrests, the article goes on to say, came just after a raid in the UK, where 19 people were arrested in connection to an online theft scheme of nearly $9.5 million. The individuals involved in the UK effort "included men and women from Ukraine, Latvia, Estonia, Belarus and Georgia"—truly a global effort (ibid.). How these conspiracies work is a combination of old and new school techniques. First, individuals called "mules" are established who set up bank accounts under false names using forged passports. At the same time, an unsuspecting computer user receives an email with a seemingly benign attachment or a link. Once clicked and/or downloaded, the attachment or website installs something called a "Zeus Trojan"—an ingenious piece of malware—on the user's computer, which sits undetected and monitors the user's computer and online activity, including web browser history and keystrokes. Once the user goes to his/her banking website and types in their user name and password, the handlers have all the information they need to transfer funds from the user's account to those set up by the mules. Then the mules either wire it overseas to the handlers, or cash out the transfer—keeping 8–10% as a kind of handling fee. In all, "the scheme allegedly defrauded five global banks and dozens of individuals and corporate defendants" (Bray et al. 2010).

Cyberwar, on the other hand, seems to lack specific cases and has only a few instances (many of which might be better understood though a cybercrime lens) and fictional scenarios. Cyberwar forecasters like Richard Clarke, the former White House national-security aide, current author, and chairman of a strategic planning and corporate risk management firm, recognize the problems of cybercrime but see the major cyber threat as coming from states that have cyber weaponry that far out-matches anything individuals or smallish groups could achieve.

One instance that cyberwar forecasters, like Clarke and former NSA director Michael McConnell, call upon to illustrate the point that cyberwar has arrived is the Russia/Georgia conflict in 2008, where Russia employed a range of techniques, including DDoS attacks, in cyberspace to shut down Georgian government websites. Another is Israel's use of "a combination of electronic attack and precision bombs" to take down Syrian air defenses prior to a military strike of an alleged nuclear facility in the Deir ez-Zor region in 2007 (UPI 2007). Others have cited the use by the U.S.

of targeted cyber-infiltrations throughout the Iraq War, including cyber attacks "on the cellular phones and computers that insurgents in Iraq were using to plan roadside bombings" (Harris 2009). Clarke (2010: 31), in his book *Cyber War: The Next Threat to National Security and What to Do About It*, sums up the general feeling when he says:

> Cyber war has begun. In anticipation of hostilities, nations are already 'preparing the battlefield.' They are hacking into each other's networks and infrastructures, laying in trapdoors and logic bombs—now, in peacetime. This ongoing nature of cyber war, the blurring of peace and war, adds a dangerous new dimension of instability.

And the state that seems to frighten the most is China. Again, Clarke (2010: 54) says, "China has systematically done all the things a nation would do if it contemplated having an offensive cyber war capability." This includes the creation of citizen hacker groups, engaging in cyber espionage, and "lacing" U.S. infrastructure with malicious code, waiting to strike. Clarke's book, along with many of the international cyberwar pushers, sees a whole spectrum of possibilities where China, through both patient and instant targeted cyber attacks, renders the U.S. (or any nation) deaf, dumb, and blind. Attacks to the power grid, to aviation controls, and to civilian and military installations and infrastructure are possible and forthcoming—in other words, cyberwar techniques not only can be included in "traditional" warfare, but can substitute for it. The message is clear: cyber security must be a military concern, especially when China, it seems, wants to hack and paralyze every modern nation on the globe.

While one cannot say that Clarke and company are wrong (China's cyber efforts *should* concern countries around the world, cyberspace *is* a new battlefield, etc.), there are a few questions that should be put to cyberwar pundits, like, for instance, why? Yes, it is true: China is amassing cyber weapons and capabilities, but so is Israel and so is the U.S., and dozens of other capable nations. Evidence of computer weapon-related stockpiling and cyber-arms racing should not be enough to add up to a looming, up-coming war. There would have to be real-world, geopolitical circumstances that would prompt countries to use these weapons.

In his book Clarke envisions a possible war between China and the U.S. (and its allies) over the island of Taiwan or the oil-rich islands in the South China Sea. Like all good prophesies, there are real-world merits to these possible situations, but it is hard to envision China using cyber attacks to knock out an electrical grid unless the countries involved were also already in a full-scale war—with the use of real-world weaponry and tactics, like air strikes and missiles. With this in mind, these cyberwar scenarios begin to crumble when one examines the dependence that countries like China have on Western economies and markets, as well as how intertwined they are in them. The industrialization and growth of China, along with other nations, are knotted to the functioning of business and commerce in the U.S. and Europe—markets that have huge influence on the global economy. This fact runs against the idea of a country like China intentionally engaging in war-like actions in cyberspace with these countries with the aim of maiming their ability to function. James Lewis, a senior fellow at the Center for Strategic and International Studies, was quoted in a November 2010 *New Yorker* article on cyberwar saying, "Current Chinese officials have told me that we're [sic] not going to attack Wall Street, because we basically own it and a cyber-war attack would do as much economic harm to us as to you" (Hersh 2010).

Interestingly, if pressed for an instance of cyberwar, one may have to go no further than July 2010 with the discovery of Stuxnet—the latest and most sophisticated instance of computer system manipulation. Stuxnet "is designed to infect a particular configuration of a particular type of industrial-control system—in other words, to disrupt the operation of a specific process or plant," as one article describes it (*The Economist* 2010). Its target seemed to be the Bushehr nuclear plant in Iran, as most of the Stuxnet infections are concentrated there, and Iran did announce that some of its systems at Bushehr were infected, but apparently no major damage was done. What makes Stuxnet so impressive and, at the same time, scary to both cyberwar pundits and critics is its ability to sit undetected in a system or network, wait until the right combination of commands is executed, and then proceed to override those commands with more destructive ones—all while relaying completely contrary information. So while it may seem that one's centrifuges are running smoothly according to one's monitoring systems, in reality, down on the plant floor, the centrifuges have ratcheted themselves into high gear and are spinning themselves into scrap metal. Here, Stuxnet falls more into the Cyber Attack category, as disruption/destruction is the aim.

Yet calling Stuxnet a "cyber-missile," capable of direct, targeted attack, is misleading and not entirely accurate (*The Economist* 2010). If Bushehr, or the refineries at Natanz, were the target—and according to a January 2011 *New York Times* article, Stuxnet was a joint U.S.–Israeli operation looking to put more time on the clock before Iran becomes nuclear-capable (Broad et al. 2011)—one cannot forget how hard hit China, India, and Germany were by Stuxnet. In some cases, harder then Iran. Stuxnet is also blamed for the failure of India's INSAT-4B satellite, the result of which was that "an estimated 70% of India's Direct-To-Home (DTH) companies' customers were without service" (Carr 2010). The openness of the Internet and its networks cannot guarantee accuracy, or even benchmarks of success, for attacks like these. Whoever is responsible for launching something like Stuxnet—if it is indeed a state or government, as is assumed owing to Stuxnet's complexity—runs the risk of being infected in return. The relatively unrestricted flow of data and information that is the Internet can be seen as a disincentive to launch so-called "cyber-weapons" because one cannot guarantee hitting the mark, but self-damage is a possibility. Regardless, "a cyber-attack is no substitute for a physical attack. The former would take weeks to recover from; the latter, years" (*The Economist* 2010).

In short, the motives for a state to fully engage its cyber weaponry are murky at best. In contrast, the motives are huge and clear for individuals or small groups to steal information, conduct espionage, trick and manipulate everyone from the single computer user to the huge multinational company. Even Clarke (2010: 59) admits this and adds a state-centric element to cybercrime/espionage when he says,

> The extent of Chinese government hacking against the U.S., European, and Japanese industries and research facilities is without precedent in the history of espionage … everything from pharmaceutical formulae, to bioengineering designs, to nanotechnology, to weapon systems, to everyday industrial products have been taken by the People's Liberation Army and been given to China, Inc.

Again, as to why "China, Inc." would cyber-attack and, in effect, destroy the source of all of these economic goodies is never really explained—possibly because too much time is taken illustrating the fallout from a cyberwar. Crime, as opposed to war, in this interconnected age has apparent purposes and a range of techniques, and runs relatively rampant, as very little regulation and enforcement, and few incentives to truly secure one's data, exist. Symantec, the world's largest maker of computer security software, cited in their Global Internet Security Threat Report (2010) that, for 2009, credit card information garnered anywhere from \$0.85 to \$30 per card (up from a max of \$20 in 2008), and bank account credentials fetched \$15–850 (up from a \$100 maximum the previous year). Incentives abound for this online ecology of crime.

Conclusion

It does not take much attention to see that societies around the world are at a crucial point in securing their digital infrastructure. How these societies address and discuss, and the metaphors used to encapsulate, this incredibly complex and multi-layered realm called cyberspace will matter greatly. There are those who see a war going on and make calls to militarize the Internet and a society's means of using it. Out of this perspective, however, is the troubling notion of ever-expanding military responsibility. If one's wallet were stolen, would the military investigate? At the same time, the risk of having one's wallet stolen is an everyday one. Similarly, having your data or personal information pilfered via cyber exploitations is now part of the online world. As opposed to war, crime is an aspect of everyday life—it is no different online. The measures taken to combat it should reflect that, be resourceful, and also be tempered by the same legal responsibilities as a typical police force.

Alternatively, being prepared for war is of course a necessity. The various CERT organizations and Cyber Command centers around the globe reflect that. However, time and time again, it may be also necessary to remind law-makers, policy-makers, military staff, and politicians that, as of yet, no one is engaging in a full-scale cyberwar. Interestingly, the U.S. and Israel, the countries reportedly behind Stuxnet—probably the closest thing to a cyber weapon yet discovered—are also claiming to be victims in the international discourse. Regardless, what many have asked for, and what many have drowned out with war-mongering, is plain, simple, and flexible cyber-security. Something like a coordinated effort that combines public organizations (like a police force or, when necessary and needed, the military) and private companies (like security software makers, Internet service providers, and telecommunications companies) with an educated populace. Easy, right?

Probably not. In the background of all this cyber-security talk are dollars and cents. With the advance of the Internet, with its blazing speed and ability to obliterate distance and time, online commerce and technological innovation have become the norm and many economies have come to depend on the ever greater advancement of communications technology. To secure it is to slow it down, to slow it down is to decrease returns. Here we have a paradox: as governments around the world decry the "cyber problem" and cyberwar as major issues to tackle, they also tout more and faster broadband, networked electricity grids, and linked air traffic control systems. With these advances in technology come new problems, and by favoring the short-term gains of, say, what a completely networked society might bring (revenue, commerce, advances in communication), the longer-term vulnerabilities are pushed down the road for the future to deal with.

For these advancements to persist and thrive, more advanced security is necessary. While no one can yet adequately articulate what this security looks like or how it operates, the first sure step towards a kind of online enforcement will come from how a society talks about getting there. Framing the need for that security in terms like "Cyber 9/11" does not help. By focusing on some future cyberwar, less emphasis is placed on the total damage being done by the smaller, multiplicitous, happening-right-now-in-reality threats that cybercrime presents. Military spending on hypothetical threats might better be used to protect citizens who use the Internet, as opposed to turning the Internet into a battlefront.

References

AFP. 2010. *Cybercrime Surge Pushes 2009 Losses to 559 Million Dollars* [Online: Agence France-Presse]. Available at: http://www.google.com/hostednews/afp/article/ALeqM5gVmzggEhc9pgpdUqMcs0CIK_xloQ [accessed: 9 October 2010].

Branigan, T. 2010. Chinese Army to Target Cyber War Threat. *The Guardian* [Online, 22 July]. Available at: http://www.guardian.co.uk/world/2010/jul/22/chinese-army-cyber-war-department [accessed: 11 October 2010].

Bray, C., Bryan-Low, C. and Gorman, S. 2010. Accounts Raided in Global Bank Hack. *The Wall Street Journal* [Online, 1 October]. Available at: http://online.wsj.com/article/SB10001424052748704483004575523811617488380.html [accessed: 12 December 2010].

Broad, W.J., Markoff, J. and Sanger, D.E. 2011. Israeli Test on Worm Called Crucial in Iran Nuclear Delay. *The New York Times* [Online, 15 January]. Available at: http://www.nytimes.com/2011/01/16/world/middleeast/16stuxnet.html?_r=2&pagewanted=all [accessed: 17 January 2011].

Byrt, F. 2010. U.S. Defense Contractors are Scrambling to Fill Massive Cyber Security Contracts. *Business Insider* [Online, 19 November]. Available at: http://www.businessinsider.com/obama-is-spending-a-ton-on-defense-spending-in-cyber-security-2010-11#ixzz181muxzmR [accessed: 19 November 2010].

Carr, J. 2010. Did The Stuxnet Worm Kill India's INSAT-4B Satellite? *Forbes* [Online, 29 September]. Available at: http://blogs.forbes.com/firewall/2010/09/29/did-the-stuxnet-worm-kill-indias-insat-4b-satellite/ [accessed: 17 January 2011].

CERT-In. 2010. Welcome to CERT-In. *CERT-In.org.in* [Online, 18 December]. Available at: http://www.cert-in.org.in/ [accessed: 18 December 2010].

Clarke, R. 2010. *Cyber War: The Next Threat to National Security and What to Do About It*. New York: HarperCollins.

Drummond, D. 2010. A New Approach to China. *The Official Google Blog* [Online, 12 January]. Available at: http://googleblog.blogspot.com/2010/01/new-approach-to-china.html [accessed: 12 October 2010].

Farivar, C. 2007. Cyberwar I: What the Attacks on Estonia have Taught us About Online Combat. *Slate* [Online, 22 May]. Available at: http://www.slate.com/id/2166749/ [accessed: 11 October 2010].

Harris, S. 2009. The Cyberwar Plan. *National Journal* [Online, 13 November]. Available at: http://www.nationaljournal.com/njmagazine/cs_20091114_3145.php [accessed: 13 October 2010].

Hersh. S. 2010 The Online Threat. *The New Yorker* [Online, 1 November]. Available at: http://www.newyorker.com/reporting/2010/11/01/101101fa_fact_hersh?currentPage=all [accessed: 2 December 2010].

I.W. Monitor. 2009. *Tracking GhostNet: Investigating a Cyber Espionage Network*. Report JR02-2009. Toronto: Munk Centre for International Studies, University of Toronto.

McConnell, M. 2010. Mike McConnell on How to Win the Cyber-war we're Losing. *The Washington Post* [Online, 28 February]. Available at: http://www.washingtonpost.com/wp-dyn/content/article/2010/02/25/AR2010022502493.html?sid=ST2010031901063 [accessed: 12 October 2010].

Moore, T., Clayton, R. and Anderson, R. 2009. The Economics of Online Crime. *The Journal of Economic Perspectives* 23(3), 3–20.

Obama, B. 2009. *Remarks by the President on Securing our Nation's Cyber Infrastructure*. White House Press Release [Online, 29 May]. Available at: http://www.whitehouse.gov/the-press-office/remarks-president-securing-our-nations-cyber-infrastructure [accessed: 12 October 2010].

Panda Labs. 2010. *Annual Report 2010* [Online, 15 December]. Available at: http://press.pandasecurity.com/wp-content/uploads/2010/05/PandaLabs-Annual-Report-2010.pdf [accessed: 14 January 2011].

Poulsen, K. 2007. 'Cyberwar' and Estonia's Panic Attack. *Wired* [Online, 22 August]. Available at: http://www.wired.com/threatlevel/2007/08/cyber-war-and-e/ [accessed: 11 October 2010].

Symantec. 2010. *Symantec Global Internet Security Threat Report Trends for 2009 Volume XV* [Online, 11 April]. Available at: http://eval.symantec.com/mktginfo/enterprise/white_papers/b-whitepaper_internet_security_threat_report_xv_04-2010.en-us.pdf [accessed: 18 January 2011].

The Economist. 2010. The Meaning of Stuxnet. *The Economist* [Online, 30 September]. Available at: http://www.economist.com/node/17147862 [accessed: 8 December 2010].

UPI. 2007. Report: Israel used Cyberwar against Syria [Online: 13 December]. Available at: http://www.upi.com/Top_News/Special/2007/12/13/Report-Israel-used-cyberwar-against-Syria/UPI-20671197559471/ [accessed: 12 October 2010].

PART II

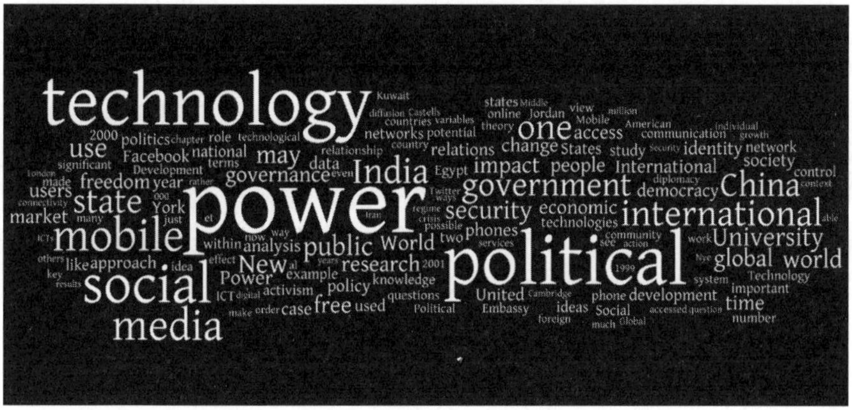
technology
power
political
social
mobile
media
international
China
government
India
one
state
University
global
world
security
public
research
New
freedom
governance
impact
people
democracy
economic
use
Facebook
national
may
relations
change
States
identity
network
society
access
communication
networks
countries
phones
approach
analysis
activism
policy
knowledge
example
Power
free
used
case
United
Embassy
ideas
Social
development
phone
time
number
important
system
Technology
control
market
users
York
Egypt
Jordan
online
states
view
American
Kuwait
diffusion
Castells
variables
theory
potential
country
relationship
data
Development
significant
politics
chapter
role
technological
study
International
technologies
community
World
two
within
like
idea
effect
questions
Political
foreign
much
Global
Cambridge
order
make
digital
ICT

Chapter 7
Web 2.0 and Public Diplomacy

Hannes R. Richter

> The effectiveness of public diplomacy is measured in minds changed, not Dollars spent or slick production packages.
>
> Joseph S. Nye, Jr

Introduction

Scholarly interest in the role of the Internet and its applications in political communication has been growing rapidly over recent years, and reached the ultimate prominence with the presidential campaign of Barack Obama. The web's role in international political communication and specifically as a tool of public diplomacy only recently began capturing wider audiences. Particularly with the rise of the social web and prominent applications like Facebook and Twitter, scholars and practitioners of public diplomacy alike became interested in how those tools can be used in the practice of public diplomacy. Recent developments have brought Twitter to the forefront of the debate; events surrounding protests in the aftermath of the Iranian election, in what has been called a "Twitter Revolution" (e.g. Berman 2009), were more often communicated through *tweets* and other new media channels than the regular media. This is not surprising as the Iranian regime tried to hinder communications and reporting on the events to the outside world, but (so far) has not managed to fully control these new communication channels. Government officials have recognized the importance of the new tools on numerous occasions; Secretary of State Hillary Clinton asked Twitter to postpone system maintenance so that Iranians could continue to feed information through it (Shater 2009). At the same time, critical voices also cast doubt on the true impact of the tool, despite the hype. Joel Schectman (2009) argued that simply not enough Iranians were able to use Twitter to reach a critical mass to actually fuel the protest, pointing out that the service has not yet operated a Farsi version. In addition, the Iranian government made efforts to block access to the site, which would have shrunk the number of Iranian users further, meaning that only the tech-savvy would know how to bypass such a blockage through the use of proxy addresses (Schectman 2009).

These and other developments and media frenzies have also brought attention to other uses of new media in international relations. In particular, the U.S. State Department has made every effort to improve their Web 2.0 smarts as part of their public diplomacy strategy. Embassies around the globe have begun embracing the new tools, and have set up Facebook pages and Twitter accounts to communicate with their audiences. I believe that these activities warrant closer observation. In this chapter, I will (1) aim to review the latest uses of Web 2.0 uses in public diplomacy, focusing on the state actor, here limited to the U.S.; (2) address obstacles and possibilities in assessing and measuring such efforts; and (3) suggest avenues for further research, drawing on evidence from the U.S. in the absence of international data. This chapter is thus intended as a small step towards a systematic, scholarly analysis of the effects of Web 2.0 as a tool of public diplomacy on audiences.

Public Diplomacy into the Twenty-first Century

Public diplomacy has long been on the agenda of nation states as a tool of their foreign policy, albeit not always under that name. The term "public diplomacy" is a relatively new one, coined in 1965 at the Fletcher School for Law and Diplomacy by Edmund Gullion (Malone 1988; for a good overview of public diplomacy research see Cull 2008). The concept itself, however, dates back to ancient times—the Roman Empire was concerned with image and reputation and invited future foreign leaders to be educated in Rome. In Egypt, Napoleon wanted the entire French army to convert to Islam in order to help establish French rule (Murphy 2008). In the twentieth century, propaganda was already omnipresent and its importance duly noted. In World War I, Woodrow Wilson created the *Committee on Public Information* as an independent U.S. government agency in 1917, shortly after declaring war on Germany. Tasked with winning public support for the war among a mostly isolationist American public, the Committee made use of all technology available at the time—film, radio, posters, etc.—to disseminate messages, and also enlisted tens of thousands of volunteers—the Four Minute Men—to speak publicly and at events. It also fabricated horror stories about German soldiers, depicting them as monsters that bayoneted babies. However, while tasked with winning public support at home, the committee also began targeting audiences abroad (Creel 1920). During World War II, both Germany and the Allies stepped up propaganda efforts, again targeting both domestic and foreign audiences in order to rally support for the War effort at home and to frame minds abroad. Technology has always played a significant role in the trade of public diplomacy and propaganda. In the Third Reich, Minister of Propaganda Joseph Goebbels made every effort to bring all media outlets under his control and quickly realized the potential of new modes of communication. The Volksempfänger was an attempt to produce an affordable radio receiver so that ultimately every German household would have one and thus could receive propaganda from the airwaves. Mobile movie screens mounted on trucks attempted to bring the propaganda on film into remote areas of Germany that did not have movie theaters (for a discussion of German World War II propaganda, see e.g. Welch 1983).

In the U.S., the Federal Communications Commission had established the Foreign Broadcast Monitoring Service at the request of the State Department before the attack on Pearl Harbor (Richelson 1999). The division originally was tasked with analyzing foreign short-wave broadcasts (Barnouw 1968). In 1942, the Office of War Information organized Voice of America, the official external radio and broadcasting service of the U.S., which still operates today. Voice of America claimed to report the truth to its audiences, which reached from Great Britain to Europe, and North Africa to Japan and the Pacific theater, stating "we bring you Voices from America. Today and daily from now on, we shall speak to you about America and the war. The news may be good for us. The news may be bad. But we shall tell you the truth" (William Harlan Hale, first VOA broadcast, quoted in Heil 2003: 32). After World War II, Voice of America, a formidable tool of public diplomacy, continued to operate as part of the State Department.

During the bipolar world of the Cold War, the idea of winning hearts and minds again moved center-stage, and Voice of America was regarded as a vital ingredient in countering communist propaganda. Consequently, Voice of America began broadcasts in Russian as early as 1947 (Whitton 1951). In 1951, the U.S. finally created what would become its premier public diplomacy agency, the U.S. Information Agency. The agency described itself as "an independent foreign affairs agency supporting U.S. foreign policy and national interests abroad, USIA conducts international educational and cultural exchanges, broadcasting, and information programs" (Electronic Research Collection of Historic State Department Materials 2010). During the Cold War, the USIA was the primary strategic and organizational vessel for U.S. public diplomacy. The agency was dissolved into the U.S. Department of State on 1 October 1999.

In a post 9/11 world more emphasis has again been put on public diplomacy as a tool of national security. Ever since, and particularly after the attacks of 9/11, voices have called for a reorganization and modernization of public diplomacy as a tool of U.S. foreign policy; some would like to see the USIA come back into existence. However, as observers of U.S. diplomacy have pointed out, the international stage has changed significantly since the days of the USIA, which was founded in the bipolar world of the Cold War. As Kiehl (2009) notes, today's public diplomacy is "field-driven and encourages egalitarianism, risk-taking and transparency" (p. 48). These new qualities and requirements of public diplomacy beg the inclusion of new tools that promise to deliver just that. Social networking applications in recent years have taken the domestic political scene in the U.S. and elsewhere by storm; however, applications in international political communication have been lagging until recently. Public diplomacy officers have come to realize that a new international environment poses new challenges, not only from a strategic perspective, but also in terms of communications. The importance of people-to-people communications has again moved center-stage when it comes to communicating values to foreign publics while aiming to correct misperceptions; today's public diplomacy requires "a sophisticated form of triangulation: diplomats from sending states use dialogue, image projection, reputation management, and the power of attraction to connect directly with foreign populations—opinion leaders, NGO representatives, businesspeople, journalists, and others—in order to advance their objectives with host governments" (Copeland 2009). These objectives must now be met through adapting to the changing information environment of the twenty-first century.

U.S. Public Diplomacy and New Media

Technological advances have always been adapted very quickly by makers of propaganda. From the printing press to radio, film, and television: each left its mark on how governments have communicated with foreign audiences. Today, we are again presented with massive technological advances that will substantially alter the way we communicate and collaborate, thus also affecting the way foreign ministries communicate with "more connected, yet more diverse and fragmented, domestic and global publics" (Potter 2008: 121).

The Rise of the Social Web

The social web, often referred to as Web 2.0, is made up of a second-generation set of software applications, enabling users to collaborate, work, and share online. It is characterized by popular web applications such as YouTube, Facebook, Twitter, Wikis, and myriad others. The exact definition of the term remains somewhat contested—it probably goes back to 2004, as Paul Graham reports that he first heard the phrase "Web 2.0" in the name of the Web 2.0 conference in 2004. At the time it was supposed to mean using the web as a platform, which he took to refer to web-based applications (Graham 2005). For the purpose of this chapter I will focus on two of the most prominent of these applications, Facebook and Twitter.

Facebook was founded in February 2004 and describes itself as a "social utility that helps people communicate more efficiently with their friends, family, and co-workers". Facebook today has some 500 million users, 70% of whom reside outside the U.S. More than 50 million users log on to Facebook any given day; each one of them on average is connected to 130 friends.

There currently exist over 3 million active pages, 3.5 million events are created each month, and users upload some 3 billion photos to the site every month. What is more, Facebook reports that the average user spends more than 55 minutes per day on Facebook, a fairly long time by web standards. Facebook has seen tremendous international growth and as a result now offers the site in over 70 languages. This international presence and growth is important for those who consider Facebook as a tool for public diplomacy. Table 7.1 summarizes the 20 countries with the highest increase of Facebook users between 2008 and 2009. Within a year's time, Indonesia saw a staggering 2,997.2% increase in Facebook users, going from just 209,760 to 6,496,960 accounts, followed by Romania, Slovakia, and the Czech Republic, who saw equally dramatic increases. Those figures are impressive and leave little doubt about the fact that such tools have grown into a force to be reckoned with.

Table 7.1 Countries with the fastest-growing number of Facebook users, 2009

Rank	Country	Number of users July 2008	Number of users July 2009	12 month growth (%)
1	Indonesia	209,760	6,496,960	2,997.2%
2	Romania	9,060	230,600	2,445.3%
3	Slovakia	27,960	588,860	2,006.1%
4	Czech Republic	51,860	1,088,020	2,005.3%
5	Italy	491,100	10,218,400	1,980.7%
6	Philippines	162,640	2,719,560	1,572.13%
7	Argentina	417,980	4,906,220	1,073.8%
8	Uruguay	40,920	395,800	867.3%
9	Taiwan	71,340	685,450	860.8%
10	Portugal	48,180	425,680	783.5%
11	Brazil	119,080	1,015,400	752.7%
12	Spain	695,900	5,773,200	729.6%
13	Paraguay	7,920	63,740	704.8%
14	Poland	83,180	619,180	644.4%
15	Bulgaria	60,240	436,480	624.6%
16	Austria	111,060	728,800	556.2%
17	Slovenia	53,740	343,320	538.9%
18	Lithuania	24,320	153,160	529.8%
19	Thailand	114,180	697,340	510.7%
20	Russia	67,760	412,840	509.3%

Source: Facebook.

Twitter describes itself as a "real-time information network powered by people all around the world that lets you share and discover what's happening now." Similar to Facebook, Twitter's growth rates, too, now continue to come from abroad. Overall, the service enjoyed an increase of 58.4 million unique visitors worldwide between August and September 2009 alone, which translates into a 949% jump, while the number of U.S. visitors has remained relatively flat during the same time at 20.9 million. In March 2009, Twitter grew by 1,382% compared with the previous year, Adam Ostrow (2009) reported. These numbers underline the claim that the Internet revolution is far from over, but rather is picking up steam. Specifically, new data from 2010 again underline the international outreach: As of January 2010, Brazil accounts for 8.8% of all Twitter users, as compared with 2.2% in June of 2009. Likewise, Indonesia's Twitter users increased to 2.5% of the total, up from 0.5%, followed by Germany (Sysomos Inc. 2010). Governments will have to continue to cope with this significantly altered media landscape on many levels, including their public diplomacy activities.

Keeping the stipulations of new public diplomacy in mind, the social web seems to fit the description well. The new web fosters interaction, as it has grown interactive itself. It encourages dialogue; never before has it been easier for governments to disseminate messages at a dramatically reduced cost, but at the same time, recipients of these messages have the ability to directly respond with just a mouse click. The new web is viral; messages are forwarded, reposted, and retweeted. As a result, "international communication, which since the dawn of the motion picture has been premised on a one-to-many broadcasting model, is now moving ineluctably towards a web-enabled many-to-many format" (Potter 2008: 123). It thus seems the web can serve as a power tool for diplomats for every one of their objectives.

With the increase in social media use worldwide, the way people receive information has changed substantially. The World Internet Project (2008) reports several key indicators that impact public diplomacy online: first, respondents in all countries covered[1] by the report indicate that the Internet is an important or very important source of information. What is more, in all countries except for Macao and Sweden, respondents "ranked the Internet as an important or very important source of information compared with television, newspapers, and radio" (World Internet Project 2008: 2), albeit with reservations about its reliability.

Data from the U.S. reinforce the trend towards the political web: in 2008, political use of social networking sites was already significant, particularly among the younger generation (see Table 7.2): 37% of 18–29 year-old social network users reported that they had discovered the political interests or affiliations of friends, 28% indicated that they had received campaign information from such sites, and some 15% said that they had started or joined a political group.

Table 7.2 Political use of social networking sites in the U.S., 2008

	Social network users age 18–29 (n = 152)	Social network users age 30+ (n = 250)
Discovered your friends' political interests or affiliations	37%	22%
Obtained any candidate or campaign information on the sites	28	17
Signed up as a friend of any candidates	16	4
Started or joined a political group	15	4
Have done any of these using a social networking site	49	32

Note: N = 409 social networking site users. Margin of error is ±5%.
Source: Pew Internet and American Life Project Spring 2008 Survey. Note that the Pew Internet and American Life Project bears no responsibility for the interpretations presented or conclusions reached based on analysis of the data.

1 Argentina, Australia, Bolivia, Canada, Chile, China, Colombia, Cyprus, Czech Republic, France, Germany, Great Britain, Hungary, Iran, Israel, Italy, Japan, Macao, Mexico, New Zealand, Portugal, Russia, Singapore, South Korea, Spain, Sweden, United Arab Emirates, U.S.A.

Given the rapid growth of these networks, particularly outside the U.S., their future impact as a tool for public diplomacy cannot be underestimated.

As a result, the U.S. State Department has increased its efforts to adapt to the changing environment while at the same time being confronted with possible pitfalls: "how should diplomats engage with the new media, can diplomats blog? Twitter? Should comments be allowed? Should they be filtered? Who can engage? Where? For what purpose?" (Graff 2009). The Department started a blog, *DipNote*, while beginning to venture into social media. Soon it had created a digital outreach team able to communicate not only in English, but also in Urdu, Farsi, and Arabic to enter the blogosphere to counter misinformation about U.S. foreign policy and the U.S. in general (Graff 2009). Within the U.S. State Department, the emphasis that is now being put on new media is evident on several levels: a new generation of Foreign Service officers is advocating changes and possibilities within the Department and its missions abroad that involve a Web 2.0-savvy approach next to structural changes (Public Diplomacy Front Line Working Group 2009). The Department since has pushed its efforts towards a digital future. Next to a substantial redesign of its websites (most notably its main site, www.state.gov), it also launched its own international social network, ExchangesConnect, in October of 2008, which encourages international users to sign up and also connects through Facebook and Twitter. The service has since enjoyed a steady increase in members (Johnson 2009). Furthermore, www.america.gov is targeted at foreign audiences and published in several languages. Its Democracy Video Project on YouTube marks another Web 2.0 outreach, calling for user-generated video submissions on democracy.

Similarly, foreign missions and diplomats increasingly are establishing a presence on Facebook and Twitter. Table 7.3 summarizes a selection of U.S. missions abroad who have established a Facebook presence and the corresponding number of "fans" (in the case of a Facebook *Page*) or the number of "members" (in the case of a Facebook *Group*). Interestingly, the country that had the largest growth rate on Facebook over the past year is also host to the U.S. Embassy currently boasting the highest number of Facebook supporters—the U.S. Embassy in Jakarta, Indonesia, with 30,207 fans at the time of the writing of this chapter. In this ranking the U.S. Embassy in Manila comes in a distant second with 3,849 fans, followed by the embassies in Podgorica, Baghdad, and Cairo.

In the light of these activities, the question remains, however: does it matter? Despite the advantage the social web might have for the dissemination of information and dialogue and its structural and strategic implications, one question must be recalled at this point: does it have the power to change minds, net of other factors, or is it just public diplomacy window dressing? Not all observers share the optimism surrounding the new digital diplomacy: that "so many governments manipulate the Internet to their advantage—all the while still practicing old-fashioned tactics like throwing bloggers in jail—suggests that those who hoped to use cyberspace to promote democracy and American ideals on the cheap may be in for a tough fight" (Morozov 2010). Thus, scholars and practitioners alike must be concerned about evaluating and assessing the impact of new media to be able to answer these questions in the future.

Table 7.3 U.S. missions abroad on Facebook *(selection)*

Mission	Number of fans/members	Mission	Number of fans/members
U.S. Embassy Jakarta	30,207	U.S. Embassy France	1,005
U.S. Embassy Manila	3,849	U.S. Embassy Nairobi	626
U.S. Embassy Podgorica	3,334	U.S. Embassy Harare	598
U.S. Embassy Baghdad	2,459	U.S. Embassy Quito	545
U.S. Embassy Cairo	2,336	U.S. Embassy Ashgabat	488
U.S. Embassy Macedonia	2,068	U.S. Embassy Warsaw	447
U.S. Embassy Tunis	1,896	U.S. Embassy Seoul	410
U.S. Embassy Dhaka	1,665	U.S. Embassy Abuja	49
U.S. Embassy Kabul	1,630	U.S. Embassy Brazzaville	10
U.S. Embassy Tirana	1,385	U.S. Embassy Mauritania	260
U.S. Embassy Gaborone	1,549	U.S. Embassy Dushanbe	292
U.S. Embassy Santiago	1,401	U.S. Embassy Alumni Bogota	280
U.S. Embassy Pakistan	931	U.S. Embassy Vienna	281
U.S. Embassy Moldova	248	U.S. Embassy Italy	733
U.S. Embassy Libreville	13	U.S. Embassy Tel Aviv	158
U.S. Embassy Bridgetown	79	U.S. Embassy Sana'a	673
U.S. Embassy Zambia	902	U.S. Embassy Kuala Lumpur	592
U.S. Embassy Prague	876	U.S. Embassy Almaty	91
U.S. Embassy London	897	U.S. Embassy Baghdad Soccer Team	31
U.S. Embassy Singapore	416		

Source: Facebook.

The Quest for Assessment

Public diplomacy effects in general are hard to measure, and empirical assessment of their impact with regard to digital media is the primary concern in this chapter. The Foreign and Commonwealth Office and the British Council have begun developing and testing an evaluation framework to assess the impact of their public diplomacy initiatives. As the authors involved in the program, Louise Vinter and David Knox, point out, "there are three inherent difficulties in measuring public diplomacy: its frequently long-term ambition; the challenge of measuring concepts that may be intangible; and the problem of attributing observable changes to one's own activities" (Vinter and Knox 2009: 163). As the authors argue, the principal problem in measuring public diplomacy is attribution: in the international environment of the twenty-first century, where multiple actors, both governmental and nongovernmental, influence issues and opinions, identifying the causes is a most difficult task. What is more, many objectives of public diplomacy are long-term goals, which pose additional challenges, as Nick Cull summarized: "Attempts to evaluate cultural diplomacy can seem like a forester running out every morning to see how far his trees have grown overnight" (Cull 2007 in Vinter and Knox 2009: 164).

If our understanding of the goal of digital diplomacy is a mind changed, then we must focus on the individual as the unit of analysis, rather than policy outcomes. Thus, it seems in order to treat social web applications as media in an empirical sense, helping us to draw on decades of scholarship and thereby bridging the gap between existing literatures on Web 2.0 in the domestic sphere and their application in international political communication. The U.S. State Department, according to Bruce Wharton, evaluates such activities "according to three criteria: reach, engagement and credibility—each of which can be measured through readership statistics and web ratings" (Wharton quoted in Johnson 2009: 24). I argue that, with the individual as the unit of analysis, survey research would be the appropriate tool to complement such findings. Within the above framework, such an analysis would fall under impact assessment, thus delivering additional insights into the effectiveness of digital tools as part of a larger effort. I will draw on descriptive international data and present evidence from the U.S., demonstrating the impact of new media during the 2008 presidential election.

Between May and June 2009, The Pew Global Attitudes project administered a 25-country survey to investigate international attitudes towards the U.S., President Obama and a number of international issues. I would like to highlight one specific aspect of the survey to illustrate the potential of attitude shifts happening as a result of a media event. In Israel and the Palestinian Territories, respondents were polled before and after President Obama's Cairo speech, Table 7.4 presents the results. While 76% of Israelis indicated that they had a positive view of the U.S. before the speech, the number dropped to 63% after the speech. Similarly, the number of Palestinian respondents indicating a positive view of the U.S. rose from 14% to 19%. Confidence in President Obama's leadership in Israel dropped from 60% to 49%, while it rose by 5% in the Palestinian Territories. While these bivariate relationships are of limited validity, they do suggest that opinions can be swayed by such messages and invite testing for such an effect in a multivariate environment. It also raises questions on the degree to which new media sources can have an effect on such opinions, if they contribute to learning about the U.S. and if they ultimately can support a long-term improvement in opinions about the U.S. In an ideal world, data to empirically test these assumptions would be readily available; as of this point, however, I was unable to locate a dataset that allows the testing of a model including such specific media variables. To illustrate the case, I resorted to the U.S., where such data is available, and present a multivariate model on new media usage and political knowledge as a proxy for democratic competence that can possibly serve as an example for future international testing.

Table 7.4 The Cairo effect

	Israel		Palestinian Territories	
	Pre-speech	*Post-speech*	*Pre-speech*	*Post-speech*
View of U.S.				
Favorable	76	63	14	19
Unfavorable	22	36	84	80
Obama's leadership				
Confident	60	49	21	26
Not confident	39	51	76	72
Will Obama consider our interests?				
Yes	58	54	27	39
No	36	43	70	57
N	800	401	804	400

Source: Pew 2009 Global Attitudes Survey. Note that Pew Internet and American Life Project bears no responsibility for the interpretations presented or conclusions reached based on analysis of the data.

New Media and the 2008 Presidential Election—A Domestic Proxy

In the absence of available international data, I draw on evidence from the U.S. regarding the impact of new media as a source of political information. The Internet today is an integral part of U.S. political campaigns. Particularly during the 2008 presidential campaign, the omnipresent web made headlines of its own (Feldman 2007; Vargas 2007); social networking and online video applications took a particularly prominent role. For the first time in history, citizens were able to submit their own questions for Democratic and Republican debates via YouTube, the web's most popular video-sharing platform, to have them aired and answered live on network television. This marked the latest milestone in the Internet's integration into the mainstream of political information. Similar to my question about the web's impact on foreign audiences, I ask if the Internet as an everyday reality of a majority of Americans does in fact alter political communication in the U.S. More specifically, do those who have access to the Internet and use it for political information tend to be better informed about politics, net of other factors? Does the medium increase information only among citizens who are politically aware in the first place, or does it in fact help bridge the information gap between the informed and the uninformed? Is the new medium an amplifier of existing patterns, an equalizer of existing divides, or does it have no impact at all? Visionaries of information technology and democracy have asserted that technological advances hold the potential to function as an equalizer for the disconnected, to flatten access to political information (Barber 1984; Dahl 1989; Morris 1999). On the other hand, past research has indicated that only a subset of the population benefits from the Internet politically; the focus was on the digital divide, the gap between the haves and the have-nots, denying notions of a cyberspace revolution (Margolis and Resnick 2000). Moreover, scholars have argued that, as the information revolution took hold, it helped form a new political elite rather than leveling the playing field (Coglianese 2007; Hindeman 2007).

I chose political knowledge as a dependent variable as it can serve as a proxy for democratic competence. Similarly, such models can be easily adapted to test for changes in issue positions and the like. The data for this model are provided by the Pew Center for the People and the Press Biennial Media Consumption Survey 2008. The sample includes 3600 adults, 2800 of whom were interviewed over their landline and 800 over their cell phone between 29 April and 31 May 2008. The best measurement of political knowledge has been subject to much debate and primarily revolves around the use of factual knowledge questions versus the use of the interviewer-evaluation of the respondent's political knowledge, particularly in face-to-face interview situations (Zaller 1985, 1992). The use of factual knowledge scales has been widespread; Levendusky and Jackman (2003) in their study of political knowledge measurement acknowledge it to be the most popular method within the discipline (next to interviewer-evaluation), but also state that it is not immune to certain drawbacks, ranging from the question of whether certain factual knowledge items should be assigned weights to address questions like "should knowing the Chief Justice of the Supreme Court count more or less than knowing which party controlled the House of Representatives before the most recent election?" (p. 6). The second possible measurement relies on the interviewer's assessment of a respondent's political knowledge measured using a five-point scale. Although there is an apparent concern that these evaluations might be biased, Zaller points out that "at least in surveys involving face-to face interviews and considerable political content, they perform extremely well [...] A fear in relying upon such interviewer ratings is that they might be systematically biased in favor of higher-status persons, notably whites and males. However, I checked carefully for evidence of such bias and was able to find none" (Zaller 1985, quoted in Zaller 1992: 338). As Levendusky and Jackman (2003) point out, the interviewer-rating measure is "arguably the strongest single-item indicator" (p. 6). In this chapter, the dependent variable, political knowledge, was measured through the available three hard-knowledge questions, asking respondents to identify the political party who has a majority in the U.S. House of Representatives, the current U.S. Secretary of State, and the current prime minister of Great Britain, respectively. These were subsequently recoded into an additive knowledge scale, coded zero for respondents who answered all three questions incorrectly, 1 for one correct answer, 2 for two correct answers, and 3 if all answers were answered correctly.

The political knowledge model can be summarized as such:

$$\mathbf{Y}(\text{Knowledge}) = \beta_1 + \beta_2\text{Newspaper} + \beta_3\text{Television} + \beta_4\text{NewsRadio} + \beta_5\text{Interest} + \beta_6\text{InternetNews} + \beta_7\text{Blogs} + \beta_8\text{Online Magazines} + \beta_9\text{Social Networks} + \beta_{10}\text{Age} + \beta_{11}\text{Education} + \beta_{12}\text{Race} + \beta_{13}\text{Sex} + \beta_{14}\text{Income} + \beta_{15}\text{PartyI.D.} + e$$

where the independent variables controlling for "traditional" news outlets are Newspaper, which measures whether a respondent regularly reads a newspaper or not, Television, measured in similar fashion to capture if a respondent regularly consumes TV news programs, and NewsRadio, capturing regular exposure to radio news programs. It is important to note that these variables provide a rather general measure of news consumption and were chosen owing to their similarity in question wording in order to provide a stable basis for comparison between them. The Internet variables capture three behaviors: first, Internet News User is coded to summarize respondents who log on at least three times a week (or more often) to obtain news online; second, Read Blogs measures respondents who stated that they regularly read political blogs as a source of political information, and third, Social Network gauges respondents who have an account with a social network site such as Facebook or MySpace. Demographic predictors of political knowledge in this model include age, education, race (coded as a white/nonwhite dummy), gender, and income, complimented by a control for party identification; *e* is the residual error term. Given the nature of the dependent variable, Ordered Probit would also be an adequate method of estimation besides ordinary least square (OLS) regression; I thus estimated the model using both techniques and did not find significant differences. For ease of interpretation, the results of the OLS regression will be presented here.

Results

The results of the multivariate political knowledge model are summarized in Table 7.5. Inspection of demographic standard predictors of political knowledge yields few surprises: age, education, and income are all significant and positively related to the dependent variable; they remain reliable predictors of individuals' levels of political information. Somewhat noteworthy, however, is the significant, negative effect of gender in this model; being female is negatively related to political knowledge. Race is barely significant at the 0.05 level, while party identification does not exercise any significant effect. Turning to the media consumption variables, one can observe the differing impact of the news source: while regularly reading a newspaper remains a positive, significant predictor of political knowledge, the missing impact of television has again been confirmed. Respondents seem not to learn much from the tube when it comes to politics; the variable is insignificant. However, it is important to note that this model employs somewhat generalized measures of media sources, so television overall does not contribute to political knowledge, thus confirming the television hypothesis. Refined measurement might lead to other insights, depending on what programming a respondent consumes—primarily and regularly watching political programming like C-Span is likely to have a different impact. The positive, significant impact of radio as a source of political information seems to be noteworthy: respondents who claim to regularly listen to political news on the radio seem to learn more than those who regularly rely on TV news programs. The Internet variables yield mixed results: while going online frequently to obtain news clearly contributes to political knowledge, other activities do not—reading political blogs and having a social network site account like Facebook are not statistically significant, while reading political magazines like *Slate* online does have a significant, positive effect. The fact that reading political magazines online potentially has more to contribute to political knowledge than uploading photos to Facebook seems obvious; yet it is also an indication that the political uses of social networking sites do potentially lie in different areas and make little contribution to levels of citizens' democratic competence. It does not quite explain, however, why reading online political magazines has a significant effect, and reading political blogs does not, while controlling for other factors.

These results pertain to a domestic political campaign in the U.S. and cannot be used to generalize the impact of new media in other countries. I include them at this point as an example from the home front and hope to be able to replicate the general idea with international data. Given the fact that we cannot assume that political behavior and information-gathering habits are universally distributed around the globe, the question of whether Facebook can contribute to a mind changed must be answered with great care, but ultimately we should gain better insights into how foreign publics receive public diplomacy campaigns employing new media, who they are, and if it can change their levels of knowledge and attitudes, while controlling for standard predictors.

Table 7.5 OLS regression results, 2008 U.S. knowledge model

Dependent variable: Political knowledge			
	Coefficient	*P > |t|*	*Standard error*
Media consumption variables			
Newspaper	0.1115199	0.014	0.045141
Television	0.0795395	0.127	0.0520798
News Radio	0.1662281	0.000	0.041913
Enjoy Keeping Up	0.130739	0.000	0.0242092
Internet News User	0.2264945	0.000	0.0456112
Read Blogs	0.0055485	0.787	0.020548
Read Online Magazines	0.1805575	0.000	0.0318495
Social Network	0.0610533	0.271	0.0554856
Demographic variables			
Age	0.1692504	0.000	0.0164835
Education	0.2719886	0.000	0.0245368
Race	0.1070845	0.050	0.0546433
Gender	−0.398015	0.000	0.0413226
Income	0.0246152	0.005	0.0088139
Party I.D.	0.0079606	0.763	0.0263814

Note: N = 2,110. R^2 = 0.3031.

Source: Pew Center for the People and the Press. Note that the Pew Internet and American Life Project bears no responsibility for the interpretations presented or conclusions reached based on analysis of the data.

References

Barber, B. 1984. *Strong Democracy*. Berkeley and Los Angeles: University of California Press.

Barnouw, E. 1968. *A History of Broadcasting in the United States: Volume 2: The Golden Web. 1933 to 1953*. New York: Oxford University Press.

Berman, A. 2009. Iran's Twitter Revolution. *The Nation* [online]. Available at: http://www.thenation.com/blogs/notion/443634 [accessed: 6 February 2010].

Coglianese, C. 2007. Weak Democracy, Strong Information: The Role of Information Technology in the Rulemaking Process, in *Governance and Information Technology: From Electronic Government to Information Government*, edited by D. Lazer and V. Mayer-Schöenberger. Cambridge, MA: MIT Press.

Copeland, D. 2009. Vitality, Diplomacy, and the Foreign Ministry: Does Foreign Affairs and International Trade Canada Need a "V Tower?" [online]. Available at: http://www.guerrilladiplomacy.com/wp-content/uploads/Virtuality-final.pdf [accessed: 4 February 2010].

Creel, G. 1920. *How We Advertised America*. New York: Harper.

Cull, N.J. 2007. *Public Diplomacy: Lessons from the Past*. Los Angeles: Figueroa Press [online]. Available at: http://uscpublicdiplomacy.org/publications/perspectives/CPDPerspectivesLessons.pdf [accessed: 23 January 2010].

Cull, N.J. 2008. Public Diplomacy before Gullion: The Evolution of a Phrase. In *The Handbook of Public Diplomacy*, edited by N. Snow and P.M. Taylor. London: Routledge.

Dahl, R. 1989. *Democracy and its Critics*. New Haven, CT: Yale University Press.

Electronic Research Collection of Historic State Department Materials. 2010. *United States Information Agency* [online]. Available at: http://dosfan.lib.uic.edu/usia [accessed: 6 February 2010].

Feldmann, L. 2007 Web 2.0 meets Campaign 2008. Podcasts and Videos are among the Features Found on the Interactive Websites of U.S. Presidential Candidates. *The Christian Science Monitor* [online May 16]. Available at: http://www.csmonitor.com/2007/0516/p01s02-uspo.html [accessed: 13 December 2009].

Graff, C. 2009. The Rise of Public Diplomacy 2.0. *The Journal of International Security Affairs*, Fall, 17 [online]. Available at: http://www.securityaffairs.org/issues/2009/17/graffy.php [accessed: 6 February 2010].

Graham, P. 2005. Web 2.0. Available at: http://www.paulgraham.com/web20.html [accessed: 15 December 2009].

Heil, A.L. 2003. *Voice of America. A History*. New York: Columbia University Press.

Hindeman, M. 2007. Open Source Politics Reconsidered: Emerging Patterns in Online Political Participation. In *Governance and Information Technology: From Electronic Government to Information Government* edited by D. Lazer and V. Mayer-Schöenberger. Cambridge, MA: MIT Press.

Johnson, J.B. 2009. The Next Generation. *Foreign Service Journal*, October, 22–8.

Kiehl, W. 2009. Addressing the Public Diplomacy Challenge. *Foreign Service Journal*, October.

Levendusky, M.S. and Jackman, S.D. 2003. *Reconsidering the Measurement of Political Knowledge* [online]. Available at: http://www.stanford.edu/class/polisci353/2004spring/reading/levendusky final.pdf [accessed: June 2008].

Malone, G. 1988. *Political Advocacy and Cultural Communication: Organizing the Nation's Public Diplomacy*. Lanham, MD: University of America Press.

Margolis, M. and Resnick D. 2000. *Politics as Usual: The "Cyberspace Revolution"*. Thousand Oaks, CA: Sage Publications.

Morozov, E. 2010. New Technology and New Public Diplomacy. *PD Magazine*, Winter, 9–12.

Morris, D. 1999. *Vote.com*. Los Angeles, CA: Renaissance.

Murphy, J. 2008. Engagement. In *Engagement. Public Diplomacy in a Globalised World*, edited by J. Welsh and D. Fearn. London: Foreign and Commonwealth Office.

Ostrow, A. 2009. Twitter Now Growing at Staggering 1,382 Percent [online]. Available at: http://mashable.com/2009/03/16/twitter-growth-rate-versus-facebook [accessed: 14 January 2010].

Potter, E.H. 2008. Web 2.0 and the New Public Diplomacy: Impact and Opportunities. In *Engagement. Public Diplomacy in a Globalised World*, edited by J. Welsh and D. Fearn. London: Foreign and Commonwealth Office.

Public Diplomacy Front Line Working Group. 2009. Speaking Out. Public Diplomacy: A View from the Front Line. *Foreign Service Journal*, October, 14–17.

Richelson, J.T. 1999. *The U.S. Intelligence Community*. Boulder, CO: Westview Press.

Schectman, J. 2009. Iran's Twitter revolution? Maybe Not Yet. *Business Week* [online]. Available at: http://www.businessweek.com/technology/content/jun2009/tc20090617_803990.htm?chan=top+news_top+news+index+-+temp_top+story [accessed: 30 January 2011].

Shater, M. 2009. From the Tumult in Iran, Twitter Emerges as a Powerful Social Tool. *The Christian Science Monitor* [online]. Available at: http://www.csmonitor.com/Innovation/Horizons/2009/0617/from-the-tumult-in-iran-twitter-emerges-as-a-powerful-social-tool [accessed: 30 January 2011].

Sysomos Inc. 2010. *Exploring the Use of Twitter around the World* [online]. Available at: http://www.sysomos.com/insidetwitter/geography [accessed: 29 January 2011].

Vargas, J. 2007. For Candidates, Web is Power and Poison. Clinton, in Particular, Draws Equal Parts Cash and Vitriol. *Washington Post*, Thursday, 8 November, p. A01.

Vinter and Knox, 2008. *Engagement: Public Diplomacy in a Globalized World*. London: Foreign and Commonwealth Office, 2008 [online]. Available at: http://www.fco.gov.uk/resources/en/pdf/pd-engagement-jul-08 [accessed: 1 August 2011].

Welch, D. 1983. *Nazi Propaganda*. Totowa, NJ: Barnes and Noble.

Whitton, J.B. 1951. Cold War Propaganda. *The American Journal of International Law* 45(1), 151–3.

World Internet Project. 2008. *Pioneering Report Finds Remarkable Similarities and Significant Differences Globally* [online]. Available at: http://www.worldInternetproject.net [accessed: 11 January 2011].

Zaller, J. 1985. *Pre-Testing Information Items on the 1986 NES Pilot Survey*. Report to the National Election Study Board of Overseers.

Zaller, J. 1992. *The Nature and Origins of Mass Opinion*. Cambridge: Cambridge University Press.

Chapter 8
Call for Power? Mobile Phones as Facilitators of Political Activism

Fabien Miard

Introduction

This chapter examines how mobile phones affect political activity. In a number of cases, the mobile phone as a uniquely easy-to-use and personal communication device has been portrayed as a key tool to facilitate mobilization and collective action, such as during the impeachment process of President Estrada of the Philippines in 2001. Taking some of these case studies as a starting point, I find a plausible theoretical framework for analysis in the literature on collective action theory, mobilization and diffusion theory, and network society theory, which I develop further to include the novel aspect of mobile telecommunications. Mobile teledensity data and three political activism indicators in over a hundred countries are then tested with negative binomial Poisson and ordinal logistic regression over a period of 16 years. The results do not support the observations of earlier case studies; I find no significant relationship between mobile teledensity and anti-government protests, riots, or major government crises.

A New Tool for Civil Society?

In 2001, the elected President of the Philippines, Joseph Estrada, had to step down after weeks of demonstrations in Manila, the capital. The protesters who demanded his impeachment were mobilized via their mobile phones, mainly by waves of text messages calling for participation in street protests. There is a tendency in the literature to give mobile phones and networks a lot of credit for shaping outcomes such as the one in Manila, calling these mobile-phone-enhanced protesters *smart mobs* (Rheingold 2002).

Mobile communication is said to enhance the autonomy of individuals, enabling them to set up their own connections, bypassing the mass media and the channels of communication controlled by institutions and organizations (Castells et al. 2007), but how much does the mobile phone really affect outcomes? Are a few calls or text messages enough to challenge the power of the state? The events in the Philippines and elsewhere were quite a sensation and have led a variety of scholars to embrace the issue and do research on the social and political impact of mobile phones. However, little systematic research beyond loose collections of case studies has been done so far. I wish to fill this gap by presenting a comprehensive theoretical discussion and extending the analysis to a larger number of cases using quantitative methods.

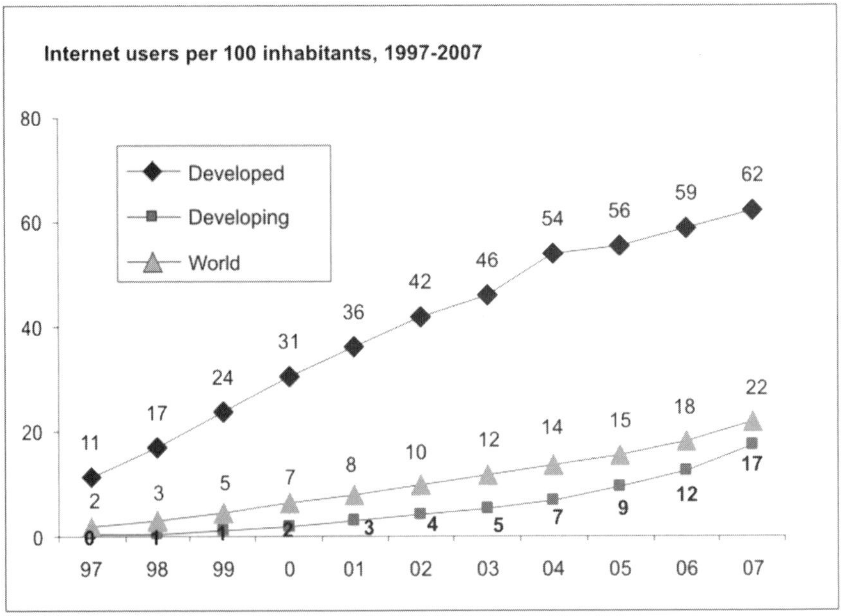

Figure 8.1 Internet usage in the world
Source: ITU 2008.

Mobile phones have, other than the Internet, only recently received increased attention by political scientists. Unfortunately, research on mobile phones in this field and in other social sciences is often being lumped together with research on the Internet, usually under the umbrella term Information and Communication Technologies (ICT). These studies often fail to capture the distinct properties of mobile telecommunications because, when they claim to analyze ICT, they do, in fact, largely deal with the Internet only (Nicholson 2005; Walker 2006; World Bank 2008).

This causes validity problems and it also completely ignores distinct inherent capacities of mobile phones and networks, treating them as if they were "a natural extension of the Internet, rather than an entirely distinct system with its own rules, a separate user base, and a completely different network structure" (Walker 2006). This is clearly unsatisfactory from an analytical perspective, especially in light of the worldwide trend that shows a rapid growth of mobile phone penetration (Figures 8.2–8.4).

There has long been a thriving body of academic literature describing the virtues of the Internet, being such a powerful and liberating tool for civil society and its activists, while there is no such resource to draw from in the case of mobile telecommunications, despite some works that will be introduced below. This lack of research is partly due to the Internet's earlier emergence compared with mobile telephony, at least with regard to its mass deployment.

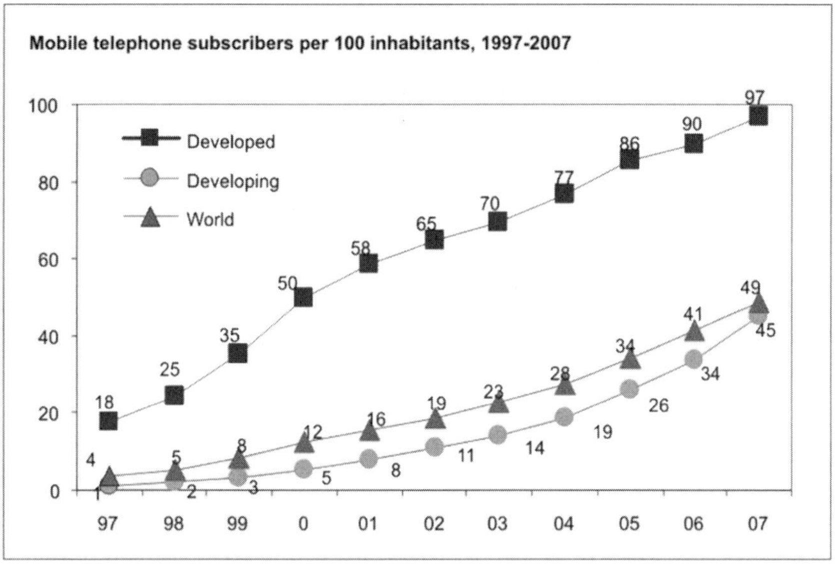

Figure 8.2 Growing mobile teledensity levels
Source: ITU 2008.

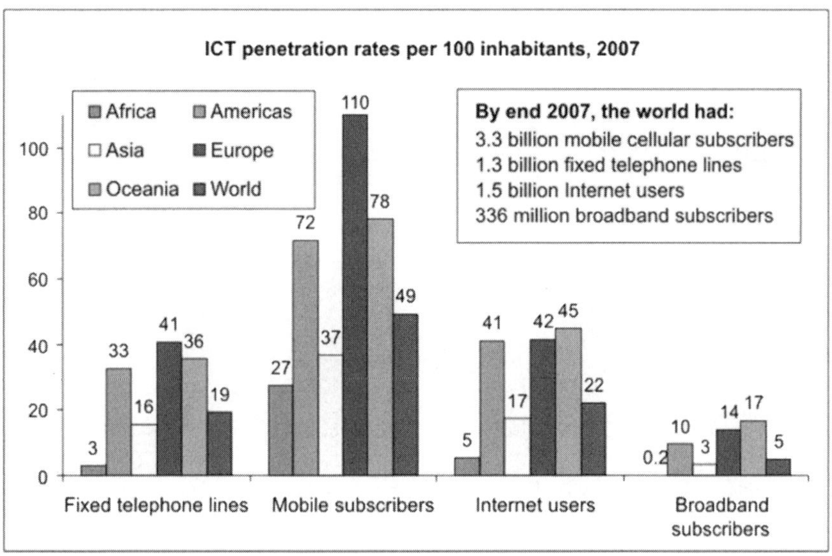

Figure 8.3 Worldwide ICT penetration rates
Source: ITU 2008.

Mobile phone networks are growing nearly everywhere. The use of mobile handsets faces almost no restriction, as the massive growth rates even outside of the OECD indicate, where more than half of these global investments in 2004 were made (ITU 2006). As some of the case studies presented later will show, mobile phones can be a powerful tool for civil society and offer possibilities the Internet cannot provide. Some of the mobile phone's functionalities deserve increased attention and research efforts by political scientists along the example of earlier Internet research.

Take for example the process of political mobilization; mobile phones can facilitate its emergence by virtue of three important factors: mobility, personalization and multimodality. Mobility adds a spontaneity factor to potential mobilization, because users can react instantly and emotionally to events. Personalization is given through the typically person-to-person and social type of contact. Finally, the mobile phone is multimodal because it can transmit voice, images, and sounds, making it a tool for live transmission of events to be shared on the network with the implications that follow from such "broadcasting" (Castells et al. 2007). These aspects can potentially turn mobile phones into indispensable tactical and organizational tools for any group or organization that wishes to mobilize people around a common cause. The case studies and interviews below present a forceful body of evidence that further research should be done.

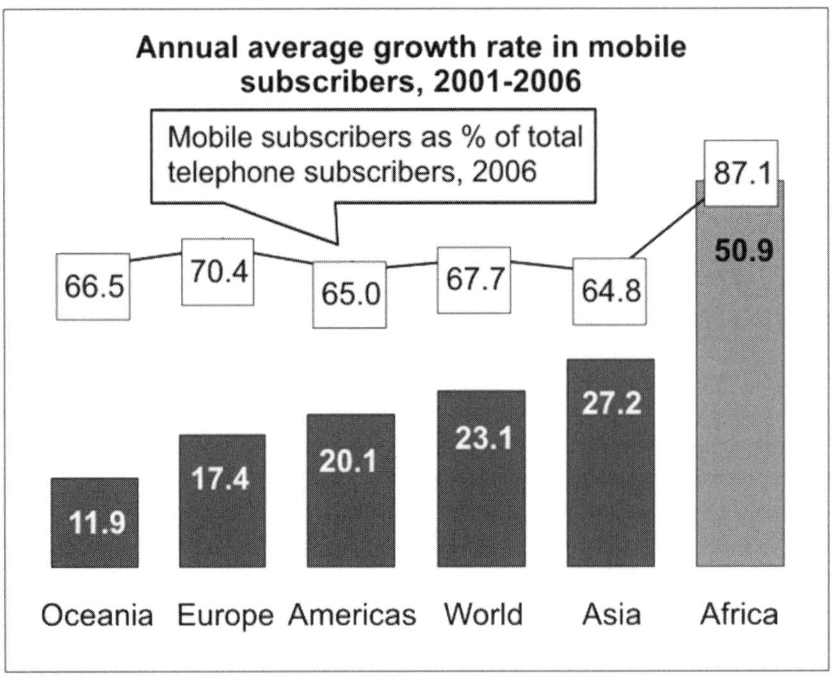

Figure 8.4 Annual mobile subscriber growth
Source: ITU 2008.

In the last decade, the world has witnessed very high telecommunications investments in almost every country. Why is this happening? Universal demand, falling costs and a profitable, competitive market appear to be the driving forces behind this phenomenon. International and home-grown mobile network operators have "worked out how to earn princely sums in the world's poorest places" (*Economist* 2006) and are fiercely competing for market share, pouring in large sums of investment in many countries.

Mobile technology, owing to its unique characteristics, is able to bypass the structural problems that inhibit the Internet in less developed countries, and has thus expanded more (see Figure 8.3). It has "enabled developing countries to skip the fixed-line technology of the 20th century and move straight to the mobile technology of the 21st" (*Economist* 2008a). This is an exception; most new technologies—the Internet and PCs are good examples—depend on existing infrastructure such as roads, electricity and fixed phone lines in order to work. In other words, "to go high-tech, you need to have gone medium-tech first" (*Economist* 2008a). If there is no reliable source of electricity, there is no point in having a computer or a fridge.

A mobile phone, however, does not need a steady, local source of electricity but can instead be recharged occasionally. Neither is it dependent on existing fixed phone lines as the Internet is. The threshold for its use is also lower in other terms: phones can be operated by users with no or minimal levels of literacy. The same cannot be said about computers (Dholakia and Kshetri 2003).

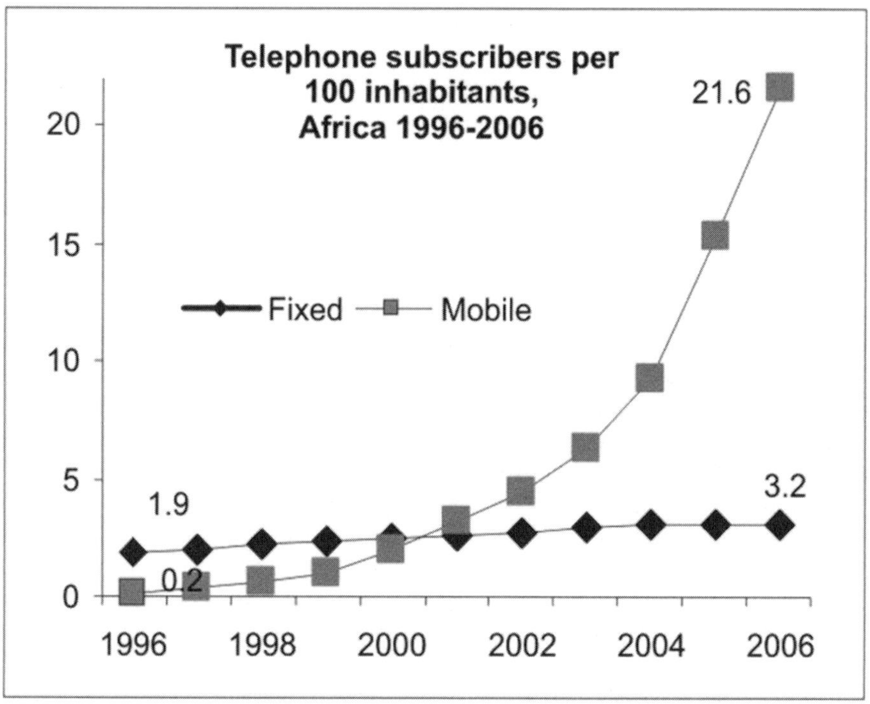

Figure 8.5 Mobile network growth in Africa
Source: ITU 2008.

This is an important factor in less developed countries with high illiteracy levels, and together with other factors, it explains mobile phone technology's swift success in connecting people in previously very isolated places. Africa is a good example of this. Infamous for extremely low penetration of telecommunication services, it has recently been able to greatly profit from the mobile phone's unique "leapfrogging" abilities. Figure 8.5 illustrates Africa's immense mobile telephony breakthrough compared with traditional fixed telephony.

More importantly, civil society in developing countries is making use of the new tool, particularly its cheap and practical text messaging function. An example is the calls for nationwide boycotts that are mass transmitted via SMS, a phenomenon that has, for example, taken place in Nigeria (Obadare 2006). As the following sections will show, the combination of quick communication and large, angry masses of people can have consequences political leaders should be wary of.

Research Question and Approach

The bottom-line question of this work is to find out what the proliferation of mobile phones, a trend observable in almost every country, means for the political sphere. Can a few calls and text messages really challenge the established powers? Will it be easier to mobilize a large number of people for street protests and other forms of political activism? Will civil society become better organized and more effective vis-à-vis the state? *Can mobile network growth be associated with increased political activism?* Is there really any effect at all? In a number of events the use of mobile phones has, perhaps too enthusiastically, been given credit for the outcomes of protest activities that have been directed against governments.

Ideally, an explanation of an outcome in one or a small number of cases should stimulate a larger-*N* analysis in order to estimate the average effects rather than explain particular cases (Mahoney and Goertz 2006). Using qualitative studies and extending the analysis to a larger number of countries is precisely the purpose of this work.

As Castells et al. (2007) note in their book *Mobile Communication and Society*, mobile communication networks can be formed and reformed instantly, and messages are often received by a known source, enhancing their credibility. At the same time, such networks provide a powerful platform for political autonomy on the basis of independent channels of autonomous person-to-person communication. The authors observe a growing tendency for people to use mobile communication to voice their discontent with their country's authorities and to mobilize protesters by inducing "flash mobilizations." Such mobilizations are thought to have "made a considerable impact on formal politics and government decisions" in a number of instances (Castells et al. 2007). In this work, I will repeatedly draw from this qualitative study that was initiated by the Annenberg Research Network on International Communication at the University of Southern California. It is to my knowledge the most comprehensive and up-to-date work on the social impact of mobile phones available.

A very illustrative case, and probably the most famous one, is the so-called *People Power II* revolution in the Philippines in 2001. Its fame is partly due to Howard Rheingold's book *Smart Mobs* (2002) and an article by Vicente L. Rafael in 2003. It is often considered the first time in history that the mobile phone has played an instrumental role in removing the ruling president of a state (Castells et al. 2007). In a nutshell, President Estrada's growing unpopularity caused by episodes of mismanagement and corruption combined with the unwillingness of the Senate to investigate evidence during a formal impeachment process caused enraged citizens to take to the streets. Many of the protesters followed "instructions" received via their mobile phones (Castells et al. 2007). Growing street pressure led most key cabinet members to abandon their posts. Eventually, the army sided with the protesters and Estrada was removed from office. By the end of the same day, the Supreme Court declared the presidency vacant, and the new president, Gloria Arroyo, was sworn in. People Power II concluded on a triumphant note. News coverage invariably highlighted the role of new communication technologies, particularly SMS and the web, in facilitating and enabling the protests. Indeed, it was texting that made the swift gathering of tens of thousands possible immediately after the crucial decision of the Senate. The demonstrators were using SMS so actively that, during the week of the protests, they "caused serious strain on the networks" that covered the protest area: Globe Telecom, an operator, reported a massive, nearly two-fold increase in SMS traffic from on average of 25 million per day to 45 million (Castells et al. 2007).

Another noteworthy case is Spain. An Al-Qaeda cell killed 192 commuters in Madrid by detonating bombs inside three trains on 11 March 2004. The attack took place just four days prior to Spain's national elections. Incidentally, these elections were dominated by the debate about Spain participating in the Iraq War. Despite broad opposition to the war, the ruling Conservative Party (PP) was expected to win the elections based on its economic record and its widely accepted tough stand on Basque terrorism (Castells et al. 2007). Ignoring the increasing evidence that Jihadist terrorists had been behind those attacks, the PP kept blaming ETA, the Basque terror organization. This was perfectly rational because "making the Basque terrorists responsible would favor the PP in the elections, while acknowledging the action to be that of Islamic terrorists would indicate to Spaniards the high price they were paying for their government's policy in Iraq, thus potentially inciting them to vote against the government" (Castells et al. 2007). An inquiry commission later produced evidence that the PP had, at the very least, deliberately delayed information and presented as proof some elements that were still under scrutiny. Regardless of the true extent of deception, thousands of Spaniards were convinced that the government was manipulating facts, and they started to disseminate their views to other citizens.

At the same time, the major TV channels, all of them directly or indirectly controlled by the government, and most radio stations supported the Basque terrorist hypothesis. The print media followed suit, after the Prime Minister had personally called editors of the main press publications to reassure them. With most of the traditional media sticking to one version, oppositional views had to turn to alternative communication channels to spread their version of the truth. The crucial aspect was the youth participation. Usually characterized by high abstention rates, the youth became politicized by these events, and their extensive use of mobile phones to disseminate information and call for demonstrations against the PP caused many voters to switch sides. The Socialist Party then unexpectedly, but clearly, beat the PP in the polls (Castells et al. 2007). SMS traffic increased by 20% over the average on the previous day, and by 40% on Election Day, an all-time record. As Castells et al. (2007) note, the critical point was that the senders were known to the receivers, making the network of diffusion increase exponentially while retaining proximity to the source. Major television channels and newspapers were soon ignored as reliable sources, but the major private radio network SER eventually started to look for the alternative Al-Qaeda explanation. Consequently, many activists referred to the SER when calling or texting their friends.

An equally interesting, but unsuccessful, case in terms of mobilization is the 2003 SARS epidemic in China (Castells et al. 2007). Families and friends of victims used mobile phones to spread the news of this strange, deadly disease, while the Chinese authorities were completely censoring information. Eventually, the Chinese government started a successful media counter-offensive denouncing the "rumors" as false and downplaying the severity of this "variant of pneumonia." Castells et al. (2007) conclude that, in contrast to the Spanish case, traditional media seem to have effectively undermined the earlier information dispersed by mobile phones "because SMS was perceived to be a medium of lower credibility and there was no other source of information." Most people, Chinese and foreigners alike, "chose to believe the official version, only to witness the SARS epidemic in full swing within weeks."

It is clear that the outcomes of the events presented above were strongly shaped by context, and that the mobile phone's facilitating aspect worked most likely in conjunction with many other factors. Castells and his co-authors do not deny this, and neither is it my point to give mobile phones too much credit for what happened. What is of interest here is a certain pattern, where mobile phones repeatedly showed their potential in shaping and facilitating the development of mass events. At the same time, the true effect of the mobile phone alone remains unclear and further analysis is needed to clarify this question; quantitative analysis may be able to do this.

Events similar to the ones above are being reported from all over the world, and they usually fall into two categories: mobile phones are either used for monitoring or reporting, or they are used for mobilization and collective action. In the former, it usually takes place at polling stations: voting results are transmitted to radio stations at once, reducing the opportunity to rig results considerably (*Economist* 2008b). Countries where such monitoring has taken place include Senegal (Abel 2000) and, more recently, Zimbabwe (Global Voices 2008; Martz 2008). My analyses, however, will focus on the second category where mobile phones have been used for mobilization and collective action.

Street Activism in Serbia and Belarus

To gain additional insight in the practical use, or "street use" of mobile phones, I interviewed two key informants. Both Ivan Marovic, a former leading member of the Serbian opposition movement Otpor, and Pavel Marozau, a Belarusian dissident, currently exiled for his media activism and involvement in an opposition movement called Third Way, have actively used and witnessed the use of mobile phones by political activists.

Originally a student movement, Otpor turned political after the NATO bombings in Serbia in 1998, waging a political campaign against Slobodan Milosevic. The campaign eventually led to a successful outcome, Milosevic stepped down in 2000 and was later extradited to The Hague for trial. In the interview, Ivan Marovic, responsible for press and PR at Otpor during the events in 2000, and one of the founding members, unequivocally confirmed the importance of mobile phones in this movement. A particularly interesting aspect that surfaced in the interview was the fact that the Internet played a rather limited role because the web was slow and not used much in Serbia in 2000. Mobile phones, on the other hand, were very common according to Marovic: "[By] 2000, almost everybody had a mobile." While the Internet was used for strategic communication—news, documents, etc.—the mobile phone was crucial for operational and tactical communication. For example, in order to transport small packages from one place to another, they would ask bus drivers to deliver them and immediately text or call the receiving party in the other town to pick up the deliveries. Marovic stated that cell phones were crucial for such operations. He also gave an example of mobile use where changing tasks in real time was critical: in a long 80 km march from Novi Sad to Belgrade in April 2000, the organizers had to coordinate tasks while walking. Food had to be supplied by volunteers from different towns, buses were needed for those who could not walk any more, and the welcome rally and press releases upon arrival in Belgrade needed to be prepared and coordinated. Marovic used up three cell phone batteries that night.

Pavel Marozau and all other activists behind Third Way, an independent youth group, eventually had to flee Belarus after charges of "insulting" the president were brought against them. In Belarus, this automatically means a guilty verdict, as President Lukashenka heads a Soviet-style police state. Third Way's goal is nothing less than reforming and modernizing Belarusian society (Third Way 2008), and they are very keen on using all kinds of technologies for their purposes. Government surveillance appears to be an overall issue in the case of Belarus, as is the need for safe communication. Pavel Marozau agreed that mobile phones are very important for his organization's activities. However, he also added that, where possible, the use of mobile phones is being avoided for "serious things." Mobile communication can be very unsafe; operators have little scope to resist governmental requests for sensitive data. Interception by state authorities is especially common in the run-up phase to state elections. Third Way has been using mobile phones to contact potential new recruits, but also for operative coordination or media reporting—for example upon having been arrested. In the case of operative coordination, it is important to use coded language or not name places while talking on a mobile phone. Marozau described a situation where he accidentally mentioned the name of a public square while talking to an activist on his mobile phone. The consequence was swift: his fellow activist was arrested within 15 minutes.

Another tactical strategy is to use reconnaissance activists in street demonstrations that report police movement. To do this, the reconnaissance activists use "clean" mobile phones with subscriber identification module (SIM) cards and phone IDs that have not yet been registered by the surveillance apparatus or that have been manipulated using illegal Russian software. The Belarusian authorities are, of course, not foolish. Marozau explained in the interview how they are well aware of the power of mass SMS and have made use of it themselves, especially prior to the presidential elections or the 2004 referendum. They routinely modify the opposition's messages, or just spread the opposite message. The Belarusian government has also created its own, well-funded youth organization, which also uses mass SMS and other communication strategies, thus copying the opposition movement's tactics. In addition to tapped phone calls, there is also the risk of *localization*; with today's technology, it is possible to localize the position of a mobile phone and thus its user even when the handset is not being used. The accuracy is 50–100 meters, according to Marozau. It has become common to simply switch off the phone or even remove the battery to be on the safe side.

Mobile connectivity can be said to both reflect and intensify social ties: without social ties, the mobile phone, predominantly used for social contact with friends and family members, is of little use. At the same time, it is a powerful tool to manage or "micro coordinate" one's social life and keep in touch with one's social network, and one that can be used to strengthen and expand social ties (Ling 2004; Livesay 2003). The concept of social ties and how mobile telecommunications are affecting these will be a recurrent theme below. In order to understand how this aspect can be understood in conjunction with existing theory, I draw from three types of theory: *collective action*, *mobilization and diffusion*, and also *network society theory*. The variant of collective action theory used mainly highlights individual motives to participate in the activities and movements of interest here. Mobilization and diffusion theory further emphasizes structural aspects of how political and social movements are generated. Finally, network society theory links the previous theories to technology both conceptually (Castells 2000a, 2000b) and more conclusively where the theory is used in connection with mobile telecommunications (Castells et al. 2007). The aim of this discussion is to advance the development of a suitable hypothesis.

Collective Action

The main point of this collective action variant developed by Roger Gould (1993, 1995) is that social ties make individuals' decisions about participating in collective action *interdependent*. If at least one actor has already made a contribution to a cause, other actors have thus according to Gould (1993) two reasons to make contributions of their own. One is *instrumental*, that is, based on how one perceives the efficacy of a cause. The other is *normative*, that is, based on how one fears, or wishes, to be perceived by others. Neither reason accomplishes much by itself: normative pressure to contribute to collective action will have little impact if elicited contributions are completely wasted, while increasing marginal returns will only reinforce the waiting game and encourage free-riding in the absence of fairness norms. Social ties, as he argues, "occupy a central role in explanations of how groups overcome the free-rider problem" (Gould 1993). A basic tenet of Mancur Olson's (1965, cited in Gould 1993) characterization of the free-rider problem is that "a rational actor will abstain from contributing to a public good if his or her contribution has a negligible impact on the total amount of the good produced and consequently a negligible impact on his or her consumption of the good." However, if these decisions are *not* independent, that is if one actor's contribution makes another actor's contribution more likely, the total benefit resulting from an individual's decision to contribute may be considerably greater than his or her cost of contributing. Introducing a normative element makes sense because, as Gould states, "few social scientists believe that individuals are pure rational egoists, particularly since collective action occurs more frequently than the rational choice framework would predict." While people may be perfectly willing to contribute something to a collective good, they are most likely to first wait and see what others do to be reasonably sure their contributions will not be wasted, before joining in. If some individuals take the initiative, it will increase the motivation of others to join in because the initiators have increased the marginal returns to the group that would arise from further contributions. Any utility maximizer would still try to get a free ride here; however, in the presence of norms of fairness, everyone with social ties to the initiators now has a reason to match the initiators' contribution. "As much as people dislike being exploited, they do not want to be perceived, and potentially ostracized, as exploitative" or to state it more positively, "seeing others contribute should motivate actors to contribute their share" (Gould 1993).

In general, one can say that the degree to which contributions are *visible* affects the level of normative social pressure noncontributors may be subjected to, thus altering their behavior (Gould 1993). This aspect of *visibility* needs to be emphasized at this point, because I will test the argument of enhanced visibility through mobile phone usage. From a theoretical point of view the concept of visibility in my context represents the collective, public demonstration of activists confronting political authority on specific grounds (Livesay 2003; Melucci 1994). Visible action, such as the waves of mass SMS described earlier, supposedly "strengthens the hidden networks, boosts solidarity, creates further groups, and recruits new militants who, attracted by the movement's public action, join its hidden networks" (Melucci 1994). Those hidden networks are the overlapping networks of small groups submerged in daily life. They make visible action possible because they can provide the solidarity resources needed and the framework within which mobilization takes place (Melucci 1994; Livesay 2003), a factor that was also pointed out by Pavel Marozau from Third Way. I will return to this aspect later, tying this conceptually to mobile phones, to analyze them as potential carriers of increased and faster-spreading visibility.

Mobilization and Diffusion

Mobilization theory and diffusion theory further emphasize structural aspects that potentially facilitate mobilization for collective action. The idea of thresholds is critical; resources, organization, opportunity and grievances must be present simultaneously at their threshold levels before a movement emerges, although deficits in some dimensions may be offset by surpluses in others (Buechler 2008; Jenkins 1983). This latter argument is particularly useful in the present case, as one can argue that mobile phones may create a surplus in, say, organization and resources.

They can do this, not necessarily through the total amount of skill or resources available, but rather through more efficient use of these factors. For instance, the real-time aspect of mobile communication means that people, supplies and money can be reallocated or redirected while a process is underway (Kwan 2007; Townsend 2000). This can be particularly effective in protest movements, for example in street demonstrations where protesters can gain the ability to quickly adapt to police movement, arrests and blockades by spreading information about them and immediately acting on it (Castells et al. 2007; Rheingold 2002). Indeed, the increase in re-allocatable discretionary resources such as time and money is absolutely central to the expansion of a social movement (Livesay 2003). Micromobilization, "that small group setting in which processes of collective attribution are combined with rudimentary forms of organization to produce mobilization for collective action" (McAdam 1988, cited in Livesay 2003), points at some other relevant arguments within mobilization theory. Nonpolitical and informal groups such as friendship networks can provide micromobilization. Such contexts can be generative of social movements for a variety of reasons. Dense social networks can increase "structural proximity," the proximity of more people to movement activity. Members of such networks are more likely to come in contact with movement activists and their flows of information. More importantly, this structural availability can operate both at the individual and group levels. "Bloc recruitment," that is on a group rather than individual basis, thus becomes possible (Livesay 2003). Such "blocs" have the potential, in turn, to increase group solidarity.

Equally important is that micromobilization contexts can make certain psychological processes that facilitate movement participation more likely. These are, for example, as Livesay (2003) notes, the "delegitimation of hegemonic ideologies, the attribution of the causes of experienced grievances to structural rather than to individual factors, and the development of the perception of the efficacy of movement participation." Social ties to movement supporters should increase the likelihood of one's recruitment. Lastly, micromobilization contexts can provide the rudiments of organization: Livesay (2003) mentions, for example, leaders and communication technologies. They are needed to translate contributions into concrete action.

The two potentially most facilitating features of pre-existing networks seem to be dense lateral ties that are social integration within the population of potential recruits as well as multiple bridging ties that link network clusters together (Livesay 2003). Proponents of diffusion theory also share this insight. This field focuses on the flows of information and ideas through various kinds of channels. As Soule (1997) notes, definitions of diffusion "almost always include the notion of connectedness" and, in relational models of diffusion, information is said to be flowing between actors through their direct network relations. She (Soule 2004) also repeatedly stresses the importance of networks to diffusion processes. Likewise, models used by network analysts reflect this in their claim that "ideas diffuse more rapidly when individuals are in direct and frequent contact," that is where the interaction rate is high (Soule 2004). Such an observation is likely to be made among users of mobile phones, where texting and calling takes very little effort and time, and can be done anywhere.

Network Society and Technology

The works of Manuel Castells, particularly his *network society theory* (Castells 2000a, 2000b) is another theoretical approach useful for the present analysis. He puts communication technologies, a virtually indispensible medium in our informational age, at the center of human action, which is to rely on processes enacted by organizational forms that are built upon networks, particularly upon information networks (Castells 2000b). While networks are to be "old forms of social organization, they are now empowered by new information [and] communication technologies, so that they become able to cope at the same time with flexible decentralization, and with focused decision-making" (Castells 2000b). Technology is omnipresent in our everyday lives. This is particularly true with mobile phones, which are highly personalized technological artifacts. Mobile telecommunications technology can modify our social structure by creating what Cooper (2002) calls the "transparency of the world", where communication is possible anytime and anywhere, virtually eradicating "communication-free pockets." The structural argument introduced earlier can be encountered again here: in the sense that technology can enhance visibility, or transparency, one could also expect it to facilitate participation boosts in the political sphere, for example through feedback loops that intensify recruitment to political and social movements. Mobile telecommunications technology also "critically affects spatiotemporal change," that is the structural dimensions that otherwise restrain human action in both distance and time. The space of social interaction becomes redefined because mobile telecommunication has the ability to change the location reference—people are "here and there, in multiple heres and theres, in a relentless combination of places" (Castells et al. 2007). The temporal dimension becomes redefined because individuals now can do "midcourse adjustments" as they "walk or travel toward their destination while deciding which destination it is going to be. [They do this] on the basis of instant communication in which they are engaged" (Kwan 2007).

This may in principle be just as true in everyday life as in a street demonstration. Places now exist as "points of convergence in communication networks created and recreated by people's purposes" (Castells et al. 2007; Kwan 2007; Ling 2004). This is an effect that a deeper analysis could reveal to work in favor of demonstrators. Communication technology can now be shifting the possibilities from place-to-place towards person-to-person connectivity. Computers and telephones are traditionally tied to a fixed location while mobile telephones are not. Owing to this phenomenon, it can become increasingly difficult to pinpoint when and where an activity begins (Kwan 2007). To relate this to an example, it will be harder to crack down on demonstrators who change plans and destinations on the go.

Conclusions and Alternative Approaches

The theoretical arguments available are concerned with issues of collective action and networking and potentially relate to the material presented in the empirical section. An example could be the recruitment and mobilization for political causes by means of mass SMS waves that call for protest participation. There are, of course, many other theories that could be used to frame these questions. However, in conjunction with the technological argument, the theories discussed above are considered the most adept to advance the chosen research focus.

Two important issues, *monitoring* and *logistics*, were briefly discussed above but are not really reflected in the theoretical literature discussed. Doing this would be beyond the scope of this work. These two aspects, together with alternative theories, are briefly addressed below for the sake of future research in this novel field.

Garret (2006) and Green (2002) have raised the issue of monitoring, calling this a "reversal of the Foucauldian panopticon." In the traditional state, the elite controls power by surveillance techniques—a central mechanism that is to generate disciplinary self-regulation by the population. This is what Foucault (1977 and 1979, cited in Garrett 2006 and Green 2002) describes with his panopticon. Modern information technologies have the ability to somewhat reverse this in today's world. The public eye, enhanced by information technologies, can thus be said to force the elite into self-regulated behavior. The cruder kinds of electoral fraud, such as the stuffing of ballot boxes, often rely on poor communications between the center and the periphery. They have now arguably become much harder to carry out, because monitoring has become so cheap and effective that it can now more easily produce considerable embarrassment for fraudulent leaders.

Mobile phone utilization for logistical purposes relates to efficiency in a more economic sense. Technology can reduce transaction costs of a certain activity, opening up new options and facilitating existing ones. The question of logistics may be better approached by strands of economic theory, and transaction cost issues may be useful to analyze the particularly restrictive conditions under which oppositionist movements operate.

An entirely different alternative approach to decision-making is the concept of *information cascades* (Bikhchandani et al. 2007). An information cascade takes place "when individuals acting in conditions of uncertainty strongly condition their choices on what others have done previously" (Drezner 2006). In repressive societies, such information cascades tend to reinforce acquiescent behavior by citizens. However, this cascade can be reversed by strong exogenous shocks that trigger acts of protest. It is not difficult to imagine what the omnipresence of mobile phones could do to boost such cascades.

Bringing in the Mobile Phone

It is increasingly becoming clear that mobile phone networks, in addition to other means of communication, are key means of social exchange (Campbell and Park 2008; Castells et al. 2007; *Economist* 2008b; Kwan 2007; Ling 2004). This is undoubtedly most pervasive in more developed countries, but as indicated previously, other countries seem to be catching up fast. This has deep consequences for social science research: "It is widely recognized that the spread of new forms of communication is likely to affect social organization in depth, and that this requires a reformulation of sociological concepts, including that of social relations" and "research on networks and participation will have to explore the impact of virtual links" (Diani 2004). I plan to do just that, using all these elements to generate a hypothesis that will be tested in subsequent quantitative analyses.

The hypothesis that is to be tested in this work boils down to the question of whether the developments in the amount of mobile phone users can be associated with anti-government demonstrations, riots, or major government crises. The degree in which political activism (such as protests) is *visible* is expected to be the key factor. The more visible a protest movement, the more likely is an individual's decision to join because of the apparent increase of participants (or contributors), and individuals will assume increasing marginal returns. However, unless there are personal friends among the protesters, the noncontributor may decide to wait and see how things develop because the normative social "pressure" is not sufficiently given. Now, with mobile networks present, the situation can be expected to change in favor of both the fairness and efficacy aspects that are central in Gould's collective action model. With regard to efficacy, the more members there are in a network, the higher the expected potential mobilization feedback loop or the "chain reaction" that can amplify any message spread within a network. Every individual is, for example, more likely to be the recipient of information spread via text messages or a phone call. As a consequence, individual expectations of marginal returns are assumed to increase because the more information and feedback one receives about a protest movement, that is, the more "visible" the joining in of others becomes, the more one will be inclined to believe in its success.

Owing to the mobile phone's ability to enhance the autonomy of individuals and to bypass mass media (Castells et al. 2007), the visibility of an issue or activity even increases when the media are not reporting it (as illustrated by the aforementioned examples of Spain and, initially, China). The effect on fairness is thought to work equally through technology-enhanced social ties: the more users there are in a network, the stronger the expected potential fairness impact on mobilization. Fairness norms are expected to have an increased effect because the mobile phone is such a personal device (Campbell and Park 2008; Ling 2004). It is assumed that nobody likes to be seen as a free rider by friends and relatives; they will on the contrary be more likely to enjoy engaging in cooperative action with friends. As mobile telecommunication increasingly gains importance for an individual's social ties, any message or call received is with great likelihood assumed to originate from a friend, work colleague, family member, fellow student, friend of a friend, and so on—in other words, from those overlapping "hidden networks" that can form trusted circuits of exchanges for information and new ideas (Melucci 1994). Individuals can therefore be expected to be more motivated to contribute to the protest activities rather than to abstain.

More mobile phones also potentially increase structural effects as described above. Drawing from mobilization and diffusion theory, it is plausible to predict that "structural proximity" and higher interaction rates through multiple bridging ties could cause faster information diffusion through dense networks of individuals directly connected to each other, and this is expected to increase the overall and interpersonal visibility of any actions planned or being taken. This, in turn, is expected to result in more effective mobilization where mobile networks are more pervasive.

Against this backdrop, it could be anticipated that an increase in mobile network users can lead to increased effectiveness of mobilization owing to *improved outreach*, *speed* and *response*. An increase in overall mobile connectivity among a country's population can thus be thought to increase political protest activity in this country. I therefore formulate the hypothesis as follows:

> An increase in mobile connectivity in a country is followed by an increase in political activism in the same country.

Here, mobile connectivity will be used as a concept that reflects interpersonal linkages enhanced by mobile telecommunication technology, while political activism is to contain protest activity. In the analysis below I attempt to identify the effect of mobile connectivity on political activism, controlling for some plausible other factors while keeping the model parsimonious. There are many plausible reasons in both the empirical and theoretical literature to formulate and test a relationship as presented above. Some caveats must be considered, however.

Counter-arguments

Next to the null hypothesis that there is no relation whatsoever between mobile connectivity and political activism, one possible alternative hypothesis could state the opposite effect—that increased mobile connectivity decreases political activism. What would be plausible arguments for these alternatives?

Much of the hypothesis developed in the previous section rests on the assumption that facilitation, provided by increased mobile connectivity, can lead to increased activism. Some authors caution against giving too much credit to technology: "[ICT technologies] influence, contextualize, facilitate, permit or inhibit courses of action, but not as first-order dynamics that change, transform, foster, impose or shape a course of action" (Mansell and Wehn 1998, cited in Wilson 2004). Such a second-order argument would create a distinction between potential and actual effects of mobile connectivity where the potential depends on first-order dynamics to unfold its impact. The tilt in the outcomes is provided by individuals' and organizations' choices as to when and how to use mobile phones, not by the device itself. It is thus important not to assume any automatisms or to jump to monocausal conclusions (Wilson 2004). For instance, increasing visibility may not automatically result in increasing response. A wave of SMS asking the receivers to join a demonstration may, for example, fail to trigger a response for a number of known or unknown reasons that cannot be offset by individual efficacy and fairness considerations. Even when the necessary structural and psychological requisites are in place, if the principal variable that is to trigger human agency does not operate, or if other variables neutralize its workings, no measurable effect will be noticed (Wilson 2004).

The dynamic perspective taken on society, while the state as a factor conceptually somewhat remaining static, could result in a potential logical flaw. Governments make use of technological progress for their own purposes. The examples described earlier allowed us to observe rapid technological adaptation of civil society actors. That government actors do not adapt to technological progress or that they do so at a slower pace than civil society actors is highly doubtful. The development of the Internet gives an indication of the ingenious ways in which governing elites are able to adapt to technologies that challenge their established power. Many countries have imposed restrictions on free Internet access. Such measures have been implemented despite the Internet's structural properties that were precisely designed to exacerbate censorship and other content interferences (Deibert et al. 2008). The same is happening with mobile telecommunications. My interview with Pavel Marozau indicates that the state increasingly asserts its power in this area as well. Finding empirical evidence of such control is more difficult owing to the secrecy typically surrounding such measures, and the less open architecture of mobile telecommunication systems compared with the Internet. Marozau highlighted the more subtle workings of such governmental counter-measures.

Castells et al. (2007) report a case where the police simply tapped into the flows of SMS between activists during a demonstration in New York and then took action based on that information. This can of course be prevented through codes, but this restricts the potential for mass mobilization. There are also more forthright variants of censorship where mobile networks are simply shut off, either in selected areas or altogether. Recent examples are Tibet during the riots prior to the 2008 Olympic Games in Beijing or Ethiopia during the violent election protests in 2005 (BBC 2007; NZZ 2008). In both cases, the authorities presumably shut down mobile networks in an attempt to prevent their use by journalists and anti-government activists. Such crude measures are no doubt highly effective, and together with other tactical adaptation by governments, may offset the advantages gained by civil society actors (cf. Meier 2009). Two possible implications of this are that increased mobile connectivity would not result in an increase in political activism, or that it may even cause a decrease if states should adapt faster to the technological progress than civil society. This is plausible if taking into consideration that new and public, omnipresent communication technologies can actually promote the state's surveillance capacities. Moreover, the same effect that could lead to increased political activism may also lead to its decrease (Kwan 2007; Townsend 2000). Mobile phones may facilitate not only mobilization, but also demobilization. Protests may be called off just as quickly and efficiently as they are initiated owing to "midcourse adjustments" and feedback loops that work in the opposite direction. Finally, changes in mobile connectivity may be part of a larger socio-economic change process that may alter civil society's interaction with the government in many ways, for example a transition to more stable forms of political activity. The downward development of political activism variables over the past 16 years may be an indication of this. With too much "noise" created by socio-economic variables, it may be difficult to identify and isolate the expected effect of mobile connectivity on political activism.

Research Design

The two key concepts in this chapter are *mobile connectivity* and *political activism*. Mobile connectivity can be understood as a specific, systematized concept within the larger conceptual background of connectivity. The background concept includes other relevant factors such as Internet connectivity, urbanization, transportation, cultural linkages and so forth, all elements that can be useful in clarifying connectivity. Discussing all these would go beyond the scope of this work. For the purpose of my research question, I will focus on the novel factor of mobile phones; the systematized concept is denoted as "mobile connectivity." This term is meant to describe interpersonal linkages via mobile telecommunication technology. Political activism, on the other hand, may draw from the underlying background concept of political participation and related ideas. I systematize this concept for my purposes by restricting "political activism" to the public expression of political discontent by members of civil society. Civil society is defined according to LSE (2004).

For the purpose of this analysis, I decided to use the proliferation of mobile phone subscriptions in a country to measure mobile connectivity. Mobile teledensity data, as it is called (see below for definitions), is considered the best available proxy to this concept. There are no other mobile phone data as comprehensive, accessible, and fit for per-country comparison I am aware of. Better still would be traffic data, which can measure the amount and location of mobile network usage; Castells et al. (2007) seem to have, in parts, been able to access some SMS traffic data, but it is not generally available to the public and much less so on a national or comparative global level in the way mobile teledensity data is. In order to measure political activism, three different variables are each tested separately: anti-government demonstrations, riots and major government crises. These were deemed good proxies for civil society's political activism. I deliberately kept out variables that would include the measurement of violence beyond riots (guerilla warfare, armed rebellion, purges, and so on). The units of measurement are country–years; therefore all definitions used below apply to such. A more comprehensive discussion of the validity as well as the reasons for including each variable are given below.

Variables Used

To measure mobile connectivity, an indicator called "mobile teledensity" is used; it is defined as *mobile cellular subscribers per 100 population*. It refers to the use of cellular-technology portable telephones subscribing to a public mobile telephone service that relies on both analog and digital cellular systems. Both postpaid and prepaid subscriptions are included. The data is collected by the International Telecommunication Union, a UN subsidiary, and provided by the United Nations Millennium Development Goals website (MDG 2008). Anti-government demonstration is used to measure political activism. It is defined as *any peaceful public gathering of at least 100 people for the primary purpose of displaying or voicing their opposition to government policies or authority, excluding demonstrations of a distinctly anti-foreign nature.* The data is provided by the Cross-National Time-Series Data Archive (CNTS),[1] a proprietary database established by the late Arthur S. Banks. According to CNTS, most of the data are derived from the *New York Times*. The variable definitions are adopted from "Dimensions of Conflict Behavior Within and Between Nations" (Rummel 1963). In order to approach the concept of political activism more thoroughly, two additional CNTS indicators, *Riots* and *Major Government Crises*, were tested as

1 http://dvn.iq.harvard.edu/dvn/dv/nds/faces/study/StudyPage.xhtml?globalId=hdl:1902.1/11448.

well. Riots are defined as *any violent demonstration or clash of more than 100 citizens involving the use of physical force* and Major Government Crises as *any rapidly developing situation that threatens to bring the downfall of the present regime—excluding situations of revolt aimed at such overthrows.* Other variables included are GDP, Population, and Time. GDP per capita is defined as *gross domestic product per capita based on purchasing power parity (PPP) in constant 2005 international dollars* and is provided by the World Bank Group's *World Development Indicators* website (WDI 2007). An international dollar has the same purchasing power over GDP as the U.S. dollar has in the U.S. Population is defined as the total population in a country divided by 1,000. This indicator is available in the CNTS database. Finally, time, measured in years, was included as a dummy variable to control for trend effects. The reasons for each variable's inclusion are discussed below.

Validity

Using mobile teledensity as a proxy to mobile connectivity was deemed straightforward and reasonably sufficient to cover the concept within the framework of this chapter. Teledensity data is considered very accurate and very reliable data (MDG 2008), but there are nevertheless some relevant issues. The dataset does not distinguish between a complete absence of networks (and hence subscribers) and missing values. In contrast, mobile teledensity of 100% and more can be found in a number of countries, suggesting that everyone there has one or more subscriptions. This is, of course, misleading, as there will always be individuals that are too young, too old or too disabled to use a phone, and those who cannot afford one, choose not to have one, or are not allowed to own one, for example in prisons and asylums (Sutherland 2008). Thus, some users own several subscriptions, while others share one. Moreover, the per-country measurement raises the issue of subscribers that are not residents of the country or countries where they are counted, and that may have further subscriptions in other countries. Mobile network operators may also have an incentive to report large numbers of subscribers, and thus deliberately inflate their customer base, especially when negotiating contracts with governments. This does, on the other hand, reduce the average revenue per user, a factor that can disappoint financial analysts and hence the value of the operator. In theory, this should restrain operators from overzealous reporting of large numbers of customers (Sutherland 2008). Why would certain individuals have several SIM cards? On one hand, wireless technology has created a proliferation of SIM cards. They can now be found in laptop computers, cars and many other devices. This is an example of wealthier customers, and some of those SIM cards may not be included in the ITU's measurement by definition. The phenomenon called "SIM switching" is more relevant: less wealthy users may use several SIM cards to take advantage of changing tariffs. Ewan Sutherland (2008) sums up the reasons for such ownership of more than one SIM card:

- overcoming patchy or poor network coverage,
- avoiding network congestion,
- saving money by making on-net calls [same operator],
- benefiting from discounted or bundled tariffs for voice or for data,
- receiving calls or voicemail [or SMS] to an older number.

The importance of such issues varies from country to country, and makes it difficult to estimate how inflated the numbers of users truly are; also, it does not allow for a more than approximate per capita definition of subscriptions (Sutherland 2008).

Using anti-government demonstrations to measure the concept of political activism as described above seems accurate. It measures the mobilization and collective action aspect I am interested in—the one that supposedly leads to protest directed against the ruling government. It excludes mobilizations "of distinctly anti-foreign nature" (CNTS 2007). Clearly, data collected through newspapers can never be truly comprehensive. CNTS acknowledges this, and also raises the issue of possible geographical bias. This means that events are being seen through the eyes of the U.S.-based media. Moreover, certain events may not be of a clear domestic nature, such as for example the Palestinian–Israeli conflict, somewhat blurring the typology used. Such data should in general only be used for macro analytic purposes as in the present case. *Riots* were considered to be a likely addition to anti-government demonstrations, insofar as these may turn violent. The dimension of nonmilitary violence is an acceptable addition to the already considered peaceful dimension to cover the concept of political activism.

However, the data provider's definition is very sparse and it remains somewhat unclear what type of event is being measured and whether the use of "citizen" is intentional (with the implications that may follow from this). *Major Government Crises* as an indicator was thought to cover some aspects of the concept as well, particularly the "rapidly developing" situation that could be associated with mobile phone-enhanced protests and the speed and magnitude of response it can facilitate. What the causes of the rapidly developing crises are and whether popular pressure (where mobile phones could play a role) or some other reason caused the downfall remains somewhat unclear, but it is reasonable enough to see it as, if not a sign, then at least a consequence of political activism, and therefore the indicator is included in the analysis. Otherwise, the same measurement reservations as above with regard to newspaper bias and comprehensiveness apply.

The underlying concept of GDP can be expressed as the (economic) development level of a country, which I intend to cover with the chosen indicator GDP per capita. Measuring economic strength with GDP is common in the social sciences; there should be little validity and reliability concerns. The choice of real (as opposed to nominal), that is inflation-adjusted dollars, which also account for purchase-power parity, should produce a valid measurement. Why include this variable? There are two reasons. The first is a possible relationship between mobile teledensity and economic development (Röller and Waverman 2001; Wilson 2004); the second is a possible positive or negative effect of economic development on political stability (for example Gates et al. 2006; Gjerde 2005). As the teledensity variable has values relative to population, I also needed to control for this to avoid picking up a spurious effect that relates to population rather than mobile teledensity levels. Time is commonly applied in time-series and panel data analysis to control for trend effects (Skog 1988, 2004). To control for the possible effect that the previous year's incidence of political activism can have on the on the following year's incidence, a lagged version of the dependent variable was included in the model, a common procedure in time-series analysis (Gujarati 2003).

Panel Data Analysis and Categorical Data

The units of analysis are country-years, thus combining cross-section and time-series analysis into so-called panel data analysis (Gujarati 2003). A total of 191 countries were repeatedly observed over a period of 16 years, from 1991 to 2006, although about a third of these dropped out owing to missing values. The scores for the dependent variables always represent the given year, while the scores for the independent variables are from the previous year ($t - 1$) to control for reverse causality (Smelser 1973). Mobile teledensity, GDP and population were log-transformed because of the effect of a unit increase that is expected to be larger for a country with a low level on the variable than for a country with a high level. The log-transformation also reduces the scenes of the variable. Panel data sets offer advantages over pure cross-section or pure time-series datasets. The number of observations is typically much larger; rather than just analyzing 191 units or 16 years of the same unit, I combined both. This is likely to generate more reliable estimates and allows one to detect effects that cannot be identified with pure cross-section or time-series data, and it also makes more sophisticated models available (Gujarati 2003).

The dependent variable determines what type of regression is adequate to analyze a given set of data. The dependent data at hand is considered to be categorical. In theory, any number of anti-government demonstrations, riots or major government crises is possible per year and per country. In practice, only a limited number of such events occur. The limit in the data seems to be no more than 24 anti-government demonstrations per country in any given year; for the other indicators, it is even less. They thus belong to the group of *discrete* variables, which have a finite number of non-negative integer values only, that is, natural numbers starting from zero and with no decimals. Such variables are defined as categorical (Powers and Xie 2000). When the outcome is not binary, as in my case, alternatives to the logistic regression are the ordinal logistic and multinomial logistic regression for ordered or nominal values, respectively. For the special case of event count data, Poisson regression should be considered. My dependent variable seems to have the properties of so-called count data, or rare event data, because the number of anti-government demonstrations, riots, or major government crises is counted on a per-year basis. Owing to the data properties, a variant of Poisson regression seems most adequate. The Poisson model requires so-called equidispersion, that is, the event counts in the dependent variable should be evenly distributed so that the distribution's variance is equal to its mean. Since equidispersion cannot be assumed here—scoring the dependent variable predominantly results in zeroes and ones—a variant of Poisson called *negative binomial Poisson regression* can instead be applied. It accounts for so-called overdispersion, that is, more observed variance than the Poisson model would predict (Liao 1994; Norušis 2008). Random events will more often than not remain unobserved, making zero event counts dominant and as a result, the distribution will be skewed. Negative binomial Poisson regression can account for this.

The rationale of Poisson distribution is that events are independent from each other. In the case of domestic protest events, this condition may not be given, that is, events in one year may correlate with those in the following year. Such occurrence dependence can result in overdispersed distributions and is common in time-series analysis (Norušis 2008). A lagged version of the dependent variable is included in the model to account for this possible effect and give a better model specification.

Regression Analysis

The results of the negative binomial Poisson analysis presented below indicate that mobile density has no significant effect on anti-government demonstrations when the control variables are included (Table 8.1). The same is true when using riots or major government crises as dependent variables (models 2 and 3, in Table 8.1). GDP per capita is small and insignificant except for riots, where it has a significant negative effect. Population has an effect on all three variants of political activism variables. The significant effects can be interpreted as follows: for a one-unit change in the predictor variable, the incidence of the political activism variable is expected to increase or decrease multiplicatively by the antilog of the coefficient (see UCLA 2008).

Table 8.1 Predictors of political activism 1991–2006. Negative binomial Poisson regression

Variables	Model 1 Anti-government demonstrations	Model 2 Riots	Model 3 Major government crises
Mobile teledensity (log)	−0.006 (0.0482)	0.092 (0.0671)	−0.018 (0.0781)
GDP per capita (log)	−0.090 (0.0748)	−0.318** (0.1035)	−0.066 (0.1276)
Population (log)	0.337** (0.0260)	0.316** (0.0362)	0.216** (0.0415)
Lagged dependent variable[a]	0.334** (0.0303)	0.448** (0.0549)	0.963** (0.1056)
[year = 2006]	−0.749 (0.4201)	−10.838** (0.5156)	−0.504 (0.8423)
[year = 2005]	−0.563 (0.4068)	−10.872** (0.4983)	0.138 (0.7915)
[year = 2004]	−0.489 (0.3969)	−10.937** (0.4889)	−0.186 (0.7903)
[year = 2003]	−0.630 (0.3911)	−20.250** (0.4928)	0.071 (0.7663)
[year = 2002]	−0.578 (0.3805)	−20.347** (0.4794)	0.551 (0.7387)
[year = 2001]	−0.964 (0.3810)	−20.160** (0.4599)	0.322 (0.7327)
[year = 2000]	−0.120 (0.3556)	−10.695** (0.4249)	0.392 (0.7169)
[year = 1999]	−0.624 (0.3559)	−10.877** (0.4274)	0.100 (0.7107)
[year = 1998]	−0.222 (0.3381)	−10.913** (0.4157)	0.362 (0.6906)
[year = 1997]	0.063 (0.3314)	−0.981** (0.3726)	10.076 (0.6711)
[year = 1996]	−0.044 (0.3376)	−10.083** (0.3866)	0.123 (0.7201)
[year = 1995]	0.243 (0.3332)	−0.718 (0.3710)	0.244 (0.7119)
[year = 1994]	−0.397 (0.3647)	−10.293** (0.4319)	0.299 (0.7189)
[year = 1993]	−0.304 (0.3830)	−10.582** (0.4951)	0.493 (0.7319)
[year = 1992]	0.065 (0.3708)	−10.098* (0.4475)	10.181 (0.6955)
[year = 1991]	0[b] (0)	0[b] (0)	0[b] (0)
Intercept	−30.011** (0.6981)	−0.967 (0.9302)	−40.023* (10.2633)
Log likelihood	−15,370.286	−8,560.620	−6,420.952
Chi-square likelihood ratio	5,350.269	3,020.938	1,790.832
N	1,913	1,914	1,914

Note: estimated coefficients are unstandardized negative binomial coefficients. Standard errors are in parentheses. All independent variables except the time dummy (year) have scores lagged by one year ($t - 1$). SPSS 16.0 for Mac was used.

Significant at the * 0.05 and ** 0.01 level.

[a] Y_{t-1}, Scores the previous year's anti-government demonstrations, riots or major government crises.

[b] Set to zero because this parameter is redundant.

Table 8.2 Predictors of political activism 1991–2006. Ordinal logistic regression

Variables		Model 1 Anti-government demonstrations	Model 2 Riots	Model 3 Major government crises
Location	Mobile teledensity (log)	0.027 (0.053)	0.088 (0.076)	−0.042 (0.078)
	GDP (log)	−0.034 (0.082)	−0.280* (0.114)	−0.078 (0.128)
	Population (log)	0.294** (0.029)	0.283** (0.039)	0.212** (0.041)
	Lagged dependent variable[a]	0.348** (0.033)	0.627** (0.063)	0.959** (0.093)
	[year = 1991]	0.375 (0.504)	0.628 (0.669)	0.396 (0.825)
	[year = 1992]	0.779 (0.433)	−0.212 (0.707)	0.912 (0.708)
	[year = 1993]	0.389 (0.431)	0.571 (0.585)	0.606 (0.681)
	[year = 1994]	0.579 (0.398)	0.659 (0.546)	0.567 (0.652)
	[year = 1995]	10.045** (0.353)	0.696 (0.502)	0.867 (0.593)
	[year = 1996]	0.851** (0.332)	0.678 (0.454)	0.434 (0.608)
	[year = 1997]	0.469 (0.329)	0.276 (0.454)	10.407** (0.517)
	[year = 1998]	0.378 (0.311)	−0.013 (0.440)	0.810 (0.507)
	[year = 1999]	0.336 (0.299)	0.264 (0.400)	0.609 (0.502)
	[year = 2000]	0.439 (0.281)	0.113 (0.380)	0.593 (0.489)
	[year = 2001]	−0.213 (0.293)	−0.425 (0.392)	0.663 (0.464)
	[year = 2002]	0.445 (0.259)	−0.278 (0.368)	0.834 (0.439)
	[year = 2003]	0.299 (0.257)	−0.374 (0.367)	0.159 (0.477)
	[year = 2004]	0.315 (0.253)	0.183 (0.311)	0.215 (0.479)
	[year = 2005]	0.174 (0.256)	0.093 (0.309)	0.463 (0.461)
	[year = 2006]	0[b] (0)	0[b] (0)	0[b] (0)
Threshold[c]	[event = 0]	40.544** (0.544)	30.189** (0.724)	40.201** (0.897)
	[event = 1]	50.375** (0.548)	40.311** (0.732)	50.895** (0.882)
	[event = 2]	50.915** (0.552)	50.150** (0.744)	70.505** (0.937)
	[event = 3]	60.637** (0.559)	50.867** (0.764)	80.899** (10.120)
	[event = 4]	70.107** (0.567)	—	90.595** (10.325)
Log likelihood		28,280.379	15,560.768	12,660.735
Chi-square likelihood ratio		3,310.004	1,810.449	1,710.335
Pseudo R^2 (McFadden)		0.105	0.104	0.119
N		1,913	1,914	1,914

Note: estimated coefficients are unstandardized negative log–log coefficients. Standard errors are in parentheses. All independent variables except the time dummy (year) have scores lagged by one year ($t - 1$). SPSS 14.0 for Windows was used.

Significant at the *0.05 and ** 0.01 level

[a] Y_{t-1}, Scores the previous year's anti-government demonstrations, riots or major government crises, respectively.

[b] Set to zero because this parameter is redundant.

[c] Intercept-equivalent term. The last category does not have an odds associated (Norušis 2008).

The same model was also tested with some modifications. A model with aggregated counts was tested but the results were not altered in any significant ways. This was done because, when there are many counts or few observations for a given count, then some aggregation of count data may be necessary. I also tested a model that excluded the lagged dependent variable, but including this significant variable was considered a better specification and the difference was small.

The insignificant results for mobile teledensity led to the question of whether this could be caused by a violation of assumptions made about the distribution. Ordinal regression can be an adequate alternative in this case, as it accounts for the natural order of count data, while assumptions of the previously tested model are relaxed. The results did not lead to significant changes compared with the previous regression model; mobile teledensity remains insignificant, while both population and the lagged dependent variable have a significant and positive effect. GDP has a significant and negative effect on riots (Table 8.2).

Discussion

One clear conclusion of my analysis is that mobile teledensity consistently remains nonsignificant throughout all types of models. At the same time, I find that population levels have a fairly strong effect on all political activism variables. Occurrence of one political activism event in the previous year appears to be a good predictor of the same event in the following year, thus indicating that occurrence independence is not given. Economic level measured by GDP seems to be negatively associated with riots. The null hypothesis stating no association between mobile connectivity and political activism cannot be rejected with 95% certainty. This conclusion is considered robust owing to the variety of models tested with the data, which did not produce notably different results.

Why are the results for mobile teledensity not significant? Although this indicator significantly correlates with the political activism variables, no significant effect can be found in a regression model that includes the control variables GDP, population and time. This suggests that the development of political activism is not dependent on developments in mobile telephony over the years in any measurable way. Running the analysis with mobile teledensity as the only predictor produced small but significant results, but these disappeared when including time and population as control variables in the model. The nonsignificant results of GDP are somewhat counter-intuitive. Gjerde's (2005) conclusion that countries with higher GDP experience more anti-government demonstrations and riots are not confirmed by my results; riots even showed a contrary result. The analysis suggests that increasing GDP reduces the probability of violent (riots), but not peaceful protest (anti-government demonstrations). Economic levels according to my results do not affect major government crises either.

Conclusion

The case studies and interviews indicate that mobile phones may have potentially gained a central function as facilitators in mobilization and collective action processes in the political sphere. Furthermore, the theoretical literature in the social sciences offers many different and productive approaches to explain these processes, and the potential function of communications technology is recognized but not very well explored. The theoretical base seems broad enough to develop a hypothesis on possible associations between mobile phone-enhanced social linkages and political activism. However, the results of my regression analyses imply that mobile connectivity can neither negatively nor positively be associated with political activism. Overall, time trends, population levels and the previous incidence of political activism appear to be better predictors of the occurrence of political activism than mobile connectivity and economic levels. It seems thus that impressions given by some of the case studies are overrated and that generalization by means of a global comparative analysis is not possible in the way conducted in this chapter. The effect of mobile phones is nonexistent, too weak to be measureable or offset by other factors. The simple assumption that mobile phones alone will create a measurable impact on political activism cannot be sustained with the methods and data used in this chapter. I will in the following suggest some amendments and outline some future work that should be done.

Outlook

One of the main counter-arguments to the hypothesis mentioned above was the issue of monocausality. Although mobile phones were not treated as causes of political activism, network society theory still claimed this communication technology (together with the Internet) to be an "indispensable medium" in the workings of twenty-first-century society. From the results achieved, one can conclude that, if mobile communication truly is a necessary condition, it may not be a sufficient one for the effects stated. What other variables could be relevant? Castells et al. (2007) repeatedly highlight their view that mobile phones, while powerful and important in the context of twenty-first-century political activism, must interact with a particular media environment to unleash their potential in the sense discussed in this chapter. Including media freedom or other media variables in the analysis may be a possible avenue to tackle this aspect. In some of the examples observed, the Internet seems to have played an important role as a backup information and dissemination source on which users of mobile phones were able to rely. It may be worthwhile to analyze the combined impact of mobile phones and the Internet, in addition to (more traditional) media variables, although the very low Internet penetration rates in many non-OECD countries may cause difficulties in extracting useful information from such data. In countries with low Internet accessibility, other media such as the radio may substitute for the Internet, a factor that can be accounted for. Broadening the set of variables included as predictors of political activism may, interestingly, return the debate to the background concept of connectivity briefly mentioned in the research design section above. This could imply that mobile connectivity is only one link in a chain of factors that amounts to connectivity effects. After all, even highly motivated would-be protesters need travel infrastructure (roads, railways, and so on) to join a demonstration, and their motivation will depend on a variety of information sources such as websites, TV channels or radio stations, and perhaps an urban setting that provides spatial proximity to high-enough numbers of other potential protesters.

A further aspect to be considered in future research is rapid adaptation, or the potential "arms race" between civil society and governing elites (see "Bringing in the Mobile Phone" section above). It seems plausible to argue that the situation under democratic and the one under oppressive regimes cannot be compared in terms of how, and how effectively, communications technology is being used. For those more concerned with authoritarian governments' dealing with citizens empowered with mobile phones, a possible way to control for this would be to separate the analysis by regime type and to check whether the mobile phone has a larger impact in freer societies compared with oppressed ones. It may also be important to keep in mind that governments, whether autocratic or not, have varying capacities in terms of resources, such as technical equipment and skilled specialists. It may be much easier to deal with an opposition newspaper than with a technically advanced communication network that everybody in a country uses, including the members of the ruling elite. To further develop this approach a distinction by regime strength may be fruitful—weak governments may be less capable of coping with "smart mobs" than stronger ones.

References

Abel, A. 2000. *A Tool for Transparency* [Online]. Available at: http://www.unesco.org/courier/2000_07/uk/connex2.htm [accessed: April 2008].

BBC. 2007. *Ethiopians get Texting in Amharic* [Online, 12 December]. Available at: http://news.bbc.co.uk/2/hi/africa/7138128.stm [accessed: 28 January 2011].

Bikhchandani, S., Hirshleifer, D. and Welch, I. 2007. *Informational Cascades and Rational Herding: an Annotated Bibliography* [Online]. Available at: http://www.info-cascades.info/ [accessed: 28 January 2011].

Buechler, S.M. 2008. Social Strain, Structural Breakdown, Political Opportunity, and Collective Action. *Sociology Compass*, 2(2), 1–14.

Campbell, S.W. and Park, Y.J. 2008. Social Implications of Mobile Telephony: the Rise of Personal Communication Society. *Sociology Compass*, 2(2), 371–87.

Castells, M. 2000a. *The Rise of the Network Society*, 2nd edition. Oxford: Blackwell.

Castells, M. 2000b. Materials for an Exploratory Theory of the Network Society. *British Journal of Sociology*, 51(1), 5–24.

Castells, M., Fernández-Ardèvol, M., Linchuan, J.Q. and Sey, A. 2007. *Mobile Communication and Society*. Cambridge, MA: MIT Press.

Cooper, G. 2002. The Mutable Mobile: Social Theory in the Wireless World. In *Wireless World*, edited by B. Brown, N. Green, and R. Harper. London: Springer, 19–31.

Deibert, R., Palfrey, J., Rohozinski, R. and Zittrain, J. 2008. *Access Denied: The Practice and Policy of Global Internet Filtering*. Cambridge, MA: MIT Press.

Dholakia, N. and Kshetri, N. 2003. Mobile Commerce as a Solution to the Global Digital Divide: Selected Cases of e-Development. In *The Digital Challenge: Information Technology in the Development Context*, edited by S. Krishna and S. Madon. London: Ashgate, 237–56.

Diani, M. 2004. Networks and Participation. In *The Blackwell Companion to Social Movements*, edited by D. Snow, S.A. Soule and H. Kriesi. Malden, MA and Oxford: Blackwell, 339–59.

Drezner, D. 2006. *Weighing the Scales: The Internet's Effect on State–Society Relations*. Paper presented to the ISA Conference: The North–South Divide and International Studies, San Diego, CA, 22–25 March.

Economist. 2006. *Out of Africa* [Online, 7 December]. Available at: http://www.economist.com/business/displaystory.cfm?story_id=E1_RPRTJTT [accessed: 28 January 2011].

Economist. 2008a. *The Limits of Leapfrogging* [Online, 2 February]. Available at: http://www.economist.com/opinion/displaystory.cfm?story_id=10650775 [accessed: 28 January 2011].

Economist. 2008b. *A World of Witnesses* [Online, 10 April]. Available at: http://www.economist.com/specialreports/displaystory.cfm?story_id=10950499 [accessed: 28 January 2011].

Garett, K.R. 2006. Protest in an Information Society: a Review of Literature on Social Movements and New ICTs, *Information, Communication and Society*, 9(2), 202–24.

Gates, S., Hegre, H., Jones, M.P. and Strand, H. 2006. Institutional Inconsistency and Political Instability: Polity Duration, 1800–2000. *American Journal of Political Science*, 50(4), 893–908.

Gjerde, C. 2005. *Political Institutions and Extreme Presidents*. Dissertation to the University of Oslo, Department of Political Science.

Global Voices 2008. Zimbabwe: *Using New Technologies to Fight for Democracy* [Online]. Available at: http://globalvoicesat.org/2008/05/06/zimbabwe-using-new-technologies-to-fight-for-democracy/ [accessed: 28 January 2011].

Gould, R.V. 1993. Collective Action and Network Structure. *American Sociological Review*, 58(2), 182–96.

Gould, R.V. 1995. *Insurgent Identities: Class, Community, and Protest in Paris from 1848 to the Commune*. Chicago, IL: University of Chicago Press.

Green, N. 2002. Who's Watching Whom? Monitoring and Accountability in Mobile Relations, in *Wireless World*, edited by B. Brown, N. Green and R. Harper. London: Springer, 32–44.

Gujarati, D.N. 2003. *Basic Econometrics*, 4th edition, international version. New York: McGraw-Hill.

ITU. 2006. *World Telecommunication/ICT Development Report 2006*. Geneva: International Telecommunication Union.

ITU. 2008. *Global ICT Developments* [Online]. Available at: http://www.itu.int/ITU-D/ict/statistics/ict/index.html [accessed: 28 January 2011].

Jenkins, J.C. 1983. Resource Mobilization Theory and the Study of Social Movements. *Annual Review of Sociology*, 9, 527–53.

Kwan, M. 2007. Mobile Communications, Social Networks, and Urban Travel: Hypertext as a New Metaphor for Conceptualizing Spatial Interaction. *The Professional Geographer*, 59(4), 434–46.

Liao, T.F. 1994. *Interpreting Probability Models: Logit, Probit, and Other Generalized Linear Models*. Sage University Paper series on Quantitative Applications in the Social Sciences no. 07-101. Thousand Oaks, CA: Sage.

Ling, R. 2004. *The Mobile Connection: The Cell Phone's Impact on Society*. San Francisco, CA: Elsevier.

Livesay, J. 2003. The Duality of Systems: Networks as Media and Outcomes of Movement Mobilization. *Current Perspectives in Social Theory*, 22, 185–221.

LSE. 2004. *What is Civil Society?* London School of Economics and Political Science, Center for Civil Society [Online]. Available at: http://www.lse.ac.uk/collections/CCS/what_is_civil_society.htm [accessed: 28 January 2011].

Mahoney, J. and Goertz, G. 2006. A Tale of Two Cultures: Contrasting Quantitative and Qualitative Research. *Political Analysis*, 14, 227–49.

Martz, L. 2008. *Surprising Africa: Interview with Ethan Zuckerman* [Online]. Available at: http://picnicnetwork.org/page/25691/en [accessed: 12 January 2011].

MDG. 2008. *United Nations Millenium Development Goal Indicators* [Online]. Available at: http://mdgs.un.org/unsd/mdg/ [accessed: 12 January 2011].

Meier, P. 2009. *From Information to iRevolution: The Tactical Use of ICTs by Repressive Regimes and Resistance Movements*. Dissertation to Tufts University, The Fletcher School.

Melucci, A. 1994. A Strange Kind of Newness: What's New in the New Social Movements? In *New Social Movements: From Ideology to Identity*, edited by E. Laraña, H. Johnston and J.R. Gusfield. Philadelphia, PA: Temple University Press, 101–30.

Nicholson, J.A. 2005. Flash! Mobs in the Age of Mobile Connectivity. *Fibreculture Journal* [Online], 6. Available at: http://journal.fibreculture.org/ [accessed: 12 January 2011].

Norušis, M.J. 2008. *SPSS 16.0: Advanced Statistical Procedures Companion*. Upper Saddle River, NJ: Prentice Hall.

NZZ. 2008. *China Will in Tibet Hart Durchgreifen* [Online, 15 March]. Available at: http://www.nzz.ch/nachrichten/international/zahlreiche_tote_bei_den_protesten_in_tibet_1.689701.html [accessed: 12 January 2011].

Obadare, E. 2006. Playing Politics with the Mobile Phone in Nigeria: Civil Society, Big Business and the State. *Review of African Political Economy*, 33(107), 93–111.

Powers, D. and Xie, Y. 2000. *Statistical Methods for Categorical Data Analysis*. San Diego, CA: Academic Press.

Rafael, V.L. 2003. The Cell Phone and the Crowd: Messianic Politics in the Contemporary Philippines. *Public Culture*, 15(3), 399–425.

Rheingold, H. 2002. *Smart Mobs: The Next Social Revolution*. Cambridge: Perseus.

Röller, L. and Waverman, L. 2001. Telecommunications Infrastructure and Economic Development: a Simultaneous Approach. *American Economic Review*, 91(4), 909–23.

Rummel, R.J. 1963. Dimensions of Conflict Behavior Within and Between Nations. In *General Systems: Yearbook of the Society for General Systems Research*, edited by L. Von Bertalanffy and A. Rapoport, Vol. VIII. New York: The Society for General Systems Research, 1–50.

Skog, O.S. 1988. Testing Causal Hypotheses About Correlated Trends: Pitfalls and Remedies. *Contemporary Drug Problems*, 15, 565–606.

Skog, O.S. 2004. *Å forklare sosiale fenomener. En regresjonsbasert tilnærming*, 2nd edition. Oslo: Gyldendal.

Smelser, N.J. 1973. The Methodology of Comparative Analysis. In *Comparative Research Methods*, edited by D.P. Warwick and S. Osherson. Englewood Cliffs, NJ: Prentice Hall, 42–86.

Soule, S.A. 1997. The Shantytown Protest. *Social Forces*, 75(3), 855–82.

Soule, S.A. 2004. Diffusion Processes Within and Across Movements. In *The Blackwell Companion to Social Movements*, edited by D. Snow, S.A. Soule and H. Kriesi. Malden, MA: Blackwell, 294–310.

Sutherland, E. 2008. *Counting Mobile Phones, SIM Cards and Customers*. Paper to the University of Witwatersrand [Online]. Available at: http://link.wits.ac.za/papers/link-Mobile_numbers.pdf [accessed: 12 January 2011].

Third Way. 2008. *Freedom. Opportunity. Success! Third Way Internet Community* [Online]. Available at: http://www.3dway.org [accessed: 12 January 2011].

Townsend, A. 2000. Life in the Real-time City: Mobile Telephones and Urban Metabolism. *Journal of Urban Technology*, 7(2), 85–104.

UCLA. 2008. *UCLA Academic Technology Services: Statistical Computing* [Online]. Available at: http://www.ats.ucla.edu/stat/ [accessed: 12 January 2011].

Walker, C. 2006. *An ICT Policy Dilemma: Ramifications on Strategic Nonviolent Social Movements and the Global Islamist Insurgency*. MALD Thesis to Tufts University, The Fletcher School.

WDI. 2007. *World Development Indicators*. The World Bank Group [Online]. Available at: www.worldbank.org [accessed: 12 January 2011].

Wilson, E.J. III 2004. *The Information Revolution and Developing Countries*. Cambridge, MA: MIT Press.

World Bank. 2008. *ICT Glossary Guide* [Online]. Available at: http://go.worldbank.org/GCEYAAZD70 [accessed: 12 January 2011].

Chapter 9
ICT Infrastructure in Two Asian Giants: A Comparative Analysis of China and India[1]

Venkata Praveen Tanguturi[2] and Fotios C. Harmantzis

Introduction

India, an emerging world power with a rising economy, is comparable with China in terms of population, geographic size, and cultural vibrancy. Also, just like China, India is striving to become a leader in the global economy. China accounts for 5% of the world gross domestic product (GDP) and 22% of the world population; India accounts for 2% of world GDP and 18% of the world population. Together they account for 40% of the world's population. In recent years, China and India have gained significant importance because of their growing role in the world economy. They have become the two fastest-growing developing economies (in the last three years especially, they have witnessed a phenomenal growth rate); India's export of goods and services were 19% of the national GDP against China's 34%. In services, India's growth rate (8.2%) was almost equal to that of China (9.8%).[3] This is one sector where India is equal to China in productivity and output: regarding telecommunications, their combined networks are among the world's largest and most promising. Ovum, an information technology (IT) consultancy, predicted that India and China will account for 30% of the world's mobile phone users by 2010. With a market of over 1 billion people (low-income and middle-income), according to the 2005 A.T. Kearney FDI Confidence Index, these two Asian giants are the most favored foreign direct investment (FDI) destinations in the world (Trinh 2006). According to the 2005 World Investment Report, among the Asian countries, China attracted U.S.$60.63 billion and India U.S.$5.34 billion in FDI inflows.[4] In the telecommunications industry alone, according to the 2006 World Development Indicators (WDI) released by the World Bank, regarding investments in the telecommunications industry with private participation, China attracted $8,495.9 million against India's $14,321.9 million (WDI 2006). India, a world power in terms of size and intellectual workforce, is striving to catch up with its close competitor in Asia, but is still not at par. In the last five to six years, India's telecommunications market has witnessed unparalleled growth. It has become the fifth-largest telephone network in the world after China, the U.S., Japan, and Germany. With substantial progress in the Information and Communication Technologies (ICT) sector, China and India have gained significant global attention and importance in the last decade. Yet the differences between the two countries are profound. Is this due to the role of technology, economy, government, or the people?

---

1 The authors are thankful to Professor James Alleman (University of Colorado, Boulder), Dr A. Curtis (Stevens Institute of Technology) and Dr Bin Song (Central University of Finance and Economics, China) for fruitful discussions.

2 The views expressed in this article are those of the author and not those of Deloitte.

3 WDI, 2006, http://data.worldbank.org/products/data-books/WDI-2006.

4 India Economic Survey 2005–2006, http://indiabudget.nic.in/es2005-06/esmain.htm.

State of Telecommunications Services in India and China

Although adoption and proliferation of the Internet is growing rapidly in the two Asian giants, China is ahead in terms of the number of subscribers. First, according to the September 2006, Telecom Regulatory Authority of India (TRAI) report, total Internet subscribers in India stood at 8.10 million and total broadband (>256 kbps) subscribers at 1.81 million. Compared with that, China has 137 million Internet subscribers with 90.7 million broadband subscribers (as of January 2007; China Internet Network Information Center 2007; Telecom Regulatory Authority of India 2006). Thus, it is clear that penetration in India is much slower than that in China. Breaking the subscribers down in terms of access methods and technologies, the gap widens further. In India, approximately 18,876 subscribers use leased lines as compared with 27.1 million in China. The vast majority of Internet subscribers in India still use dial-up connections against China's 39 million. Second, they differ in the number of Internet hosts, i.e. computers that are directly connected to the worldwide Internet network, measured in terms of country-specific domain names registered; India[5] (.IN) has 200,000 versus 1,803,393 in China (.CN) (China Internet Network Information Center 2007). Third, India's recent phenomenal growth in the telecommunications industry has become a great success story. This is evident from the fact that India's teledensity had reached 18.26%[6] at the end of February 2007, up from 1% in the late 1990s. Furthermore, at the end of February 2007, India had a total of 202.74 million telephone subscribers (40.40 million fixed line users and 162.53 million wireless users) against China's 740 million users (350 million fixed line users and 390 million mobile users) at the end of 2005. The growth of main telephone lines in China between 2000 and 2005 was 19.3% against India's 8.95% during the same period. In India, during the same period mobile subscribers grew at a rate of 90.6% against China's 35.8%.[7] Fourth, at the level of competition, the Indian mobile market is much more competitive than China's (Telecom Regulatory Authority of India 2006). Fifth, the Network Readiness Index ranking, measuring the propensity for countries to exploit the opportunities offered by ICT, based on the 2005 World Information Technology Report, ranked India at 40 whereas China was ranked at 50 (Telecom Regulatory Authority of India 2006). This shows more opportunities in India as compared with China. It is clear that, in the recent past, the mobile market in India grew at a faster rate as compared with China, but in the case of fixed services, China is still ahead. Furthermore, India continues to lag behind China in terms of broadband penetration. If we compare the statistics of China and India with the S-curve of growth, perhaps India is on the lower but faster growing portion of the curve whereas China is at a more mature stage.

This brings forth some fundamental questions: why there is such a stark difference between India and China with regard to telecommunication services? Is it due to the affordability, availability, or the lack of awareness and knowledge? Does lack of knowledge play a part in the adoption of a technology? How significant is knowledge or rather the lack of it in the adoption of technology?

The lack of knowledge has a significant impact on the effectiveness of the adoption of technology. The use of information services in recent years has changed the way people connect, learn, share knowledge, and do business. Academics, consultants, and research organizations have argued over the years that development of infrastructure and its associated services has an immense impact on

5 INRegistry, The .IN Domain Name Registry, http://www.registry.in/.

6 TRAI press release available at: http://www.trai.gov.in/trai/upload/PressReleases/443/pr16mar07no29.pdf.

7 World Telecommunications Development Report 2006, http://www.itu.int/newsroom/wtd/2006/survey/charts/index.asp.

individuals, societies, businesses, and the overall growth of the country. Infrastructure development (road, power, transportation, and telecommunications) helps improve the attractiveness, adoption, proliferation, and competitiveness of markets, businesses, and the workforce. Recent studies by Press et al. (2003), Kshetri (2002), Dholakia et al. (2003), Kshetri and Dholakia (2003), Hong (2004), Malik (2004), Indjikian and Siegel (2005), Tallon and Kraemer (1999), Hollifield and Donnermeyer (2003), and Rai and Lal (2000) offer insights into the factors contributing to success. Factors such as *awareness*, *availability*, and *affordability* will all have different (yet relevant) impacts on the penetration and acceptability of a technology. It is worthwhile mentioning that the key factors and variables are interrelated and overlap, but the idea is to highlight the individual factors that are critical in understanding the growth patterns in China and India.

Awareness

The elementary examples of social networks we come across in daily life are, for example, groups of friends, nongovernmental organizations, associations, societies, and the government. It is common to all that they communicate verbally but within themselves, or within their small network, and rarely with other societies. Some of the reasons that contribute to this weak link are the overall objectives, security, information flow, education, and availability of physical infrastructure. If technology is introduced, one can observe the differences in the organization and communication of these societies that were once connected verbally. The first and the foremost question is whether technology can help them to learn, communicate, and share knowledge. There are certain requirements such as education, knowledge of the technology and how to use it, and knowledge of its purpose. India and China are rivals in IT and in IT-related services, and China is ahead in terms of proliferation of Internet services. China is known for being the production house of the world, while India is recognized for its service industry, i.e. information technology-enabled services. In China, it is the availability of a well-developed physical infrastructure that contributes to the growth, whereas in India, it is the availability of millions of low-cost English-speaking professionals. To reap the benefits of technology, the simple requirement is the creation of a workforce to use and convey the benefits associated with being connected.

The prime factor that contributes to the adoption of technology is education. To put things into perspective, India's biggest advantage is the availability of skilled labor and qualified engineers. Yet the availability of such a workforce can be a problem—illiteracy rates in India are above 35% while they are only 4.9% in China; India has a significantly higher education dropout rate. According to the National Sample Survey Organization (NSSO),[8] India, at least 26% of rural families in India and 8% of urban families have no literate member over the age of 15. There is a considerable difference between the two countries when one looks at gross education enrolment ratio (as a percentage of the relevant age group). Furthermore, looking at the secondary and tertiary education gross enrollment ratios, the difference is clear, as shown in Table 9.1. As is evident from the 2006 Human Development Report, India's public expenditure on education dropped from 12.2% in 1991 to 10.7% in 2004. China also ranks higher than India in terms of the Gender Development Index;[9] this shows the higher gender disparities in India than in China. The female literacy rate in China (87%) is much higher than that in India (48%). According to the United

8 See "No Literate Adult Among 26 Percent of Rural Families", http://www.hindustantimes.com/StoryPage/Print.aspx?Id=67049cca-0141-401c-a987-e5be023229ca.

9 A Gender Development Index of 1 indicates that parity exists between the sexes.

Nations Development Program, the global 2006 Human Development Report ranked India 126th and China as 81st in terms of a composite Human Development Index (see Table 9.1).

The next important dimension is the use of technology in the education system. Tallon and Kraemer's (1999) study suggests that it is not just attracting investments in building infrastructure that is important, but also the creation of awareness and the development of an education system that is tailored to the needs of industry, along with encouraging its use. How many schools and universities are connected to the Internet? In both China and India, an initiative to connect schools and universities to the World Wide Web was launched by their respective governments. However, differences still exist. In the case of India, the government launched the Education and Research Network (ERNET, http://www.ernet.in/index.htm) in 1986 with the objective of providing state-of-the-art infrastructure and service to academics and research institutions. The ERNET[10] backbone is a mix of terrestrial- and satellite-based wide area networks. Other initiatives launched through ERNET include Vidya Vahini (IT in education), which was launched in seven districts in six states and enrolled 167 schools into the program; Gyan Vahini (computer-aided techniques into the learning environment); ICAR-Net (Indian Council for Agriculture Research–Net), in which 274 institutions have been connected through VSAT and terrestrial link; AICTE–Net, with 48 institutions connected so far; and UGC-Infonet. In the case of China, the China Education and Research Network (CERNET, http://www.edu.cn/.), established in 1994, supports "1500 universities and institutions connected and about 20 million end users."[11] In terms of international connectivity, ERNET's global connectivity is far less as compared with that of CERNET (see Table 9.1). In short, China has been successful in networking universities, institutes, schools, and other organizations serving professors, researchers, and students. These indicators are key to differentiating between the availability of skilled and qualified engineers in India and China.

10 See The ERNET Backbone; http://www.ernet.in/backbone.htm.

11 See About Cernet; http://www.edu.cn/introduction_1378/20060323/t20060323_158626.shtml.

Table 9.1 Awareness

	India	China
Education index		
Literacy rate	64.84% (according to 2001 census)	95.1%
Expenditure on education as a proportion of GDP	2.78 (as of 2003–04)	NA
Expenditure per student, primary (% GDP per capita)	9.1 (as of 2005)	NA
Public expenditure on education (% total government expenditure)	12.2 (1991) 10.7 (2004)	12.7 (1991) NA
Gross enrollment ratio		
Secondary	52%	70%
Tertiary	11%	15%
Gender disparity		
Gender Parity Index, gross enrollment in tertiary education	0.66 (as of 2004)	0.85 (as of 2004)
Development Index		
Human Development Index	126 (as of 2004)	81 (as of 2004)
Gender Development Index	98 (as of 2003)	64 (as of 2003)
Academic Internet Backbone		
International capacity	6.64 Mbps (ERNET)	800 Mbps (CERNET)
Traffic generated	20 GB (ERNET)	800 GB (CERNET)

Source: United Nations Development Program, Human Development Report, 2006; World Development Indicators 2006; International Telecommunications Union (ITU); and India Budget (2005–2006).

Affordability

Affordability measured in terms of income and cost of a service (Internet, mobile phone, fixed line) is a good indicator of the adoption of a technology, irrespective of whether it is available or not. According to the 2006 Human Development Report, India's GDP per capita (purchasing power parity, U.S.$) is $3,139 against China's $5,896 (see Table 9.2). China's per capita income is almost twice that of India. When compared in terms of the price basket for a residential fixed line, mobile phone, and Internet services, i.e. dollars per month, the difference is negligible in the case of fixed line and mobile phone services, whereas in the case of Internet services, they are cheaper in India than in China (see Table 9.2).

Table 9.2 Affordability

	India	China
Cost of service ($ per month)		
Price basket for residential fixed line	$3.2	$3.6
Price basket for mobile	$3.2	$3.7
Price basket for Internet	$8.7	$10.1
Income		
GDP per capita (purchasing power parity, U.S.$)	$3,139	$5,896

Source: 2006 World Development Indicators.

Availability

Moving from indicators measuring awareness and affordability, one has to look at the availability, i.e. infrastructure. Availability of services such as fixed, mobile phone, personal computers (PCs), and Internet are as important as awareness and affordability. India has only 12.67 total telephone subscribers per 100 inhabitants against China's 56.53 (World Telecommunications Development Report (WTD); International Telecommunication Union 2006). Breaking it down, in the case of fixed line services, India has 4.5 main telephone lines per 100 inhabitants against China's 26.63 (International Telecommunication Union 2006). The difference is also visible in the case of mobile phones: India has 8.16 cellular mobile subscribers per 100 inhabitants against China's 29.90 (International Telecommunication Union 2006). In terms of coverage, 41% of the population[12] in India is covered by mobile telephony against China's 73% (The World Bank Group 2006). Rural coverage telephone services are available in 97% of villages in China against 87% in India.

As far as information technology is concerned, access to and availability of PCs is also critical, as they enable access to Internet. China has the lead in PCs, according to the ITU WTD 2006 report: as of 2005, China had approximately 53 million PCs versus 17 million in India, and the *Computer Industry Almanac* estimates approximately 64 million PCs in China and 17 million in India. Thus, the two industry group estimates are different in terms of China's number of PCs, but the fact remains that not only is the gap already wide, it is widening even more. Two of the reasons are the availability of locally manufactured computers and cost. Furthermore, in terms of international connectivity, i.e. international Internet bandwidth for transmitting Internet traffic contracted between countries, China overwhelms India five-fold. The broad picture is that India invests 4% of its GDP back into infrastructure development against China's 9%. Regarding ICT expenditure (which includes computer hardware, software, services, and wired and wireless communications equipment), China spends 4.4% of GDP as compared with India's 3.8%; also, when compared in U.S. dollars spent per capita, China spends more than India (The World Bank Group 2006). This contributes to China having superior access and services as compared with India. China is not only well-positioned in terms of telecommunication infrastructure, but it also has a huge availability of hardware (PCs, phones, etc.) owing to their local manufacturing base.

12 This is the percentage of people within range of mobile cellular signal regardless of whether they are subscribers.

Table 9.3 Availability

	India	China
Telephone lines		
Total telephone lines/100 inhabitants	12.67	56.53
Main telephone lines/100 inhabitants	4.51	26.63
Mobile subscribers/100 inhabitants	8.16	29.90
Information age		
Personal computer (as of 2005) (in millions)	17	53
International Internet bandwidth bits per capita (2004)	11	57
Information and communications technology expenditure		
Percentage of GDP (2004)	3.8	4.4
Per capita epnt (U.S.$, 2004)	24	66
Television		
Households with television (%, as of 2005)	37	91

Note: The Computer Industry Almanac estimates.

In a nutshell, China has a substantial lead over India in the development of infrastructure and the subsequent creation of its awareness. The International Telecommunication Union (ITU)'s Digital Access Index (DAI) takes into account factors such as infrastructure (availability), affordability, knowledge, and quality in classifying countries as high, upper, medium, and low ICT access. Based on ITU's DAI[13] results, China and India are listed under countries with medium-level ICT access, but overall, China's (0.43) performance is better than India's (0.32) (International Telecommunication Union 2003). The e-readiness rankings of *The Economist*'s Intelligence Unit (EIU) capture variables such as connectivity, citizens' ability to utilize technology skillfully, the transparency of the business and legal systems, and the extent to which governments encourage the use of digital technologies (*The Economist* 2006). Based on the 2006 e-readiness rankings, India (53) ranks higher than China (57). The two indices show a different picture but what remains common is bottlenecks with technology infrastructure and access to ICTs.

Other Factors

Moving from the information age to other physical infrastructures that indirectly contribute to the growth of the society, China enjoys a much better physical infrastructure as compared with India (see Table 9.4). The problem with infrastructure in India is that the infrastructure deficit continues to impede its progress. According to the recent article, "The Trouble with India," in *BusinessWeek* (Hamm 2007), India is where China was a decade ago. According to T.V. Mohandas Pai, Director of Human Resources for Infosys, "India has underinvested in infrastructure for 60 years, and we're behind what we need by 10 to 12 years" (Hamm 2007). This is clearly visible when you compare the two giants in terms of road networks; as of 2006, India has 3,700 miles of national highways against China's 25,000. With the road networks in disarray, India's woes with power production

13 A total of 178 economies, on a scale of 0–1 where 1 = higher access.

and consumption are continuing (see Table 9.4). It is unsurprising that international companies choose China over India when setting up manufacturing plants.

Table 9.4 Other infrastructure

Other	India	China
Roads network, paved (percentage of total roads) (as of 2001)	46%	91%
National Expressways[a] (thousands of miles)	3.7	25 (data for 05)
Electric power (consumption/capita kWh, as of 2001)	365	893
Electric power production (billion kWh)	654	2,500

Note: [a] Hamm (2007), p. 55.

Summary and Discussion

Based on the qualitative analysis of key variables such as awareness, availability, and affordability, it is clear that India has substantial challenges to overcome to catch up with China. Today, India's huge pool of low-cost English-speaking professionals is attracting business process outsourcing services. However, high illiteracy rates and a dearth of qualified engineers can hinder India's growth in the long run. Analysis shows that huge gaps exist in the education system of the two countries. Access to education needs to be improved in India. The usage of technology in the education system needs to be stressed. Along with this usage, schools and universities should be provided with broadband coverage, enabling them to interact and share knowledge. Furthermore, India needs to focus on delivering customized educational content in local languages via ICT.

China's self-dependence on home-grown hardware, its superior infrastructure, and the availability of higher regional and international bandwidth make it more attractive for FDI as compared with India. Furthermore, China's higher per capita income coupled with superior access to infrastructure help in driving telephone (fixed and mobile) and broadband penetration levels. In order for India to reach the same levels, it needs to push its manufacturing base to offset its dependence on importing hardware, and increase network coverage and user acceptability, which will, in turn, help in creating jobs. Apart from the investments in telecommunications, huge investments are needed in the power sector as well as road development, which indirectly impact the level of foreign investment and attractiveness.

References

China Internet Network Information Center (2007). *The 19th Survey Report*. Available at: http://www.cnnic.net.cn/en/index/0O/index.htm [accessed: 1 August 2011].

Dholakia, N., Dholakia, R.R. and Kshetri, N. (2003). *Internet Diffusion*. Working paper. Available at: http://ritim.cba.uri.edu/wp2003/pdf_format/Wiley-Encycl-Internet-Diffusion-v12.pdf [accessed: 1 August 2011].

Hamm, S. (2007). The Trouble with India. *BusinessWeek*, 19 March, 48–58. Available at: http://www.businessweek.com/magazine/content/07_12/b4026001.htm [accessed: 1 August 2011].

Hollifield, A.C. and Donnermeyer, F.J. (2003). Creating Demand: Influencing Information Technology Diffusion in Rural Communities. *Government Information Quarterly*, 20, 135–50.

Hong, W. (2004). An Empirical Study on Telecommunications Development in the Rural Areas of China's Western Provinces. *Proceedings of the International Telecommunications Society 15th Biennial Conference*, Berlin.

Indjikian, R. and Siegel, S.D. (2005). The Impact of Investment in IT on Economic Performance: Implications for Developing Countries. *World Development*, 33(5), 681–700.

International Telecommunication Union (2003). *World Telecommunications Development Report 2003: Access Indicators for Information Society, Executive Summary*. Available at: http://www.itu.int/ITU-D/ict/publications/wtdr_03/index.html [accessed: 1 August 2011].

International Telecommunication Union (2006). *World Telecommunication Development Indicators 2006*. Available at: http://www.itu.int/ITU-D/ict/statistics/ [accessed: 1 August 2011].

Kshetri, N. (2002). What Determines Internet Diffusion Loci in Developing Countries: Evidence from China and India. *Pacific Telecommunications Review*, 23(3), 25–34.

Kshetri, N. and Dholakia, N. (2003). Broadband Potential in Asian Giants: A Comparison of China and India. Working paper, available at: http://ritim.cba.uri.edu/wp2003/pdf_format/PTC-2003-Broadband-Kshetri-Dholakia-Final-v2.pdf [accessed: 1 August 2011].

Malik, P. (2004). *Indian Telecommunications Policy and Regulation: Impact on Investment and Market Structure*. Working Paper. Available at: http://regulateonline.org [accessed: 1 August 2011].

Press, L., Foster, W., Wolcott, P. and McHenry, W. (2003). The Internet in India and China, *Information Technologies and International Development*, 1(1), 41–60.

Rai, P.L. and Lal, K. (2000). Indicators of the Information Revolution. *Journal of Technology in Society*, 22, 221–35.

Tallon, P.P. and Kraemer, L.K. (1999). The Impact of Technology on Ireland's Economic Growth and Development: Lessons for Developing Countries. *HICSS-32, Proceedings of the 32nd Annual Hawaii International Conference on System Sciences*. Available at: http://ieeexplore.ieee.org/servlet/opac?punumber=6293 [accessed: 1 August 2011].

Telecom Regulatory Authority of India (2006). *Study Paper on Financial Analysis of Telecom Industry of China and India*. Study Paper no. 1/2006, 1–13. Available at: http://www.trai.gov.in/StudyPapers_list_year.asp [accessed: 1 August 2011].

The Economist (2006). *The Economist Intelligence Unit 2006 e-Readiness Rankings*. Available at: http://www.eiu.com/site_info.asp?info_name=eiu_2006_e_readiness_rankings [accessed: 1 August 2011].

The World Bank Group (2006). *World Development Indicators 2006*. Available at: http://devdata.worldbank.org/wdi2006/contents/home.htm [accessed: 1 August 2011].

Trinh, S. (2006). India a Study in Contrast. *Deutsche Bank Research*. Available at: http://www.dbresearch.com/ [accessed: 1 August 2011].

Chapter 10
Information (without) Revolution? Ethnography and the Study of New Media-enabled Change in the Middle East[1]

Deborah L. Wheeler

Introduction

The headlines read, "In Egypt, Twitter Trumps Torture" (Eltahawi 2010b: A13). While the coercive excesses of the Egyptian regime are well known, the new media-enabled "micro-coups" committed by publics armed with mobile phones and Internet-linked computers are not as well publicized. On the surface, new media technologies have given states, especially authoritarian ones, more complete, panoramic views of their subjects' (oppositional) imaginations. Censorship, cyber-spying, misinformation campaigns, cyber sting operations; all of these tools and more have been used by Middle Eastern states, to "better" police their publics in the twenty-first century. The story behind this story, however, suggests that Internet empowerment is a double-edged sword. Citizens, it seems, are also empowered by new media tools in creative ways, some of which are explored in this chapter.

Most of my fieldwork has concentrated on interpreting the meaning of Internet cultures in Kuwait, Egypt, and Jordan, and thus observations drawn from these three cases form the basis for this chapter. There is clearly more democratic access to media than there is political access to democracy in the case studies examined below. Thus in these cases, are we seeing "information (without) revolution?" The question mark suggests that "information revolution" remains a distinct possibility for the region. From Twitter-enabled election protests in Iran, to angry bloggers in Egypt, to youth unemployment protests in Sidi Bouzid neighborhood in Tunis (January 2011), the masses are increasingly using tools like the Internet to carve out spaces for empowerment in the face of what Jason Brownlee calls "durable authoritarianism" (Brownlee 2007), in other words, authoritarianism that is creative in neutralizing opposition, even when mass-based, resilient in maintaining the status quo, and unyielding, even when public demands for greater accountability, and increased opportunities for employment and public goods, are reasonable and well articulated. This chapter argues that surface maintenance of the status quo, however, should not mask the study of Internet-enabled turmoil and change at the grass roots.

One of the key findings of my ethnographic research of new media power struggles is that culture and context help to shape the meaning of new media practices, in terms of both their

1 Author's note: This chapter was completed in January 2011, one month before Twitter trumped the Egyptian regime, so to speak. While the chapter anticipates the possiblility of major political changes sweeping the region, at the time of its completion, this was more about intuition than evidence, or following small changes to their logical conclusions. The chapter, although dated by subsequent events, provides a first-hand account of the kinds of micro transformations that made the Egyptian revolution possible.

perceived utility and the impact of use. Part of the analysis to follow also focuses specifically on ethnographic research methods.

Starting Points: Theories and Expectations of New Media-enabled Change

A recent study of the Arab blogosphere observes, "In a part of the world where print and broadcast media traditionally have been controlled by the government, digital networked spaces offer the possibility of a much richer public sphere than existed before" (Etling et al. 2009: 46). Thus new media networks in the Arab world have the potential to reshape relations between citizens and the state, but will they? And if so, at what cost? Mona Eltahawi, in an interview with Voice of America, explains how social media are re-tooling relations between state and society in the Middle East. She observes:

> I find social media to be one of the few tools in the Middle East that keep me optimistic about the region. Social media have given the most marginalized groups in the region a voice … So they finally have a place now to express themselves, and it's not just for "stress relief," because there are many examples I could give you from the region of how social media, for example, have helped convict police officers of torture; of how social media were used to organize the victims of police torture within Egypt; of how social media were used to help a hunger strike in Saudi Arabia in support of political dissidents; of how social media—again in Egypt—were used to raise awareness about sexual harassment against women in public, to the extent that the Egyptian Parliament is discussing a draft law that would both define and criminalize sexual harassment; and, in a country like Morocco, social media have been used to expose police corruption. (Eltahawi 2010a)

The death of Neda Agha Soltan ("angel of Iran") during the Iranian election protests in 2009 (Fathi 2009) and the brutal beating to death (by plain clothes police officers) of Khalid Said, who dared to post a video on-line of Egyptian police splitting money obtained during a drug bust (Eltahawi 2010b), suggest that blood will be spilled in the state's effort to maintain the status quo.

As we already know without in-depth research, the expected "wave of democratization" promised by the Internet revolution's earliest prophets (Barlow 1996; Gore 1994) has not materialized in the Middle East. Authoritarian rule persists, leading one scholar to coin the phrase "stalled democracy" (Bellin 2002) to characterize political reform in the region. The most significant transformations in political development thus far are located in the residual people's power that emerges when wiring a country to communications networks (Faris 2010). New information and networking capabilities give netizens the ability to consume and share new information resources, and sometimes to organize and to contest power. These voices expressed in chat rooms, in emails, in tweets, or through the simple sharing or consuming of new information resources, by forwarding a link or "friending" on Facebook, create transformations in individual lives according to the more than 1,400 participants interviewed or surveyed in Kuwait, Jordan and Egypt between 2004 and 2010 for this study. Collectively these narratives illustrate how cyberspace presents "opportunities for new forms of communicative action which have emancipatory potential" (Murphy 2009: 1131).

Ethnographic Adventures: What do Ethnographies of New Media Add to the Interpretive Mix?

In spite of the fact that "ethnography has been generally under-appreciated in academic political science," I cannot think of a better way to be on the cutting edge of knowledge than to be the first to discover some new political process taking place in remote but nonetheless strategically important locations (Schatz 2009: 17). One of the reasons I prefer ethnographic research methods is that spending time in the field makes it easier to be a pioneer. Those of us who do ethnography tend to be "an open minded lot" and less wedded to any particular approach or method of inquiry (Schatz 2009: 16). For those of us who study other countries, and are interested in mining data at the peripheries of political, social, and geographic power, with the intention of finding the seeds of change in undiscovered territory, ethnography is the best method of inquiry. The subjects we study more than likely have not yet been topics in extant secondary sources. Statistical data on specialized communities (like women, youth and the opposition) in the developing world tends to be sparse. Therefore, we are ethnographers not just out of desire, but also out of necessity.

Using ethnographic research methods to study new media-induced change gives observers access to the story behind the story, where enhanced state repression sometimes yields to digitally empowered citizens, albeit on a selective basis. Ethnography means "spending an extended period of time immersed in a field setting, taking account of relationships, activities, and understandings of those in the setting and participating in those processes" (Hine 2000: 4). Ethnographers, "care" to "glean the meanings that the people under study attribute to their social and political reality" (Schatz 2009: 5). Ethnographic research methods applied to the question of new media-enabled change gives observers "previews" of potential storylines as they unfold, or even before they unfold. Moreover, ethnography enables political scientists to "track down the exercise of power within the interstices of official structures, behind the veil of various officialdoms, and in ostensibly apolitical spaces and domains" (Kubik 2009: 31). The reason it is important to use ethnographic methods when studying the development and impact of the Internet is that "the Internet is not a monolithic or placeless 'cyberspace'; rather it is numerous new technologies, used by diverse people, in diverse real-world locations" (Miller and Slater 2001: 1). Thus, "ethnography of the Internet can look in detail at the ways in which technology is experienced in use" (Hine 2000: 4).

Establishing Relevance: Technology Diffusion and the Emancipatory Potential of IT

The fact that an estimated 3.4 million Egyptians have a Facebook page is indicative of the new spaces for networking, communicating, and sometimes protesting government action emerging in Egypt and beyond. Add to this mix new websites where people's stories and pictures of government torture can be posted, and the link between new media and oppositional imaginations becomes clearer.[2] One increasingly irrelevant counterargument for the limited importance of the Internet as a tool for oppositional behavior in the Muslim Middle East is the question of access. There was a time, not too long ago, when Internet access was growing and spreading more slowly in the Middle East and North Africa than any other place in the world. This gave power to the view that the Internet was mainly an elite technology, giving increased networkability to the already connected and empowered. This argument was supported by facts such as that, in 2001, Egypt was among the countries with the lowest Internet diffusion rates, with only 0.85% of the

2 http://www.monaeltahawy.com/blog/?p=302.

population having access! Kuwait, in 2001, even though it was an oil-rich community, only had 8.9% Internet penetration. With technology diffusion patterns, the passage of time changes circumstances, often in revolutionary ways, so that what was once a duck becomes a rabbit. By 2008, as depicted in Table 10.1, the Internet's global diffusion rates showed that the Internet was surprisingly spreading more *quickly* in the Middle East than anywhere else on the planet except Africa.

Table 10.1 Internet penetration rates in the global context (2010)

Region	Percentage population penetration	Growth 2000–2010	Percentage of world population	Percentage of Internet users worldwide
Middle East	28.8%	1,825.3%	3.1%	3.3%
Africa	10.9%	2,357.3%	14.8%	5.6%
Asia	21.5%	621.8%	56%	42%
Europe	58.4%	352.0%	11.9%	24.2%
North America	77.8%	146.3%	5%	13.5%

Source: Internet World Stats www.Internetworldstats.com.

With Internet access increasingly reaching a critical mass of citizens in the region (as depicted in Table 10.2), expectations for Internet use to matter in some detectable way politically are also on the rise, whetting the ethnographer's appetite. How will these new media capabilities affect local politics? Social media provide publics with an increased ability to organize and mobilize in mass numbers, without the repressive state finding out until the opposing public has reached critical mass. This amassing of public protest can stall the state's potential for coercive resource use in ways dangerous to an authoritarian state's fear-based legitimacy, as was the case in the Lebanese Cedar Revolution, the Kuwaiti Orange Revolution, and the Iranian election protests.

Table 10.2 Internet penetration rates for the Middle East and North Africa (2009)

Country	Population 2009 (estimated)	Internet use/2000	Internet use/2009	Percentage of population with access	Percentage growth 2000–2009	GNP (puchasing power parity) in US$
Bahrain	728,290	40,000	155,000	21%	287.5%	38,400*
Iraq	28,945,569	12,500	300,000	1%	2,300.0%	3,300*
Jordan	6,269,285	127,300	1,500,500	23.9%	1,078.7%	5,530
Kuwait	2,692,526	150,000	1,000,000	37.1%	566.7%	52,610
Iran	66,429,284	250,000	32,200,000	48.5%	12,780.0%	10,840
Lebanon	4,017,095	300,000	945,000	23.5%	215.0%	10,880
Oman	3,418,085	90,000	465,000	13.6%	416.7%	20,650
Qatar	833,285	30,000	436,000	53.3%	1,353.3%	121,490*
Saudi Arabia	28,686,633	200,000	7,700,000	26.8%	3,750.0%	22,950
Syria	21,762,978	30,000	3,565,000	16.4%	11,783.3%	4,350
UAE	4,798,491	735,000	2,922,000	60.9%	297.6%	41,800*
Yemen	22,858,238	15,000	370,000	1.6%	2,366.7%	2,210
Algeria	34,178,188	50,000	4,100,000	12.0%	3,740.0%	7,940
Egypt	78,866,635	450,000	12,568,900	15.9%	2,693.1%	5,460
Libya	6,324,357	10,000	323,000	5.1%	3,130.0%	15,630
Morocco	31,285,174	100,000	10,300,000	32.9%	10,200.0%	4,330
Tunisia	10,486,339	100,000	2,800,000	26.7%	2,700.0%	7,070

Source: Internet World Stats, www.Internetworldstats.com, World Bank (www.worldbank.org) and * CIA World Factbook (2009) (www.cia.gov).

Introducing the Cases

Understanding where Internet use in Kuwait, Jordan and Egypt fits in the spectrum of regional connectivity, politics, and public culture is important in contextualizing the cases' meaning for the study of new media-enabled socio-political change. Thus, some things should be established about each case before the analysis proceeds. In terms of freedom, Jordan and Egypt are ranked as "not free" by Freedom House, 2010 estimates, while Kuwait is ranked as "partially free" given democratic parliamentary elections, recent successes in terms of women's rights and a relatively free and open press. Moreover, all three countries are known to be "semi-democratic" with active, popularly elected parliaments that provide a relatively weak check, if any, on the power of the ruler. The fact that, in each case, the ruler can suspend or dissolve parliament at will means that the head of state's power outweighs public consent. There is little accountability between ruler and ruled in any of these cases, especially because the head of state is not popularly elected, but also because there are few if any checks on the head of state's power, outside of revolution, of which there have been many in the Middle East, including Iran in 1978; Egypt in 1919 and 1961; Syria in 1925 and 1963; Iraq in 1920 and 1959; Yemen in 1962 and 1963; and Oman in 1962.

If rulers in Jordan, Egypt and Kuwait do not like the pressure they are getting from public representatives, they just dissolve parliament. For example, Jordan's king dissolved parliament in 2009 and decided not to allow re-elections until the end of 2010. The move was designed to check the rising voice and power of Islamist elements in Jordanian politics. Jordan also has one of the strictest press laws in the region, and has used it to prosecute people who are too free with their oppositional words in print, and on-line. Jordan also has a high rate of honor killings for the region, which implies that women who experiment with cyber dating, as was found in my ethnographic research to be common among Internet users, take big risks to do so, given tribal norms and laws that do not effectively protect women from threats from family members if they act in ways that "tarnish" family honor.

In spite of clear constraints on democratic politics in Jordan, recent scholarship suggests that significant processes of change are occurring at the grass roots. For example, King Abdulla's "Jordan First" initiative aims "to increase political participation" and "to advance democratic dialogue" (Baylouny 2005: 40). Part of the Jordan First initiative is a USAID-sponsored project to make Jordan a regional IT hub. Computers and e-learning are being introduced to the educational curriculum to prepare youth for the digital economy. Telecenters that provide low-cost Internet access and training have been built throughout the country, including poor and rural areas. Jordan is also in the Guinness Book of world records for having the most Internet cafés on a single street, University Ave, across the street from Yarmouk University. State efforts to get new media technologies diffused throughout Jordanian society are having an impact on social and political behavior in Jordan, as examined in this chapter.

Egypt is also rated as "not free" by Freedom House, politically, while at the same time new media diffusion is giving Egyptians new political and social agency. Egypt has an active parliament that has only been dissolved twice by the ruler, once in 1987, and once again in 1990 (Morrow and al-Omrani 2009). President Hosni Mubarak has other ways of manipulating politics, such as his National Democratic Party, controlling four-fifths of all the parliamentary seats, and suppressing opposition politicians by making their movements illegal. This has been true especially for the most popular and best-organized opposition movement, the Muslim Brotherhood. After the 1981 assassination of President Anwar Sadat, a state of emergency rule was instituted. These emergency laws have been in effect since 1981 and have been used by President Hosni Mubarak to suppress civil rights, including press freedom, freedom of association and freedom of speech, even on-line. The number of opposition politicians in prison, especially those from the outlawed Muslim Brotherhood, always rises before elections, even when such candidates try to run as "independents." In spite of state repression of the opposition, and an entire branch of the Ministry of the Interior dedicated to policing cyber space, activism in Egypt is on the rise, especially in light of increased economic instability and hardship for the majority of Egyptians. This economic unrest matched with a state policy of introducing IT access and training to most Egyptians as a means of stimulating foreign direct investment and economic opportunity for the society, means that the stage is set for tension (Wheeler 2003a).

In Egypt, a tug of war is developing between a public increasingly making demands for greater government accountability and more economic opportunities using IT as a vehicle for their voices and their emerging social networks. For example, it is not surprising that "although the Muslim Brotherhood is technically illegal in Egypt, it has a very active presence in the blogosphere" (Etling et al. 2009: 4). Similarly, a Ph.D. thesis by David Faris about the role of blogs and social networking technologies in Egyptian politics more widely, argues that new media technologies reshape public discourse by making what is fit to print in the official press broader and less muzzled by censorship. As a result, social media networks have "placed new tools and resources in the hands of the political opposition" (Faris 2010: 22). Faris demonstrates ways in which new media break stories, stimulate mobilization, and sometimes encourage government reform in cases of torture, sexual harassment, land grabs and human rights abuses of Sudanese refugees. While he is careful not to over-sell the impact of social media, he does skillfully demonstrate how new media practices "change the context of the relationship between the regime and its people" in Egypt (Faris 2010: 78).

Kuwait seems to be the case that holds out the most promise for new media-enabled change, both in terms of the data yielded by this study, and by demonstrations of the impact of IT use on actual government policy. For example, in 2006, what became known as the Orange Movement used information technology to network for political change. A Master's thesis by Jon Nordenson (May 2010), written at the University of Oslo about the 2006 Orange Movement in Kuwait, argues that this Kuwaiti reform project used the Internet "to convey unfiltered news, discuss, agitate, expose corruption, mobilize", making it possible to "engage each other in ways impossible offline" (Nordenson 2010: iv). The main political impact of the Orange movement was to get the Kuwaiti government to change the number of electoral districts from 25 to 5. The reduction in the number of districts was said to favor women's chances of getting elected to parliament (four women succeeded in getting a seat in the 2009 elections, after redistricting) and was said to reduce the possibilities of corruption through vote buying (Bowles 2007: 1). Similarly, in the 2009 Kuwaiti elections, many candidates used the web to campaign and to widen their base of support. Four candidates in particular, all of them female, were highly successful in this enterprise of e-campaigning—to the degree that they overcame local cultural norms that discount the effectiveness of women as leaders, to win parliamentary seats.

These observations are backed up by a survey of Internet users conducted by students at the American University of Kuwait in 2009. The survey of more than 350 Internet users revealed that more than 80% of participants felt that the Internet was having an impact on power and politics in the region. Emerging patterns in the earlier research in Jordan and Egypt show that, even as early as 2004, people surveyed were articulating how the technologies opened their minds, changed their thoughts, and encouraged them to be more actively engaged with the world around them, but they were a minority voice within the survey group (34% of those surveyed). In the Kuwait case, however, we have more than 80% of those surveyed telling us in their own words exactly how the Internet matters politically. Collectively these narratives suggest that "political change doesn't always begin with a bang; it often starts with just a whisper" (Goldfarb 2006: 1) It is not by accident that, as Goldfarb observes, "The Internet favors a democratic politics of small things" (Goldfarb 2006: 141). It allows for the pooling of whispers, the collective, yet often uncoordinated, redefinition of new information relationships, and new forms of power, localized in individual lives, congealing changes in norms and behaviors one click at a time.

One puzzle yielded by this study is the fact that each Internet user studied for this project identified important changes created by the technology in their individual lives. At the same time, Internet diffusion and increased use by Arab publics seems to have had little effect on formal institutions of power. I call the situation one of "information without revolution." This project is not the first to argue that authoritarian regimes will be resistant to Internet-enabled publics making demands for political liberalization (Albabtain 2008; Kalathil and Boas 2003; Norton 1999). What is unique about this analysis, however, is that it dives beneath the surface of politics as usual to highlight important transformations in individual Internet users' lives, which cumulatively could challenge political and social norms in the region. By using ethnographic research methods, this analysis is able to "see and question political relations and political sites that are generally unseen, or 'unidentified' by mainstream political science but which are nonetheless meaningful for local political actors" (Jourde 2009: 201). In user accounts of how Internet use has changed their lives, their thinking and their activism, we see nascent forms of political change, not observable if we keep our eyes firmly fixed upon formal institutionalized power and policy-making. Especially in authoritarian contexts, where the risks of opposition are high, the use of ethnographic methods to study political change is particularly revealing. This is because, as Jeffrey Goldfarb observes, "when people freely meet and talk to each other as equals, reveal their differences, display their distinctions and develop a capacity to act together, they create power" (Goldfarb 2006: 4). It does not take a great deal of imagination to understand how cyberspace would be a particularly suitable realm for citizens in the Arab world to leverage this kind of power. It is to the concrete details of this power struggle that we now turn.

Lessons from the Field

Jordan

The circumstances that enabled me to conduct fieldwork on the Internet and its impact in Jordan (2004) were multi-layered. First of all I had a fellowship from the Oxford Internet Institute and, with their support, I was able to travel to the field for data collection, then return to Oxford periodically to share findings with colleagues at the Institute (between 2004 and 2005 I returned to Oxford twice for research briefings, and to teach in the Summer Doctoral Thesis seminar). Secondly, while in Jordan, I was hired by three different aid organizations to consult on various aspects of IT and development: the Queen Zein Al-Sharaf Institute for Development, for whom I served as an editor for their production of Jordan's Arab Human Development Report 2005; the United Nations Development Program, Jordan, with whom I worked to create a number of new project documents, most of which had a crosscutting IT for Development element; and the Digital Opportunity Trust of Canada, who hired me to perform an impact assessment of the Netcorp Jordan project. Netcorp Jordan was an IT for Development project that leveraged King Abdullah's Knowledge Station initiative to build IT access and training centers in 150 remote locations throughout the kingdom. By training trainers who would be placed in knowledge stations in their communities, versed in community development strategies and the role that IT could play in such processes, Netcorp Jordan attempted to build new media-enabled pathways out of poverty and lack of opportunity.

While in Jordan, and armed with my initial questions of how and why new media use would (or would not) impact the lives of Jordanian Internet users and the Jordanian state, I decided to hire a research assistant to help me in generating ethnographic data with which to answer these questions. This meant that, in the Jordanian case, I was both ethnographer and supervisor of an ethnographic research team of two, my research assistant and me. The hiring of a research assistant was not a matter of wanting someone else to do the dirty work for me. On the contrary, given the growing tensions between the US and the Muslim Middle East following the US military campaign to oust Saddam Hussein (many of whose family members had taken refuge in Amman where I was conducting research) from power in Iraq, and the growing suspicion among the Jordanian public that any American researcher who spoke Arabic and was asking potentially sensitive questions must be a spy, I had no choice but to take this approach in the field. Creating a barrier between the subject and me was necessary in order to get people to participate. To supplement, however, I constructed my own ethnographies of Internet use by participating in and observing emerging Internet cultures and interviewing Internet users whenever and wherever I could find them, if they were willing to talk.

Following a lead I had gained in Egypt in 2000 that revealed that the majority of the region's Internet use took place in an Internet café (and perhaps explained the low numbers for Internet penetration—it is hard to count who goes on-line only at a café), my research assistant and I decided to make a systematic sweep of Internet cafés in neighborhoods, rich to poor, located throughout Amman and Zarqa, where more than three-quarters of Jordanian society lives. While in these cafés, my research assistant and I would conduct interviews with willing participants, during which we would ask them a series of about 30 questions about their surfing habits, attitudes, and how such practices were impacting on their lives, if at all. We also interviewed Internet café managers, and asked them similar questions, since they could provide a general overview of the communities of users located in their café, as well as generalize about the uses and meanings of new media tools. What we found was that, on average, Jordanians were spending about 14.5 hours a week in an Internet café; that more than 55% of those interviewed were using the technology to obtain wider access to information; that more than 62% stated that the Internet was expanding their social networks; and that more than 42% of those interviewed were spending time in Internet cafés in order to alleviate severe boredom. Both widening social networks and severe boredom are two potential triggers to activism that deserve further investigation.

One finding that specifically clarifies the importance of Internet use for transgressing socially conservative norms in the kingdom is the fact that Jordanian women are using the tool to meet with members of the opposite sex, both on-line and in person. This risk-taking behavior is particularly unexpected, given that Jordan has one of the highest rates of so-called "honor killings" in the region. Of the 100 women interviewed for this project, a surprising 66 said that they had made a friend on-line. Perhaps more striking is the fact that 45% of those who had made a friend on-line had also met this person in real life. Surprisingly, 76% of those women who had met their cyber-pals in real life stated that the person whom they had met was a man. This number is striking given the conservative nature of Jordanian society, especially when it comes to gender issues, and Jordan's rate of honor killings. Yet, many women are meeting men on-line and then meeting them in real life too.[3] The majority of those engaging in this counter-cultural practice were Muslim, not Christian as one might expect. Moreover, all of the women who had met male cyber-pals in real life were between the ages of 20 and 27 and were single.

Among the women who had met men on-line and off, clear spillover effects of these encounters are present in their narratives. For example, a 24-year-old, single, Muslim woman from Zarqa who spends on average 8 hours a week in an Internet café, is a sales girl with a community college degree and is not comfortable speaking or surfing the net in English, observes:

> The Internet has clearly changed my life. It made my life full. I enjoy my free time and I got to know many girls and made good female friends in Amman and Madaba. I also made a relationship with a man that was my friend in chat. I became more open minded and less conservative since I started talking with people in chat. (Interview, Zarqa, 20 May 2004)

Similarly, a 21-year-old, single Muslim college student majoring in Pharmacology who spends on average 7 hours a week on-line in an Internet café observes:

> The Internet has changed my life in a positive way. It changed my character and I became more social, and less reserved in my relationships with the opposite sex (males). I became more relaxed;

3 A recent BBC news story states that in Jordan, "approximately every two weeks, a woman is killed by a male relative because of the shame she has brought upon her family by an alleged sexual transgression." See Clare Murphy, "Jordan's Dilemma over 'Honor Killings'," BBC News Online, 2003/09/10 (http://news.bbc.co.uk/go/pr/fr/-/2/hi/middle_east/3094736.stm), accessed 9/12/2006.

> before I used to feel shy. Chat teaches a person to be more relaxed and open with people. It's great! (Interview, Amman, 10 May, 2004)

Once again stressing the spill-over effects of on-line encounters with the opposite sex, a 25-year-old, single Christian with a community college degree who is employed as a telemarketer and spends about 10 hours a week surfing the Internet in an Internet café, surfing only in Arabic states said:

> The Internet has changed my life. It made me more social, less closed-minded. I also met a friend that I chatted with. He came to Jordan from Saudi Arabia to meet me, but the relationship didn't work out between us. I made many other friendships. It's a good way to communicate with people. (Interview, Zarqa, 17 May, 2004)

If women in Jordan are increasingly willing to risk interrupting patriarchal social relationships that govern their private lives, could the political arena of contest with a patriarchal state be next? We will all need to stay tuned, with our ethnographic tools ready, to see these processes unfold. The King of Jordan often repeats that he wants to build an information society where no Jordanian is left out. The narratives above suggest that many Jordanian women are taking full advantage of the technologies made available to them through such national strategies, and in ways the state might not like in the long run—altering norms, demanding more control over their lives. When asked if the Internet was enabling Jordanians to experiment in ways that expanded their civic engagement and activism, only 30% said yes among both men and women interviewed. In Jordan, social experimentation trumped political experimentation at this stage. As suggested by the Kuwaiti case, however, social experimentation seems to lead naturally to more engaged forms of citizenship and political engagement over time. A repeat visit to Jordan is needed to see if the Kuwaiti pattern is shared across cases.

Egypt

My initial interests in the Egyptian information revolution stemmed from my desire to see how new media use and impact was affecting nonoil-rich societies. The Egyptian government was vocal about its hopes to use information technology to build new jobs, new opportunities and more significant links to the global economy. The Egyptian state is also burdened with the need to create more than half a million new jobs a year, just to absorb the new entrants into the labor force. Thus far, in spite of an open attitude towards IT diffusion, the government has not been able to meet the challenges of the youth bulge. A large community of educated, unemployed and IT savvy youth has created new challenges for the state. Social media allow for the pooling of anger and resources, thus producing the conditions necessary for a showdown between state and society that is increasingly visible and violent, in the blogosphere and beyond.

A fieldwork opportunity presented itself in 2000 through which I could begin to satisfy my initial curiosities. My spouse had received an ARCE grant to spend time studying Islamic manuscripts in Dar al-Kutub and Al-Azhar libraries for a project he was completing on Moses' representation in the Quran. During this time, I was able to obtain a visiting researcher position in the Department of Political Science at the American University in Cairo. This initial phase of research was rather top-down-oriented as I attempted to meet with those in the government and private sector who were most responsible for bringing the Internet revolution to Egypt. I visited the Ministry of Information and Communication Technology, and research institutes such as RITI,

Regional Institute for Technology and Innovation; I also met with members of the Information Decision and Support Center, which was responsible for both upgrading the government's IT capabilities and thinking about the most beneficial and safest ways to close IT gaps at the grass roots. The head of IBM Egypt and entrepreneurs like the young men who established Career Egypt.com, a "Monster"-like on-line job search service, were important to my ethnography. At the time that I began this research in 2000, Egypt had only an estimated 250,000 Internet users out of a population of 68 million, another reason for the top-down design to the ethnography. The results of this initial phase of research were two publications that detailed the government's efforts to turn Egypt into an Information Society (Wheeler 2003a, 2003b). As a political scientist, my question even at that time was what the impact on power and agency would be if Egypt wired its citizens to new media tools. Would this prepare the ground for significant changes in institutionalized power? In the words of Richard Norton, would the state "slowly retreat?" While the introduction to this chapter illustrates that the Egyptian state is not retreating, the effectiveness of the state's bark and bite to ward off socially networked challengers is in retreat.

Phase 2 of my research on the development and impact of the Internet in Egypt took place four years later when, inspired by the Jordanian case study, which revealed that, even though institutionalized power was not directly transformed by new media users, these Internet users were documenting significant impacts that the technology was having on their everyday lives, political awareness and civic engagement. Bayat has told us that this process whereby citizens become actively engaged in shaping the course of their own lives and political consciousness is a necessary step in preparing the ground for democracy (Bayat 2010). So, were these same processes happening in Egypt; and if so, to what degree?

The 2004 ethnography in Egypt mirrored the method used in Jordan. The same research assistant I employed in Jordan had spent significant time in Cairo and was anxious to apply her skills and lessons learned to a new context. In May and June of 2004, she would spend time participating and observing and talking with Internet café users in Cairo, throughout rich and poor neighborhoods, to try to obtain an idea about who was using the technology, how frequently, and with what impact, just as we tried to assess in Jordan. Given the great difficulties in conducting survey research in Egypt (it is illegal without a license from the state), she only "talked" with people, asking them a shorter list of the same questions we asked in Jordan. Our key interests were (1) how many hours they were spending on-line; and (2) what impact their surfing was having (if any) on their life. In the end, she was able to interview 50 people, 25 women and 25 men. The interviews took place in Garden City, Dokki, Muhandiseen, downtown Cairo, and Zamalek. When follow-up research is done, we would like to expand this study to Imbaba, a poor neighborhood on the West bank of the Nile, and to add locations outside of Cairo.

The findings were similar to the Jordanian case, even though only one-quarter of the number of people were interviewed for this second case. For example, the average number of hours spent on-line in an Internet café was 13.5 (one hour less per week than the Jordanian case). In terms of the impact on Internet users' lives, a substantial 84% said that they used the tool to expand their access to information not readily available in Egypt (as opposed to 53% in Jordan). Even more impressive, 94% of those interviewed said that Internet use was expanding their social networks both in Egypt and beyond (as opposed to 62% in Jordan). Surprisingly, only 16% of those interviewed stated that they used the Internet to alleviate boredom (as opposed to 42% in Jordan). Most importantly for this study about the potential impact of new media use on people's political identities and practices, 50% of those interviewed stated that they were using the tool to intensify their civic engagement and political awareness, from reading the news to joining political debates on-line, to networking with like minded individuals. (Only 30% of those surveyed in Jordan agreed that Internet use was re-tooling their political engagement and identity.)

One month after my research assistant returned to Jordan from Cairo, I left for Egypt to conduct two months of follow-up ethnography. I visited Internet cafés to participate in and observe emerging new media cultures, meet with government officials, visit aid organizations involved with bridging the digital divide, read the press and follow leads, attend conferences and meet with members of the private sector. I interviewed students at American University in Cairo (where I would once again obtain visiting research professor status) and met with faculty there who shared a common interest in the development and impact of new media in Egypt. The end results of this analysis were the conclusions that Internet use had increased greatly over the four years since my last visit to the and field; that the state was being more proactive in punishing opposition forces that pressed too hard for democratic reform. The words of one Internet café manager interviewed for the 2004 ethnography summarize the research findings:

> There is no way to compare the Arab world before or after the net, of course it has made a huge difference, especially for the younger generations. The Internet is a door to the outside world. If we cannot have the chance to travel and live abroad, at least through the net people have access to get in touch with the world through chat discussions. These discussions are making people in the Arab world more open minded, regardless of the negative influence of chat and porn sites. It's also educating people, adding to their knowledge and exposure to new ideas. In chat people have the freedom to express themselves. (Interview with Internet Café Manager in Zamalek, Cairo, May, 2004)

Oppositional imaginations and actions in Egypt have grown in part because people are armed with new social media tools. Once again, this case invites further exploration. The writings of David Faris begin where this study leaves off. He has performed the most complete study on the political importance of new media in Egypt to date (Faris 2010).

Kuwait

The Kuwaiti case is the most important for this chapter, first, because it is the place where I have done the most ethnographic research, and over the longest time period. Second, it is important because the findings are most relevant for understanding the new political relationships supported by new media technologies. My first ethnographic experiences in Kuwait began back in 1996 when, beaten up and intellectually bloodied by my analysis of the role of the media and popular culture in the Palestinian–Israeli conflict (Wheeler 1993), I sought refuge in Kuwait, where I had received a Fulbright Post-Doc (under urging to apply by Susanne Rudolph). In Kuwait, my plan was to study the development and impact of new Internet cultures. I was inspired by a 1994 speech by VP Al Gore at an International Telecommunications meeting in Brazil, in which he stated that the whole world would soon witness the widespread construction of Athenian-style democracy, free markets and the closing of the gap between opportunity-rich and -poor, in addition to the transformation of the globe into a global village with all of us interconnected and looking out for each other, sharing our culture, resources, and concerns. All of this would be made possible by the Information Superhighway. I wanted to see what would happen when conservative Islamic societies, with authoritarian political and patriarchal social structures, transitioned to this new media era. What would happen to local values and perspectives if something illegal, like porn, became readily available? What would happen if new media tools enhanced citizen agency? Would the public make better-organized demands for states to open new avenues for citizen participation, government transparency, and ruler accountability? Would states listen, and act in accordance with citizen demands, or just lash out, with more ferocity, to maintain complete control over public life and politics?

My initial ethnographic research on Kuwaiti Internet cultures yielded a rich body of knowledge with which to explode many techno-deterministic myths about the alleged importance of new media tools. For example, just because people had access to the Internet did not mean that they would all become liberal democrats. Moreover, free market economic values were not automatically promoted by ecommerce abilities, given state control over entrepreneurialism. Similarly, the Internet did not automatically cause users to shed their cultural and political specificity. Instead, the Internet seemed to be enhancing whatever issues, concerns, and ways of being were characteristic of "the locale." Yes, the technology made new relationships, new ways and modes of being and thinking possible, but at the end of the day, these new relationships, modes and thoughts were distinctly Kuwaiti, in this case, or Jordanian or Egyptian in the others.

The end result of my Fulbright research was a book that analyzed three trends in Kuwait's emerging Internet culture: (1) use of the technology by women; (2) use of the technology by youths; and (3) use of the technology by Islamists. These were the communities who took the most active, overt expressions of interest in new media tools.

Twelve years would pass before I would be afforded another visit to Kuwait to do follow-up research. Those of us who perform ethnographies of the developing world are often surprised by how quickly the context is subject to change: developing countries are not the same place twice.

Rare opportunities for annual visits to a field site over a sustained period of time give ethnographers better data and thus greater credibility. My field entries from the return visit to Kuwait in 2010 reveal the clear impact on one's psyche as the foreign location becomes more familiar. Additionally, sometimes a change in neighborhood produces new insights into the field. Finally, it is worth noting, we do not always get to control the circumstances of our visit, especially when one accepts a job in the field.

The field research conducted in Kuwait 2009 while teaching an Arab Human Development class at the American University of Kuwait revealed keen insights into the meaning and implication of Internet access. The findings discussed in this section were all made possible by a research project conducted with assistance by students at the American University of Kuwait in 2009. Each student interviewed people both inside and outside their friend and family networks, asking the same questions posed in Jordan and Egypt several years earlier. The goal, they were told, was to interview a broad range of Kuwaiti sources. The project yielded 267 interviews with Internet users in Kuwait. The most important finding is that more than 80% of those interviewed stated that the Internet has had a definite impact on Arab politics.

Interviews reveal that the average number of hours per week spent on-line for both Kuwaiti men and women was 20. Just shy of 100% owned a mobile phone and sent on average 34 SMS messages a day. Nearly 100% of those surveyed had Internet access at home, while more than 75% had Internet access on their mobile phones. This wireless access distinguishes Kuwait, as even in the U.S., regular access to the Internet on a mobile phone remains below 20% according to a 2009 survey by the Pew Internet and American Life project (Horrigan 2009: 1). More than 65% of those Kuwaitis interviewed had a Myspace or Facebook page and 30% of those surveyed visited blogs regularly. At the same time, only 4.5% of the Kuwaitis surveyed actually blogged themselves. This is not necessarily unique to Kuwait. A study of the U.S. blogosphere found that, while 27% of the U.S. public reads blogs, only 7% actually maintain a blog (Hassan and Adamic

2007: 1). In terms of activities pursued on-line, again Kuwaiti Internet practices parallel more global use patterns as demonstrated in Table 10.3.

Table 10.3 The six most common Internet uses among Kuwaiti men and women (2009)

Use	Women (%)	Men (%)
Email	98.4	97.1
Chat	78.9	72.7
Music	82	74.8
Study	76.3	78.9
Shopping	73.4	51.1
News	58.6	67.6

The 80.5% of Kuwaitis surveyed who felt the Internet was significantly impacting local politics explained their assessment in the following ways. Some argued that the Internet "opened Arab minds." Others stated that, with Internet use growing in the region, "states can no longer hide political information from their publics." Some pointed out how the Internet enabled greater capacities for users to organize themselves, while others pointed to the Internet's role in campaigns for the 2009 Kuwaiti elections. Some attributed great political power to bloggers, while others pointed to the Iranian election protests, the mobilization of which, in their assessment, would not have been possible without new media tools. From the outside looking in, however, it is difficult to see such "transformations" affecting policy-making and the institutions of state. Moreover, in addition to giving publics more information access and networking abilities, the Internet has likewise given more power to the authoritarian state, especially enhanced powers of surveillance.

As Hannah Arendt observed, "no revolution is even possible where the authority of the body politic is truly intact" (Arendt 1963: 112). Since the Internet increases the power of publics and states simultaneously, and Middle Eastern state authority has not crumbled (even if legitimacy has waned in some cases), we are seeing significant transformations in public engagement and risk-taking, while at the same time, little change has occurred in the formal institutions of power. This puzzle deserves further investigation beyond policy predictions parading as fact. The argument that, in the words of a White House official, "we want to make sure the information flows," as "it will obviously have political implications in a range of ways" may be true, as the survey of Kuwaiti Internet users reveals (Landler 2010b: 8), but it may not necessarily "support the democratic aspirations" of Middle Eastern citizens in search of a greater impact on policy-making, more evenly applied rule of law, and enhanced state accountability (Landler 2010b: 8).

Conclusion

This chapter illustrates the fine line between (information) revolution and no revolution. New media increasingly support oppositional politics and social practice in the region. The fact that regimes have not fallen, nor have oppositional practices (both virtual and real) had deep impacts on institutionalized power, does not mean that these technologies are not having an impact on politics. This is because, as illustrated above, new media uses are supporting more subtle and widespread forms of change, including increased risk-taking, transgressions of social norms, and sometimes collective action, easily detectable through the ethnographer's view. At this stage we see that "social media won't [necessarily] overthrow regimes." (Eltahawi 2010b: A13) At a minimum, however, they "give a voice and platform to young people long marginalized by those regimes" (Eltahawi 2010b: A13). This "virtual revolution" is "affecting Egypt's tightly controlled society" by "connecting Egyptians and amplifying their voices as never before" (Eltahawi 2010b: A13).

This chapter illustrates that forms of the Twitter-based change occurring in Egypt are commonly replicated in other Middle Eastern societies, including Jordan and Kuwait. In all three cases, new forms of citizen empowerment compete with consolidated and retrenched state power. The spread of networked forms of citizen opposition make it increasingly difficult for Arab states to control public records, imaginations, and subtle acts of defiance. Increased risk-taking within society is breeding new civic cultures and transforming norms of both public and private behavior. Determining where these processes lead as they intensify and spread (evidence of which is already overtly observable) animates the ethnographic imagination and pulls one to the field for more up-close glimpses of change in action.

Some questions for future research are:

1. As stories go viral on the web via text messages and beyond, are oppositional imaginations inspired to be the change they want to see in the world? Is this how a handful of protesters mobilize from 5 to 5,000 to 5 million in a matter of hours? In other words, is new media the vehicle for intensified collective action in the Middle East, or is some other variable (like increased public hardship, reduced state legitimacy) the cause? Isolating exactly how new media matter politically is best discovered by asking the participants in the trenches if and why the technology draws them into oppositional politics—from chat room discussions to street protests and beyond. Rather than guessing, and relying on secondary research, why not pack a bag, and join the subject, letting the participants narrate their views on processes of change in the region?
2. Once protests or social networks reach 5,000 or 5 million, does this limit a state's repressive capacity? In other words, what is critical mass in this equation? How many protesters or networked individuals does it take to stall the state's ability to contain oppositional behavior? If oppositional critical mass is maintained over time, growing and spreading as quickly as new media access in the region (how long does it take to friend someone on Facebook, or link to a blog or send/receive a tweet—organizational expansion on the cheap, relatively hidden and expeditious too), how will the state maintain the status quo? Answers to these questions are best collected through interviews with government officials who are on the receiving end of new media protests, as well as organizers of and participants in new media-inspired campaigns at the grass roots. The question of access to these individuals and collectives will limit the ability to answer these questions. A supplement to these ideal conversations could be provided by participant observation, but possibilities to directly participate are limited by the need to be in the right place at the right time, and the risks involved if the state becomes aggressive. The costs of this kind of direct knowledge may be too high. As a result, these questions might be best explored using "virtual ethnography" (Hine 2000).
3. If the status quo cannot be maintained, and citizen empowerment increases in the new media age (two big ifs in and of themselves), then when, how and why will new ways of being political take fixed institutional form? I am afraid that answers to these questions will take the most time and energy to solve. One missing element in this formulation is a focus on the role that culture and the public play in aiding state attempts to maintain the status

quo. Just because "new and improved" is a good marketing tool in the U.S., it does not mean that the frame sells everywhere (Tedlow 1996). For more tradition-loyal places, could it be that "new and improved" is a misnomer? Could "new" mean "scary, unproven, untested, unreliable, something to avoid?" Like the advice that one should avoid buying a car the first year that major design changes have been made, until car companies have worked out the kinks, could public fear of the unknown keep the new media revolution from coming? These questions require ethnographies of cultural practice; detections of risk aversion; attitudes towards change; and locations of those places where collectives are pushing for a new era of politics (we know they exist, because increasingly large, vocal and viral street protests throughout the Muslim Middle East tell us they do).

I hope this analysis has inspired a few to join in the ethnographic study of politics and Internet practices. The job can seem overwhelming, as the pace of change in the field is break-neck fast. The complexities and intervening variables are seemingly endless, but the spirit of discovery and pioneering ethic should draw some to the virtual gold rush. If the U.S. congress is now dumping millions of dollars into programs to make the Internet more freely and widely available to citizens in the Muslim Middle East with the hopes that regime reform will be enabled, we should at least be ready to predict how and why this program will or will not succeed.

References

Albabtain, Afraa Ahmed (2008) "Downloading Democracy: Bloggers in the Gulf." *Arab Insight* Fall, 53–65. Available at: http://www.arabinsight.org/aishowarticle.cfm?id=193 [accessed: 1 August 2011].

Arendt, Hannah (1963) *On Revolution*. New York: Viking Press.

Barlow, John Perry (1996) *Declaration of the Independence of Cyberspace.* Available at: https://projects.eff.org/~barlow/Declaration-Final.html [accessed: 1 August 2011].

Bayat, Asaf (2010) *Life as Politics: How Ordinary People Change the Middle East* (Stanford, CA: Stanford University Press).

Baylouny, Anne Marie (2005) "Jordan's New 'Political Development' Strategy." *Middle East Report* 236 (Fall), 40–43.

Bellin, Eva (2002) *Stalled Democracy: Capital, Labor and the Paradox of State Sponsored Development* (Ithaca, NY: Cornell University Press).

Bowles, Henry (2007) "Kuwait's Women's Rights Pioneer Talks Religion and the Future." *Kuwait Times*, 30 November. Available at: http://www.kuwaittimes.net/read_news.php?newsid=MTAxNzI5MDkwMw== [accessed: 1 August 2011].

Brownlee, Jason (2007). *Authoritarianism in an Age of Democratization* (New York: Cambridge University Press).

Eltahawi, Mona (2010a) "Can Social Media Bring Democracy to the Middle East?" *Voice of America*, 17 August. Available at: http://www.voanews.com/english/news/middle-east/Will-New-Media-Bring-Democracy-to-Middle-East-100898544.html [accessed: 1 August 2011].

Eltahawi, Mona (2010b) "In Egypt Twitter Trumps Torture." *New York Times*, 7 August, A13.

Etling, Bruce, Kelly, John, Faris, Rob and Palfrey, John (2009) "Mapping the Arab Blogosphere," 16 June. Available at: http://cyber.law.harvard.edu/publications/2009/Mapping_the_Arabic_Blogosphere [accessed: 1 August 2011].

Faris, David (2010) "Revolutions and Revolutionaries: Social Media Networks and Regime Response in Egypt". Ph.D. Thesis University of Pennsylvania Department of Political Science. Defended 19 April.

Fathi, Nazila (2009) "In a Death Seen around the World, a Symbol of Iranian Protests." *New York Times* 23 June, A1.

Goldfarb, Jeffrey C. (2006) *The Politics of Small Things: The Power of the Powerless in Dark Times* (Chicago, IL: University of Chicago Press).

Gore, Al (1994) "Information Superhighways." Speech delivered 21 March at the World Telecommunications Development Conference, Buenos Aires, Argentina. Available at: http://vlib.iue.it/history/Internet/algorespeech.html [accessed: 1 August 2011].

Hassan, Noor Ali and Adamic, Lada (2007) "Expressing Social Relationships on the Blog through Links and Comments." Paper presented at the *International Conference on Weblogs and Social Media*, Boulder, CO, 26–8 March.

Hine, Christine (2000) *Virtual Ethnography*. London: Sage.

Horrigan, John (2009) "Wireless Internet Use." Pew Internet in American Life Project, 22 July. Available at: http://www.pewInternet.org/Reports/2009/12-Wireless-Internet-Use.aspx [accessed: 1 January 2011].

Jourde, Cedric (2009) "The Ethnographic Sensibility: Overlooked Authoritarian Dynamics and Islamic Ambivalences in West Africa." In *Political Ethnography: What Immersion Contributes to the Study of Power*, ed. Edward Schatz (Chicago, IL: University of Chicago Press), 201–14.

Kalathil, Shanthi and Boas, Taylor C. (2003) *Open Networks, Closed Regimes: The Impact of the Internet on Authoritarian Rule* (Washington, DC: Carnegie Endowment for International Peace).

Kubik, Jan (2009) "Ethnography of Politics: Foundations, Applications, Prospects." In *Political Ethnography: What Immersion Contributes to the Study of Power*, ed. Edward Schatz (Chicago, IL: University of Chicago Press), 25–52.

Landler, Mark (2010a) "U.S. Hopes Exports will Help Open Closed Societies." *New York Times*, 7 March, A4. Available at: http://www.nytimes.com/2010/03/08/world/08export.html [accessed: 1 August 2011].

Landler, Mark (2010b) "Spreading Freedom with Twitter or Facebook." *International Herald Tribune*, 9 March, 8.

Marvin, Carolyn (1988) *When Old Technologies Were New: Thinking about Electronic Communications in the Late Nineteenth Century* (Oxford: Oxford University Press).

Miller, Daniel and Don Slater (2001) *The Internet: An Ethnographic Approach.* Oxford: Berg.

Morrow, Adam and al-Omrani, Khalid Moussa (2009) "Father Still Knows Best." *IPS* 17 July. Available at: http://ipsnews.net/news.asp?idnews=47700 [accessed: 1 August 2011].

Murphy, Emma C. (2009) "Theorizing ICT's in the Arab World: Informational Capitalism and the Public Sphere." *International Studies Quarterly*, 53(4), 1131–53.

Nordenson, Jon (2010) "We Want Five! Kuwait, the Internet and the Public Sphere". Master's Thesis in Arabic. Department of Culture Studies and Oriental Languages, University of Oslo.

Norton, Augustus Richard (1999) "The New Media, Civic Pluralism, and the Slowly Retreating State." In *New Media in the Muslim World: The Emerging Public Sphere* (Bloomington, IN: Indiana University Press), 19–28.

Schatz, Edward (2009) "Ethnographic Immersion and the Study of Politics." In *Political Ethnography: What Immersion Contributes to the Study of Power*, ed. Edward Schatz (Chicago, IL: University of Chicago Press), 1–22.

Tedlow, Richard (1996) *New and Improved: The Story of Mass Marketing in America* (Cambridge, MA: Harvard Business School Press).

Wheeler, Deborah (1993) "Deconstructing Revolution: The Intifada in the Shadow of '68." Ph.D. thesis, University of Chicago, Department of Political Science.

Wheeler, Deborah (2003a) "Egypt: Building an Information Society for International Development." *Review of African Political Economy* 30(98), 627–42.

Wheeler, Deborah (2003b) "Living at E.Speed: A Look at Egypt's E.Readiness." In *Economic Challenges and Opportunities in the MENA Region* (Cairo: Economic Research Forum).

Chapter 11
The Political History of the Internet: A Theoretical Approach to the Implications for U.S. Power

Madeline Carr

Introduction

During the 1970s, global financial challenges including the failure of the Bretton–Woods system and the world oil crisis brought into sharp focus the complex interplay of politics and economics. Attempts to better understand the intricacies of this relationship led to the emergence of the sub-field of international political economy (IPE). In a similar manner, the disruptive effect of information and communications technology (ICT) on international affairs has provided impetus for a more integrated inquiry into the connections between the fields of technology and politics. Working to better comprehend this complex relationship has highlighted the fact that some questions are not easily addressed by existing international relations theories and concepts.

In seeking to better understand the relationship between state power and new technology, this chapter focuses on the political history of the Internet in America. Despite states' increasing dependence and interdependence upon the global network, the political history of how this technology was initially conceived, developed, governed and managed over time is not adequately understood. Although "histories of the Internet" abound, they are almost exclusively concerned with documenting key technicians and developers and attributing their achievements and contributions to the code and architecture now in use. However, the political forces surrounding those developments are rarely referenced in these accounts and given no substantive place in understanding the progression of the Internet from a military project to an open global network. Key enabling legislature, policy mandates, the role of the state in enabling or dissuading Internet governance and the influence of governmental perceptions and intentions in shaping the technology are largely absent this work, leaving an important aspect of the development and ongoing management of the Internet unexamined.

In designing this chapter, it became apparent that existing international relations theories cannot provide an adequate framework for comprehending this multi-faceted and important issue. Although international relations has a range of theories about power, it has not yet developed a corresponding research project to explain approaches to technology. Just as a lack of economic literacy restricted the discipline prior to the emergence of IPE, the lack of technological literacy is having a similar effect by hampering efforts to move beyond existing paradigms which largely address industrial rather than information technology. Understanding how to incorporate new technologies like the Internet into international relations theory is increasingly being recognized as an important research project (Eriksson and Giacomello 2006; Mayer-Schöenberger and Brodnig 2001; Rosenau and Singh 2002; Weiss 2005).

One solution to this theoretical impediment can be found within the discipline of the philosophy of technology. Primarily concerned with the interaction of technology with every aspect of the human experience, the philosophy of technology articulates a range of "approaches" that frame our understanding of and response to technology. Each of these approaches leads to a methodological framework. This study finds that two of these approaches dominate current international relations literature, but it is in fact the third approach that can help to expand the breadth and depth of studies dealing with power and new technology.

The following brief introduction to the philosophy of technology will lay a foundation for the application of central concepts and approaches that can be observed and integrated into international relations literature. The second section of this chapter identifies two dominant paradigms within international relations for understanding the relationship between technology and power. These paradigms comprise self-consciously articulated theories of power coupled with (generally) unself-conscious but clearly evident approaches to technology. Neither of these two paradigms is proving consistently effective for understanding the relationship between power and technology in the information age as they either remain embedded in industrial age concepts and theories or fail to effectively engage with complex technical issues. Finally, this chapter will explain how the application of the third approach—the social construction of technology—can be applied to the study of the political history of the Internet in the U.S. to better understand the complex relationship between power and new technology.

Philosophy of Technology

The emergence of the philosophy of technology as a discipline was a response to rapid changes in technology and science. Prior to the industrial revolution, the pace of change was not generally sufficient to radically affect the wider social fabric during the course of an individual's lifetime. However, the past two centuries have been a time of fairly constant, rapid and profound technological development. This has led to what Norman Vig calls "a dominant paradigm of adaptation to changing technology" (Vig 1988). Attempts to better comprehend the impact of technology on the human condition have emerged as a coherent study now referred to as the philosophy of technology.

The philosophy of technology asks questions like "how does technology impact upon social structures?," "how and why do social groups seek to shape technology?," "does technology follow a pre-ordained developmental path?," and "if so, are we powerless to stop it?" These questions have as much relevance in the context of information technology as they did to industrial technology. Indeed, it is these questions and others like them that need to be applied to international relations literature attempting to understand issues of the complex relationship between power and technology. Instead, much of the literature addressing these issues remains tied to paradigms developed within the context of industrial technology and specially suited to those issues that arise from it. The philosophy of technology can provide a conceptual bridge for moving beyond those paradigms.

Within the philosophy of technology, there are various approaches that have been articulated by a number of scholars. Although the nomenclature may differ, the concepts are relatively stable across the discipline. This chapter adopts the definitions offered by Norman Vig of *instrumentalism*, *technological determinism*, and *social construction* (Vig 1988). These three "approaches" to technology will later be linked to existing international relations literature demonstrating the prevalence of instrumentalism and technological determinism, and explaining why the social construction of technology provides a means of arriving at new questions and answers to the problem of power and technology.

Approaches to Studying Technology

The approach referred to as *instrumentalism* regards technology is a means to address a human-defined problem or need. In this approach, technology is morally neutral and disconnected from its social consequences. Dominant in the commercial sector, instrumentalism justifies continuous innovation while also implying that, if any negative social outcomes arise, the answer to them probably lies in a technologically based solution.

In studying two concepts of a fundamentally social nature like power and the Internet, an approach that disengages from the social is not appropriate. In this study, an instrumental approach would lead to questions about whether the design is "good"—that is, does it address the problem or purpose it was intended for? Is it being used for its intended purpose and is that *purpose* socially acceptable? Interesting though they are, these questions fail to engage with the profound impact of the Internet, which goes far beyond its originally intended purpose and also makes it difficult or impossible to engage with changing perceptions of American power.

Technological determinism (or autonomous technology, as it is sometimes referred to) is a social view of technology; however, it is based on a mono-directional relationship. That is, technology has an impact on society—in many cases, a profound impact—but it is an external force over which society has minimal control or influence. It is the story of Frankenstein, of technology running along a predetermined evolutionary path which may or may not be beneficial for society but which is largely unstoppable. A determinist approach certainly does not see technology as "value neutral." Rather, it is regarded as imbued with values like a desire for power, the quest for efficiency, and the profit motive—"over other human needs (including those of future generations) and against the integrity of nature" (Vig 1988: 17). The fear of technological determinists is that, once large systems are in place, it becomes very difficult to alter or reverse them—they become so embedded in society that they are not necessarily respondent to changed human perceptions about their value or use. In this context, an elite group of "technocrats" control what Lewis Mumford called the "megamachine" leaving the rest of society vulnerable to its effects (Mumford 1967). This view negates social choice—it does not take into account the many decisions that societies do make about how they will develop and use technology. Technological determinism could provide a methodological framework for one-half of this study. If the research aim were simply to examine the impact of Internet technology on political ideas of U.S. power, this approach may have been adequate. However, it is irreconcilable with an epistemological position of constructivism that underpins the other half of the research aims—how ideas of U.S. power have shaped and influenced the development of the Internet. An essential starting point for this study is that states do make decisions about how they believe the Internet should best promote their national interest and enhance state power, but technological determinism would refute that claim.

Problems of the previous views led some scholars, particularly historians and sociologists, to adopt a new approach—the *social construction of technology* (SCOT).[1] For these scholars, technology is neither a neutral instrument for problem-solving nor a value-laden force that threatens

1 As this chapter is adopting the nomenclature of Norman Vig, this approach should perhaps be referred to as "contextualism," which is his term. However, for consistency with the rest of the chapter, it will be referred to here as the "social construction of technology." The two terms are interchangeable.

human autonomy. Rather, it is an *expression* of social, political, and cultural values. Vig writes, "decisions about which technologies are developed and who benefits from them are shaped more by cultural preferences and the distribution of financial and political power than by specific problems or technical opportunities" (Vig 1988: 15). The social construction of technology rejects the premise that a particular technology succeeds simply because it was "superior" to other competing options. Trevor Pinch and Wiebe Bijker illustrate this theme through a sociological history of the development of the bicycle, citing a range of social, judicial, and moral influences that combined with the application of science to favor certain bicycle models over others (Pinch and Bijker 1989: 17–50). Superiority, of course, is a subjective term and dependent upon the articulation of stated priorities. In addition—and particularly relevant for the Internet—adoption changes technology. Those who use it improve, exploit, adapt, and shape technology. In this process, priorities and the means by which success is measured may change. Therefore, SCOT argues that the emergence of any new technology needs to be understood in the context of social and political forces at work that influence choices and preferences.

A SCOT approach to technology leads to questions such as, how are technological priorities ordered and by whom? What happens to technology when those priorities are altered? And, fundamentally for this project, what role do ideas play in this process of shaping technology?

In the next part of this chapter, these approaches will be contextualized within the frameworks for understanding power and technology that currently exist in international relations. By merging these two conceptual fields, it becomes apparent that international relations literature is dominated by paradigms that adhere most closely to either instrumentalism or technological determinism and that the introduction of SCOT may provide a theoretical bridge for moving beyond the existing stalemate in the literature.

Existing Frameworks in International Relations

Understanding power in international relations is an ongoing and unresolved academic project. A key shift in recent years has seen scholars more comprehensively explore the social aspects of power as opposed to the previously dominant theoretical view that regarded power more narrowly defined as material. In part, this shift has been necessitated by key systemic changes within the international system as a consequence of globalization and the conclusion of the Cold War. Recent developments in information and communications technology have played an important role; however, the relationship between power and new technologies remains under-theorized.

The following section of this chapter will demonstrate that ideas about power have changed over time but understandings of its relationship with technology have remained remarkably stable despite the recent introduction of very different technology. This would pose no problem if the theory retained its explanatory capability; however, there are compelling reasons to argue that it does not. The first section, entitled "The Industrial Age: Technology and National Power" brings together realist notions of power and an instrumental approach to technology which (largely) dominated international relations literature from World War II to the late 1980s and (for some) the early 1990s. As noted earlier, a key characteristic of instrumentalism is a view of technology as a morally neutral means to an end. This approach dovetails with political ideas of the state as morally neutral, compelled to survive in a self-help system by any means necessary. The second section entitled "The Information Age: Technology and Social Power" brings together the changes in approaches to power that have emerged largely since the conclusion of the Cold War, with the information revolution. Much of the literature in this section is characterized by a technologically determinist view which (often owing to insufficient technical knowledge) tends to regard new technologies as value-laden and autonomous. This view aligns more comfortably with ideas about American power that emphasize moral responsibility not only to its constituents, but to a broader global community as well.

Through a discussion of the dominant frameworks extant within international relations literature, this section will elucidate the problems with each view, thereby justifying the adoption of a new framework for examining these issues. Essentially, these two competing frameworks arrive at a stalemate based on an unquantifiable question. Does new technology enhance state power more than it undermines it? This project argues that it does both and, therefore, it would be more useful to ask some different and more enlightening questions. Those questions include *how do states influence the emergence and management of new technologies to address their national interest? How does technology itself influence perceptions about state power? What role do ideas play in the political shaping of social technology?* These questions cannot be asked or answered within the two paradigms that currently dominate international relations theory. The first does not engage with technology as a social construct and the second does not fully account for the political influence and shaping of technology. A social construction of technology methodology that focuses on these very issues will consequently prove more useful.

The Industrial Age: Technology and National Power

> The healthy functioning of cyberspace is essential to our economy and our national security. (Bush 2003: 1)

For much of the twentieth century, scholars of international relations have approached the relationship between power and technology in a relatively stable and consistent manner.[2] Through the dominant lens of realist theory that views the state as a self-interested, power-maximizing unit in an anarchical system, technology has been regarded as a constitutive element of state power. Its military and economic relevance has made technology a mechanism through which power- (or security-) seeking states pursue relative advantage by the development of more efficient production methods (economic power) as well as advanced weaponry (military power) (Morgenthau 1978: 322). Having explained something of the philosophy of technology and instrumentalism, it is possible now to explain how that scholarship intersects with realist power theory to produce what is referred to here as the "nation-state" approach to the relationship between power and technology in international relations.

Realist power theory argues that power must be narrowly perceived as material capabilities owing to their relative importance in determining the outcome of conflict and also their quantifiable nature. The realist adherence to this view of power coupled with neo-realism's emphasis on system structure underpinned the importance of technology, as (despite the acknowledgement of other factors) material capabilities continued to be viewed as the most important and decisive element in ordering the system structure. Indeed, the twentieth century witnessed a growing emphasis on technology as material capability while other more conventional resources such as population and

2 Within realist thought, there is a range of views on how power should be defined, i.e. whether as a means to an end or an end in itself. This chapter will not provide a comprehensive catalog of variations in realist approaches to power. It is concerned here only with understandings of the relationship between technology and power in international relations and as such is proposing two broad conceptual approaches—the first of which—the nation-state power view, is most closely associated with a broadly realist approach.

territory came to be regarded by some as diminishing in relevance. Employing a Fordist approach, Alastair Buchan wrote of the decline of territory and population as a form of power with emphasis instead placed on states' technical and scientific base. In his view, "power, influence, or prestige can now be increased by the better organization of existing domestic resources and the application of science and technology to them" (Buchan 1972: 177).

A material view of power sits comfortably with an instrumental view of technology—indeed, they complement one another. The combination of an instrumental view of technology as a value-free tool employed to achieve the ends of a state with only one moral objective, survival, results in the "nation-state" approach to the relationship between power and technology. In this framework, technology is a mechanism to enhance state power and thereby has implications for world order.

Despite more recent theoretical and empirical challenges, the nation-state view continues to resonate in contemporary international affairs as states persistently attach a high value to advanced technology as it relates to state power. By continuing to regard ICT as an artifact like other forms of industrial technology, the vulnerabilities that come hand in hand with the rapid integration of ICT into contemporary state affairs are surmountable. States simply need more—more ICT capabilities, more rapid advances in the development of these technologies, and more doctrine for their application. This perspective resonates with the instrumental approach that regards technology as morally neutral and able to address negative social consequences of technology with a "techfix." In this context, militaries the world over are rapidly developing "information warfare" or "cyberwar" capabilities. The U.S. Department of Defense now views information as a "realm, a weapon, and a target of warfare" (Wilson 2006: 1). Information and communication in the nation-state view become commodities to be weaponized in the same way that previous industrial-age technologies were. There is a general sense that ICT is becoming a significant factor in conflicts and that militaries need to adapt and be prepared to project state power throughout this new sphere. Thus dominance in "cyberspace" is equated with dominance in other international commons such as space or sea lanes (Tanji 2007).

However, operationalizing these capabilities in a conventional conflict situation remains difficult. Under both domestic and international law, responding to aggression with reciprocal force over the Internet is highly problematic. The determination of what constitutes the use of force in the context of a cyber attack remains unclear—one of the key problems highlighted in 2007 when Estonia turned unsuccessfully to NATO for help while undergoing a massive cyber attack (Grove et al. 2000). Although ICT has certainly been applied to enhance existing warfare technologies, regarding information and communication technology simply as another commodity fails to acknowledge its distinct nature and the complexities of operationalizing it in the context of state to state conflict.

While a material view of power and technology may have been useful in understanding the dynamics at work in conventional conflicts, ICT lends itself to unconventional conflict characterized by anonymity, geographical dislocation, low-ranking actors on a par with states and the interdependence of industrialized states on a vulnerable global network. Just as nuclear technology prompted a shift from wars of destruction to a strategy of deterrence, ICT is being understood more clearly as a technology of "disruption" (Demchak 2003; Shimeall et al. 2001). The impact of disruption is at the heart of a key paradox of ICT—states that have been most successful in adopting new information age technologies are also most vulnerable to disruption (Christensen 1999; Markoff 1991). This is the central power/technology paradox that the nation-state approach is unable to address.

While new technologies have certainly had a positive impact on existing industries and security, the theoretical challenge to international relations has been the emergence of fundamentally social rather than industrial technologies. Unlike the early part of the twentieth century, which was characterized by a strong realist practice and fundamentally industrial technology, the latter decades saw a growth in a theoretical reassessment of power coupled with the emergence of revolutionary social technology. The relationship between social technology and concepts of political institutions like power and sovereignty appear to be distinct from those of industrial technology. Not surprisingly, theories predominantly concerned with material power have not easily synthesized emerging social technology. To date, more ideationally inclined theoretical frameworks have generally been used to examine the relationship between new technology and power, and it is to these that this chapter turns next.

The Information Age: Technology and Social Power

> The realpolitik of the new era is cyberpolitik, in which the actors are no longer just states, and raw power can be countered or fortified by information power. (Rothkopf 1998: 326)

From the beginning of the 1990s, applications for ICT expanded exponentially. Simon Rogerson and Terrell Ward Bynum (1995) describe computer technology as "the most powerful and most flexible technology ever devised." Access to the Internet rapidly moved from a small band of academic and military clients in the mid 1980s into the public domain. In a very short space of time, ICT has become ubiquitous in advanced industrial states and integral to the delivery of essential public services, including national security. Newly industrialized and industrializing states regard ICT as a mechanism to "leapfrog" generations of technological development and move more quickly towards modernization and competitiveness in the international system. In addition to the innumerable applications of ICT to enhance essentially industrial technology, the social aspect of ICT has impacted significantly on civil, economic, and political relations. Coinciding with the advent of social technology was a theoretical shift in international relations scholarship to considering issues of power as socially constituted rather than primarily material.

The combination of these factors contributed to the emergence of the second dominant paradigm for understanding the relationship between power and technology in international relations—referred to here as the "information-age" approach. This approach encompasses many of the theoretical shifts that have arisen to challenge realism, material power, and the immutability of the state. In addition, it often exhibits a determinist approach to technology—one that regards technology as imbued with values (democratization, freedom of speech, and transparency of government, or conversely, invasive surveillance and lack of personal privacy). It generally regards the Internet as anarchical, user-driven, and beyond the dominance of the state. Essentially, this is a view characterized by change and re-evaluation of power in which ICT more broadly is frequently cited as a catalyst or even the driving force for those changes. This view engages with new technology and generally regards it as breaking down old power structures by redefining both the players and the playing field of international relations. However, it often does so without engaging adequately with technical issues, leading to utopian or dystopian readings—dependent largely upon the perception of which values, positive or negative, reside in Internet technology.

Two broad questions have preoccupied the academic debate addressing these issues. Scholars have worked to understand, first, how technological change has impacted on power relations between individuals and the state (or the idea of the state; Drezner and Farrell 2004; Slaughter 2004; Smith and Naim 2000), and second, what implications those changes have for conceptual approaches to state power (Aronson 2002; Hachigian 2002; Nye 2002). Many studies have concentrated on the manner in which social technology has impacted on state power by eroding or undermining the institution of sovereignty. The general emphasis in these debates is that social technology is dissipating power from the state in a variety of ways. Prominent among these is the proliferation and organization of nonstate actors that compete for power with states and the challenges of state control over extra-territorial issues which stem from interconnected networked systems (Castells 2000; Langman 2005).

A dominant concern for theorists of social power is legitimacy (Lebow 2005). Through an analysis of the U.S. neo-conservative approach to power, Christian Reus-Smit (2004) concludes that social capital is an integral element of political power and effective influence relies on social legitimation. Although a social view of power can be understood independently of technology—either old or new—social technology has significant relevance for issues of legitimacy, "soft power" and other social aspects of power in international relations. A 24-hour news cycle, unrestricted access to satellite footage, and the rapid dissemination of information and images have intensified awareness of state behavior and made it much more difficult for states to conceal events detrimental to their international standing. As demonstrated by the mobile phone generated images of torture inside Abu Ghraib and the Wikileaks release of diplomatic cables, states have difficulty escaping surveillance even in the most remote and guarded situations. Thus, intersubjective relations between states are heightened by social technology and outcomes are difficult to subvert to capabilities in this context.

For these scholars, changing ideas about power and emerging technology combine to bring about a substantially changed system, transforming from one comprising simply states to one comprising multiple and diverse actors (Nye 2002: 60). In this new system, states are relinquishing or losing control with obvious implications for the relationship between technology and power.

While these studies make a significant contribution, they do contain impediments to a richer understanding of how new technology interacts with power. In explicating the manner in which state power is undermined by new technology, this literature frequently fails to make informed distinctions between aspects of the technology that are the consequence of state decisions, and those that are beyond the immediate control of states. Of particular relevance here is Donald MacKenzie and Judy Wajcman's observation that technological determinism "focuses our minds on how to *adapt* to technological change, not on how to *shape* it. It removes a vital aspect of how we live from the sphere of public discussion, choice and politics" (MacKenzie and Wajcman 1999: 5). This leads to a focus on "adaptation" that has been a dominant feature in recent work attempting to understand political change in the context of the Internet. Although there are some intractable technical issues that pose real challenges to state power, there are no natural or scientific laws that make it imperative that the Internet function in the way it does. By failing to make accurate distinctions between what states choose and what they have imposed upon them, this "information age" view relies upon a technologically determinist approach.

Both the industrial age approach and the information age approach are able to contribute to understanding of the relationship of ICT to power in international relations. However, although technology infrastructure and the use of ICT applications to enhance industrial power are significant, the complexities of state responses to social technologies such as the Internet necessitate a broader approach which moves beyond twentieth-century conceptualizations of power in the international system. A social view, which places the role of information, culture, identity and knowledge at the center of its analysis, is able to engage with the more complex and compelling issues. Despite this better conceptual fit, the polarizing debates within this literature about whether ICT enhances or diminishes state power coupled with the prevalence of a technologically determinist approach also place limits on theoretical development.

The Social Construction of Technology

Having introduced the basic premise of the social construction of technology (SCOT) in the first part of this chapter and having demonstrated that existing approaches to the relationship between technology and power in international relations literature are failing to accommodate new social technologies like the Internet, the next part of this chapter will explain in some detail how a SCOT methodology can be applied to the study of the relationship between power and technology in international relations.

The social construction of technology is fundamentally about looking beyond the impact of a particular technology on society in order to understand how society itself shaped the evolution and adoption of that technology. The following four concepts are essential to understanding and employing a social construction of technology methodology and they also provide a means of conveying how this methodology can be implemented in a study such as this one.

"*Interpretive flexibility*" refers to the understanding that there were *alternatives* to the design of a particular technology (Pinch and Bijker 1989: 40). In other words, there was no natural law or predetermined outcome for a technological development. Rather, the manner in which it was perceived and responded to played a role in shaping it. Interpretive flexibility is linked to priorities and allows for an analysis of how changes to priorities may influence both how technology is interpreted and how it continues to evolve in a design sense.

In the context of Internet technology as it relates to ideas about U.S. power, interpretive flexibility is a key concept in understanding how changing political circumstances have impacted upon the technological evolution of the Internet. Over the course of its development, there have been a number of unintended consequences—both positive and negative—of Internet technology. Questions about how these second- and third-order consequences have been perceived politically leads to insight into values and priorities held externally to the technology itself—values and priorities that interact with technology but are not a direct product of it.

A second key concept is that of "*closure*." Pinch and Bijker define closure in technology as "the stabilization of an artefact and the 'disappearance' of problems" (Pinch and Bijker 1989: 44). In other words, it is not necessary to "solve" problems—rather closure relies on key social groups regarding the technology as stabilized. A particular technology, then, may achieve closure through social rather than technological means by redefining the problem or through the transfer of power to a social group that disregards that problem. Closure is a social construct and is a significant factor in understanding the relationship between technology and the human condition.

Understanding how U.S. politicians regard the resolution of a range of "problems" with the Internet is essential to an analysis of its relationship to U.S. power. In a SCOT approach, problems with the Internet exist only if the relevant social actor believes they do. Some problems may be tolerated because of the advantages they provide or because immediate solutions would transgress other firmly held beliefs or values. This is illustrated by the range of state approaches to censorship on the Internet—something that is regarded as inappropriate in the U.S. where values of freedom of speech and access to information are highly valued social norms. Other problems arising from the Internet may pose difficulties for some actors but not others. For example, credit card transactions over the Internet favor banks over vendors but collective apprehension about the (in)security of banks reinforces that problem. Finally, closure can be achieved by *redefining* the problem—an approach that proves relevant in an examination of changing American strategic priorities and views of power.

A third SCOT concept of relevance to this study is the "*reverse salient*." Thomas Hughes (1989: 73) defines a reverse salient as "components in the system which have fallen behind." They create lag and are often considered points of weakness that must be addressed before the system as a whole can effectively develop. Reverse salients are of particular significance to a large technical system like the Internet, and Hughes suggests that they can often be points of innovation. However, when reverse salients cannot be corrected within an existing system, they can lead to the evolution of a competing system (Hughes 1989: 75). This concept underlines the notion that systems are not pre-determined to either success or survival.

Reverse salients are important to this study because they can help to identify issues that are understood to impact negatively upon U.S. power and help explain responses to those perceived weaknesses. This will lead to questions in the study about how U.S. politicians understood reverse salients in the context of Internet technology and how those perceived reverse salients translated into policy and legislative responses. There is nothing naturally definable about reverse salients. Rather, they are a product of priorities and perceived goals and, as such, they can reveal much about the views of the social group—far beyond the technology to which they relate.

One final concept, which will be integral to the methodology of this chapter, is that of the "*relevant social group*." SCOT deals with the subjective and as such it is necessary to be clear about the source of subjectivity. Some SCOT studies focus predominantly on this issue—seeking to ascertain who exactly the relevant social group is and how it influences and shapes technology. In some cases, the relevant social group is found to be other than that which was expected or anticipated, in which case this variable leads to insightful findings.

However, in this study the relevant social group has already been defined as U.S. political decision-makers. While the study acknowledges that there are wide ranges of social groups who have influenced and shaped the Internet in profound and important ways, this particular social group is considered here to be both highly relevant and under-researched. In studies of the Internet there is a tendency to define the relevant social group as the broader community, the commercial sector, or the technical community (which is generally understood to privilege the best interests of the other two groups). This project is an attempt to bring the state back in to these debates. In order to research the manner in which ideas about U.S. power influence Internet technology, this study will focus on those ideas that emanate from the state apparatus through policy documents, key speeches, and legislature.

In an attempt to move beyond the previously articulated competing paradigms, this project proposes a deeper engagement with the *relationship* between new technology and power. Rather than assess these issues exclusively through a determination of the positive or negative effects of technology, this study asserts that the Internet both enhances and undermines state power in complex and important ways. The SCOT concepts discussed above generate a set of questions that move beyond the conceptual and empirical stalemate of whether ICT enhances state power more than it undermines it or vice versa. Asserting that there is nothing determined or fixed about either of these outcomes, it moves on to more enlightening questions about how political ideas and technology interact.

Criticisms of SCOT include the assertion that it reduces technology to simply another form of cultural expression, along with art and literature. Also, as Vig points out, the "chain of causation between social context and technology is difficult to establish" (Vig 1988: 16). However, the first criticism is only an issue for those studies that are primarily concerned with the development of technology. This study is not compromised by an understanding of technology as a form of cultural expression—indeed, such a reading is fundamental to the conceptual framework here. Second, causation *is* difficult to establish but this study does not assert that ideas of power *caused* the Internet to develop in the way it has. Rather, it seeks to better understand the *relationship* between ideas of U.S. power and Internet technology in an intersubjective manner. Ultimately, this project takes the position that a meaningful understanding of technology cannot be achieved in abstraction from its human context.

The empirical research for this project is underway through the following case studies. Each of these periods brought with it a range of technical and political factors that interacted to shape Internet technology and these are currently being examined using a SCOT methodology.

Case Study One—Developing it: TCP/IP and the Expansion of the Internet (1960s to early 1980s)

Established in 1958 in response to the Soviet launch of Sputnik, Advanced Research Projects Agency (ARPA) was charged with ensuring that the U.S. maintained a leading role in the application of state-of-the-art technology to military capability. With a view to connecting large computer systems in order to maximize their capabilities, ARPA began to fund and support work on networking protocols, both from within its own research institute and through funded association with key computer scientists working in academia. As work progressed, more specific applications were conceptualized, including the establishment of a secure communications system necessary to enhance the second-strike capability of the U.S. in the event of nuclear attack. Although there were alternatives (Clark 1988), the technology adopted in response to ARPA's requirements was the "transmission control protocol/Internet protocol"—or TCP/IP—the foundational technology of the Internet developed by Vinton Cerf and Robert Kahn.

Superficially, the development and implementation of TCP/IP technology to address ARPA's priority of providing a more robust communications system can be understood within the paradigm of nation-state power. However, throughout this design phase, security of the network and accountability appear to have been low priorities—possibly owing to the fact that access was restricted to defense, science and academia. TCP/IP was conceptualized from the beginning as an open and flexible architecture that ultimately provides a rich environment for both innovation and exploitation. Given that the code prioritizes redundancy and flexibility over security and accountability, how did ARPA and U.S. policy-makers conceptualize the impact on American power of making the Internet globally available? How did ideas and expectations about the future direction of American power coalesce with the Internet transforming from a communication system designed to protect and enhance U.S. military capability to a global system open to the ideas, innovations, and requirements of a broader community?

Case Study Two—Expanding it: Commercializing the Web (mid 1980s to late 1990s)

The second research phase for this project covers the mid 1980s to the end of 1990s. During this period, the Internet was commercialized and became widely accessible. Initially distinguished by the rapid growth in email traffic, the defining technological development of this phase was arguably the emergence of HyperText Transfer Protocol (HTTP) and HyperText Markup Language (HTML) and their application to the development of the World Wide Web, largely credited to British physicist Tim Berners-Lee. The subsequent commercialization of web browsers that provided a user-friendly graphical interface was instrumental in the widespread take-up of Internet technology. This period covers the "dot-com" economic boom and bust, transformation of news media, and developing notions of the democratizing potential of the Internet. The rapid escalation in use of the Internet during these years brought the U.S. face-to-face with difficult decisions about whether or how to loosen their grip on controlling factors such as the assignment of names and numbers, the development of a legal framework that balanced freedom of speech and privacy of the individual with national security issues, the encryption debate, and how to manage the global spread of the physical infrastructure of the Internet.

The political context for these decisions was distinct from that of the first phase discussed previously. With the Cold War over, small government was in vogue and economic power was coming to be regarded as an increasingly significant aspect of foreign policy strength. President George H. Bush's foreign policy doctrine was premised on a "new world order" that projected a period of peace and stability founded upon the predominance of liberalism, free markets, and the rule of international law. The Clinton administration followed up by emphasizing American global economic leadership based on free markets and projection of an enlargement policy that promoted democratization and human rights. The dominant political paradigm of liberalism, free market force, and minimizing government provided an ideological platform for U.S. decisions to disallow any state-led governance structure for controlling the Internet during this critical period of growth. Former vice-president Al Gore was a key political force during this period, introducing the High Performance Computing and Communication Act of 1991 while still a senator during the Bush Administration. The passing of this bill had a number of important effects on the development of Internet technology including the funding of the first commercial web browser, Mosaic, and the establishment of the National Information Infrastructure. Significantly, the National Information Infrastructure was legislative acknowledgment of a view that would become increasingly important in emerging ideas of state power and its relationship to new technology—the notion of information as a form of state power.

These views largely resonated with prevailing ideas of U.S. power. The emphasis on less government left the Internet to govern itself; market forces would ultimately prevail and result in a healthy and stable system; the Internet could have a democratizing effect similar to economic factors; and the positive economic impact of the IT boom reinforced the mutual and symbiotic benefit of this approach. However, the problems of security and accountability across the network were both increasingly apparent and intractable. The economic bubble was about to burst, and state-to-state conflict was about to be overtaken by wars of asymmetry and disruption. How had the decisions taken during this stage prepared the U.S. for the problems to emerge in the new millennium? To what extent were ideas about the relationship between U.S. power and new technology dependent upon the positive outcomes of the 1980s and 1990s? How were these ideas challenged, reinforced and/or amended during the years to follow? And how would changing ideas about American power influence the way Internet technologies further developed, especially in terms of geopolitical security issues and international codes of conduct?

Case Study Three—Controlling it: The Changing Role of the ISP (the Previous Decade)

The third period covered in this study looks at changes to ideas about U.S. power and technology since 2001. The foreign policy doctrine of George W. Bush was initially conceived in terms of a selective and discriminate national interest to be pursued through enhanced military capability. This doctrine was comprehensively articulated in a *Foreign Affairs* journal article written by U.S. Secretary of State, Condoleezza Rice (2000) and by U.S. Secretary for Defense, Donald Rumsfeld in the 2001 *Quadrennial Defense Review Report* (2001). However, post-911 this was significantly reworked with the new strategic framework fundamentally based upon a more expansive view of the American national interest that now faced a range of emergent globalized threats less responsive to conventional military power (Jervis 2003; Rumsfeld 2006). Changing conceptions of conflict, the role of nonstate actors, the doctrine of pre-emption, high-tech versus low-tech, asymmetry, and the erosion of some aspects of geopolitics have all come to the fore in this phase. Changing ideas about U.S. power have had significant implications for changing conceptions of the Internet—from a system largely driven by fundamental tenets of economics and democracy to one more focused on the vulnerabilities of misuse and disruption.

In the political context of the "war on terror" that subverts conventional sources of power and elevates social power, the Internet takes on new meaning. The rapid migration of information systems connected to the Internet during the course of the late 1980s and 1990s made Internet commentator John Perry Barlow's insistence that "you of the past leave us alone" (1996) less tenable now that 1.5 billion people or 23.5% of the world's population were online—as well as 85% of critical infrastructure of the U.S. (Deloitte Touche Tohmatsu 2004; *Internet World Stats* 2008). Some of the previously acknowledged vulnerabilities of the Internet have enhanced relevance in an era marked by unconventional threats from determined individuals. The growing realization that universal software platforms like Microsoft Windows and the Office suite are highly vulnerable—particularly when coupled with the open architecture of the Internet—highlighted a range of possible threats to the state (Geer et al. 2003). The cross jurisdictional nature of cyber-crime that may be committed from a state with laws divergent from the state in which the crime actually occurs, greatly complicates the exercise of power (Krebs 2007). Certainly, one of the distinguishing features of the Internet is that it remains difficult to moderate behavior through conventional institutions and regimes such as state or international law. Given that some unintended or unanticipated consequences arise from the adoption and implementation of new technology, how has the U.S. responded and how have changing ideas about U.S. power influenced this phase of Internet development?

In some ways, the original military approach to the Internet that drove development in the 1960s and 1970s has risen again to prominence during this period. The Department of Defense has increasingly focused on cyberwar or infowar strategies and doctrine, largely through a dedicated unit within the Air Force, which now regards domination of airspace to include cyberspace. A U.S. congressional report published in 2006 notes, however, that reciprocating against a cyber attack might lead to "possible accusations of war crimes if offensive military cyber-weapons severely disrupt critical civilian computer systems, or the systems of other non-combatant nations." The report concludes that the U.S. Department of Defense believes that it lacks "sufficient policy and legal analysis for guiding appropriate responses to intrusions or attacks on DoD networks" (Wilson 2006: 5). Increasingly, the U.S. faces a "strategic paradox" whereby it is forced to balance the often contradictory computer security requirements of its economy with military strategies that increasingly involve the capacity to disrupt the infrastructures of rival nations (Rathmell 2003). Additionally, cyber-espionage has become a significant issue, with many allegations directed against China—arguably America's key strategic challenger. With the expected democratizing effect of the Internet still to eventuate, the U.S. has instead focused attention on China's use of the Internet as a weapon and as a tool of suppression—notably the U.S. Congressional hearing on Yahoo over the divulgence of the contact details of a Chinese journalist charged with revealing state secrets (Kahn 2005; Marquand 2005). This takes place in the context not of the closed system of ARPAnet, but rather in a globally accessible and open network that necessitates a modified approach to that employed during the 1960s and 1970s.

Changing ideas about American power impact on conceptions of the Internet and, in this phase, the disruptive capacity of the technology has increased resonance, leading to a "re-militarized" view of the Internet. This re-conceptualization allows for a range of policy discussions that would have been difficult during the previous phase, including those surrounding the need to rebalance the security/privacy aspect of the Internet (Mueller 2007; Singel 2008). It also leads to a paradox. How does the U.S. reconcile a re-militarized approach to the Internet with suggestions that Internet challenges are not particularly responsive to military power? How has the re-conceptualization of U.S. power influenced the progressive development of Internet technology since 2001? How has the U.S. sought to minimize Internet vulnerabilities in the context of an expanded view of the U.S. national interest? How has the national security community responded to and influenced changing perceptions about the Internet? Finally, what future consequences for state power does the U.S. anticipate in relation to the Internet?

Conclusion

In summary, then, this chapter proposes that a more engaged and conscious approach to technology needs to be integrated with international relations theories of power in order to better understand the relationship between power and technology. In attempting to move beyond the debate in international relations about whether new technology like the Internet enhances state power more than it undermines it, the philosophy of technology provides a conceptual framework for better understanding the intricacies of the relationship between the political and technological realms. Specifically, the social construction of technology allows for the analysis of the ways in which states seek to shape and influence emerging technology and also the manner in which changing technology can impact on political ideas. This leads away from a simple quantitative equation to a more complex reading of how political processes are affected by and also impact upon the evolution and implementation of new technology like the Internet. Ignoring this complexity can lead to an over-simplification of important issues and questions. Asking and answering these questions is essential to the development of theories equipped to deal with the relationship between power and technology in the information age.

References

Aronson, J. 2002. Global networks and their impact. In *Information Technologies and Global Politics: The Changing Scope of Power and Governance*, edited by J.N. Rosenau and J.P. Singh. Albany, NY: State University of New York Press, 39–62.

Barlow, J.P. 1996. *A Declaration of the Independence of Cyberspace* [online]. Available at: http://homes.eff.org/~barlow/Declaration-Final.html [accessed: 1 August 2011].

Buchan, A. 1972. Technology and World Politics. In *The Aberystwyth Papers—International Politics: 1919–1969*. London: Oxford University Press.

Bush, President G.W. 2003. *National Strategy to Secure Cyberspace*. Washington, DC: USGPO.

Castells, M. 2000. Toward a Sociology of the Network Society. *Contemporary Sociology*, 29(5), 693–9.

Christensen, J. 1999. Bracing for Guerrilla Warfare in Cyberspace. *CNN Interactive*, 6 April. Available at: http://edition.cnn.com/TECH/specials/hackers/cyberterror/ [accessed: 1 August 2011].

Clark, D.D. 1988. The Design Philosophy of the DARPA Internet Protocols. *Computer Communication Review*, 18(4), 106–14.

Deloitte Touche Tohmatsu. 2004. *2004 Global Security Survey*. Available at: http://www.deloitte.com/dtt/cda/doc/content/GFSISE.pdf [accessed: 1 August 2011].

Demchak, C.C. 2003. Wars of Disruption: International Competition and Information Technology-driven Military Organizations. *Contemporary Security Policy*, 24(1), 75–112.

Drezner, D.W. and Farrell, H. 2004. Web of Influence. *Foreign Policy*, 145, 32–40.

Eriksson, J. and Giacomello, G. 2006. The Information Revolution, Security and International Relations: (Ir)relevant Theory? *International Political Science Review*, 27(3), 221–44.

Geer, D., Bace, R., Gutman, P., Metzger, P., Pfleeger, C.P., Quarterman, J.S. and Schneier, B. 2003. Cyber*In*Security: The Cost of Monopoly, How the Dominance of Microsoft's Products Poses a Risk to Security. Published by the Computer and Communications Industry Association, 24 September. Available at: http://cryptome.org/cyberinsecurity.htm [accessed: 1 August 2011].

Grove, G.D., Goodman, S.E. and Lukasik, S.J. 2000. Cyber-attacks and International Law. *Survival*, 42(3), 89–103.

Hachigian, N. 2002. The Internet and Power in One-party East Asian States. *The Washington Quarterly*, 25(3), 41–58.

Hughes, T.P. 1989. The Evolution of Large Technological Systems. In *The Social Construction of Technological Systems: New Directions in the Sociology and History of Technology*, edited by T.E. Pinch and W.E. Bijker. Cambridge, MA: MIT Press, 51–82.

Internet World Stats, December 2008. Available at: http://www.Internetworldstats.com/stats.htm [accessed: 1 August 2011].

Jervis, R. 2003. Understanding the Bush Doctrine. *Political Science Quarterly*, 118(3), 365–88.

Kahn, J. 2005. Yahoo Helped Chinese to Prosecute Journalist. *New York Times*, 8 September. Available at: http://www.nytimes.com/2005/09/07/business/worldbusiness/07iht-yahoo.html [accessed: 1 August 2011].

Krebs, B. 2007. Shadowy Russian Firm seen as Conduit for Cybercrime. *The Washington Post*, 13 October. Available at: http://www.washingtonpost.com/wp-dyn/content/article/2007/10/12/AR2007101202461.html [accessed: 1 August 2011].

Langman, L. 2005. From Virtual Public Spheres to Global Justice: A Critical Theory of Internetworked Social Movements. *Sociological Theory*, 23(1), 42–74.

Lebow, R.N. 2005. Power, Persuasion and Justice. *Millennium: Journal of International Studies*, 33(3), 551–82.

MacKenzie, D. and Wajcman, J. 1999. *The Social Shaping of Technology*. Philadelphia, PA: Open University Press.

Markoff, J. 1991. Dutch Computer Rogues Infiltrate American Systems with Impunity. *The New York Times*, 21 April. Available at: http://www.nytimes.com/1991/04/21/us/dutch-computer-rogues-infiltrate-american-systems-with-impunity.html?src=pm [accessed: 1 August 2011].

Marquand, R. 2005. Yahoo, Chinese Police, and a Jailed Journalist. *The Christian Science Monitor*, 9 September. Available at: http://www.csmonitor.com/2005/0909/p01s03-woap.html [accessed: 1 August 2011].

Mayer-Schöenberger, V. and Brodnig, G. 2007. *Information Power: International Affairs in the Cyber Age*. John F. Kennedy School of Government Harvard University Faculty Research Working Papers Series. Available at: http://papers.ssrn.com/sol3/papers.cfm?abstract_id=292949 [accessed: 1 August 2011].

Morgenthau, H. 1978. *Politics Among Nations: The Struggle for Power and Peace*, 5th edn revised. New York: Alfred A. Knopf.

Mueller, R.S. 2007. Director Federal Bureau of Investigation, Speech to Penn State College, Pennsylvania, 6 November. Available at: www.fbi.gov/pressrel/speeches/mueller110607.htm [accessed: 1 August 2011].

Mumford, L. 1967. *Techniques and Human Development*. New York: Harcourt.

Nye, J.S. 2002. *The Paradox of American Power: Why the World's Only Superpower Can't Go It Alone*. Oxford: Oxford University Press.

Pinch, T.E. and Bijker, W.E. 1989. *The Social Construction of Technological Systems: New Directions in the Sociology and History of Technology*. Cambridge, MA: MIT Press.

Rathmell, A. 2003. Controlling Computer Network Operations. *Studies in Conflict and Terrorism*, 26, 215–32.

Reus-Smit, C. 2004. *American Power and World Order*. Cambridge, MA: Polity Press.

Rice, C. 2000. Campaign 2000: Promoting the National Interest. *Foreign Affairs*, 79(1), 45–62.

Rogerson, S. and Bynum, T.W. 1995. Cyberspace: The Ethical Frontier. *Times Higher Education Supplement*, 9 June.

Rosenau, J.N. and Singh, J.P. 2002. *Information Technologies and Global Politics: The Changing Scope of Power and Governance*. Albany, NY: State University of New York Press.

Rothkopf, D.J. 1998. Cyberpolitik: The Changing Nature of Power in the Information Age. *Journal of International Affairs*, 51(2), 325–59.

Rumsfeld, D.H. 2001. *2001 Quadrennial Defense Review Report*. Washington, DC: U.S. Department of Defense, 30 September.

Rumsfeld, D.H. 2006. *2006 Quadrennial Defense Review Report*. Washington, DC: U.S. Department of Defense, 30 September.

Shimeall, T., Williams, P. and Dunlevy, C. 2001. Countering Cyber War. *NATO Review*, 49(4), 16–18.

Singel, R. 2008. NSA must Examine all Internet Traffic to Prevent Cyber Nine-eleven, Top Spy Says. *Wired Magazine*, 15 January. Available at: http://www.wired.com/threatlevel/2008/01/feds-must-exami/ [accessed: 1 August 2011].

Slaughter, A.M. 2004. *A New World Order*. Princeton, NJ: Princeton University Press.

Smith, G. and Naim, M. 2000. *Altered States: Globalization, Sovereignty and Governance*. Ottawa: International Development Research Centre.

Tanji, M. 2007. Buccaneer.com: Infosec Privateering as a Solution to Cyberspace Threats. *Journal of Cyber Conflict Studies*, 1(1), 4–10.

Vig, N. 1988. Technology, Philosophy and the State. In *Technology and Politics*, edited by M.E. Kraft and N.J. Vig. Durham, NC: Duke University Press, 8–32.

Weiss, C. 2005. Science, Technology and International Relations. *Technology in Society*, 27(3), 295–313.

Wilson, C. 2006. *Information Operations and Cyberwar: Capabilities and Related Policy Issues*. Washington, DC: Congressional Research Service, 14 September.

Chapter 12

U.S. Identity, Security, and Governance of the Internet

Ryan Kiggins

In 1997, the U.S. government claimed ownership of the root file database and the domain name system (DNS) on which the functioning of the Internet depends. In short, no root file or domain names, no Internet. This claim of ownership by the U.S. government was incompatible with alternative visions of Internet governance championed by other Internet stakeholders including nation-states, international intergovernmental organizations, nongovernmental organizations, corporations, and global civil society activists. Some of these stakeholders called for free, inclusive, collaborative, and global ownership and management of the root file database (root) and the DNS.

Others called for an Internet governance regime that took their commercial and intellectual property interests into account. Calls for alternative normative visions continue despite the formation of the U.S. backed Internet Corporation for Assigned Names and Numbers (ICANN) that serves as the current Internet governance regime. The U.S. government supported the formation of ICANN in order to secure the Internet within the current liberal economic and political order. Proponents of alternative normative visions viewed the U.S. government claim of root and DNS ownership as unfettered and unwelcome hegemony. How to structure Internet governance was and continues to be a controversial global issue.

Conceptually, an Internet governance regime can be structured in a number of ways to accord with alternative political, economic, or social visions so long as the root and DNS are efficiently managed. Why did the U.S. government promote the Internet as a new global market in which to expand commercially instead of as a global community for communications and information exchange? I will argue that U.S. government identity, anchored in the ideas of freedom and expansion held by U.S. policy-makers, precluded any alternative to the Internet as a platform for commercial and political expansion from emerging as a viable Internet governance solution. The U.S. acted to incorporate and secure the Internet into market-oriented normative and legal frameworks in a way that reflected and reproduced America's self-image as a champion of freedom and a leader of the community of the world's capitalist-democratic nations. The relative success of the U.S. in shaping the Internet as a commercial medium means that the Internet is free in the predominant sense in which "freedom" is discursively constructed by U.S. policy-makers; it is not "free" in the more radical sense implicitly associated with the term by champions of the global community vision of the Internet, which predominates in the extant literature on the subject.

In order to fully explain U.S. identity towards Internet governance one must excavate the concretized discourse within the U.S. government security policy-making apparatus to uncover how security is intertwined for the U.S. with the issue of Internet governance. I will demonstrate the link between U.S. security identity and Internet governance by examining U.S. national security strategy reviews, policy statements, and U.S. policy-maker statements concerning Internet governance. I will then move to show how U.S. identity towards Internet governance directly shaped the current international regime for governance of the Internet. Broadly speaking, the controversy over Internet governance, "is not 'state intervention or not?' but 'what kind of state intervention?' And this is true politics: the struggle to define the conditions that govern our lives" (Zizek 2008; also see Finnemore 1996; Hall 2003; Mattern 2005; Neumann 1999; Wendt 1999; Weldes 1999). By examining U.S. identity towards Internet governance, the question concerning who controls the Internet can be re-conceptualized as a controversy over ontology. More broadly, the controversy over Internet governance reflects the continuous struggle over the meaning of democracy, the structural place of governance, and the role of the state in the information age.

Theory and Method

Constructivist studies of the Internet and politics have focused on the social construction of cyber threats (Dunn-Cavelty 2008; Giacomello 2005; Hansen and Nissenbaum 2009) or focused on the development of Internet policy within their sovereign borders (Franda 2001; Pare 2003). Other studies have argued that the extent to which the global Internet governance regime reflects the interests of great powers (Bach and Newman 2007; Drezner 2004), is an example of state actors forming regimes in order to reduce transaction costs (Keohane and Nye 2001), which represents a new form of regime structure (Farrell 2003; Mathiason 2009), or reflects efforts on the part of states to control the Internet (Lessig 1999, 2004; Mueller 2002). No study has investigated the formation of U.S. Internet governance policy from a constructivist perspective; this study is a first step towards filling that lacuna.

Although I hang my hat on the constructivist hook for the purposes of this study, I nonetheless understand theories of international relations as conceptual lenses, that is, "as expressions of an historically specific understanding of the character and location of political life in general," and "as a crucial site in which attempts to think otherwise about political possibilities are constrained by categories and assumptions that contemporary political analysis is encouraged to take for granted" (Walker 1993: 5). Checkel (1998) argued that constructivism could be seen as a bridge between realist and liberal approaches to international relations. Following in that spirit, my study gestures towards Bach and Newman (2007) and Drezner (2004) by demonstrating the link between the ideas held by policy-makers and the formation of U.S. Internet governance national interest. This study also gestures towards Finnemore (1996), who examined the formation of national interest from a constructivist perspective, arguing that the international organizations help state actors learn what is in their interest. In effect, Finnemore argued that structure shapes the interests of agents but did so while acknowledging the mutual constitutiveness between agent and structure. My study is able to demonstrate how agents shape structures through ideas. I am also able to show how ideas held by U.S. policy-makers concerning the appropriate normative structure for global politics and the global economy were shaped by concerns over the economic performance of the U.S. economy and especially over the relative position of U.S. high-technology companies in the emerging digital economy of the twenty-first century. Foremost on the minds of U.S. policy-makers was spurring job creation for U.S. high-technology workers. Job creation, preserving the relative dominance of U.S. high-technology companies, and positioning the Internet as a platform for the global expansion of commerce and freedom are important cogs in broader U.S. national security policy. Policy-makers within the U.S. government engaged in a well-planned and executed strategy to discursively construct the Internet as the lynchpin for future global and domestic economic growth. Within that discourse, the idea of freedom played the starring role.

Constructivism, in general, treats international relations as a social condition in which actors form and reform ideas and structures of meaning by which actor social practices are shaped. The focus of the approach is the identity of political actors. Beyond this point, there remains much discussion over what precisely comprises a theory of constructivism (Adler 1997; Checkel 1998; Fierke and Jorgensen 2001; Hopf 1998; Onuf 1989; Reus-Smit 2005; Ruggie 1998; Wendt 1999; Zehfuss 2002). I take the core assumption of the constructivist approach to be that, "Constructions of reality reflect, enact, and reify relations of power. In turn, certain agents or groups of agents play a privileged role in the production and reproduction of these realties" (Weldes 1999: 13). If there is a singular contribution to international relations theory by constructivists, it is that ideas matter (Finnemore 1996; Wendt 1999).

The issue for constructivism has been how to investigate identity formation. This has led some constructivists to focus on structure in an attempt to demonstrate how identities are exogenously constructed by the structure in which those identities are embedded (Wendt 1999). In effect, the structural variant of constructivism constructed a dichotomy in which structure was privileged as an explanatory variable over agency. However, discounting the role that agency plays in the processes of identity formation is to commit the error of complex cause. That is, to ascribe causality to one variable when another or multiple variables contribute to the outcome being investigated. Agents are not only influenced by the structures in which they are embedded but also participate in the construction and reconstruction of those very structures and, accordingly, of themselves. Onuf (1989) argues that it is through words and deeds that humans construct their realities. I shift the focus of analysis from structure to agent in this study, utilizing discourse analysis as a method.

Discourse analysis is a recent addition to the toolbox of methods for scholars of international relations. Milliken (1999) offers an excellent review of the method while engaging criticisms. For my purposes at hand, discourse is understood, "as structures of signification which construct social realities. Underlying this … is a constructivist understanding of meaning—things do not mean (the material world does not convey meaning); rather, people construct the meaning of things, using sign systems (predominately, but not exclusively linguistic)" (Milliken 1999: 229). In formulating policy, key decision-makers construct worldviews or ontologies on past experience, memory, and cultural norms. It is through the lens of ontology that framings of meanings are filtered and rendered intelligible. The combination of key decision-maker ontology and framings of meanings are ingredients in the construction and projection of the identity of nation-states. Ontological framings of meaning assist decision-makers in discursively constructing binary oppositions, which define a nation-state in relation to another nation-state and policy direction in relation to other policy directions. Derrida's contribution to discourse theory is that discourses are structured as binary oppositions—us/them, developed/undeveloped, objective/subjective—in which one term is always privileged over the other term (Derrida 1981). It is within binary oppositions that the power relations among subjects can be illuminated, analyzed, and critiqued. Discourse analysis leads the researcher to focus on "subjects authorized to speak and to act" (Milliken 1999: 229).

Authorized subjects within foreign policy discourse include heads of state, department or ministry heads and officials, or NGO and IGO officials. In the case of Internet governance, authorized speakers include Presidents of the United States and their policy advisors. Speakers articulate written and spoken texts that are subjected by the researcher to analysis in order to identify intertextual links between texts, binary oppositions, and reflections, constructions, and reifications of identity. It is through discourse that meanings concerning what practices are legitimate are defined and redefined (Howarth 2000; Milliken 1999). Discourse analysis explores "how, in what forms, and for what reasons social agents come to identify themselves with particular systems of meaning, as well as the constitution, functioning and transformation of systems of discursive practice" (Howarth 2000: 128). The social agent focused on in this study is the U.S. Government. Yet, governments are composed of institutions and the individuals—policy-makers—that occupy positions of authority within those institutions. In what follows I peel back the cover of the U.S. government to illuminate the core idea for U.S. national security policy laying the foundation for the claim that U.S. Internet governance policy is shaped by U.S. national security discourse.

U.S. Security Discourse: Democracy, and Free Market Enterprise

Security has undergone and continues to experience focused conceptual analysis concerning the meaning of the term (Baldwin 1997; Buzan, et al. 1998; Campbell 1998a, 1998b; Dillon 1996; Edkins 2003; Huysmans 1998; Krause and Williams 1997; Lipshutz 1995; Mitzen 2006; McSweeney 1999; Walker 1993; Weldes 1999; Wight 2006; Zehfuss 2002). For my purposes, I shall treat security as an ongoing discourse concerning what we hold to be ethical and what we perceive as threats to what we hold as ethical. The discourse of security offers an explanation of the social construction of identity/difference in which identity is secured against the insecurity represented by difference. In what follows, I describe how U.S. identity is anchored in the idea of freedom and articulated through the discourses of democracy and free market enterprise. I argue that security for the U.S. means constructing global institutions and organizations, and supporting change within other nation-states in the image of the U.S. (Oren 2003).

On 7 April 1950 the National Security Council published NSC 68. This document laid the foundation for U.S. national security policy in the post-War era and represents a reformulation of U.S. national security policy in response to the perceived threat from the Union of Soviet Socialist Republics (U.S.S.R.). The U.S.S.R. was a former World War II ally of the U.S., more a "frenemy" in the sense that both nation-states, while globally championing alternative political and economic arrangements with evangelical zeal, set aside ideological differences to combine against the threat posed to both by Nazi Germany. Once the war ended, the U.S. and the U.S.S.R. squared off in a 40-year struggle over whose ideas would ultimately win out as the basis for politics. NSC 68 anchors U.S. identity in the idea of freedom and appropriates the responsibility to expand "freedom" globally. As part of that responsibility, preserving "freedom" included appropriating the role of global leader of the free world. "By the same token, in relations between nations, the prime reliance of the free society is on the strength and appeal of its idea, and it feels no compulsion sooner or later to bring all societies into conformity with it" (NSC 1950: Section IV-a). In this statement the claim is made that the strength, resilience, and attractiveness of the U.S. resides in the idea of freedom. Indeed the association of the term "freedom" with "society" implies that political and economic institutions and social practices are brought into accord with the idea of freedom. The statement concludes by asserting that the U.S. will endeavor to bring other nation-states into "conformity" with what the U.S. holds to be "freedom." Such an assertion can be interpreted as utilizing any means necessary whether those means are categorized as soft power, economic power, or hard power to achieve the global expansion of freedom.

The strategic imperatives of the U.S. shifted dramatically after the fall of the U.S.S.R. The threat of communism to U.S. identity ceased and the U.S. entered a searching-for-meaning phase because of the lack of an other. The national security strategy text (NSS 1991) represents an attempt to construct the other that a self is dependent upon in order to construct identity for the self. The U.S. begins the document by (re)asserting the need on behalf of the "world" for American leadership and justifies the assertion with the notion that the U.S. is the country that all others turn to when in need. The U.S. constructs "the world" to replace the U.S.S.R. as the other to the U.S. self. However, the self constructs the other as being in need of stewardship, a radical difference between the construction of the U.S.S.R. as a direct menacing threat in NSC 68. In the post-Cold War era, the U.S. constructs the other as having the potential to become as the self.

The recently (at the time) concluded Gulf War to expel Iraq from Kuwait is used as the prime example in support of the claim to world leadership. This "leadership" is to be used to support and extend a free and broadly inclusive global economy that supports "free society." The notion "free society" is where the idea of freedom enters in NSS 1991. It is here, with and through the carryover of the idea of freedom from NSC 68 to NSS 1991, that an intertextual link is stitched between NSC 68 and NSS 1991. Once the U.S. has (re)established the import of the idea of freedom and constructed its identity as the leader and champion of the "free" world, the text moves to develop discursive strategies anchored in the idea of freedom. The discourses of free market enterprise and democracy are forcefully intertwined with the idea of freedom in the NSS 1991 text.

After 40 years of cloaking security of the self in the idea of freedom, U.S. identity has congealed in more concrete terms in the discourse of democracy and the discourse of free market enterprise. The discourses of democracy and free market enterprise actuate the idea of freedom in political and economic practice.

In 1996, 1998, and 2000 the Clinton administration issued national security strategy studies and reports (NSS 1996; NSS 1998; and NSS 2000, respectively) in which the idea of freedom and discourses of democracy and free market enterprise remain the determinants of U.S. identity. It was during this time period that the controversy concerning Internet governance was in full force. Little is mentioned concerning the Internet or information technology beyond the need to secure U.S. information infrastructures against hacking or state-sponsored cyber attack. There is acknowledgment that the global economy of the time was being changed as information was becoming more fungible and accessible globally. Concomitant to this acknowledgement is the claim that the U.S. must make economic changes that reflect the demands of the information age. Yet no specific policy initiatives are given concerning what sort of economic changes are to be undertaken. It is important for my purposes here that in a national security text is articulated the ontological position that the global political economy is changing in consequence of the spread of Internetworking technology. As we will see with later U.S. Internet governance policy texts, this ontological position forms part of the foundation for U.S. identity towards governance of the Internet. The articulation within NSS 1991 of this ontological position also represents an intertextual link between U.S. national security texts and U.S. Internet governance texts such as the Framework for Global Electronic Commerce issued 1 July 1997 by the Clinton Administration (Clinton 1997). This is a crucial point to which I will return in the next section. For now, I return to showing that the identity of the U.S. is constructed and articulated through the issuance of national security texts, that the idea of freedom represents the binding agent among national security texts in the post-World War II era, and that the discourses of democracy and free market enterprise are the concrete articulations of the idea of freedom that serve to structure political practice reflective of U.S. identity.

What remains consistent in NSS 1996, NSS 1998, and NSS 2000 with NSC 68 and NSS 1991 is the idea of freedom, the articulation of the discourses of democracy and free market enterprise, and the claim to global leadership. The following, taken from NSS 1996, is representative of the construction of U.S. identity on the idea of freedom and articulated through the discourses of democracy and free market enterprise to be found in NSS 1996, NSS 1998, and NSS 2000 texts:

> We believe that our goals of enhancing our security, bolstering our economic prosperity and promoting democracy are mutually supportive. Secure nations are more likely to support free trade and maintain democratic structures. Free market nations with growing economies and strong and

> open trade ties are more likely to feel secure and to work toward freedom. And democratic states are less likely to threaten our interests and more likely to cooperate with the United States to meet security threats and promote free trade and sustainable development. These goals are supported by ensuring America remains engaged in the world and by enlarging the community of secure, free market and democratic nations. (NSS 1996: Preface)

In the 1990s, the meaning of security for the U.S. is to be found in projecting the self onto the other. Attaining security means using all facets of power available to the U.S. to maintain its military and economic position relative to other nation-states while also engaging in cooperative frameworks that produce absolute gains so long as those relative and absolute gains transform the identity of the other into that of the self. Absolute gains need not be equal and indeed most often are not (Keohane 1984). In the post-9/11 world, remaking the world in its free market and democratic image took on an added sense of urgency for the U.S. The 2002 and 2006 national security strategy reviews (NSS 2002 and 2006, respectively) remain dogmatically anchored to the idea of freedom, but both texts reflect the shift in U.S. identity to hard power in the post-9/11 era. In NSS 2002, the U.S. is committed to accelerating the transformative aim of its foreign policy through the use of force to impose the desired change to the other through the Bush Doctrine of pre-emptive application of military force. NSS 2006 strikes a more conciliatory tone by acknowledging that the U.S. must be more committed to multilateralism. Both articulate the discourses of democracy and free market enterprise as solutions to the question concerning how to structure meaningful political practice.

In conclusion, U.S. identity is most concisely and forcefully articulated in national security strategy reviews and papers. In NSC 68, the U.S. anchored its identity in the idea of freedom. By NSS 1991, the idea of freedom had become concretely articulated through the discourses of democracy and free market enterprise. The discourses of democracy and free market enterprise serve to structure political practice reflective of U.S. identity. Political practice reflective of U.S. identity forms the basis of security for the self against the other. When engaging in relative gains-seeking, absolute gains-seeking, or a combination of relative and absolute gains-seeking, U.S. practice is shaped by its identity and insatiable pursuit to secure its identity through constructing a world of free market and democratic clones hung in webs of regimes spun by the discourses of democracy and free market enterprise. In the case of Internet governance, alternative visions of governance did not win out precisely because those alternatives threatened U.S. identity. So long as the normative structure of the Internet governance regime was consistent with U.S. identity and security aims, an Internet governance regime would have U.S. support. I now turn to developing this claim.

Linking U.S. Security and Internet Governance

On 1 July 1997, the U.S. issued the Framework for Global Electronic Commerce in which U.S. identity towards Internet governance was plainly articulated. In announcing the framework, President Clinton succinctly described the U.S. view of the Internet, "It should be a global free-trade zone." We can observe in this statement that the Internet is understood by key policy-makers in the U.S. government through the lens of free market enterprise. The Internet is to be the province of commerce and trade precisely because the Internet holds out the promise of collapsing geographic barriers to market entry. Meaning that the sort of barriers to market entry observed in international trade (distance, tariffs, customs duties, and quality standards) enforced and imposed on the global market by states are to be nonexistent where electronic commerce is concerned—a key aim of U.S. security and aspect of U.S. identity. However, combined with U.S. security identity is an ontological position, articulated in NSS 1996, concerning the transformative effects of Internetworking technology on the global economy. This ontological position represents an intertextual link between U.S. national security strategy texts and U.S. Internet governance texts.

The perception held by Ira Magaziner, the key Internet governance policy-maker within the Clinton administration, was that the global economy was experiencing a significant structural shift on a par with shifts from agrarian-based economic organization to industrialized economic organization. His structural shift view held that the global economy was shifting from the industrial age to the information or digital age. The ontology of Ira Magaziner is largely responsible for this aspect of U.S. identity towards Internet governance. Magaziner in a published interview in 1997 described the ontological position that directly shaped U.S. identity towards Internet governance in response to a question concerning the role of government:

> The context here is that we believe that the digital age is going to be profoundly different than the industrial age in ways that we don't yet understand fully. With the coming of the industrial age from the agrarian age, you had changes in commercial and political philosophy, legal frameworks, economic paradigms. And something similar is happening today. My sense is—and this is just a personal feeling—that, philosophically, part of what this will involve is a different role for government.
>
> To be clear, I'm one who believes that government has important roles to play in society. I believe, for example, that the government should guarantee all citizens access to affordable health care, something that a lot of people probably disagree with. But with respect to the digital marketplace—because I think government legislation and regulation is too slow moving, too inflexible and too centralized to match the digital age—I think a model of industry self-regulation and of industry codes of conduct and decentralized governance fits better for the Internet age. (Harris 1997)

If one holds the view that the global economy is fundamentally and structurally changing, then ensuring that the core organizing aspect of the emerging digital economy remains anchored in the idea of freedom is of paramount importance. Especially for securing an identity constructed on the idea of freedom and articulated through the discourses of democracy and free market enterprise. Even more telling is Magaziner's explanation for the role of government in the information age, that government should have a minimal role in regulating the Internet. The notion that the role of government should be minimized in the market place is a core norm within the discourses of democracy and free market enterprise that reflects the idea of freedom. U.S. policy-makers discursively constructed the Internet as a free and open domain to counter the global community vision of the Internet that relied on robust government involvement in defense of community.

Elliott Maxwell, a former Department of Commerce official who served as a member of the interagency taskforce chaired by Magaziner charged with developing U.S. Internet governance policy, echoes Magaziner in the following statement, "Best shield for an open and free Internet was the presence of the U.S. and U.S. authority to protect the nascent potential of the Internet for communications, exchange of information, electronic commerce, and innovation in general. A regulated utility like Internet would impede the spread of free speech norms and electronic commerce" (Maxwell 2010).

The approach the U.S. government took to government oversight of the Internet Corporation for Assigned Names and Numbers (ICANN), the private market-based not-for-profit corporation charged with managing the domain name system, was characterized by Dr John Marburger, former head of the White House Science and Technology Policy Office during the George W. Bush Administration as reflecting concerns that the idea of freedom would be hindered by heavy-handed government oversight. Dr Marburger (2010) states that:

> The U.S. was concerned that oversight authority for ICANN by any governmental entity would ultimately lead to interference with the open nature of the Internet that gave it flexibility and allowed it to grow rapidly. The Department of Commerce oversight was very light-handed, permitting the rather free-form governance structure to evolve in response to market forces. In a sense, the arrangement with the Department of Commerce was regarded as the most benign form of oversight possible.

A key component of checking heavy-handed government oversight of the Internet for U.S. Internet governance policy was to ensure that the Internet would be treated as a duty-free trade zone in which governments would be prohibited from assessing tariffs, duties, or levies to goods and services exchanged through the Internet. Accordingly, U.S. policy-makers successfully negotiated an amendment to World Trade Organization agreements to that effect in May 1998 (Abelson 2009). By keeping government at bay, U.S. policy-makers ensured that U.S. high-technology companies could maintain and leverage their competitive advantage on the Internet. According to Magaziner (2010), "U.S. [IT] companies, at that time, were dominant and we wanted to ensure economic growth." On Magaziner's view, U.S. policy-makers were successful at designing a global Internet governance regime based on the idea of freedom that preserved the Internet as a platform for commercial and political expansion. On the view of Dr Michael Nelson (2009), who spent 15 years in the federal government working on computer and networking technology policy as a senate staffer and a special assistant in the White House, culminating with his appointment as Director for Technology Policy at the Federal Communications Commission in January 1997, U.S. Internet governance policy was, "All about jobs. All about local. Nothing motivates the political process like providing high paying jobs for voters." The policy-maker that succeeded Magaziner as the U.S. coordinator for Internet governance policy was Ambassador Richard Russell, Deputy Head of the White House Office of Science and Technology Policy during the George W. Bush Administration. Ambassador Russell (2010) shows the continuity of U.S. Internet governance policy as he describes the overarching objective of U.S. policy-makers concerning the Internet, "The overall goal was to keep the Internet expanding. The Internet was not only a powerful commercial force but also a powerful democratizing force." Discursively constructing the Internet as a medium for commercial and political expansion while grounded in the idea of freedom was materially about job creation in the U.S. economy and protecting the competitive advantage of U.S. high-technology companies in the emerging digital economy of the twenty-first century. Providing jobs for U.S. voters and protecting the competitive advantage of U.S. industry have long been U.S. national security objectives, usually couched in terms of "economic growth," "free and open," "democracy," or "limited government."

The texts issued on U.S. security strategy and U.S. identity towards Internet governance are all anchored in the idea of freedom. The intertextual link between national security strategy reviews and the framework for global electronic commerce is the idea of freedom. The idea of freedom and the discourses of democracy and free market enterprise are threads that weave and stitch together U.S. national security aims with U.S. identity towards Internet governance. The identity that the U.S. constructed towards Internet governance was no different than U.S. security identity. The U.S. acted to secure its economic and political position in the emerging digital age when it backed a private market governance vision. In doing so, the U.S. preserved its capacity to promote transformative change in nation-state institutions in accord with the idea of freedom and the discourses of democracy and free market enterprise. The grand strategy of the U.S. has been to construct a security community between sovereign, democratic, and free market states. Security communities rely on shared identities among states as a primary catalyst for and sustaining their security (Adler and Barnett 1998). The international regimes that develop within security regimes serve to reinforce shared identities (Katzenstein and Social Science Research Council (U.S.). Committee on International Peace & Security 1996; also see Jervis 1983; Russett and O'Neal 2001).

For the U.S., maintaining the free market enterprise economic model and the international regimes which support that model is essential to the maintenance of the security community on which the U.S. depends. The U.S. framework for global electronic commerce was the opening move by the U.S. to ensure that any Internet governance regime was to be incorporated into the already existing free market structure of the global economy. ICANN was to ensure that the Internet developed in accord with market norms and legal frameworks in order to thwart any destabilizing effects social practice on the Internet may have towards the current liberal economic order.

Given U.S. identity as the hegemonic guardian of freedom and quintessential democratic and free market institution and society, U.S. identity towards Internet governance was a forgone conclusion. In other words, the U.S., in the role of market hegemon, acted to preserve the embedded liberal economic order that had prevailed during the post-war era and served as the basis not only for U.S. power and prestige but also for global prosperity and wealth—long a core aim of U.S. security identity (Ikenberry 2000). The U.S. was simply fulfilling the essential role of the hegemon for preserving economic stability in the face of rapid and potentially destabilizing change in the market (Ruggie 1983). In staking claim to the root and DNS, the U.S. positioned itself relative to other nation-states as the most powerful actor on the issue of Internet governance. Yet such an action can be interpreted as a hegemonic act on behalf of community. The potential absolute gains derived from e-commerce, the spread of Internetworking communications technology, and the democratization of information would have been unavailable had existing market regimes and legal frameworks not been institutionalized on the Internet. The erosion of value as the result of intellectual property rights not being enforced on the Internet would be economically destabilizing on a massive scale. There was no other alternative, from the perspective of economic stability and desire not to squelch technological innovation through bureaucracy, except for a private market-based regime over the short term. Such actions by the U.S. are altogether consistent with U.S. security identity dependent on a security community populated by democratic and free market enterprise societies (Nau 2000; also see Ikenberry 2000). Such actions can be interpreted as being in defense of subjective framings of meanings for democracy, the market, and the role of the state in global governance.

Conclusion

I have tried to show that the idiosyncratic framings of meanings attached by the U.S. to the concepts of freedom, democracy, and free market enterprise directly shaped the present outcome to the Internet governance controversy. National idiosyncrasies matter to the construction of international regimes, but only to the extent that a nation-state has the power to infuse the processes of regime construction with subjective framings of meanings for the principles, norms, rules, and decision-making procedures that ultimately make up regimes.

The U.S. in seeking to sustain, expand, and secure the current liberal-capitalist structure of politics and economics moved to ensure that social practices on the Internet would be shaped by existing market norms and legal frameworks. In doing so the U.S. employed its power and prestige to construct a regime structure consistent with its self-image as champion of freedom and leader of the world's capitalist-democracies. While such an outcome can be easily interpreted through a realist lens that relies on relative gains seeking, doing so obfuscates the absolute gain-seeking that the U.S. sought to achieve and ensure for other members of the democratic and free market security community. The U.S., as market hegemon, acted out of concern for relative and absolute gains in the construction of an Internet governance regime that preserves market norms and legal frameworks on which its security community of capitalist-democratic states depends. In doing so, certain global marketplace preferences and frameworks of meanings were privileged over global public community preferences. This is an outcome of politics that is more often than not unavoidable and reflects the Foucauldian insight that power shapes knowledge (principles, norms, rules, and decision-making procedures), and becomes the basis for political practice. Two very different meanings of democracy, community, and freedom can be identified in the Internet governance discourse as vying for hegemony—in the Gramscian sense of the term.

The global public community (internationalist/transnationalist) position concerning Internet governance reflects a very different meaning of politics from that of the U.S. For the U.S., the controversy over Internet governance is about the role of government in the marketplace, which is linked to the view that in democracy the role of government in the life of the individual should be minimal. However, for a global public community, the controversy over Internet governance is about the prospect for global democracy with the Internet being the catalyst for the emergence of global democracy. Global democracy for the global public community position means that international regimes play a more prominent role in governance than the state. The reverse view is held by the global marketplace standpoint of the U.S. It seeks to avoid any governance arrangement that stamps out the potential commercial and technological innovation of the Internet.

For the U.S., the structural location of Internet governance must remain at the level of states so that the marketplace, democracy, and shared identities of the democratic and free market security community can be protected. The role of the state in the marketplace is to enforce contracts and rules of exchange in order for individuals to share relative equal opportunity to engage in profitable enterprises. In the global economy, the role of the state is filled by the market hegemon on behalf of other states. For the global public community, the enforcement of contracts and rules of exchange would reside at the systemic level in regimes. Within regimes, stakeholders would be able to deliberate concerning the best course of management of the Internet public resource. Were the current configuration of global politics a post-hegemonic configuration, the global public community regime would be optimal. In a world of post-hegemony, the prospect of competition among actors for control over public resources is potentially reduced through the construction of regimes and international intergovernmental organizations (Keohane 1984). However, during a phase of hegemony, as in the current period of global politics, the hegemon acts to manage public resources on behalf of the security community it has constructed. Indeed, according to the regime literature, a hegemon ensures the efficient functioning of the regime (Keohane 1980; Kindleberger 1986; Krasner 1983). This is precisely what happened in the case of Internet governance with the formation of ICANN as a U.S. government contractor charged with efficiently managing the root and DNS on behalf of all Internet stakeholders. Governance for the U.S. means that the U.S., as market hegemon, protects market norms and legal frameworks to ensure efficient and stable market functioning. Securing the commercial potential of the Internet for capitalist-democracies was an act of hegemony on behalf of global governance. In addition, staking claim to ownership of the root and the DNS was an act of hegemony in defense of subjective meanings of freedom, democracy, and the marketplace that reflect and reinforce U.S. identity, which were under threat of redefinition by the global public community vision of Internet governance. On these grounds the controversy over Internet governance can be re-conceptualized as being about framings of meaning for democracy, community, freedom, and the marketplace. It is also a case that serves to affirm the role of the hegemon in the politics of regime formation (Jervis 1983; Young 1983).

Beyond re-conceptualizing the Internet controversy, my study also makes an important contribution to the literature concerned with how state identity is formed. Key policy and decision-makers with the government apparatuses of nation-states, marshal their experiences, knowledge, and cultural norms in articulating what the image of the nation-state is and ought to be. Their idea of what the identity of the collective self or nation-state is serves to shape preferences, constrain choices, and construct desire for the sort of outcomes in global politics that square with the image of the self. Identity formation occurs through the discursive articulation of the ideologies of key policy- and decision-makers in official government texts. This does not mean that structure does not matter to the formulation of identity. Certainly, structure contributes to identity formation by constraining the location and choices of identity. In the current configuration of global politics, the location of identity is dictated by the normative structure of sovereignty—identity, at least those that matter to outcomes in global politics, is located at the level of states. It is on this structural template that the self projects the ideal image and meaning of politics. Ideas and structure matter, for each constructs and reconstructs the other.

The security of the U.S. relies on the vitality of its economy, capacity to project force, the attractiveness of its ideals, and in (re)constructing the world to reflect its identity. Sometimes maintaining its economic position comes into conflict with its ideals. In the case of the controversy concerning Internet governance, preserving the economic power of the U.S. was deemed more critical to the security of the U.S. rather than the attractiveness of its ideals. The cost has been damaging to the soft power of the U.S., but the gain has been to position the U.S. as the center of the Internet governance regime and of the new digital economy going forward. A shift in the underlying power configuration among states or within the hegemon may serve as the catalyst for change from the current U.S./ICANN regime (Puchala and Hopkins 1983). With the change in presidential administrations in the U.S. government, the moment may be ripe for pursuing change to the U.S./ICANN Internet governance regime in favor of a global public community regime.

References

Abelson, D. (2009). Phone Interview of Ambassador Donald Abelson with author, 23 September 2009.

Adler, E. (1997). Seizing the Middle Ground: Constructivism in World Politics. *European Journal of International Relations*, 3, 319–63.

Adler, E. and Barnett, M.N. (1998). *Security Communities*. New York: Cambridge University Press.

Bach, D. and Newman, A. (2007). The European Regulatory State and Global Public Policy. *Journal of European Public Policy*, 16(6), 827–46.

Baldwin, D.A. (1997). The Concept of Security. *Review of International Studies*, 23, 5–26.

Buzan, B., Wæver, O. and Wilde, J.D. (1997). *Security: A New Framework for Analysis*. Boulder, CO: Lynne Rienner.

Campbell, D. (1998a). *National Deconstruction: Violence, Identity, and Justice in Bosnia*. Minneapolis, MN: University of Minneapolis Press.

Campbell, D. (1998b). *Writing Security: United States Foreign Policy and the Politics of Identity* (revised edition). Minneapolis, MN: University of Minnesota Press.

Checkel, J.T. (1998). The Constructivist Turn in International Relations. *World Politics*, 50, 473–95.

Clinton, W.J. (1997). *A Framework for Global Electronic Commerce, July 1, 1997*. Available at: http://clinton4.nara.gov/wh/new/commerce/read/html [accessed: 1 August 2011].

Derrida, J. (1981). *Writing and Difference*. London: Routledge.

Dillon, M. (1996). *The Politics of Security: Towards a Political Philosophy of Continental Thought*. London: Routledge.

Drezner, D.W. (2004). The Global Governance of the Internet: Bringing the State Back In. *Political Science Quarterly*, 119(3), 477–98.

Dunn-Cavelty, M. (2008). *Cyber-security and Threat Politics: U.S. Efforts to Secure the Information Age*. London: Routledge.

Edkins, J. (2003). Security, Cosmology, and Copenhagen. *Contemporary Politics*, 9(4), 361–70.

Farrell, H. (2003). Constructing the International Foundations of e-Commerce: The EU–U.S. Safe Harbor Arrangement. *International Organization*, 57(2), 277–306.

Fierke, K.M. and Jørgensen, K.E. (2001). *Constructing International Relations: The Next Generation*. Armonk, NY: M.E. Sharpe.

Finnemore, M. (1996). *National Interests in International Society*. Ithaca, NY: Cornell University Press.

Franda, M.F. (2001). *Governing the Internet: The Emergence of an International Regime*. Boulder, CO: Lynne Rienner.

Giacomello, G. (2005). *National Governments and Control of the Internet: A Digital Challenge*. New York: Routledge.

Hall, R.B. (2003). The Discursive Demolition of the Asian Development Model. *International Studies Quarterly*, 47(1), 71–99.

Hansen, L. and Nissenbaum, H. (2009). Digital Disaster, Cyber Security, and the Copenhagen School. *International Studies Quarterly*, 53, 1155–75.

Harris, B. (1997). *Interview of Ira Magaziner*. Available at: http://www.govtech.com/gt/print_article.php?id=95442 [accessed: 1 August 2011].

Hopf, T. (1998). The Promise of Constructivism in International Relations Theory. *International Security*, 23, 171–200.

Howarth, D.R. (2000). *Discourse Theory and Political Analysis: Identities, Hegemonies, and Social Change*. Manchester/New York: Manchester University Press/St Martin's Press.

Huysmans, J. (1998). Security! What Do You Mean? From Concept to Thick Signifier. *European Journal of International Relations*, 4(2), 226–55.

Ikenberry, G.J. (2000). America's Liberal Grand Strategy: Democracy and National Security in the Post-War Era. In M. Cox, G.J. Ikenberry and T. Inoguchi (eds), *American Democracy Promotion: Impulses, Strategies, and Impacts* (pp. 103–26). Oxford: Oxford University Press.

Jervis, R. (1983). Security Regimes. In S.D. Krasner (ed.), *International Regimes* (pp. 173–94). Ithaca, NY: Cornell University Press.

Katzenstein, P.J. and Social Science Research Council (U.S.). Committee on International Peace and Security (1996). *The Culture of National Security: Norms and Identity in World Politics*. New York: Columbia University Press.

Keohane, R.O. (1980). The Theory of Hegemonic Stability and Changes in International Economic Regimes, 1967–77. In O.R. Holsti, R.M. Siverson and A.L. George (eds), *Change in the International System*. Boulder, CO: Westview Press.

Keohane, R.O. (1984). *After Hegemony: Cooperation and Discord in the World Political Economy*. Princeton, NJ: Princeton University Press.

Keohane, R.O. and Nye, J.S. (2001). *Power and Interdependence* (3rd edn). New York: Longman.

Kindleberger, C.P. (1986). *The World in Depression, 1929–1939* (revised and enlarged edn). Boston, MA: Little Brown.

Krasner, S.D. (1983). Structural Causes and Regime Consequences: Regimes as Intervening Variables. In S.D. Krasner (ed.), *International Regimes* (pp. 1–22). Ithaca, NY: Cornell University Press.

Krause, K. and Williams, M.C. (1997). *Critical Security Studies: Concepts and Cases*. Minneapolis, MN: University of Minnesota Press.

Lessig, L. (1999). *Code and Other Laws of Cyberspace*. New York: Basic Books.

Lessig, L. (2004). *Free Culture*. New York: Penguin Press.

Lipshutz, R.D. (1995). *On Security*. New York: Columbia University Press.

Magaziner, I. (2010). Phone Interview of Ira Magaziner with author, 5 April 2010.

Marburger, J. (2010). Interview of Dr. John Marburger with author via email, 5 April 2010.

Mathiason, J. (2009). *Internet Governance: The New Frontier of Global Institutions*. London: Routledge.

Mattern, J.B. (2005). *Ordering International Politics: Identity, Crisis, and Representational Force*. New York: Routledge.

Maxwell, E. (2010). Phone Interview of Elliott Maxwell with author, 18 January 2010 and 3 February 2010.

McSweeney, B. (1999). *Security, Identity and Interests: A Sociology of International Relations*. Cambridge: Cambridge University Press.

Milliken, J. (1999). The Study of Discourse in International Relations: A Critique of Research and Methods. *European Journal of International Relations*, 5(2), 225–54.

Mitzen, J. (2006). Ontological Security in World Politics: State Identity and the Security Dilemma. *European Journal of International Relations*, 12(3), 337–41.

Mueller, M. (2002). *Ruling the Root: Internet Governance and the Taming of Cyberspace*. Cambridge, MA: The MIT University Press.

Nau, H. (2000). America's Identity, Democracy Promotion, and National Interests: Beyond Realism, Beyond Idealism. In M. Cox, G.J. Ikenberry and T. Inoguchi (eds), *American Democracy Promotion: Impulses, Strategies, and Impacts* (pp. 127–50). Oxford: Oxford University Press.

Nelson, M. (2009). Phone Interview of Dr Michael Nelson with author, 21 September 2009.

Neumann, I.B. (1999). *Uses of the Other: "The East" in European Identity Formation*. Minneapolis, MN: University of Minnesota Press.

NSC (1950). *NSC 68: United States Objectives and Programs for National Security*. Available at: http://www.fas.org/irp/offdocs/nsc-hst/nsc-68-4.htm [accessed: 1 August 2011].

NSS (1991). *A National Security Strategy of the United States*. Available at: http://www.globalsecurity.org/military/library/policy/national/nss-918015.htm [accessed: 1 August 2011].

NSS (1996). *A National Security Strategy of Engagement and Enlargement*. Available at: http://www.globalsecurity.org/military/library/policy/national/nss9602.htm [accessed: 1 August 2011].

NSS (1998). *A National Security Strategy for a New Century*. Available at: http://www.globalsecurity.org/military/library/policy/national [accessed: 1 August 2011].

NSS (2000). *A National Security Strategy for a Global Age*.

NSS (2002). *The National Security Strategy of the United States of America*. Available at: http://www.lib.umich.edu/govdocs/pdf/nss02.pdf [accessed: 1 August 2011].
NSS (2006). *The National Security Strategy of the United States of America*. Available at: http://www.whitehouse.gov/administration/eop/nsc/ [accessed: 1 August 2011].
Onuf, N.G. (1989). *World of Our Making: Rules and Rule in Social Theory and International Relations*. Columbia, SC: University of South Carolina Press.
Oren, I. (2003). *Our Enemies and U.S.: America's Rivalries and the Making of Political Science*. Ithaca, NY: Cornell University Press.
Pare, D.J. (2003). *Internet Governance in Transition: Who is the Master of this Domain?* Lanham, MD: Rowman and Littlefield.
Puchala, D.J. and Hopkins, R.F. (1983). International Regimes: Lessons from Inductive Analysis. In S.D. Krasner (ed.), *International Regimes* (pp. 61–92). Ithaca, NY: Cornell University Press.
Reus-Smit, C. (2005). Constructivism. In S. Burchill (ed.), *Theories of International Relations* (3rd ed., pp. x, 310). Basingstoke: Palgrave Macmillan.
Ruggie, J.G. (1983). *The Antinomies of Interdependence: National Welfare and the International Division of Labor*. New York: Columbia University Press.
Ruggie, J.G. (1998). *Constructing the World Polity: Essays on International Institutionalization*. New York: Routledge.
Russell, R. (2010). Phone Interview of Ambassador Richard Russell with author, 16 April 2010.
Russett, B.M. and O'Neal, J.R. (2001). *Triangulating Peace: Democracy, Interdependence, and International Organizations*. New York: Norton.
Walker, R.B.J. (1993). *Inside/Outside: International Relations as Political Theory*. Cambridge: Cambridge University Press.
Weldes, J. (1999). *Constructing National Interests: The United States and the Cuban Missile Crisis*. Minneapolis, MN: University of Minnesota Press.
Wendt, A. (1999). *Social Theory of International Politics*. Cambridge: Cambridge University Press.
Wight, C. (2006). *Agents, Structures and International Relations: Politics as Ontology*. Cambridge: Cambridge University Press.
Young, O.R. (1983). Regime Dynamics: The Rise and Fall of International Regimes. In S.D. Krasner (ed.), *International Regimes* (pp. 93–114). Ithaca, NY: Cornell University Press.
Zehfuss, M. (2002). *Constructivism in International Relations: The Politics of Reality*. Cambridge: Cambridge University Press.
Zizek, S. (2008). Don't Just do Something, Talk. *London Review of Books*. Available at: http://www.lrb.co.uk/v00/n03/print/zize01_.html [accessed: 11 January 2011].

Chapter 13
Information and Communications Technologies and Power

Jeffrey A. Hart

Introduction

The politics of information and communications technologies (ICTs) frequently centers on questions of power. How does the diffusion of these technologies affect the distribution of power? In particular, does the spread of ICTs empower individuals and small organizations or does it favor large organizations and institutions such as governments and multinational corporations? Does it undermine existing hierarchies or reinforce them? Does control over the "architecture" of computing systems and networks affect the distribution of power?

How does the spread of ICTs affect the distribution of power internationally? Starting from an initial state of growing economic inequality among nations, does the diffusion of these new technologies result in increases or decreases in inequality? This is the question that motivates the literature on the "global digital divide" (see Compaine 2001; Norris 2001; van Dijk 2005). In brief, we are interested in the impact of ICTs on both domestic and international power distributions.

To answer these questions to our satisfaction, we need to review what scholars have said about power: how they define it, measure or observe it, and explain shifts over time. How does technology and technological change affect the distribution of power? Only if we have a clear understanding of these issues, will it be possible to address more specific questions about the power implications of the spread of ICTs.

Defining Power

Dictionary definitions of power are helpful in suggesting the way words are used in ordinary language. In Dictionary.com (which assembles definitions that are located in various place on the World Wide Web), one can find the following definitions:

> http://dictionary.reference.com/browse/power.
>
> ***–noun***
>
> 1. ability to do or act; capability of doing or accomplishing something.
>
> 2. political or national strength: the balance of power in Europe.
>
> 3. great or marked ability to do or act; strength; might; force.

4. the possession of control or command over others; authority; ascendancy: power over men's minds.

5. political ascendancy or control in the government of a country, state, etc.: they attained power by overthrowing the legal government.

6. legal ability, capacity, or authority: the power of attorney.

7. delegated authority; authority granted to a person or persons in a particular office or capacity: the powers of the president.

8. a document or written statement conferring legal authority.

9. a person or thing that possesses or exercises authority or influence.

10. a state or nation having international authority or influence: the great powers held an international conference.

11. a military or naval force: the Spanish Armada was a mighty power.

From this list, it is apparent that, in common parlance power, control, influence, and legal or legitimate authority are closely related to one another, and that power is associated with both potential and actual control over others. In the social sciences, and particularly in political science, the concept of power has taken on a set of more specific meanings as part of an effort to achieve greater conceptual clarity, but also to serve as the basis for systematic inquiry.

Political philosophers have attempted to define power in various ways, and their efforts to do so have certainly influenced social scientists. Steven Lukes (1986) provides an excellent overview in an introduction to a volume he edited on power. According to Lukes, Bertrand Russell defined power as "the production of intended effects." Max Weber defined it as "the probability that an actor in a social relationship will be in a position to carry out his own will despite resistance, regardless of the basis on which this probability rests." Unlike Russell, Weber stressed the importance of achieving results in the presence of resistance. In a frequently cited article, Robert Dahl argued "A has power over B to the extent that he can get B to do something that B would not otherwise do" (Dahl 1957). Dahl apparently agreed with Weber that an exercise of power required overcoming resistance.

Weber and Dahl cast their definitions in terms of an abstract relationship between two actors (or two sets of actors). Other scholars preferred to see power defined in terms of social aggregates or communities. Talcott Parsons, for example, wanted power to connote a "generalized facility or resource in the society." Hannah Arendt argued that power is "not the property of an individual" but "corresponds to the human ability not just to act but to act in concert" (Lukes 1986: 3).

In an effort to improve upon the efforts of his predecessors, Lukes argues that "to have power is to be able to make a difference in the world. Those interested in power are interested in two questions: in the difference that is made, and in the making of the difference. Let us call the first an interest in the outcomes and the second an interest in the locus of power." He asks other scholars to keep this distinction in mind (Lukes 1986: 5).

Nagel vs Lukes

In his attempt to build on the work of his teacher, Robert Dahl, Jack Nagel defines power as a relationship in which A is able to get B to do something that A preferred initially but that was initially against B's preferences (Nagel 1975). This definition incorporates the idea that B may initially resist A's efforts, but allows that B might change his/her mind about a preferred outcome. So there are two possible ways for A to get B to do what A prefers: (1) to use coercion (the threat or actual use of force); or (2) to persuade B to change his/her mind about what B prefers. B's preferences may remain unchanged after an act of coercion, but not after successful persuasion. Nagel's definition, in short, allows for the possibility of a noncoercive form of power.

In subsequent work, Lukes develops a notion of power similar to Dahl's and Nagel's, but different in one important way. Instead of defining power in terms of *preferences*, Lukes defines power in terms of the *interests* of social actors. According to Lukes, "power must serve the interests of the powerful" (Lukes 1986: 5). Therefore, A has power over B if A is able to get B to act according to A's interests and against his/her own interests and implicitly regardless of A's and B's preferences. This allows Lukes to argue that the power that he is interested in is guaranteed to be more objective than the power that can be observed using the Dahl/Nagel approach in that it is less subject to an arbitrary selection of conflicts over preferences that may not matter that much.

Under Lukes's definition of power, however, an outside observer would have to be able to assign interests to two social actors and then observe their behavior in terms of those interests. If one adheres to the Marxist or neo-Marxist school of thought, this is not problematic: indeed it is an advantage of the Lukes approach over the Dahl/Nagel approach. The key conflict of interest in Marxist thought is class conflict: so interests are determined by class membership. If one adheres to a more liberal philosophical tradition, however, the assignment of objective interests to individuals or groups by outside observers is considered both impossible and undesirable.

My own preference is to apply the Dahl/Nagel approach to relational power and so I will not use the Lukes approach here. Still, one needs to bear in mind the criticism of Lukes and others that not just any outcome where initial resistance is overcome can be used to assess relational power.

The Second and Third Dimensions of Power

Soon after Robert Dahl published his influential article on power, two scholars, Peter Bachrach and Morton Baratz, argued that Dahl's definition excluded a type of

> power that was harder to observe but which was still important. This type of power produced "non-decisions," where there was no debate and no apparent conflict over preferences. The reason for this was that the powerful had suppressed debate and the powerless had no opportunity to voice their preferences. (Bachrach and Baratz 1962, 1963)

Bachrach and Baratz called the analysis of nondecisions the "second face of power." Steve Lukes renamed it the second dimension of power and added a third in the first edition of *Power: a Radical Analysis* (1974). The third dimension concentrates on the power that arises from agenda formation and agenda control. To overt and covert struggles, Lukes adds latent conflicts that are submerged only to re-emerge at a later time. In short, Bachrach and Baratz and Lukes consider Dahl's approach to power to be too narrow. They want a broader conception even if that introduces additional difficulties for the empirical observation of power relationships.

Lukes's third dimension of power has much in common to what later came to be called "structural power" or "metapower." For example, Susan Strange writes that:

> structural power … confers the power to decide how things shall be done, the power to shape frameworks within which states relate to each other, relate to people, or relate to corporate enterprises. The relative power of each party in a relationship is more, or less, if one party is also determining the surrounding structure of the relationship … What is common to all four kinds of structural power is that the possessor is able to change the range of choices open to others, without apparently putting pressure directly on them to take one decision or to make one choice rather than others. Such power is less "visible."
>
> Today the knowledge most sought after the acquisition of relational power and to reinforce other kinds of structural power (i.e. in security matters, in production and in finance) is technology. The advanced technologies of new materials, new products, new systems of changing plants and animals, new systems of collecting, storing and retrieving information—all these open doors to both structural power and relational power. (Strange 1988: 25–31)

Later in the same work, however, Strange argues that "Structural analysis suggests that technological changes do not necessarily change power structures. They do so only if accompanied by changes in the basic belief systems which underpin or support the political and economic arrangements acceptable to society" (Strange 1988: 123).

Soft and Smart Power

Joseph S. Nye's concept of "soft power" may be seen as a way of talking about noncoercive power. Soft power, according to Nye, is the ability to achieve desired outcomes through attraction rather than coercion. According to Nye, the primary currencies of soft power are an actor's values, culture, policies, and institutions. Soft power depends upon the extent to which these currencies are able to attract or repel other actors, to make them "want what you want" (Nye 2004). Soft power depends on the appeal of ideas and an actor's ability to set the agenda in ways that shape the preferences of others (Nye 1990).

Nye's approach suggests that ICTs may matter because of the connection between them and the ease or difficulty of the diffusion of cultural ideas and artifacts. The easy access to digital text, audio and video means that anyone connected to the Internet, if not subject to local censorship, may be exposed to ideas and cultural products of other cultures. The attractiveness of these ideas and products may win over hearts and minds of people who previously did not have access to them and thereby build sympathy for the culture that created them.

In later work, Nye argues that a judicious combination of hard and soft power is more effective than the application of hard or soft power alone. Hard power is not strictly coercive in Nye's view since it can rely on "inducements" as well as threats. Nye calls the combination of hard and soft power "smart power" (Nye 2008: chapter 2).

Nye has used these concepts to criticize the policies of the Bush administration, which he believes neglected soft power entirely (Nye 2002). He also argues that the Bush administration's neglect of soft power resulted in a failure to take advantage of opportunities for using multilateralism in diplomacy. Not only were international organizations and regimes under-used during the Bush presidency, but also traditional alliances: unilateralism replaced multilateralism.

In addition, Nye uses the concepts of soft and smart power to argue that the U.S. had not declined in relative power as much as other scholars claimed, in part because of the growing importance of ICTs. According to Nye, the U.S. still had much potential soft power:

> The values of democracy, personal freedom, upward mobility, and openness that are often expressed in American popular culture, higher education, and foreign policy contribute to American power in many areas. (Nye 2002: 11)

Klaus Knorr argues in *Power and Wealth* (1973) that inducements work as instruments of power because they either are or are perceived to be contingent upon certain actions by the recipient. Inducements involve an implicit threat to end the rewards when the desired behavior changes. Realist scholars such as Kenneth Waltz, John Mearsheimer, Robert Kagan and Niall Ferguson have criticized Nye's ideas on soft power. These scholars question the effectiveness of soft power in determining the outcomes of strategically important conflicts. They tend to downplay the role of ideas in politics in general, and particularly the ideas that are embodied in international regimes, focusing instead on the predominant role of military force in world affairs and facts imposed by placing "boots on the ground."

While Lukes agrees with Nye about the evils of focusing exclusively on force and coercion, he criticizes Nye for implying that certain means of noncoercively winning hearts and minds (by persuasion or attraction) are better or more legitimate than others. He argues instead that it is difficult empirically to distinguish between "indoctrination and that ideal form of persuasion that consists in securing conviction through the freely exercised judgment of others" (Lukes 2007: 94). So Lukes is dubious about the empirical usefulness of Nye's concepts while still entertaining the possibility that ideas and persuasion are important.

He is also skeptical about what he calls Michel Foucault's 'ultra-radical' view of power in which forms of subjugation are embedded deeply in all social institutions and arrangements. Lukes does not adhere to the Foucauldian premise that "rationality itself, enabling one to distinguish between what is true and what is false, is itself internal to alternative 'regimes of truth'" (Lukes 2007: 96) Of course, if an actor or a group of actors could control a "regime of truth" for a given society, as Foucault implies, that actor would be enormously powerful. The argument rests on the plausibility of the assertion that such control is possible.

In short, the concept of power remains contentious and the debates go on. In the meantime, we can productively relate these various definitions of power and attendant theories about power to the question of the impact of the diffusion of ICTs by focusing on what can be observed and measured empirically, remembering that this may not be the whole story.

Observing Power

There are basically three different approaches to observing power empirically: (1) power as a resource or capability; (2) power as a relationship; and (3) power as a structure (Hart 1976).

Observing Capabilities

"In the power as capabilities approach, power is measured in terms of control over a resource (potential power) which can be converted in some manner into control over others or over outcomes (actual power). These resources, also called capabilities, may be connected with measurable phenomena such as economic wealth or population" (Hart 1989: 3). The literature on community power in the 1960s that stimulated Robert Dahl and others to formulate the relational approach to power relied on this type of power assessment. One could identify local elites by focusing on variables that measured potential influence such as wealth, education, and prestige.

Realist theories of international relations and works on "geopolitics" often rely on a power as resources approach. Power is measured or assessed in terms of certain "capabilities" that are a function of control over specific types of resources, e.g. land area, population, GNP, energy production.

In recent years, besides the usual set of capabilities indicators used to measure power, technological capabilities are now viewed as potential power resources. Contemporary governments, for example, increasingly focus on measures of national investments in research and development (R&D), numbers of scientists and researchers, and patenting activity as indicators of potential technological capability (National Science Foundation 2010: Overview). The relative success of a country in producing or selling ICT-related goods and services is also becoming a part of many national inventories of technological capability (National Science Foundation 2010: chapter 6). Access to technology on the part of the citizenry is another indicator. The number of landline and cellular telephones and Internet users and Internet hosts is monitored by the Central Intelligence Agency in its annual publication, *The World Factbook* (2010).

For example, in recent years, *The World Factbook* has highlighted the fact that the absolute number of cell phone subscribers (600 million) and Internet users (over 300 million) in China is greater than that in the U.S. This fact came up at the beginning of 2010, when it was reported that Google might be forced to leave the Chinese market because of its objections to being required to censor the results of searches performed on its Chinese website. The size of its domestic market for ICT-related projects gives the Chinese government some leverage over Google, although the growth in consumer preference for Google over Baidu (its main competitor in China) suggests the reverse, but only if the Chinese government decides to listen to those consumers instead insisting upon its right to censor Internet content.

The OECD Division of Science and Technology has been measuring indicators of ICT-related capabilities of its member states on an annual basis. It reports the household penetration rates of broadband services, for example, which have been widely reported in the press, especially because those statistics reveal that the U.S. is not generally in the top 10, but is in fact rather far down the list. Within the G7, the U.S. is not first. In fact, it is behind Canada, Germany, France, and the UK in broadband penetration. In the OECD, the U.S. is also behind the Netherlands, Denmark, Norway, Switzerland, Korea, and Iceland. For the U.S. not be first in this area provides ammunition to those political actors who want the U.S. government to more actively promote the diffusion of broadband networks.

Opponents of such a strategy, including members of the Bush administration, cite factors such as the geographic distances between population centers in the U.S., the lower cost of broadband services to consumers, and other factors, in explaining away apparent U.S. backwardness in this area. The Obama campaign made broadband access an issue in the 2008 presidential election and the Obama administration included some broadband funds in the stimulus bill that was passed just after the election.

ICTs clearly have had an impact on power assessment using the capabilities approach. The assumption is that, if a country possesses a vigorous computing and telecommunications equipment industry, then it can more easily access the benefits of ICT-related business activity. This is not just an assumption anymore, since there is increasing empirical evidence that investment in ICTs stimulates growth and economic productivity. Also, it is assumed that, if a country has developed information networks that many citizens can use, then the country as a whole will have informational advantages over others and may be better able to compete internationally.

Like all observational approaches that rely on measures of capabilities, the use of capabilities to assess ICT-related power depends more broadly on the assumption that potential power as indicated by control over resources can be translated into actual power either in the relational or the structural sense. Such translations are never perfect, however, so the appropriateness of the translation assumption remains a potential weakness of the capabilities approach.

For example, despite the evident inability of the U.S. to remain in the top position among the industrialized countries in all areas of ICT-related business activities, U.S. firms remain powerful and sometimes dominant players in key areas. In microprocessors, for example, Intel and AMD are the dominant firms, even though in other areas of the semiconductor market, such as memory devices, U.S. firms are not dominant. In PC operating systems and desktop packaged software, the largest share of the market is still dominated by Microsoft. Microsoft and Apple, as a result, have a lot to say about who can do what and how in the PC business. This leads some observers to speak about a new form of power peculiar to ICTs: the power to determine technical aspects of an ICT *platform* or *architecture*.

Observing Relational Power

Relational power approaches allow us to think about the domestic distribution of power in terms of the power of individuals *vis-à-vis* the government or other large institutions. Thomas Friedman (2005) has argued that individuals have been empowered *vis-à-vis* both governments and other large institutions because they now have access to information and knowledge via the Internet (helped by search engines). In arguing this, he joins a broader group of authors such as John Perry Barlow (former member of the rock band The Grateful Dead), who believe that the Internet, as well as the information it carries, "wants to be free" (Barlow 1996). By that, they do not mean that access to information will be without economic cost, but rather that individual users will push hard for minimal barriers to access once they see the potential for free speech and individual empowerment. Barlow advocates a policy for governments of nonregulation. Instead, he argues that the Internet is inherently self-organizing and self-regulating. The school of thought associated with this argument has come to be called "Cyber Anarchism."

In contrast, some authors argue that ICTs present new opportunities for both governments and large corporations (among others) to centralize control and to consolidate their pre-existing power over others. Lawrence Lessig (2006), for example, argues that the technology itself has the potential to either empower individuals or to empower large institutions. In the absence of organized efforts to preserve individual rights, the latter is more likely. An entire school of thought, the Surveillance School, starts from the premise that ICTs make it easier and cheaper for governments and corporations to spy on individuals and to act against those they consider to be threats (see, for example, Foucault 1975 and Lyon 2001).

One area of relatively intense research in recent years is the impact of ICTs on journalism and opportunities for free speech. There is considerable evidence that the diffusion of ICTs is undermining traditional print publishers while enabling a proliferation of on-line publications of various sorts. The flight of advertisers from newspapers, magazines, and network television to digital media is forcing a major restructuring of the world of journalism.

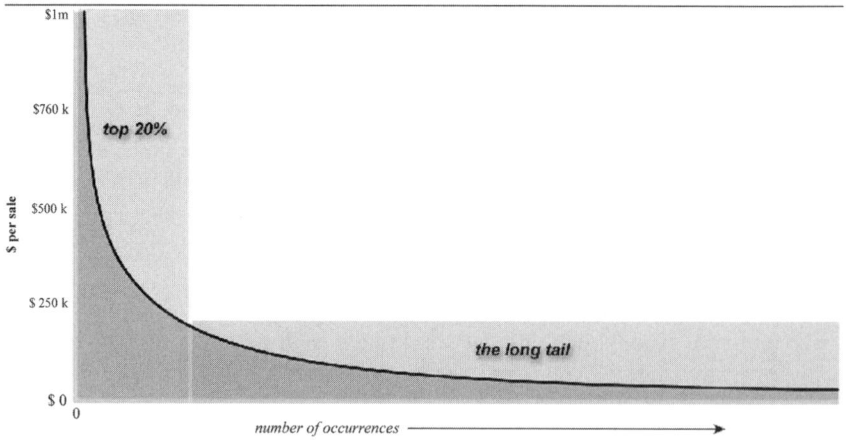

Figure 13.1 The long tail (Pareto distribution)
Source: http://blogs.idc.com/ie/wp-content/LongTail_01.jpg.

Some effort to measure the informational impact of ICTs has been associated with the analysis of the so-called "Long Tail" phenomenon. Popularized in a best-seller by Chris Anderson (2006), the long tail is simply an expected distribution curve called a Pareto Distribution (or power law) where the highest ranked services in terms of audience dominate the total but where, as the ranking declines, there are still many services commanding smaller and smaller audiences (see Figure 13.1). If the distribution has a "fat tail"—i.e. if a large percentage of service providers are in the right-hand half of the tail—then that is a sign of market diversity, even if a small number of large providers dominate the market.

Therefore, the argument would be that, if the diffusion of ICTs results in more fat tails in audience shares, then there will be greater diversity of viewpoints expressed in the associated media. This should be a plus for free speech and the relative power of individuals and small groups relative to larger institutions. It should be noted, however, that there might not be a direct association between empowering smaller media outlets and genuine improvements in free speech and individual empowerment. One line of criticism stems from a comparative analysis of the content of smaller media outlets, where some analysts claim that that content is "edgier," but only in that it contains more sensational and salacious, not politically controversial, content. Indeed, scholars like Neil Postman have argued that the proliferation of media outlets results in so much entertainment that we are amusing ourselves to death (Postman 1986).

Relational power at the international level also has been affected by the diffusion of ICTs. Nongovernmental organizations (NGOs), for example, have been quick to use email, blogs and other websites to connect with their supporters and to use information and other resources to lobby governments and international organizations for their preferred policies. ICTs are being used more and more intensively during political campaigns to inform supporters, raise funds, and increase the number of votes cast. Transnational political movements have new tools to connect their far-flung members electronically. While governments and corporations have also jumped on the ICT bandwagon for disseminating information, they generally have not taken advantage of the interactive capabilities of ICTs, preferring instead to emphasize one-way flows from themselves to their audiences.

With the end of the Cold War, power relationships that were previously based on bipolar enmity or alliances were redefined to take into account the absence (with the notable exception of the People's Republic of China) of a Communist bloc. Part of that adjustment was an increased interest in avoiding the commitment of military resources in attempts to influence specific other actors in the international system. Thus, there is greater interest in economic sanctions as an alternative response to various forms of bad behavior, and we predict that sanctions involving a deprivation of access to informational resources will become another possible alternative to military threats as the information economy develops.

Observing Structural Power

International actors seem to be thinking more these days about the larger set of norms, rules, and procedures that govern the world political and economic systems now that the Cold War is over. They are more interested in exercising structural power. Part of this is due to the impact of economic globalization, itself a consequence of a series of policy decisions at the national and international level that resulted in reduced barriers to trade and investment flows. The stakes connected with control over the international regimes that embody globalization are clear to all, including the growing number of opponents of globalization.

In addition to the question of influencing the character of international economic regimes, there is the question of how to build international governance systems for ICT- related activities. There has been some excellent research on the domain name system and the international body that was put in charge of overseeing registrars of domain names, the Internet Corporation for Assigned Names and Numbers (ICANN). The pioneering work of Milton Mueller (Mueller 2002) seems in particular to have stimulated other IR scholars to delve more deeply into this subject (see, for example, Braman 2006; Drezner 2007; Singh 2008).

Information technologies embed institutional and cultural practices into the technology itself. Thus, a certain amount of structural power is implicit in the transfer of information technologies across national boundaries. The country that is the source of key new technologies, such as microprocessors, fast digital switches, operating system software, and the like, frequently gets to impose its institutional and cultural arrangements on others. For example, Microsoft and Intel now dominate the personal computer market with the Windows operating systems on computers using Intel microprocessors. Apple currently dominates the markets for portable audio devices and smart phones. Google dominates the market for search engines and on-line advertising.

ICT companies and users in Europe and Asia have tried to compete directly with these firms, but have been mostly unsuccessful and now are forced to adapt to the technological solutions that the dominant firms have imposed on them (as well as the rest of the world). This causes a certain amount of resentment and irritation that sometimes percolates up to the level of national governments. Yet this is arguably a result of the success of Microsoft, Intel, Apple and Google in anticipating the demands of the marketplace, and also, to some extent, making concessions to overseas users so that they will continue to buy their products even though they are not of domestic origin.

Authority and Legitimacy in Cyberspace

It would be wrong to talk solely about power and the distribution of power without at least mentioning that power does not necessarily equate with authority and/or legitimacy.

Conclusions

The purpose of this chapter was to review the literature on power and the distribution of power and to apply the concepts from that literature to assess the impact of the diffusion of ICTs on domestic and international distributions of power. While such an assessment gets to the heart of much of the political science literature on ICTs, it is clear that the definition and observation of power still comprise a contested terrain. Nevertheless, it is possible to use those concepts for systematic observation and even quantitative measurement of changes in the distribution of power as long as everyone remembers their limitations.

Here are some of the lessons from this exercise:

- The diffusion of ICTs has resulted in the use of new capabilities indicators to assess potential power domestically and internationally connected with access and use of technologies. These indicators already have had some affect on policy debates, such as the debate over broadband infrastructure in the U.S.
- The diffusion of ICTs has altered the power relationships between citizens and their governments and other large social institutions, including multinational corporations. It is now easier to organize and mobilize people for political purposes who are separated by great distances.
- The diffusion of ICTs has helped to create or reinforce new types of relationships between governments and other international actors, including the establishment of international regimes that have adopted a "multi-stakeholder approach" to international governance.

Some important modifications in received notions of power need to be made in order to successfully apply the lessons of power analysis to ICT-related activities. For example, the political science literature does not talk much about the role of technology in general and technological architectures or platforms in particular on the distribution of power. Similarly, whereas control over conventional resources is often a zero-sum game, control over informational and cultural resources may not be. Power rivalries in the realm of knowledge and culture may be less dangerous and destructive than rivalries that center on territory or economic wealth. On the other hand, knowledge and cultural artifacts tend to be very close to the heart of what people care about, so the monopolization of control over these resources may be much more threatening than other types of power concentration.

We are not finished with the long discussions about how power should be defined and observed. As political scientists, we should not shy away from the task, otherwise we might as well belong to some other branch of the social sciences. Greater clarity has been achieved in conceptualizing power over the decades, and even greater clarity can be obtained by returning to the basics of power analysis. The diffusion of ICTs provides an opportunity to do this once again and a chance to revise the concepts and theories so that they can be applied fruitfully to a new set of human activities.

References

Anderson, Chris (2006) *The Long Tail: Why the Future of Business is Selling Less of More*. New York: Hyperion.

Bachrach, Peter and Morton Baratz (1962) "Two Faces of Power," *American Political Science Review*, 56 (December): 947–52.

Bachrach, Peter, and Morton Baratz (1963) "Decisions and Non-Decisions: An Analytical Framework," *American Political Science Review*, 57 (September): 632–42.

Barlow, John Perry (1996) *A Declaration of the Independence of Cyberspace*. Published online from Davos, Switzerland.

Braman, Sandra (2006) *Change of State: Information, Policy, and Power*. Cambridge, MA: MIT Press.

Central Intelligence Agency (2010) *The World Factbook*. Available at: https://www.cia.gov/library/publications/the-world-factbook/ [accessed: 1 August 2011].

Compaine, Benjamin (2001) *The Digital Divide: Facing a Crisis or Creating a Myth?* Cambridge, MA: MIT Press.

Dahl, Robert (1957) "The Concept of Power," *Behavioral Science*, 2 (July): 202–15.

Drezner, Daniel W. (2007) *All Politics is Global: Explaining International Regulatory Regimes*. Princeton, NJ: Princeton University Press.

Foucault, Michel (1975) *Surveillir et punir: Naissance de la prison*. Paris: Gallimard.

Friedman, Thomas (2005) *The World is Flat*. New York: Farrar, Straus, and Giroux.

Hart, Jeffrey A. (1976) "Three Approaches to the Measurement of Power in International Relations," *International Organization*, 30(2): 289–305.

Hart, Jeffrey A. (1989) "ISDN and Power," Discussion Paper 7, Center for Global Business, the Business School of Indiana University.

Knorr, Klaus (1973) *Power and Wealth: The Political Economy of International Power*. London: Macmillan.

Lessig, Lawrence (2006) *Code: And Other Laws of Cyberspace, Version 2.0*. New York: Basic Books.

Lukes, Steven (1974) *Power: A Radical View*. London: Macmillan.

Lukes, Steven (1986) "Introduction." In Steven Lukes, ed., *Power*. New York: New York University Press.

Lukes, Steven (2005) *Power: A Radical View*, 2nd edition. London: Palgrave Macmillan.

Lukes, Steven (2007) "Power and the Battle for Hearts and Minds: On the Bluntness of Soft Power." In Felix Berenskoetter and M.J. Williams, eds, *Power in World Politics*. London: Routledge.

Lyon, David (2001) *Surveillance Society: Monitoring Everyday Life*. Philadelphia, PA: Open University Press.

Mueller, Milton (2002) *Ruling the Root: Internet Governance and the Taming of Cyberspace*. Cambridge, MA: MIT Press.

Nagel, Jack (1975) *The Descriptive Analysis of Power*. New Haven, CT: Yale University Press.

National Science Foundation (2010) *Science and Engineering Indicators*. Available at: http://www.nsf.gov/statistics/seind10/ [accessed: 1 August 2011].

Norris, Pippa (2001) *The Digital Divide*. Cambridge: Cambridge University Press.

Nye, Joseph S. Jr (1990) *Bound to Lead: The Changing Nature of American Power*. New York: Basic Books.

Nye, Joseph S. Jr (2002) *The Paradox of American Power: Why the World's Only Superpower Can't Go It Alone*. New York: Oxford University Press.

Nye, Joseph S. Jr (2004) *Soft Power: The Means to Success in World Politics*. New York: Perseus Books.
Nye, Joseph S. Jr (2008) *The Powers to Lead*. New York: Oxford University Press.
Postman, Neil (1986) *Amusing Ourselves to Death: Public Discourse in the Age of Show Business*. Harmondsworth: Penguin.
Singh, J.P. (2008) *Negotiation and the Global Information Economy*. New York: Cambridge University Press.
Strange, S. (1988) *State and Markets: An Introduction to International Political Economy*. New York: Basil Blackwell.
Van Dijk, Jan (2005) *The Deepening Divide: Inequality in the Information Society*. Thousand Oaks, CA: Sage.

Chapter 14
Social Media and Iran's Post-election Crisis

Lida Khalili Gheidary

Introduction

Social media or social media websites, alternatively referred to as Web 2.0, are supposedly second upgraded versions of the web that are more open, collaborative and participatory by virtue of enabling users (peers, grassroots or back-channel) to actively generate content. As noted by Dellarocas (2003), social media websites are unique in offering the opportunity for users to "make their personal thoughts, reactions and opinions easily accessible to the global community." Instances of these media include wikis, blogs, mashups and in particular Social Network Sites (SNS) as the most recent development in the field. The way these tools are used alters many practices, including communication, collaboration, information dissemination and social organization (Benkler 2006; Castells 1996); hence, they have the potential to alter how societies are organized. As these media are evolving in terms of design, the circumstances of their deployment by users are taking new shapes. As an instance, after the 2007 Virginia Tech shootings people gathered online, participated in list-building activities and identified the names of victims in advance of official news releases (Palen and Vieweg 2008; Vieweg et al. 2008).

In this chapter, deployment of social media during Iran's post-election crisis is explored. In this crisis the pervasive use of SNS by members of the public widened the virtual participation opportunities; hence, virtual investigation of the emergent phenomena became feasible by taking a virtual ethnography approach and an information science perspective. In the rest of this chapter, following relevant background information, the online interactions of grassroots are spelled out in the same way that they were observed, in an attempt to characterize the emergent activities by placing them in organizational context.

Background

The latest Iranian presidential election was held on 12 June 2009, in which Ahmadinejad, the incumbent president, ran against three other candidates. According to Iran's constitution, which is often viewed as a peculiar hybrid of authoritarian, theocratic and democratic elements, no president can serve more than two consecutive four-year terms, and so Ahmadinejad was presumably highly determined to win his second term. This hybrid system had led to national TV and most official publications favouring Ahmadinejad in such a way that Ahmadinejad's government would enjoy a decisive advantage in the management of public information. Within hours of the 2009 election the national TV announced Ahmadinejad as the winner with 62.63% of the votes, and Mousavi as the runner-up with 33.75% of the votes. This statistic brought supporters of Mousavi as well as two other candidates to a state of shock and distress as, in particular, Mousavi's supporters strongly believed that he would be the next president of Iran. Mousavi quickly released a statement claiming that he would not surrender to this charade and declared the election to be engineered and rigged.

Following this dispute, the streets of Tehran witnessed massive numbers of protesters rallying against the perceived rigged election, resulting in severe clashes and casualties, and creating news headlines around the globe. According to several official reports, the Iranian government quickly attempted to control the flow of public information in reaction to the ongoing national crisis. They disconnected the SMS system, reduced the landline facilities to national calls and on 13 June completely cut Internet access; however, the traffic was gradually allowed through again at a reduced level. The Internet censorship that was already in effect was made more rigid, and most SNS were blocked.

Prior to the election, Mousavi's campaigners had opened blogs on Facebook and Twitter, with green icons as chosen campaign colour, and disseminated information about his agenda by those means. By 20 June, at least 24 correspondents had been detained in custody, including CNN's official correspondent; however, most of the foreign journalists were later released and then expelled. The only media that were not disrupted were those fully controlled by government. As observed by other researchers, the use of social media in activities such as facilitating discussion and debate (Kolbitsch and Maurer 2006) and organizing on a large scale has already become an established phenomenon; yet Iran's unique circumstances raised the question of what forms of communication would be used in support of information generation, seeking and sharing among the participants.

In an analysis for CNN, Clay Shirky mentioned that shutting the SMS service probably radicalized another part of the population who had previously thought that they were not part of the fight. This probably acted as an impetus for them (Iranians) to employ any communicative tool they had available, which led them, and subsequently the world, to turn to social media technology. On 16 June, the U.S. State Department said that it had contacted Twitter to urge it to delay a planned upgrade that would have cut daytime service to those who were disputing their election inside Iran (Source: Reuters, CNN, BBC and others). As will be outlined below, Iran's crisis provided a great opportunity for social media, in particular SNS, to increase their prominence to an unprecedented level.

Method

In this interpretative research, virtual ethnography was carried out for a period of at least two months starting from 12 June 2009 through Facebook and Twitter, as these two were the most crucial social media used during the crisis period at both grassroots and official levels. Collectively through three Facebook accounts (the author's and two other contributors' accounts), 600 users were observed, of which more than 60% were Iranians and the rest were of a variety of nationalities. The visible online interactions of these users regarding Iran's crisis were monitored several times a day. The Facebook groups and micro-blogs that formed during the crisis were monitored and the comments and discussions left in each were read. All the shared files and links related to the crisis were observed carefully. On Twitter, #Iran Election was searched on a daily basis and those users who had the largest numbers of followers sending tweets on #Iran Election were followed. Additionally, for secondary or external data, BBC World News, CNN, BBC Persian, Voice of America (VOA) Persian, Reuters website, Guardian website and Youtube.com (which is already embraced by most users inside SNS), and others were continuously followed several times a day. Moreover, a number of interviews were conducted with around 20 grassroots contacts and two correspondents from CNN and the *Huffington Post*.

Power of Seduction

The previous Iranian presidential election (2005) had not enjoyed large citizen participation, and thus the initial forecasts for the 2009 election were not high. Comments and status updates from a few weeks before the election through Facebook show a variety of views on the distribution of materials about the election through SNS. Some condemn their peers for sharing the materials on the basis that such activities publicize the election and encourage people to vote for candidates who are deemed incapable of reform by most. Not only the presidential debate videos but also plenty of elaborately edited photos from Mousavi's offline campaigns were shared, and led to the formation of ephemeral virtual communities around the "either to vote or not" issue. A new fashion emerged at this time when some of Mousavi's supporters started to edit their Facebook display photos, producing green shadowed photos of themselves. The responses to this fashion, found through Facebook comments, ranged from anger to praise. As time passed the number who subscribed themselves to this photo fashion increased. One of the interviewees said in this regard:

> I didn't even know about these candidates nor did I want to vote. I just used to wander in Facebook occasionally and got attracted by these emerging activities, symbols and photo editing and hence decided to experiment (with) the things myself. I was apathetic to vote but after a while I felt this is a different case. I can't say what exactly happened but I think I very much got seduced by the excitement which was generated around the whole thing in my Facebook community.

In the end it was reported that 84% of the electorate participated in this election, which was a notable increase over the 2005 election. It is not claimed that such colossal participation took place merely because of the application of social media, but it is reasonable to claim that the virtual *flâneur* who was wandering without destination in SNS found a destination, arriving in a political arena in response to seduction. The audience was seduced by experimenting with the green (Marres 2009) photo editing in a networked public, and thereby engaged with politics.

Organizing and Information Pathways

By 20 June, as the street clashes became more violent and more correspondents were disrupted, the fear of information dearth became more widespread among protesters (Mousavi's supporters), since the remaining stable media inside Iran were in favour of Ahmadinejad. On the occurrence of nonroutine events during crises, nonroutine behaviours and new social arrangements, including self-organization by members of the public in response to emergent needs, may emerge. In this crisis, prior to any other needs, the need for accurate information was pivotal. During the protests, opportunities for creating new and ephemeral organizations/communities frequently arose. When communities were formed during the protests (i.e. a group of people who had escaped from armed forces to a narrow street), their peers would converse with each other, make sense of the situation and generate information related to their situation; thus the *first* information pathway (Palen and Liu 2007) would run between peers in the crisis zone. As an instance, if a peer was seen shot and injured, other peers and local groups, in an improvised act, would video record the peer by mobile handset and thus generate information that was not perishable and was traceable. Then a *second* information pathway would run between affected peers and those citizens outside the crisis in the sense that peers would upload the information to the SNS as soon as they could access high-speed Internet (scarce in those days); those (i.e. most Iranian diaspora) outside the main site of crisis would receive the images, make sense of them, and share or re-produce them. In this way, information entered the distributed networks and arrived at many destinations where ephemeral virtual communities formed around it. The *third* information pathway that was automatically created during this crisis ran between the grassroots actors and formal global media members who were also watching the SNS alongside the grassroots outsiders. The *fourth* information pathway probably ran between grassroots actors from outside the crisis zone and those inside the zone, mainly through SNS communities regarding the opposition groups' activities.

Several other intertwined information pathways ran between various communities during this crisis, and limited access to Internet connection would often disrupt these pathways, at least for a while. In regard to being connected to the crisis, one of the interviewees said:

> The first thing I did, after I heard the election results were disputed, was to check news agencies such as BBC, and VOA Persian. The next thing was to check my Facebook. After a while I figured out that I could find better and untouched information straight from the reports in Facebook. Everyday after work Facebook was the first place I was checking to get the latest videos and rumours.

Although digital messages can easily be transmitted, this may result in the loss of context or a level of distortion, and therefore the generation of an opportunity for subversive voices. In fact, in this case, two or more social networks that were meant to be separate collided. Government sympathizers could enter from a point (i.e. an open group) and access the information generated by opposing groups, then reproduce them, distort them and disseminate them from scratch. Evidence of this can be traced through many English-language blogs, where each of them have provided a different version of one specific story that was supposedly initially picked from SNS.

Rise of Global Activism

When SNS became the main platform for information aggregation about the crisis event, an opportunity for connecting to friends' friends who also were affected by crisis arose. This suggests that relationships that may not have otherwise existed between people who had had similar experiences became achievable (Palen et al. 2007), and resulted in large participation in demonstrations both inside and outside Iran, mainly in front of Iranian embassies in major capital cities.

Coordinated information technology support (SNS) enabled non-Iranians from outside the affected communities to merge and take part in generating and reproducing information, even in the English language, as opposed to the unidirectional model of information dissemination from Iranian officials to the public. In fact, by such inexpensive communication, easy linkages across diverse organizations were achievable through the SNS, and they facilitated network-building based on affinities or relatively loose identifications (Bennett 2004) of international dimensions. A common theoretical assumption is that such networks are flexible, easy to join and leave, and capable of relatively fluid reorganization following the addition or loss of organizations (Castells 1996). The problem of language (in Iran's case most materials were in Persian) delays reorganization and results in reduced decision-making coherence across temporary organizations. These decentralized organized protest groups, i.e. in Facebook, of thin ideological ties enabled the virtual *flâneur* to join them from various points of entry. They often harboured intellectual contradictions, leading to the formation of epistemic communities fundamentally questioning the Iranian regime.

The groups took the shape of temporary organizations that sometimes fell apart as a result of thin ties, lack of clarity and unstable coalitions, but then refigured themselves (Bennett 2004). The groups in Facebook that were formed for organizing protests, after experiencing a few clashes and losses, merged into a centralized organization for an organized worldwide protest announced for 25 July (http://united4iran.org/).

Collective Intelligence

As the clashes were going on in Iran, the online interactions in Facebook, apparently, conformed to what was going on in the offline zone, or perhaps the direction of conforming was the reverse if not bidirectional. Early communications on Facebook included changing display photos to "Where is my vote?" drawings in green. The following famous Persian poem, which carries the concept of collectivity at its core, circulated among the users in a variety of forms, supposedly in an attempt to call for solidarity and support:

> Human beings are members of a whole, In creation of one essence and soul. If one member is afflicted with pain, Other members uneasy will remain.
>
> If you have no sympathy for human pain, The name of human you cannot retain.

In the offline zone, communications appeared in the form of posters of "Where is my vote?," banners of the aforementioned poem, candles, green shawls, green objects and Allah Akbar chanting, which would collectively resemble an assemblage of human interaction, communications and cultural symbols. Other kinds of persistent communications that emerged were messages written on the walls and the proliferation of caricatures related to the crisis in the online zone by caricaturists. As the videos that were posted throughout Facebook and Twitter became highly graphic, showing disturbing content, the users added a red stain to their "Where is my vote?" display photos. As more protesters and political dissidents were arrested and jailed in Iran, a fearful environment was created throughout Facebook. In response to the fear of being identified for anti-government activities through Facebook, temporary communities were formed to discuss the issue. This can be marked as a form of distributed problem solving activity for which the solution was name change. Within a short time many users had changed their names. The same trend was evident in Twitter, which allows "username" change in addition to display name change. Following this, more online communities were formed criticizing this name change behaviour, saying that "people in Iran are being killed and in this virtual space we are worrying for our own selves."

Similar temporary communities emerged following each shared video. Comments left under these videos (or links) showed on each occasion that at first a few users tried to make sense of the content and then questioned the authenticity of the sources or the videos; after a few discussions and confirmatory sort of comments, some considered the shared information as an authoritative source (Sutton et al. 2008). More activities, such as those that resemble collective intelligence learnt from disaster scenarios (i.e. through work of Vieweg et al. 2008), happened frequently during the Iranian crisis. The next sequence of the "Where is my vote?" photo display was "Where is my friend?" in reaction to the arrest of more dissidents. Or in case of name change, the next action was to change the surnames to "Irani" (Iranian), supposedly as a nationalist and unifying gesture. When the death of Michael Jackson, on 25 June, coincided with crucial days of Iran's crisis, within a few hours of his death, fusion works including videos of "violence against protesters in Iran" mixed with Michael Jackson's songs as the background music were distributed along these networks.

Implications for Social Media

As SNSs became the primary platform for aggregation of information about the Iranian crisis, members of official media adapted themselves to these services more than before, especially through the third information pathway described above. Previously researchers had observed during the Virginia Tech shooting in 2007 that the related news was directly picked up by CNN from the peer-generated information in the SNS, but during the Iranian crisis, the extent to which this phenomenon occurred was unique. Such unique reliance of official media on SNS can be associated with the co-occurrence of another sub-phenomenon, the rise of widespread usage of new media in covering the recent presidential elections (i.e. the 2008 U.S. election), after which the U.S. media had maintained their usage of these new technologies on all stories. Here the archetype of directing the events to official media is provided:

> On the 20th of June the footage of the last two minutes of the life of an Iranian girl called Neda Agha Soltan, shot during street rallying, was captured on video by mobile phones of bystanders and was virally distributed across SNS. Within a few hours of her death #Neda tweet became one of the top trending topics in Twitter and then the video went on air through CNN. Iranian official media later confirmed her death but accused foreigners of plotting such a murder for political gain. She quickly became an international heroine and a symbol of the Iranian Green movement. A Street in Rome was also named after her.

These phenomena are not entirely new, but they are taking new shapes and are altering formal practices. During this crisis many in-depth talks were held on the BBC and CNN, discussing "the verification of footage," "what should be picked by official media" and "to what extent is the collaboration of official media with absolute grassroots achievable given ethical journalism." As the CNN correspondent who was interviewed for this chapter noted, "Iran's crisis pushed the news verification debate to a serious stage."

Conclusion

The exploration of the context suggests that wide-scale employment of social media during Iran's crisis, reflecting what was happening inside Iran, augmented the public's and officials' awareness of the existence of social media and the potential of this technology. The way they were embraced by officials and grassroots actors reveals how new forms of social media can be incorporated into the activities of citizens in crisis and complicates formal practices, or re-shapes them. This draws attention to how this technology should be incorporated into formal responses, i.e. official media, in an effective way. The study can provide lessons for future SNS designers, i.e. that they better understand the potentials of this medium in the context of political engagement. Last but not least, the study suggests that the widescale adaptation to social media by back-channels (grassroots) in a country with a perceived authoritarian regime acted as a catalyst for social media to enter a new phase of their history, and supplied the impetus for the official world to use the technology in a different manner.

Acknowledgments

I acknowledge inspiration for my research from research papers on Crisis Informatics by ConnectivIT Laboratory team at the University of Colorado, Boulder. I would like to thank all the interviewees and Information Systems Group of the London School of Economics, Dr Susan Scott and Ofer Engel in particular, who generously gave their time to my research. Also, many thanks go to ISCRAM organizers and reviewers for their hard work.

References

Benkler, Y. (2006) *The Wealth of Networks: How Social Production Transforms Markets and Freedom*. New Haven, CT: Yale University Press.

Bennet, L.W. (2004) "Communicating Global Activism," in Win van de Donk, Brian Loader, Paul Nixon and Dieter Rucht, eds, *Cyberprotest: New Media, Citizens, and Social Movements*. Abingdon: Routledge, pp. 123–46.

Castells, M. (1996) *The Rise of the Network Society*. Cambridge, MA: Blackwell.

Dellarocas, C. (2003) "The Digitization of Word of Mouth," *Management Science*, 49(10), 1407–24.

Kolbitsch, J. and Maurer, H. (2006) "The Transformation of the Web: How Emerging Communities Shape the Information We Consume," *Journal of Universal Computer Science*, 2(2), 187–207.

Marres, N. (2009) "Testing Powers of Engagement: Green Living Experiments, the Ontological Turn and the Undoability of Involvement," in "What is the Empirical?," special issue edited by L. Adkins and C. Lury, *European Journal of Social Theory*, 12(1), 117–33.

Palen, L. and Liu, S. (2007) "Citizen Communications in Crisis: Anticipating a Future of ICT-Supported Participation," *Proceedings of the ACM Conference on Human Factors in Computing Systems, CHI 2007*, 727–36.

Palen, L. and Vieweg, S. (2008) "Emergent, Widescale Online Interaction in Unexpected Events: Assistance, Alliance and Retreat," *Proceedings of Computer Supported Cooperative Work Conference*, November, San Diego, CA.

Palen, L., Vieweg, S., Sutton, J., Liu, S. and Hughes, A. (2007) "Crisis Informatics: Studying Crisis in a Networked World," *Proceedings of the Third International Conference on E-Social Science*, Ann Arbor, MI, 7–9 October.

Sutton, J., Palen, L. and Shklovski, I. (2008) "Backchannels on the Front Lines: Emergent Use of Social Media in the 2007 Southern California Fires," *Proceedings of the Information Systems for Crisis Response and Management Conference (ISCRAM 2008)*.

Vieweg, S., Palen, L. Liu, Hughes, A. and Sutton, J. (2008) "Collective Intelligence in Disaster: an Examination of the Phenomenon in the Aftermath of the 2007 Virginia Tech Shooting," *Proceedings of the 5th International ISCRAM Conference*, Washington, DC, May.

Chapter 15
VIEWPOINT: Combating Censorship Should be a Foreign Policy Goal

Hannes Steen-Thornhammar

Never in history has the flow of information been greater. The rapid development and ubiquity of information and communication technologies (ICT) have turned digital information into a commodity, whether as key words, wiki entries or financial instruments. As the world is becoming increasingly wired, and as more people have access to information and communication technologies, the gains from controlling that information have never been greater. The stakes have been raised precisely because there is so much information available, and because so many people depend on it. Information empowers, but it also dethrones. This will be obvious not just between corporations that fight for profits, but also between sovereign nations and private individuals, whose values will be tested in the growing flatness of the world. The tension between those who want to accelerate the proliferation of information and those who want to control it will rise in the years to come. The tension will test the strength of political and economic entities, ideologies and cultures. It will also show itself in the growing gap between those who have access to the latest technological developments and those who do not. Legal systems will have to accommodate these rapid changes and, in the vast sea of digital change, censorship will acquire new meaning.

When the political theorist, Francis Fukuyama, declared that the end of history had arrived with the triumph of Western liberal democracy, he did not account for the political complexity of such countries as China, Russia and Saudi Arabia, where economic success has occurred at tremendous rates with little progress in political freedom. In these countries, censorship is continuously employed as a tool to curtail individual expression and to support the powers that be. Whether or not these political systems will be successful in the long term remains to be seen; what is clear is that the ideals of democracy, the institutions and values that it represents, have found competition in the global economic system. It appears that economic progress and the spread of prosperity can occur while freedom of expression is curtailed and, despite what was previously true of market-based western liberal democracy, political and economic freedom may not necessarily be aligned; material progress can occur without moral progress.

Thus, the question of censorship becomes a question about liberty and the pursuit of a common humanity. Censorship rests on the shoulder of Kantian autonomy, referring "to the capacity to be one's own person, to live one's life according to reasons and motives that are taken as one's own and not the product of manipulative or distorting external forces" (Christman 2009). The capacity to live one's life distinct from external influence and the right to freedom of expression are negative liberties. The liberty to express oneself freely must be ascertained in the absence of external constraints; for without individual human autonomy, there can be no freedom of expression. Without allowing freedom of expression, there can be no form of legitimate power. The argument, then, for why "we are in this together" resides in individual choice. However, regardless of what one believes to be right, censorship should not be employed if it constrains human autonomy. This is one of the foundational aspects of democracy and it is neatly summarized by Evelyn Beatrice Hall, who chronicled the philosophy of the French Enlightenment thinker, François-Marie Arouet, better known under his pen name, Voltaire: "I disapprove of what you say, but I will defend to the death your right to say it."

And so it was. The moral choice was made when the Western liberal democracies—after the extraordinary sacrifices and the atrocities of the Second World War—decided once and for all that the International Covenant on Civil and Political Rights had to establish and formalize the fundamental and unalienable rights of every citizen. Among the some 30 articles, the Universal Declaration of Human Rights stated that the right to receive, seek and impart information represents one of the cornerstones of a free society and that every person has "the right to hold opinions without interference" from others. Expecting the political elites in China, Russia and Saudi Arabia to accept democracy as byproducts of economic integration is naïve, but by the same token, the argument for why combating censorship should be a foreign policy goal is to be made in the light of the history that brought democracy to life.

Since the early formations of democracy, free speech has been an integral component of the political process. The very foundation of democracy demands that individuals have equal access to power and every individual has the right to certain unalienable freedoms and liberties; the means of accessing power occurs through an independent individual voice—the ability to express an opinion—and the unalienable right of equality in law and protection. Freedom of speech is an incentive—the incentive to acquire power by means of participation, involvement and collaboration within the political sphere and in the public space. In the small democratic enclaves that emerged 500 BCE around Athens and the Greek islands, active participation became the leading thread of political viability. The *agora*—"the public sphere"—became the center for political dissemination and discourse. In particular, the *agora* took on a central role in Athenian society, where it became the meeting place for political and commercial transactions and ensured the active participation of the suffrage, the actual architectural space where opinions could be exchanged, ideas and laws debated, and legislations to be brought forth to the ruling assembly, the *ecclesia* (Hansen 1989).

The centrality of a public marketplace for opinions, ideas and thoughts is widely recognized between scholars of Ancient Greek democracy as one of the main reasons for the emergence of a decentralized, semi-egalitarian, and cohesive political system (Athenian Constitution, Wikipedia 2010). Understanding both the limits and the underlying premise within which these were formed is crucial, not just for the development of Anglo-Saxon inspired liberal democracies, but also for active participation in the political process, the development of human rights, and the value of free speech: "In Athens, all adult male citizens were admitted to the *ecclesia*, and every citizen was entitled to address the assembly and make proposals. A decree passed by the assembly was—in theory—a decision made by all sovereign Athenians" (Hansen 1989).

The connection between democracy and technology follows henceforth. The etymology of these words uncovers the importance of speech—and other forms of communication—to the democratic process. Democracy, meaning "popular government" was coined from δῆμος (dēmos), "people" and κράτος (kratos), "rule, strength" signifying the hopes of communion and dialogue within the population. The link between ICTs and democracy becomes apparent once the connotations of the word "technology" are explored and put into this context. Technology is a term with origins in the Greek "technologia:" "techne," "*τέχνη*" ("craft") and "logia," "*λογία*" ("saying"). Technology then literally refers to the "craft of saying" which posits a dynamic relationship between the importance of free speech and the ability to voice and share opinions, thoughts, and ideas.

There is a strong history of these ideas rooted in the liberal tradition. John Milton politicized the Greek *Areopagus* in one of the seminal works on the universal value of free speech, *Areopagitica: a Speech of Mr. John Milton for the Liberty of Unlicensed Printing to the Parliament of England.* As a commemoration to the orator Isocrates—whose speech became one of the leading tracts for the undivided importance of a "Court of Appeals" in civic society—Milton stressed that censorship was never a requisite of either Greek or Roman society. That any form of censorship should be imposed on the British Isles was an insult to those qualities that distinguish a free and prosperous society. "Give me the liberty to know, to utter, and to argue freely according to conscience, above all liberties," Milton wrote in the *Areopagitica* (Milton 2009).

The polemic of the *Areopagitica* traces the history of Athenian democracy to contemporary society. Free speech is central for man's quest to reach his or her full potential; it is through language that we communicate. Therefore, it is through language that we connect with fellow citizens, and that we make our differences or similarities explicit. It is also through language that we record and communicate those differences. Allowing this liberty to flourish was in Milton's view one of the ways in which free speech could transpire into a higher good for society. Of course, this could only occur when the statutes of justice are upheld and censorship abolished. The actual function of the *agora* and the *ecclesia* within a democratic framework is an interesting analogy to the way users today engage with modern ICTs, particularly social networking sites. The link between the *agora* and social networking sites may seem far-fetched, but the increased integration of commercial platforms with e-government initiatives in Northern Europe and in North America suggests otherwise—precisely because censorship is not immediately exercised. The presence of physical platforms dedicated to social and political discourse today draws a parallel to the slopes of the Parthenon more than two millennia ago, suggesting that the need for a public space is shared throughout history, and stands as one of the foundations of democratic participation.

Yet this does not automatically mean that Western democracies should allow complete transparency and unlimited freedom. Some measure of secrecy and censoring must still be employed and, undoubtedly, will be employed, but this is often a good thing. Pun intended, the Prussian statesman, Otto von Bismarck, reportedly cautioned lovers of democracy with the following quotation: "laws are similar to sausages; it is best not to see how they are made." The unevaluated and unedited truth is left to the mercy of interpretation, and to have no filtering mechanism is not always beneficial. Sometimes, the truth is better served in small doses, rather than in a giant cake. In the Western world, there are media, journalism, NGOs and such to keep an eye out for any wrongful censoring, but in most parts of the world, the ability to voice contrary opinions to the power construct is too often prohibited. The former Canadian diplomat, Scott Gilmore, addressed this topic in light of the leaked cables by the website, WikiLeaks. Making a case for the benefit of freedom of speech, Gilmore also suggests that one must exercise a balance between idealism and reality (Gilmore 2010):

> When we sent the reporting cables back to the Department of Foreign Affairs, they were secret for a reason. If they were published in *The Globe and Mail* instead, I would have been thrown out of the country in 24 hours and the Indonesian officials would not have permitted a replacement. The local politicians would have hired a rent-a-mob to stone the Canadian embassy. Their leaders would have told the Jakarta media I was a liar and would have blamed the Timorese for feeding me calumny. And the police would have arrested and killed the young teacher before the week was out.

One of the advocates for the proliferation of information is the search-engine giant, Google, whose mission statement is "to organize the world's information and make it universally accessible and useful." The company left mainland China after its email service, Gmail, was attacked by what was believed to be hackers sanctioned by the Chinese government in order to acquire information on political dissidents. As a result, the search engine stopped filtering search results and moved its operations to Hong Kong. Google's executives have argued since the incident that China's censorship constitutes an actual economic sanction and nothing short of a trade barrier. This argument is not unfamiliar to Washington. The U.S.–China Economic and Security Commission drafted a report to Congress, quoting Google Executives on the unfair conditions for the businesses operating in Chinese information services (U.S.–China Economic and Security Review Commission 2010). Through the Google-China affair, it has become increasingly obvious that censorship has major implications for international trade. One official made the point, saying that, if a foreign country placed broad restrictions on "physical trade, we'd all be saying this violates trade agreements. If you want to be part of the community of free trade, you have to let the Internet be open" (Greenberg 2010).

Google's legal chief David Drummond offered a similar comparison and argued that economic activity and human rights run tandem (Greenberg 2010):

> In our view at Google it's high time for us to start really sinking our teeth into this one ... We have great opportunities now with pending trade agreements to start putting some pressure on countries to recognize that Internet freedom not only is a core value—that we should be holding them to account from a human rights standpoint—but also that if you want to be part of the community of free trade, you are going to have to find a way to allow the Internet to be open.

Google is not alone in voicing its concerns over Chinese censorship. The U.S. foreign secretary, Hillary Clinton, delivered a speech in Washington for the Council of Foreign Relations that criticized China for the way it censors the Internet. The Chinese government continues to detain and harass journalists, and even though the economy is bourgeoning, allowing for greater diversity in the mainstream media coverage, the government is still controlling media in order to maintain power (Clinton 2010). A senior fellow at the Council of Foreign Relations, Elizabeth C. Economy, says that the various forms of censorships reflect a state of "schizophrenia" in the Chinese government about how to handle media policy—"[it] goes back and forth, testing the line, knowing they need press freedom—and the information it provides—but worried about opening the door to the type of freedoms that could lead to the regime's downfall" (Baldwin et al. 2010).

The extent of Chinese censorship runs contrary to expectation. Many have suspected the Chinese President Hu Jintao of pushing the liberal agenda and relaxing the Chinese monitoring of Internet activity. Under his administration, the Chinese media have undergone a process of increased commercialization, growing competition, greater entertainment, diversification, and modern investigative reporting. China's Internet users are approaching several hundred millions and the number is growing at tremendous speed. However, despite this development, only government-sponsored agencies can own media in China. Privatization is happening at dismal rates, and under Hu's leadership, the government has instead pursued a media policy that involves increased regulation as well as the arrest and prosecution of dissidents and journalists. The Asia Program Director for the Committee to Protect Journalists, Bob Dietz, says this "hard swing to the conservative side" is likely to be the direction as long as Hu is in power (Baldwin et al. 2010).

This theory is also confirmed by James Fallows. What appears to be a soft attitude to increased liberalization is in fact a phantom menace that is carefully thought out, planned and executed (Fallows 2008):

> In reality, what the Olympic-era visitors will be discovering is not the absence of China's electronic control but its new refinement—and a special Potemkin-style unfettered access that will be set up just for them, and just for the length of their stay.

Fallow depicts a state that is at once meticulous, soft and determined. The Internet was always designed to re-route packets of information around any given obstacle, but in China, this is not so: the Chinese Internet architecture comes with built in choke points.

Andrew Lih, professor of journalism at the University of Southern California and director of the New Media Institute, has documented the ways in which Chinese government can monitor online activity on the various fiber optic cables that direct Internet traffic. There is the DNS block that prohibits the browser from recognizing the IP address of a "harmful" site. There is the "connect phase" that informs the gateway servers when someone is connecting to a "undesirable" site, usually producing "site not found" or "connection lost" messages. Then there is the "URL keyword block" and sophisticated scanning of website content against sensitive keywords. Whenever keywords like "falun gong" or "Chinese mining accident" are discovered, the mirroring software disrupts the connection and the content window becomes invisible. In this way, big Western sites do not have to be blocked entirely, but whenever suspicious content appears, the surveillance software notifies the authorities and instigates some form of censorship (Fallows 2008).

Yet if censorship in China is deliberately deceptive, in Syria it is actual policy. Most of the Syrian news, media, and broadcasting are controlled by the state. Only family members, top government officials and a hand-picked oligarchy are allowed to operate media industries. The founder of All4Syria.info, Ayman Abdel Nour, left Syia to set up an independent news site for Syrian emigrates. He concludes that, in Syria, "the first level is censorship," where no contrary view may be voiced, "the second level is when they send you statements and force you to publish them" (Worth 2010). There can be no criticism of the president or the security services, or how Syria's Kurdish minority is treated. Foreign journalists are regularly banned from the country and any realistic attempt at monitoring the internal politics of the country has proved difficult under such harsh regulations.

The Internet and its numerous blogs were once hailed as the new media of change, but bloggers in Syria are frequently subjected to bullying and harsh treatment. Tal al-Mallohi, a 19-year-old female blogger, was arrested for encouraging the Syrian government to protect Palestinians. The blogger Osama Kario was jailed for 28 days and, when released, refused to speak to fellow journalists about his experiences (Worth 2010). The progressive Orient TV, owned by a Syrian businessman and broadcasted from Dubai, was abruptly shut down without explanation. Mohammad Ali Abdallah, whose brother received a five-year prison sentence for his contribution to an Internet forum that the government found hostile, says that "the Internet in Syria is a bit like the samizdat publications were under the Soviet Union" (Worth 2010). Yet, at the same time, social networking sites such as Facebook have become powerful outlets for anonymous journalists, who can broadcast news across the world and gain social media traction. In Damascus, foreign proxy server numbers sell well.

In India, censorship transcends security concerns. The terrorists who orchestrated the Mumbai attacks utilized a variety of ICT to communicate with their Pakistani cohorts. There is still speculation as to how Chinese hackers gained access to India's military computer networks. The government of India has adopted a harsh approach to combating these threats, but critics remain concerned about the government's security efforts in blocking or monitoring peer-to-peer services. Combating illegal activities by aiming for individual service providers may sometimes have the reverse effect. Ajay Shah, an economist who writes frequently on topics related to security and technology explains that "they will do damage by blocking highly visible systems like BlackBerry or Skype ... this will shift users to less visible and known platforms. Terrorists will make merry doing crypto anyway. A zillion tools for this are freely available" (Austen and Vikas 2010).

At the same time, Senior Indian officials argue that perpetrators and technology companies leave them with little choice. Government security agencies, they demand, must have access to the data that could help secure the prevention of cyber and terrorist attacks. The secretary of India's Home Ministry, Gopal Krishna Pillai, who oversees domestic security, explains that access to data is critical: "All communications which is done by Indians or coming to and from into India—and where we have a concern about national security—we should have access to it" (Austen and Vikas 2010). He receives a good deal of popular support from security officials who, during the Mumbai attacks, had difficulty accessing the communication between terrorists. Legal experts also indicate that Indian law offers little protection for individual privacy. Pavan Duggal, a lawyer who practices regularly before the Supreme Court and who specializes in issues regarding technology, explains that "the concern of corporate users and general users of BlackBerry is that if this is allowed, the government will become the single biggest repository of information ... and we have no idea how this information will be used and misused in the future" (Austen and Vikas 2010).

Balancing the need for greater national security while maintaining individual privacy will become one of the hallmarks of twenty-first-century policy. Fear of cyber attacks will prompt officials to ask for greater control, and some are already demanding that network operators and service providers allow government agencies access to private data. Monitoring data may protect national security, but it might also cripple technological innovation and business investment. India and dozens of countries in the Middle East have attempted to block encrypted BlackBerry services. Popular services such as Skype and Gmail have also been under scrutiny by governments who view these open services as repositories of encrypted data. However, critics say that these moves could further hurt business relations. India, with its large outsourcing industries, is obviously vulnerable to policies that could disrupt the flow of information. Peter Sutherland, the former Canadian ambassador to India and now consultant for European and North American companies who want to invest in India, has suggested that maintaining secure data transmissions is critical for business relations: "If there is any risk to that data, those companies will look elsewhere" (Austen and Vikas 2010). Similarly, the vice chairman of one of India's largest outsourcing companies, Tata Consultancy Services, has also suggested that policies that undermine the integrity of service providers are likely to be detrimental in the long term: "Bans and calls for bans aren't a solution ... they'll disconnect India from the rest of the world" (Austen and Vikas 2010).

The debate regarding censorship is heating up, and not just in India. Government initiatives designed to instill a certain measure of control over the flow of information are not limited to the Middle East and Asia. In the U.S., security officials and law enforcement agencies have voiced similar concerns. As the ICT infrastructure becomes more finely integrated across nations, those in charge of protecting national interests from terrorist activities are forced to adjust and enhance their practices. New regulations for the Internet are beginning to emerge. While wiretapping, once a popular method for law enforcement, is coming to be viewed as an outdated form of surveillance, digital decryption is becoming standard practice for most sophisticated security agencies. Similar to the government of India, Congress has suggested that all service providers, including encrypted BlackBerry exchanges, Facebook conversations, and peer-to-peer interactions must comply with digital decryption orders, forcing service providers to decrypt intercepted messages between users. As consultants and business specialists point out, this kind of legislation will not only affect business relations, but will also affect the Internet architecture (Savage 2010):

> They are really asking for the authority to redesign services that take advantage of the unique, and now pervasive, architecture of the Internet … they basically want to turn back the clock and make Internet services function the way that the telephone system used to function.

Thus, the argument for greater security is often made in the context of protection of national interests. However, the vice president of the Center for Democracy and Technology, James X. Dempsey, has been critical of the government's handling of ICT, democracy, and security, maintaining that, while private, corporate, and state interest intersect, the government has failed to accommodate the rapid development of technology with the right legal structures that would bridge these disparate interests: "Today, it is clear that the balance among these three interests—the individual's right to privacy, the government's need for tools to conduct investigations, and the interest of service providers in clarity and customer trust—has been lost as powerful new technologies create and store more and more information about our daily lives" (Savage 2010). The reality is that ICT law enforcement and security concerns are trapped in a cat-and-mouse game, continuously hampered by a slow bureaucratic process; ICT develops at much greater speed than legal frameworks.

Thus, the power structure has shifted. Technological prowess is increasingly within private hands and outside government control. Encryption methods are fast becoming increasingly sophisticated and the ability to generate new code keys takes far less time than finding ways to unlock them. Companies such as Google have improved their encryption methods, making it harder for governments to intercept and monitor messages. The maker of BlackBerry smartphones, R.I.M., has said that it is willing to meet "the lawful access needs of law enforcement agencies" (Austen and Vikas 2010). However, the company also says that it does not disclose unencrypted copies of messages of corporate users. The company has been quoted saying that "strong encryption has become a mandatory requirement for all enterprise-class wireless e-mail services today … and is also a fundamental commercial requirement for any country to attract and maintain international business" (Austen and Vikas 2010).

When WikiLeaks published some 220 cables of confidential material from embassies, officials and foreign ambassadors on nuclear and security threats from around the world, it not only sent shivers down the spines of the diplomatic establishment, it also proved that the interconnectedness of the twenty-first century transcends domestic concerns. The cables made headlines everywhere and exacerbated meetings between foreign leaders from the world's leading nations. The power balance between nations was turned upside down by a single website, and this is a good thing. The state's use of power should be monitored. Otherwise, how can it be held accountable? (*The Economist* 2010).

> Organisations such as WikiLeaks, which are philosophically opposed to state secrecy and which operate as much as is possible outside the global nation-state system, may be the best we can hope for in the way of promoting the climate of transparency and accountability necessary for authentically liberal democracy. Some folks ask, "Who elected Julian Assange?" The answer is nobody did, which is, ironically, why WikiLeaks is able to improve the quality of our democracy. Of course, those jealously protective of the privileges of unaccountable state power will tell us that people will die if we can read their email, but so what? Different people, maybe more people, will die if we can't.

Effective monitoring of state power and commitment to democracy makes websites such as WikiLeaks powerful and necessary components of societies that protect and promote free speech. The ubiquity and the availability of information afforded by ICT have leveled the playing field for nations, forcing the urgent need for transparency, containment, or outright censorship. The right of free speech should therefore be enforced internationally. Without the right to express concern, to assess, or to critique, the use of power cannot be legitimate, for it is through citizenship that one willfully grants the state legitimate use of power. However, if this power cannot be subject to scrutiny, then free individuals cannot grant it. They have no autonomy by which to give that right. Thus, the right to freedom of expression must be made to ensure that the individual's rights are protected, not just by Western democracies, but also by a common cause for human rights as most ICT transcends mere national concerns.

Yet while this is being debated in most Western nations, it is almost entirely ignored in the Middle East. The Iranian government frequently blocks access to YouTube (Deibert and Rohozinski 2008). As one of the most visited sites in the world, YouTube provides a valuable platform for controversy, discussion, and dialogue. Repressive governments have an easy time curtailing the supply of dissent, especially in countries where power is concentrated in the hands of few and where service providers are complicit in the act of censoring. Nevertheless, the massive reach and the commercial appeal of YouTube must be highlighted; the site has been instrumental in fostering a culture on the web that is committed to democratic forms of sharing information. The White House's private YouTube channel is littered with offensive commentary, but it does not censor and it does allow for a diversity of interests to be reflected as fairly as the technology makes possible—staying true to the ideal of freedom of speech.

In 2008, the media-broadcasting network CNN began to use YouTube for the presidential debates. Partnering with the site and announcing that it would be gathering questions from "viewers like you" through the site and then directing those questions to the contending candidates, the level of democratic interaction changed dramatically. Appropriating social media in order to reach out to politicians, users, viewers, and the entire electorate, what the broadcasting network did was pertinent and previously unheard of. Much of the reporting during the showdown of presidential nominees was conducted through YouTube, and this propelled private businesses such as CNN and YouTube to serve the principles of democracy in a way that brought the etymology of the word "democracy" alive.

People rule. And what we see is something not unlike the relationship between the *agora* and the *ecclesia* and the early formations of practiced participation—the supply of information, thoughts and opinions through the marketplace of the local town-square and how these concerns were then passed on to the ruling assembly, the *ecclesia*. The information flow between CNN, YouTube, and the Capitol is not unlike that of the *agora* to the *ecclesia*. What is beginning to emerge in the U.S. is something structurally similar. Certainly, the democratic process is not without flaws, but initiatives like these signal empowerment, uniquely so when speech can be distributed at a minimal cost and the freedom of expression favors all those who participate. Social media communities are shorthand for news-broadcasting units, independent marketing, and promotional agencies where ideas, opinions, and thoughts are freely recorded and distributed (Helft 2009):

> As a result of those discussions, the White House first switched from a YouTube video player that installs a cookie on a user's computer whenever it is loaded, to a player that installs a cookie only when a user clicks to watch a video. YouTube also developed a version of that player that does not have the YouTube logo. And it began embedding its own privacy policy on videos that are streamed from government sites to alert users that YouTube was collecting information about them.

This trend—wherein the centers of government appropriate consumer technologies for the sake of increasing political participation—represents a positive change in how the popular connections between business, media, ICT, and government interact, and the grass-roots participative phenomenon is not to be underestimated. When the election ended, all YouTube videos mentioning Senator Obama had received a total of 1.9 billion views compared with those mentioning Senator John McCain, which had received 1.1 billion views. TubeMogul, a measurement service, estimates that just the videos that ran on Obama's YouTube channel were watched for the equivalent of 14.5 million hours, with McCain's channel racking up about 488,152 hours (Ramirez 2008). After all, it was sites such as YouTube and the clever use of other social networking services that helped bring President Obama into office (Nagourney and Rutenberg 2009):

> Mr. McIntosh's uncertainty suggests just one of the many obstacles the White House faces as it tries to accomplish what aides say is one of their most important goals: transforming the YouTubing–Facebooking–texting–Twittering grass-roots organization that put Mr. Obama in the White House into an instrument of government. That is something that Mr. Obama, who began his career as a community organizer, told aides was a top priority, even before he was elected.

Organizing communities, rallying people, and distributing ideas go back to the idea of the public space—the *agora*. These things can only be accomplished when freedom of speech is guaranteed. Censorship is thus antithetical to a free society and constrains the autonomy of mankind. The idea of the *agora* is the incentive and a powerful metaphor for the development of democratic participation, political communion and legitimate power. Applications such as YouTube, Facebook, Twitter and similar social media technologies have in today's Western societies become tools for liberty in ways that are unimaginable in authoritarian regimes. Free expression is not a loaded term in the context of Anglo-American societies, but for dissidents across the globe, the term is a hallmark of life. The new developments in ICT are empowering citizens to voice opinions outside the monopoly of traditional power structures.

As free citizens we do not have an obligation to combat censorship, but we have a choice and we recognize the enormous value that, when abolished, it bestows not just on politics, but also on business, technology and culture. The ancient *agora* in the heart of Athens was the hub of free expression and informational exchanges that propelled the structural function of democracy into practical existence. As the marketplace of announcements, discussion and rulings brought forth a tradition that empowered Western societies to achieve an unprecedented level of technological innovation, the foundational elements of a free society were born. In the growing polarity of an interconnected age, those awesome qualities are now challenged, and if we are to continue to enjoy the fruits of those achievements, we must protect that which made it possible. Censorship represents a trade barrier, but also a barrier to greater cooperation, collaboration, and consensus between nations. For this reason, censorship should be a foreign policy goal, but not for the sake of a common humanity, but rather for our separate, and entirely unique, individual autonomy.

References

Austen, Ian and Bajaj Vikas. "India's Surveillance Plan Said to Deter Business." *The New York Times*, 27 September 2010.

Baldwin, Corinne, Preeti Bhattacharji and Carin Zissis. *Media Censorship in China*. Council of Foreign Relations, 27 May 2010.

Christman, Jon. "Autonomy in Moral and Political Philosophy." *Stanford Encyclopedia of Philosophy*, 11 August 2009.

Clinton, Hillary. *Internet Freedom*. Speech. Council of Foreign Relations, 21 January 2010.

Deibert, Ronald and Rafal Rohozinski, *Access Denied: The Practice and Policy of Global Internet Filtering*. Cambridge, MA: MIT Press, 2008.

Fallows, James. "The Connection Has Been Reset." *The Atlantic*, 28 March 2008.

Gilmore, Scott. "Wikileaks Just Made the World More Oppressive." *The Globe and Mail*, 30 November 2010.

Greenberg, Andy. *Congress Commission Echoes Google: China's Censorship is Trade Barrier*. Forbes, 18 November 2010.

Hansen, Mogens Herman, *The Athenian Ecclesia: A Collection of Articles 1976–83*. Viborg: Museum Tuscalanum Press, 1989.

Helft, Miguel. "White House Denies Shunning YouTube." *The New York Times*, 2 March 2009.

Milton, John. *Areopagitica: A Speech of Mr. John Milton for the Liberty of Unlicensed Printing to the Parliament of England*. WLC books, 2009.

Nagourney, Adam and Jim Rotenberg. "Melding Obama's Web to a YouTube Presidency." *The New York Times*, 25 January 2009.

Ramirez, Jessica. "The Big Picture." *BusinessWeek*, 10 November 2008.

The Economist. "In Defence of Wikileaks." 12 March 2010.

Savage, Charlie. "U.S. Tries to Make it Easier to Wiretap the Internet." *New York Times*, 27 September 2010.

U.S.–China Economic And Security Review Commission. *Report to Congress*." November 2010. Available at: www.uscc.gov [accessed: 1 August 2011].

Wikipedia. *Constitution of Athenians in the 4th Century BC*, 2010. Available at: http://en.wikipedia.org/wiki/File:Constitution-of-the-Athenians-in-the-4th-century-BC.png [accessed: 1 December 2010].

Worth, Robert. "Web Tastes Freedom Inside Syria, and It's Bitter." *New York Times*, 29 September 2010.

Chapter 16
VIEWPOINT: An Alternative Perspective on Cyber Anarchy for Policy-makers

Eddie Walsh

Introduction

Cyberspace as we know it today exists independent of the modern international political system. Despite the serious threat posed by computer network operations to international peace and security, the global community has been unwilling or unable to develop and adapt norms and institutions to govern cyber interactions between state and nonstate actors. This is in stark contrast to other transnational issues, such as terrorism, weapons proliferation, outer space, and nontraditional security issues, which have been subsumed into the existing system. The consequence is a general state of strategic anarchy within cyberspace, which imparts both risk and opportunity for the U.S.

Strategic Threat

The threat of attack and exploitation by state and nonstate actors in the cyber domain remains the primary risk. At least 10–20 state actors already possess the capabilities to carry out sophisticated cyber attacks.[1] Furthermore, state actors lack the monopoly on violence over cyberspace that they maintain over the traditional battlespace. Nonstate actors, including well-known computer groups such as Anonymous, have demonstrated an ability to prosecute operations that exceed the present capabilities of many state actors.

As a consequence, this complex environment promises a new set of winners and losers whose means of acquiring power, prestige, and wealth are not inextricably tied to traditional gaps in military and economic capabilities. Computer network operations thus provide a means for both state and nonstate actors to alter the current distribution of power within the international system.

Strategic Opportunity

In the absence of law and order, state actors inevitably seek assurances for their security in order to preserve political legitimacy. Their preference is to secure new violent interaction capabilities through domestic development or technology transfer. In the absence of this ability, the history of state behavior demonstrates an almost universal willingness to secure such assurances through

---

1 See "UN Chief Calls for Treaty to Prevent Cyber War," AFP; http://www.google.com/hostednews/afp/article/ALeqM5h8Uvk-jpSvCWT-bqYSg1Ws4I4yAA.

other means, including procurement of foreign weapons, acquisition of mercenary forces, and execution of strategic defense alliances.

Lack of governance and other associated risks also lead nonstate actors to seek out means to personally protect themselves and their economic well-being. Assuming the somewhat free flow of goods and people, this encourages a net inflow of savings and investment to states that possess the means to best ward off the known threats present in the system. It also promotes the sheltering of important commercial and personal information in these "secure" states.

Holding these propositions to be true, continued anarchic conditions in cyberspace will probably lead both state and nonstate actors to seek additional assurances for their security. This presents a unique opportunity for any actor who can demonstrate dominant capabilities to extract payments and prestige for their products and services. One can argue that this is especially true for cyber security—given that many state and nonstate actors lack the required infrastructure to develop the necessary capabilities themselves.

Inflection Point

The threat posed by anarchic cyberspace can be viewed as an unwelcome challenge for a dominant power like the U.S. Following this line of analysis, one could advocate for the U.S. to impose governance and order in the cyber domain through the codification of new norms vested in international institutions. Unfortunately for those who would advocate such a position, cyberspace presents serious rule-making, monitoring, and enforcement challenges that could render such institutions incapable of properly mitigating cyber threats. In fact, such institutions could actually disadvantage signatories by restricting their ability to counter noncompliant parties, especially rogue states and nonstate actors.

One apparent alternative to multilateral cooperation is for the U.S. to unilaterally leverage its cyber security capabilities to advance its own national interests. Despite strong competition from rising powers, the U.S. remains uniquely endowed with the public and private infrastructure necessary to dominate cyberspace. Its academic, civilian, and military institutions and private sector ecosystem continue to play a central role in the advancement of cyberspace.

If the U.S. elected to purposefully mobilize these resources, it could probably sustain the development of cyber security capabilities that exceed those of its strategic competitors—at least for the foreseeable future.[2] The long-term payoff of such investment promises to transform American foreign and domestic policy:

- the acquisition of a "Cyber Defense Shield" would be a major diplomatic boost for American treaty alliances—on a par with the National Missile Defense Shield;
- new cyber tools and technologies would generate innovation and a new generation of exportable security products and services capable of growing and strengthening the domestic economy;

2 Strategic dominance requires more than just the allocation of resources. It also necessitates, among other things, a complete overhaul of cyber security doctrine, the redoubling of science and technology education programs, a critical rethinking of the continued privatization of cyber security, a restructuring of the existing military industrial complex, and the passing of a new generation of cyber legislation and policy. These changes could be delivered in an executive mandate, similar to that which President Kennedy delivered for the space program.

- the investment in improved quality in education across science and technology would help ensure that American higher education remains a gold standard.

An Alternative Strategy

While the international call for a cyber treaty may be growing louder, the U.S. must first consider what best serves its national interests. A new national security strategy grounded in strategic dominance of cyberspace does not ameliorate the concerns of the majority of state and nonstate actors. This is especially true for those entities with the least ability to ensure their own cyber security. Alternatively, the exploitation of cyber anarchy provides one of the clearest mechanisms by which the U.S. can prevent the further systemic erosion of its global strategic dominance. Cyber anarchy therefore may serve as a strategic imperative that the U.S. must accept and act upon if it hopes to preserve its status—and the benefits that status entails—as the preeminent guarantor of international security. Until the international community can better resolve the serious challenges to rule-making, monitoring, and enforcement, American policy-makers consequently should not seek to enter into an international treaty for cyber security.

PART III

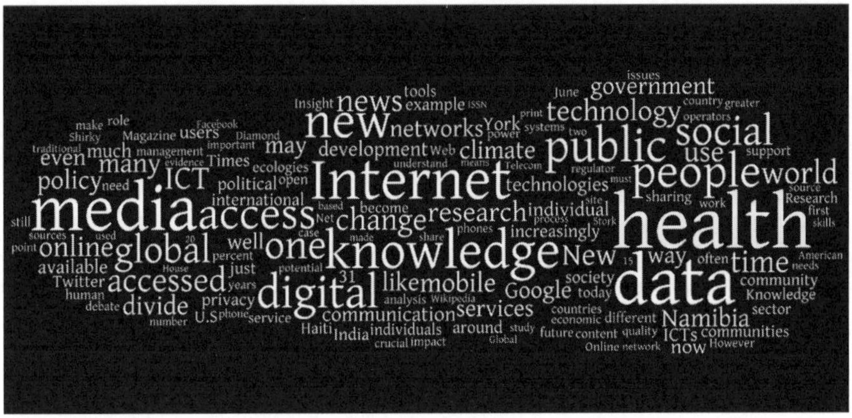
media
Internet
health
knowledge
data
digital
access
public
people
social
new
global
online
news
technology
government
accessed
research
change
one
world
policy
ICT
many
climate
mobile
Google
Namibia
networks
development
communication
services
divide
privacy
time

Chapter 17
Digital Divide: The Reality of Information Haves and Have-nots

Natalya Sverjensky

> More Americans than ever have access to telephones, computers, and the Internet … however, NTIA has found that there is still a significant "digital divide" separating American information "haves" and "have nots." Indeed, in many instances, the digital divide has widened in the last year … We should be alarmed by this news. (NTIA 2004)

Introduction

The Internet is the fastest growing technology in human history. Between 2005 and 2010, the number of Internet users doubled and will soon surpass 2 billion, including 1.2 billion in developing nations (ITU 2010). By the end of 2010, half a billion households worldwide (or 29.5%) will have access to the Internet, but these extraordinary figures hide a troubling story that has implications for social, political, and economic development around the world in the twenty-first century: the deepening digital divide.

The OECD defines the "digital divide" as the gap between individuals, households, businesses, and geographic areas in terms of both their opportunities to access information and communication technologies (ICTs) and their use of the Internet. Broadly speaking, the digital divide can be classified into two areas: the old divide and the new, or "second" divide. The old divide expressed the division between those who had the physical technology and those who did not. The emerging new divide expresses the division between those who have the digital skills to use this technology, and those who do not. That is, as computers and the Internet continue to evolve, a significant section of the global populace is being left behind.

Many of the drivers of the digital divide—geography, income level, race—are drivers of other forms of inequality and barriers to consumption. In our current economic and political systems, they might be somewhat expected consequences. For example, penetration of Internet in developing countries remains low—4.4 subscriptions in 100 people—compared with the developed world, which averages 24.6 subscriptions per 100 people (OECD 2010).

Yet the impact this divide is having on the world, and will have in the future, cannot be overstated. The healthy growth and success of our emergent knowledge economies both depend on adequate and equitable distribution of digital skills and technologies. At the same time, we face a world where billions of people lack access to essential everyday resources, such as water and food, let alone computers. The spread of digital skills and Internet technologies could help lift these people out of poverty and provide radically improved quality of life. The potential of ICTs should not be underestimated.

So why do some insist on denying the existence of a digital divide, downplaying its importance and dismissing the scale of the policy challenges associated with bridging it? These arguments will be explored later, but many have their foundation in ideological politics, technodeterminism or general ignorance of the statistics. In addition to these drivers, there is also a powerful optimism associated with the rise of the Internet and networked technologies that tends to overshadow the people who have been left behind by the Information Age. Van Dijk and Hacker (2003) summarize the interests that underpin the conversation:

> There are heated debates occurring in the United States and in Europe concerning questions of whether there is a so-called "digital divide" and if there is, how important it might be. In turn, the question is whether it will close or widen in future years. Much of this discussion is politically charged. Old views reappear about markets and people who are supposed to solve all problems by themselves, or not, and about the need or rejection of government intervention.

Increasingly, it proves beneficial to look at the divide in terms of those who can benefit from information technologies, and those who cannot. As the OECD (2010) explains, "The digital divide in education goes beyond the issue of access to technology. A second digital divide separates those with the competencies and skills to benefit from computer use from those without."

Van Dijk (1999) identifies four different elements of the digital divide, which he frames as barriers to access: mental access, material access, skills access, and usage access. The first of these, mental access, refers to the resistance many people experience towards adopting new technologies. This idea of "computer anxiety" or pure lack of interest disproportionately affects the elderly or disabled, for obvious reasons. Yet it is also evident in a wide spectrum of people who worry about their privacy and security online. A 2010 study by the U.S. Federal Communications Commission found that nonadopters of broadband Internet are almost 50% more likely than broadband users to say it is too easy for personal information to be stolen online. Likewise, over 50% of current broadband users agreed that there is too much pornographic or inappropriate content readily available online.

The second barrier, material access, has up to this point been the primary focus of policy-makers and corporations. The question of "who owns a computer" or has access to broadband Internet is relatively easy to measure and attempt to solve. Yet even here the story is a more complex one than might be expected. Indeed, the developing world—especially African countries—suffers from extremely low levels of Internet penetration and computer distribution compared with their developed world counterparts. Consider that, in Benin, the cost of a basic PC is the equivalent of eight months of a teacher's salary (World Bank 2010). This statistic captures the failure of many development programs, such as One Laptop Per Child (OLPC), to come to terms with what the digital divide means for poor countries across the developing world. The UN described the failure of the program as not providing tech support for the machines, or training in how to incorporate them into education. Teachers did not understand how to use the laptops in their lessons; some resented them. Kids liked the laptops, but their learning did not actually appear to be aided by them.

These kinds of policy interventions, designed to address the material access barrier, fail to take into account the other types of barriers that Van Dijk and Hacker (2003) identify. Of course, many are also designed from a Western and philanthropic perspective that carries more benefits for the designer than for those the intervention is attempting to benefit.

As the Internet and methods of access continue to evolve, a further complication underpinning the material access debate arises: the gap between those who enjoy access to high-speed Internet, and those who cannot afford it. Many of the most beneficial services available on today's Internet, as well as much of the entertainment, require a fast network connection.

The U.S. Federal Communications Commission found in 2010 that over a third of Americans lacked access to broadband Internet, with the main dividing lines being along levels of income and education. Some 52% of Americans in households with annual incomes of $50,000 or below had broadband at home, compared with 87% of those in households with incomes above that level. Of the 35% of Americans who did not use broadband at home, 22% did not use the Internet at all and lacked high school degrees. A smaller portion relied on dial-up connections, usually living in rural areas. Another small portion did use the Internet, but not at home, ostensibly for reasons of cost or a perceived lack of relevance to their everyday lives.

The current FCC Chairman, Julius Genachowski, has been clear about what the results of this survey, which it is worthwhile noting was the first of its kind, actually mean. "We need to tackle the challenge of connecting 93 million Americans to our broadband future," he noted in an accompanying statement to the survey. "In the 21st century, a digital divide is an opportunity divide."

It is a similar story in the UK, where broadband speeds in rural areas have actually been falling over the past two years, rather than improving. Ofcom, the independent regulator and competition authority for the UK communicatons industries, has stated that this divide will probably worsen before it gets better.

The third and fourth barriers, skills and usage access, are at the center of the deepening divide. Digital skills are the competencies, and educational and social support necessary to make the best use of ICTs. Complementary to this barrier is usage access, or lack of opportunities to actually implement ICTs. Van Dijk and Hacker (2003) describe how the digital divide has gradually moved towards these last two barriers and the broad consequences this shift entails:

> [A]ccess problems of digital technology gradually shift from the first two kinds of access to the last two kinds. When the problems of mental and material access have been solved, wholly or partly, the problems of structurally different skills and uses become more operative … [thus] the appearance of a usage gap between parts of the population systematically using and benefiting from advanced digital technology and the more difficult applications for work and education, and other parts only using basic digital technologies for simple applications with a relatively large part being entertainment.

If Van Dijk and Hacker's (2003) argument is true, which I believe it is, we are facing a complex and long-term set of challenges associated with increasing equitable distribution of ICTs around the world. Providing material access and breaking down mental barriers are only the beginning of an effort that will be further complicated by the exponential pace of growth and evolution of ICTs.

In particular, the rise of what is being termed the Information Age, or the Information Society, is an entirely new political, social, cultural, and economic landscape for people to navigate. The divide over the use of new technologies increasingly reflects whether people are capable of understanding the Information Society that surrounds them. For the first time in human history, we are capable of producing, storing, and consuming information ourselves.

In this fast-paced environment, learning is a continuous process and not a static achievement. The "early adopters" of many new technologies or applications, such as social media, are automatically poised to benefit. For those who are new to using a computer, let alone navigating the information overload of the Internet, the benefits are much more difficult to reap.

In this sense, the type of usage being pursued is key. It is not difficult to use a mobile phone to send a text message, for example. However, what about setting up your own website or blog, or creating a digital presence for your small business? The digital divide is in many ways the gulf between the ends of this technological continuum, and it is affecting every country around the world, some more disproportionately than others. There are several key drivers of the previously outlined barriers of the digital divide. The first, and logically most crucial, is income inequality.

According to the Pew Research Center's Internet and American Life Project, while 95% of high-income households in the U.S. use the Internet at home in some fashion, just 57% of the poorest do. Some 79% of those higher-income households own laptops, compared with 47% of those living in less well-off homes. Predictably, the wealthiest households are also more likely to own mobile phones, computers, e-readers, and other entertainment devices.

In addition to material access, income is also a sound predictor of usage. As the Pew study concludes, Internet users in high-income households tend to use the web several times a day, rather than as a single point of access. They are more likely to go online to get news, conduct research before purchasing a product or service, or to search for maps and directions. It is not difficult to surmise that, because of the greater options available to a savvy Internet user for all of the above activities, wealthier individuals with superior digital skills enjoy a better quality of life and probably save more money too.

As more and more government services move online and increasingly require a digital component for participation, the inequitable distribution of digital skills is only increasing the distance of those marginalized by society from the health and well-being services they desperately need. Many of those who could benefit most from information and services available on the Internet—such as seniors looking for Medicare—cannot use it or do not understand what is available to them online.

This is in many ways one of the most tragic impacts of the digital divide on a developed, rich country like the U.S. The promise of the Internet is that it will make basic products and services, especially government ones, more widely available to a greater sector of the populace that has traditionally been underserved. How can we expect these marginalized people to access the Internet just because it exists? Yet, many of the current policies in place to increase material access assume just that.

The other missing piece of the usage debate is employment and the future of work. In a world where even the most basic jobs now carry some requirement for digital skill, this is unquestionably a huge question for governments, businesses, and educators alike. People without adequate digital skills will find themselves severely debilitated in the job market and operating on the fringes of society.

Long gone are the days when those out of work would look through the classifieds in a printed newspaper to find their next job. Today, a wealth of online job aggregators have taken the place of printed material. The average job seeker has a much better chance of finding several jobs to apply for online than offline.

The implications of the digital divide on employment, and the relationship of these with broader issues, are well summarized by Campbell (2001):

> As a meta-technology, ICTs' pervasive effects hold implications not just for the labour market but also for access to learning and health care, for cultural and political awareness, for the transparency and accountability of organizational governance structures (including government agencies), and for social cohesion.

Given the connection of ICTs to nearly every aspect of economic, social, cultural, and political life, it is unsurprising that race also continues to be a driver of the deepening digital divide in the U.S. The National Telecommunications and Information Administration (NTIA) has found that, in addition to income, race is one of the key determinants of Internet access in America. Over the past decade, a consistent trend across the U.S. is that whites are more likely to have access to the Internet from home than blacks or Hispanics have from any location.

The issue has also been publicly raised in the UK Chandler (2002) has written eloquently about what the digital divide means for traditional divisions between developed and developing countries, and the role that accusations of racism in the U.S. play therein:

> The Internet is slow to recognise its responsibilities as an ethical player. If we have racism, a digital divide is its new colonial frontier … Among African Americans in the U.S., the best-educated people of African descent, a digital divide exists. The scenarios re-circulate—poverty, lack of access, unequal educational opportunities, and the absence of family property … In tracking the arrangements that brought about the structural inequalities precipitating the digital divide, the path leads back to globalisation's ubiquitous projects of free trade, development and colonialism.

Chandler's point about critical underlying sources of inequality that pre-date the digital divide is key and I will revisit it later. However, clearly if there is a silver lining to the emerging digital divide, it is the sober challenges it poses to the traditional developed vs developing country debate. Generating the skills needed to maximize use of the Internet and evolve economies is a challenge that is now just as prevalent in India as it is in the UK While the risk of digital exclusion is, as expected, much higher in African countries than in the West, this leveling is still an interesting question, especially as the global balance of power shifts to accommodate the increasingly powerful economic interests of BRIC (Brazil, Russia, India, China) countries.

The U.S., for example, despite its wealth and power, is behind many European countries in providing equitable Internet access. In fact, it remains the only industrialized nation without a national policy promoting high-speed broadband. This leads to the reality that, in the U.S., there is a nationwide average of four students to a computer. Using an average to express computer access is obviously an inadequate measure, as clusters of richer areas will skew it with multiple computers per student in contrast with large rural areas with no computers at all. Nonetheless, this statistic comes as a shock to many in a country that is the proud home of Silicon Valley.

In many ways, the greatest driver of the digital divide for a country like the U.S. is a hugely unequal and inefficient educational system. The NTIA has found that those with a college degree are more than eight times as likely as those with an elementary school education to have a computer at home, and nearly 16 times as likely to have Internet access at home. If the key barrier here is a college education, then the U.S. has a long and challenging path ahead to bridge the digital divide, which will clearly not be solved overnight. Computers may be rapidly decreasing in cost, but the cost of a college degree in America is rising rapidly.

This educational barrier being further exacerbated by socioeconomic inequality between races and geographic areas, a deepening digital divide should hardly come as a surprise in the U.S. Yet what about European countries that have traditionally pursued a larger role for government in ensuring a well-distributed educational system, especially with regards to the cost of post-graduate education?

The story remains largely the same. Ten million people in the UK, for example, have never used the Internet. Four million of those who are offline are society's most disadvantaged, including a large share that are unemployed, and many of those are adults in families with children. The majority of the rest either live in rural areas that are underserved in terms of the physical infrastructure necessary for access, or are elderly and disinterested in new technologies.

It is not unfair to say that, in the light of these kinds of facts, in today's ICT landscape every country is a developing country. Yet there is an increasingly hostile debate over whether or not a digital divide even exists, let alone what to do about it. Van Dijk and Hacker (2003) describe how ideological interests skew the debate:

> The data concerning the digital divide have come to constitute a political battlefield. Statistics are freely selected and judged according to political interests or subjective perspectives.

Many who doubt the existence of a serious and deepening digital divide do so on the grounds that those who are being left behind are largely the elderly, or people who are uninterested in new technologies. While certainly these groups are among those with barriers to entry in the Information Age, the digital divide affects a much wider spectrum of people.

So who will play a role in addressing this increasingly complex and globally distributed challenge? The most obvious place to start is policy-makers, although that immediately poses a host of issues from a practical standpoint. Despite gaining a higher profile in recent years, the digital divide is an issue competing for policy-makers' attention on the same level as environmental protection. While it is an increasingly critical driver of economic health and international competitiveness for governments, it inevitably remains secondary to other political priorities. The challenge remains in convincing government to elevate the issue of bridging the digital divide to the top of the agenda where it belongs.

It is also worth emphasizing that government and the business world, now that they are paying an increased amount of attention, have mixed motives for pursuing solutions to the digital divide. As Natriello (2001) points out:

> Although both governmental and corporate leaders have voiced support for digital initiatives to improve education, they have often cast these initiatives in limited economic terms … Clearly, leaders in all sectors have an interest in bringing those left behind by the digital revolution into the fold to allow not only for greater participation and individual opportunity, but for greater administrative efficiency (as when the Internal Revenue Service seeks to encourage more taxpayers to file electronically) or greater market penetration (as when businesses offer free computers and Internet connections in exchange for placing advertising on their screens).

These motives often conflict with what the greater priority should be in bridging the digital divide. Policy initiatives are also complicated by the reality that government moves more slowly than the business world, and that both of the previous institutions are nowhere near as fast as the growth of technologies we are currently experiencing. Policy is destined to play a game of "catch-up" that could have serious consequences for the so-called information have-nots if education, for example, is reoriented to focus on the wrong kinds of software or the digital skills that would accompany its use.

Likewise, the market will inevitably play a role in determining which businesses and even entire industries succeed and which fail in the emerging knowledge economies. What must be of concern is the health, livelihood and security of the workers who are negatively affected by this form of economic creative destruction. If we are moving towards a future where everyone is online and has adequate digital skills to maximize ICTs, then policy-makers and corporations have a responsibility to aggressively prepare for the fallout that will occur in the meantime.

A second critical issue when crafting policy solutions that can keep up with the momentum of emerging technologies is that much of the evidence for the digital divide has come from in-depth ICT studies. These academic investigations, while extremely important, have largely been conducted from a highly technical perspective that is difficult to translate into practical legislative or regulatory terms. Thus, much of the expertise necessary to create appropriate policies can be considered "buried treasure," which is problematic for those in charge of implementing legislative priorities on the ground to access.

This roadblock is summarized by Natriello (2001):

> The rush to create more compliant citizens and more willing consumers by connecting them to the digital economy may lead to patterns of digital development that exacerbate disparities by both shaping what kind of computing students engage in and by disproportionately consuming resources that would be better put to other purposes. Each of these processes could make it more difficult to address the use divide even after we solve the access divide.

Natriello's last comment is worth exploring, because a crucial question remains: which should come first—expanding access, or expanding digital skills? Or for a third option, how do you pursue enhancing both at once?

Addressing the access gap first, both to computers and broadband connections, is a tempting priority for policy-makers and corporations alike. It is a simple equation of purchase and distribution that looks good to the general public and is a relatively easy expenditure to justify. Likewise for corporations, contributing to increasing access is an opportunity to enhance image as a philanthropic and responsible gesture.

From an ideological perspective, in the U.S. conservatives are far more likely than their liberal counterparts to espouse material access as a market-driven answer to bridging the digital divide. This is due in no small part to deep-seated resistance from conservatives to increasing the role of government in addressing the socioeconomic inequality that underpins the first, and especially what is being called the second, digital divides. Take as an indicative example this research summary from the conservative think-tank the Heritage Foundation:

> As the public policy debate over America's "digital divide" intensifies, federal, state and local policymakers are considering steps to solve this apparent gap between the technological "haves" and "have-nots" ... Before policymakers make rash decisions on these proposals or create an expensive new government program to address America's supposed digital divide, they would be wise to take a closer look at the current market for personal computers and Internet access ... Free computers and free Internet access are helping to filling the digital gap. Clearly, the vibrant PC market is doing more than an adequate job of speeding computing technology to every American.

This abuse of the abundance argument to dismiss the existence of a digital divide is classically misguided. Just because the market for personal computers is accelerating, as with any consumer product, that trend hardly guarantees an equitable distribution of those technologies—let alone the skills that are expected to accompany their use.

There is yet another route to promoting access that in some ways transcends the material vs usage and skills barriers debate. An increasing number of countries has deemed Internet access a human right. First proposed by the UN, those countries now include Estonia, Finland, France, and Greece. Laura Vilkkonen, the legislative counselor for the Finnish Ministry of Transport and Communications, described the country's decision in the following terms, "We think it's something you cannot live without in modern society. Like banking services or water or electricity, you need Internet connection ... Universal service is every citizen's subjective right."

These initiatives may seem radical, but they accord with popular opinion around the world. A BBC World Service poll in early 2010 found that nearly four out of five people in countries across the globe agreed that access to the Internet is a "fundamental human right." It seems reasonable to assume that any progress made towards closing the digital divide will also represent progress made towards human rights for the global population.

The debate over the digital divide, like so many others sparked by the emergence and rapid growth of the Internet and new technologies, is representative of deep-seated social, economic and political issues. This is why arguments against the importance of the digital divide by otherwise genius technological thought leaders like Kevin Kelly are so frustrating. Here Kelly (2009) describes broadly why he is not worried about the current information haves and have-nots:

> In every technology's lifespan then, there will be a period of "haves" and "have nots." Clear advantages may flow to the individuals or societies who first risk untried guns, or the alphabet, or electrification, or the Internet, over those who do not. The distribution of these advantages may depend on wealth, privilege, or lucky geography as much as desire … During the 1990s when technologists such as myself were promoting the advent of the Internet, we were often asked what we were going to do about the digital divide? My answer was simple: nothing. We didn't have to do anything, because the natural history of a technology such as the Internet was self-fulfilling.

On a fundamental level, Kelly is right. There are always early adopters of technology who reap the benefits before the wider population is able to participate, but Kelly's argument inherently dismisses the deep-seated global issues that underpin the current digital divide, as they have previous divides, in favor of an ambiguous technological prophecy. The Internet may very well become ubiquitous—it probably will. Yet despite the rapid pace of growth, it is impossible to ignore the people who are being left behind owing to traditional disparities of income, education, race, and geography, as Kelly is so content to reject them.

The critical issue that Kelly's argument feeds into is the technodeterminism that so easily sways high-level decision-makers and the thought leaders who influence them. If these decision-makers listen to Kelly, then we will all sit back and trust that the Internet will continue to grow at a rapid fire pace, supported by ever-cheaper hardware, and achieve total ubiquity. At the same time, we will fail to address the critical host of issues that divide the world into haves and have-nots for nearly everything: essential everyday resources like food, water and shelter, protection from the impact of environmental challenges like climate change, sound political systems, social stability, and economic opportunity. Trusting in the growth and ultimate ubiquity of the Internet is like placing a huge band-aid over these issues. It is indeed a band-aid that will lessen the pain and create opportunity for many people, but inevitably leave many more behind.

Here is the most problematic statement Kelly then makes, "The have-nots were a temporary imbalance that would be cured (and more so) by market forces." Kelly's argument, like so much of technodeterminism, is not just rooted in faith in ubiquity. It rests upon the belief that the market will solve the inequalities we are currently experiencing on a global scale. However, if the past decade has shown us anything, let alone the past two years of devastating financial crisis, it is that we literally cannot afford to place our trust in market forces alone.

Tapscott (1999) provides an excellent explanation of why market-based arguments are wholly inadequate when it comes to the new ICTs:

> By the time—if ever—the "free market" catches up to the [have-]nots, they will no longer be children. Denied the opportunity to assimilate the new media in their youth, they will, instead, have to adapt to it. They will be on the wrong end of the generation lap—lapped by those of their own generation. Moreover, their employment prospects in a knowledge economy, their potential income levels, their prospects for stable families, and their potential for a fulfilling life will all be greatly diminished. This is a downward spiral.

It is probably fair to say that authors like Kelly are not concerned with the plight of one, two, or even three generations resulting from an unsolved digital divide. What matters from the technodeterminist perspective is the long-term trend towards Internet ubiquity, the net benefits of which can ostensibly cancel out the short-term suffering any disadvantaged populations will experience as they are shut out of the Information Age.

To go back to the point Natriello (2001) has made about the mixed motives of government, corporates and other actors in attempting to solve the digital divide, it is worthwhile here to note that not just these actors but literally everyone will unquestionably benefit from helping to close it. This is to be expected, and it also gives hope that decision-makers and the general public alike will act because of these benefits, as long as they are made aware of them. As Van Dijk and Hacker (2003) describe it,

> Corporations look for a large electronic marketplace. Politicians want extended reach for political persuasion and a grip on new channels of political communication bypassing traditional mass media. Military people and security agencies want everybody to be connected for purposes of control and surveillance, as the off-liners of the future will create unknown risks. Educators are concerned about universal and public access to all learning resources. Community builders want every citizen to be involved in online communications linked to offline local activities.

Like so many of the complex, interconnected and global challenges we face in the twenty-first century, bridging the digital divide will probably require an integrated set of solutions from a variety of sources. Academia, policy-makers, corporations, NGOs, and civil society will all have roles to play. While this may seem obvious, it is a reality that is difficult for many who are pursuing silver-bullet solutions, or relying on trust in technological progress alone, to accept.

References

Campbell, Duncan. "Can the Digital Divide be Contained?" *International Labour Review*, 140(2), 2001. Available at: http://www.ilo.org/public/english/revue/download/pdf/campbell.pdf [accessed: 13 August 2011].

Chandler, Robin. "Digital Divide: Racism's New Frontier." *The Guardian*, 17 January 2002. Available at: http://www.guardian.co.uk/technology/2002/jan/17/comment.onlinesupplement [accessed: 13 August 2011].

ITU. *World Telecommunication/ITU Indicators Database 2010*, 1 December 2010. Available at: http://www.itu.int/ITU-D/ict/material/FactsFigures2010.pdf [accessed: 18 February 2011].

Kelly, Kevin. "Increasing Ubiquity," 2009. Available at: http://www.kk.org/thetechnium/archives/2009/05.increasing_ubiq.php [accessed: 13 August 2011].

Natriello, G. *Bridging the Second Digital Divide: What Can Sociologists of Education Contribute?* Columbia University, 2001. Available at: http://edlab.tc.columbia.edu/files/EdLab_Bridging.pdf [accessed: 18 December 2010].

NTIA. *National Telecommunications and Information Administration Report*, 2004. Available at: http://www.ntia.doc.gov/legacy/newarchive2004.html [accessed: 13 August 2011].

OECD. *Information Technology Outlook*, 2010. Available at: http://www.oecd.org/document/20/0,3746,en_2649_33757_41892820_1_1_1_1,00.html [accessed: 30 December 2010].

Tapscott, Dan. *Growing Up Digital: The Rise of the Net Generation*. New York: McGraw-Hill, 1999.

Thierer, Adam. "How Computers are Filling the Digital Divide," 2000. Available at: http://www.heritage.org/Research/Reports/2000/04/How-Free-Computers-Are-Filling-the-Digital-Divide [accessed: 13 August 2011].

Van Dijk, Jan A.G.M. *The Network Society, Social Aspects of New Media*. London: Sage, 1999.

Van Dijk, Jan A.G.M. and Hacker, K. *The Digital Divide as a Complex and Dynamic Phenomenon*, 2003. Available at: http://web.nmsu.edu/~comstudy/tis.pdf [accessed: 13 August 2011].

World Bank. *The World Bank Annual Report*, 2010. Available at: http://siteresources.worldbank.org/EXTANNREP2010/Resources/WorldBank-AnnualReport2010.pdf [accessed: 18 February 2011].

Chapter 18

Using ICT Research to Assist Policy-making and Regulation: The Case of Namibia

Christoph Stork and Tony Vetter

Introduction

Research ICT Africa (RIA) fills a strategic gap in the development of sustainable information societies and knowledge economies in Africa by supporting evidence-based information and communication technology (ICT) policy and regulation through research. The research comprises household and business surveys, sector performance reviews and telecom regulatory environment assessments (Table 18.1). The research arising from a public interest agenda is available in the public domain. The public and private sector and civil society are encouraged to use it for teaching, further research or to enable them to participate more effectively in national, regional and global ICT policy formulation and governance.

Table 18.1 RIA research in Namibia

Year	Research title	Number of African countries
2003	ICT Sector Performance Review	7
2004	Household e-Access and e-Usage Survey	11
2005	Small Medium Enterprise e-Access and e-Usage Survey	14
2006	ICT Sector Performance Review and Telecom Regulatory Environment	17
2007	Household e-Access and e-Usage Survey	17
2009	ICT Sector Performance Review and Telecom Regulatory Environment	19

This chapter demonstrates how donor-funded ICT research contributed to evidence-based policy-making and regulation in Namibia. First, sustainable development and ICTs, inefficient operators, information asymmetry and the role of regulators will be discussed in the background section of the paper. Then background on Namibia's Telecommunication sector will be provided. The third section links research-based publications and emerging recommendations to sector outcomes.

Background

The term "sustainable development" was first popularized by the publication of the 1987 report of the Brundtland Commission, also known formally as the World Commission on Environment and Development (IISD, 2006). Most working definitions of sustainable development refer to development that meets our needs without compromising our ability to do so in the future, highlighting in particular "the essential needs of the world's poor" (WCED 1987). The original Brundtland report also states that "meeting essential needs depends in part on achieving full growth potential, and sustainable development clearly requires economic growth in places where such needs are not being met" (WCED 1987). Over time the global understanding of sustainable development had broadened and, in some ways, been redefined to promote "the integration of the three components of sustainable development—economic development, social development and environmental protection—as interdependent and mutually reinforcing pillars" (WSSD 2002). Many have also come to view good governance as a fourth pillar of sustainable development. The 2002 World Summit on Sustainable Development (WSSD) Plan specifically singles out "sound environmental, social and economic policies" and "democratic institutions responsive to the needs of the people," among others, as "the basis for sustainable development."

When considering the role of ICTs in sustainable development, linkages with these pillars are being convincingly demonstrated. In the case of economic development, there is mounting anecdotal, econometric and theoretical support for the role of information and communication technology in growth and development, particularly in the case of developed economies. Mobile communications have a particularly important impact in rural areas, which are home to nearly one-half of the world's population and 75% of the world's poor (World Bank 2007). A widely cited study by Vodafone found that mobile phones in less developed economies are playing the same crucial role that fixed telephony played in the richer economies in the 1970s and 1980s. The study also found that mobile phones substitute for fixed lines in poor countries, rather than complementing fixed lines as in rich countries, implying that they have a stronger growth impact in poor countries (Vodafone 2006).

In considering social development impacts, it has been found that mobile phones fulfill basic human needs for physical, economic and social security more than any other ICT to date. One study by LIRNEasia revealed how mobile phones can play a role in helping to meet the basic needs of the world's poor, observing that "the biggest and most widespread impact of access to telephones at the Bottom of the Pyramid (BOP) is in creating a sense of security, owing to the ability to act in an emergency" (LIRNEasia 2007). Other surveys carried out by Research ICT Africa have produced evidence that mobiles improve relationships with friends and family and help small businesses operate more effectively (ITU 2006).

No technology has ever spread faster around the globe than the mobile phone. Adoption rates of mobile phones have consistently exceeded analysts' predictions. Private sector investment and favourable enabling legal and regulatory environments have played a critical role in the rapid expansion of access to mobile networks. Competition has been particularly effective among wireless mobile operators, resulting in the rapid rollout of networks across urban areas and, more recently, into rural areas at constantly declining cost (World Bank 2009). However, despite the rapid penetration and adoption of mobile services, several billion people, primarily in developing countries, still lack access to affordable telecommunication services that address their basic communication needs. Certain approaches to the governance of telecommunication services, forming the fourth pillar to sustainable development for communication technologies, are proving instrumental to overcoming these challenges. In 2006, the World Telecommunication Development Conference in Doha declared that:

> Governments play a key role in the development of ICTs and telecommunications, and are urged to establish an enabling environment that promotes reasonable and affordable access to basic telecommunication services for all, so as to pave the way for the active participation of other stakeholders in the ICT sector. Such an environment should also create a stable and transparent framework and promote fair competition, while protecting network integrity and the rights of users, operators and investors. (WTDC 2006)

Studies have shown that effective policy-making and regulation, drawing on global best practices, like those suggested in the above declaration, and adapted to local conditions, are critical for expanding affordable access to, and effective use of, ICTs and services as tools of broad-based development and poverty reduction in developing countries (infoDev 2008). However, the capacity and willingness of relevant institutions to make informed and appropriate decisions and policies remains challenged in most developing countries.

Policy-making and regulation for the ICT sector is already a complex endeavour. Add to this the political economy of ICT sector reform where many vested interests are reluctant to accept the implications of restructuring, privatization and competition, and several challenges commonly emerge. Three examined here that present barriers to effective policy-making and regulation in developing countries are: inefficient operators; information asymmetry between regulator and operators; and where the role of the regulator to balance the interests of consumers, competing enterprises and investors is not being fulfilled.

Inefficient Operators

Given the significant costs associated with establishing and maintaining telecommunications infrastructure, monopoly or oligopoly markets are common in this sector. In the absence of an effective regulatory framework, operators in such markets have low incentives for promoting static cost efficiency, leading to market failure. These operators commonly know how they might improve on efficiency, both in terms of effort and in terms of technology. This suggests that, if the operators are called on to use this information, efficiency can be enhanced. The regulator cannot enforce these improvements top-down since it lacks the information to do so, i.e. the agents have what is called "private information" (CPB 2000). These conditions set the stage for the challenge of information asymmetry between operators and regulators.

Information Asymmetry

Good regulation seeks to successfully balance the interests of consumers, operators and investors while promoting broader public interests. Several variables such as prices, quality of service, profits, cost of investment, and fair competition need to be taken into account by regulators. However, operators often feel it is in their best interests to conceal the assets, costs and profits of their business. In a study into difficulties faced by regulators when operating price caps and rate of return regulation in developing and transition economies, information asymmetries or inadequate information on the firm's cost and revenues, and enterprises providing misleading information were identified as primary difficulties (Kirkpatrick et al. 2005).

In monopoly or oligopoly markets harbouring inefficient firms where information asymmetry is a barrier to effective regulation, the use of 'benchmarking' or 'yardstick competition' in economic regulation is increasingly considered as a solution (Dassler et al. 2006). Shleifer (1985) first argued that a regulated firm's revenue needs should be assessed by looking at costs in comparable firms or industries to identify 'some relatively simple benchmark, other than the firm's present or past performance, against which to evaluate the firm's potential' (Dassler et al. 2006). Such an approach is an attractive solution to the regulatory challenge of information asymmetry where the firm in question refuses to share profit and cost information, or the information it provides is deemed intentionally misleading.

Role of the Regulator

Information asymmetries with operators can have a significant influence over whether a regulator effectively balances the interests of consumers, competing operators and investors. When major information asymmetries are present, "hold up" threats and regulatory and political capture are likely to occur (Cook and Mosedale 2007). "Hold up" is a situation where either side tries to take unfair advantage of the other after an agreement is established. Once an operator has heavily invested in network infrastructure, the regulator can hold the investor to ransom by forcing price reductions. To protect against this, operators often demand state guarantees or contracts that reduce efficiency incentives. In situations where operators are the sole service provider, they can demand price increases in their favour, knowing the government has no alternative supplier. "Regulatory capture" is prone to occur when consumers are not well organized, and operators encounter little resistance to lobbying the regulator for concessions leading to the regulator becoming biased in their favour. "Political capture" occurs when regulatory goals become distorted to serve political ends (Cook et al. 2007).

However, it can also be the case that the resources available to the regulator to carry out their mandate are simply inadequate for the task, as is often the case in developing countries. Even if a regulator understands how strategies such as benchmarking could be employed to foster effective competition in their monopoly or oligopoly markets, they are likely to lack the capacity to marshal and analyse the appropriate information and establish an appropriate regulatory framework informed by such a strategy. It has even been suggested that the effectiveness of competition as a regulatory tool to contribute to public interest outcomes of access, affordability, quality and choice of service is dependent on the existence of capacities and resources to implement, monitor and enforce the relevant policies. If these conditions do not exist, as they do not in many developing countries, the adoption of privatization and liberalization strategies could be counterproductive (Gillwald 2002).

Clearly, creating appropriate enabling environments for expanding affordable access to ICT in developing countries is highly dependent on developing country policy-makers and regulators having adequate capacity to analyse policy and regulatory issues, and adapt global experience to their local realities. It has been noted, however, that while government policy-makers and regulators have been a priority target of ICT capacity-building programs, and their key role in effective policy and regulation is undeniable, there are other stakeholders—the private sector, civil society, researchers—whose capacity to engage intelligently in policy and regulatory debates and decisions is crucial to effective, locally appropriate policy and regulatory outcomes that will promote the expansion of affordable, appropriate ICT infrastructure and services.

Research and analysis carried out by independent civil society actors, when combined with effective communication strategies, can inform and influence policy and regulatory debates and decisions to dramatic effect. Such efforts can bring transparency to negotiations between regulators and operators with impartiality and effectively defuse "hold up" threats described above, thus leading to greater market efficiencies and more affordable access. In markets where consumers do not have an effective voice for their concerns, research and analysis carried out by independent civil society actors can also act as a proxy for consumers' interests and discourage regulatory and political capture as neither operators nor government officials wish to tempt negative publicity.

What follows is arguably a textbook example of how independent research and communication efforts from civil society researchers were translated into useful information and advice for policy-makers and regulators, informing and influencing policy and regulatory debates and decisions to dramatic effect. Such efforts demonstrate their effectiveness to shoring up the fourth governance pillar of sustainable development in the context of expanding affordable access to ICT in a developing country, significantly contributing to the achievement of economic and social sustainability objectives for telecommunications services in the process.

Namibia's Telecommunication Sector

The Namibian Communications Commission (NCC), established in 1992, reports to the Ministry of Information and Communication Technology, and is solely funded by the government. The NCC will become a fully fledged independent regulator for the entire ICT sector with the passing of the new Communications Bill. The new Bill makes the regulator financially independent of the government, allowing it to collect licence fees to fund its own operation and the universal service fund. The Bill was passed by parliament in July 2009 and is still expected to become an Act in 2009.[1] New ICT policies dealing with broadcasting, telecommunications, information technologies, licensing and ICTs in general were finalized in early 2009.

Namibia's telecommunication sector is likely to develop from a fixed monopoly and mobile duopoly to a converged oligopoly in 2010. A second mobile licence was awarded in 2006 to CellOne. The market entry of CellOne and the resulting competitive pressure has reduced access and usage prices for consumers and led to a rapid increase in subscriber numbers. However, the institutional set-up and the regulatory environment have been everything but ideal. Two different ministries were responsible for the regulatory supervision of the sector, one for fixed-line telephony and one for mobile telephony. The absence of an independent regulator with authority to regulate the entire sector meant that CellOne's market entry was a risky endeavor. Namibia has since then accelerated telecommunication sector reform, with an ICT ministry responsible for the entire sector established in 2008. In 2009, parliament passed a Telecommunications Bill which is expected to become an Act still in 2009. An interconnection dispute was also resolved in 2009. The year 2010 will most likely see the conversion of existing licences of Mobile Telecommunications Ltd (MTC), CellOne and Telecom Namibia into service and technologically neutral licences. This will increase the competition within the sector, which in turn will lead to lower prices, expanded service delivery

1 The Act only commenced in May 2011. The licence conversions need to be completed within six months of the commencement. The expectations for 2010 have hence shifted to 2012.

and more investment. In particular, broadband access and usage and international calls can be expected to drop by a large percentage in price.

Currently, Telecom Namibia is the only fixed-line operator in Namibia and is owned by Namibia Post and Telecom Holdings (NPTH), which in turn is owned by the State. NPTH is also a majority shareholder of MTC, which was awarded a mobile telecommunication licence in 1996. In July 2006, 34% of MTC was bought by Portugal Telecom. MTC still has about 87% market share and subscriber numbers are increasing. CellOne launched its services in April 2007. Telecel Globe, a subsidiary of Orascom Telecom, bought 100% of CellOne in January 2009.

Telecom Namibia launched a mobile service in late-2006/early-2007 called Switch, based on code division multiple access (CDMA). Switch was restricted to fixed-wireless until May 2009 owing to political pressure. CellOne and MTC had argued that Switch would be illegal and lobbied the government to stop Telecom Namibia from providing mobile services. However, this is not the case, and Telecom Namibia "voluntarily" restricted its service to fixed-wireless owing to the political pressure. MTC and CellOne use the global system for mobile (GSM) to provide mobile telephony, while Telecom Namibia uses CDMA.

Telecom Namibia has a statutory licence but not a statutory monopoly. It remains a *de facto* monopoly until an additional fixed-line licence is awarded, breaking Telecom Namibia's monopoly. The new Telecommunications Act, expected for the end of 2009, and the expected licence conversion, is likely to end Telecom Namibia's monopoly and allow CellOne and MTC to also offer fixed-line services. Neither MTC nor CellOne are likely to enter the fixed-line market. They would, however, be likely to establish their own international voice and data facilities. MTC's home phone, launched in 2009, is a fixed-wireless product that is based on GSM.

End-user Internet access is available in the form of modem dial-up, integrated services digital network (ISDN), asymmetric digital subscriber line (ADSL), leased lines, Wi-Fi hotspots, line-of-sight wireless, WIMAX and mobile third generation (3G) or EVDO. Telecom Namibia provides Namibia with international bandwidth through the SAT3 cable via the Cape Town landing point and via satellite. Namibia is a nonlanding consortium member of SAT3. Telecom Namibia joined the West African Cable System consortium. MTC and CellOne are expected to join Telecom Namibia as sub-consortium members and Botswana might join as well. VSAT satellite is used by MTC and MWeb (an Internet service provider), among others, to provide additional bandwidth. Further international bandwidth is obtained by Internet service providers leasing capacity from South Africa. MTC and CellOne were awarded international data licences in 2008. Potentially, this will further increase Namibia's international data capacity.

Key challenges for the years ahead include building the institutional capacity of the new independent telecommunications regulator. The sector currently relies heavily on international management and technical expertise. The regulator would be well advised to seek secondment from a well-established regulator in another country as well to build up the institution and sustainable capacity on a staff and institutional level.

Creating a market structure that creates access opportunities for all Namibians at affordable costs will be a formidable task. The existing laws and policies state that as an objective but provide little guidance on how to attain it.

Support for Evidence-based Policy-making and Regulation in Namibia

The initial household survey on e-Access and Usage of 2004 opened the door to writing an ICT column for *Insight* magazine. This ICT column became a tool for discussing pertinent issues in the ICT sector. The household survey data of 2004 together with the sector performance reviews for Botswana, South Africa and Namibia of 2006 also allowed the benchmarking of Namibia against Botswana and South Africa. In a presentation to Cabinet by Research ICT Africa on behalf of the NCC in March 2006 this benchmarking convinced Namibia's government to open the telecommunication sector to competition and start the telecommunication sector reform process in earnest. The presentation to Cabinet recommended opening up the market, creating an independent effective regulator, creating a ministry responsible for the entire ICT sector, creating a universal service fund and increasing Namibia's international bandwidth. A second mobile licence was subsequently issued in the following month and the process of formulating a new Telecommunications Bill and new ICT policies was re-started.

Table 18.2 NEPRU Policy brief no. 17, July 2006, telecommunication sector reform for development

Description	Benchmarked Namibia against Botswana to convince policy-makers and regulators that telecommunication sector reform is urgently needed
Recommendations	Three key steps: (1) a new telecommunications act (2) a strong resourced and independent regulator for the entire ICT sector (3) clear policy guide lines for the regulator Subsequent steps: (1) lifting the restriction on Voice over IP (2) international voice and data gateways for CellOne, MTC (3) number portability (4) service-neutral licences for CellOne, MTC and Telecom Namibia (5) regulating interconnection (6) annual reviewing of the ICT environment and the possibility of new entrants (7) universal service fund
Media response	1 August 2006, Die Nachbarn hängen uns ab, Allgemeine Zeitung 3 August 2006, Drei kurze Schritte zur Reform, Allgemeine Zeitung 3 August 2006, Haal politiek nier uit se NEPRU, Republikein 3 August 2006, Namibia needs to dial into reform on telecoms sector, Namibian 4 August 2006, Die ICT Dämme brechen, Allgemeine Zeitung 4 August 2006, More calls for Telecommunications Bill, New Era 21 February 2007, Draf telkom se taal 1-2-3 kaf, Republikein
Outcome	The new Telecommunications Bill was passed by Parliament and is expected to become an act still in 2009. The new Bill establishes a strong resourced and independent regulator for the entire ICT sector. New ICT policies were formulated in the beginning of 2009. However, they are fairly general and the minister will need to provide more concrete policy guidelines for the regulator in future. The new Communications Bill also addresses number portability and service neutral licences, establishes a universal service fund, and regulates interconnection. CellOne and MTC have both applied for an international voice gateway and are likely to be awarded it in 2009.

Research ICT Africa and NEPRU, as the Namibian nodal partner, had by then established themselves as neutral and credible research organizations. Research results were communicated through various channels, including academic research reports, glossy books, articles in magazines, contributions to quarterly economic reviews, policy briefs, media interviews, parliamentary training sessions and presentations at workshops.

The combination of communication channels has been the secret of the success, although the four- to eight-page policy brief with five key messages on the front page seems to reach the widest audience. Tables 18.2–18.6 give example of policy briefs, their recommendations and media coverage. The tables also link the recommendations to sector outcomes. The outcomes cannot be attributed to the policy briefs. However, indications are that they have indirectly contributed.

Table 18.3 NEPRU Policy brief no. 18, January 2007, SWITCH to competition—regulatory challenges for Namibia's telecommunication sector

Description	Addressed a dispute between CellOne, MTC and Telecom Namibia concerning the mobile service SWITCH launched by Telecom Namibia
Recommendations	(1) Service and technologically neutral licences for Telecom Namibia, MTC and Cell One (2) Replace licence fees for telecommunication licences with sales or turnover fees
Media response	11 January 2007, Belchaos staat se skuld, Republikein 13 January 2007, MTC reaches out to remote areas, Namibian 15 January 2007, Switch is just fine: Nepru, Namibian 15 January 2007, Telestryd nader aan oplossing, Republikein 15 January 2007, Verwirrung laehmt Entwicklung, Allgemeine Zeitung 16 January 2007, Verwirrt mit SWITCH, Allgemeine Zeitung 17 January 2007, Switch is legal says study group, http://wireless-watch.com 19 January 2007, NEPRU raps MTC for alleged "profiteering", Informante 24 January 2007, Bel-oplossing vertraag, Republikein 26 January 2007, NEPRU calls for neutral telecoms licence, Economist 30 January 2007, Die geswets oor Switch—Die geswets oor Switch Wat 'n oop telkommark behels, Republikein 2 February 2007, Nepru raps MTC for alleged profiteering, Informante 2 February 2007, Vertraagde wet kon swaar straf, Republikein 16 February 2007, Die nuwe kommunikasiewet, Republikein 21 February 2007, Ken jou terme, Republikein 03/02/2007, Beltwis onbeslis, Republikein
Outcome	The restriction of Switch to fixed-wireless was only lifted in May 2009. The new Telecommunication Bill entails service-neutral licences and licence fees based on turnover.

Each policy brief was covered by the main Namibian newspapers and mostly on the front page. Timing for the release of policy briefs for that is important. Fridays and Mondays are usually not good days for releasing policy briefs in Namibia. Tuesday, Wednesday and Thursdays are more likely to yield front-page coverage. On Tuesday the news from the weekend has been digested, and Thursdays are ideal too since Friday's editions have more pages.

Table 18.4 NEPRU Policy brief no. 20, November 2007, impact of VAT on prepaid telecommunication services

Description	The aim was to prevent the ministry of finance from scrapping VAT exemption for prepaid airtime
Recommendations	(1) Keep VAT exemption for prepaid telecommunication services (2) A new Telecommunications Act (3) A strongly resourced and independent regulator for the entire ICT sector (4) Clear policy guide lines for the regulator
Media response	11 April 2007, Hof toe met telkomwet, Republikein 15 January 2008, Bekgeveg, Republikein 30 January 2008, Belmark staal hom vir BTW-slag, Republikein 30 January 2008, Wrong approach on prepaid telcoms VAT, Namibian 1 February 2008, Cost of Pre Paid Calls o Rise, New Era 1 February 2008, Telecom dra BTW namens bellers, Republikein 1 February 2008, VAT on airtime likely to hurt consumers, Economist 7 March 2008, Kommunikasietegnologie 'n swak skakel, sê Mbumba, Republikein 31 July 2008, NEPRU suggests alternatives to VAT exemption, Informante
Outcome	The policy brief and the resulting press coverage and lobbying of operators using the policy brief could not stop the Ministry of Finance from levying VAT on prepaid airtime

Table 18.5 NEPRU Policy brief no. 21, September 2008, draft telecommunications bill 2008: lessons from South Africa

Description	Policy brief following a presentation at the Telecom Namibia's ICT Summit that addressed shortcomings of the draft Telecommunications Bill
Recommendations	Improve definitions Simplify licensing: (1) avoid another agency (Universal Service Agency) and host universal service fund at regulator (2) clear role for minister is to provide policy guidance and not intervene with the regulatory process (3) interconnection regime that is implementable immediately
Media response	2 October 2008, Communication Bill is loophole prone, Informante 3 October 2008, New Communications Bill may be difficult to implement, The Economist 8 October 2008, NEPRU Slams draft Telecoms Bill, Namibian 17 October 2008, Belstryd by kruispad, Republikein 20 October 2008, Openheid kosbaar, Republikein
Outcome	The draft Communication Bill that went to parliament was corrected in all points raised in the policy brief except the clear role of the Minister

Providing five key messages on the front page of the policy brief improves the accuracy of reporting by the media. Newspaper articles often only quote from these five key messages. A further important point is to be helpful to journalists and develop a constructive relationship, assisting in breaking down complex topics and jargon. It helps to think like a journalist when compiling a policy brief for media release—what information do I need to write a good story?

Table 18.6 NEPRU Policy brief no. 22, November 2008, price transparency for Namibia's telecommunication sector

Description	Sequence of 12 policy briefs in 2008 and 2009 comparing retail prices of mobile operators
Recommendations	Introduction of per second billing for CellOne's post paid products Lowering of MTC's prepaid products Offering converged Fixed-mobile solutions for Telecom Namibia
Media Response	12/03/2008, Price transparency for Nam's telecoms sector, Namibian 12/08/2008, Prysmandjies laat belmark roer, Republikein 01/29/2009, Belmark propvol opwinding, luidens verslag, Republikein 07/08/2009, Belskale kry balans, Republikein
Outcome	The monthly price comparison increased the competition between telco operators and led to concessions being made to subscribers such as free SMS, free Internet access during night time, call special, doubling of free on-net minutes for post paid subcribers, etc. CellOne moved to per second billing for is post paid products. Telecom Namibia is expected to launch converged services still in 2009.

Instead of thinking like a researcher and justifying use of methodology and stressing statistical significance, being clear about the recipient's needs is critical for getting the message across.

The ICT column in *Insight* magazine served the purpose of starting discussions about pertinent issues, issues of importance to the regulator and the private sector. Price comparisons between Namibia, Botswana and South Africa based on OCED price basket methodology that were published in *Insight* in 2005 led to mobile monopolists stating that their costs were too high to reduce prices owing to the low population density.

The Namibia sector performance review of 2006 then proved MTC wrong based on financial ratio analysis. Returns on equity of around 50% clearly demonstrated that retail prices could be brought down and that costs could not possibly be too high. The 2007 e-Access and Usage household survey also demonstrated the cost sensitivity of Namibians and that the lower prices would lead to greater usage. The accumulated research then led to one of the main arguments for the interconnection study, that competition is not bad but in fact good, not only for Namibia, but also for the incumbent monopoly, increasing the efficiency addressed in the background paper.

Research ICT Africa was awarded the Interconnection Benchmarking Study in January 2009, precisely because of its research track record and impartiality. The study was put on the webpage of the regulator to increase the transparency of the regulatory process. This led to it being picked up by the media and the private sector in South Africa. The subsequent press coverage, public seminars, parliamentary training courses, TV and radio interviews might have started a process that will bring termination rates down in South Africa as well.

Table 18.6 summarizes the recommendations of the study, some of the press coverage and the outcome. Table 18.8 provides a breakdown of the articles written for magazines. The Background section discussed the effect of inefficient operators, asymmetry of information and the role of the regulator; all three aspects can be demonstrated for the case of Namibia.

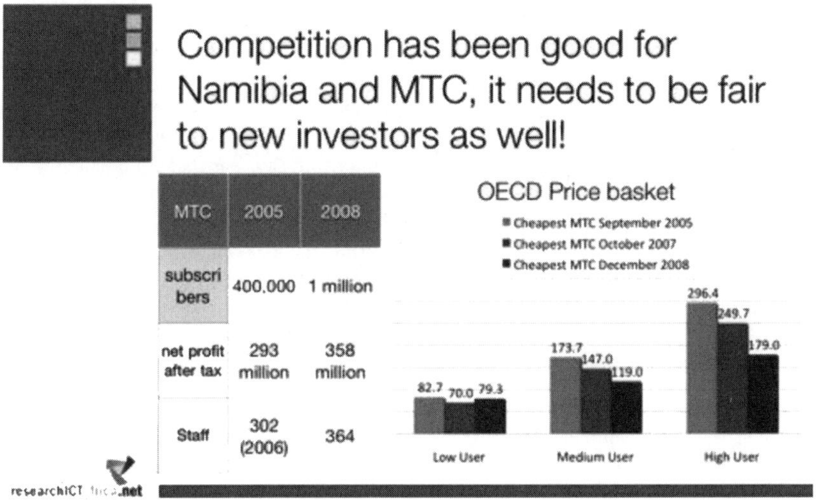

Figure 18.1 Interconnection presentation to Minister for ICTs, 13 May 2009

Inefficient Operator

MTC gained efficiency through competition, which led to lower prices, more employment, higher subscriber numbers and more usage. MTC initially argued that all that was not possible. Issuing a second mobile licence and the implied competitive pressure changed their choices of technology (they moved immediate to 3G instead of first rolling out EDGE), the design of their products and their approach to customer service. That all might have happened anyway eventually; however, competition made those changes urgent.

Asymmetry of Information

The regulator had to take MTC at face value when it said that the costs where too high to reduce retail prices. The NCC was not able to assess the cost of termination either. The regulatory capacity and legal powers were not sufficient to overcome the information asymmetry between operators and regulator. Benchmarking prices and costs helped to overcome this information asymmetry to some extent. Fairer competition that results from cost-based termination rates is likely to reduce prices and increase access and usage again for Namibia. This will contribute to economic growth and employment generation. The research hence allowed the regulator to balance consumer interests and the return on investment of the operators, in particular the new entrant CellOne.

Table 18.7 Research ICT Africa research report for the Namibian communications commission: Namibian benchmarking study, June 2009

Description	*Research ICT Africa* was commissioned by the NCC to conduct the benchmarking study in January 2009 and gave its recommendation in June 2009.
Recommendations	The initial recommendation emerging from this was that the new termination target rate should be N$0.30 based on the cost of termination of the most efficient operator.
Media response	07/06/2009, Namibia: Regulator Reduces Mobile Interconnection Charges, Intelcon 07/06/2009, ICT and Telecom: Namibia: NCC Slashes Mobile Charges, AllAfrica News 07/08/2009, Belskale kry balans, Republikein 07/08/2009, NCC slashes mobile charges, Namibian 07/08/2009, Namibia: NCC Slashes Mobile Charges, allAfrica.com 07/10/2009, MTC gets a whipping, Namibian 07/10/2009, MTC Gets a Whipping, tmcnet.com 07/11/2009, NCC slashes mobile interconnection fees by 43% (Namibia), Wireless News 07/11/2009, NCC slashes mobile interconnection fees by 43% (Namibia), WirelessFederation 07/13/2009, Fairness will benefit economy, expert says, Namibian 07/23/2009, How to reduce telecoms costs, ECN Telecoms 07/23/2009, De Lille urges probe into cellphone costs, The Star 07/23/2009, Competition chief "shares De Lille's concerns", Mail and Guardian Online 07/23/2009, We are not anti-competitive, say cellular operators, MyBroadband 07/28/2009, Namibia cuts phone fees before SA, Business Day 07/28/2009, South Africa: Namibia Cuts Phone Fees Before Nation, allAfrica.com 07/31/2009, Call It Crazy, Mail and Guardian 07/31/2009, Icasa agrees to look into high cellphone rates, Mail and Guardian Online 08/01/2009, NCC to resolve interconnection dispute between Namibia's three mobile operators., HYPERLINK "http://goliath.ecnext.com/coms2/gi_0199-9827542/NCC-to-resolve-interconnection-dispute.html" http://goliath.ecnext.com/coms2/gi_0199-9827542/NCC-to-resolve-interconnection-dispute.html or HYPERLINK "http://www.highbeam.com/doc/1G1-191150065.html" http://www.highbeam.com/doc/1G1-191150065.html 08/01/2009, Namibia's Telecom Regulator to Settle Interconnection Fee Dispute, Cellular News 08/01/2009, Namibia cuts phone fees before SA, HYPERLINK "http://www.bizcommunity.com" http://www.bizcommunity.com 08/03/2009, Lower call rates won't be easy to achieve, MyBroadband.co.za 08/06/2009, Interconnection fees reduction begins to bite, Informante 08/06/2009, Inter-connection rates lowered, Informante 08/16/2009, Why can't talking be cheaper?, Timeslive 09/01/2009, Will the ceiling interconnection cellular rate like Namibia work in South Africa?, tech4law 09/03/2009, Telecom to earn N$10 million dollar from interconnection rate cut, Informante 09/13/2009, TV. Carte Blanche on Interconnection, Mnet Carte Blanche 09/16/2009, Vodacom ready to reduce its rates, Timeslive 09/26/2009, NAMIBIA CUTS PHONE FEES BEFORE NATION, tmcnet.com
Outcome	CellOne, MTC and Telecom Namibia agreed on a compromise model with an immediate drop of termination rates to N$0.60 and an 18 months glide path to N$0.30.

Role of the Regulator

The independent research conducted by Research ICT Africa over the years provided the regulator with the data to convince government to open up the market and pass a new Telecommunications Act. It also provided the tools to resolve interconnection disputes and regulate retail tariffs (see Table 18.7).

Table 18.8 *Insight* magazine ICT column and *Business Namibia*

Title	Date	Publication
A tax against progress	December 2007	*Insight*
VoIP: why is it illegal?	2007	*Business Namibia*
Telecommunications: review and economic outlook	2007	*Business Namibia*
Broader and faster	June 2007	*Insight*
Airtime and cash	December 2006	*Insight*
Kick-starting telecom reform	May 2006	*Insight*
Here comes the cyber SME	February 2006	*Insight*
A summit of solutions: WISIS	December 2005	*Insight*
The costs of monopolies	October 2005	*Insight*
Introducing Namibia's new currency—airtime	August 2005	*Insight*
Half a G behind and way too expensive	May 2005	*Insight*
Satellites can bridge Namibia's digital divide	April 2005	*Insight*
Least-cost routing: who wins, who loses	March 2005	*Insight*
Power talking: transforming the good old power grid into a 21st century ICT network	February 2005	*Insight*
Narrowing the digital divide: it's policy not technology that counts	December 2004	*Insight*
Convergence still buzzes: how fixed-line operators can win back traffic from cellular operators	November 2004	*Insight*
Talking up the economy: if legalized, Internet telephony could slash the cost of communicating	October 2004	*Insight*
An open and closed case: telecommunications liberalisation will open new business opportunities in Namibia	September 2004	*Insight*

Conclusion

Most of the sector outcomes strived for have been met or are about to be met in Namibia. Five years of independent quantitive and qualitative research have contributed to provide the data for policy-makers and regulators to make better decisions. They also delivered the tools to resolve interconnection disputes and analyse the sector performance. Feeding research into policy and regulatory processes is a complex task. It requires that credibility and impartiality be established. It also requires a combination of communication strategies that break down research into useful information for various players in the sector.

Benchmarking countries, whether retail prices, cost of termination or regulatory environment perception, has proven to be useful to overcome information asymmetry and strengthen the role of the regulator. The demand-side research by Research ICT Africa provided an alternative data source to the data provided by operators.

References

Cook, P. and Mosedale, S. (2007). *Regulation, Markets and Poverty*. Cheltenham: Edward Elgar.

CPB (2000). *Yardstick Competition. Theory, Design, and Practice*. Netherlands Bureau for Economic Policy Analysis, The Hague. Available at: http://www.cpb.nl/nl/pub/cpbreeksen/werkdoc/133/wd133.pdf [accessed: 1 August 2011].

Dassler, T., Parker, D. and Saal, D.S. (2006). "Methods and trends of performance benchmarking in UK utility regulation." *Utilities Policy* 14:3, 166–74.

Gillwald, A. (2002). "Policy and regulatory challenges of access and affordability," in *Networking Knowledge for Information Societies: Institutions and Intervention*, eds Robin Mansell, Rohan Samarajiva and Amy Mahan (Delft: Delft University Press, 2002), 101–102. Available at: http://lirne.net/resources/netknowledge/gillwald.pdf [accessed: 1 August 2011].

IISD (2006). *The Sustainable Development Timeline*. Available at: http://www.iisd.org/pdf/2006/sd_timeline_2006.pdf [accessed: 1 August 2011].

infoDev (2008). *Building Local Capacity for ICT Policy and Regulation: A Needs Assessment and Gap Analysis for Africa, the Caribbean, and the Pacific—Supply Analysis*. infoDev Working Paper no. 16. Available at: http://www.infodev.org/en/Publication.508.html [accessed: 1 August 2011].

ITU (2006). *World Telecommunication/ICT Development Report 2006: Measuring ICT for Social and Economic Development*, March. Available at: http://www.itu.int/dms_pub/itu-d/opb/ind/D-IND-WTDR-2006-SUM-PDF-E.pdf [accessed: 1 August 2011].

Kirkpatrick, C., Parker, D. and Zhang, Y. (2005). "Price and profit regulation in developing and transition economies: methods used and problems faced: a survey of the regulators." *Public Money and Management* 25:2, 99–106.

LIRNEasia (2007). "Teleuse at the bottom of the pyramid: Findings from a five country study," Background paper prepared for *3rd Global Knowledge Conference*, Kuala Lumpur, 11–13 December 2007. Available at: http://www.gkpcms.com/GK3/documents/07.12.12-GK3-ET8-Ayesha%20Zainudeen.doc [accessed: 1 August 2011].

Shleifer, A. (1985) "A theory of YC." *Rand Journal of Economics* 16: 319–27.

Stork, C. (2004a). An open and closed case: telecommunications liberalisation will open new business opportunities in Namibia. *Insight* 1, September.

Stork, C. (2004b). Convergence still buzzes: how fixed-line operators can win back traffic from cellular operators. *Insight* 3, November.

Stork, C. (2004c). Narrowing the digital divide: it's policy not technology that counts. *Insight* 4, December.

Stork, C. (2004d). Talking up the economy: if legalised, Internet telephony could slash the cost of communicating. *Insight* 2, October.

Stork, C. (2005a). A summit of solutions, *Insight* 14, December.

Stork, C. (2005b). *e-Access and Usage Index Survey 2004*. NEPRU Research Report no. 35, 52 pages.

Stork, C. (2005c). Half a G behind and way too expensive. *Insight* 8, May.

Stork, C. (2005d). Introducing Namibia's new currency—airtime. *Insight* 11, August.
Stork, C. (2005e). Least-cost routing: who wins, who loses? *Insight* 6, March.
Stork, C. (2005f). Narrowing the digital divide in Namibia. *NEPRU Quarterly Economic Review* 59.
Stork, C. (2005g). Power talking: transforming the good old power grid into a 21st century ICT network. *Insight* 5, January/February.
Stork, C. (2005h). Satellites can bridge Namibia's digital divide. *Insight* 7, April.
Stork, C. (2005i). The costs of monopolies. *Insight* 13, October.
Stork, C. (2006a). Airtime and cash. *Insight* 26, December.
Stork, C. (2006b). Here comes the cyber SME. *Insight* 15, February.
Stork, C. (2006c). Kick-starting telecom reform. *Insight* 18, May.
Stork, C. (2006d). When Apple met Windows. *Insight* 17, May.
Stork, C. (2007a). A tax against progress. *Insight* December/January.
Stork, C. (2007b). Broader and faster. *Insight* 26, June.
Stork, C. (2007c). *Impact of VAT on Prepaid Telecommunication Services*. NEPRU Policy Brief no. 20.
Stork, C. (2007d). Telecommunications: review and economic outlook. *Business Namibia.*
Stork, C. (2007e). VoIP: Why is it illegal?, *Business Namibia*, 2007 edition.
Stork, C. (2008a). *Draft Telecommunications Bill 2008: Lessons from South Africa*. NEPRU Policy Brief no. 21.
Stork, C. (2008b). Telecommunication—the untapped market. *NEPRU Quarterly Economic Review*, 59.
Stork, C. (2008/2009). *Price Transparency for Namibia's Telecommunication Sector*. NEPRU Policy Brief no. 22/1, series of 12 briefs.
Stork, C. (2009). Information communication technology—towards fairer competition in the sector. *NEPRU Quarterly Economic Review*, 68.
Stork C. and Deen-Swarray M. (2007). *Switch to Competition*. NEPRU Policy Brief no. 18.
Stork, C. and Esselaar, S. (2006). *Telecommunication Sector Reform for Development*. NEPRU Policy Brief no. 17.
Vodafone (2006). *Africa: The Impact of Mobile Phones*. London: Vodafone. Available at: http://www.vodafone.com/etc/medialib/attachments/cr_downloads.Par.78351.File.tmp/GPP_SIM_paper_3.pdf [accessed: 1 August 2011].
WCED (1987). *Our Common Future, World Commission on Environment and Development (WCED)*. Oxford: Oxford University Press, 43. Available at: http://www.un-documents.net/wced-ocf.htm [accessed: 1 August 2011].
World Bank (2007). *World Development Report 2008: Agriculture for Development*. Washington, DC: World Bank. Available at: http://go.worldbank.org/ZJIAOSUFU0 [accessed: 1 August 2011].
World Bank (2009). *Information and Communications for Development 2009: Extending Reach and Increasing Impact*. Washington, DC: World Bank. Available at: http://go.worldbank.org/NATLOH7HV0 [accessed: 1 August 2011].
WSSD (2002). *Plan of Implementation of the World Summit on Sustainable Development*. Available at: http://www.un.org/esa/sustdev/documents/WSSD_POI_PD/English/WSSD_PlanImpl.pdf [accessed: 1 August 2011].
WTDC (2006). "Doha Declaration," in *The World Telecommunication Development Conference*, Doha. Available at: http://www.itu.int/ITU-D/wtdc06/DohaDeclaration.html [accessed: 1 August 2011].

Chapter 19
Leveraging Information and Communication Technologies for Global Public Health

Shriya Malhotra

Introduction

We live in an information- and data-driven world, increasingly defined by visuals. Global connectivity is being driven by a revolution in information and communication technologies (ICTs). Vast networks of people across the world communicate, share and collaborate unlike ever before. Concurrently, population growth and concentration in urban areas is creating a range of multidimensional health concerns. With global public health challenges constantly arising, the networks of knowledge-sharing enabled by ICT are more crucial than ever. This chapter discusses ICT trends and its applications to improve community and human health.

Rapid advances in ICTs combined with applications for knowledge sharing and management have created several opportunities to improve people's health. They have facilitated an increase in the quantity as well as the quality of data and information shared worldwide. As of 31 December 2009, an estimated 1,802,330,457 people were using the Internet worldwide (Internet World Stats 2009).

From an international affairs perspective, the advent of the Internet and mobile phone networks can have positive as well as negative implications for public or population health. Many argue that the lack of knowledge surrounding the health impact of technologies is risky; the impact of exposure to radiation from mobile phones, for instance, is not known with scientific certainty. A recent article in the *New York Times* explores the impact of technology on human behavior and how it often decreases focus and increases stress (Richtel 2010). The opposite of technological "skeptics," however, completely embrace technological developments, relying on them almost exclusively to solve problems. The way forward seems to be thoughtfully utilizing the power of ICT to fill gaps in public health services delivery, community education and data management.

Applying ICT is not a blanket solution to the lapses in public health services delivery, disaster preparedness or knowledge management. However, it is a valuable tool that links people with information that can improve and protect their lives. It has inherent risks and can potentially exacerbate inequalities, compromise security and individual privacy. Therefore, the practical and theoretical pros and cons of the impact of ICTs on global public health must be carefully analyzed. From activating virtual social communities to facilitating expert networks, sharing knowledge amongst communities or engaging constituents to participate in data gathering, the possibilities enabled by ICTs seem endless.

ICTs have the potential to improve lives despite technological curves, infrastructure lapses and a "digital divide." They enable visual and spatial tools to form connections in order to address global public health. At the same time, the impact and potential complications must be weighed.

Electrical blackouts can render all electronic-based ICT networks ineffective, for example. How can safeguards be put in place to allow the greatest overall benefit for the most people? Can technological solutions drive research and policy requirements into actions that address human health?

In the International Affairs contexts, ICTs facilitate engagement and creative applications to solve complex problems. Information is easily and reliably transmitted across borders and distances. Emergency situations are easier to respond to by the international community, as evidenced in the 2004 Asian tsunami and the 2008 earthquake responses in Haiti. Applications like advanced mapping, data management and widened social and communication networks raise issues of quality and reliability of information, given the democratization of information sources. The question becomes: how can individuals best manage the growing wealth of information and data to achieve sustainable, healthy communities? The response could be that lateral and technological solutions need to be integrated to improve global public health. Examples in this chapter will demonstrate how technological solutions and visual/spatial representations of health information can advance research, inform policy, and communicate the information necessary to educate individuals and empower communities.

ICT and Data

ICTs have had a significant impact on the creation, sharing, analysis and management of data over the last 20 years. With the advent of the Internet, mobile phone technologies and innumerable data management systems, millions of individuals create and share information. From credit card users submitting personal details, to government data gathering projects, to private sector giants like Google, IBM and GE leveraging the power of technology for consumer market research and analysis—knowledge gathering and sharing increasingly define modern life. The impact is faster, easier data gathering, sharing and storing *en masse*. So, how can we ensure communities and individuals are equipped to properly use the information and how can misuse and misinformation be prevented? Can ICT solutions maximize benefits to human health, for example, by generating knowledge to create awareness of preventative health?

ICT and Visualization

Information and communication technologies allow comprehensive and faster analysis of complex data comparatively, over time and dynamically, in real time. Data modeling and visualizing multiple variables facilitate holistic comprehension and inform health planning and preparedness. Visualization allows several variables to be analyzed or modeled in their space and conveys information in the form of static, interactive or participatory maps. It also enables improved education and communication of information to engage and inform communities. The concern over using these technologies is the rate of adoption—are communities equipped to analyze and understand the visual display of data? How much information can actually be comprehended without a complete educational overhaul?

ICTs, Community and Human Health

The health of populations, a science referred to as "public health," links individual behaviors with community health. ICT facilitates faster data gathering, analysis and communication that inform public health systems. Sharing information and creating participatory knowledge facilitate a preventative approach towards health, one that is based on educated and informed individuals, as well as shared local and international knowledge. Disease preparedness and prevention, disaster relief and risk management are different components of contemporary public health systems. Through the improved communication and transmission of information, ICT can link and strengthen the role of health systems and organizations. It thus facilitates improved health services delivery by targeting issues and allocating resources. It also engages individuals and activates communication networks as emergency and alert systems. Allowing information gathering, storing and analysis of different types of health data and information creates a comprehensive picture of population health.

Theoretical Assumptions

Viewing population and human health as policy and security priorities means re-thinking several paradigms in which international affairs operates.

Development as Community and Human Health

The field is dominated by discussion of international and human development that revolves around a broader definition of economic growth and security. By most definitions, development is a means of improving the lives and freedoms of people, but is problematically rooted in economics. The argument states that, by creating freer markets and generating economic growth, a trickle-down effect will eventually even out the benefits. However, defining development as community health or well-being instead of an expanded version of economics is more effective. This is the first assumption that underlies discussion in this chapter. Development expertise remains segregated and inaccessible for many stakeholders looking to engage in projects to improve communities. Many of the issues faced in the field of development, including the definitional limitations, can be overcome by ICT-facilitated collaboration and experience. Furthermore, measuring development impact in terms of health indicators is perhaps more in line with its underlying goals.

Collaboration and Participation for Improved Community and Human Health

A second assumption that underlies this discussion is that collaboration fostered between international entities, individuals and communities provides comprehensively informed and holistic health knowledge. Sharing information and experiences, and participating in virtual communication or mobile networks is a crucial component of global public health preparedness. ICTs facilitate rapid emergency responses and disaster/disease outbreak preparedness, as well as creating a dialogue amongst the numerous international actors involved in global health. It is of crucial importance that communities become engaged in ensuring their well-being and addressing population health requirements.

Sharing Knowledge = Power

Finally, it is important to reconsider the time-old saying, "knowledge is power." Given the advances in ICTs, common sense dictates that now knowledge sharing is a source of power. There is potential to generate knowledge and share information via the Internet and mobile phones, among other means—and this has important implications. ICT also has the potential to support and integrate health and education, the cornerstones of Amartya Sen's idea of human development and expanded capabilities (Sen 1999).

Public Health

Public health is defined as "the art and science dealing with the protection and improvement of community health by organized community effort and including preventive medicine and sanitary and social science" (*Merriam Webster Online Dictionary* 2010). As a tool to promote public health research, services and education, ICTs have several applications. These technologies can engage and communicate health information for citizens to protect themselves. They can be leveraged to gather, store and analyze complex data and information. However, the effectiveness of these networks and technologies requires a careful delineation of their aims and end goals. There are several competing interests, even in the international affairs realm, unless the consensus is that health and well-being are ultimate priorities. Private and medical organizations may use ICT for confidential data collection and gathering, while governments might apply this information to inform policies. Individuals may use multiple sources to gain health information.

ICTs can overcome these limitations by empowering individuals to prevent poor health and protect themselves. Smart phone applications, for instance, now offer free, tailor-made nutrition and exercise regimens. Meanwhile, they also offer up-to-date information on the seasonal flu. Alternative sources of data and dissemination networks with a greater reach than any government have the potential to inform communities and individuals. This also entails several risks depending on the supply and quality of information.

Global Public Health

Global public health, by definition, aims to save lives by improving health worldwide in response to global and local determinants of health, while addressing the apparent trade-offs between the environment and urbanization. Global health governance and local management is an emerging challenge, combined with the localization for urban health needs. IT can be leveraged to improve the health of communities around the world. It is in this context that we find contemporary global health at the fore of international affairs agendas and research across the world. From anticipating the health impact of climate change in cities to the spread of HIV/AIDS and its intrinsic link to individual behavior, global public health is increasingly recognized as multifaceted and requiring multidimensional approaches.

ICT can fill the gaps in global public health by enabling global information sharing across borders, oceans and cultures, and creating multiple opportunities for collaboration. It does so in real time, transmitting information and populations faster than ever. Apart from supporting the health systems in urban spaces, it forms a crucial and often missing link for communication and information to be shared between rural and urban areas. This crucial link is increasingly blurred and misunderstood, but stands to benefit from trends and advances in ICTs.

Urban Public Health

Because of the economics of scale, living in urban areas can facilitate better health because of cheaper transportation costs and access to numerous clinics and hospitals. The Internet and mobile phones reduce the "distance" between individuals and experts such as doctors and medical professionals. Urban life, however, comes with its own risks—stressful lifestyles and mental health issues. These can be addressed through analysis and research of site-specific health requirements and issues. Cities as network or information hubs can avail themselves of the multiplier effects and available infrastructure. The future goal should perhaps be towards creating networked urban ecosystems that inform and share knowledge on topics of public health.

ICTs can fill knowledge gaps; they form links between rural and urban populations and relate individual behaviors to community health. Their implications for global health encompass multiple dimensions of well-being, centered on human development. Real-world examples, such as using geographic information systems (GIS) to map out vaccine availability or concentrations of malaria-causing mosquito sites, demonstrate applications to improve global health. There are on-going efforts worldwide to empower individuals with ownership of their medical records and data. Whether by nutrition education, infectious disease prevention or HIV/AIDS awareness, the first line of preventative health is individual empowerment and access through information and knowledge. ICT enables basic education, improved engagement and avenues of communication for urban communities. The issues that arise stem from regulation and standardization of information to ensure quality. Global and urban public health therefore stands to benefit from ICT trends of communication and increased participation in data gathering. ICT can target and solicit information, disseminate knowledge amongst experts and nonexperts, visualize data to help users to grasp concepts and create dialogues to increase understanding in a participatory manner.

These advances in information gathering and sharing, visual research and spatial analysis support and reinforce efforts to meet the public health needs of urban communities, while strengthening global health systems and networks. Cities are ideal sites to form collaborative networks and hubs of knowledge. Inter-city networks can be created to learn about and manage the health of constituents. However, they have much to learn from more sustainable and rural lifestyles. ICTs can prepare cities to protect populations for the future, which is crucial given that, by 2050 almost two-thirds of people will live in cities (UN HABITAT 2009). The next section will use real-world examples and practical applications of ICTs towards improved public health.

Theory to Practice: Leveraging Visual and Virtual Networks

ICT is not a panacea for public health concerns, which are diverse and multifaceted. The possibility of large-scale disruption of telecommunication networks, for instance, poses a security, privacy and health risk. There are also innumerable practical considerations surrounding the transfer and rate of adoption of technology. Given the gap between developed and developing countries, issues like accessibility, infrastructure, hardware/software compatibility and language barriers continue to persist. ICTs do, however, hold the potential to gather and extrapolate valuable information to educate, allocate and communicate knowledge for people and policy-makers to improve health.

The practical impact of ICTs on public health encompasses the following:

1. knowledge sharing and management;
2. health data visualization and mapping;
3. health services delivery and resources allocation;
4. disease outbreak preparedness and resilience building;
5. disaster preparedness, risk management and mitigation;
6. health education and communication.

ICT allows wider access to preventative health information, which is crucial for timely responses to different health concerns. The Internet can be a crucial tool for improving and informing global health. Apart from facilitating communities, online interaction and participatory mapping, it is a major repository of health information. People often use Google search engines to analyze their symptoms instead of immediately consulting with doctors. The Mayo Clinic's website (www.mayoclinic.com) offers comprehensive health information online relating to many allergies, diseases, and medical conditions which is openly and freely accessible.

At the same time there are websites that lure people into purchasing medicines or remedies, the efficacy of which may or may not be verified. The Internet can be a marketplace for misinformation, scams and poor health information. The concern is that people may incorrectly self-diagnose or medicate themselves, thereby instigating widespread myths, rumors and panic. Ensuring that populations are equipped with basic awareness and media literacy or setting regulatory standards may be ways to prevent that from happening.

The Internet has innumerable websites and web-based applications that facilitate the sharing and analysis of personal data. Websites like IBM's Many Eyes—http://manyeyes.alphaworks.ibm.com/manyeyes—offer "a social aspect to data visualizations like maps, network diagrams, and scatter plots." Similarly, there are many publicly available online surveys, mapping and data gathering tools. An example of a data visualization website for individuals is Daytum (www.daytum.com), designed by information designer Nicholas Feltron to allow users to visualize their personal data, specifically to "collect, categorize and communicate your own data." Another website, www.data.gov, is the U.S. government portal to share official data from innumerable sources and with an array of mash-up and visualizations tools.

There are many examples of mapping and spatial representation tools enabled by the Internet and new generations of smart phones. Geo-tagging information online and making it public is a defining element of Web 2.0 and its links with mobile phone networks. Phones enable linking, sharing and immediate access to information from almost anywhere. People can identify local environmental risk spots or track the spread of seasonal allergies in their local communities. Websites like habitatmap.org and Google maps allow individuals to geo-tag their images and data while disseminating it online.

ICT engages new audiences and communities with their health and well-being by enabling transparency via participation, availability of open data and open source software. Increased participation has been key to data-gathering efforts. The website www.oasisnyc.com, for example, specifically stores NYC asthma and environmental health data that can be visualized and explored by zip code. This geographic insight forms a crucial dimension of urban environmental and public health.

The Internet and mobile networks facilitate global, urban–urban as well as urban–rural data sharing. In many countries, municipal and state health departments maintain websites with up-to-date information and updates via SMS alerts. Mobile networks, in addition to facilitating voice conversations and connectivity, now support a slew of data services such as SMS messages, email, mobile Internet, Bluetooth, picture/video sharing and GPS. The most commonly used data application on mobile phones is SMS text messaging, and it can facilitate alerts, reminders and instant information. Phones themselves are now data-collecting tools, storing notes, information and even basic medical information.

A major barrier to the benefits of the Internet and mobile networks use lies in infrastructure and hardware differences between developed and developing countries. Telecommunication and infrastructure penetration rates vary by region and within countries, so it is difficult to assume that in the near future everyone will have a computer or a phone and that there could be benefits to this as a source of data. Although ICT enables the tools to communicate information and gather and share knowledge, people have to acquire and then use these facilities in order to generate data and information. Programs that can support literacy and distribution of such tools are one way of enabling greater global connectivity. Through education, massive sharing and engagement, communities can be involved to address their own health.

Table 19.1 Practical examples of how ICT facilitates new knowledge connections and networks

Individual health	Social networks; SMS health reminders, smart phone health maps; manage own data; locate and communicate directly with healthcare professionals.
Population health	Epidemiological mapping and data visualization to understand health determinants; inform and promote disease outbreak responsiveness preparedness.
Built environment health	Map infrastructure maintenance, electrical lines, wi-fi networks, noise pollution, potholes.
Environmental health	GIS for water quality, environmental management; flora and fauna research; natural disaster preparedness.

Case Study 1: GIS and Advanced Mapping

In 1857, English epidemiologist Dr John Snow used a simple, hand-drawn map to prove that London's cholera epidemic was being spread through a contaminated water pump. Given ICTs and advances in mapping technologies combined with the increased availability of such tools, there is immense room for epidemiological mapping to inform community health.

Snow's map is an historic example of information and data visualization, as is Charles Booth's "Poverty Map," which revealed the spatial dimension of poverty. Mapping and geo-locating data and information visualizes the context, making it more valuable. Advanced mapping technologies enable faster, easier and more accurate mapping on a bigger scale, as well as the ease of sharing results.

Spatial representation and mapping used to be time-consuming, 2D, expert-driven endeavors. With the advent of Internet based mapping tools, computer-assisted design and open source GIS, multiple data variables can be layered and understood in their specific geographic contexts. These layers of information add further relevance to health research and policy efforts.

As a result of advances in technology and participation of communities, mapping is no longer the expert science it was once. It can be interactive, participatory and even subversive. With the advent of Web 2.0 have also emerged a plethora of mapping tools, freely available online. More advanced interactive maps are now easy to create and update. They can be dynamic and comprise large sets of complex data. They hold the potential to communicate information in a powerful way and serve as a means of analysis.

Applying advanced mapping software for epidemiological mapping has been particularly important to global public health. It is now presumed that "the visualization of geographic patterns could predict the spread of diseases" (Penn State 2010). Apart from "epi maps," however, there are several other kinds of maps that communicate valuable information about a range of health determinants. An exploration of the potentials of health mapping is available at ehealthmap.com and healthmap.wordpress.com.

Technologies like GIS evidence the potentials of advanced open source software for health. In the field of public health, GIS is a research and analysis tool. It can be used to correlate medical research data and environmental information such as air pollution modeling, urban land use and ground water quality issues. This type of spatial analysis for health is important in understanding the extent and speed at which infections spread in specific geographic locations and in relation to several variables, like population density and transportation networks. It is also crucial for disaster preparedness, which is of increasing importance given the increasingly visible impacts of climate change.

GIS allows users to view, understand, question, interpret and visualize data for disease surveillance among other public health applications. It enables land use analysis and tracing of water sources, for instance. The extent to which it can be used in health research and to promote disease surveillance, preparedness and response while supporting community health projects is still being explored. The consensus and proliferation of websites such as healthmap nevertheless reflect that there is much room to leverage GIS to promote better health.

Open source software enables the visualization and increases the visibility of multiple interlocking components of health. The urban dimension, for instance, stresses the importance of mental wellness and looking at factors such as noise pollution. All these interlocking and site-specific factors are best understood using advanced mapping and modeling tools as well as increased participation with data, revealing latent information.

Mapping with GIS or through simple, participatory cartography, can visualize and make visible infection sources, epidemic clusters and transmission routes. Overlaying maps with socioeconomic data can highlight the varied factors contributing to disease outbreaks as well as the location of resources to address them. Visuals easily communicate information for preventative health behaviors, such as washing hands or getting vaccines. They also provide evidence for better-targeted health policy and advocacy efforts.

Users who submit information, opinions, photographs and ratings frequently use free and publicly accessible online maps such as Google Maps, Yahoo and Wikimap. These online tools engage communities and encourage them to geospatially record and interact with information. Having publicly available but varied points of view is a democratic and participatory means of creating and disseminating knowledge.

Maps can be used to efficiently allocate resources and communicate information to communities. In Yemen, for example, USAID has used GIS to map vaccine stocks and dispensing locations. Another example of visualizing and mapping online search query trends was the Google Flu tracker, which showed the relationship between flu queries and prevalence. The output visuals, i.e. maps, engage new audiences and effectively communicate valuable information.

For several years the World Health Organization (WHO) has employed GIS for global public health programs. The *Global Health Observatory* "provides critical data and analyses for key health themes, as well as direct access to the full database" (WHO 2010). It contains data from all WHO programs, including the WHO Statistical Information System (WHO 2010). Apart from data management, the WHO has also developed a "Communicable Disease Global Atlas" which enables "analysis and comparison standardized data and statistics for infectious diseases at country, regional, and global levels" (WHO 2010).

The WHO has been using GIS programs and public health mapping techniques since 1993 to assess decisions for a range of diseases and health programs (WHO 2010). According to its website,

> GIS provides ideal platforms for the convergence of disease-specific information and their analyses in relation to population settlements, surrounding social and health services and the natural environment. They are highly suitable for analyzing epidemiological data, revealing trends and interrelationships that would be more difficult to discover in tabular format. Moreover, GIS allows policy makers to easily visualize problems in relation to existing health and social services and the natural environment to more effectively target resources. (WHO 2010)

The website outlines the following uses of GIS for public health: calculating the geographic distribution of diseases; analyzing spatial and temporal trends; mapping and stratifying risk factors; informing resource allocation; planning targeted interventions; and monitoring diseases and health interventions over time (WHO 2010). These examples of basic and advanced mapping applications demonstrate the importance of exploring the possible role of ICTs to improve global public health.

Case Study 2: Health Data Visualization and Management Systems

Visualizing data entails not only the end product (i.e. the information visual), but also analyzing, educating and communicating information. It allows comparison to be shown over time, dynamic changes to be shown and hidden correlations and patterns to be revealed. Meanwhile, advanced mapping tools and maps enable real-time modeling and interactive analysis. Data visualization is crucial to inform evidence-based decision-making and convey crucial, basic health knowledge to populations.

It is reported that, "an emerging set of tools is making it easier than ever to track and compile all sorts of 'data' and display it in a way that's relatively easy to understand" (CNN 2010). ICTs enable communities to address future concerns about global health through data visualization, knowledge management and sharing. They support the advent of advanced data modeling, projections and analysis; information sharing and management; and communication for preventive health education—the bases of a comprehensive health system (CNN 2010).

Visualization plays a role as both a process and an output. On the one hand, it is defined as the visual and spatial display and analysis of information. The process of visualizing is both research and analysis, while the output visuals are able to educate and communicate. The quality of the methods used to display, understand and reveal knowledge through data, etc., as well as the systems that manage and share this information cannot be underestimated. This is why ICT is crucial for health decision-makers and individuals.

As a process, data visualization can have enormous potential benefits:

1. facilitating research and analysis;
2. educating populations and experts, facilitating dialogue and bridging their divide;
3. communicating information and creating new knowledge;
4. building shared communities (local + global);
5. informing evidence-based policymaking and resource allocation;
6. facilitating disease outbreak preparedness and disaster risk management.

Visualizing epidemiological data and using information diagrams to educate populations and inform decision-makers is crucial to urban public health research. Maps and visuals can disseminate complex information in a clear, concise manner, while educating populations and raising awareness—a key component of public health preparedness.

Community health is informed by multiple factors and different components that affect individuals and even cities. Health data highlight that health determinants are all kinds of sources—not just medical and epidemiological statistics, but also environmental and occupational health factors, like proximity to trees and green spaces. Socioeconomic determinants influence the location of households and access to fresh foods and parks, which are essential to quality of life. By participating and sharing information about their lives, people are inadvertently informing health knowledge and well-being.

Data visualization includes spatial representation as well as mapping. Mapping as both a tool and a process is of crucial importance to data visualization and the field of global health. Hans Rosling's Gapminder is an online tool that visualizes statistics in real time, organizing and representing historical data for advocacy purposes. According to the website, it unveils the hidden power of data and "the beauty of statistics for a fact based world view" (Gapminder 2010). Rosling is known for making public health statistics interesting and engaging for new audiences.

IBM's "Many Eyes" is an endeavor by the tech giant to add the social and networking dimension to data visualization (*MIT Technology Review: Indian Edition* 2010). Similarly, Processing is an open source software application that visualizes data and information into patterns, which can then be analyzed. Created by Ben Fry and freely available at www.processing.org, it offers insights through visualizing data. Another website, healthymagination.com is a partnership between GE and the website to look at health gaps and intricacies over time. GE's "Health Visualizer" states that "looking at the data in new ways like this can help us understand health and gain new insights about how to take better care of ourselves." Google Lab's Public Data Explorer is a project that "makes large datasets easy to explore, visualize and communicate (Google 2010). As the charts and maps animate over time, the changes in the world become easier to understand. You do not have to be a data expert to navigate between different views, make your own comparisons and share your findings."

With so much data being generated, submitted and shared, and so many available tools to understand it, the question that arises is what constitutes health data? The good news is that health statistics go beyond just medical information. The bad news is that they can incorporate innumerable lifestyle, economic and environmental factors. With the advances in ICT, the hope is now not only for increased and varied health data, but also for health management systems that have improved methods of management and analysis.

The proliferation of data tools online and mobile phones in the hands of so many is one reason why we are seeing more data visualization in popular culture and explains why data visualization itself is becoming simpler and more innovative (CNN 2010). The costs of hardware like computers and phones have been reduced, and "the technology needed to build applications is now in the hands of more people. Meanwhile, data is becoming increasingly digital and thereby easier to parse and catalog … Finally, through the advent of social media applications like Facebook and Twitter, coupled with the rise of increasingly sophisticated mobile phones, a cultural shift is seemingly under way" (CNN 2010).

Information graphics, visuals and diagrams can engage and educate patients and citizens. Data analysis is complex, but by making it visual and using software and information technologies to marry the vast amounts we create in their contexts can be a gold mine of knowledge. Google is collaborating with the World Bank to expand the "data sharing partnership, to include 54 World Development Indicators and visualization tools" (Google 2009). Users of the site can interact with a range of environmental and population statistics, using visualization tools like graphs and maps to track change over time (Google 2009). ICT thus facilitates improved accessibility, research and analysis of health data and information. Ease of comprehension and interaction seems to remove the "fear" and complexity of data, making it more usable and user friendly.

Case Study 3: Communication and Social Networks for Public Health

Cities are assumed to facilitate healthier communities via their concentrated networks and proximity to care systems. Urban spaces are knowledge and information hubs that can increasingly leverage virtual communication networks. Mobile phone technologies and the Internet are gearing towards global health services delivery while forming crucial links with rural areas. Mobile phones are increasingly being used to support community health services. By disseminating information and forming communication linkages, ICT is facilitating a smaller world and a smaller rural–urban divide. It enables the formation of networks to share information and build shared knowledge communities across barriers of all kinds. It can also put remote populations in touch with doctors and hospitals that are a long distance away.

Trends toward individual ownership of personal medical histories would not only empower patients vs medical practitioners but would also ensure their engagement in their own well-being. Sermo.com, for instance, is an attempt to bridge the gap between experts and medical professionals, compromising privacy for health. It is described as a "forum to share latest medical insights for physicians," and allows experts to stay in direct contact while sharing knowledge amongst each other. The formation of such collective knowledge networks directly link experts and populations. Social networks of experts and caregivers allow people to communicate, inform and share medical histories with the doctors they select.

Sites like the website Hello Health are examples of the leveraging of the power of social networks and communication to directly link practitioners and patients. HelloHealth.com allows public ratings and direct contact with and choice of practitioners. The site claims, "If you're ready for a real physician/patient relationship—one that's built on trust and what's best for you—then you're ready for Hello Health" (Hello Health 2010). This type of informed decision-making is crucial for well-being.

ICT has played a crucial role in humanitarian relief efforts, which are also central to global health. SMS and voice over Internet protocols connected Haiti's earthquake victims with the requisite medical attention and resources. These networks facilitated faster responses and helped to target health and relief support for these communities. Social networking websites like Twitter helped to ensure that funds were effectively allocated. Bloggers posted news and visuals from their smart phones, sometimes before the news media could understand and communicate what was occurring on the ground. These visuals informed global communities of what was happening and what was required to help people on the ground in Haiti. The directness of the link helped overcome the logistical delays and other inefficiencies of going through third party aid agencies.

The Internet and mobile phones are building a global network that fills in the gaps in government and international responses. Despite physical distances, the aftermath of disasters in Haiti and elsewhere reveal how the collapse of physical infrastructures lead virtual networks of individuals to spread information, share and communicate. Rapid and timely crisis responses and humanitarian relief can in this way be aided by ICT.

Social networks are crucial to good health, providing support, interaction, information, and access to medical histories and care givers. Virtual social networks that connect caregivers, experts, doctors and patients are therefore as important, constituting requisite knowledge ecosystems. Using their mobile phones, patients can transmit photos and get treatment without traveling a long distance for an expensive consultation.

For individual health, online social networks inform and support crucial human behaviors. Research shows that healthy habits like condom use, not smoking and reducing obesity can be socially contagious. This raises the question—when it comes to health knowledge, who do people listen to? Global health can take advantage of the interconnectivity facilitated by ICT to identify people with answers, solicit the right kinds of input and share knowledge.

The benefits of ICT are tremendous—improved connectivity, dynamic information analysis and updates, real-time responses, emergency alerts, reminders and increased information access. The applications of ICT for global health concerns seem immense. We now have large amounts of data that are open source and freely available. The pros seem to outweigh the cons, but effectiveness has yet to be shown. Systems, standards and regulations need to be in place for these benefits to be truly felt and to ensure that goals are all adequately met.

ICTs can inform and allow more effective responses to global health concerns, through:

1. education and communicating information (and health information);
2. participatory urban policy and planning for effectiveness;
3. disaster preparedness and relief;
4. better-targeted resource allocation.

There are also many risks involved in using ICT for public health. Allowing ownership of medical data, for instance, means that patients try to take treatment into their own hands or misunderstand what is being shown. This is an obvious drawback, but empowering individuals to know when to ask for expert advice and have basic control over their medical history and lives is also crucial. ICTs raise issues of ownership and legitimacy of data, intent, risks of sharing, privacy and access concerns, identity theft and risks of profiling.

To maximize the benefits of ICT one must consider:

1. Privacy concerns of how much and what information can and should be gathered and shared. How is privacy—medical and personal—to be maintained in the interest of the individual? What about security concerns of leaking information to pharmaceutical companies that try to prey on consumers by marketing drugs that can prolong illnesses? These risks must be mitigated through governance and management of information, as well as transparency and accountability of data gatherers—what is being collected/documented and for what reason?
2. Oversimplifying information for ease of communication or comprehension. When visualized, for the sake of coherence, information is often taken out of context. Meanwhile, correlations may become skewed when the users do not understand what the data indicates. Similarly, when the public cannot understand or contextualize information and are skeptical of the data it can lead to confusion and panic, at which point the issue of responsibility arises. Maintenance of transparency and accountability by the owners of data is important.

Conclusion

ICT impacts global public health by enabling information-sharing, improved communication and tools to analyze and respond to challenges, while generating participatory knowledge. The changing international arena supports the potential preventative health strategies enabled by ICT. The future will be dominated by people living in cities, and urban communities will continue to be bombarded by millions of ads per second. The most effective way to quickly communicate information appears to be through visuals and communication networks. Aesthetically displayed information can engage new audiences and inform or educate them on relevant health-related topics. Since we live in a data-driven world, everything is also becoming increasingly quantifiable—from food and nutrition to lifestyles. There is growing recognition that the display of public health information is crucial to its understanding. For example, online portals are available to guide users trying to understand public health data (NHS Public Health Network 2010). So how can we make the most of the opportunities presented by ICTs?

Global public health stands to benefit from technological adoption and recognition of improved health infrastructure and services. Building on arguments by Peter Evans, ICTs and transnational global networks can be leveraged to form social networks, which are oriented towards social achievements (Evans 2005). Given advances in social media, there is room for social marketing as a tool to encourage healthier behaviors. The possibilities to improve global public health using the tools and opportunities enabled by ICTs are immense.

The advantage of diverse data and information is that global public health is informed by a multitude of determinants, operating on different levels, concerning individual behavior, human development, environmental health, community health, health security and disaster preparedness. It relies on the ability of countries and municipalities to be equipped in order to detect, investigate, communicate and contain events that threaten the public. ICTs can enable timely responses and preparedness to concerns that could impact population health in a large way. Climate change in cities, for instance, can be informed by data-led social marketing campaigns that encourage walking instead of driving, to reduce greenhouse gas emissions.

The Internet, smart phone networks, the mobile web, SMS features and wireless radio are facilitating greater connectivity and flows of information than ever before. The quantity of information is proving to be an opportunity and a burden. *Wired* magazine's 2009 Smart List suggests a unique idea—giving up a little individual privacy for greater overall well-being (Koerner 2009). It describes how, in 2004, Jamie Heywood co-founded PatientsLikeMe, a website for users to easily access their own health data (Koerner 2009). The ultimate goal of these online portals and communities is to empower individuals with their personal medical and health data. Giving up privacy in a regulated and systematic way enables a crucial, but lacking, link between individual and population health.

Thus, ICTs can address lapses in global and urban public health. They can inform and create urban resilience, by linking environmental, population and individual health. Efforts should focus on strengthening, improving and reinforcing the role of ICTs without entirely relying on it. Dr Kevin Cahill has written extensively about the benefits of IT and its role for humanitarian relief. The consensus is that "information technology can shift our focus from costly late-stage disease management to a proactive investment in keeping people healthy" (Mundie 2006). For improved health, the mantra of "prevention is better than cure" has remained constant. The advent of ICTs in support of advanced mapping, visualization, social and communication networks can deepen global preventative health methods.

The state of international affairs and the actors involved in global health are changing. No longer is global health comprised exclusively of development agencies, governments and NGOs. Corporations and businesses are also increasingly involved through public and private partnerships as well as individuals who are acting in their own interest. Health should be defined by collaboration and driven by recognition that development paradigms and processes of the past have not been successful. Although involving multiple stakeholders can be difficult, mapping, data visualization and social networks allow the flexibility of preparing for different levels of interpretation and address the multitude of population health needs.

Major companies are becoming involved in the grab to generate and share data—GE's health visualizer, IBM, Google, Microsoft, even the U.S. government, are making resources available along with free visualization tools and data sets. The "grab" for data and sharing it is not only becoming a means of competition amongst these entities, but also fosters collaboration amongst a greater number of people. While health knowledge was previously relegated to experts, the power of decentralized sources of data from voluntary submission of information to involuntary threats to individual privacy could change this dynamic towards greater overall benefits.

It is crucial to remember that data is uni-dimensional and not 100% reliable; it can be manipulated to tell whatever story we want it to—and without numbers, stakeholders are often difficult to convince of different benefits. The aims and purposes with which data is gathered are often completely separate from its use. The priority lies therefore in exploring what we are targeting and how it informs knowledge when contextualized. Data, therefore, needs to be viewed with healthy skepticism, in the way that people listen to the media and ad campaigns with a degree of hesitance. Education must be geared towards holistic understanding and recognizing the relevance, and sometimes irrelevance, of numbers. The skepticism surrounding ICTs should promote securing reliable back-up systems rather than entire dismissal.

In the U.S., websites like data.gov are fast becoming a dumping ground of open source data and all U.S. municipal agencies are now opening up their data vaults. In New York City the Health and Human Services department has opened up its health data and is devising online and smart phone applications (Howard 2010). Their goal is to make community data "as useful to the world as weather data or other types of data is to other parts of American life" (Howard 2010). In response to this move by municipal government, innovators have reacted and built remarkable and valuable tools for citizens, enabling them to access and better understand the data (Howard 2010).

Mobile phones facilitate improved service delivery in several ways beyond forming links. Smart phones like Apple's iPhone allow instant access to drug databases, and calorie and nutrition calculators. These gadgets hold the potential to store and access electronic health records and medical images, or directly receive medical laboratory results. Thus, ICTs enable instant communication between patients and hospitals, doctors and their medical information. Smart phones can be used to schedule reminders for doctor visits and allow access to search engines as well as medical databases. This direct communication and information link between experts and users facilitates better information and can empower individuals.

ICT allows us to connect and share unlike ever before, thereby facilitating improved global public health. ICTs hold the potential to do so in terms of better and responsive health services delivery, improved knowledge management and knowledge communities. The proliferation of blogs gives voice to many and goes beyond the sharing of knowledge by adding an experiential layer of what works and what does not. There are innumerable hoaxes and scams that people need to be wary of, which raise questions surrounding the legitimacy, quality and reliability of information. With the proper systems and standards in place, however, these can be alleviated.

It is important to consider the quantity versus the quality of information and knowledge enabled by ICT. Under President Obama, the U.S. government has undertaken an open government data project, making everything available on data.gov. U.S. Centers for Disease Control are developing techniques to visualize health data and support research efforts. This will also enable users to make interactive or dynamic images, diagrams and displays as well as improved ways to display public health data. Interactive maps give users the ability to engage with and better understand public health science. An interactive flu map developed for the 2007–2008 influenza season compared cases over time and included data updates to educate constituents.

For our urban future, we need to anticipate challenges and address them in a preventative way to ensure healthy and sustainable population health. Issues of water quality, efficient energy security and the costs of development to the environment and for individual health are part of the urban public health equation. All these issues are mitigated when we start to think of development as well-being or health. Individuals, governments and businesses need to collectively avail themselves of the opportunities and advantages presented by ICT. Disseminating information has never been so easy; the large-scale disruption of ICT networks poses a big risk, but the potential benefits outweigh the costs. This also raises issues of information governance—whose responsibility is health? How are individuals accountable and to whom? Efforts should target building a global network of urban health knowledge ecosystems—harnessing technology to provide essential services, share experiences, improve well-being and save lives.

Apart from forming direct linkages and social networks for support, health knowledge can directly benefit from ICTs. They facilitate data visualization and systems to manage and store health information. This in turn generates health knowledge and improved access to experts and tools via social networks and communication links. Misinformation and fraud can be addressed by creating standards to tag information and present it in standardized or formatted way. They can be also structured for filtering, sorting and cross-tabulation. We live in a data-driven world, but unlike before, now it is all about knowledge sharing being power. The data we create and share will be passed onto future generations; it therefore needs to be systematized in a sustainable and useful way.

ICT can address some of the most pressing global public health concerns, linking the local and global in terms of health services delivery, health security, health systems and data management, sharing and gathering research and information, health education, and the effective allocation of resources. It allows for communication and knowledge collaboration and supports intricate relationships, participatory creation of data, and dissemination of findings. Without relying on it entirely, it should be leveraged for the benefits of education, collaboration and research, and provide basic information that can empower and protect the well-being and health of communities while maintaining a dose of skepticism.

The way forward seems to be by adopting a careful optimism towards a health system of empowered educated and informed individuals that constitute knowledge networks and relationships with experts and institutions that gather data. Visual research and spatial analysis can support the healthcare needs of urban communities and strengthen public health systems. Visualizing epidemiological data and health statistics while using information diagrams to educate populations and inform decision-makers is crucial for urban public health. Creative application of ICTs can facilitate improved public health resilience, preparedness and responsiveness. ICT promotes mapping, which is one way to improve urban public health, enabling visual and spatial analysis that informs populations as well as researchers (Malhotra 2009). The possibilities for applying advanced technologies for global public health are thus immense and ought to be carefully explored and thoughtfully applied.

References

CNN. 2010. *A New Way of Looking at the World.* [Online]. Available at: edition.cnn.com/2009/TECH/11/02/data.viz/index.html [accessed: 27 January 2011].

Daytum. 2010. [Online]. Available at: http://www.daytum.com [accessed: 27 January 2011].

Evans, P. 2005. Counter hegemonic globalization: transnational social networks in the contemporary global political economy. In *Handbook of Political Sociology: States, Civil Societies, and Globalization*, Thomas Janoski, ed. Cambridge: Cambridge University Press.

GE. 2010. *Health Visualizer.* [Online]. Available at: http://www.ge.com/visualization/health_visualizer [accessed: 27 January 2011].

Gapminder. 2010. [Online]. Available at: http://www.gapminder.org [accessed: 27 January 2011].

Google. 2009. *World Bank Public Data now in Search*, 11 November. Press Release. [Online]. Available at: http://googleblog.blogspot.com/2009/11/world-bank-public-data-now-in-search.html [accessed: 27 January 2011].

Google. 2010. *Data Visualizations for a Changing World.* Google Labs. [Online]. Available at: http://www.google.com/publicdata/home [accessed: 27 January 2011].

Health Map. 2010. [Online]. Available at: http://www.healthmap.wordpress.com [accessed: 27 January 2011].

Hello Health. 2010. [Online]. Available at: http://www.hellohealth.com [accessed: 27 January 2011].

Howard, A. 2010. Making community health information as useful as weather data. *O'Reilly Radar*, 2 June 2010. [Online]. Available at: http://radar.oreilly.com/2010/06/unlocking-innovation-through-d.html [accessed: 27 January 2011].

IBM. 2010. *Many Eyes*. [Online]. Available at: http://manyeyes.alphaworks.ibm.com/manyeyes [accessed: 27 January 2011].

Internet World Stats. 2009. [Online]. Available at: http://internetworldstats.com/stats.htm [accessed: 27 January 2011].

Koerner, B.I. 2009. Jamie Heywood: forget medical privacy. *Wired.* [Online]. Available at: http://www.wired.com/techbiz/people/magazine/17-10/ff_smartlist_heywood [accessed: 27 January 2011].

Malhotra, S. 2009. Mapping the way to better health. *ISN Special Report.* [Online]. Available at: http://www.isn.ethz.ch/isn/Current-Affairs/Special-Reports/Preparing-for-a-Pandemic/Public-Health-Gaps [accessed: 27 January 2011].

Mayo Clinic. 2010. *Medical Information and Tools for Healthy Living*. [Online]. Available at: www.mayoclinic.com [accessed: 15 June 2010].

Merriam-Webster Online Dictionary. 2010. [Online]. Available at: www.merriam-webster.com/netdict/public%20health [accessed: 15 June 2010].

MIT Technology Review: Indian Edition 2010. *Sharing Data Visualization*. [Online]. Available at: http://www.google.com/url?q=http%3A%2F%2Fwww.technologyreview.in%2Fcommunications%2F18516%2F&sa=D&sntz=1&usg=AFQjCNHw7X7w5kxJmJHaVQaj_-XLAyD7KQ, www.technologyreview.in/communications/18516 [accessed: 15 June 2010].

Mundie, C. 2006. Information technology: advancing global health. *NBR Analysis*, 17(2), 5–26.

NHS Public Health Network. *Understanding Public Health Data.* [Online]. Available at: http://www.avon.nhs.uk/phnet/PHinfo/understanding.htm [accessed: 27 January 2011].

Penn State. 2010, April 16. Visualization of geographic patterns may predict spread of disease. *ScienceDaily*. [Online]. Available at: http://www.sciencedaily.com/releases/2010/04/100415141130.htm [accessed: 27 January 2011].

Richtel, M. 2010. Attached to technology and paying a price. *The New York Times*. [Online]. Available at: http://www.nytimes.com/2010/06/07/technology/07brain.html [accessed: 27 January 2011].

Sen, A. 1999. *Development as Freedom*. New York: Knopf.

UN HABITAT. 2009. *State of the World Cities*. [Online]. Available at: http://www.unhabitat.org/pmss/listItemDetails.aspx?publicationID=2562 [accessed: 27 January 2011].

WHO. 2010. *Global Health Observatory*. World Health Organization. [Online] Available at: www.who.int/gho [accessed: 15 June 2010].

Chapter 20
Knowledge Ecologies in International Affairs: A New Paradigm for Dialog and Collaboration

Sean S. Costigan and Chris Pallaris

> Knowledge is information that changes something or somebody—either by becoming grounds for action or by making an individual (or an institution) capable of different or more effective action.
>
> Peter Drucker, *The New Realities*

Introduction

To have command over increasingly complicated social, political, economic and environmental challenges, fragmentary knowledge, or rather the simple accumulation of basic research, is inadequate (Kim 2007). International affairs professionals operating in government, academia and the private sector are progressively more aware that access to, and the blending of, interdisciplinary policy-related knowledge are critical to effective problem solving and decision-making. Yet how can one do so effectively?

This paper examines the concept of knowledge ecologies as a means of addressing this challenge. Although still in their infancy, knowledge ecologies (or knowledge ecosystems) are enabling innovative research, learning and policy solutions. While their intellectual origins can be traced back to the 1990s, it is only in the last few years that we have witnessed the emergence of viable ecologies dedicated to supporting the research and policy process. This pace is certain to increase as the international affairs community embraces new information and communications technologies and reappraises its approach to knowledge creation, management and exchange.

The study of knowledge ecologies covers a broad range of disciplines. In keeping with our subject, so does our paper. We readily acknowledge that, in sketching our ideas, we do not do justice to any of the disciplines we borrow from. Clearly, more work of both a qualitative and quantitative nature is needed to fully appreciate what impact knowledge ecologies will have on the study of international affairs and the conduct of its community.

In the pages that follow we explore a series of definitions, examine the elements shaping today's knowledge ecologies, and briefly introduce a number of online examples for the reader's reference. Our intention here is not to suggest that knowledge ecologies are a panacea for the real-world challenges we face. Instead, we hope to provoke a wider discussion among our peers as to their value and utility.

Defining our Subject

The study of knowledge ecologies has grown out of several intellectual and academic disciplines. These have been summarized by Pór (2001) and include complexity science, epistemology, systems thinking, organizational learning, evolutionary science, cognitive science and knowledge management. The study of knowledge ecologies also owes a debt to concepts such as memetics and the noosphere.

The term lends itself to a variety of definitions. Let us begin with a scientific approach. The term "knowledge" dates from the fourteenth-century Middle English *knowlechen*, or acknowledge, and today is used to describe the fact or condition of knowing something with familiarity gained through experience or association, acquaintance with or understanding of a science, art or technique, and no less than the body of truth, information and principles acquired by humankind. The term ecology is derived from the Greek words *οίκος* (ecos), which means household or institution, and *λόγος* (logos), which means dialogue or discourse. By extension, knowledge ecologies can be seen as *a discourse that takes place within a physical or virtual institution*. Just as an ecology is made up of a diversity of inter-connected organisms, minerals and processes that evolve according to their environment, so too does a knowledge ecology consist of a diversity of interdependent and interconnected technologies, processes, entities, strategies, tools, methodologies and communities that adapt to changing circumstances (Young 2007). Inevitably, the greater the diversity of knowledge, the greater the ecology's adaptability and its resilience to external shock.

From the perspective of an information scientist, a knowledge ecology can also be seen as a dynamic alternative to a traditional ontology, wherein knowledge is created and recreated in multiple contexts and at various points in time (Malhotra 1999). To the business leader the term is used to describe a community of practice that generates knowledge using collaborative applications and a bottom-up approach (Magnan et al. 2007). Such ecologies can be seen in the "skunk works" and "innovation cells" that exist in major industrial concerns, where teams of people are given freedom to work without the fetters of bureaucracy. Until recently the tools they used to interact have been domain-specific, and sometimes secret, restricting participants to closed environments of collaboration and knowledge exchange. Increasingly, however, software developers and information architects are pioneering ways to connect disparate communities and the ideas they share, thus enriching these ecologies as well as the innovative and profit-making capabilities of the organization further.

Finally, to an international relations (IR) scholar, as to anyone active in a wide-ranging field, knowledge ecologies consist of the individuals, institutions and ideas that contribute to the production, collection, analysis, disputation, management, distribution and consumption of research or policy-relevant knowledge. Indeed, the international affairs community is itself a knowledge ecosystem, relying as it does on distinctive academic disciplines for inspiration, ideas and action and, increasingly, on information technologies to develop the disciplines.

Why do these definitions (or perspectives) matter? We would argue that their variety captures the increasingly idiosyncratic nature in which knowledge is generated and shared. Across the board, traditional models of knowledge creation and exchange are being undone. Peer-reviewed journals may contain the best research librarians' money can buy, but their impact is proportional to the audience they receive, and these audiences are likely to dwindle. On the institutional level, the "knowledge capital" of an organization is determined not only by the quality of its research, but also by its willingness to nurture the knowledge commons. Further, a recent report titled *University Publishing in a Digital Age* (Brown et al. 2007) argues that the trend towards open access publishing will nurture new knowledge ecologies, foster new research environments and overhaul the means by which we create and consume educational resources.

The forces driving such processes are interrelated and irresistible. Indeed there is a vast literature—no longer exclusively science fiction—that argues that the creation and adoption of information technologies is an evolutionary step for humanity. Information and our attempts to control it are defining life itself (Beniger 1986). Just as we now accept the web as a symbiotic part of our natural existence, so too are we apt to accept newer knowledge ecologies as a matter of course.

With this in mind, it is critical to understand the properties of knowledge ecologies and the forces shaping their emergence. By doing so, one can anticipate how these might shape the study of international affairs.

Dissecting the Ecology

Broadly speaking, these properties can be examined on both the macro and micro levels. On the micro level they consist of the individual nodes that engage in the business of knowledge creation and exchange. Closer analysis here reveals the interests and motivations of these nodes, which can be personal or professional in scope and driven by any number of perspectives from selflessness to self-actualization.

The macro level, however, is concerned with those elements consistent to knowledge ecologies in general. These include, *inter alia*, their culture, organization and design; the technology they employ; their system of collaboration and communication; and the language they employ to achieve their ends. To understand how a knowledge ecology functions from an international studies perspective, it is necessary to consider these elements in greater detail.

Technology

Technology is the primary driver behind the creation of dynamic web-based ecosystems. The explosion of user-generated content, coupled with the dialectic process of data synthesis and atomization, is allowing us to identify patterns and relationships between different disciplines and ideas, which in turn foster new cognitive and semantic approaches to long-standing global problems. Elsewhere, the use of common standards is enabling greater interoperability and information sharing within and between individuals and institutions, as well as improved manipulation, searching, browsing, storage and visualization. Data that was once the preserve of different academic disciplines (e.g. geospatial indices of environmental decay) can now be integrated into a basic text document as a means of underlining policy recommendations, overlaid over maps, merged into ever more revealing mash-ups with multiple and various data sets, and perused and simultaneously modified by parties the world over. Knowledge ecosystems need not invest in expensive technology in order to develop community. In fact, studies show that some of the least costly technologies have proven to be the most fruitful; investments in outreach to potential community members are more critical (Worthen 2008). Twitter is but one (albeit extraordinary) example of a low-cost, highly integrated ecology. While some might argue that Twitter, at 140 characters a tweet (or feed), is not expressly in the business of creating new knowledge, a counterpoint may be made that the Library of Congress's acquisition of every Twitter feed since 2006 represents an attempt to capture the widest collection of interconnected sentiments, musings and ideas ever in human history.

Technology is also empowering the architectures of participation, communication and collaboration. Although there are persistent tensions from social networking giants, particularly from Facebook and its ever-changing privacy settings, the overall trend here is toward ever-greater openness, the purpose of which is to generate not only convergent and consensus-oriented solutions, but also diverse interpretations of information based on previously unpredicted contexts and unforeseen assumptions (Malhotra 1999). Indeed, many technologists argue that the closed architectures being built today stem from previous *technical limitations* and therefore are not to be considered part of the natural way of the world.

Language and Understanding

The languages we use to address global challenges are also evolving, albeit at different paces. English is universally acknowledged as the *lingua franca* of international affairs, and for good reason. A shared language augments shared cognition and the search for common solutions to problems such as climate change and weapons proliferation. Moreover, its growth is unfettered by a national academy dedicated to its preservation. As knowledge of the English language evolves, so too will the impetus to communicate in it. This will compel even native English speakers to accommodate new terms and definitions so that they might engage and grow the knowledge ecosystems to which they belong. The essential democratic elements of the English language, as well as its relative simplicity and substantial speaking population, also add strength to its position as the language of the Web.

Societal Context

Knowledge is invariably a social construct. As ideas jump from one community to another, and from one country or region to the next, they must adapt to prevailing social circumstances if they are to have any currency. It is all very well preaching energy conservation to several million affluent Europeans. How should one do so to a billion plus South Asians, many of whom receive only a couple of hours of electricity a day? In a similar vein, democracy may be the best form of government we have; it may also be the one form of government people everywhere aspire to. Nonetheless, recent events in Iraq, for example, have demonstrated at terrible cost that it cannot be transplanted wholesale.

"Biological" Design

All ecologies adhere to certain biological principles. Most are self-generating and self-organizing; they form of their own volition and evolve according to internal and external pressures. Second, they operate as networks of relationships. These networks are sustained by communication and the exchange of information, knowledge and ideas. This exchange furnishes the network's meaning and purpose which, in turn, allows the network to define its boundaries. Invariably, these boundaries are permeable. In order to sustain themselves and meet their purpose, networks must remain open to the ideas and influence of others. The intellectual vitality of a knowledge ecosystem serves as a reliable indicator of its future performance, as well as its potential to meet rapidly moving strategic challenges and opportunities (Pór 2001). In a successful biological ecosystem, genes mutate, organisms are selected, and populations evolve—and in a successful economy, business plans are generated, businesses evolve, and a global economy emerges (moreover, failure to share information and market opacity can lead to economic crashes; Bray et al. 2008).

Organizational and Cultural Drivers

Knowledge ecologies are a reflection of emerging organizational structures in both the public and private sector. These structures are engineered to ensure maximum resilience and flexibility in environments of high turbulence and uncertainty, as well as to encourage new attitudes and behaviors, especially with regard to knowledge creation and exchange. Thus, to address complex global challenges, the IR community is being compelled to establish analytic nodes across the physical and digital globe. Virtual think tanks will move from being the exception to the norm. As part of the process of adaptation and survival, the IR community will take on a growing range of organizational functions, from policy advocacy to intelligence gathering and analysis (one could go so far as to argue that web-based knowledge ecologies will evolve into the intelligence enterprises of the future). This will require a cultural framework that is as open and flexible as its structure. Academic stovepipes will have little real-world utility. It also requires incentives to encourage greater engagement in the creation and development of new ecosystems.

Existing incentives, especially in academia, appear to be inadequate. A recent study in *Nature* (2006) noted that feedback and peer review tools do not do much to encourage the active sharing of knowledge. In fact, the study noted "most comments were not technically substantive. Feedback suggests that there is a marked reluctance among researchers to offer open comments." In a knowledge ecology, comments and ideas are more likely to be scrutinized constructively. This is because relations between the various analytic nodes are not based on power and authority but rather on a collective sense of curiosity, engagement and survival based on co-dependence.

The Virtues of Openness

Further to the above, the present decade can be called the "open decade" (open source, open systems, open standards, open archives, open everything) just as the 1990s were called the "electronic" decade (e-text, e-learning, e-commerce, e-governance). However, as Peters (2008a, 2008b) argues, the decade of openness has been accompanied by a change of philosophy and ethos that has transformed the marketplace of ideas and the modes of production, collaboration and participation. The drive towards ever-increasing transparency and openness is essential not just to scientific inquiry and progress, but also to the healthy functioning of democracy. However, as Nielsen (2008) points out, to create an open scientific culture that embraces new online tools, two challenging tasks must be achieved: (1) build superb online tools; and (2) cause the cultural changes necessary for those tools to be accepted.

This culture of openness is remaking traditional markets and domains. According to Pór, some governments appear to be waking up to the fact that web-enabled technologies make the function of "information gate-keeping" obsolete (Pór 2001). However, recent work by the OpenNet Initative has shown that governments, particularly in Asia, have expanded their mandate to filter sensitive content both technically and through "soft controls" such as legal regulation and delegated liability (Deibert et al. 2008). The basic tension between control and flow remains, even if the most technically savvy are able to procure open information on the web that governments have attempted to filter.

In an example of the growth of openness that relates to the IR community, the growing popularity of open source intelligence appears to be evidence of a cultural and organizational shift that values knowledge as an imperative to action rather than occlusion. We are witnessing the emergence of an intellectual commons, one that is sustained by the efforts of researchers, writers, academics, bloggers and encyclopedists, as well as a global telecommunications network.

Knowledge is increasingly seen as a public good. Similarly, those who nurture the commons by enabling the sharing of ideas are increasingly seen as *public servants*. Their role will only grow in importance as we begin to tackle problems of a global, systemic nature. While their motivations may differ, as we have seen with Wikipedia and other online communities, most will be committed volunteers. As Benkler (2007) reminds us:

> Together, these three characteristics [ubiquitous computing, knowledge as a public good, modularity of technical architectures and social dynamics of knowledge production] suggest that the patterns of social production of information that we are observing in the digitally networked environment are not a fad. They are, rather, a sustainable pattern of human production given the characteristics of the networked information economy.

Without access to a global knowledge commons governments and individuals can only address problems from necessarily narrow (and sometimes selfish) perspectives rather than through a process of collective understanding and a shared responsibility for the outcomes. The networks that furnish the commons are moving towards ever-greater openness and transparency. Only by doing so can the network's purpose be communicated and its knowledge ecology nurtured and sustained.

The Convergence of Work and Learning

It seems almost trite to acknowledge that a Master's or PhD is no guarantee of lifetime employment. And yet, thousands of IR students graduate each year with little or no knowledge of the twenty-first-century literacies vital to their places of work. For those in the business of training and hiring, the skills shortage is palpable. Efforts like the American Library Association's Information Literacy Competency Standards for Higher Education (2000) go far, but only if educators are willing to assign value to this type of competency.

Knowledge ecologies are alerting participants not only to the theoretical trends shaping their disciplines, but also to the practical skills they must acquire in order to succeed. Looked at differently, knowledge ecologies operate as biological sensors, alerting their constituents to the properties they must adopt to ensure their relevance and survival. Leveraging knowledge and experience into a process of continuous learning and thoughtful reflection moves us toward insight. And insight is one of the ingredients of true innovation (Mamprin 2006), whether in research or policy-making.

Changing Work Patterns

Changing work patterns are a consequence of the organizational and cultural changes outlined above. A virtual think tank can work on a perpetual cycle of data collection and analysis. Field research need not be packaged into edited volumes (whose utility to the international studies community may be negligible by the time they reach the library's bookshelf). Similarly, insights gleaned from the morning's headlines need not wait for a conference paper or presentation. Assumptions, hypotheses, opinions and facts can be uploaded to the web and scrutinized in near real time by individuals populating the same knowledge ecologies.

The Culture of Knowing

Knowledge ecologies are emerging thanks to our individual and collective desire to know. Their advocates are noted for the passion with which they consume and discuss ideas from disparate fields. Indeed, the local and global contexts within which knowledge ecologies evolve necessitate greater intelligence, awareness and understanding on the part of its members. Thus, knowledge ecologies are expeditionary in nature; they are inspired by the prospect of discovery and shaped through exploration. As they become smarter, so too do they become more capable and effective.

Just as the world of work will not forgive a graduate lacking in practical skills, so too will the culture of knowing refuse to forgive willing ignorance of scientific advances or sociological trends. Knowledge ecologies compel us not only to know more, but also to *know knowledge* and the forces that enable its creation and exchange. Introductory epistemology would not be out of place on a progressive IR syllabus eager to encourage younger scholars to know the world through multiple perspectives. Indeed, it is imperative that we understand how concepts and ideas are interpreted in different settings. Knowledge ecologies teach us that global challenges can be understood in different contexts at the same time. Thus, when speaking of climate change, one must also ask *whose climate*? And *what change*? In a knowledge ecology, the basis for cooperation and survival is differentiation *and* similarity between the individuals and perspectives that exist within it (Malhotra 1999).

Shifting Lines of Power and Authority

Today's knowledge dynamics will continue to undermine traditional power structures. Knowledge ecologies demonstrate how ideas, insights and opinions flow to where they are most needed or best appreciated. No doubt, this will shape the loyalties of those who have knowledge to contribute. The maverick policy-maker may find more use for his or her ideas in an ecology of strangers than in the stilted environment they work in. Thus, knowledge ecologies will become marketplaces for ideas and cohesive mechanisms of change for institutions and professions.

Ecologies as the Evolution of Knowledge Management

Knowledge ecologies are both a compliment to, and the successor of, traditional knowledge management (KM) approaches. KM remains a powerful enabler of organizational efficiency and effectiveness. Its value is all too apparent to those organizations that have succeeded in implementing effective KM practices. Regrettably, most have failed to do so, assuming that solutions lie in the technologies they adopt rather than the people they employ. Much remains to be done here. However, no discipline stands still for too long. Knowledge ecologies are slowly supplanting knowledge management as the principle by which the international studies community will increasingly marshal its knowledge assets. Why?

In an era of discontinuous change, it is necessary to move beyond technological frameworks designed around predictive rules of engagement to complex adaptive systems engineered to anticipate surprise (Malhotra 1999; Bray et al. 2008). Put differently, knowledge ecologies move towards *adaptation* while knowledge management systems tend toward *optimization*. The former enables responsiveness; the latter inevitably spells redundancy. Whereas knowledge management seeks to harness know-how and know-what, knowledge ecologies provide the context and enable trust and collaboration.

Knowledge Ecologies in Practice

So much for the theory; what of ecologies in practice? A number of international affairs-related websites can be identified as emerging knowledge ecologies. While they may have started life as static web services, they are beginning to demonstrate many of the macro elements noted above. These ecologies are emerging as a result of a turbulent international environment. According to Dumaine (2008), this environment is characterized by:

- the emergence of nonstate actors as drivers of global security challenges;
- the proliferation of alternative information sources and communication tools;
- the unpredictability and volatility of world events;
- the blurring of foreign and domestic issues;
- greater complexity and interconnectedness in the physical and virtual environments we inhabit;
- asymmetries affecting strategy and conflict;
- organizational disabilities.

Managing these challenges requires as yet unseen levels of research, cooperation, coordination, and information sharing at the international, regional and national level (Nielsen 2008). The basis for much of this will inevitably be realized online. The services we examine below demonstrate some of the macro characteristics outlined above. As time passes, we suspect they will evolve into fully fledged ecologies dedicated to leveraging the insights and expertise of their users.

One of the oldest active international affairs portals on the web, Relief Web (www.reliefweb.net) actively encourages the participation of the IR community. The site welcomes contributions from NGOs, UN agencies, governments, think tanks and the media. Drawing on the contributions of others, Relief Web publishes situation reports, appeals, policy documents, analyses, press releases and maps in support of the humanitarian affairs community and their operations worldwide. By encouraging greater information sharing on the part of its users, Relief Web hopes to improve the collective understanding and response capacity of the community as a whole. While Relief Web does a great service collecting and pushing content, it would benefit from greater community involvement and sense-making tools.

In 2004, The Centre for International Governance Innovation launched IGLOO (www.igloo.org), which operated as a "network of networks." IGLOO enabled the creation of subject- and region-specific communities of practice by inviting participants to make use of its community development software. To date, dozens of academic and policy-oriented communities comprising thousands of members have been developed using this tool. IGLOO's strength lay in the motivation of its users and the usability of its software tools. Anyone could launch a network and, depending on the access restrictions they define, open participation to as broad or as narrow a community of participants as they deem necessary. Naturally, the more open the network, the greater the ecology of input and ideas they will sustain. Inevitably, one must engage the networks they are interested in if they are to benefit from, or contribute to, their work. This is an inevitable trade-off that ensures both user commitment and transparency. In 2008, IGLOO was spun off as a commercial venture (http://www.igloosoftware.com/) with the mandate to overcome information trapped in silos.

The International Relations and Security Network (ISN; www.isn.ethz.ch) is an altogether different ecology. Established in 1994, it operates as an information, IT and educational services provider to the international affairs community. The ISN has also developed communities of its own, many of which are openly accessible to individual users. Here too, however, collaboration is oriented on an institutional rather than an individual level. The more engaged the institutional partner, the likelier it is to profit from its membership in the ISN's communities of practice. The effectiveness of these communities as incubators of innovative research and policy solutions will need to be addressed in time.

Pushing the envelope further was the Global "Energy and Environment Strategic Ecosystem" (EESE; http://globaleese.org/). In 2007 the U.S. Department of Energy's Office of Intelligence and Counterintelligence established an Energy and Environmental Security Directorate. In order to understand future problems and consequences more fully, this Directorate initiated the formation of a truly global, interdisciplinary, collaborative and adaptive network to obtain the necessary insights on complex connections and dependencies associated with energy and environmental concerns.

Given the complex scientific and societal issues associated with today's energy and environmental concerns, formulation of an effective policy solution requires a global strategic intelligence capability that employs an ecosystem approach to identifying present and future challenges, as well as potential solutions to these encroaching dilemmas. The Global EESE network was thus designed to increase dialogue and openness, surface unanswered questions and amplify weak signals related to energy and environmental concerns. However, despite its initial successes, Global EESE was not able to anticipate political shifts that would undermine its funding.

Inviting people to "join the dialogue" and "brag a little," the developers' corner of Data.gov, the flagship of the Obama Administration's Open Government Initiative, is fostering a knowledge ecology around machine-readable datasets that are generated and held by the Federal Government. By sharing mash-ups and other visualizations that were not possible just a few years earlier, Data.gov has become a focal point for participatory democracy and creative use of data to further policy goals and societal understanding. Helping to further evolve Data.gov, Ideascale (http://datagov.ideascale.com/) offers a service for developers of all stripes to share and vote on new uses of government data. While initially criticized by some as a data-dumping ground, it seems now that Data.gov is both a catalyst and emerging knowledge ecology.

Conclusion

The services outlined above are in various stages of development. However, they all demonstrate the properties of emergent knowledge ecologies and are evolving rapidly to meet the broader needs of the communities they serve. To ensure their continued relevance, they must increase incentives for participation while at the same time enabling a shared sense of community and purpose, despite the geographical distribution of community members, as well as their anonymity to one another.

References

American Library Association's Information Literacy Competency Standards for Higher Education (2000) Available at: http://www.ala.org/ala/mgrps/divs/acrl/standards/informationliteracycompetency.cfm [accessed: 1 January 2011].

Beniger, J. (1986) *The Control Revolution* (Cambridge, MA: Harvard University Press).

Benkler, Y. (2007) *The Wealth of Networks: How Social Production Transforms Markets and Freedom*. Available at: http://www.benkler.org/Benkler_Wealth_Of_Networks.pdf [accessed: 1 January 2011].

Bray, D.A., Croxson, K. and Dutton, W. (2008) *Information Markets: Feasibility and Performance*. OII DPSN Working Papers.

Brown, L., Griffiths, R. and Rascoff, M. (2007) *University Publishing in a Digital Age*. Available at: http://www.ithaka.org/strategic-services/university-publishing [accessed: 1 January 2011].

Deibert, R., Palfrey, J., Rohozinski, R. and Zittrain, J. (eds) (2008) *Access Denied: The Practice and Policy of Global Internet Filtering*. Cambridge, MA: MIT Press.

Drucker, P. (2003) *The New Realities*. Piscataway, NJ: Transaction.

Dumaine, C. (2008) "Global Intelligence, Developing a Globally Networked Intelligence Capacity." Presentation to the *DNI Open Source Conference*, 11–12 September 2008.

Kim, S. (2007) *Ecosystem of Policy-related Knowledge*. United Nations Public Administration Network. Available at: http://unpan1.un.org/intradoc/groups/public/documents/unpan/unpan026271.pdf [accessed: 1 January 2011].

Malhotra, Y. (1999) "Knowledge Management for Organizational White-waters: an Ecological Framework." *Knowledge Management*, March, 330–51.

Magnan, F., Habel, G. and Fournier, N. (2007) *Building Knowledge Ecosystems in Web 3.0*. Available at: www.lornet.org/Portals/10/I2lor07_Proceedings/Tuesday/Papers/5-1.pdf [accessed: 1 January 2011].

Mamprin, A.N. (2006) "Designing Knowledge Ecologies for Associations." *Journal of Association Leadership*, Fall. Available at: http://www.asaecenter.org/Resources/JALArticleDetail.cfm?ItemNumber=19976 [accessed: 1 August 2011].

Nature (2006) Peer Review Trial and Debate. Available at: http://www.nature.com/nature/peerreview/ [accessed: 1 January 2011].

Nielsen, M. (2008) *Building a Better Collective Memory*. Available at: http://michaelnielsen.org/blog/?p=448 [accessed: 1 January 2011].

Peters, M.A. (2008a) "Education and the Culture of Openness: New Architectures of Collaboration." Presentation to the *Conference on Education, Culture and the Knowledge Economy*, 6 June.

Peters, M.A. (2008b) "Globalization and the Virtues of Openness in Higher Education." *Global e-Journal*. Available at: http://global-ejournal.org/2008/08/29/globalization-and-the-virtues-of-openness-in-higher-education/ [accessed: 1 January 2011].

Pór, G. (1997) Designing Knowledge Ecosystems for Communities of Practice. Presentation to the *Conference on Advancing Organizational Capability via Knowledge Management*, 29–30 September.

Pór, G. (2001) *Management Education and Knowledge Ecology*. Available at: www.providersedge.com/docs/km_articles/Management_Education_and_Knowledge_Ecology.pdf [accessed: 1 January 2011].

Worthen, B. (2008) *Why Most Online Communities Fail*. Available at: http://blogs.wsj.com/biztech/2008/07/16/why-most-online-communities-fail/ [accessed: 1 January 2011].

Young, R. (2007) *Knowledge Ecologies*. KM Consulting Blog. Available at: http://km-consulting.blogspot.com/2007/04/knowledge-ecologies.html [accessed: 1 January 2011].

Chapter 21
Environmental Politics: How Information and Communication Technology have Changed the Debate

Erica Dingman

> Climategate almost immediately caused climate scientists to lose control of the media narrative … Almost instantaneously, many in the press switched into "cover the conflict" mode, with stories portraying climate scientists as scheming to rig scientific data and prevent the publication of dissenting opinions from the scientific literature.
>
> Andrew Freedman, *Washington Post*

Introduction

Despite the vast body of scientific evidence suggesting that climate change is the result of human-induced greenhouse gas emissions, skepticism of the evidence is a growing trend within American society. Coupled with this phenomenon are the implications of the media in general, and new media specifically, for the social structure of society. This question gained significance in the 1960s when Marshall McLuhan, the acclaimed and controversial Canadian literature professor and communications theorist, coined the term "the medium is the message." He also stressed that, as a result of improvements in communication technologies and media, society was organizing social patterns that shaped the formation of a "global village." Technologies and media had decreased and even eliminated factors relating to both time and space. Despite criticism of McLuhan's work, I would argue that, together, these concepts are as applicable today as they were half a century ago.

Because distances in space and time are continuously diminishing, society is further exposed to a deluge of information 24 hours a day, 7 days a week. The fact that technology improves access to information does not, however, result in unmediated knowledge—knowledge remains open to the manipulations of individuals and groups alike with a specific agenda in mind.

Marshall McLuhan suggested that the importance of a new technology was not the technology in and of itself. Additionally, changes associated with technology were not of the greatest importance. What was significant, however, was how the technology or medium actually shaped and controlled "the scale and form of human association" (McLuhan 1964). The two cases that follow attempt to link this idea of scale and form to the primary question: how have the Internet and mobile devices impacted societies' responses to (1) environmental events of catastrophic magnitude, and (2) the American debate on climate change?

The first example, the 2010 Haiti earthquake, attempts to explain some of the motivating factors behind American public support for the victims of this devastating environmental crisis. Text-messaging, social media and government intervention all contributed to the expression of human sympathy and financial support exemplified by a message that went viral. The message was clear and the technology provided the means by which the individual had the power at their fingertips to make a small difference.

The second example is focused on an environmental issue that is substantially larger and potentially epic in scale—climate change. Climate change, often still referred to as global warming is debated far and wide, causing political divides that sometimes resemble a political battlefield—soldiers falling and others emerging with the dogged persistence of a Navy Seal. While the term 'global warming' has largely fallen out of favor, it remains prominent in the language of skeptics, who that claim climate change is naturally occurring rather than resulting from human-induced greenhouse gas emissions.

Indeed the message conveyed by climate change skeptics is so effective that a recent Pew poll shows that there has been a sharp decline in the percentage of Americans who believe there is "solid evidence that global temperatures are rising" (Pew Research Center: For the People and the Press 2009). Thrown onto this battlefield are the numerous climate scientists whose reputations were the focus of punitive investigation after emails were suspiciously leaked just prior to the 2009 U.N. Panel on Climate Change conference in Copenhagen. In what came to be known as "Climategate," "public ridicule was unleashed" against some scientists providing evidence for the ensuing climate talks. Furthermore, numerous journalists jumped into the fray, smelling fodder for headlines and intrigue (Freedman 2010).

In his final days in Washington, John Inglis, the former Republican representative from South Carolina, warned scientists that they should prepare to be called to Washington for Congressional hearings planned for 2011. Lines had been drawn, sides taken and many were on the firing line.

Common to both of these case studies is the pervasive rise of new technology and how it relates to an evolving underlying societal shift. In the case of Haiti, society organized quickly and effectively, showing that indeed at moments we act as a "global village." However, as I will show, the American public has shown limited taste for the greater debate of climate change, in part because it is mired in conflicting information pouring along the highways and byways of an increasingly networked community.

Defining the Parameters

Some of the sources presented below will perhaps raise eyebrows among some who define the validity of a source by the author's credentials. Does the author present a biased perspective? Have primary sources been interpreted accurately and reliably? Are the views expressed plausible? Indeed, all these factors are important considerations for evaluating evidence.

Yet, one often has to look outside traditional sources of information to explain how public opinion is formed. For this reason some sources included here would normally not be considered acceptable. Because this piece attempts to explain the reasons why there is a decline in the percentage of Americans who believe that the U.S. needs to address the effects of climate change, it requires investigation of sources that some may dismiss as inaccurate and biased.

Media and technology have always had an indelible effect on public opinion. More recently, new media (for example, the Web) and new technology (for example, mobile phone technology) have catapulted society into a potentially boundless world of information, adding to the existential database of mass knowledge. Clay Shirky notes, "Society is not just the product of its individual members; it is also the product of our constituent groups" (Shirky 2009). Furthermore, Shirky explains, "when we change the way we communicate we change society" (Shirky 2009). When a message is channeled it needs to be understood as plausible and "achievable enough to inspire confidence" (Shirky 2009). With the tools of new technology, groups that were once fragmented now have the means to associate freely and coordinate the production of knowledge through a collaborative process (Shirky 2009).

Two sources mentioned below, Wikipedia and Conservapedia, are examples of the collaborative production of information. Each represents constituencies that have the ability to affect public opinion.

Wikipedia

In January 2001 Jim Wales and Larry Sanger launched Wikipedia, a free encyclopedia built collaboratively using wiki software. It was born out of a belief that the process of collaboration would result in successfully edited articles. On average, Wikipedia's world ranking stands at around no. 7 based on the number of individual visits to the site (Alexa 2010a). Within three years of its founding, Wikipedia had more than 1,500,000 articles, outnumbering all other encyclopedias (Voss 2005).

Studies of Wikipedia's standing as a reliable source have revealed some interesting facts. Andrew Lih noted, "Some of the decisions are strikingly similar to those of other professional news organizations. For example, the Wikipedia community's tendency to avoid the use of the word 'terrorist' is similar to a policy adopted by the Reuters news agency."[1] Indeed, journalists often cite Wikipedia and several evaluations have concluded that it is a very good source. The strongest criticism is found within the Wikipedia community. The primary feature of openness is continually evaluated against the need for stricter policy (Voss 2005). Furthermore, in 2003, a Colorado court dismissed a case based on a Wikipedia article (Lih 2004).

Conservapedia

Conservapedia was launched in November 2006 by conservative author and Harvard-educated attorney Andy Schlafly. In his capacity of home-school teacher, he started this source in conjunction with a high school class of New Jersey students. He sees the website as "a much-needed alternative to Wikipedia, which is increasingly anti-Christian and anti-American" (Calore 2007). Although the website receives considerably fewer visits than Wikipedia, it is estimated that 64% of traffic is from the U.S. (Alexa 2010b).

In comparison to Wikipedia, Conservapedia defines some of the differences as quoted below:

> 1) We are an educational resource, including lectures and study guides … Wikipedia has no lectures or study guides and many of its entries and discussions are anti-intellectual in nature.
>
> 2) We do not attempt to be neutral to all points of view. We are neutral to the facts. If a group is a terrorist group, then we use the label "terrorist" but Wikipedia will use the "neutral" term "militant."
>
> 3) We do not allow liberal censorship of conservative facts. Wikipedia editors who are far more liberal than the American public frequently censor factual information. (Conservapedia 2010)

In terms of who informs public knowledge, it is a matter of complex connections circulating in cyberspace. Sources will rise and fall and some may seem impotent yet have an impressive impact on public thinking and reaction as a cumulative result of collective knowledge.

1 Working paper: citeseerx.ist.psu.edu/viewdoc/download?doi=10.1.1.117.9104.

This article will first explore the highly successful effort to accumulate donations for the Haiti earthquake crisis. Second, I will investigate the climate change debate with a focus on the perspective of the conservative right. Unlike the Haiti example, the climate change debate does not have a definitive beginning and end. However, like the Haiti case, it illustrates the power of technology and the resulting flow of information moving ever more quickly through time and space.

Haiti: Technology Success

> So many people recognize they can use their mobile phones to donate. It's an impulse give. You don't have to be sitting at [a] computer and can donate a small amount of money. (Tony Aiello, Senior Vice President, mGive Foundation)

Minutes before 5 p.m. on 12 January 2010, Haiti was struck by a devastating earthquake measuring at a magnitude of 7.0 on the Richter scale (CNN 2010a). According to the U.S. Geological Survey, 222,570 people were killed and 1.3 million displaced (U.S. Geological Survey 2010). CNN's iReport Haiti reported 8322 people missing as of 28 January 2010 (CNN 2010b). Haitian society was thrown into chaos, the earthquake's epicenter being located in a highly populated area a mere 10 miles from the capital, Port-au-Prince.

By 9 p.m. that same evening, the American Red Cross (ARC) had launched a text-to-give campaign. By 10 a.m. Thursday, 14 January, the ARC raised an unprecedented $3.4 million from text message donations alone (Travers 2010). Within a month, the text-to-give campaign had raised $32 million for the relief of an estimated 3 million Haitians affected by the quake (Mobile Marketing Watch 2010); and by June 2010, the Red Cross had raised $41 million through the mGive campaign (Mobile Accord 2010).

The philosophy was simple, clean and required a minimum of thought. Simply by texting the phrase "Haiti" to the number 90999 donors could contribute $10. The donation was charged to the donor's mobile phone bill. Coordinated by the mGive Foundation, an organization linking charities with mobile carriers, the ARC corralled the power of technology with a potential donor population of 270 million mobile subscribers nationwide. Tony Aiello, senior vice president of mGive noted: "It's microdonations by millions of people, adding up to an amount that can make a difference" (Travers 2010).

In another campaign, Haitian-born hip hop artist Wyclef Jean chose Twitter to urge people to donate as little as 5 dollars to his charity, Yéle Haiti. Jean's website crashed on the morning of 13 January 2010 owing to the volume of traffic (Clark 2010).

Why was this human response to Haiti's environmental crisis such a success? One of the most discernible qualities is the increased capability of communication technology: 91% of Americans are mobile subscribers (Foresman 2010) and text messaging is considered the preferred method of communication (CTIA 2008). Indeed, the technology maximized the power of civil society by galvanizing public support around a common concern. In a 2005 study, *Electronic Communications and Socio-Political Mobilization: A New Form of Civil Society*, Manuel Castells et al. found that: "The communication networks that mobile telephony makes possible can be formed and reformed instantly, and messages are received from a known source, enhancing their credibility" (Castells et al. 2005).

In the case of the Haiti mGive campaign, the U.S. State Department initiated the effort by contacting Mobile Accord, the parent company of mGive. In turn, the State Department designated the ARC as the funding recipient (Denard 2010). The process was streamlined and centrally managed by mGive. Government backing provided the credibility that substantiated the efforts of individual politicians, actors and corporations collectively throwing their weight behind Haiti's environmental crisis. Numerous actors including Angelina Jolie, Brad Pitt and George Clooney contributed their popular acclaim to galvanizing public support. Jolie and Pitt donated $1 million from their foundation to Doctors without Borders and Clooney hosted an MTV fund-raising campaign, joined by musicians and fellow movie stars (Maestri 2010). President Obama also immediately pledged the government's "full support" for the people of Haiti, further galvanizing public support.

In the immediate aftermath the White House blog announced "The Help Haiti" initiative and Twitter and Facebook created a flurry of social network activity that went viral (*New York Times* 2010). The ease with which the individual could respond to the crisis was a "direct response to the medium it [was] transferred through" (Gross 2010). Yet, traditional media were also put to use: as an example, the National Football League ran ads during the playoffs urging people to text donations to the Red Cross (Strom 2010a). In the past, technologies such as television and radio provided only a linear experience whereby the individual was merely an observer of news. In the Haiti case traditional media augmented the technology of mobile phones and texting.

James Eberhard, founder of Mobile Accord explains: "If you want to communicate with the generation under 30 text messaging is the way to build a relationship, and nonprofit fund-raising is all about building relationships" (Strom 2010a). The majority of the text-to-give donations came from individuals aged 19–29 (Denard 2010). Notably, after the initial success, within six weeks of the Haiti earthquake, "donations to the ARC text message campaign slowed significantly" (Denard 2010).

Technology and publicity alone were not the only contributing factors in the resounding success of the mGive campaign. In general, perception is an important contributor to the extent of public support. In this case the reputation of the ARC presents an interesting case. One fund-raising professional noted that the ARC's "reputation in the last eight years has been really checkered." It was a question as to whether they could "effectively use all of this money that they [were] raising?" (Strom 2010b). Beyond the gut reaction to human suffering, donors respond to organizations that they perceive as trustworthy and honest with finances (Denard 2010). Because of this, it is questionable as to whether or not the ARC would have enjoyed the success that they did this time around on their own. "The ARC had experimented with mobile fund-raising in the past with limited success, but this was the first time the State Department initiated such a program" (Denard 2010). To start, the mGive Foundation believed that, because the White House was behind the campaign, "there would be … sufficient support and outreach to media and individuals" (Denard 2010). Indeed, government backing was most likely the catalyst in not only linking the ARC with mGive but also providing the perception of credibility that this all-out campaign needed.

On the other hand, texting as a means of rallying public interest is often met with limited support. A 2005 study found that text messaging, as a means of mobilization was not successful when the message lacked clarity because of conflicting reports. For instance, at the start of the SARS epidemic victims and families of victims used text-messaging to alert the public. Word spread quickly to residents of Guangdong, China and then throughout the countryside. China's government countered by launching a mass media campaign claiming that the "infections were no more than a variant of pneumonia, that it was already under control, and that the public panic partially induced by text messages was groundless" (Castells et al. 2005). Initially this undermined the texting campaign initiated by citizens "because SMS was perceived to be a medium of lower credibility and there was no other source of information. As a result, most people, including experienced foreign analysts living in south China, chose to believe the official version—to witness a few weeks later the horror of SARS in full swing" (Castells et al. 2005).

The effectiveness of electronic communications (largely mobile phones and texting) in mobilizing civil society is strongest when an event is strong enough to arouse emotion and there is "support from respected institutions." Furthermore, "supplementary information from mainstream media and/or Internet information" is critical (Castells et al. 2005). "Arguably," the study noted, "other media such as wired phones, radio or TV could perform the same rallying function as wireless methods, but not in as timely a manner, not with the ability to reach people wherever they are, and not free of the production constraints associated with traditional media" (Castells et al. 2005).

Indeed, the rate of acceptance of mobile technology has been dramatic. In 2010 Morgan Stanley released a report showing an extensive shift towards the use of mobile web technology. Based on the current rate of change and adoption, it is believed that mobile web use will surpass Internet use by 2015 (O'Dell 2010). The mGive campaign was an early indication of this trend.

The Haiti mGive campaign allowed "instant communication at any time, anywhere, [and] it is most suited to assembling large-scale demonstrations immediately after emergent political events" (Castells et al. 2005). Although the mGive campaign was not associated with political motivations, the extent of American outpouring did raise doubts in Haiti. The intention to send 10,000 troops reportedly for humanitarian purposes caused old grievances to resurface in Haiti (Laing 2010). Haitians feared that the Americans were returning as an occupation force, recalling the U.S. occupation of Haiti from 1915 to 1935. As increasing numbers of troops entered Haiti, American commanders had to repeatedly reassure Haitians that they were there not as an occupying force but to provide humanitarian aid and to intervene in the spiraling violence (Laing and Leonard 2010).

Climate Change: An Evolving Debate

The debate around climate change presents vastly different parameters than does the Haiti earthquake crisis. However, in common with the Haiti case is the application of technology to disseminate information and harness public support. In this case information is fragmented, institutional legitimacy is questioned and it is decidedly political.

At no time has the climate change debate been as politicized as it was in November 2009 when a large number of stolen emails were released into cyberspace, raising doubt about the scientific evidence supporting anthropogenic climate change. In what came to be known as "Climategate," the scandal was certainly a highly influential moment, providing substantiating evidence for the opposing side.

Journalists jumped onto the bandwagon, smelling headlines: one UK *Telegraph* headline read, "Climategate: the final nail in the coffin of anthropogenic global warming." The reporter, James Delingpole, unleashed accusations of "manipulation of data, suppression of evidence and attempts to disguise the inconvenient truth of the Medieval Warm Period." He warned his readers that anyone who owns "shares in alternative energy companies … should start dumping them NOW" (Delingpole 2009).

In retrospect, Andrew Freedman of the *Washington Post* opined that journalists had fed the frenzy because they "love conflict" and most were "ill-equipped to read and interpret the approximately 1,000 emails" regarding climate science (Freedman 2010). However Climategate did not shape the origins of the dissenting view.

In October 2009 the Pew Research Center conducted a survey on global warming, less than two months prior to the United Nations Climate Change Conference in Copenhagen. Findings showed that 57% of Americans thought that there was solid evidence that the earth is warming. Significantly, these results showed a considerable drop from 2008. Between 2006 and 2008 the percentage of Americans who believed there was solid evidence of global warming had remained largely constant at 77%, dropping to 71% in 2008. Additionally, when asked if global warming was the result of human activity, in 2009, 36% of Americans answered yes, down from 47% in 2008. In 2009, 16% said it was caused by natural patterns.

Statistical changes occurred across partisan lines. Not surprisingly, the percentage of Republicans agreeing with the statement that there is evidence of global warming declined the most. In 2009, 35% of Republicans believed that there was solid evidence, down from 49% in 2008 and 62% in 2007. Of Democrats polled, 75% believed that there is solid evidence of global warming, down from 91% in 2006.

In January 2009, global warming ranked dead last of the public's list of policy priorities. However, equally surprising, the survey found that "Half of Americans favor setting limits on carbon emissions and making companies pay for their emissions, even if this may lead to higher energy prices" (Pew Research Center: For the People and The Press 2009).

Given the results of this Pew poll showing evidence of declining public acceptance of global climate change, it is not unexpected that Washington consensus is shifting likewise. A growing faction of Republican politicians mirror public opinion. However, what the poll does not show is why people now view the scientific evidence with suspicion.

> A View from the Right: God Said Climate Change isn't a Threat
> The earth will end only when God declares its time to be over.
> Man will not destroy this earth.
> This earth will not be destroyed by a flood. (Congressman John Shimkus)

Perhaps you are inclined to think that little or no evidence suggests the existence of anthropogenic climate change, attributing at least part of your view to God's will. Without a doubt there is ample information to substantiate this claim. To begin with, simply Google the search terms "climate change" and "God." Like any Google search a plethora of websites are at your disposal from which you can pick and choose news articles, blogs or webcasts that are likely to directly align with your point of view. Added to that, after conducting research on the websites of "Conservapedia" and the Christian-based "Institute for Creation Research," evidence of the biblical accuracy supporting creation science could be a deciding factor. Instantly you have gained a level of expertise on "A New Theory of Climate Change" (Vardiman 2008). Accordingly, you will read the view that reducting the levels of carbon dioxide will have little impact on climate change (Vardiman 2008).

After prodigious study some will emerge with a wide body of evidence supporting the idea that climate change is an act of God. Others who have decided to search elsewhere will gain expertise on human-induced climate change. However, a large number of Americans will find themselves confused and overwhelmed by conflicting information. Indeed, the percentage of Americans who view global warming as either real or consider the issue as "very serious" is dropping significantly. Yet at the core of this issue is a growing reaction against what some perceive as unbridled secularism.

The Science According to Creationism

In 1993, *USA Today* ran a front-page story titled "Church, State and School Boards." Robert L. Simonds, founder and president of the Christian-based groups National Association of Christian Educators and Citizens for Excellence in Education, claimed that his organization had helped elect 3611 Christian candidates in 1992 (Kelly 1993). Rather than running for office at the state and federal level, candidates ran for lower-profile positions on local school boards and in local governments (Kelly 1993). In turn, Simonds penned an article for the Institute for Creation Science (ICS), entitled *Teachers Can Teach Creation Science in the Classroom* (Simonds 1989).

The ICS, a Christian-based institute, claims authority because the information provided is "Biblical • Accurate • Certain." It aims to equip "believers with evidence of the Bible's accuracy and authority through scientific research educational programs and media presentations, all conducted within a thoroughly biblical framework" (Institute for Creation Research 2010).

Larry Vardiman, Ph.D., chairman of the Department of Astro-Geophysics at the Institute for Creation Research's Graduate School since 1989, is a creationist scientist and educator, and has contributed extensively to the ICS. He has authored numerous books and articles on a variety of issues from evolution to climate change. In all he has published 133 articles on the ICS website (Creation Wiki 2010).

In Vardiman's 2010 article, "Climategate: Begging the Question," Vardiman laments the woeful behavior of scientists connected to Climategate. Reflecting on this perception of misdirected climate science, he notes that, to the embarrassment of the scientific community, they displayed "inappropriate behavior and scientific malfeasance [leading to] the global warming fiasco." Yet he attributes this to a "logical error," originating in the 1950s. Attributing this contemporary "error" to earlier incorrect data, he cited the work of oceanographer Roger Revelle and a junior scientist, Charles Keeling. He points out that Revelle inspired Al Gore's views on global warming, expressed by the film *An Inconvenient Truth*.

The National Oceanic and Atmospheric Administration explains the story a little differently. Early work conducted by Revelle suggested that the burning of fossil fuels had far-reaching implications for the earth's atmosphere (National Oceanic and Atmospheric Administration 2010). Yet when Charles Keeling sought to establish a system for monitoring carbon dioxide in one location alone, atop Hawaii's Mauna Loa volcano, Revelle opposed his methods. Regardless, Keeling went ahead, with his research resulting in the now well-recognized barometer of CO_2 emissions, known as the Keeling Curve. Revelle conceded that "the data proved fossil fuels were causing global warming" (Brand 2007).

Vardiman insists, however, that fundamental scientific errors were made. "Unfortunately" he says, "most climatologists were so convinced by the data … that they insisted that man-caused global warming had to be occurring."

Although Vardiman's primary critique is directed toward climate science, in conclusion he forewarns that the "economies of nations" and credibility of science is in jeopardy if climate change is not regarded as a naturally occurring phenomenon (Vardiman 2010). For the most part, Vardiman's work is not widely read. Yet one can assume that his views of creationism have contributed to the accumulation of information that is increasingly influencing Washington's debate on the economy, energy and climate change.

The Politics

When President Barack Obama took office on 20 January 2009, his supporters believed that Washington would finally establish meaningful policy to enact climate change policy. In his inaugural speech Obama said: "We will restore science to its rightful place … We will harness the sun and the winds and the soil to fuel our cars and run our factories … and roll back the specter of a warming planet" (Obama 2009). Yet after two years the Obama administration has made little progress on climate change policy. When the midterm elections resulted in a Republican majority in Congress, climate change skeptics felt empowered to undermine future debate on ways to limit future U.S. greenhouse gas emissions.

In the immediate aftermath, ranking members of the Republican Party prepared to take their positions. John Shimkus (Republican, Illinois) put in his bid to chair the House Committee on Energy and Commerce (Merrion 2010); Darrell Issa (Republican, California) was poised to chair the House Oversight and Reform Committee; and John Boehner (Republican, Ohio) was ready to take over Nancy Pelosi's place as House Speaker.

John Shimkus gained prominence in March 2009. Speaking before the House Energy Subcommittee on Energy and the Environment, chaired by Representative Ed Markey (Democrat, Massachusetts), Shimkus famously quoted the Book of Genesis, Chapter 8, Verse 22: "As long as the earth endures, seed time and harvest, cold and heat, summer and winter, day and night, will never cease." Does he believe in the existence of climate change? After his trip to Greenland, "the answer is yes." However, taxpayers should not be responsible for "something that cannot stop versus the changes that have been occurring forever" (Samuelsohn 2010). Beyond the fallacy of his phrasing, the meaning of "versus" being either a part of the falsehood or mere folly, Shimkus clearly favored a do-nothing, business as usual energy and economic strategy.

He testified that the current rate of "388 parts per million in the atmosphere," presumably of CO_2 emissions, is minimal compared with pre-historic times. "I think in the age of dinosaurs," he argued, "when we had the most flora and fauna, we were probably at 4,000 parts per million." Shimkus suggests that the planet is carbon-starved: "If we decrease the use of carbon dioxide, are we not taking away plant food from the atmosphere? … So all our good intentions could be for vain. In fact, we could be doing the opposite of what the people who want to save the world are saying" (Sheppard 2010b). Arguing against cap-and-trade, he contends that it would result in undue burden on the poor (Mail Online 2010).

By running for chair of the House Committee on Energy and Commerce, Shimkus strove to play a central role in formulating policy on climate change. Also speaking before Markey's Subcommittee, Calvin Beisner of the Cornwall Alliance for the Stewardship of Creation warned that restrictions on carbon emissions would cause undue harm to the impoverished. Beisner maintains that Americans are "morally obligated to provide access for the poor to affordable, abundant fossil fuels" (Sheppard 2010b).

Darrell Issa (Republican, California), then ranking minority member of the House Oversight and Reform Committee, accepted the reputation of Barack Obama's "annoyer-in-chief." Poised to become the Committee chair, Issa aimed to go after the source of where he saw the real malfeasance—an investigation of climate scientists. At the top of his list were researchers whose emails were hacked in 2008 from the computer system of Britain's University of East Anglia. Although their work had been subject to three separate Climategate inquiries, all of which rejected the allegations of data manipulation, Issa wasn't satisfied. "We're going to want to have a do-over," he said (Kolbert 2010).

Fellow Republican John Boehner (Ohio), the 2011 House Speaker, was equally focused on rejecting climate change legislation. When asked in 2009 about his Party's plans to address climate change by ABC's George Stephanopoulos, Boehner answered: "The idea that carbon dioxide is a carcinogen, that it is harmful to our environment, is almost comical" (Kolbert 2010). Notably, climate scientists do not claim that carbon dioxide is a carcinogen, rather the concern is that CO_2 and other greenhouse gases will be trapped in the earth's atmosphere and raise "global temperatures to potentially dangerous levels" (Rudolf 2010). Boehner has targeted the Environmental Protection Agency (EPA) for its regulations that "open the door to the Democrats 'cap and trade'," which he claims will "destroy jobs and threaten family farms" (Boehner 2010).

Indeed, in late 2010 House Republicans switched strategy from ignoring the science to actively pursuing a complete overhaul of existing policy. Republicans who once sought to eliminate the House Select Committee on Energy Independence and Global Warming then viewed it as a tool to go after the EPA. James Sensenbrenner (Republican, Wisconsin), the likely chair of the Committee, saw it as an ideal platform for "harassing the Environmental Protection Agency" (Kolbert 2010). Sensenbrenner wrote, "Now that Republicans have retaken the House, the Select Committee is more qualified than any other Congressional institution to ensure the administration doesn't bend to unrealistic international demands—and that the EPA doesn't attempt to do what Congress wouldn't" (Geman 2010). In the absence of legislative action, the EPA is the only body with the power to regulate carbon emissions (Kolbert 2010).

Politically, the climate change debate creates divisions, not just along party lines but within the Republican Party itself. Bob Inglis, the South Carolina Republican Representative and then member of the House Science and Technology Committee, who lost his seat to a Tea Party-backed Republican, Trey Gowdy, in the 2010 primary runoff, did not spare his scorn of climate deniers. He scoffed: "I would also suggest to my free enterprise colleagues—especially conservatives here—whether you think it's all a bunch of hooey, what we've talked about in this committee, the Chinese don't." Suggesting that those who ignore global warming put the U.S. in a disadvantaged position, he assured his colleagues: "And they plan on eating our lunch in this next century" (Sheppard 2010a).

On reflection, Inglis singled out his position on climate change as the primary reason for defeat: "For many conservatives, it became the marker that you had crossed to Satan's side—that you had left God and gone to Satan's side on climate change." He added, "because many evangelical Christians in our district would say that it's up to God to determine the length of Earth, and therefore, you are invading the province of God." In contrast to Shimkus and many other Republicans, Inglis wanted to end the strategic importance of oil (Lehmann 2010). However, for the majority of Republicans, according to Inglis and Representative Vern Ehlers (Republican, Michigan), who retired after eight terms in government, much of the disdain for environmental legislation has to do with money. Inglis, as a self-designated member of the Republican minority, said, "The majority, I think, view is it's not real, we don't need to do anything about it, it will harm our economy" (Lehmann 2010).

Likewise, Sherwood Boehlert, a former Republican Congressional Representative from New York State and past Chair of the House Science and Technology Committee agreed with Inglis. Speaking almost with a sense of nostalgia, Boehlert recalled the bygone days of bipartisanship when Democrats and Republicans alike based the decision-making process on insights gained from climate scientists. In his 19 November 2010 article penned in the *Washington Post*, Boehlert noted that, "many newly elected Republican House members take the stance that defies the findings of our country's National Academy of Sciences, national scientific academies from around the world and 97% of the world's climate scientists" (Boehlert 2010). Boehlert comes down on the side of climate change debate that supports the National Academy of Science view of anthropogenic climate change. In what would seem as a highly unlikely scenario, Boehlert looked to former President Reagan as a Republican who did not deny the existence of global environmental problems. He noted that Reagan "was proud of his role in helping to phase out ozone-depleting chemicals" (Boehlert 2010). For decades successive governments—Bush I, Clinton, Bush II, and Obama—have been officially committed to avoiding "dangerous" climate change, even though it has resulted in minimal policy to mitigate the effects of climate change (Kolbert 2010).

The Church

Representative John Shimkus, a Lutheran, stands in direct opposition to the official position of the Lutheran Church. Quoting the same passage as Shimkus, Genesis 8:22, the Lutheran Church paints a far different picture of climate change. "Many of the problems associated with climate change," notes the Church, "have arisen because of how human beings have misused that which God has created for the benefit of all creatures" (Bloomquist and Machila 2009). As a result, humans are suffering, urban areas are polluted and life as we know it is in jeopardy. Central to the Lutheran Church's stance are the findings by the Intergovernmental Panel on Climate Change. Unlike climate change skeptics such as Shimkus, the Church claims that, not only is climate change attributed to "acts of God," but we must also look to science for answers. Yet, Shimkus looks at science in far different terms. In a true display of obfuscation Shimkus wants to "really focus on science." Shimkus continues to conceal the fact that unbridled energy use is at the heart of his argument (Samuelsohn 2010).

In a report by Karen Bloomquist and Rolita Machila representing the views of the Lutheran Church, they give a vastly different theological perspective. "The accumulation of money and goods has displaced the liberating economy of the Creator, based on synergy, cooperation and life-enhancing justice for all of creation." As for what has occurred in some religious circles, the Lutheran Church takes the position that "some human beings have acted as if they were demigods," ordering and controlling the environment for their own self-interest (Bloomquist and Machila 2009).

Conclusion

For many Americans the pervasive web of information on climate change has added to an already cloudy understanding of climate science. As it is, understanding scientific analysis and data is difficult at best and daunting at worst for most laymen, whether they admit it or not. Also thrown into this stockpile of information is a political dynamic divided mostly along party lines, but further complicated by a growing offshoot of the Republican Party formed out of a strategy devised in the 1980s by a consortium of Christian fundamentalist organizations. What appears to have started as a localized effort to take back public school systems from those who are perceived to teach "immoral sex education," now has far-reaching implications. In 1994 the liberal leaning think tank, People for the American Way had it right when they said the Christian-right were using "stealth" tactics. Yet, at that time those tactics were conditionally limited to redirecting the curriculum of a handful of public school systems toward an agenda that taught creationism and sought to mandate school prayer. Today this agenda seems mild.

In light of the success of climate change deniers in the 2010 mid-term election and the ensuing dividing line developing within the Republican Party, the Christian right has amassed enough popular support to potentially change already limited regulation on climate change.

On understanding the relationship between technology and the public, Dr Kim Veltman, Scientific Director of Virtual Maastricht McLuhan Institute, has reflected on the social implications of technology for decades. He says, "We need a system that reflects distinctions between truth and viewpoints." (Veltman 2005). Yet understanding the ingredients associated with "our all-too-fragile planet … is largely an abstraction" (Veltman 2005). Abstraction indeed. The Pew Center on Global Climate Change (2009) concedes: "The issue of climate change has received so much attention in recent years that it has become difficult for interested citizens and policymakers to separate facts from fiction."

As we work our way through conflicting stories, ultimately the direction of national and global climate change policy may come down to who owns the debate. New technology has admittedly given us the tools to be authors and interact with the medium in ways that Marshal McLuhan only imagined, but the underlying element is how technology changed society in a manner that we are yet to perceive.

References

Alexa. 2010a. *Wikipedia.org*. Available at: http://www.alexa.com/siteinfo/wikipedia.org [accessed: 28 November 2010].

Alexa. 2010b. *Conservapedia.com*. Available at: http://www.alexa.com/siteinfo/conservapedia.com# [accessed: 28 November 2010].

Bloomquist, K.L. and Machila, R. 2009. *The Lutheran World Federation*. Geneva: Department for Theology and Studies.

Boehlert, S. 2010. "Can the Party of Reagan accept the Science of Climate Change?" *The Washington Post*, 19 November. Available at: http://www.washingtonpost.com/wp-dyn/content/article/2010/11/18/AR2010111805451.html [accessed: 20 November 2010].

Boehner, J. 2010. *EPA Opens Door to National Energy Tax, Threatens Jobs, Farms*. Available at: http://www.johnboehner.com/?p=734 [accessed: 20 November 2010].

Brand, M. 2007. "Climate Change is Clear Atop Mauna Loa." *National Public Radio*, 1 May 2007. Available at: http://www.npr.org/templates/story/story.php?storyId=9885767 [accessed: 15 November 2010].

Calore, M. 2007. "What Would Jesus Wiki?" *Wired*, 28 February 2007. Available at: http://www.wired.com/techbiz/it/news/2007/02/72818 [accessed: 20 November 2010].

Castells, M., Fernandez-Ardevol, M., Qiu, J.L. and Sey, A. 2005. "Electronic Communication and Sociopolitical Mobilization: A New Form of Civil Society." In *Global Civil Society*, 266–85. London: Sage.

Clark, M. 2010. "Wyclef Jean Haiti Earthquake: Singer Leads Charge to Help through Yele Haiti charity—and Twitter." *Christian Science Monitor*, 13 January. Available at: http://www.csmonitor.com/World/Global-News/2010/0113/Wyclef-Jean-Haiti-earthquake-Singer-leads-charge-to-help-through-Yele-Haiti-charity-and-Twitter [accessed: 20 November 2010].

CNN. 2010a. *Haiti Earthquake: Relief Efforts*. Available at: http://www.cnn.com/interactive/2010/01/world/google.map.haiti/index.html [accessed: 18 November 2010].

CNN. 2010b. *Haiti Earthquake: People Reported Missing via iReport 2010*. Available at: http://www.cnn.com/interactive/2010/02/world/map.ireport.missing/ [accessed: 18 November 2010].

Conservapedia. 2010. *Conservapedia: How Conservapedia Differs from Wikipedia*. Available at: http://www.conservapedia.com/Conservapedia:How_Conservapedia_Differs_from_Wikipedia [accessed: 15 November 2010].

Creation Wiki. 2010. *Larry Vardiman*. Available at: http://creationwiki.org/Larry_Vardiman [accessed: 20 November 2010].

CTIA. 2008. *CTIA—The Wireless Association® Releases Latest Wireless Industry Survey Results*. Available at: http://ctia.org/media/press/body.cfm/prid/1772 [accessed: 10 September 2008].

Delingpole, J. 2009. "Climategate: the Final Nail in the Coffin of 'Anthropogenic Global Warming'?" *The Telegraph*, 20 November. Available at: http://blogs.telegraph.co.uk/news/jamesdelingpole/100017393/climategate-the-final-nail-in-the-coffin-of-anthropogenic-global-warming/ [accessed: 10 November 2010].

Denard, T. 2010. *Text Haiti to 90999: The Future of Relationship Fundraising for a Nonprofit Organization*. Paper to the Association for Education in Journalism and Mass Communication, Denver, CO, 4 August.

Foresman, C. 2010. "Wireless Survey: 91% of Americans use Cell Phones." *ARS Technical*. Available at: http://arstechnica.com/telecom/news/2010/03/wireless-survey-91-of-americans-have-cell-phones.ars [accessed: 15 November 2010].

Freedman, A. 2010. "A Year after Climategate, Applying Lessons Learned." *The Washington Post*, 22 November. Available at: http://voices.washingtonpost.com/capitalweathergang/2010/11/a_year_after_climategate_apply.html [accessed: 25 November 2010].

Geman, B. 2010. "Sensenbrenner: Keep House Climate Panel as a Check Against EPA." *E-Wire*, 8 November. Available at: http://thehill.com/blogs/e2-wire/677-e2-wire/128229-sensenbrenner-keep-house-climate-panel-as-a-check-against-epa [accessed: 15 November 2010].

Gross, J. 2010. "Understanding the Medium as a Message." *Jason Gross.com*, 11 June. Available at: http://jasonagross.com/?p=143 [accessed: 20 November 2010].

Institute for Creation Research. 2010. *Explore ICR*. Available at: http://www.icr.org/discover/ [accessed: 20 November 2010].

Kelly, D. 1993. "Church, State and School Boards." *USA Today*, 4 May.

Kolbert, E. 2010. "Uncomfortable Climate." *The New Yorker*, 12 November. Available at: http://www.newyorker.com/talk/comment/2010/11/22/101122taco_talk_kolbert#ixzz162s5r7qX [accessed: 25 November 2010].

Laing, A. 2010. "Haiti Earthquake: Thousands more U.S. Troops Arrive in Haiti." *The Telegraph*, 19 January. Available at: http://www.telegraph.co.uk/news/worldnews/centralamericaandthecaribbean/haiti/7018877/Haiti-earthquake-thousands-more-US-troops-arrive-in-Haiti.html [accessed: 15 November 2010].

Laing, A. and Leonard, T. 2010. "U.S. Accused of 'Occupying' Haiti as Troops Flood in." *The Telegraph*, 18 January. Available at: http://www.telegraph.co.uk/news/worldnews/centralamericaandthecaribbean/haiti/7020908/US-accused-of-occupying-Haiti-as-troops-flood-in.html [accessed: 15 November 2010].

Lehmann, E. 2010. "Republicans Learn the Perils of being Politically Incorrect on Climate Change." *The New York Times*, 22 November. Available at: http://www.nytimes.com/cwire/2010/11/22/22climatewire-republicans-learn-the-perils-of-being-politic-3326.html [accessed: 25 November 2010].

Lih, A. 2004. Participatory Journalism and Asia: From Web Logs to Wikipedia. Paper for the 13th Asian Media Information and Communications Centre Annual Conference: ICT and Media Inputs and Development Outcomes Impact of New and Old Media on Development in Asia, July 1–3.

Maestri, N. 2010. *Update 1-U.S. texting raises $11 million for Haiti*. Reuters, 15 January. Available at: http://www.reuters.com/article/idUSN1517056920100115?pageNumber=1 [accessed: 12 November 2010].

Mail Online. 2010. "'The Planet Won't be Destroyed by Global Warming because God Promised Noah,' says Politician Bidding for Chair U.S. Energy Committee.' *The Daily Mail*, 10 November. Available at: http://www.dailymail.co.uk/news/article-1328366/John-Shimkus-Global-warming-wont-destroy-planet-God-promised-Noah.html [accessed: 20 November 2010].

McLuhan, M. 1964. "The Medium is the Message (from Understanding Media)." In *The New Media Reader*, edited by N. Wardrip-Fruin and N. Montfort. Cambridge, MA: The MIT Press. Available at: http://www.newmediareader.com/book_contents.html [accessed: 1 August 2011].

Merrion, P. 2010. "Rep. Shimkus Aims to be House Energy and Commerce Chairman." *Chicago Business.Com*, 9 November. Available at: http://www.chicagobusiness.com/article/20101109/NEWS02/101109853/rep-shimkus-aims-to-be-house-energy-and-commerce-chairman [accessed: 25 November 2010].

Mobile Accord. 2010. "Mobile Accord's mGive Platform Raises More Than $41 Million for Red Cross to Help Earthquake Victims in Haiti." *Mobile Accord*, 19 January, updated June 2010. Available at: http://mobileaccord.wordpress.com/2010/01/19/mobile-accords-mgive-platform-raises-more-than-22-million-for-red-cross-to-help-earthquake-victims-in-haiti/ [accessed: 20 November 2010].

Mobile Marketing Watch. 2010. "SMS Donation Answer The Call For Gulf Oil Spill Relief." *Mobile Marketing Watch*, 7 June. Available at: http://www.mobilemarketingwatch.com/sms-donations-answer-the-call-for-gulf-oil-spill-relief-7223/ [accessed: 10 June 2010].

National Oceanic and Atmospheric Administration. 2010. *Mauna Loa Carbon Dioxide Record: An Atmospheric "Experiment" on a Global Scale*. National Oceanic and Atmospheric Administration. Available at: http://celebrating200years.noaa.gov/datasets/mauna/welcome.html [accessed: 15 November 2010].

New York Times. 2010. "$2 Million in Donations for Haiti, via Text Message." *The New York Times*, 13 January. Available at: http://bits.blogs.nytimes.com/2010/01/13/1-million-in-donations-for-haiti-via-text-message/ [accessed: 10 June 2010].

Obama, B. 2009. *President Barack Obama's Inaugural Address*. The White House, 21 January. Available at: http://www.whitehouse.gov/blog/inaugural-address/ [accessed: 20 November 2010].

O'Dell, J. 2010. "New Study Shows the Mobile Web Will Rule by 2010 [STATS]." *Mashable.com*, 13 April. Available at: http://mashable.com/2010/04/13/mobile-web-stats/ [accessed: 15 November 2010].

Pew Research Center: For the People and The Press. 2009. *Modest Support for "Cap and Trade" Policy: Fewer Americans See Solid Evidence of Global Warming*. Pew Research Center, 22 October.

Pew Center on Global Climate Change. 2009. *Realities vs. Misconceptions about the Science of Climate Change*. Pew Center on Global Climate Change, August. Available at: http://www.pewclimate.org/science-impacts/realities-vs-misconceptions [accessed: 19 November 2010].

Rudolf, J.C. 2010. "Climate Cues From the Next House Speaker." *The New York Times*, 3 November. Available at: http://green.blogs.nytimes.com/2010/11/03/climate-cues-from-the-next-house-speaker/ [accessed: 20 November 2010].

Samuelsohn, D. 2010. "John Shimkus cites Genesis on climate change." *Politico.com*, 10 November. Available at: http://www.politico.com/news/stories/1110/44958.html#ixzz15OZIfeZh [accessed: 20 November 2010].

Sheppard, K. 2010a. "Outgoing GOPer Slams Climate Denying Colleagues." *Mother Jones*, 18 November. Available at: http://motherjones.com/mojo/2010/11/inglis-slams-gop-climate-deniers [accessed: 20 November 2010].

Sheppard, K. 2010b. "House Republicans Bring Strange Theories and Wacky Witnesses to Climate Hearings." *Grist*, 20 April 2010. Available at: http://www.grist.org/article/2009-04-20-house-republicans-bring [accessed: 20 November 2010].

Shirky, C. 2009. *Here Comes Everybody*. New York: Penguin Books.

Simonds, R.L. 1989. *Teachers Can Teach Creation Science in the Classroom*. Institute for Creation Research, 1 October. Available at: http://www.icr.org/article/teachers-can-teach-creation-science-classroom/ [accessed: 15 November 2010].

Strom, S. 2010a. "Nonprofits Rush to Solicit Donations via Text, but the system is flawed." *The New York Times*, 31 October. Available at: http://www.nytimes.com/2010/11/01/business/01text.html?pagewanted=all [accessed: 25 November 2010].

Strom, S. 2010b. "Haiti Crisis Prompts Fresh Talk of Pooling U.S. Relief Money." *The New York Times*, 2 February. Available at: http://www.nytimes.com/2010/02/02/us/02charity.html [accessed: 12 November 2010].

Travers, K. 2010. "Haiti Relief: Text Messages Speed Donations." *ABC News/Politics*, 14 January. Available at: http://abcnews.go.com/Politics/HaitiEarthquake/haiti-earthquake-donations-haiti-relief-efforts-text-message/story?id=9551199&page=1 [accessed: 10 June 2010].

U.S. Geological Survey. 2010. *Magnitude 7.0—Haiti Region*. US Geological Survey, 12 January 2010. Available at: http://earthquake.usgs.gov/earthquakes/recenteqsww/Quakes/us2010rja6.php#summary [accessed: 15 November 2010].

Vardiman, L. 2008. "A New Theory of Climate Change." *Acts & Facts*, 37(11), 10. Available at: http://www.icr.org/article/new-theory-climate-change/ [accessed: 15 November 2010].

Vardiman, L. 2010. "Climategate: Begging the Question." *Acts & Facts*, 39(5), 12–13. Available at: http://www.icr.org/article/climategate-begging-question/ [accessed: 15 November 2010].

Veltman, K.H. 2005. Understanding New Media: Augmented Knowledge and Culture (with Corrections until 3 February 2005 by KHV). Available at: http://sumscorp.com/book_understanding_new_media:_augmented_knowledge_and_culture_/ [accessed: 15 November 2010].

Voss, J. 2005. "Measuring Wikipedia." In International Conference of the International Society for Scientometrics and Informetrics: 10th, Stockholm (Sweden), 24–8 July. [Conference Paper].

Chapter 22
VIEWPOINT: Privacy—There is Not Enough and it is Shrinking Fast

Hannes Steen-Thornhammar

The invasion of privacy has only just begun. As a society and as individuals, we are addicted to information technology. The exchange of information between social, economic and political entities is fast becoming increasingly sophisticated, and at the same time, also increasingly complex. While information technology allows more people to connect, share and trade—spawning new levels of efficiencies—it also allows for a new destructive potential. Online fraud, cyber-warfare and identity theft have become increasingly common as a result of the growing presence of the Web in public and private domains. Individual privacy is at the heart of this development. The explosion of social media has propelled an unprecedented change in digital behavior. The creation of online profiles is signaling a new era of socio-digital interaction.

The era that we are fast approaching will be defined to a large extent by how the digital players can come to protect privacy and identity, and how governments can create the digital regulations necessary to ensure individual rights and the democratic foundation within the context of the virtual sphere. The net is vast, mostly disorganized, and only in its infancy. We have no way of predicting the future, but we do have a way of influencing it. The task of accommodating these rapid and overwhelming changes represents an enormous task for the judicial and technological community. Accompanying frameworks must be reconsidered and re-evaluated from the point of view of the "cybercitizen." Difficult questions about national and global jurisdiction will have to be resolved. The spread of cloud computing and software as service technologies makes this increasingly pressing, and so too does the increased divide between software and hardware, between those with access and those without, those with technological literacy and those without. Yet, the rate of change is occurring at great speed. More and more people wire up as technological prowess follows tandem with emerging economies. In addition, the amount of time spent online is multiplying at staggering rates.

One thing that is often overlooked in this debate, and which may be the most important question of all, is the recognition of privacy as a nonfixed entity; privacy is an issue that is being crafted in real time, by service providers, software manufacturers, local and national governments, and, privacy is also heavily dependent on context. The flexibility and the amount of privacy differ for example between countries and obviously between applications. Understanding how and why is therefore critical. What are the stakes involved and what are the long-term consequences of regulating privacy? What effect will this have on future social momentum and financial opportunity? How much should be the task of government, and how much should be left to individuals and service providers?

These are not easy questions to answer, but, one can see how the debate around privacy traces its roots to a classic debate within political philosophy—what constitutes the private and the public? To what extent does the virtual world distinguish between these? Indeed, as of yet, the Internet infrastructure has made it difficult to make distinctions between the private and the public. The distinctions may be there, but they are blurry. Without venturing too much into the technical domains of the Internet architecture, this chapter will attempt to illustrate the complexity of the privacy debate. One thing is clear—there is no one-size-fits-all solution; your interests are likely to differ from, let us say, someone who works for Google or a government official. Recognizing the complexity at hand sheds light on how acutely individuals differ in their perception on privacy. This chapter will highlight some of these interests facing individuals, service providers and governments. Nevertheless, however one may decide to view the situation, the invasion of privacy has only just begun—there is not enough, and it is shrinking fast.

For most of human history, people's identities were fixed in a rigid social hierarchy. The idea that one could somehow reinvent or reshape identity was mostly inconceivable. Social and geographic mobility was at a minimum, and one's identity was closely interlinked with one's town, village, class, job or guild. Starting with the Middle Ages and the Renaissance, a growing sense of individualism began to infiltrate Western society. The first ideas of human achievement as a defining element of one's humanity began to take hold amongst the educated classes. Slowly, identity began to be viewed as less about inheritance and increasingly about the function of one's effort within society. Pierre Beaumarchais popularized this new conception in the wake of the French revolution in the controversial play of *The Marriage of Figaro* (Beaumarchais 1964):

> Just because you're a great nobleman, you think you're a great genius! Nobility, riches, a title, high positions, that all makes a man so proud! What have you done for such fortune? You went to the trouble of being born, and nothing else. Otherwise, a rather ordinary man; while I, good grief! lost in the obscure crowd, I had to use more skill and planning just to survive than has been put into governing all of Spain for the last hundred years.

The American Constitution expropriated this new conception of man's quest for greater participation in society. The American ideal of the self-made man, as a constituent autonomous from the monarchic sovereign, was adapted to the pursuit of happiness. The European migration to America opened up what the historian Fredrick Jackson Turner called, "the significance of the frontier," where pilgrims gradually made their way from Ellis Island to California. The attitude embodied by most newborn Americans was a sense of exploration. Hierarchy based on anything except entrepreneurial zeal was quickly disbanded and the sense of exploration blended with the idea of individual reinvention and transformation.

In the twentieth century, however, most land of the American wilderness has been tamed and the idea of seeking out a clean slate had been lost. Yet, with the new information technology of the Internet, the digital equivalent of the American wilderness re-emerged. This was, perhaps, on a different scale, a new type of frontier. The digital world created a new landscape, the virtual landscape of endless possibilities. If the sense of escape had been lost with the urbanization of California, the Internet promised a new beginning, because, if you could not physically escape the conventions of everyday society, the Internet provided its users with the possibility of finding an interesting chat-room or the creation of a new screen name; this protean quality of the Internet spawned a number of identity modalities in the form of pseudonyms, avatars, forums, social networking profiles and email addresses. Suddenly, one could instill a measure of control over the shifting nature of identity.

Yet, the increased segmentation of our identities has finally caught up with reality (Rosen 2010). The ubiquity of information technology (IT), the prevalence of social networking and the force of media technologies have amalgamated the construction of the Self. It is not easy to segment one's identity. The increased connectivity between major services has created standards and formalities that force users to become increasingly transparent in their Internet usage. By many accounts, this represents a positive development, but, at the same time, the Internet binds us in ways we never could have predicted. Everything that we do online is recorded, and it never goes away. Jon Kleinberg, who spends his time studying social networks and who teaches computer science at Cornell University, has plenty of advice for ardent networkers: "When you're doing stuff online, you should behave as if you're doing it in public—because increasingly, it is" (Lohr 2010).

The idea of providing a stranger with one's email address or Social Security number appears unintelligent and contrary to any sustainable logic. Yet, most people give out a ton of information on the Internet, not realizing that all kinds of personal data can be easily deduced. Information that is being exchanged on friendly services like Twitter, Facebook and Flickr may appear innocent, but in the wrong hands it could potentially be perilous. What is the likelihood that two strangers who meet on the street would exchange intimate information about their professional and personal lives? Not very strong. Yet on the Internet, this is common behavior. "Technology has rendered the conventional definition of personally identifiable information obsolete," said Maneesha Mithal, associate director of the Federal Trade Commission's privacy division—"You can find out who an individual is without it" (Lohr 2010).

Since social networking services arrived on the scene, it has become obvious that, even though meticulous privacy controls are made available, friends and colleagues may easily disclose information such as gender, employment, location, friends, and interests. In this interconnected world, individual actions are just as empowered as they are insignificant. They can either reverberate or fade away. "Personal privacy is no longer an individual thing," said Harold Abelson, professor of computer science at MIT. "In today's online world, what your mother told you is true, only more so: people really can judge you by your friends" (Lohr 2010). Social patterns have become easy to identify. Digital behavior discloses specific use patterns that can provide detailed instructions about individual identities. In a study by researchers that broke through Netflix's database, more than 30% of users on Twitter and Flickr could be positively identified even though the account names and email addresses of the accounts researched were hidden. "When you link these large data sets together, a small slice of our behavior and the structure of our social networks can be identifying," one of the researchers suggested (Lohr 2010).

Perhaps even more unsettling is the paper published last year by two researchers from Carnegie Mellon University asserting that they could accurately predict the full, nine-digit Social Security numbers for 8.5% of the people born in the U.S. between 1989 and 2003—nearly 5 million individuals (Acquisti and Gross 2009). Social Security numbers play an important role in online fraud. Identities are stolen to authenticate financial transactions. What was specifically unnerving about the report was its use of publicly available information. Most of the base research was taken from social networking profiles by merely acquiring birthdays, cities, and state of birth. All of this information represents some of the first digits on the Social Security number; the remaining numbers were deduced from the government's number assignment system that could be re-engineered based on cycles of statistical correlations.

Yet, as most of us know, getting through a privacy policy document on a popular networking site is needlessly time-consuming. These texts are usually long, poorly designed and virtually incomprehensible for anyone without a law degree. It was reported that Facebook's privacy policy document was actually longer and contained more text than the American Constitution. Most major companies have begun a process of amendment, making the privacy policies more amenable to a wider public. At the same time, most of the popular Web services have come under attack for the way in which they handle consumer data and for the way that the digital imprint is tracked on third-party servers. Consumer Watchdog released a report that accused Google of acquiring too much customer information and not allowing users to freely opt out from Google's data collection software program that runs on its software and applications. Google's defense has been duly noted, "Since contacts are shared between services like Gmail, Talk, Calendar and Docs, it makes sense for those services to be governed by one privacy policy" (Bilton 2010a).

Stephen Colbert, a popular media satirist, reminded the CEO of Google, Eric Schmidt, that "now you famously said, and I completely support this, the idea that someday, young people, instead of having privacy for the things they put up on Facebook ... they'll just erase their histories and change their names and they'll be scot-free." Mr. Schmidt's responded that, "it was a joke." To which Mr. Colbert replied, "I guess it was too hip for the room" (Bilton 2010b). Yet, what was left out of the debate was the crucial notion that most Web service companies are beginning to treat their applications as part of larger integrated platforms. As more of these Web services are intertwined with commercial and professional circuits, the domino dangers are continuously present and, indeed, heightened.

This too is equally present at a social level. A 25-year-old teacher, Stacy Snyder, in training at Conestoga Valley High School in Lancaster, PA, posted a photo of herself on her Myspace page wearing a pirate hat and drinking, with the caption, "Drunken Pirate" (Rosen 2010). Eventually, the dean of Millersville University School of Education accused the teacher of promoting underage drinking in view of her peers. Subsequently, she was then denied her teaching degree. A lawsuit against the school was denied based on the claim that the photo was not protected speech since it did not relate to matters of public concern (Rosen 2010).

Stacy Snyder is not alone. Her problem may very quickly become our own. Everything on the Internet is recorded, and almost nothing is forgotten. Photos on Flickr, tweets on Twitter, and posts on Facebook may well haunt their users for years to come. The recent reports on the subject are increasing daily. It has now become quite common to hear of individuals fired from work for illicit comments on social networking sites. The story of the Canadian psychotherapist barred permanently from entering the U.S. after an article was discovered on her experiments with LSD has become a classic example of this taunting development (Rosen 2010).

At the same time, advances in information technology have always elicited some form of fear of change. Facebook surpassed Myspace in 2008 to become the largest social networking site in the world. The site boasts more than 500 million visitors and directs the posts, pictures and interactions of 22% of all Internet users. In a sense, these cases are bound to occur, and as the traffic of exchanges increases, so too should the reports of misuse. In an 1890 article with the Harvard Law Review, Samuel Warren and Louis Brandeis complained in their seminal work on "The Right to Privacy" that technological advances had meant that "gossip is no longer the resource of the idle and of the vicious but has become a trade" (Warren and Brandeis 1890). When the Library of Congress recently decided to acquire—for permanent storage—the entire history of public Twitter posts since 2006, it granted the social networking site a measure of legitimacy that was previously the domain of professional journalism.

As social media transitions from the private to the public sphere, federal law enforcement and national security officials are adjusting their practices to accommodate this development. New regulations for the Internet are gradually introduced. Wiretapping is increasingly seen as an outmoded form of surveillance as most communication is conducted by online means rather than by fixed landlines. Congress have suggested that all service providers, including encrypted BlackBerry transmission, closed-community-based communication such as Facebook and peer-to-peer technologies like Skype must comply with authorized wiretap orders. This would force service providers to decrypt intercepted messages between users. This kind of legislation has implications that transcend the dynamics of the Internet's decentralized design. The vice president of the Center for Democracy and Technology, James X. Dempsey, has raised concerns of what this means in practical terms. "They are really asking for the authority to redesign services that take advantage of the unique, and now pervasive, architecture of the Internet," he said. "They basically want to turn back the clock and make Internet services function the way that the telephone system used to function" (Savage 2010).

However, depending on the perspective, these measures are seen as the necessary bulwarks for the protection of democracy. Law enforcement officials continuously contend that these mandates are reasonable given the Internet's corrosive effect over traditional investigative powers. As the Internet matures, so too must law enforcement. "We're talking about lawfully authorized intercepts," said Valerie E. Caproni, general counsel for the Federal Bureau of Investigation. "We're not talking expanding authority. We're talking about preserving our ability to execute our existing authority in order to protect the public safety and national security" (Savage 2010). James X. Dempsey has documented the tension between information and communication technology and the current legal structure, often claiming that the interests between private, corporate and legal paradigms are not necessarily aligned (Dempsey 2010):

> Congress have sought to balance two critical interests: the individual's right to privacy and the government's need to obtain evidence to prevent and investigate crimes, respond to emergency circumstances and protect the public. More recently, as technological developments have opened vast new opportunities for communication and commerce, Congress has added a third goal: providing a sound trust framework for communications technology and affording companies the clarity and certainty they need to invest in the development of innovative new services. Today, it is clear that the balance among these three interests—the individual's right to privacy, the government's need for tools to conduct investigations, and the interest of service providers in clarity and customer trust—has been lost as powerful new technologies create and store more and more information about our daily lives.

What is evident from the rapid technological development is the need for the legal structures to develop at the same rate as technology. Unfortunately, this is not a reality. Dempsey adds on his blog on the website for the Center for Democracy and Technology, that: "In the absence of judicial protections, it is time for Congress to respond, as it has in the past, to afford adequate privacy protections, while preserving law enforcement tools and providing clarity to service providers." Officials from the Justice Department, the National Security Agency, and the FBI, including the White House, have been working on a solution that would satisfy all parties and that could work in broader, more realistic terms. However, this has put manufacturers of Blackberry devices in direct conflict with national governments—illustrating the difficulties of conducting surveillance of messages that use encryption software.

The trend has been somewhat reversed. In a landmark 1967 case, the court explained, "wherever a man may be, he is entitled to know that he will remain free from unreasonable searches and seizures" (*New York Times* 2010). The ruling included evidence from a wiretap on a phone booth that was considered unconstitutional. Under the Fourth Amendment, the wiretap directly violated the defendant's privacy. However, under the 1994 Communications and Assistance to Law Enforcement Act, phone and broadband networks are subject to regular interception (CALEA 1994). Particularly promising is the technology of Flash cookies—a type of software that creates data profiles of users with or without their consent. Flash cookies have clashed with privacy activists, who have also brought a number of federal lawsuits against media and technology companies (Vega 2010). Regular HTML cookies can be managed through settings on browsers, whereas Flash cookies are stored in off-site directories that users are unlikely to be aware of or know how to control. In the Clearspring Technologies and Walt Disney lawsuit, it was reported that these companies "knowingly authorized" the use of online tracking devices that would "allow access to and disclosure of Internet users' online activities as well as personal information" (Vega 2010).

Flash cookies, and even regular HTML cookies, are hot business amongst advertisers, who use the information to create detailed consumer profiles. With enough time and effort, strategic information regarding ethnicity and age can be predicted with uncanny accuracy. Peter Eckersley, a developer at the Electronic Frontier Foundation, explains that "the core function of the cookie is to link what you do on Web site A to what you do on Web site B … the Flash cookie makes it harder for people to stop that from happening" (Vega 2010). Privacy activists have recently illustrated their discontent with Google's online practices. Mounting a 540-square-foot video advertisement in Times Square in New York City, the whole ploy is a protest against Google's use of user profiling. Google's CEO, Eric Schmidt, is depicted as a greedy capitalist offering ice cream in exchange for invisible full body scans. The advertisement is meant to symbolically illustrate Google's approach to privacy; in exchange for free online services, they scan our personal information in order to sell more advertisements. Ironically, the video is available on the social networking site, YouTube, which is owned by Google, whose corporate slogan—"don't be evil"—has come to define the newfound power of online service providers.

Originally, Flash cookies were intended to save a user's volume or language preferences. According to Adobe, one of the major manufacturers of Flash technologies, more than 75% of online videos are delivered with Flash technologies (Vega 2010). The company has made public statements against the wider use of Flash technologies and also provides an online tool that gives the user control over and the possibility to erase Flash cookies. The company condemned the practice of restoring cookies in a letter to the Federal Trade Commission. The criticism centers on the fact that controls are not easy to reach and, if they are reached, they are still difficult to maneuver. John Verdi, senior counsel at the Electronic Privacy Information Center, critiqued the Federal Trade Commission (FTC) for being passive on following up on the rapid development of information technology: "The F.T.C. has been inactive on this front and has failed to present meaningful regulation … There's wide evidence that online tracking is not being controlled by self-regulation" (Vega 2010).

Equally pertinent are Internet-connected mobile phones. Location, email, and credit-card numbers are all stored through smartphones connected to the Web in one way or the other. Given the ease with which transmissions can be hijacked by third parties, new software has emerged providing websites with privacy approval ratings. Sites like Wikipedia and Google have often left people tarnished from misrepresentation. Michael Fertik, a Harvard Law School graduate, has started a service that cleans up misrepresentations online: "I was seeing articles about the 'Lord of the Flies' behavior that all of us engage in at that age," he told me, "and it felt un-American that when the conduct was online, it could have permanent effects on the speaker and the victim. The right to new beginnings and the right to self-definition have always been among the most beautiful American ideals" (Rosen 2010). The company monitors your online reputation, contacting websites individually, requesting the removal of offending pieces of information. Alternatively, it bombards search engines, like Google, with neutral information about its clients, creating new Web pages or replacing offending ones all together. These types of services are becoming increasingly common.

This development is not confined to the U.S. In Europe and Asia, people are beginning to seek practical measures to curtail privacy infringement. Germany is particularly cautious. Given its history, individual privacy is considered an important cornerstone of a free, democratic society. The German government has investigated Google's Street View service—panoramic street scenes on Google maps —alleging that it represents a series of privacy breaches in the way that it collects data for mapping. Google has already acknowledged that it collected 600 gigabytes of information from around the world as it was building out its service (Minder 2010). Similarly, Apple's data-collection policies for the iPhone have been carefully investigated and a draft is in the making for laws on governing workplace privacy where employers would be restricted from using Facebook profiles when recruiting talent (Jolly 2010). The bill provides detailed guidelines for how managers are allowed to screen prospective employees. Professional services like LinkedIn or Xing are allowed, but social networking services like Facebook are prohibited for professional recruitment. Also, the bill states that employees have the right to conduct secret investigations if they suspect that the company had made a privacy breach (Jolly 2010).

Germany is not alone in Europe. Spain, Denmark, Ireland and Austria have already criticized Google for the way it collects data, using unsecured wi-fi networks to build out its Street View application. Investigations are ongoing in Spain, and through official requests, Google has destroyed data that was collected in the same way in Ireland, Denmark and Austria (Minder 2010). As part of a global strategy, Google has dispatched cars, bicycles, and other vehicles mounted with cameras to digitally record every big city environment for its service. This new form of commercial penetration of public life has caused particular annoyance—precisely because of the manner in which the data was collected. In Seoul for example, Google's offices have been raided by South Korean police as part of a similar investigation of Google's Street View service. At the same time, however, the Street View Service is going live in the 20 biggest cities in Germany, including Berlin, Munich, and Frankfurt (Sang-Hun 2010).

It is not just Google. The United Arab Emirates have made continuous threats to shut down the mobile services on smartphones, like the BlackBerry (Helft 2010). The tensions between privacy and national security are mounting. Terrorism plays a critical part in this development. IT and communications companies want to give their customers the best service, shielding users from those who want a sneak peek, whereas governments insist on gaining electronic access to monitor suspicious behavior and track down criminal activity. This is a conundrum. Most countries have laws and the regulatory frameworks available that require IT and communications companies to comply with government agencies for some form of interception.

With the ubiquity of IT and the spreading of increasingly sophisticated cloud services, the balance between private, commercial and government interests will remain strenuous. Most of the cases found in this chapter highlight the complexity at hand. The reason why these are important is because they touch at the very heart of what it means to have an identity—an identity that is defined, not by others, but by the volition of the Self. It is just text and images one might easily say, but Stacy Snyder would disagree. No, this is real, and the digital realm of a cyber identity is here to stay. Indeed, with deep integration of socio-political institutions and economic activity online, we are slowly witnessing a duplication of society as we have previously come to know it (Rosen 2010):

> We've known for years that the Web allows for unprecedented voyeurism, exhibitionism and inadvertent indiscretion, but we are only beginning to understand the costs of an age in which so much of what we say, and of what others say about us, goes into our permanent—and public—digital files. The fact that the Internet never seems to forget is threatening, at an almost existential

> level, our ability to control our identities; to preserve the option of reinventing ourselves and starting anew; to overcome our checkered pasts.

This is at the heart of the debate. For the Internet is no longer the escape that web developers of the Bay area once foresaw it to be. The Internet and its multitudes of webscapes are becoming part of the mainstream, ushering in entirely new dimensions of responsibility for those who engage with it. The Web is not about forgetting anymore. It is about remembering. This is not a new concept. The Argentinean writer, lecturer, and librarian, Jorge Luis Borges—although an unlikely figure in the great drama of the Internet—wrote in his short story, "Funes the Memorious" (1999):

> I was struck by the thought that every word I spoke, every expression of my face or motion of my hand would endure in his implacable memory; I was rendered clumsy by the fear of making pointless gestures.

Privacy, as the world is gradually coming to realize, is a thing of the past. The financial incentives and the political necessity—in terms of surveillance—are above and beyond individual private concerns. These will be continuously squeezed and, to some extent, marginalized. So it follows that disconnection is the new counter culture. For those deciding to opt out, they will indeed lose out on some of the opportunities and novelty emanating from the latest trends and developments affecting hundreds of millions (soon billions) of people. However, at the same time, one will be left with the sense of freedom that only those who stand at the margins can know and appreciate. It is rare that people stop reading the news, but surprisingly, those that do will not have it any other way.

Caveat emptor! For those who wish to retain a measure of integrity as part of their online identities, a significant dose of balance and tact must be employed and exerted. It is possible to see how, in the future, the most interesting journeys for privacy, solitude and, subsequently, identity will increasingly take place at the margins of the Web and not within it. Why? Because the Web is representing the fully integrated mainstream and individuals at the center can never have the same perspective as those standing in the peripheries. The Googles, Facebooks and Twitters of the future, and those that replace them, will have to play ball with democratic principles that made them prosper in the first place. This is all good and well, because by recognizing that the mechanisms gave them life, they also need to protect those that might have them undone. The quest for privacy comes at the cost of transparency. Ultimately, all of this comes down to a choice: a choice about one's place and interest in society—what position one might want to hold and what one wants to fight for or possibly defend. There is nothing dramatic about all of this. In a sense, it is just as it has always been.

References

Acquisti, Alessandro, and Gross, Ralph. *Predicting Social Security Numbers From Public Data.* Pittsburg, PA: Carnegie Mellon University, 5 May 2009.

Beaumarchais, Pierre-Augustin. *The Marriage of Figaro*. London: Penguin, 1964.

Bilton, Nick. "Google to Simplify its Privacy Policies." *The New York Times*, 3 September 2010a.

Bilton, Nick. "Google's Chief Defends his Privacy Comment—or Joke." *The New York Times*, 22 September 2010b.

Borges, Jorge-Luis. "Funes the Memorious." In *Collected Fictions*. Penguin U.S.A., 1999.

CALEA. *Communications Assistance for Law Enforcement Act of 1994.* House Report no. 103-827, Part I. Online, 17 November 2010. Available at: http://www.calea.org/ [accessed: 1 August 2011].

Dempsey, Jim. The Electronic Communications Privacy Act: Promoting Security and Protecting Privacy. Center for Democracy and Technology, 22 September 2010.

Helft, Michael. "For Data, Tug Grows Over Privacy vs. Security." *The New York Times*, 2 August 2010.

Jolly, David. "Germany Plans Limits on Facebook Use in Hiring." *The New York Times*, 26 August 2010.

Lohr, Steve. "How Privacy Vanished Online." *The New York Times*, 16 March 2010.

Minder, Raphael. "Google Sued in Spain Over Data Collecting." *The New York Times*, 17 August 2010.

Rosen, Jeffrey. "The Web Means the End of Forgetting." *The New York Times*, 21 July 2010.

Sang-Hun, Choe. "Police in South Korea Raid Google's Office." *The New York Times*, 10 August 2010.

Savage, Charlie. "U.S. Tries to Make it Easier to Wiretap the Internet." *The New York Times*, 27 September 2010.

The New York Times. Editorial. "An Illegal Search, by GPS." *The New York Times*, 5 October 2010.

Vega, Tanzina. "Code That Tracks Users' Browsing Prompts Lawsuits." *The New York Times*, 20 September 2010.

Warren, Samuel D., and Brandeis, Louis D. "The Right To Privacy." *Harvard Law Review*, IV(5), 15 December 1890.

Chapter 23
VIEWPOINT: Information Overload: Real and Growing by the Minute

Natalya Sverjensky

> A century ago the average person could only create and access a small amount of information. Now, ordinary people not only have access to huge amounts of data, but are also able to create gigabytes of data themselves and, potentially, publish it to the world via the Internet, if they choose to do so.
>
> Lyman et al. 2000

Introduction

We live in the age of information. From the moment we wake up in the morning to when we turn off the light at night, we are exposed to more information than at any other time in human history. We can produce and store vast amounts of data more quickly, and more cheaply, than ever before, and for the first time, we are also beginning to ask a critical question: are we suffering from information overload? Are all the emails, text messages, blogs and websites providing us with a net benefit? Or are we facing an exponential growth in flows of information that is hurting us more than it is helping?

The concept of information overload pre-dates the rise of the Internet and personal computers. Alvin Toffler first popularized the term in his groundbreaking 1964 work, "Future Shock." Toffler (1970) discussed the idea in a behavioral context, reasoning that the individual's ability to make an informed decision is threatened and even paralysed by too much information. This challenge, Toffler believed, was crippling life in the emergent information society.

> When the individual is plunged into a fast and irregularly changing situation, or a novelty-loaded context … [h]e can no longer make the reasonably correct assessments on which rational behavior is dependent … Incompatible demands [are] now producing a decision-making crisis in the techno-societies. Taken together these pressures justify the term "decisional overstimulation", and they help explain why masses of men in these societies already feel themselves harried, futile, incapable of working out their private futures.

Toffler (1970) identified several different ways the individual could respond—"maladaptions"—to information overload. The first he termed "The Denier," someone who ignores the information entirely. The second is "The Specialist," someone who focuses on a niche and aggressively gathers information that is exclusively relevant to that niche. The third is "The Reversionist," someone who takes a dogmatic approach to pursuing their previous habits and the status quo.

Regardless of the response, Toffler (1970) shows that each is little more than a short-term coping mechanism with long-term repercussions. It is easy to see how his writing on the negative impacts of information overload are still relevant today, if not even more so. These impacts are shaping the future of our social, political and economic systems, and challenging how we are going to thrive—and not just live—in a fast-paced knowledge economy.

When we talk about "information overload" today, it is almost always in the context of the digital realm. As Lyman et al. (2000) points out, digital information is both the largest source of information in the world and the most rapidly growing. While unique content on print and film are nearly static, optical and digital magnetic storage shipments are doubling each year. This makes sense because they are cheap, accessible and storage is quickly diminishing in price.

According to Lyman et al. (2000), in 2000 the World Wide Web consisted of about 21 terabytes of static HTML pages, and is growing at a rate of 100% per year. This figure becomes even more staggering in the face of the reality that only 20% of the world is on the Internet.

We expect to see the amount of digital content produced by individuals stored on hard drives increase dramatically. This democratization of data is quite remarkable.

Can we assume the rate of information growth will continue? If so, what does this democratized landscape of digital information look like with a billion more users? And how will we navigate it?

These questions address what can be seen as two different levels of information overload. The first is the impact on everyday life so eloquently described by Toffler: how the individual operates in a rapidly changing information landscape. The second is the higher-level impact on decision-makers in government and key institutions, and the degree to which information overload poses a threat to progress on the global stage.

The rise of networked technologies has radically intertwined these two levels. This chapter examines several of the negative impacts of information overload that are relevant on both levels. Perhaps the most fundamental place to start is with the trend of attention deficit and the role information plays in driving it.

The average American now consumes 34 GB worth of content a day, including 100,000 words of information.[1] A common response to this extraordinary statistic is that we are already expected to multitask in a fast-paced society, and have the skills necessary to navigate the landscape. Bargh (2009) makes the argument that these skills even become less necessary as time evolves:

> We are already and have long been multitaskers, in other words, we just do it (so well) unconsciously, not consciously. It is conscious multitasking (talking on the phone while driving) that we are so bad at because of the limits of conscious attention, but multitasking per se—we are built for that. As we gain skills those skills require less and less of that conscious attention.

This explanation is reasonable enough until you actually start asking people if, and how, the Net and information technologies are affecting their lives and jobs. A recent survey by LexisNexis (2010) of white-collar workers around the world found that information overload is becoming a widespread issue that is affecting productivity and morale. Some 62% of respondents said that the caliber of their work had suffered because they were not able to navigate or find the information they need quickly enough. A further majority agreed that, if the amount of information they received continued to increase, they would soon reach a "breaking point," at which they would be unable to handle any more. Unsurprisingly, the survey also found that between 30 and 50% of all the information that professionals received at work each day was not relevant to their job.

The rise of the Net, email and other technologies has transformed everyday life at work and at home for those living in the emerging knowledge economies. Most jobs now require the use of a computer, and the information management skills that go along with it. The LexisNexis survey

---

1 Lehman 2003, http://hmi.ucsd.edu/howmuchinfo.php.

makes it clear that, if the flow of information continues at its current pace, accompanied by an ever-expanding array of sources, people will not be able to handle it with the management tools that are available now.

Progress has been made since the introduction of email over a decade ago, when spam quickly became a widespread problem. Basic email services, such as Gmail, offer highly effective spam blockers that help people to manage the constant tide of unwanted information. However, these are incremental improvements that, while helpful, do little to address the critical issues with information management in everyday life: how people find and process information necessary to conduct their jobs, how people process the news they need to understand national and global affairs, and how people gain the digital skills necessary to do all of the above.

At the same time, we are seeing the rise of "social media addicts" and "online gaming addicts"—people who are so deeply immersed in the realm of digital information that their mental health is threatened. In early 2010, statistics from Nielsen confirmed that the average American Internet user spends more time on Facebook than on Google, Yahoo, YouTube, Microsoft, Wikipedia and Amazon combined. This absorption with social media is one side of the information overload problem—an increasing obsession with information that is personally relevant so that one fails to take advantage of the extraordinary array of sources available on the Net.

Many who dismiss the idea of information overload do so on the grounds that the phenomenon has been present since the Gutenberg Press first made the technology of the printing press—and thus the power to spread the word—available to the average consumer. Still others contend that it can even be traced back to the advent of writing in the Roman empire, when Plato decreed in The Republic that poetry could have no place in the ideal state.

These arguments certainly ring true at a fundamental level, but in reducing the concept of information overload to a broad historical trend, they miss the real context of the transformative change we have experienced over the past decade. The ways we encounter, capture and process information in the emergent knowledge economy today are radically different from those experienced by previous generations. The attention of the individual is stretched across an unprecedented number of directions because of it.

A prime example of attention deficit from information overload is the digital press. A few decades ago most people received their news through a single newspaper or TV program. On any given day now, the volume of news available to the average consumer is immense, whether via the digital outlets of traditional sources like *The New York Times* or blogs or aggregators like Google News.

It is worth emphasizing that this sea change in access to information sources has huge potential benefits, but as Nicolas Carr (2008) so effectively points out, the idea of attention deficit owing to information overload is less about what the individual reads than about how the individual subsequently processes or acts on the information:

> what the Net seems to be doing is chipping away at my capacity for concentration and contemplation. Whether I'm online or not, my mind now expects to take in information the way the Net distributes it: in a swiftly moving stream of particles.

As Carr (2008) describes it, the act of reading on the Net is necessarily superficial because of the volume of information available. It changes the expectations of the individual when reading something as simple as a news article. Why read a single article thoroughly and contemplate it when there are likely to be thousands of others describing the same topic from different perspectives?

In this sense, news aggregators hold the promise of breaking down some of the traditional media barriers and helping the individual access this spectrum of perspectives. For example, searching for a key term on Google News yields the top stories relating to that issue, providing the possibility of rapidly comparing coverage of the same issue across outlets.

However, the key question is, how many people even read all the way through a single article on the Internet any more? And if all the average consumer does when examining the news digitally is skim through multiple articles, without thinking critically about what they are encountering, they are arguably worse off than before.

This leads to a second trend in the way we are processing information online. The Net, especially the blogosphere, enables like-minded individuals to form communities of dialogue more rapidly than ever before. It is arguable that these small congregations of people with the same values, opinions and thoughts are driving less exposure to new information and perspectives and more pursuit of personal ideologies. Farhad Manjoo (2008) sums it up as a shift occurring across channels:

> On the Web, television, radio and all manner of new devices, today you can watch, listen to, and read what you want, whenever you want; seek out and discuss, in exhaustive and insular detail, the kind of news that pleases you; and indulge your political, social or scientific theories, whether sophisticated or naïve, extremist or banal, grounded in reality or so far out you're floating in an asteroid belt, among people who feel exactly the same way … it is more convenient than ever before for some of us to live in a world built out of our own facts.

This is indeed what the landscape of digital information often seems to look like today: a vast network of small groups of people trading commonly held ideas. Readership is concentrated on a small number of these small groups and opinion formers, such as TechCrunch and Mashable. There are certainly exceptions to this trend, but overwhelmingly it seems like Toffler's Specialist has won.

The consequences of this deepening ideological processing of information are obvious. The Net may have radically changed the amount of information we have access to, and our ability to produce and consume it, but it has not achieved the potentially groundbreaking democratization and acceleration of progress. We can now build our own universes of truth without having to encounter other perspectives.

Some opinion formers are rebelling against this ideological approach. Aidan Henry (2008) describes why he no longer reads go-to blogs like TechCrunch "A combination of thoughtless articles and copycat posts just isn't compelling to me … I used to enjoy reading many of these blogs 'back in the day'. Back then, a single author posted quality content. Those days are long gone and priorities have shifted. Breaking the news ahead of everyone else is the main objective at the expense of value and insight."

Henry's point about quality is key. Even laudable institutions on the Net, such as Wikipedia, continue to be plagued by unverifiable information. Googling simple topics often turns up pages which, while popular, are not necessarily reliable sources for unbiased perspective. This poses significant issues for academia and education in general. Many schools already ban Wikipedia as an official source for writing papers, on the basis that the information it contains, while remarkably sound for a collective effort of amateur writers around the world, is far from constituting a sound secondary source.

Yet many ask, so what? Wikipedia is nearly always a good starting point for learning about any issue. Furthermore, it is of course no longer necessary to rely on a single news source. The individual could easily source all of their news through the blogs and niche sources of people just like them. Popular applications like Facebook are deepening this trend as its members access news articles recommended by friends.

However, it is impossible to ignore the reality that the Net has not delivered at a macro level the kind of change through access to information that we hoped for. Yochai Benkler frames this argument as a comparison between traditional media and the potential for the Internet to improve or break down those barriers: "Both infrastructure and, more fundamentally, patterns of attention are much less distributed than we thought. As a consequence, the Internet diverges from the mass media much less than we thought in the 1990s and significantly less than we might hope."

Yet, ironically, it can also be argued that this landscape is evolving too rapidly for us to meaningfully analyse its impact on basic information processes like personal news consumption. However, without question, the rapidity with which the average news story—such as a visit by President Obama to India—is translated into the politicized poles of the digital news sphere makes it entirely possible for the average user of the Net to absorb only the politics and none of the context.

This becomes especially relevant when we move a level above the average consumer to examine who the opinion formers are on the Net and how they are interacting. Especially in political and technological circles, it seems that the blogosphere collectively swarms around one or two topics at a time. This cycle is also relentless. It operates at such a breakneck pace that taking one day off from it means missing an insurmountable volume of commentary, even for the most organized individual who uses the best available means of managing these streams of information.

For example, the introduction of a new technology like Amazon's Kindle e-book reader is guaranteed to dominate the blogosphere for days at a time as opinion formers weigh in on the product. In these periods, the Net tends to resemble the hyper-concentrated 24-hour cable news cycle more than it does a bounteous sea of proliferating new ideas and new thoughts. Manjoo (2008) frames this issue as the difference between thinking about issues and the "unthinking" cycle of focusing on current events as they unfold (his italics):

> No longer are we merely holding opinions different from one another; we're also holding different facts. Increasingly, our arguments aren't over what we *should* be doing—in the Iraq War, in the war on terrorism, on global warming, or about any number of controversial subjects—but instead over what *is happening*.

The information overload of the Net is forcing us into a cycle where we fail to think critically about the global issues we are facing, and instead engage in iterative debates over the facts of daily news. As Manjoo begins to articulate, the issues we face economically, socially and environmentally are unprecedented in their complexity and scope. Climate change, for example, demands that we each play a role in both mitigation and adaptation. Yet it is a prime example of a topic that has been distorted into a rampant debate across the blogosphere over "the facts" of its existence.

Social media and its associated applications that encourage duplication of content are exacerbating this cycle. Many blog posts are already little better than regurgitations of other popular posts. The advent of Twitter has only intensified this as people are encouraged to consistently "retweet" items they consider newsworthy or relevant.

How much content on the Net can really be classified as original, and how much is just replicated? This is a distinction that needs to be made and is much more subtle than measuring originality in an absolute sense. Individual bloggers, for example, can always create a new post by rewording the language on someone else's popular post, meanwhile retaining essentially the same content.

In that sense, a complementary key question that needs to be asked is how much of the information being created is actually valuable. The promise of Web 2.0 and social media was that the individual's ability to publish their opinion could radically alter the balance of power. The Net was supposed to enhance individual liberties, but we are finding that the Net has a limited potential to drive this kind of change, mostly because a lot of the information and social media commentary has little value or originality. Few people have the time or the inclination to go through the overwhelming amount of information available to find what is of value.

As Amity Shlaes (2010) writes, "there is a certain kind of person who is able to efficiently sift through a flood of information, pulling out nuggets that matter and presenting them in a compelling way ... that person is called an editor." So the Net brings the average consumer back to square one: relying on someone else to decide what is worth reading, watching or even writing about.

As described above, this editorial force can indeed be an individual source—such as Slate—or it can just be the aggregate effect of navigating the blogosphere's concentrated discourse. Benkler (2006) describes this consequence as a kind of Babel effect that necessitates editing, pointing out that "when everyone can speak, the central point of failure becomes the capacity to be heard—who listens to whom, and how that question is decided."

This Babel effect is a critical issue. The romance of the Internet's potential as a sweeping force of democratization has overshadowed much of the information overload debate. In some senses, this is a good thing. The escalation and growth of digital information is bound to continue, indubitably with tangible benefits to most of society. On an absolute basis, people have access to kinds of information they never could have even a decade ago. The advent of institutions like WikiLeaks, which are radically disrupting the elite political and business circles in favour of populist access, are a case in point of this potential benefit (although doubtless they will cause harm too).

The example of WikiLeaks is worth lingering on because it has created extraordinary rifts through nearly every discourse on the future of the Net. The vast majority of these conversations paint a sinister picture of WikiLeaks as a dangerous institution that threatens the fragile stability of international diplomacy. In the first week of the leaks, which are becoming known as "Cablegate," key sites including Amazon and Paypal withdrew their hosting support for WikiLeaks in response to intense pressure from the White House and other governments and stakeholders.

It is difficult to imagine a more disappointing response to the leaks from these major institutions on the Net. Although we know the volume of digital data is growing exponentially, the kind of top-secret information WikiLeaks is making available to the global public is unprecedented and in extremely short supply. George Dyson (2010) puts the problem in perspective neatly:

> The problem is that as more and more information has been classified, those classes have become very, very large. Apparently (although the amount of classified information is classified information) the United States Government now produces more classified information than unclassified information. Since no information can be useful unless it is shared, we have developed a vast and unwieldy apparatus for sharing classified information.

It is not unreasonable to say that, in a supreme case of irony, the U.S. government is probably experiencing *classified* information overload. If it is indeed true that more classified information is being produced than unclassified information, that amount of data would probably be useless to the average federal employee trying to conduct their job effectively on a day-to-day basis. It makes the whole concept of classification essentially null and void, which only intensifies the case for institutions like WikiLeaks to publish the allegedly classified material that it has, and to continue to do so.

However, championing the pure availability enabled by events like Cablegate is not enough. Just because information exists for the public to access, this does not mean it will have any discernible impact. In fact, in the case of WikiLeaks, the critical harm may come in assuming that political and economic change will be affected because the information has been exposed. In this case, the information overload inevitably present in a volume such as 250,000 leaked cables is enough of a barrier to the average journalist—let alone the average citizen—to be essentially impenetrable. The information might as well not even exist.

Here we come to an important lens through which to assess the impact of WikiLeaks. Adam Weinstein (2010), a reporter for *Mother Jones* and former contractor in Iraq, points out that the majority of the data from an earlier leak in July 2010 was already available to thousands of people through the military's basic intranet for sensitive data, the Secret Internet Protocol Router Network (SIPRNet): "I haven't been through everything yet, but most of what you see on WikiLeaks are military SIGACTS (significant activity reports). These are theoretically accessible by anyone in Iraq, Afghanistan, or the Tampa, Florida-based U.S. Central Command—soldiers and contractors—who have access to [SIPRNet]."

The key point here is that theoretically the access to this data already existed. Not to a general public audience, but in fact to the people who actually have the capability to analyse and understand it—those actively involved in the military. So why did few people proactively seek it out? It is not difficult to surmise that there is so much data available on SIPRNet that spending the time investigating and finding the important or newsworthy content would be nearly impossible for most people with access to the intranet. So WikiLeaks serves the invaluable purpose of raising the public awareness that this information exists—but it can do little more in the supersaturated landscape of digital information we are encountering.

As Weinstein (2010) continues, "[WikiLeaks is] a great bibliographic resource for reporters with time on their hands to file a FOIA request for the actual orders ... but in the meantime, it's not much by itself." Indeed, from the two to three stories which dominated the media landscape in the wake of Cablegate, it is painfully clear that few reporters even have time to delve into the wealth of information. What could have been a breakthrough in dismantling long-standing international diplomatic manoeuvring is distorted by the one or two stories that dominate the media landscape. The reality is that, despite incredible breakthroughs in the types of information being disclosed to the public, the actual penetration of the information is severely compromised by overload.

Theoretically it is possible that radical change will be effected simply because WikiLeaks will show politicians and major corporations that there is no such thing as private or "safe" information anymore. Yet it is hardly the beacon of light which proponents of the Net as a democratic force have hoped for, and if recent reactions from government in response to Cablegate are any indicator, it is likely that the radical change will be in the direction of more security and less transparency, and not the opposite.

Yet the overall trend for government thus far has been to make more and more data available to the public. From the Obama White House's Open Government Memorandum to the Department of Energy's Open Energy Information, government has been implementing initiatives that are both voluntary and driven by regulation.

In one interesting example, the U.S. Federal Reserve posted the details of more than 21,000 of its transactions with financial firms and other businesses during the financial crisis in early December 2010. The disclosure was mandated by a new Dodd-Frank law overhauling financial regulation and has been considered an important step forward to improving the public's access to allocation of taxpayer funds, but is the average citizen really going to parse through thousands of technical financial transactions and gain any understanding of them? What about the average academic?

David Karger (2010), a professor at MIT in computer science and artificial intelligence, has described the multitude of recent open government initiatives as daunting and a potentially critical case of too much meaning "nothing at all"—even for someone like him whose entire academic interest revolves around such initiatives:

> [T]here's too much going on here for a single interested academic to keep up with. We can hope that there are enough people looking to actually keep it all in our collective awareness, and spread anything really important to all of us, but is there any evidence that this is actually true? We face network effects meaning that a given government channel will only become useful if it achieves a critical mass of users … we have a classic tragedy of the commons where the commons is public attention.

The point Karger (2010) makes is a crucial one. On the one hand, we have the issue that competing initiatives to release information are themselves causing information overload. On the other hand, we are confronted with the reality that the general public is barely aware of these initiatives and may have very little interest in them, therefore defeating their entire purpose as democratic resources. Furthermore, much of the data used in the open government initiatives is data that was never intended for public consumption: it is complex, it is highly technical, and it is jargon-filled.

To return to the problem of attention deficit, the key issue is that, despite the fact that the financial crisis has affected nearly everyone around the world, most people would probably rather visit Facebook than examine troves of transactional data which they are poorly equipped to understand. It is increasingly impossible to ignore the fact that most people use the Net to do relatively mindless things. The Net is in many ways a Candyland of distractions, from online games to social networks to shopping. In this supersaturated environment, some of the most important flows of information and information sources are destined to go ignored by the vast majority of the global population.

The question remains how to weigh whether the sheer volume of information being made available is helping or harming us, regardless of whether it is being understood. Benkler (2006) correctly points out that the appropriate benchmark for today's information society is the mass media of the twentieth century, not the utopia of the nineteenth century, "everybody a pamphleteer." In that sense, on a fundamental level the amount of information we have access to, and the number of news sources available, represent tremendous progress from the past.

It is perhaps useful to question if we can think outside both of these benchmarks. After all, if information overload is the new reality, we are going to have to find a way to transcend it. In a world where only 20% of the global population is online, the quest to navigate the Net effectively is only going to become more challenging as billions more users enter into the digital fray. As Lyman concludes, "it is clear that we are all drowning in a sea of information … the challenge is to learn to swim in that sea, rather than drown in it" (Lyman et al. 2000).

Clay Shirky (2008) is one of an increasing number of proponents for collectively intelligent filtering systems to manage the chaos:

> The real question is, how do we design filters that let us find our way through this particular abundance of information? And, you know, my answer to that question has been: the only group that can catalog everything is everybody. One of the reasons you see this enormous move towards

> social filters, as with Digg, as with del.icio.us, as with Google Reader, in a way, is simply that the scale of the problem has exceeded what professional cataloguers can do.

This faith in our collective power to catalogue and make sense of the Net's vast stores of information is tempting. As Shirky (2008) points out, this group filtering system is already happening, but the question remains whether we have the intellectual and scientific foundations to implement this kind of filtering at the necessary scale. Jaron Lanier is one of the most vocal critics of filtering today:

> The usual answer these days … [is] that we need to create "intelligent" filter technology that will serve up only the best information for you. The problem with that is that we don't have adequate scientific understandings of meaning or thought, so we can't actually write software that does the job. We can only pretend to write such software, so that you can pretend it's working, thus lowering your standards and lessening your personhood.

The other element of critique in this debate that is missing from both authors is the question of whether "the best information for you" is what we are aiming to achieve as the Net evolves. Is the ultimate personalization of digital information the right goal? In an increasingly complex world with extraordinary social and economic inequality, global challenges like climate change and financial meltdowns, and political instability, do we want the average Net user to be focused on information that is entirely personalized and relevant? Or do we desperately require a Net that offers unprecedented and intelligent access to information that at once meets personal needs and helps increase understanding of the global challenges we face?

The evolution of the Net over the past decade has both met and failed to live up to many of our expectations. We face a critical juncture in how average consumers and opinion formers alike will produce and consume information on the Net in the future. If we continue on the current path, which assumes information overload for nearly everyone on a fundamental level, the prospects are not good for progress on the global stage. By progress I mean benefits such as more political, social and economic liberties for people; less inequality; better and fairer access to information.

The radically increased transparency we are experiencing through data availability in the Information Age should be welcomed, but it should not be touted as a harbinger of democratic freedom or boundless opportunity for personal expression. As we well know, data is useless until it becomes information, and information is not relevant until context enables it to take the form of knowledge.

What we really need in this tornado of information overload is more knowledge, and the Net in its current form, and current modes of usage, is not fulfilling that. Information overload is a reality and it needs to be overcome.

References

Bargh, John. "Response: The Age of the Informavore." *Edge Foundation*, 5 November 2009. Available at: http://www.edge.org/documents/archive/edge303.html [accessed: 1 August 2011].

Benkler, Yochai. *The Wealth of Networks: How Social Production Transforms Markets and Freedom*. New Haven, CT: Yale University Press, 2006.

Carr, Nicholas. "Is Google Making Us Stupid?" *The Atlantic*, July 2008. Available at: http://www.theatlantic.com/magazine/archive/2008/07/is-google-making-us-stupid/6868/ [accessed: 16 February 2010].

Dyson, George. "Response: Who Gets to Keep Secrets?" *Edge Foundation*, 9 December 2010. Available at: http://www.edge.org/documents/archive/edge335.html [accessed: 12 January 2011].

Henry, Aidan. "Why I Stopped Reading TechCrunch and Mashable." *Mapping the Web Blog*, 7 April 2008. Available at: http://www.mappingtheweb.com/2008/04/07/why-ive-stopped-reading-techcrunch-and-mashable/ [accessed: 13 August 2011].

Karger, David. "Open Government: Will Too Much Mean None at All?" *MIT CSAIL Haystack Blog*, 2010. Available at: http://groups.csail.mit.edu/haystack/blog/2010/05/11/open-government-will-too-much-mean-none-at-all/ [accessed: 30 December 2010].

Lanier, Jaron. *You are Not a Gadget*. New York: Vintage, 2010.

Lehman, Peter and Hal R. Varian 2003. How Much Information? 2003. Available at: http://www2.sims.berkeley.edu/research/projects/how-much-info-2003/ [accessed: 1 August 2011].

LexisNexis. 2010 *International Workplace Productivity Survey*, 20 October 2008. Available at: http://www.lexisnexis.com/media/press-release.aspx?id=128751532767689 [accessed: 14 December 2010].

Lyman, Peter et al. 2000. "Reprint: How Much Information." *Journal of Electronic Publishing*, 6(2).

Manjoo, Farhad. *True Enough: Learning to Live in a Post-Fact Society*. New York: Wiley, 2008.

Nielsen, "Facebook Users Average 7 hrs a Month in January as Digital Universe Expands." *Nielsen Online*, 16 February 2010. Available at: http://blog.nielsen.com/nielsenwire/online_mobile/facebook-users-average-7-hrs-a-month-in-january-as-digital-universe-expands/ [accessed: 12 January 2011].

Shirky, Clay. "Interview with Clay Shirky: Part I." *Columbia Journalism Review*, 19 December 2008. Available at: http://www.cjr.org/overload/interview_with_clay_shirky_par.php?page=all [accessed: 24 September 2011].

Shlaes, Amity. "WikiLeaks Plus Fed Disclosures Are Data Overload." *Bloomberg News*, 2 December 2010. Available at: http://www.bloomberg.com/news/2010-12-03/wikileaks-plus-fed-s-dump-equals-data-overload-commentary-by-amity-shlaes.html [accessed: 13 August 2011].

Toffler, Alvin. *Future Shock*. New York: Random House, 1970.

Weinstein, Adam. "WikiLeaks' Afghan Documents and Me." *Mother Jones*, 25 July 2010. Available at: http://motherjones.com/mojo/2010/07/wikileaks-afghan-documents-and-me-source [accessed: 13 August 2011].

Chapter 24
VIEWPOINT: PageRank and Perceptions of Quality

David Millman

Introduction

As scholars and researchers we take for granted that the papers and books we read and cite are the products of a shared research process, part of a decades-long tradition that includes going to the library, sorting through references, and building bibliographies. However, of course that is not necessarily true anymore. Now we can just use Google for everything.

Is that a problem? Does the direction of academic research now depend on what appears on the first page of a search result?[1] This chapter will examine how research habits and scholarship have been affected by the Internet and Web technologies in the twenty-first century. It will also examine the changing nature of academic libraries, as they have historically been the source of authoritative scholarly information. The experiences reported are primarily from the U.S. and the UK.

Current Practice

A number of recent studies have attempted to document the behaviors of students and professional academics as they do research. In their summary of 12 studies conducted in the U.S. and the UK over the last five years, Connaway and Dickey (2010) identified several consistent patterns. Their findings indicate that Google and other search engines do now play a central role in the discovery of materials, but the materials found and used are often from scholarly sources. Researchers claimed that e-journals are increasingly important to their work, and journal publishers reported that over a third of the requests for their articles are referrals from Google (Research Information Network 2009).

Researchers continued to value the imprimatur of traditional publishers. In certain disciplines, different publication vehicles have also gained acceptance, for example the "arxive.org" e-print service for physics and mathematics. The studies also indicate consistently that recommendations by colleagues and peers remain important ways of learning about information sources. Thus, while Google is a useful way to quickly survey the literature, it is often a starting point into an otherwise traditional scholarly research process.

However, the widespread use of Google may also explain the following findings. While researchers now considered themselves confident in their ability to search for information on the Internet, measures of their actual searching indicated that they spent little time evaluating search

1 The order of Google search results is based on a method called "PageRank," named for co-founder Larry Page (Wikipedia 2010).

results, were not expert searchers, and that their skills have not kept pace with current notions of digital literacy.

Researchers were frustrated when an article, once identified, could not be immediately retrieved. They increasingly want instant access to content from their personal computer. Going to the library is considered an inconvenience. Researchers' perception is that libraries are about books, and they are spending less and less time there.

Librarians could address some of researchers' concerns by improving their communication about more advanced search strategies ("information literacy") and about their existing services. Research libraries are now spending over 50% of their materials budgets on electronic content (Kyrillidou and Bland 2009: 21). Many researchers appear unaware of how to use their own libraries to obtain that material.

Implications for Libraries

The role of the academic library has changed dramatically in recent years. Once the sole authority of research materials, based in their physical collections, libraries are increasingly focused on their services. While core library services have essentially remained the same, to curate and facilitate access to information, they are taking on new forms. Because today's culture is increasingly information-based, library services are arguably more critical than ever. Indeed, the Connaway and Dickey surveys indicated that libraries need to make many of their existing services more widely publicized and to perform more of them.

One way to understand trends in research library services is to examine how new libraries, with no historical service commitments, are creating them. In profiles of seven recently founded libraries (Spiro and Henry 2010), a few common strategies emerge. First is a re-examination of the library's core mission. For example, rather than asking "Where should the reference desk go?," the University of California's new Merced campus library asked "What is the purpose of reference? How do we fulfill that purpose?" In their case, reference services are now being performed by phone, email, and online chat.

Another strategy is a more flexible approach to delivery of content. All of the libraries profiled emphasized electronic delivery, but each also recognized the appropriate role of print-based materials, often offering print materials through collaborations with other libraries. Each of the new libraries also re-examined the roles of the librarians. Freed of many tasks related to handling physical materials (such as cataloging, processing, and circulating), librarians could, for example, help scholars create, manage, and manipulate their own research materials.

While these profiles of new libraries were focused on U.S.-based institutions, they offer insight in how new libraries may emerge in the developing world as well. Emphasizing digital formats and being creative in organization and strategy can be helpful models in many settings. These trends are underway in more established research libraries too. Faculty and librarians at Harvard University, for example, have expressed the librarian's role as primarily a broker of information (Shaw 2010). In the large research university, creation of and access to quality information are the most important activities. Librarians participate in all aspects, from insuring that scholars have the skills to mine all relevant data sources to insuring that newly created research products are themselves trustworthy and findable.

Librarians have generally become more active in guaranteeing the authenticity and integrity of newly created scholarship. In a recent presentation, a library-school-trained data archivist described the information systems design and processes used to capture contextual information that insures provenance and authenticity to accompany research data collected at the UCLA Center for Embedded Networked Sensing. Using the librarian-designed processes, the raw data and the associated context were stored together in their digital library, thus enabling meaningful use by future researchers (Wallis 2009; Mayernik et al. 2008).

This type of librarian intervention is of course not limited to the curation of scientific data sets. In the Preserving Digital Public Television project, sponsored by the Library of Congress, NYU and WNET-TV New York captured contextual information from a television news production process in order to make it available, along with the news production itself, to future scholars (Rubin 2010).

Libraries also understand their physical spaces in new ways. For instance, in 2005 the University of Texas at Austin removed practically all of the books from its undergraduate library (Blumenthal 2005).

Based on their study of faculty and graduate student needs for research and teaching (Marcus et al. 2007), New York University has reconfigured a number of areas within its library to accommodate a variety of research needs. While different particular environments were desired, a common theme was to "have a place to study and work that is comfortable, aesthetically pleasing, and welcoming." Spaces were created for group study, for multimedia viewing, for long-term quiet study, for informal instruction, and for flexible configurations. Many spaces were near windows with good natural light. All offered power and network access for laptops.

A more experimental model is the "Unlibrary" space in the Crouch End district north of London (Evans 2010). While it appears to be still defining itself, the space is intended for informal social gathering to discuss the intersection of the libraries, the arts, and the Internet. These examples counter the perception raised above that the library is about books. The popularity of these spaces demonstrates that this perception may be shifting.

Of course, libraries have no particular monopoly on the design of physical spaces to encourage social interactions around Internet resources. Other facilities, inside and outside of the academy (Miller 2007), may also accommodate this need, but in today's universities, the library unit is frequently the most sensitive to implications of the changing information environment, not only in finding and using digital materials but also in preserving them.

While the preservation of paper and film are relatively well understood, preservation of digital material is still an active area of research in the library profession. The devices on which information is stored become obsolete quickly; the software to interpret information (such as a PDF viewer or a media player) becomes obsolete as file formats evolve. Scholarly archives, intermediate drafts of academic papers, and personal correspondence exist largely on individual scholars' current workstations or within their institutionally based email systems. When the materials are digital, libraries no longer collect their own copies of journals, and journal publishers have little incentive to engage in aggressive preservation programs themselves. Repositories such as *Portico* and the *Hathi Trust Digital Library* have emerged recently to store and care for digital files representing primarily books and journals (Hathi Trust 2010; *Portico* 2010). These efforts have been led and executed by librarians.

Increasingly, the cultural record exists on highly dynamic websites, which are often transitory, with boundaries that may be hard to determine, and which are technically difficult to copy for archival purposes. For example, it is not at all clear how to preserve the *Vectors* or *MediaCommons* publications described below.

New Methods

Activities on several fronts are also shifting the territory in which research is happening. Some researchers are using the most current technologies and, based on that experience, are inventing new methods in which to conduct scholarship. One or two examples may illustrate these directions.

The *Vectors* journal, based at University of Southern California (*Vectors* 2010), is organized like a traditional journal, with regularly published, peer-reviewed issues and "projects" within each issue. No print version is produced. Each project employs sophisticated design and interaction techniques, often to visualize cultural data in ways that involve the active participation of the reader. *Vectors* projects often raise questions around the meaning of authorship, as the creators' "narrative" is typically the design and organization of a database. As each reader may approach the data with different questions, their experiences can be unique.

The *MediaCommons Network,* a joint project of the Institute for the Future of the Book and the NYU Libraries, hosts several publications that depart from the traditional publishing model (MediaCommons 2010). In some *MediaCommons* publications, a community of scholars each publishes pieces that are somewhat shorter than traditional journal articles and then they publicly comment on each other's work. The form of the publication resembles a typical "blog" rather than a journal. No print equivalent is produced. In other *MediaCommons* publications, scholars offer article- or chapter-length material and then other scholars publicly comment on specific portions, down to individual paragraphs. The publication cycle also happens at web speed: in one *MediaCommons* publication a set of related articles is published on a 6- to 12-week cycle; in another of its publications a new article appears every day. Because the social network of scholars' comments on each others' work itself constitutes a form of academic review, *MediaCommons* raises questions about the traditional peer review process and has received prominent attention for doing so (Cohen 2010).

Another promising development in access to information, and one where librarians may play a unique role, is the establishment of specialized databases, so-called "linked open data," that allow the automatic correlation of related digital items on the Internet. While they take different forms, most current instances of such databases perform the functions usually understood as indices, structured vocabularies, or ontologies. Using this information, automated processes may traverse related topics on the Internet and dynamically reassemble them in arbitrary ways. For example, *The New York Times*' "Times Topics" service, http://topics.nytimes.com, offers a way for people to browse the continually changing indices offered by that publication. *The New York Times* also offers this index data freely in dynamic, machine-readable form and so computer programs may also browse and "remix" it on one's behalf (Miller 2009). Many other information sources are beginning to offer such index data, including Wikipedia and the Library of Congress (Simonite 2010; Library of Congress 2010).

These technologies are often characterized as part of a forthcoming "semantic web," suggesting that new intuition and meaning will arise in automated ways, but the initial construction of these linked data indices is still a largely human process, relying on such skills as "subject analysis" and "authority control" that have been routine in librarian training for generations and, for now, remain the foundation and are prerequisite to successful "linked data" benefits. Librarians have a significant opportunity to enable more, and more effective, access to their collections by their contributions to these efforts. The library can become, rather than a destination itself, a source of particular materials and the information by which those materials can be reused in other contexts.

Forward-thinking scholars and library professionals find themselves in a vibrant environment and are making strong contributions that support scholarship now, that are pushing technological and academic boundaries, and that are preparing new ground for the scholarly record. Search engines and the Internet do not appear to be making serious scholars any less thorough. Indeed, scholars have more resources than ever.

While there is reason to be optimistic, the long-term impact of the changing information environment is of course hard to predict. As one *MediaCommons* editor remarked, "We know what we're trying to do. But we don't know what we're trying to do will do."

References

Blumenthal, Ralph. 2005. "College Libraries Set Aside Books in a Digital Age." *The New York Times*. Available at: http://www.nytimes.com/2005/05/14/education/14library.html [accessed: 23 September 2010].

Cohen, Patricia. 2010. "Scholars Test Web Alternative to Peer Review." *The New York Times*, 24 August 2010, p. 1.

Connaway, Lynn Silipigni and Dickey, Timothy J. 2010. *The Digital Information Seeker: Report of Findings from Selected OCLC, RIN, and JISC User Behavior Projects*. JISC: UK.

Evans, Rhiannon. 2010. "Unlibrary launches in Crouch End." *Hampstead and Highgate Express*, 27 November 2010. Available at: http://www.hamhigh.co.uk/news/unlibrary_launches_in_crouch_end_1_737520 [accessed: 10 December 2010].

Hathi Trust. 2010. *Hathi Trust Digital Library*. Available at: http://www.hathitrust.org/ [accessed: 1 December 2010].

Kyrillidou, Martha and Bland, Les. 2009. *ARL Statistics 2007-08*. Washington, DC: Association of Research Libraries. Available at: http://www.arl.org/stats/annualsurveys/arlstats/arlstats08.shtml [accessed: 23 September 2010].

Library of Congress. 2010. *Library of Congress Authorities and Vocabularies Service*. Available at: http://id.loc.gov/authorities/about.html [accessed: 23 September 2010].

Marcus, Cecily, Covert-Vail, Lucinda and Mandel, Carol A. 2007. *NYU 21st Century Library Project: Designing a Research Library of the Future for New York University*. Available at: http://library.nyu.edu/about/KPLReport.pdf [accessed: 23 September 2010].

Mayernik, Matthew S., Wallis, Jillian C., Pepe, Alberto, and Borgman, Christine L. 2008. *Whose Data do you Trust? Integrity Issues in the Preservation of Scientific Data*. Proceedings of iConference, Los Angeles, CA, 28 February to 1 March 2008. Available at: https://www.ideals.illinois.edu/handle/2142/15119 [accessed: 23 September 2010].

MediaCommons. 2010. Available at: http://mediacommons.futureofthebook.org/ [accessed: 1 December 2010].

Miller, Kerry. 2007. "Where the Coffee Shop Meets the Cubicle." *Businessweek*. Available at: http://www.businessweek.com/smallbiz/content/feb2007/sb20070226_761145.htm [accessed: 23 September 2010].

Miller, Paul. 2009. "New York Times Embraces Linked Data." *ZDNet*, 18 June 2009. Available at: http://www.zdnet.com/blog/semantic-web/new-york-times-embraces-linked-data/309 [accessed: 23 September 2010].

Portico. 2010. Available at http://www.portico.org/ [accessed 1 December 2010].

Research Information Network. 2009. *e-Journals: Their Use, Value and Impact*. UK. Available at: http://www.rin.ac.uk/system/files/attachments/E-journals-report.pdf [accessed: 10 November 2010].

Rubin, Nan. 2010. *Preserving Digital Public Television: Final Report*. June. Available at: http://www.digitalpreservation.gov/partners/pdpt/high/pdpt_finalreport0610.pdf [accessed: 10 November 2010].

Shaw, Jonathan. 2010. "Harvard's Libraries Deal with Disruptive Change." *Harvard Magazine*, May–June, p. 36.

Simonite, Tom. 2010. "Wikipedia to Add Meaning to its Pages." *MIT Technology Review*, 7 July 2010. Available at: http://www.technologyreview.com/web/25728/ [accessed: 1 December 2010].

Spiro, Lisa and Henry, Geneva. 2010. "Can a New Research Library Be All-Digital?," in *The Idea of Order: Transforming Research Collections for 21st Century Scholarship*, edited by C. Henry. Washington, DC: Council on Library and Information Resources, p. 5.

Vectors. 2010. Available at: http://www.vectorsjournal.org/journal/index.php?page=Introduction [accessed: 1 December 2010].

Wallis, Jillian. 2009. *A Virtual Compass: Digital Technology and Resources as an Impetus for Change in Higher Education*. Presentation to Council on Library and Information Resources 2009 Sponsors' Symposium, Washington, DC, 16 December 2009. Available at: http://www.clir.org/activities/registration/09sponagenda.htm [accessed: 18 August 2010].

Wikipedia. 2010. *PageRank*. Available at: http://en.wikipedia.org/wiki/PageRank [accessed: 23 September 2010].

Chapter 25
VIEWPOINT: Citizen Change: How Technology and New Media have Turned us all into Digital Freedom Fighters

Anthony Lopez

Introduction

In mid-January 1998, Matt Drudge was sitting in his Hollywood apartment and working by his computer. On this particular evening he was finishing dotting the i's and crossing the t's on a breaking news story he planned to post on his political news website The Drudge Report, an endeavor which he had begun only a year ago. Drudge was by no means a reporter, but he also was not endowed with any special super computer science degree that made him any sharper than the next man in trying to build a political website from the ground up. In fact, up to that point Drudge's career had been irrefutably a farce, a makeshift resume consisting of nothing more than a handful of graveyard shifts at 7-Eleven and a position as a gift shop manager at CBS Studios. If you knew Drudge then, there was very little evidence that would have led you to believe that he was somebody who was on the verge of making history; and you most certainly would not have put your life on him being about to get rich and famous by typing up a few words on a website. But then again, none of us were Matt Drudge; and none of us were about to outfox every media organization in the country and break the news to the world that the President of the U.S. had been having an affair with a 23-year-old intern.

Over a decade later, history has come to confirm to us the impact of Drudge's revelation, as the Monica Lewinsky scandal has no doubt gone down in infamy as one of the most notorious moments in White House history. However, what is often left out of the narrative is what that scandal meant for Drudge and the many other budding web tacticians who would become inspired by his groundbreaking scoop. Although Drudge's days as an obscure bit player are long behind him thanks to the windfall of credibility spawned by the Lewinsky story, to digital revolutionists, his legacy will not be measured by the Drudge Report's meteoric rise or his impact on election campaigns. Instead, he will be best remembered for arguably becoming one of Internet's first prominent blogger forefathers; he was a regular Joe who cracked the initial chinks in the armor of the media establishment and gave palpability to the prospect that technology could help everyday citizens take back ownership of what they were being exposed to.

Today the idea of a more democratic media experience is now being realized in stunning ways that even Drudge himself probably could not have imagined. On a domestic level, more Americans now receive their news from the Internet than any other form of media, including long-time fixtures such as newspapers and radio outlets (Gross 2010). Globally, news aggregation sites operated by companies such as Google and Yahoo are outpacing the traffic of recognized organizational websites run by the likes of CNN and *The New York Times* (Schonfeld 2009). These deductions, while arguably broad and varying to some degree, call to attention a massive shift in behavior, one that, with the rise of Web 2.0 and the phenomenon of social media, has opened up the feasibility of a more informed and incessantly connected society. Furthermore, this change highlights an immense modification in the relationship between those who consume the media and those in the press who have traditionally held the power to produce it (Bowman and Wills 2003; Shirky 2009). In the digital age, consumers no longer adhere to being just sideline observers; they instead also increasingly assume the duty of contributors and producers as well (Bowman and Willis 2003; Shirky 2009). Using the enhanced capability of mobile phones and smart applications, people now have the ability to react and report what they see to massive audiences in little or no time at all, on occasion even breaking a few of them in a Drudge-like fashion before mainstream news organizations get the chance (Bowman and Willis 2003; Shirky 2009).

Whether we are vlogging (blogging a video), tweeting or posting a picture, or tagging and poking a friend, the digital actions that we have come to embrace so effortlessly are readily transforming the way we understand our world, and moving beyond functioning as merely leisurely diversion (Bowman and Willis 2003; Shirky 2009). In media-starved countries, these tools of innovation are creating important levers against censorship and refashioning spaces for political organization and debate (Diamond 2010). In democratic environments, these same tools are challenging media organizations to be held more accountable, while furthermore inducing a mandate to produce valuable journalistic collaboration between citizens and professionals (Bowman and Willis 2003; Carr 2010). With so much new freedom at our disposal, and an unbridled treasure trove of information within our grasp, the era of a media and information system piloted by the people and for the people is clearly here. All we need to do now is simply sit back and enjoy the Wi-Fi.

"Easy Does It"

When we try to visualize the history of media and how they have evolved overtime, there is always a technological dimension that can be accounted for that pushes the needle forward and consequently revolutionizes how people acquire and share their knowledge (Bowman and Willis 2003; Shirky 2009). According to tech guru Clay Shirky (2009), most media and communication devices used throughout the twentieth century have been disseminated by "one-to-one" and "one to many" distributions. Print publications, television programs, or films, Shirky (2009) says, were considered "one-to-many" media because they were viewed and absorbed by many people, but only could be consumed exclusively over the course of one sitting. Inventions such as the telephone or its predecessor the telegraph, on the other hand, were by contrast "one-to-one" media, since they involved the one-on-one communication between two people (Shirky 2009). The subsequent invention and evolution of the Internet over the past 20 years has by Shirky's (2009) estimations eradicated those patterns of distribution we all came to recognize as the standard modes of communication and knowledge acquisition. Where once before the distribution of information was either "one-to-one" or "one-to-many," the Internet in its consolidated form had in effect created a new "many-to-many" paradigm of communication and conversation (Shirky 2009). This development Shirky (2009) states has created a situation where the media we gain knowledge from are now right "next door" to the devices we use to communicate with one another. It is a defining moment that Shirky (2009) says had led to "the largest increase of expressive capability in human history," an era where infinite number of people are able to experience more than one medium simultaneously, and can communicate and share their sentiments about those experiences all in one huge hub.

As technology and the Internet have matured, the efficiency of the "many-to-many" pattern has no doubt turned the net into an open forum for public self-expression and uninhibited idea generation (Shirky 2009). The introduction of new innovations as well as the evolution of Web 2.0 have furthermore also altered societal perceptions of the value of the net as an informational tool and reputable outlet for knowledge sharing (Anderson and Wolff 2010). In recent years the explosion of the web log, or as it is otherwise known in today's lexicon, the "blog," has given online users new personalized media to both express themselves and interact with others through the sharing of thoughts and common interests (Bowman and Willis 2003). As the mainstream appeal of blog culture has risen, the demand for more online environments driven around social connection and conversation has also naturally grown as well, with them eventually making their way into the practical technologies of daily living (Anderson and Wolff 2010). The transformation of the Internet and the Web itself, from strictly an item of the domestic home into one accessible through devices such as touch screen tablets and multipurpose mobile phones, has no doubt aided in the evolution of the net as a tool for newsgathering and individual self-expression (Anderson and Wolff 2010). Seminal inventions such as Apple's iPhone have clearly set the standard in this regard, institutionalizing through its ubiquity the feasibility of absorbing and creating multiple forms of media on the go and at all waking moments of the day (Anderson and Wolff 2010). With smart phone technology swiftly turning into a societal addiction, the act of documenting life has now become cultural activity, and with it has taken the workflow of self-expression completely into the realm of social convention (Anderson and Wolff 2010).

As a result of the smart phone insurgency, the value of social media platforms as viable online centers for more consolidated content sharing experiences has become more widely accepted as both leisure devices and the go-to forums for communication and informational exchange. At 550 million users and growing, Facebook is the undisputed Big Kahuna of the social media movement, a network that, when you put it in perspective, has taken Shirky's "many-to-many" pattern and amalgamated it even further into a network experience comprising strictly the people we know or are acquainted with (Bosker 2010). The success of Facebook has been accredited to a number of things, but its strongest selling point is that it offers users the virtues of a media experience built around the social experience, and it does it in an addicting and entertaining way (Friedman 2010). Interestingly enough, in many respects Facebook and the social network in general are the optimization of Internet maturation, a homogenization of not just the best of what the net has to offer, but of what technology and Web 2.0 have given us over the years as well (Friedman 2010). To the die-hards who use Facebook, the site is not just a network; it is a community, a place where you can practically explore your infatuations at will and by the same token seemingly learn through osmosis from the people who you aspire to be in the company of the most (Bowman and Willis 2003; Shirky 2009).

Citizen Change

By now we have already dwelled on some of the advantages that a more Internet-driven media has had in cultivating a society more prone to informational conversation. However, what exactly are its advantages as an actual journalistic practice? Unlike civic journalism, which involves more collaboration between professionals and the general public, acts of citizen journalism are entirely independent (Bowman and Willis 2003). Under these conditions, average Joes and Joans are completely in charge of "collecting, reporting, analyzing and disseminating news and information" all on their own, without the presence of any higher authority or editorial oversight (Bowman and Willis 2003). Owing to the varied scope of responsibility and the lack of resources available at the genesis of the Internet, leisurely taking on the role of a citizen journalist was considered a daunting and aggravating task. Today, however, thanks to the wealth of knowledge available on the Internet and the speed with which it can be attained, the gap between the corporate-bred journalist and the stay at home opinion-maker is no longer as Brobdingnagian as it once was (Bowman and Willis 2003).

As people with no monetary attachment or brand name affiliation, citizen journalists operate entirely on their own volition, motivated by the freedom of free speech and inspired by the opportunity to share their passions with a broad audience (Bowman and Willis 2003). This development and expansion in human effusion has not necessarily made the job of media professionals expendable in terms of breaking news, but what it has done rather is give under-reported issues greater exposure and larger stories an opportunity to be revitalized and refashioned in an entirely new approach for online audiences (Bowman and Willis 2003). As soon as the mainstream media reports on a story, citizen journalists can turn to a number of platforms to disseminate an opinion or add depth to an existing piece produced by commercial media (Bowman and Willis 2003). If the networks in which they share these opinions are vast, other readers might catch wind and contribute their own insights and perspectives to the post, enriching both the learning experience of the readers and those of the users who took the time to build on the initial information.

This is of course an action frequently seen in the blog format, where one photo or a blurb can elicit a chain of responses from anonymous users and interested parties. Although there is no circumventing the occasional ineptitudes effused by the obnoxious rant, anonymous feedback can be quite productive in online debate, as people not only can express their feelings to the blog's author on that particular subject, but can also draw that blogger's attention to other dimensions related to that story (Bowman and Willis 2003).

How Tweet it Is

While the blog format does offer tremendous potential for joint collaboration among citizens, an offspring phenomenon that has emerged in recent years as an even greater example is the ascendance of the social networking site Twitter. In terms of membership, Twitter by no means supersedes the size and diversity of a network such as Facebook; however, what it lacks in numbers, it clearly makes us for in the niche role it has taken on as an informational tool for citizen bloggers and working journalists alike.[1] In contrast to the cumbersome nature of standard text-driven blogs, micro-blogs such as Twitter require brevity (you cannot post anything longer than 140 characters). Although users do have the ability to customize their background, add a photo, or change the color of the text that appears on their page, Twitter requires very little in the way of advanced web design skills or expert understandings of HTML5. In Twitterverse, the appeal lies in the minimalism and intuitiveness. All of the posts that appear available to a user materialize in a constantly updating news stream, a feed that is composed strictly of organizations, people, and groups that a given user has chosen selectively to subscribe to or "follow." While there are private accounts that do require a user's approval beforehand, most people who use Twitter take fun from the fact that

1 As of October 2010, Twitter had an estimated 175 million users. It had reportedly gained 70 million users since April of that year (Rao 2010).

anyone, even if they do not know them, can follow whatever they say or publicly subscribe to their musings; an advantage that is noticeably absent from more privatized forums of communication such as email (Grossman 2009). On Twitter it is not out of the ordinary to see someone tracking the likes of President Barack Obama or Miley Cyrus, while on the same page receiving updates from groups such as Amnesty International or news organizations such as Al Jazeera. From a journalistic standpoint, the resulting payoff is a resource *à la carte* of information and opinion, an environment where the headlines from media organizations and publications from all over the world are just as accessible as the personal ruminations and announcements of public figures, celebrities, and corporate entities.

The dynamic of the Twitter experience, however, is not just defined by the amount of information available and how it is presented, but by its inherent features and unique rules of engagement. Perhaps the most essential trademark of the site is a feature called the "retweet," an ode of attribution that allows users to forward and republish headlines, statements, and stories they come across to other Twitter users in and out of their network. Shameless self-promotion and frivolity notwithstanding, retweeting by all intents has become the contemporary equivalent of what used to be a radio news flash or a TV network's interruption of a regularly scheduled program. Retweets are most visible especially when executed by established reporters and tweeters, particularly when they involve the promulgation of breaking news events such as natural disasters or terrorist attacks. At the end of retweets, regular users will sometimes "hash-tag" their contributions by adding a pound sign followed by the desired subject of their post. The zeitgeist of the practice derives from the notion that every tweet can be classified or cataloged by one word or a mash-up of expressions. If given enough play, the subjects that are the most retweeted and hash-tagged make their way into Twitter's trending topics list, a curated top-10 directory that reflects what users in a specific city, country, continent, or even around the world are talking about. The trending topics list, although on occasion fickle and trivial, more often than not serves as a virtual barometer for the cultural pulse of various societies, acting as a source for citizen journalists and working professionals aiming to keep tabs on a story.

Besides "retweeting" and "hash-tagging," Twitter's value as an informational search engine is emboldened by the presence of a classification tool called Twitter Lists, a feature that allows tweeters to organize users by directories according to specific interests. It is the kind of idiosyncrasy that makes triaging messages from political reporters at *The Washington Post* or gathering tweets from, let us say, only emerging market business writers in the UK, literally a walk in the park. What makes "Lists" furthermore significant is that it is not just an apparatus being embraced by nonprofessionals, but an asset that is additionally being adopted by news organizations and industry professionals. The upshot has been a dynamic that has been doubly advantageous to both seasoned veterans and news junkies alike, giving wannabe bloggers an opportunity to collectively mine the thought stream and headlines of their favorite professionals while vice versa giving mainstream media producers a chance to connect and converse with the people who share an interest in their work.

Today Twitter's place as a media staple has reached such a threshold that it is nearly impossible to find a person, especially one working in journalism, who is not at least casually mindful of its potential for tapping into dialogue imparted by colleagues and citizens across the globe. Unfortunately, owing to the nonchalant nature of the platform and the overall nascent novelty of social media, consensus regarding the journalistic efficacy of using posts found in networks such as Twitter remain tendentious, especially in view of the capricious and anonymous nature of average tweeters and the lack of veracity surrounding various posts.

Despite the controversies that may exist, the significance of social media and their penchant for producing invaluable citizen media particularly during moments of crisis have already proven to have their merits (Shirky 2009). When speaking of watershed moments, media observers often reference the Mumbai terrorist attacks of 2008 as a turning point for citizen journalism (Stelter and Cohen 2008).[2] A few days after the start of the crisis, writers Brian Stelter and Noem Cohen of *The New York Times*, described citizen journalism as a surprise blessing that filled the gap for a mainstream media in flux.[3] All over the net residents and tourists in Mumbai blogged about the events on personal sites, posting videos of the disaster on YouTube, and photo streams from the ground on websites such as Flickr (Schachtman 2008; Stelter and Cohen 2008). The most compelling coverage of all, however, came remarkably from trapped victims inside the hotel Taj Mahal, who in spite of duress, courageously managed to send photos and videos to news networks, and text messages to reporters on the outside (Stelter and Cohen 2008). The imagery and reporting produced by these individuals were so captivating that big name outlets such as CNN and mainstream blogs such as Wired's Danger Room, had no choice but to run some of the material themselves on their own platforms (Schachtman 2008; Stelter and Cohen 2008). The wave of social media dominance during these wild moments was particularly a coup for Twitter, which all of a sudden found itself to be as much of a crucial news source to "Hasidic Jews in Brooklyn tracking the fate of a rabbi held hostage" as to "students in Britain with loved ones back in India" (Stelter and Cohen 2008).[4]

Fun and Gains?

As we become more proficient in our ability to access and spread information, there is an existing theory that persists that a more connected citizenry does not necessarily always translate to a more conscious and socially active one (Gladwell 2010). Even as phenomena such as Mumbai reveal to us the auspicious potential of these technologies, the overall capability of social media and citizen reporting as viable instruments for organizing authentic activism remains tempered by the perception that in the end they are no more than devices of mere recreation (Gladwell 2010; Gurak and Antonijevic 2008; Nordenson 2008). In fact, when abstracting the contemporary Internet and social media experience, rarely do we ever arguably come across tasks online that are devoid of any semblance of leisure or do not eventually lead to an engagement that somehow tempts us to diversion (Bowman and Willis 2003; Nordenson 2008). It is for precisely this reason that best-selling authors such as Malcolm Gladwell (2010) have come to doubt the true power of online communities and social media as legitimate tools for organizing social mobilization. According to Gladwell (2010) these platforms are useful only in "low-risk" situations, where anonymity and "weak ties" between community members can work to the benefit of a particular cause. This is part of the rationale behind why he believes we join a Facebook group on human rights suggested to us by a friend or are out of the blue compelled to make a "Cause" page for starving kids in Africa (Gladwell 2010; Gurak and Antonijevic 2008). We obviously do so because on some level we do

2 Interestingly enough, writer James Surowiecki (2005) has suggested that the 2005 photo and video documentation of the Indonesian tsunamis was one of the first appearances of citizen journalism in the post Web 2.0 environment.

3 During the third day of the crisis, CNN's transmission license ran out and could only allow for live updates to be given via the phone (Stelter and Cohen 2008).

4 Reportedly, at the height of violence, "more than one message per second with the word Mumbai in it was being posted onto the site" (Stelter and Cohen 2008).

care, but we also choose to make these efforts because, at the end of the day, there really is no commitment demanded of us (Gladwell 2010; Gurak and Antonijevic 2008). Social networks and online media, after all, are typically informal stages (Gladwell 2010; Gurak and Antonijevic 2008). Similar to the beginnings of a new relationship, they are normally uncomplicated, easy, and more than ever driven by innocent fun (Gurak and Antonijevic 2008). Thus, as much as we might like to believe that the entire universe would fall apart if we did not post a new blog entry or write a new status update on Facebook, any conscious and realistic user of these media understands that ultimately nobody really dies if you decide to abandon your page for a day or neglect it entirely for the rest of your life (Bowman and Willis 2003; Gurak and Antonijevic 2008).

Gladwell (2010) asserts that this lack of emotional investment or feigned solidarity that is often evident in social media and online communities simply cannot fly when put under the pressure of more "high-risk" affairs, particularly in mobilizations where "stronger ties" are much more crucial against stalwart opposition. He explains that, over the long haul, tangible and more invested forms of organization apparent in eras such as the American civil rights movements of the 1960s are far more potent when juxtaposed with the inadequate and feigned communities of contemporary Internet culture (Gladwell 2010).

Boycotts and sit-ins and nonviolent confrontations—which were the weapons of choice for the civil-rights movement—are high-risk strategies. They leave little room for conflict and error. The moment even one protester deviates from the script and responds to provocation, the moral legitimacy of the entire protest is compromised. Enthusiasts for social media would no doubt have us believe that Martin Luther King's task in Birmingham would have been made infinitely easier had he been able to communicate with his followers through Facebook, and contented himself with tweets from a Birmingham jail. However, networks are messy: think of the ceaseless pattern of correction and revision, amendment and debate that characterizes Wikipedia. If Martin Luther King Jr had tried to do a wiki-boycott in Montgomery, he would have been steamrollered by the white power structure. And of what use would a digital communication tool be in a town where 98% of the black community could be reached every Sunday morning at church? The things that King needed in Birmingham—discipline and strategy—were things that online social media cannot provide (Gladwell 2010).

That said, Gladwell's denigrators, although admittedly cognizant of the narcissist and self-serving festival that social media often promulgate, are still not ready to paint every person who logs on to Facebook with the same brush (Popper 2010). In spite of every status update that harps on about American Idol results or is planted for the sole purpose of ramping up sympathy over a bad hair day, there are still instances when social media and new technology can offer us impassioned opinion or contribute something worthwhile (Diamond 2010; Shirky 2009). In fact, when we start to scrutinize it on a global level, one does not have to look very far to find instances where the viability and versatility of contemporary technology has revolutionized the way people are participating in original forms of activism (Diamond 2010).

Over the course of the last decade, the utilization of cellular phones and text messaging services in politically charged countries such as Ukraine and the Philippines has already displayed the basic feasibility of technology as a credible medium for organizing large-scale protests against fraudulent government (Barry 2009; Diamond 2010). The use of cell phones and text messaging proved to be effective in organizing post-election protests in countries such as Ukraine in 2004 and Belarus in 2006 (Barry 2009). In 2001, massive rallies organized via SMS texting were also credited in helping oust then Philippine President Joseph Estrada, who at the time refused to give up his seat despite widespread allegations of corruption (Burton 2001; Diamond 2009). Since then, technological evolution has dramatically continued to improve, and with it so have the means by which citizens have been able to mobilize in various societies throughout the world (Diamond 2010). One prime example of a unique undertaking can be found in the African nation of Kenya, where in 2008, citizen bloggers and software developers put their heads together and launched *Ushahdi*, a website dedicated to mapping post-election violence (Diamond 2010; Giridharadas 2010). *Ushahdi*, which in Swahili means "witness," became a popular destination in the weeks following the presidential election, as it became a "crisis-map" constructed mainly from the violations reported by Kenyan citizens via text message and email (Diamond 2010; Giridharadas 2010). The information transmitted on *Ushahdi* proved to be a blessing for the Kenyan authorities and citizens, as it provided a digital canvas of reported rapes and murders and served as a vital tool for geo-tagging the locations of displaced refugees (Diamond 2010; Giridharadas 2010). Since its success in Kenya, the site has eventually gone on to be adopted to monitor potential hotbed elections in countries like Afghanistan and Mexico, while also serving as a useful geo-tagging apparatus for detecting the whereabouts of trapped victims during the 2010 earthquake in Haiti (Diamond 2010; Giridharadas 2010).

Enemy of the State

One of the bedrocks of Gladwell's (2010) critique of social media and informational technology revolves on the notion that productive activism cannot be produced in an ethos where offhand conversation and anonymous interaction are constants. Nevertheless, one should consider that the same traits that make these interactions seem so trivial to nonbelievers such as Gladwell are by nature the same characteristics that make them pliable and invaluable in countries where dissenting opinion is often suppressed (Diamond 2010). No event epitomized the zenith of this influence more than the 2009 Iranian presidential elections, where following the announcement of incumbent Mahmoud Ahmadinejad's unanimous victory, social networks became one of the core centers of post-election organization and protest (Diamond 2010; Stone and Cohen 2010). In fact, the importance of Twitter as a source of unfiltered media reached such a level that at one juncture the U.S. State Department reportedly requested that the company delay performing overnight maintenance on the site, so that Iranians and interested parties around the globe could continue to log on and keep track of the developments (Musgrove 2009). Just as it had done less than a year before in the aftermath of the Mumbai attacks, Twitter once became a focal gateway site for real-time citizen updates, media coverage, and personal accounts of the ensuing violence (Diamond 2010; Stone and Cohen 2010). What made Twitter's impact more meaningful this time around, however, was that the environment in which the conflict was occurring happened not in a nascent democratic country such as India, but in a state such as Iran, where the promotion of democratic ideals had been historically easy to quell (Diamond 2010).[5] Over the years, the Iranian government had grown accustomed to squashing opposition movements, routinely finding success in controlling the lines of communication between organizers and their associates by shutting down

5 Despite widespread media proclamations that the success of Iran's Green Revolution was aided by Twitter, it must be noted that various journalists have insinuated that this assumption has been greatly exaggerated (Esfandiari 2010). Foreign Policy writer Golnaz Ensfandiari claims that many of the key news breakers and organizers who received major attention on Twitter were unfortunately stationed outside of the country and rarely relayed their information in Farsi, a communicative failure that certainly would have impeded those in Iran who lacked English fluency. Esfandiari (2010) furthermore mentions that information purported to be by insiders on Twitter in the midst of the crisis, was lacking in credibility and accuracy.

mobile phone lines, putting a screeching halt to text message services, and furthermore blocking websites used by rival groups to disseminate opposition rhetoric (Musgrove 2009).

When post-election protests picked up steam in 2009 and everyone began turning to websites such as Twitter, few in Iran's government doubted that there would be any real difficulty in ultimately censoring the site (Musgrove 2009). Unfortunately for them and to the benefit of Iran's cyber activists, the social network's setup proved to be far more resilient than initially perceived (Musgrove 2009). To aid matters, people did not have to log on to Twitter's homepage to post; they could do so through mobile text message, or by virtue of various software apps that allowed users to post from partner-owned sites (Musgrove 2009; Stone and Cohen 2009). Although Iran did have the ability to disable text messaging in certain parts of the country, blocking off Twitter's reach completely required that the government either shut down text messaging throughout the entire country, or specifically weed out rebel texters individually, two procedures that in the midst of a large-scale revolution were laborious challenges (Musgrove 2009). Of further detriment to Iran's IT armies, was the anonymous and brazen conduct of pro-Twitter freedom fighters, who at the height of the protests kept opening up new proxy servers where Twitter and other social media sites could be accessed from (Kralev 2009).

Besides tweeting, Iranian citizens found other unprecedented ways to use technology to circumvent the censors of state-run media. With the lack of international outlets able to report from the country at the time of the protests owing to state restrictions, many Iranians filled this void by using the basic technology of mobile phone cameras to document the unfolding drama (Diamond 2010). One of the more prominent and seminal pieces of footage to surface from these pursuits was a 37-second mobile phone clip taken of an Iranian woman being gunned down by a state sniper during the middle of a protest (Diamond 2010; Stelter 2010). As the story goes, the clip went viral after a doctor in Iran who had obtained the video supposedly sent it to several friends he knew abroad who he believed could sidestep the auspices of Iran's Internet filters and post it to popular sites such as YouTube and Facebook (Stelter 2010). The dissemination of the killing, which within days was picked up and broadcasted by major organizations like CNN and the BBC, became a harrowing reminder to the rest the world that the tensions had indeed hit a boiling point (Diamond 2010; Stelter 2010). Further, the video instantly also made a martyr of the victim, Neda Agha-Soltan, and in succession further inspired the opposition cause (Diamond 2010; Stelter 2010). Although to this day the identity of the doctor and the actual cameraman who shot the film, as well as those of his accomplices who distributed and uploaded the file, remain undisclosed, the legacy of the video continues to live on as a reminder of the power of citizen activism and what can be achieved within the panorama of new media (Diamond 2010; Stelter 2010).

Another country that often is lumped into the same category as Iran when it comes to censorship and informational control is obviously China, a territory that in the realm of the Internet has earned a reputation for its stringent and efficient methods of content filtration (Diamond 2010). Throughout the last 10 years, China has invested hundreds of millions of dollars in keeping its net borders clean of content incongruent to the state's message, with the end product being the Golden Shield Project, or as it has been coined in cultural lexicon, China's "Great Firewall" (August 2007).[6] While the government would probably choose to describe Golden Shield's directives with a euphemism akin to net purification, the "Great Firewall," make no mistake about it, was invented for the sole purpose of seeking and destroying (August 2007). With thousands of scanners and an endless supply of human eyes at its disposal, China's surveillance of the web is a finely tuned

6 The Golden Shield project reportedly cost $700 million dollars and took eight years to make (August 2007).

machine, an around the clock panopticon where the slightest mention of the word "democracy" and the smallest flirtation with hot buttons topics such as Tibet or Tiananmen Square are quickly subject to adjustment (August 2007; Diamond 2010). Under the watchful eye of the firewall, dissenting bloggers are targeted, probed, and jailed; emails are scanned with careful deliberation; and suspicious posts do not live for more than two days (August 2007; Diamond 2010). Add to that the fact that social media titans such as Facebook, Twitter, and YouTube have already been banned or obstructed from public access, and the issue of China's Internet freedoms has in short order become a topic of great international intrigue and debate (August 2007; Diamond 2010; Singel and Kravets 2010).

Regardless of these hardline measures, China's quest for draconian control of the net within recent years has become much more difficult owing to the globalization of social media and the increasingly egalitarian disposition of contemporary technology (Diamond 2010; Ramzy 2010). As China's Internet faithful have learned to adapt to the government's techniques, citizen activism on the net, whether it is in protest for online freedoms or in relation to politically sensitive subjects, has progressively found its way, even if only ephemerally, onto the screens of laptops and PCs all over the country (August 2007; Diamond 2010). Hackers and brave engineers have helped the movement by creating specialized software that evades censors and establishes "secure connections" from which people can communicate (August 2007). In certain instances, some software tools are even developed by embargoed religious groups in China, such as Tibet's Falun Gong (August 2007). Nowadays bloggers and organizers are continually using the speed of the net and strength in numbers to exploit loopholes around the sensors, keeping conversation alive by re-blogging and reposting major news stories from site to site (Diamond 2010). After the 2008 earthquake in Sichuan province, online activism of this kind was especially evident, as Chinese activists took to the net as a way of exposing corruption amongst local officials that had resulted in the shoddy construction of dozens of schools, which collapsed in the earthquake and killed thousands of children (Ford 2010). Tan Zuoren, a Chinese activist and one of the leaders of the investigation, set up an online database that listed the names of all the school children who perished in the earthquake; stoking resentment amongst one-child-policy parents who had lost their only heir that the government had indeed left their children for dead (Ford 2010; Shirky 2009). The reaction and protests that ensued were so immense that officials began offering compensation to families to prevent them from suing, but at the end of the day, online transparency had won (Ford 2010; Shirky 2009). In a sad testament to the effectiveness of his efforts, Zuoren was eventually sentenced in February 2010 to five years in prison for what Chinese officials called "incitement to subversion" (Ford 2010).

The actions of people like Zuoren have no doubt proven that China's citizenry has exhibited a resilient fearlessness in their attempts to attain a more democratic society. Moreover, what we are also witnessing is that, as the stakes grow higher, they are gradually receiving a huge vote of support from the companies whose systems they have come to be liberated by (Diamond 2010; Singel and Kravets 2010). In January 2010, the plausibility of this axiom was fully realized when reports surfaced that China had hacked into the systems of search engine giant Google and stolen intellectual property (Diamond 2010; Zetter 2010). Even more glaring a discovery than the breach itself was that Google had not only been hacked, but the G-mail accounts of two human rights activists who had used the service were also compromised in the attack (Zetter 2010). In an act of protest and defiance, Google put their relationship with the Chinese government on the line and allowed uncensored searches on its Chinese site, a move that signified that Google was not afraid to issue payback for the contravention of its systems (Singel and Kravets 2010). Following the back and forth backlash, concerns began to surface that Google would have no choice but to leave

China entirely, rendering the biggest pool of Internet users (384 million and counting) in the world abandoned and once again victimized by government policy (Singel and Kravets 2010). Reaction to these rumors set off a huge wave of panic and protests among China's web faithful, as in its short time in the country, Google had indeed come to establish itself as a more benevolent expurgator of information compared with other search engines available in the country (Diamond 2010; Singel and Kravets 2010).[7] Although Google did eventually agree to stay in China for at least the short term, its future as a result of the fiasco currently still remains in the air (Diamond 2010; Singel and Kravets 2010). Nevertheless, to the cheerleaders of new media, Google's response was interpreted as a sign that large corporations were ready to stand in allegiance next to the common "netizen" in the war on censorship, and moreover be willing to sacrifice dollars to do so (Diamond 2010; Singel and Kravets 2010).

Wiki or Won't He?

Owing to the vast evolution of technology, it goes without saying that our expectations regarding what citizens are able to accomplish on a macro scale has been significantly redefined amidst the digital revolution (Carr 2010). Perhaps no man is more of the moment in pushing this envelope than WikiLeaks founder Julian Assange. For those who have been sleeping under a rock for the past year and have only woken up yesterday, Assange is a former hacker turned pioneer truth seeker, turned government enemy no. 1 (Carr 2010). In 2006, Assange and a devoted team of hackers/specialists started WikiLeaks, a whistle-blowing website, with the sole purpose of acquiring and publishing classified government documents, images, and videos on the Internet (Khatchadourian 2010). In the beginning, Assange's releases were an entertaining grab bag of provocative content, with reports ranging from the exposure of Kenyan president Daniel Erap Moi's funneling of government funds, to the hit-worthy postings that were Sarah Palin's emails (Khatchadourian 2010). In April 2010, Assange made his first mainstream media splash when he leaked footage of a U.S. Apache helicopter attack in Baghdad in 2007 (Carr 2010; Thompson 2010). Assange titled the video "Collateral Murder," a label that brought as much attention as it did YouTube hits (Thompson 2010). The footage, which shows the Apache brutally firing on unarmed bystanders and what turned out to be two employees who worked for the international news organization Reuters, was a shocking reminder to the public of the raw nature of war, but to the Pentagon and others within the U.S. government it was a sign that Assange was about to become a headache (Thompson 2010). In July and October Assange followed the Apache release up with the controversial publishing of confidential field reports from Iraq and Afghanistan, releasing the names of the informants in the leak and shedding exclusive light on two of the most hotly debated wars in U.S. history (Coll 2010). The trepidation had barely worn off from the previous seven months of leaks when Assange moved forward on his biggest coup to date, a November 2010 release of select documents from a collection of over 250,000 U.S. diplomatic cables (Coll 2010). The cables, which in exhaustive detail essentially aired America's intimate sentiments about the rest of the world, came to be pegged by media observers as the most important journalistic leak since the Pentagon Papers in the 1970s (Carr 2010). The release of the cables set off a plethora of polarized reactions, garnering Assange a mix of vitriol and praise (Alford 2010). To American detractors and the techie elite, he

7 Google also gained support for tagging all forbidden searches with a pop up notification that told users that the topic in question had been blocked, a feature that over time turned into a dependable advisory for China's users on what the government was censoring from the public (Singel and Kravets 2010).

was a God, a vigilante who had used the gifts of the new media landscape to convey the truth to the masses and bring big government to its knees (Carr 2010; Collett-White 2010). After Assange released the cables, the funding future of WikiLeaks came into question with many companies such as Amazon, Mastercard, and Paypal backing out from allowing payments and donations to the site. In a extraordinary development, hacker activists reacted by attacking and blocking access to the sites allegedly involved in boycotting donations (Vance and Helft 2010). To those at the top in Washington, however, Assange was nothing more than a rogue provocateur, a man who was putting not only national security at risk, but was also endangering the people he exposed to retaliation and retribution (Carr 2010).

Since the release of the cables, the prospect of prosecuting Assange and trying him for treason has become ardent legal and constitutional fodder. Nevertheless, contrastive arguments from the journalism community, in particular, have voiced concern about the slippery slope that could be crossed if that day indeed comes (Carr 2010). Long-time writers such as George Packard believe that prosecuting Assange would "set a terrible precedent," since it would be legally too much of a challenge to try to delineate the "difference between what WikiLeaks did and what news organizations do" on an everyday basis (Carr 2010). Additionally, there is also an issue of complicity that must all be considered, since Assange shared the cables with international publications such as *El Pais*, *La Monde*, *The Guardian*, and *Der Spiegel* before their release (Carr 2010). All in all, from a journalistic perspective, Assange's work no matter the means, is generally viewed as yet another seminal chapter in the movement known as citizen journalism and Internet activism (Carr 2010). Although some people do not know what the future holds for WikiLeaks organizationally, especially in light of Assange's legal troubles and recent arrests for alleged rape and sexual assault, tech pundit Evgeny Morozov hopes that the site will ultimately serve as example of what collaborative citizen and mainstream investigative journalism could be in the future (Carr 2010; Morozov 2010). In Morozov's optimal paradigm, leakers and news organizations will constantly be finding ways to share documents between each other, so that regional experts and journalists can interpret their meanings and write about them in greater depth (Carr 2010; Morozov 2010). This relationship, just like in the case of "Cable-Gate," could in turn be extremely beneficial for the overall publicity and coverage of the leaks themselves, allowing the information to be packaged in a more commercial way to broader audiences (Carr 2010).

Conclusion

Our current digital revolution, which in many ways is a phenomenon of both societal acceptance and technological brilliance, has brought with it a new spirit of possibility and optimism. Human communication and socialization through these new mechanisms, although at times consuming and overwhelming, have put a cultural premium on knowledge sharing and individual gratification. The aftermath of a society more open to transparency and new forms of media, has galvanized those who have embraced their adoption, while seemingly antagonizing and frustrating the conventional classes of the vanguard, who are constantly bewildered by the strength of egalitarian fortitude and the originality of citizen activism.

The profession of journalism, which so long held the onus of being the watchdog pillar of the general public, has not so much been replaced by the techie generation as it has been forced to adapt because of it; whether each side wants to admit it or not, the futures of the unofficial reporter and the mainstream media member both hinge on their abilities to accept the presence of the other. As social media platforms continue to grow and technologically fluent enterprisers like

Julian Assange proceed to redesign the framework of what we can consider tenable journalism, the need for mainstream organizations to verify and legitimize these works on a commercial level will always be a necessity in helping separate fiction from fact. On the other side of the coin, traditional news outlets must be willing to seek out and understand these technologies and the people who use them more extensively, so that story opportunities are not lost and greater depth of coverage can be obtained.

Moving forward, many challenges seemingly lie ahead for us as we continue to constantly adapt and acclimatize ourselves to an environment where the rules of social interaction and public communication are constantly being re-written by innovation and human valor. Although the days of total privacy and latent secrecy may be behind us, there is an exciting sense of affection for the new and unprecedented ways technology has glocalized our existence. No system can ever be perfect nor can it ever be permanent, but right now, at this very movement, you would be hard pressed to find someone that is not greatly liberated by the fact that today the opportunities to know what we want to know, how we come to know it, and our abilities to express why they matter to us; are greater than they have ever been at any point in history. If that is not cool, I really do not know what is.

References

Alford, C. 2010, "Whistle-blowing, redefined," *The New York Times*, 9 December. Available at: http://www.nytimes.com [accessed: 31 December 2010].

Anderson, C. and Wolff, M. 2010, *The Web is Dead. Long Live the Internet*. Available at: http://www.wired.com [accessed: 31 December 2010].

August, O. 2007, *The Great Firewall*. Available at: http://www.wired.com [accessed: 31 December 2010].

Barry, E. 2009, "Protests in Moldova explode, with help of Twitter," *The New York Times*, 7 April. Available at: http://www.nytimes.com [accessed: 31 December 2010].

Bosker, B. 2010. *Facebook Tops Google as Most Visited Website of the Year*. Available at: http://www.huffingtonpost.com [accessed: 31 December 2010].

Bowman, S. and Willis, C. 2003. *We Media: How Audiences are Shaping the Future of News and Media*. American Press Institute.

Burton, S. 2001, *People Power Redux*. Available at: http://www.time.com [accessed: 31 December 2010].

Carr, D. 2010, "WikiLeaks taps power of the press," *The New York Times*, 12 December. Available at: http://www.nytimes.com [accessed: 31 December 2010].

Coll, S. 2010, *Leaks*. Available at: http://www.newyorker.com [accessed: 31 December 2010].

Collett-White, M. 2010, *WikiLeaks, Web to Revolutionize Reporting: John Pilger*. Available at: http://abcnews.go.com [accessed: 31 December 2010].

Diamond, L. 2010, *Liberation Technology*. Baltimore, MD: The Johns Hopkins University Press, 21(3), 69–83. Available from: Project MUSE database [accessed: 31 December 2010].

Drudge Report: Blog. Available at: http://www.drudgereportarchives.com/data/2002/01/17/20020117_175502_ml.htm [accessed: 31 December 2010].

Esfandiari, G. 2010, *The Twitter Devolution*. Available at: http://www.foreignpolicy.com [accessed: 31 December 2010].

Ford, P. 2010, *China Sentences Quake Activist Tan Zuoren*. Available at: http://csmonitor.com [accessed: 31 December 2010].

Friedman, D. 2010. *The Viral Me*. Available at: http://www.gq.com/ [accessed: 31 December 2010].

Giridharadas, A. 2010. "Africa's gift to Silicon Valley: How to Track a Crisis," *The New York Times*, 13 March. Available at: http://www.nytimes.com [accessed: 31 December 2010].

Gladwell, M. 2010. *Small Change: Why the Revolution will not be Tweeted.* Available at: http://www.newyorker.com [accessed: 31 December 2010].

Gross, D. 2010, *Survey: More Americans get News from Internet than Newspapers or Radio*. Available at: http://articles.cnn.com/ [accessed: 31 December 2010].

Grossman, L. 2009. *Iran Protests: Twitter, the Medium of the Movement*. Available at: http://www.time.com [accessed: 1 August 2011].

Gurak, L. and Antonijevic, S. 2008, "The psychology of blogging: you, me, and everyone in between," *American Behavioral Scientist*, 52(1), 60–68. Available at: Academic Search Premier, EBSCO*host* [accessed: 31 December 2010].

Khatchadourian, R. 2010. "No secrets," *The New Yorker*, 7 June.

Kralev, N. 2009. "U.S. backs Iranian Web use," *The Washington Times*, 18 December.

Morozov, E. 2010. "Why it's hard to duplicate," *The New York Times*, 11 December. Available at: http://www.nytimes.com [accessed: 31 December 2010].

Musgrove, M. 2009. "Twitter is a player in Iran: State Dept. asked to keep site running," *The Washington Post*, 17 June. Available at: http://www.washingtonpost.com/ [accessed: 31 December 2010].

Nordenson, B. 2008, "Overload!," *Columbia Journalism Review*, 47(4), 30–32, 35–7, 40, 42. Available at: ABI/INFORM Global [accessed: 31 December 2010].

Popper, B. 2010. "Malcolm Gladwell compares Twitter activism to civil rights". *The New York Observer*, 27 September. Available at: http://www.observer.com/ [accessed: 31 December 2010].

Ramzy, A. 2010. *The Great Firewall: China's Web Users Battle Censorship*. Available at: http://www.time.com [accessed: 31 December 2010].

Rao, L. 2010. *Twitter Added 30 Million Users in the Past Two Months*. Available at: http://techcrunch.com [accessed: 31 December 2010].

Schachtman, N. 2008. "Mumbai attack aftermath detailed, Tweet by Tweet," 26 November. *Danger Room: Blog*. Available at: http://www.wired.com/dangerroom/2008/11/first-hand-acco/ [accessed: 31 December 2010].

Schonfeld, E. 2009. *More People Around the World get their News Online from Google News than CNN*. Available at: http://techcrunch.com [accessed: 31 December 2010].

Shirky, C. 2005, "Clay Shirky on institutions vs. collaboration" (video file). Available at: http://www.ted.com/talks/clay_shirky_on_institutions_versus_collaboration.html [accessed: 31 December 2010].

Shirky, C. 2010. "Tapping the cognitive surplus," *Futurist*, 44(6), 21–2. Available at: Business Source Premier, EBSCO*host* [accessed: 31 December 2010].

Singel, R. and Kravets, D. 2010. *Only Google Could Leave China*. Available at: http://www.wired.com. [accessed: 31 December 2010].

Singh, T. 2009. *How Social Media Was Used During the Mumbai Attacks*. Available at: http://www.ngonlinenews.com [accessed: 31 December 2010].

Stelter, B. 2010. "Honoring Citizen Journalists," *The New York Times*, 21 February. Available at: http://www.nytimes.com [accessed: 31 December 2010].

Stelter, B. and Cohen, N. 2008. "Citizen journalists provided glimpses of Mumbai Attacks," *The New York Times*, 30 November. Available at: http://www.nytimes.com [accessed: 31 December 2010].

Stone, B. and Cohen, N. 2010. "Social networks spread defiance online", *The New York Times*, 15 June. Available at: http://www.nytimes.com [accessed: 31 December 2010].

Surowiecki, J. 2005. "James Surowiecki: when social media became news" (video file). Available at: http://www.ted.com/talks/lang/eng/james_surowiecki_on_the_turning_point_for_social_media.html [accessed: 21 February 2010].

Thompson, M. 2010. *Combat Video: The Pentagon Springs a WikiLeak*. Available at: http://www.time.com [accessed: 31 December 2010].

Vance, A. and Helft, M. 2010. "Hackers give web companies a test of free speech," *The New York Times*, 8 December. Available at: http://www.nytimes.com [accessed: 31 December 2010].

Zetter, M. 2010. *Report Details Hacks Targeting Google, Other*. Available at: http://www.wired.com [accessed: 31 December 2010].

Chapter 26

VIEWPOINT:
Old and New Media: Picket Fences Until the End

Sujit Bhar

Introduction

The news media today can rarely afford to try to change society. It has to change *with* it. The media needs to transform itself, adapt, change, reinvent, and look around for inspiration. These are the basic assumptions of my essay here, and in making them I have chosen interchangeable backdrops of old media standards (or the print media), current economic situations, external relations and internal security aspects, as well as the sheer survival of the media as we know it today. There is also the impact of bad politics (or politicians) to be seriously considered.

When the New Media are taken into consideration, there comes a weak suggestion: let the old media—as we have known them for so long—finally down shutters and leave this increasingly youthful world. Such views, of course, lie only in the very extremities of Julian Assange-like mindsets.

In the midst of it all sits the Internet, and a part of the world (India and many parts of South Asia) where even old media have failed to penetrate fully. Will we forget the architecture of the wheel in our endeavor to not reinvent history?

The Media of Trust

The basic precept of all media activity is trust. Never break it has been the rule. Early in my career, one editor took pains to explain to me how lucky I was to have "access to the printed word." Wow! I thought, what a break I had made. I read books on journalism, and they dictated the sterile function of a reporter and I tried to stick to the spirit of the word. The result was a series of "reports" that would anyway have been transmitted by agencies. Was I doing the right thing by just reporting the bare facts? If I had been there (and the reader was not around), was my duty as a reporter restricted only to telling the reader just what happened and not the whys of the case?

Such rules, of course, came to be laid down through experience. Any level of localized excitement is bound to influence the reporter's mind, it had been concluded. Rumours were to be feared. Hence it was best to let the reporter bring back the bare-bone details of the happening. "Experts" could step in immediately after and dissect the issue at hand in opinion pieces. That left a big gap between what the reader read and what he assumed (read: heard).

Rumour, however, can remain sensitive to its localized urges: there is nobody to force-structure a rumour. Thus all investigative reporters are pretty aware of the maxim "never undermine the power of the grapevine." You simply cannot ignore it.

In the corporate world this grapevine phenomenon has been analysed in detail, and many managers have found utility in its existence, rather than in stifling it. Two seemingly unrelated findings arise from such analyses.

1. The amazing speed with which information is dispersed through the grapevine can be utilized in a fruitful manner.
2. Information from the grapevine can act as an indicator of the employees' sense of belonging with regard to the company.

Hence any sensible CEO would not overlook the grapevine, and would want to get the best out of it. As for politics, U.S. President Franklin D. Roosevelt had a fine ear for such grapevine talk, and he benefited immensely from it.

When the traditional media came face-to-face with the Internet, there was apprehension that its credibility would be rapidly eroded in the huge number of conflicting sources of information arising from so many sites claiming so many alternatives. When blogs came into the picture, they presented a big, individualized source of trouble. There is a media grapevine blog in India (Sans Serif)[1] that regularly disseminates "information" on what goes on inside media houses—who is leaving, who has joined where, who has been unceremoniously sacked and who is the evil boss. Such information will, in all probability, never be given by the traditional media (and television, for all practical purposes, has now become "traditional"). "Churmuri"—obviously a pen name—runs this blog and, since it is read mainly by the media hacks, it is popular. There is another site, exchange4media.com, that also carries media-related activity (it also includes the advertising world, hence diluting the impact somewhat for journalists), but there is much more staid old-media hangover visible on this site, with unconfirmed "news" items rarely being reported. Of course, there is also The Hoot (thehoot.org), a site very stoutly defending old rules of journalism and keeping all activity above board, while trying to keep to straight reportage. This site, sadly, is now in financial trouble.

It is the inherent desire of humans to know "what is really going on" that drives them to these grapevines. I must say, through experience, that I have benefited immensely from following many a grapevine story (not Sans Serif). Follow-up stories can often be structured into excellent "scoops," even if the seed of the information started elsewhere.

Thus, if a journalist happens to be following a particular story, say in the Department of Defence, through "sources" (a formal name in the media for grapevine nodes), he would want to believe them *before* checking out the story. Here, the seed of trust starts to germinate. If such information is available regularly in a blog, traffic to the site would increase exponentially and could even financially benefit the blogger. One concludes that a parallel broadcast of news always existed; only the Internet has made it easier and more formal. Therefore, it is to the benefit of all media houses to be able to follow such Internet grapevines and benefit from them, instead of trying to fight them.

I think the Internet today is acting as a handmaiden for traditional media. Treat it as a stepping-stone, not as a hurdle. In one amateurish effort to widen the definition of media, I tried to incorporate within its realm all activity that can be called a "medium" of disseminating information. I ended up with much of society in general, including print media, television, cinema, snail mail, email, chain mail, advertising, the radio, telephones, text and multimedia messages, water-cooler interactions, parlour chats, pub discourses, all educational institutions, social networking (physical and cyber),

1 See http://wearethebest.wordpress.com/.

legal institutions, the government, confined societies, the many grapevines, the stock markets, libraries, Kindle/iPad, etc.

Each medium, interactive or not, serves its purpose in telling us something. Hence each is, first, a storehouse of information. In the absence of early-day whistle blowers and today's WikiLeaks, such information is carefully considered, edited and formatted for different sections of recipients. That has always been the case. Even if it is a rumour, it will take different shapes, shades and sizes as it is related to different sets of listeners. That also means that certain sections of society may never really get to know what really passes through the grapevine. This was the corollary.

I needed to establish the above inferences and assumptions first, to be able to, then, gain a narrow focus. What I realized was that media are only rarely about journalists and media houses. They are more about common perceptions, outside the beat of newshounds. When one talks about newshounds and media houses, one has to keep that in mind.

Old Media and Digital Media

With the print media, you go right back to that one word: *trust*, or interchangeably, *credibility*. Every "respectable" newspaper has gone through decades of growing up pains. I was involved in the formative stages of *The Telegraph*,[2] today's leading English language newspaper, in the eastern Indian city of Kolkata (earlier Calcutta). In 1982, Aveek Sarkar, chief editor of the Ananda Bazar Patrika Group (ABP) of publications, decided to bring out a new format English daily, under the editorship of M.J. Akbar. M.J., as he was called (and still is), was among the Young Turks of Indian journalism and he went about every aspect of the process in earnest, as the ABP house, professional that it is, played along.

The idea was to present to readers with a fresh morning paper, complete with new ideas, daring news coverage and entertainment. There remained a small problem, however. It was *The Statesman*, a hugely popular, venerable brand in Indian newspaper industry, that was the leader of the city's informant and informed society. People trusted the daily. We grew up being "ordered" at home to read the daily to enrich our knowledge of society and the language. It was the last word in ramrod-straight, independent and unbiased reportage. *The Statesman* was trusted like no daily in the country was; it also demanded the highest advertisement rates.

M.J. moved away from existing formats of reportage. He designed with passion, he wrote scathingly, and once sent a reporter and photographer quietly inside a city jail and splashed those pictures (against the administration's wishes) across the centrespread in a major exposé—Insight. Insight became a common name for exposé in capital letters. Political reportage was raised from the audience to the dais, columns ran circles around establishments, and you got all this in a neat, bright package every morning.

The Telegraph soon beat *The Statesman* in popularity and resultant circulation, and Aveek Sarkar's active support in the venture earned plaudits and respect. Down the years *The Telegraph* was no longer a rabble-rouser publication, but a highly respected daily. Of course, the contributing factor to this success was the army of termites eating away at *The Statesman*'s woodwork and not a finger raised in remedying this.

It was hard work for all of us, but trust comes at a price. It also pays: today *The Telegraph* is the largest circulated eastern Indian English daily, and its advertisement rates are eons ahead of the city's other publications—*The Times of India*, *The Statesman* and *The Hindustan Times*. One must

2 *Telegraph, India* (Calcutta). http://www.telegraphindia.com/section/frontpage/index.jsp.

also be reminded that the management had agreed to try out *The Telegraph* as an "experiment" for around 11 months or so before deciding whether it deserved to be a fully financed project. Not that we cub reporters knew about this "deal" (or the morale may not have been as it was), but in the end it turned out to be an unqualified success. This was the management's way of estimating the credibility factor gained in quick time, while putting in place a risk management circuit-breaker that could act quickly if we failed. The company would have been saved further losses and embarrassment. In the event, we grew up to be pretty wholesome children.

When television invaded homes, the newspapers quickly cashed in on this trust factor and reportage became more objective, carrying more intrinsic value than any amount of video footage on television can. There were strong views to be read, along with background research that was missing in television's instant-noodle dispatches. The daily also had the advantage of being read throughout the day and even in crowded public transport. Dailies also generated "scoops" more regularly than television. In India, at least, the battle was even.

The Internet quickly changed many beliefs. Initial website structures and designs loaned ideas from the print media (because they were expensive, then, to put up). With that loan also came a fraction of the trust that the print media had built up over decades. That is how early scamsters could earn a quick buck—a well-designed website sort of represented a well-appointed office on the Net—and that was why the remnants of trust soon disappeared. The Internet was deemed to be a tool for transmitting data that would then be vetted by the old media before the public cared to believe it. It was a settlement of sorts, reached between the operators and promoters of the media.

Until then, the Internet was an expensive proposition and bandwidth was that which a poor dial-up connection could afford. It was not really worth the time for a busy professional or a student under examination pressure to log on and wait for the front page to load or the links to activate before the connection went on the blink. He/she had deadlines to meet. However, the off periods of us newsmen were devoted to surfing the Net and valuable inputs were snipped off the pages, to be followed up over the telephone. Working the phone still remains a must for beat reporters.

Trust was still within the exclusive confines of the print media. Those were the days when television was wreaking havoc with deadlines and breaking news. The government was warming up to news channels and quick calls to them for important press briefings were answered with quick responses. Our editors whipped us up with verbal volleys, and the night car pool was beefed up.

So far, so good. It was a fair fight, a hard battle, but every bit enjoyable. Then two things happened: broadband (or more bandwidth) and the mobile phone. Emails were a fad and mobile phones (even though they were expensive then) intercepted our "sources" at odd hours. The good news was that we were getting around faster without having to move much. The bad news was that soon the novelty wore off and the phones were left unanswered—caller line identification has its major disadvantages as well.

Meanwhile, the websites took shape in their dozens. Funding was available, and the net was getting cheaper. Web designers were being absorbed as fast as they could graduate. There was a huge spread of competition and large numbers of journalists left established print media jobs to join the dotcom bandwagon.

Then the bubble burst: twice. With the advertisers remaining laggards in moving out of their comfort zones, Indian and the sub-continent's major sites quickly disappeared, leaving many jobless. The bigger problem was with those hanging on. Their reportage reached a nadir: unconfirmed rumors were highlighted, then stripped off; they failed to follow up stories and, with tight budgets, failed to reach the spot.

That was the big depression. The obsession with design also left their sites too heavy to load, even with bandwidth increasing. That was lost opportunity, because the print media were slow in putting their newspapers online. Even today, with all media houses having their newspapers on the Net (with some pretty fancy sites), traffic has grown, but consequent ad revenue remains minimal.

A case in point is that of a news website, Tehelka.com, which became a legend of sorts with its "sting" exposés of bribe-taking. Hidden cameras were used in recording top government officials in the act of taking bribes and the resultant pictures and added transcripts were uploaded. It was an instant hit. Ex-print media editor Tarun Tejpal (once also associated with M.J.) led a team of very motivated young journalists to produce a series of scoops. Newspapers simply had to follow up such stories, but in the end a fund crunch and the establishment forced Tehelka out of business. That experiment remains a legend in the Indian journalistic world. Tehelka is now a print periodical, and somewhat less scathing in its stories.

Advertisers failed to see Tehelka.com gaining any measure of "credibility" or trust among peer groups and probably saw biased references that stopped them from advertising on the site and getting into the bad books of those who matter. In retrospect, had Tehelka.com developed its credibility over a period before conducting those "sting" operations, there would have been the weight of those years of solid credibility to fall back on for the promoters. Of course, it was also true that, for a new website to become popular in those days (with Net connections still pretty expensive and access to the public limited), certain explosive content was immediately necessary to draw traffic and funds. Sadly, it did not turn out as planned, and the debate on it continues.

Print Media Growth, Internet Penetration and the Mobile Age

India (and the sub-continent) is one of the few nations in the world where the growth of the print media (especially newspapers) remains unabated. The growth has been noted across the spectrum, but the biggest movements have been in the regional language dailies. Away from the metropolitan cities and Tier II cities of the country, the newspaper industry has found safe havens, for the time being at least, and with the economic condition of those cities and sub-cities improving fast, ad revenue is not hard to come by.

According to the Indian Readership Survey of the top 10 Indian publications (circulation) of 2010, Q1, a Hindi daily, *Dainik Jagaran*, tops the list with robust growth year on year. If you go down the list, you will see the top five slots booked by Hindi dailies from different states of India—Maharashtra, Gujarat, Tamil Nadu, etc. Slot 6 belongs to a Marathi daily (the language of the state of Maharashtra, where the metropolis of Mumbai is), with a Tamil daily at no. 7. The English language daily *Times of India* (published from all over India) comes in at no. 8. Slot 9 goes to a Malayali daily (from the southwestern state of Kerala) and 10 to another Hindi daily, from Rajasthan. Also, the only daily showing a distinctive negative growth year on year that same quarter was the *Times of India* (in English). *Rajasthan Patrika*, at slot 10, showed a movement downwards of just one point in the second decimal. The rest saw healthy growth.

Why is this happening in this online age? Ramananda Sengupta, Chief Editor at India.com, an info portal from Mumbai, and a former print media journalist, believes that this is the direct fallout of the government's mass education drive. "As more people move into the literate world, with their children taking up engaging occupations, they dig into information/news. English language newspapers are not the need here. Your content must be more localized and of use to you. And the advertising world still believes that the impact factor of ads in the print media and on television far outreaches anything that can be placed online."

A major chunk of this growth is happening outside cities, in rural areas. This might sound ironic, until you look at some totally unrelated data. Famously, Mahatma Gandhi said "India lives in its villages," which meant that most of India's population lived in rural areas. Sixty-two years after the Mahatma's death, India still lives in its villages, with over 72% residing in rural areas. However, here are some really radical figures:

- 46% of all soft drinks sales in the country are in rural areas;
- motorcycle manufacturers sell 49% of their products in rural India;
- 53% of FMCG sales happen in rural India;
- 25% of rural India uses talcum powder;
- 11% of rural women wear lipstick;
- Maruti Suzuki (India's largest passenger car maker) sells close to 10% of its cars in rural India;
- and the clincher—rural India has 58% of India's total disposable income, and nearly 60% of all-India produce is consumed by rural India.

As the trickle-down factor of national economics takes hold, the interests of farmers grow. They look to the "respectability" of city folks and soon the printed media make headway, aided by huge corporate bodies that see big markets in these areas. This has been a financial win–win situation so far for the print media.

However, if there is that much progress, and if education is a big helping hand, and if access to the Internet is so cheap in India, why are not online information dissemination systems gaining ground, especially in the news category? Ramananda and I agree on three reasons:

1. Internet penetration in India hovers around a poor 6% of the population.
2. The Indian population seems to have leapfrogged the Internet, into the mobile phone era—there are more phones per capita in India today than there are toilets. "Handheld devices are taking over, and Internet access on such devices is growing exponentially, even off city limits. The sale of personal computers and laptops has, thus, not taken off as predicted when Net access became easy."
3. News, as we have seen earlier, is consumed in local languages. Translation on the Net is still poor, and dynamic fonts are either not available or cannot be loaded onto the systems.

It is easy to understand the importance of this to the advertisers, who make the wheels of the news industry turn. "In a newspaper, the ad is in your face, whether you like it or not. You can read the lead news item in the page, or you can concentrate on the anchor, but that display ad covering a third of the page remains, in your face, and you do not even have to waste time clicking on it to get to the bigger picture. That IS the bigger picture," explains Ramananda.

It (the advertisement) comes home with you with the daily, and hangs around for anybody to see, the whole day and days on end until the newspaper disposed of. If you decide to make a book cover out of it, you see it all over again, for many more months. The impact is terrific.

The Cityscape, Bad Politics and Closer Views

In the cities, however, the picture is a little different. This is where the decision-makers of the country live, and this is where major issues are, well, major issues. Here is the prevalence of blogs, of Twitter tweets, of Facebook societies and of emailed spam.

If I may go back to my many definitions of media as a whole, the entire gamut of media functions plays out boldly, and each affects the news media in more ways than one. The English language media remain elitist in the general perception, and the Net has the right to interfere anywhere. That is not happening, and the reason might be less economical than political.

One media watcher was very clear in his perception of why the media are slipping.

> The youth of today receives her/his education at a high cost. She/he is not willing to throw it away on 'useless' political information. The youth of today seeks specific, often personalized information in the media jungle and, Google-willing, moves away immediately after. The intelligentsia of India, especially the youth, will not touch politics with a nine-foot bargepole if they can afford it. And the print media is still full of it.

The reason for this is the general perception of Indian politicians as being either extremely corrupt or very incompetent, or both: generally both. "If the guardians of a decent student have toiled hard to put her/his ward through good schooling, the student will stay away from garbage. And for the educated Indian youth of today, politics in India today is garbage," says a media watcher, who refuses to be identified. I can believe that this sentiment—right or wrong—does echo around all walls of educational institutions and of society.

So does that mean the newspaper is losing ground in cities to blogs and to social media? Not really. As digital media grew exponentially (in cities), media houses rearranged their content. Presentation was simpler, articles were shorter, headings and captions were smarter and more pithy, pictures were more dramatic, and news was more analytical. There was a slow movement away from politics, except in hardcore newspapers such as *The Indian Express*. Columns increased in number, "experts" arrived by the dozen, and everything was about news behind the scenes, and more talk revolved around issues of society than of politics.

The scope of content was also narrowed down to cater to specific interest groups, such as technology, or food, or the cinema, or even lifestyle. Surveys show that, while general, news-oriented periodicals have seen steep circulation and ad cuts, special category periodicals have seen good growth. Politics is slowly getting to be seen as "an illiterate's and a hoodlum's prime activity" and "no self-respecting young man would think twice about politics." "It is a sad chronicle of our people in public life, and it is also a sad chronicle of the news media's insistence on showing unabashed support of one party of radicals or the other. Either way, the people don't care," says the media watcher.

Vivek Sengupta, Founder and Chief Executive at Moving Finger Communications, does not agree. "Political news content anyway has decreased in the print media," he says, "except in some pockets. But the youth of today are not as interested in information as we were, just because information exists. If I may say so, we were sort of information junkies in our time, but the youth of today just want what they need: you either call it tunnel vision or focused vision."

Not long back the print media and television had the responsibility of informing and educating. Today this credibility factor has seen extraordinary dilution. A city youth, brought up in a somewhat educated family, stays on his path. Science columns/pullouts in dailies, for example, have been reduced to a pathetic once-a-week "page," with content sourced mostly from international publications (except for *The Hindu*, headquartered in Chennai, which has remained faithful in its originality and richness of content). With the Net providing easy access to such information and much more in real time, newspaper credibility slips further.

Ramananda has a point when he says that the print media (read newspapers) in India have remained a one-way information street with hardly any scope for interactivity. The websites of these newspapers look good, but are so badly maintained that responses are hardly ever vetted and/ or highlighted. Such elitist attitudes of newspapers, which today mostly cater for "Page 3 people" (as Sunanda K. Dutta Ray, former editor of *The Statesman* and a respected political commentator, believes), easily put off today's educated youth.

A Forward-looking Youth Population

One must understand what the educated youth of today look ahead to. India today is not only the second-fastest growing major economy of the world (after China), but experts also believe that India has a better economic model that will better survive the test of time and keep growing. Consider this bit of seemingly unrelated data:

> China will grow old before it gets richer. India will have more employable bright youths than China by the years 2016–2020. The India growth model, according to many experts, bears a long-term view of staying power, combined with innovation. These are the horizons the youth is looking towards, not towards a quagmire of irresponsible politics.

Give me one sensible reason why even a semi-educated, moderately intelligent youth would want to think about the stink of politics in this atmosphere?

That is why voices of protest come through blogs and in social networks and at the pub and even around water-coolers. Technology has also helped. Quite in the way that the rural areas seem to be leapfrogging the Internet era, the cities are refusing to read that most important page 1. "It is as if biased journalism is helping irresponsible politicians survive. We don't need either," points out Mehraj Ahmed, a graduate student of economics at a New Delhi institute.

So where do they get their daily fix of information? "Define information—for you it could be the political hokum of India, for us, believe me, it is the development news of a country, of the opportunities that the youth have and may still not have been sullied by politics. I have friends to support me, and I support them, and even if it's often crowd-sourcing of information, we have the ability to sift and decide for ourselves."

The hate for politics is deep, very deep. Thankfully, they have the confidence to live independent lives. The distrust for the media is growing apace. It is as if the print media (especially that in English, which mostly cater to the intelligentsia) are actively putting themselves out of business by aligning themselves with one political party or another.

So is the country looking forward to an Assange-like "leak"? Or will sense prevail before the pandemonium? "Can't say," is the general view, but consensus exists in the area where each would want her blog to be read and responded to, and each would want to put up a portal that would not only generate revenue, but overall, would improve the credibility of information to the public.

The Effect on Newspapers, Reportage and Photographers

For newspaper owners, the digital explosion is a dilemma. If you dilute and compress content, bringing in less politics and more "light reading," you lose the weight that a serious newspaper should carry into corridors of power and influence. If you go overtly political, you lose the youth. Financial considerations seem to be snipping away at available options, and quality erosion cannot be avoided.

The first "victims" have been top-notch photography and photographers, their brilliant 1,000-word essays proving to be less incisive these days. Robert Nickelsberg, a former contract photographer for *Time* magazine based in New Delhi from 1988 to 1999, believes that the world is about information, but not actually about the quality of information.

That was one assignment (actually I was a happy lackey to Bob, hanging around his photo assignment while picking up raw information for my story on the Ganges pollution and Kanpur's tanneries) that put me very close to a top-level photographer. Our own photographers would dream of situations where they would be allowed to use as much film as they wanted to capture the right mood in maybe just one or two pictures. Bob was clicking away in that northern Indian town in the state of Uttar Pradesh, and in black and white too (he loved those pictures better than color, and surely they *were* better). He used a prodigious number of rolls and finally maybe arrived at a few brilliant pictures. He would not stop till he did: he was a perfectionist.

For a person of his dedication, it is sad when he says:

> There's no doubt the new digital era has broadened the world's viewership and overall access to information. One effect of this has been the lower financial return to photojournalists for images which in print form would receive close to ten times the money or compensation than a web-generated download fee. News photographs on some websites are nearly free and with the high number of quality phone cameras in circulation web-based publishing has managed to circumvent the traditional higher priced photo agency archive where a professional photojournalist would offer his/her images for resale.

This is the downside of news photography, and even photojournalists of the calibre of Nickelsberg have not escaped that. Quality has been deserted for quantity and easy availability. There are places of excellence still around, but they are rare. "Images of high quality can still fetch a fair market price, but the number of photographers flooding the Web from any given event has diluted the pool of quality imagery normally created by professionals," says Nickelsberg.

Newspapers today have little option but to choose from a rather low-quality pool when they think of the cost factor. However, that is not the competitiveness of the Net in that. As a news photographer, Nickelsberg cannot but appreciate what new devices can do.

> During the Mumbai attack in 2008 and the street protests in Tehran over the rigged presidential elections in 2009, news coverage depended on the social networking sites that were essentially free ... These images would not have been transmitted had it not been for the number of electronic devices on the streets able to access the Web or phone lines for texting and for MMS. The general public has shown that they care less for high quality resolution images than in the past.

Where does that lead? Are the young of every nation happy with mere speed of access even though quality is no more than mediocre? There are places around the world where this may be true, but in India probably a double system is on show. Newspapers have a lag time of 12–24 hours (depending on the number of editions) following an event. If the reader is scanning the paper for that news item, the electronic media and the Internet and other platforms may have already informed her of the basic facts. She is then looking for further analysis, and information. If, then, she finds low-quality pictures accompanying sketchy reports, she is not impressed. Similarly, if she is buying a periodical for the same reason—where the lag time is about a week at least, and even more for large-circulation magazines—she expects to be delivered even better presentations, even better analyses and reportage and even better pictures.

The nature of the demand seems to change with time because, by the time the periodical has managed to encapsulate the entire content of what has happened in a fine package, the world outside has already sped ahead to the next event, which has been reported (probably again in low quality) by other media available to today's youth. In theory, then, newspapers can only report behind-the-scenes, and periodicals should talk about life in general.

In India the dip is taken care of, for the time being, through hinterland demand, and we can expect this to be steady, because the Internet's movement is far slower than mobile platforms and handheld devices are getting cheaper. Mobile connectivity in India is anyway among the cheapest in the world.

Multiplatform Dilemmas

That brings us to multiplatform presentations, a sort of idealistic one-size-fits-all ambition. The India Today Group is one of the largest media conglomerates in India that does not have a broadsheet newspaper (one tabloid: *Mail Today*). The group's primary focus is its many focused and general periodicals, led by Aroon Purie. Along with the print versions, each publication is also on the Internet and on various other platforms. Purie's daughter Kalli is now head of India Today Group Digital, an amalgamation of all the digital versions of the many publications. In a recent interview, Kalli mentioned to the interviewer a very interesting aspect of what she intends to do:[3]

> India Today Group, as a company, is platform agnostic. We believe that we need to be present on every platform possible. We started with print and now we are on TV, radio and also the Internet. On Internet also, the strategy remains the same. If we are available on Internet, we are there on mobile, iPad, Blackberry, HP DreamScreen and any other device or platform that is out there.

Sounds pretty. Only the problem seems to be in content sourcing. It is true that India Today's periodicals and its television channels (*Aaj Tak* in Hindi and *Headlines Today* in English) do generate prodigious quantities of content. However, all content is tailored to the particular dissemination medium and it is unlikely that a common-platform content situation can be arrived at without compromising on quality.

The plus of course, is the trust factor, and that can have a big effect. The credibility of the India Today group is huge. This goodwill and trust will automatically transfer itself to every platform when content flows through the many available media portals. This can be a high leverage point for users, and if back-reference points exist (such as hyperlinks to print media content), each receiver is a potential traffic generator/sales promoter for "old" media.

However, that is the idealist's prognosis. As Kalli herself points out, a saleable and scalable business model is not on the table yet:

> The business is evolving but I think in a couple of years, there will emerge a concrete business model. Presently, there is none. This is an experimental phase and one needs to be present on every platform and hence India Today Group Digital is aggressive on being present on every platform. I do not believe in doing hygiene. I mean putting an RSS feed on the mobile phone is something you need to do. I am talking about new things and new ideas.

---

3 See http://www.youtube.com/watch?v=1mKkTzWARZ.

Coming from a top media house, that is not a very encouraging state of affairs. However, if we draw a parallel with diversified industrial groups, one may see the value of being able to draw sustenance from, say, a group's thermal power plants in pushing new, sustainable energy projects. Carbon credit benefits apart, a new, fresh endeavour can be supported until it can find its feet. Meanwhile, the overall health of the company may not suffer that much.

In the early stages of *The Telegraph*, the ABP group's mother publication, its Bengali (the tongue of Bengal as well as of Bangladesh) daily *Ananda Bazar Patrika* kept its newborn English sibling in its palm. *Ananda Bazar Patrika* is the largest selling language daily in the eastern part of the country and is hugely profitable. This was a case in point. Looking at the growing regional language figures of the country, this is a sustainable point of reference that exists. Meanwhile, the new media experiments can go on unhindered.

As Nickelsberg points out: "The curiosity remains for photojournalism, fine art photography and visual story telling. The trend for smaller devices able to transmit higher quality images will continue. Any image appears to be more important than waiting for the high resolution images print magazines traditionally offer. There's a growing audience for photographers and reporters covering the conflict in Afghanistan with an iPhone." That means it does not essentially follow that all traditional craft needs to be given up for the new. In reality, a bit of reworking can work fine in fitting it into the new era. This applies to accepted norms of journalism and newspapers as well, at least in this part of the world where tradition, interestingly, has remained the bulwark of progress.

The Pitfalls

That brings us to the firewalling of information, which is basically how you decide not to let unwanted external stimuli dilute content. Sashi Tharoor gained immense credibility in India through his books. His senior position at the United Nations was only a bonus for Indians. Frankly, until Tharoor returned to claim his son-of-the-soil dividend, his defeat in the race for the Secretary General's post was not the top discussion point of society: it was merely among one of the news items at hand. He probably became more famous back home (among those who were not in the habit of picking up Tharoor books in their leisure hours) in his defeat than he was when he ruled in New York.

Tharoor is a culture junkie, and possesses an open mind—he has stayed abroad for too long, some say. So when he tweeted "cattle class" (as he was flying during one of the Union government's many strange austerity drives), he meant no disrespect to anybody. In any yesterday, in the print media, this would have been treated with the nonchalance that Tharoor himself thought it should have been. Not so by the new peckers in the new media world. All hell broke loose and an apology was asked for. It was quite like having to call an ass a donkey, because ass seems politically incorrect.

The problem was with the many excellent decisions that Tharoor had taken as a junior minister for external affairs of India. Those remained on the sidelines of daily, boring reportage.

Sensationalizing a news report may not be the best way to deliver information. For a moment I return to the cub reporter who was directed to bring back bare-bones information that could later be followed up. There is, still, a lot of sense in looking back at the scene of the act and pausing for a moment to review, before putting things into print or delivering instant gratification over new media portals.

One has to also debate whether correspondents are acting within their sacred limits when they start their own blogs, which, in turn become popular. What is the difference between a reporter's column/article and her blog? Is she repeating herself in them, or is she providing fresh inputs to an already mentioned issue? If she has fresh inputs then why did she not mention them in the first place, in her column/article? Does she feel there is not enough freedom in the media house she works for, or is this simply personal gratification?

Then there are personal blogs of celebrities, key political figures, businessmen, etc. Today, the standard response by celebrities to a newspaper or television allegation is a quick reply through their blogs, which has also graduated to Twitter tweets. One can empathize with this, because in having to talk to the reporter, the person in question was simply abiding by the dictates of the interviewing media. In his blog, there is freedom of expression, translating into freedom of denial. There is a saying in Indian media today that all that is reported is false until an official denial comes in. That is when it becomes sanctified, blessed into truism. Thus, scandalous, scurrilous, downright lies and outrageous blogs that have been pulling traffic need to be studied in detail before they are believed. One need not apply Chinese methods, but it is well within the rights of the reader to ask the blogger to establish his credibility first. Newspapers are way ahead of the field in this regard, having spent hard years and harder decades simply trying to establish this.

Cloud Reporting

Quality and credibility gaps are dangerous issues, as I have pointed out and as has been qualified by Nickelsberg and others. The first casualties in the new media world have been foreign correspondents. They are too expensive for media houses, and do not present an appreciable return on investment. Great argument, one must say.

I remember once, *The Telegraph* involved in its modernization drive an international business consultancy firm to streamline activity. Reporters were asked to show how many column centimetres of news they had generated in a week and this was to be used to adjust their remuneration. When we told them it was maybe several hundreds in one week but nothing in others, they were aghast. How could that be? How does one judge a reporter's output? Thankfully, laughter had already been invented. And thankfully, such "yardsticks" were quickly thrown out of the window by our very experienced and able management.

Measuring quality through financial leveraging is not always a good idea, at least in journalism. So when citizen reporting came into being there was a hue and cry over quality, but it is probably here to stay. However, one hopes that such reportage is restricted to local school exhibitions and local musical soirées. Quite like cloud computing, where one can draw on compatible software and storage from the Web instead of using one's computer, the media house/editorial headquarters will have to stay in constant touch with hundreds of un-vetted, semi-reliable sources of information. Then it has to crosscheck each peice of information for reliability. The salary overhead may be down several notches, but the brows will remain permanently creased.

Foreign correspondents are deputed to provide very close reportage, conforming to the policies of the house or the country. In their absence, agencies can fill up space quickly, but it is again a case of one-size-fits-all.

The Assange Effect

Continuing from the cloud, you will bump into the Julian Assanges of the world. Debates will continue as to his own credibility and viability in news distribution. For one thing, he wanted to break open Fort Knox, but then he had no control over who plundered what and for what reason. That is not civil society's way of handling issues. Yes, you will argue, that is why Tunisians are free today from the oppressive regime of Zine el Abidine Ben Ali and his in-laws, the Trabelsis. And you will argue about how much the Americans really knew about the Pakistani ISI's intransigence and failed to do anything, and you will argue how 9/11 may have been prevented. Yet what if potentially explosive international relations material is released? What if state secrets are no longer state secrets? A modest explanation for Julian Assange's act would be a lack of sense and maturity.

I am sure the news media do not want to dive to such obtuse depths. If it does, its already decaying edifice of credibility and trust will crumble to dust. Anarchy is a good word to describe the ensuing situation.

The print media remain the last bastion of public faith. New media are welcome, but need to keep their side of the deal—not be in denial, be responsible, be educated, and be mature. Old media must show the maturity to adopt new ideas and use the new media to best effect. Until such a time when new media envelope the world, old media picket fences will be respected, read, followed and emulated. Sense shall survive in social moderation, and lies will still be uncovered for a long time to come.

Chapter 27
Postscript

Sean S. Costigan and Jake Perry

While putting the finishing touches on this book, world-changing events occurred in North Africa and the Middle East: popular uprisings in Tunisia and Egypt drove out entrenched leaders, while Bahrain and Libya, to name but two other Arab countries, descended into violent unrest. Many argue that these unanticipated developments were due, in large part, to information and communication technologies (ICT)—in particular to social media. Much like the cyberspaces this book covers, attempting to delve comprehensively into how ICT affected each event and situation would only serve to enumerate a small fraction of ICT's effect on global affairs. However, in each recent case the nexus of people, media, and technology created a highly charged atmosphere, leaving the international community at turns surprised, activated and, perhaps, slightly apprehensive.

New Media in the Arab World

Experts agree that the rise of social media in the Arab world represents incredible unforeseen change. As Jeffrey Ghannam, an independent analyst, put it, the changes were the most "dramatic and unprecedented improvement in the freedom of expression, association, and access to information in contemporary Arab history."[1]

Underpinning the changes are these facts about ICT in the regions:

- In 2004 a Carnegie Endowment for International Peace study tallied 2,854,800 Internet users in the Arab world. In 2009 the UNDP Arab Knowledge Report numbered Arabic-speaking Internet users at 60 million.[2] In 2010, a Google executive at the Google Days conference anticipated that 100 million people in the region will be online by 2015.
- From 2000 to 2009, the Middle East witnessed an impressive Internet usage growth rate of 1648.2%.[3]
- In 2010, Facebook penetration was estimated at 17 million in the region and 5 million in Egypt alone.[4]

1 CIMA, p. 4. Available at: http://cima.ned.org/publications/social-media-arab-world-leading-uprisings-2011-0 [accessed: 1 August 2011].

2 "Arab Knowledge Report 2009, Toward Productive Intercommunication for Knowledge," Mohammed bin Rashid Al Maktoum Foundation and United Nations Development Programme, October 2009. Available at: http://content.undp.org/go/newsroom/2009/october/the-arab-knowledge-report-2009-towards-productive-intercommunication-for-knowledge.en [accessed: 18 April 2011].

3 Available at: http://www.internetworldstats.com/middle.htm [accessed: 18 April 2011].

4 Arab Crunch. Available at: http://arabcrunch.com/2010/12/google-mena-ad-spending-is-between-110-130-million-usd-in-2010-100-million-arab-users-will-be-online-in-2015.html [accessed: 18 April 2011].

- Kzalek, the first Arab-language Twitter interface was launched in 2009;[5] Twitter included Arabic into its language possibilities in 2011.
- More than 50% of the populations of Yemen, Oman, Saudi Arabia, Jordan, Morocco, and Egypt are currently estimated to be under 25 years of age.[6] For the rest of the Arab region, the age group under 25 makes up between 35 and 47%.
- The average unemployment rate in some countries of North Africa and the Middle East is 25%.[7]

Bursting at the Seams

If, as some have said, demography is destiny, then much of the recent developments should have been predictable. A youth bulge is changing the landscape and will continue to do so. In these recent instances, tech-savvy youth—some educated, some not—created ways to make new media their ally. Politically and economically, what they held in common was shared lack of opportunity; and culturally they shared not inconsiderable engagement with the outside world through social media.

So, it could be said that the cultural and political fabric of these regions is being refashioned, in no small part owing to ICT. The uprisings were cut from this very cloth, and so were the methods and tactics. Consider the flash mob, or video clips of police brutality uploaded in real-time, or the names of the missing posted on Twitter: without these, what would the revolutions have resembled? Indeed, it appears that there is a positive feedback loop at work: the media helps to shape the worldview of the individual and the group, and changes in media cause shifts in worldviews.

What New Media "Did" in early 2011

From the "Facebook" revolutions in North Africa and the Middle East to the use of social networking technology in the aftermath of disasters such as the earthquake in Japan, to the spread of mobile phones throughout the developing world: all of these developments are part of how social networking applications are profoundly altering global affairs in this still new century.

With the rise of the social web and applications like Facebook, YouTube and Twitter, scholars and practitioners of global change are adapting to this new information space across a wide range of issue areas: in conflict resolution, dialogues and communication are taking the form of open social networks, while in the legal realm, where cyberspace appears as a largely lawless space, states are stepping up policing efforts to combat online criminality and programmers are finding new ways around increasingly sophisticated censorship. Militaries are moving to deeply incorporate information technologies into their doctrines, and protesters are developing innovative uses of technology to keep one step ahead of the authorities. Parallel to all this, mobile technologies are changing the nature of work, education, and lifestyle with especially significant implications for the developing world.

In the Middle East and North Africa, new media allowed for coordinated action without imposed or pre-existing structures. As historians will reveal, no doubt there were organizations

5 Available at: http://twitsmag.com/kzalek-first-twitter-arabic-desktop-app-beta-launched-supports-all-platforms-farisi-ui-planned/ [accessed: 18 April 2011].

6 Arab Media Outlook, 2008–2012, Dubai Press Club. Available at: http://www.slideshare.net/AlHaqqNetwork/arab-media-outlook-20082012 [accessed: 18 April 2011].

7 The Challenge of Arab Unemployment. Available at: http://www.middle-east-online.com/english/?id=35690 [accessed: 18 April 2011].

pushing the protesters and actively encouraging change, but participation—the definition of which has changed—meant that people could now follow a friend on Facebook, or a Twitter feed, retweet, or—if actually there—act. In effect, whether physically there or not, individuals around the world *became* the effort. Loose coordination with groups paved the way for an alignment of disparate interests, from human rights, to regime change, to economic opportunism. Young, progressive types protested alongside more conservative elements—all for the same outcome. Shared ability was found because it was broadcast from the bottom up, in real time, with collective awareness of the opportunities, technical and political.

Division by Zero?

Yet critics will rightly note that *over*emphasis on technologies serves to blind analysts to the conditions and causes that lead up to any event, leaving only its aftermath and so many digital breadcrumbs. One thing we can certainly be sure of is that the pace of change is increasing, with unpredictable results. A sort of political fission is now taking place across both wide and narrow spaces with never before imagined ease: a person may self-align with a shared goal, pushing that cause a bit further by a measurable unit (one Facebook page, one tweet), moving from there to the community then to the regional aggregator, moving further to news outlets, finally being picked up by large media distribution channels. We also know that technology alone does not make a revolution. As Alec Ross, U.S. Secretary of State Hillary Clinton's Senior Advisor for Innovation, stated "[technology] did not make the dissent movement successful … technology served as an accelerant."[8]

As of this writing, some of the populations involved in "The Arab Spring" are now grappling with the hardest part of social upheaval and revolution: how to piece together a new form of government and society, often without the pieces perceived to be necessary, like a technocratic class or stable infrastructure. Time will tell if the methods and tools used to achieve change (technology, open communication) and the beliefs that inform some (transparency and free expression) will also influence the forms and structures of the future of these societies. Undoubtedly it seems as if these changes are now creating new societal expectations, supporting new amendments in the contract between governments and the governed, media and the mediated. While this might not be new, the pace of change is startling and is increasing geometrically, a fitting corollary to Moore's law, but this time for political change.

Despite these events, and perhaps—in some instances—because of them, Internet freedom throughout the world may be on the decline. Bloggers in Egypt are still being arrested by the interim military government that replaced Hosni Mubarak. In China authorities have pre-emptively struck out at critics, arresting prominent individuals, most notably the artist and activist Ai Weiwei, and are suppressing potential sites of dissent. Furthermore, as the OpenNet Initiative shows, across the globe vast efforts are underway to deploy technologies to *enhance* censorship, all while many of these same countries seek to bolster access to the Internet for economic gain. Where all of this is heading is impossible to ascertain, but to paraphrase Antoine de Saint Exupéry, perhaps our task is not to foresee the future, but simply to enable it.

8 "Social media, cellphone video fuel Arab protests." Available at: http://www.google.com/hostednews/afp/article/ALeqM5gudZE43cbT0n7FKFrf95m7quvylQ?docId=CNG.fe8ee2026cbc31267697a46821cc7ecf.41 [accessed: 18 April 2011].

Index

Page numbers in *italics* refer to figures and tables.